# Switzerland

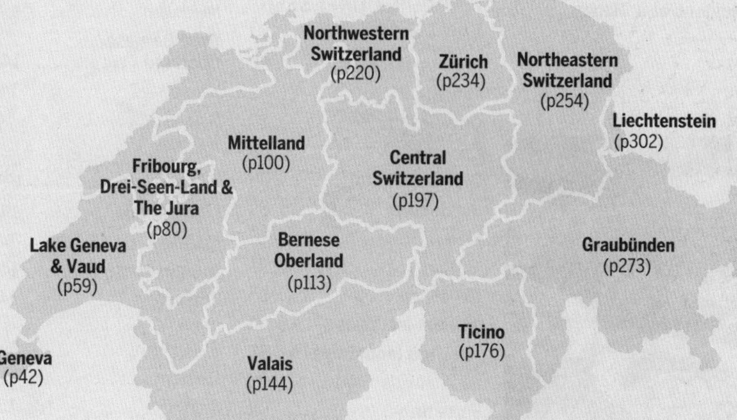


Kerry Walker,
Gregor Clark, Craig McLachlan, Benedict Walker

## PLAN YOUR TRIP

ALEXANDER CHAIKIN/SHUTTERSTOCK ©

SWISS CHOCOLATE P322

HERACLES KRITIKOS/SHUTTERSTOCK ©

KINDLIFRESSERBRUNNEN P105

## ON THE ROAD

# Contents



**COVID-19**

We have re-checked every business in this book before publication to ensure that it is still open after the COVID-19 outbreak. However, the economic and social impacts of COVID-19 will continue to be felt long after the outbreak has been contained, and many businesses, services and events referenced in this guide may experience ongoing restrictions. Some businesses may be temporarily closed, have changed their opening hours and services, or require bookings; some unfortunately could have closed permanently. We suggest you check with venues before visiting for the latest information.

Right: Matterhorn, Zermatt (p162)

PATHARA BURANADILOK/SHUTTERSTOCK ©

## WELCOME TO

# Switzerland

*Switzerland for me has always meant the Alps. For years when I lived in the Black Forest, they were the closest proper mountains. Sighting them on the horizon brought the promise of winter snow and happy days spent cross-country skiing, snowshoeing in silent, frozen forests and curling up in a log cabin. Or else the joy of summer: bell-swinging cows, high pastures and rising with the first pink light to crest a summit. This idiosyncratic little land hooked me 20 years ago and I'm still in love with its wild places, and the great railways and never-ending trails that make reaching them a breeze.*

**By Kerry Walker, Writer**

@kerryawalker

For more about our writers, see p352

# Switzerland

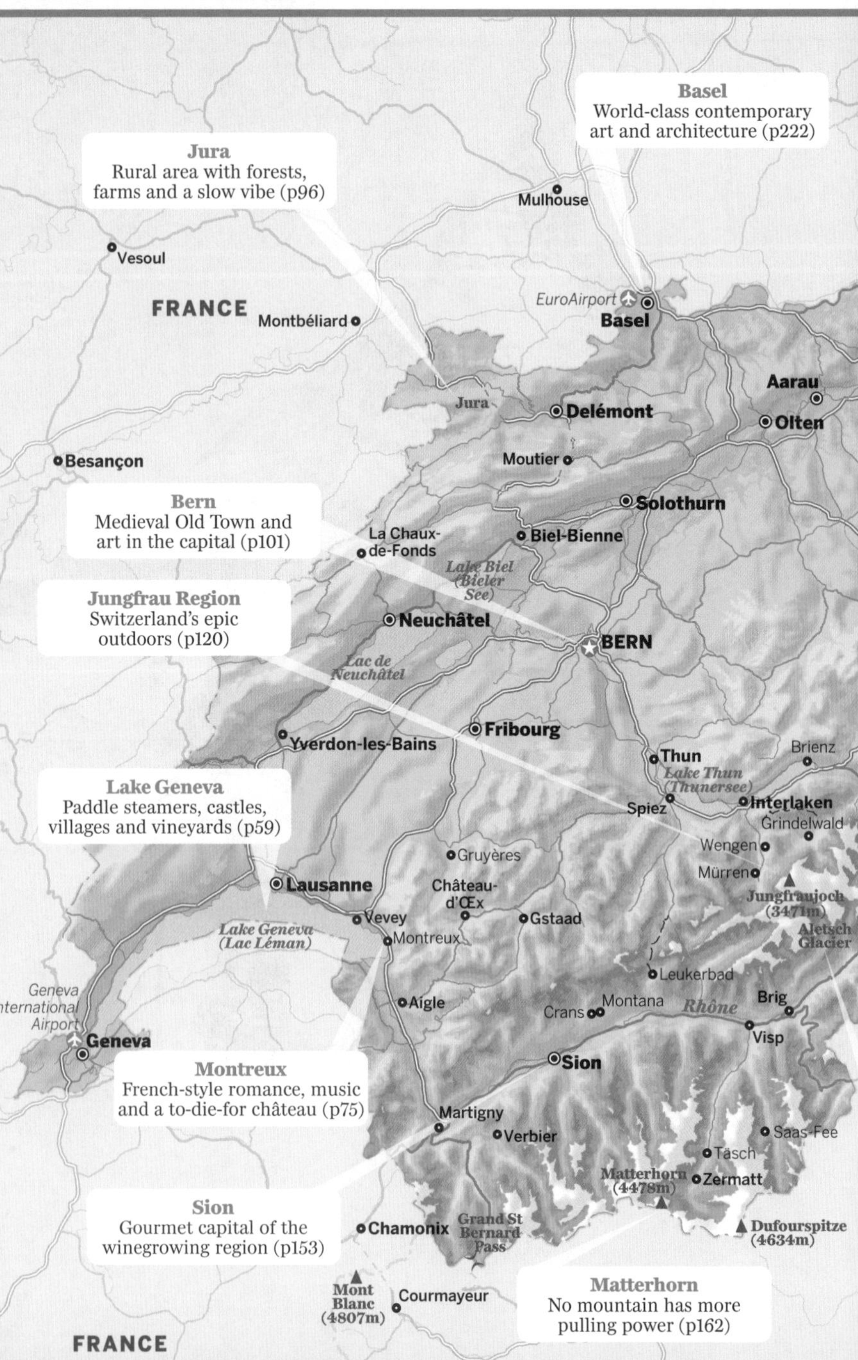

0 — 50 km
0 — 25 miles

**Zürich**
One of Europe's most liveable cities (p234)

**Rheinfall**
Europe's largest waterfall and Rhine cruises (p259)

**Lucerne**
Sparkling vistas and Victorian curiosities (p199)

**Swiss National Park**
Magnificent 'n' mighty, high-altitude national park (p298)

**The Glacier Express**
One of the world's great train journeys (p163)

**Lago di Lugano**
Switzerland's flamboyant, Italian-speaking heart (p187)

**Aletsch Glacier**
Ancient and awe-inspiring 23km-long glacier (p172)

ELEVATION
3000m
2500m
2000m
1500m
1000m
500m
200m
0

GERMANY
AUSTRIA
LIECHTENSTEIN
ITALY
Schaffhausen
Rheinfall
Waldshut
Lake Constance
Konstanz (Constance)
Lake Constance (Bodensee)
Rhine River
Frauenfeld
Winterthur
Baden
Zürich Airport
Zürich
St Gallen
Appenzell
Lake Zürich (Zürichsee)
Rapperswil
Zug
Buchs
VADUZ
Lucerne
Lake Lucerne (Vierwaldstättersee)
Schwyz
Glarus
Landquart
Altdorf
Chur
Klosters
Davos
Scuol
Arosa
Engelberg
Mt Titlis (3239m)
Oberalp Pass
Vorderrhein
Andermatt
Engadine
Swiss National Park
St Gotthard Pass
San Bernardino Pass
St Moritz
Bernina Pass
Valle Maggia
Locarno
Bellinzona
Gravedona
Sondrio
Tirano
Domodossola
Lago di Como
Lugano
Lago di Lugano
Lago Maggiore
Verbania
Como

# Switzerland's Top Experiences

## 1 EPIC MOUNTAINS

Der Berg ruft...The mountain calls. With the Alps rippling across much of the country, Switzerland has serious altitude and, come winter, snow. Insanely beautiful views set spirits soaring, making you want to grab your boots, pop on skis or leap into a bike saddle. Then there are the mountains of myth: fierce peaks punching above 4000m, where rock climbers have for centuries grappled for fame and a foothold in the realms of eternal ice.

## Matterhorn

No mountain has more pulling power than the Matterhorn (4478m), Switzerland's perfect pyramid of a peak. Whether ensnared in mist, dusted with snow, or glimpsed by the first pink light of day, this ferocious fang of a mountain will keep you utterly gripped as you climb, hike or ski in Zermatt. p162

## Eiger, Jungfrau & Mönch

The Jungfrau Region's 'Big Three', Eiger (Ogre), Jungfrau (Virgin) and Mönch (Monk) hit the mountain spot every time, with sky-high hiking trails and slopes, Europe's highest railway station and views of the 23km-long icy swirl of the Aletsch Glacier. p172

Above: View of Mt Eiger (p126) ;
Left: Jungfrau Railway (p127)

## Rigi

Other mountains might beat it for height, but few are as steeped in legend and enshrined in romance as this crag rearing up above shimmering Lake Lucerne. In the 19th century, Turner painted its many moods and Queen Victoria trotted up here on horseback. p207

# 2 ROAD TRIPS

Switzerland might look tiny on paper, but whopping great Alps mean this little nation packs in a lot of vertical. Wherever you go, you're in for one hell of a drive: roads unfurl along the shores of great lakes to glaciers, mountain passes corkscrew up to fairy-tale medieval castles and, on the high roads, every glorious bend makes you want to screech to a halt and yodel in delight.

## Furka Pass

The Alps never leave your rear-view mirror on this astonishingly steep, snaking, stop-the-car-and-grab-the-camera drive (picture below right) from the remote valley of the Goms in Valais to mountain-encrusted Andermatt in Uri. p175

## Gotthard Pass

If it's Alpine highs you're after, the old road over the 2108m (6196ft) Gotthard Pass (pictured above left) enthralls. Buckle up, roll down the window and prepare for a feast of wild, lonely, bleakly beautiful scenery on this serpentine road between Italian-speaking Ticino and German-speaking Uri. p219

## Grand Tour of Switzerland

Wrapping up the entire country is the 1600km (994-mile) Grand Tour of Switzerland (pictured right): an efficiently-signposted lap of the country that strings together 12 Unesco World Heritage Sites and shows off the Alpine nation from its most flattering angles.

# 3 ART & ARCHITECTURE HIGHS

LAURAVR/SHUTTERSTOCK ©

UROŠ MEDVED/SHUTTERSTOCK ©

BENNY MARTY/SHUTTERSTOCK ©

With the mountains never more than a whisper away, Switzerland's landscapes are limelight-stealers, but the country deserves to be better feted for its outstanding cache of art museums and galleries, which can easily rival some of the world's best. Cities like Zürich, Basel, Bern and Geneva are big-hitters, but you'll also unearth wonders in the least-expected places: from rural mansions to revamped factories.

## Zürich

Once the stomping ground of the Dada crowd, Zürich sets the artistic bar high with its cavernous, fine arts-filled Kunsthaus (recently expanded by David Chipperfield Architects) and contemporary arts–focused Kunsthalle. p234

## Bern

Beyond its World Heritage, arcade-woven medieval heart, Bern manages to woo art lovers with Switzerland's oldest fine arts collection, Kunstmuseum, and the city's own wavy Guggenheim, Zentrum Paul Klee. p101

## Basel

Finger-on-the-pulse Basel deliver's Switzerland's biggest international art fair and Pritzker Prize winner–designed architecture. Top billing goes to its Frank Gehry Vitra Design (pictured above) Museum and Renzo Piano–designed Fondation Beyeler. p222

# 4 OFF-PISTE WILDERNESS

Focus solely on the central Alps and you'll be missing a trick. Switzerland saves its most endearing villages, riveting wildernesses and heart-quickening views for those who go the extra mile beyond map and app. From tucked-away national parks where you can hike hut-to-hut at eye level with ibex, to wildflower-freckled meadows you can hole up in a log cabin and live the Swiss dream.

## Jura

Snuggling up to the dark forests of France, the ever-so-peaceful Jura Mountains (pictured below) have their own beauty: lush meadows, ancient woods, rocky outcrops overlooking a trio of lakes, Alpine backdrops and slow-the-pace villages that have remained largely unchanged for centuries. p96

IRIS KURSCHNER/GETTY IMAGES ©

KARL ALLEN LUGMAYER/SHUTTERSTOCK ©

SASKIAACHT/SHUTTERSTOCK ©

## Swiss National Park

Huddled away in the country's southeast, Switzerland's one-and-only national park (picured above left) is a ravishing, nature-gone-mad, trail-laced spectacle of snow-frosted peaks, waterfalls, canyons and Alpine wildlife - all barely touched by human hand. p298

## Appenzell

Switzerland's rural, folksy heart beats at its loudest in the Appenzell region, sidling up to Liechtenstein in the northeast. It's a terrifically unsung area, with rolling dairy country giving way to lavishly frescoed towns. p267

Above right: Apenzell's historic quarter

# 5 PURE INDULGENCE

Few nations are as downright indulgent as the Swiss. Here chocolate is considered an essential part of the daily diet (the Swiss scoff 9.9kg per capita each year), cheese comes in a world of varieties - holey Emmental, nutty Gruyères, stinky Appenzeller, and hot and bubbling fondue. Swiss wine is having a moment, too - enjoy it in situ as precious little travels beyond these borders.

## Lavaux

Vineyards stagger down steeply terraced hillsides to brilliant-blue Lake Geneva (pictured below right) in the Unesco-listed Lavaux, cultivating wine since medieval times. Taste flinty Chasselas whites and fruity Pinot Noir reds with a dégustation (tasting). p71

OF BARMALINI/SHUTTERSTOCK ©

## Emmental

How does Swiss cheese get its holes? Find out with a spin of this deliciously mellow, rural, cow-grazed region. Buy from the farm door or see cheese in the making at the Emmentaler Schaukäserei. p110

## Maison Cailler

Creamy, melt-in-your-mouth Swiss chocolate is everywhere today, but François-Louis Cailler (1796-1852) first perfected the art. Create the chocolate bar of your dreams during a hands-on workshop at this chocolate factory in Broc. p87

# 6 RAILWAY ROMANCE

EVA BOCEK/SHUTTERSTOCK ©

WESTEND61/GETTY IMAGES ©

YURI TURKOV/SHUTTERSTOCK ©

You've got to hand it to the Swiss, their trains are the dream: efficient, slickly modern, eco-friendly and with views that keep you glued to the window for the entire duration of the journey – come rain or shine, summer or winter. The famous panorama trains (with the big windows) are just tip-of-the-iceberg stuff: regular scheduled services can be just as enjoyable and significantly less expensive.

## Glacier Express

The wow never leaves your lips on this legendary Alpine train journey between Zermatt and St Moritz. The Brig–Zermatt Alpine leg makes for pretty powerful viewing, as does the area between Disentis/Mustér and Brig. p163

Above: Landwasser Viaduct (p163)

## Bernina Express

This beauty strides through 55 tunnels and over 196 bridges as it travels between Engadine one-way from Chur to Tirano in four hours, hitting its high point at 2253m above sea level. p277

## Gotthard Panorama Express

This rail-boat combo starts with a wonderful 2½-hour cruise across Lake Lucerne to Flüelen, where a train winds its way through ravines and past mountains to Bellinzona or Lugano. p335

# 7 CASTLES & ABBEYS

Castles and abbeys entice at every corner in Switzerland. Perching on hilltops, clinging to crags and hugging lake shores, they are often in fantasy settings. With great Benedictine abbeys that gave Switzerland a foot up the celestial ladder in the Middle Ages and Gothic castles that touched the likes of Turner, Lord Byron and Mary Shelley, Switzerland has history, heritage and views that inspire towards the lyrical and the profound.

CGE2010/SHUTTERSTOCK ©

KEITMA/SHUTTERSTOCK ©

## Château de Chillon

Château de Chillon (pictured above top) is Switzerland's medieval pin-up castle, with its moat, double ramparts, riot of turrets and towers and knockout views of Lake Geneva and the French Alps. p77

## Bellinzona

With a trio of medieval fortresses rising high and the Alps rearing beyond, Bellinzona, capital of Ticino, is an instant heart-stealer. Kick off your castle crawl at Castelgrande (pictured above left). p178

## Stiftsbibliothek St Gallen

Religious or not, you can't help but heaven gaze and fall silent upon entering St Gallen's rococo feast of an abbey library (above), erstwhile the beating heart of one of Europe's finest Benedictine monasteries. p264

# 8 OUTDOOR THRILLS

OLEG V ZINCHENKO/SHUTTERSTOCK ©

IMAGNO/GETTY IMAGES ©

PETE SEAWARD/LONELY PLANET ©

One look at Switzerland's skip-inducing meadows, cloud-shredding peaks, rainbow-kissed falls, raging rivers, exquisitely blue lakes and glaciers will have you itching to hit trail, slope, ice, water or rock. The Alps have the adventure edge, naturally, with hiking, skiing, mountaineering and extreme sports galore. But you don't have to go hardcore: more gentle paths unspool along lake shores and through vineyards. And even most cities have a local peak to climb and river to swim.

## Aletsch Glacier

One of the world's natural marvels, this 23km-long, five-lane highway of ice (below left) makes your heart sing, especially when hiking alongside its crevasses or skiing above the glacier in Bettmeralp. p172

## Interlaken

With 1001 ingenious ways to make you scream and get your Alpine groove on, Interlaken is the world's second biggest adventure hub. Ice climb, white-water raft, go canyoning or skydiving in the face of Eiger (top left). p115

## Basel Rhine Swim

Basel chills out with wild swims in the Rhine. Hire a Wickelfisch (a fish-shaped waterproof bag) , strip off and go with the flow, floating downstream past the city's landmarks. p226

# Need to Know

For more information, see Survival Guide (p325)

### Currency
Swiss franc (official abbreviation CHF, also Sfr)

### Languages
German, French, Italian, Romansch

### Visas
Generally not required for stays of up to 90 days. Some non-European citizens require a Schengen Visa.

### Money
ATMs are at every airport, most train stations and on every second street corner in towns and cities; Visa, MasterCard and Amex widely accepted.

### Mobile Phones
Most mobile phones brought from overseas will function in Switzerland; check with your provider about costs. Prepaid local SIM cards are widely available.

### Time
Central European Time (GMT/UTC plus one hour)

## When to Go

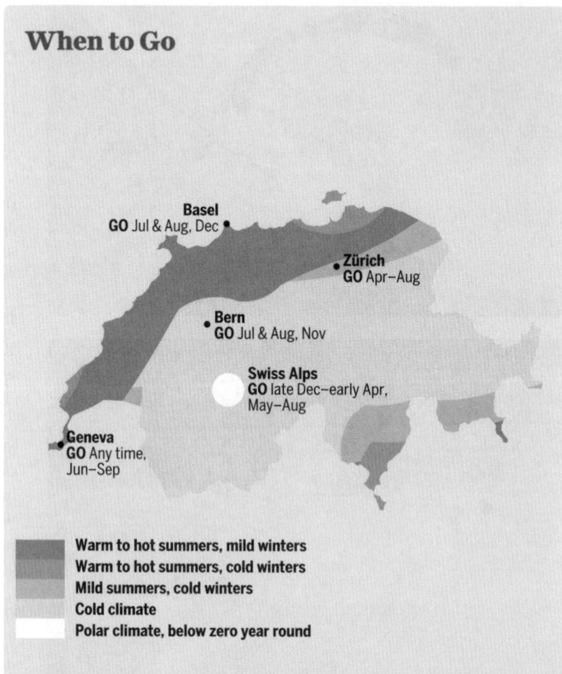


### High Season
(Jul, Aug & Dec–Apr)

- In July and August walkers and cyclists hit high-altitude trails.
- Christmas and New Year see serious snow-sports action on the slopes.
- Late December to early April is high season in ski resorts.

### Shoulder
(Apr–Jun & Sep)

- Look for accommodation deals in ski resorts and traveller hotspots.
- Spring is idyllic, with warm temperatures, flowers and local produce.
- Watch the grape harvest in autumn.

### Low Season
(Oct–Mar)

- Mountain resorts go into snooze mode from mid-October to early December.
- Prices are up to 50% lower than in high season.
- Sights and restaurants are open fewer days and shorter hours.

## Useful Websites

**My Switzerland** (www.myswitzerland.com) Swiss tourism.

**ch.ch** (www.ch.ch) Swiss authorities online.

**Swiss Info** (www.swissinfo.ch) Swiss news and current affairs.

**Lonely Planet** (www.lonelyplanet.com/switzerland) Destination information, hotel bookings, traveller forum and more.

**SBB** (www.sbb.ch) Swiss Federal Railways.

## Important Numbers

Swiss telephone numbers start with an area code that must be dialled every time, even when making local calls.

| | |
|---|---|
| **Switzerland's country code** | ☎41 |
| **International access code** | ☎00 |
| **Police** | ☎117 |
| **Ambulance** | ☎144 |
| **Swiss Mountain Rescue** | ☎1414 |

## Exchange Rates

| | | |
|---|---|---|
| **Australia** | A$1 | Sfr0.73 |
| **Canada** | C$1 | Sfr0.73 |
| **euro zone** | €1 | Sfr1.09 |
| **Japan** | ¥100 | Sfr0.88 |
| **UK** | UK£1 | Sfr1.23 |
| **US** | US$1 | Sfr0.97 |

For current exchange rates, see www.xe.com.

## Daily Costs

### Budget: Less than Sfr200

- Dorm bed: Sfr30–60
- Double room in budget hotel: from Sfr100
- Lunch out and self-catering after dark: from Sfr25

### Midrange: Sfr200–300

- Double room in two- or three-star hotel: from Sfr200 (Sfr150 at weekends)
- Dish of the day *(tagesteller, plat du jour, piatto del giorno)* or fixed two-course menu: Sfr40–70

### Top End: More than Sfr300

- Double room in four- or five-star hotel: from Sfr350 (Sfr250 at weekends)
- Three-course dinner in upmarket restaurant: from Sfr100

## Opening Hours

Each Swiss canton currently decides how long shops and businesses can stay open. With the exception of convenience stores at 24-hour service stations and shops at airports and train stations, businesses shut completely on Sunday. High-season opening hours appear in listings for sights and attractions; hours are almost always shorter during low season.

**Banks** 8.30am–4.30pm Monday to Friday

**Restaurants** noon–2.30pm and 6pm–9.30pm; most close one or two days per week

**Shops** 10am–6pm Monday to Friday, to 4pm Saturday

**Museums** 10am–5pm, many close Monday and stay open late Thursday

## Arriving in Switzerland

**Zürich Airport** (ZRH; www.zurich-airport.com) Up to nine SBB trains run hourly to Hauptbahnhof from 5am to midnight; taxis cost around Sfr60 to the centre; during the winter ski season, coaches run to Davos and other key resorts.

**Geneva Airport** (GVA; www.gva.ch) SBB trains run at least every 10 minutes to Gare de Cornavin; taxis charge Sfr35 to Sfr50 to the centre; in winter coaches run to Verbier, Saas Fee, Crans-Montana and ski resorts in neighbouring France.

## Getting Around

Switzerland's fully integrated public-transport system is among the world's most efficient. However, travel is expensive and visitors planning to use inter-city routes should consider investing in a Swiss travel pass. Timetables often refer to *Werktags* (work days), which means Monday to Saturday, unless there is the qualification *ausser Samstag* (except Saturday). For timetables and tickets, head to www.sbb.ch.

**Bicycle** Switzerland is well equipped for cyclists. Many cities have free-bike-hire schemes. Bicycle and e-bike rental is usually available at stations.

**Bus** Filling the gaps in more remote areas, Switzerland's postbus service is synchronised with train arrivals.

**Car** Handy for hard-to-reach regions where public transport is minimal.

**Train** Swiss trains run like a dream. Numerous discount-giving travel cards and tickets are available.

For much more on **getting around**, see p334

# What's New

The Green Party storming ahead in elections, floating solar farms and minimal-impact skiing – the Swiss have always had an eye on the eco ball, but now they are seriously upping their sustainable game. And since voting yes for same-sex marriage in 2021, the country has its sights set on a more egalitarian, liberal future.

## Million Stars Hotel

Switzerland Tourism shines bright with Million Stars Hotel, a repertoire of imaginative open-air sleeps in the country's remotest reaches. From a converted gondola in Alpine Engelberg to an alfresco bed under an apple tree in Thurgau and a pine-clad 'beehive' with views of Eiger's mile-high North Face, these clever, comfortable glamps all have one thing in common – they offer an unrestricted view of starry night skies.

## Eiger Express

Reaching Jungfraujoch (3463m; p127) is now a breeze since the recent launch of the new fast-track, tri-cable Eiger Express gondola, which has slashed journey times to Europe's highest train station. The 15-minute ride from Grindelwald to Eigergletscher station gets so close to the mountain's fierce north face, it feels like you're going to slam right into it.

## Plateforme 10

Lausanne is storming ahead culturally since the recent completion of its Plateforme 10 arts district (p66). Former train sheds have been revamped as a forward-thinking gallery space, harbouring the Musée Cantonal des Beaux-Arts (Cantonal Fine Arts Museum or MCBA), the Musée de l'Elysée (Cantonal Museum of Photography) and the MUDAC (Museum of Contemporary Design and Applied Arts), as well as a library, restaurants and event spaces.

## Subspirit

With its fjord-like twists and turns and mountain backdrop, Lake Lucerne always looks extraordinary. But what lies above the water is only half the story. Now you can journey to depths of 100m and explore mysterious wrecks with Switzerland's only passenger **submarine** (www.subspirit.ch), equipped with state-of-the-art technology and offering trips for up to three lucky, intrepid-minded people.

## Tell Trail

This new long-distance trail (www.luzern.com/en/things-to-do/summer-hiking/hiking/tell-trail/) from Altdorf to Brienzer Rothorn follows in the footsteps of the nation's freedom-loving, apple-shooting rebel hero, William Tell. Heading through flower-flecked meadows and sublimely pretty villages beading the shores of Lake Lucerne and cresting six mountains, this eight-day, 156km yomp takes a deep dive into Central Switzerland's one-of-a-kind history, heritage and landscapes.

## Kunsthaus Extension

Zürich now rivals Basel in the art stakes since the 2021 opening of the Kunsthaus Extension (p236), bearing the boldly geometric hallmark of David Chipperfield Architects Berlin. With a strong focus on creatively interpreted urban space and outdoor sculpture, the gallery zooms in on 1960s and modernist art. The new central hall (inspired by Tate Modern's Turbine Hall) hosts events and rotating exhibitions, while the café showcases the largest-surviving work by Max Ernst.

## Kumme Gondola

The ski resort of Zermatt, where the mighty fang of the Matterhorn looms large, is having its moment in the limelight thanks to the recent launch of Switzerland's first autonomous, 10-person gondola, which runs entirely without staff as it whizzes up to Rothorn. Featuring cutting-edge technology, the minimal-impact lift is environmentally sound, too, designed in harmony with its Alpine surrounds.

## Hotel Noël

Everyone loves an advent calendar, but now Zürich has a new festive surprise. **Hotel Noël** (www.noelzurich.com/en), spotlights 10 rooms at 10 different hotels across the city during the Christmas period. Graphic designers, storytellers, photographers, concept artists and illustrators have pooled their creativity to come up with out-of-the-ordinary designs for lucky visitors to stay in.

## Senda dil Dragun

At eye level with the birds and squirrels, the new 1.5km **Senda dil Dragun** (Way of the Dragon; www.flimslaax.com) in the resort of Laax in Graubünden is the world's longest treetop walk. Snaking through the spruce and larch canopy, the trail also offers snapshot views of the Alps. A spiral slide, towers and lookout platforms open up the forest in a playful way.

## Lindt Home of Chocolate

Chocolate lovers are in for an enormous treat at Lindt's new museum (www.lindt-home-of-chocolate.com/en) near Zürich. This architect-designed, white-and-gold wrapped wonder hits the sweet spot with tours dunking you into Swiss chocolate history, master chocolatier workshops and (the clincher) the world's biggest chocolate fountain, where 1500 litres of real chocolate pour down from a height of 9.3 metres at a speed of one kilo per second.

## What's Happening in Switzerland

Sustainability is the hot topic of the moment. Switzerland Tourism's environmentally game-changing campaign Swisstainability provides a platform where travellers can plan eco-friendly holidays and carbon offset at the touch of a button.

In 2021, the world's first high-altitude floating solar farm opened in the Swiss Alps, setting a precedent for more to come. Swiss trains draw 90% of their energy from hydropower (they're aiming for 100% by 2025). Ski resorts are also cleaning up their act: Zermatt with plastic roads, the Jungfrau Region with hybrid cable cars, and Laax on target to become the world's first self-sufficient Alpine resort. Winters traditionally meant downhill skiing, but now the emphasis is shifting to off-piste activities like ski touring, ice climbing, fishing and swimming, cross-country and snowshoeing.

Same-sex marriage got the Swiss vote in 2021, and Switzerland Tourism has launched 100% Women, which encourages women into tougher outdoor sports like mountaineering, which involved a peak challenge of all 48 of Switzerland's 4000m peaks in 2021.

### LISTEN, WATCH & FOLLOW

For inspiration and up-to-date news, visit www.lonelyplanet.com/switzerland.

**My Switzerland** (www.myswitzerland.com) Switzerland Tourism's up-to-the-minute site is a terrific first port-of-call for planning a trip.

**Newly Swissed** (www.newlyswissed.com) On-the-ball blog covering culture, design, food and events.

**Schweiz Mobile** (www.schweizmobil.ch) SwitzerlandMobility's ultra-handy resource for getting around the country on foot or skates, by bike or canoe.

**SWI** (www.swissinfo.ch) The latest Switzerland news, opinions, podcasts and videos in 10 languages.

**Time Out Switzerland** (www.timeout.com/switzerland/blog) City guides, news and the inside scoop on arts, shopping, restaurants, music and nightlife.

### FAST FACTS

**Food trend:** insect-based food

**Number of peaks above 3000m:** 437

**Annual consumption of chocolate:** 9.9kg per capita

**Population:** 8.7 million

# Month by Month

**TOP EVENTS**

**Lucerne Festival**, April

**Montreux Jazz**, July

**Swiss National Day**, 1 August

**Zürich Street Parade**, August

**L'Escalade**, December

## January

**The winter cold empties towns of tourists, but in the Alps the ski season is in full swing. Glitzy celebrity station, lost Alpine village – Switzerland has a resort for every mood.**

### Harder Potschete

What a devilish day it is on 2 January in Interlaken when warty, ogre-like *Potschen* run around town causing folkloric mischief. The party ends on a high with cockle-warming drinks, upbeat folk music and merrymaking. (p117)

### Vogel Gryff

An old folkloric celebration, this street party sees a larger-than-life savage, griffin and lion chase away winter in Basel with a drum dance on a city bridge. The savage sails into town on a raft afloat on the Rhine. (p226)

### World Snow Festival

Grindelwald glitters with astonishing ice sculptures during this six-day festival in late January. Sculptors from across the globe gather to flaunt their ice-carving skills, with everything from giant animals to abstract creations. (p122)

## February

**Crisp, cold weather in the mountains translates to ski season in top gear. Families mob resorts during the February school holidays and accommodation is at its priciest.**

### Fasnacht

Never dare call the Swiss goody two-shoes again: pre-Lenten parades, costumes, music and all the fun of the fair sweep through Catholic cantons during Fasnacht (Carnival). Catch the party – stark raving bonkers – in Lucerne or Basel. (p226)

## March

**The tail end of the ski season stays busy thanks to temperatures that no longer turn lips blue and, depending on the year, Easter holidays.**

### Engadine Ski Marathon

Watching 11,000 cross-country skiers warming up to the rousing sound of 'Chariots of Fire' is unforgettable – as is, no doubt, the iconic 42km cross-country marathon for the athletes who ski across frozen lakes and through pine forests and picture-perfect snow scenes in the Engadine.

## April

**Spring, with its pretty, flower-strewn meadows, suddenly pops into that magnificent Alpine vista and the first fair-weather walkers arrive.**

### Lucerne Festival

Easter ushers in this world-class music festival, with chamber orchestras, pianists and other musicians from all corners of the globe performing in Lucerne. (p202)

## June

**As the weather heats up, so Switzerland's events calendar increases the pace with a bevy of fabulous arts**

**Top**: Fasnacht Festival, Lucerne (p226).

**Bottom**: Montreux Jazz (p76)

**festivals. In the mountains, chalet hotels start to emerge from hibernation to welcome early-summer hikers.**

### Pride

Zürich sings a rainbow at this huge LGBTIQ+ street festival. Expect a high-spirited roster of parties, parades, concerts, shows and events. (p240)

### St Galler Festspiele

It's apt that Switzerland's 'writing room of Europe', aka St Gallen, should play host to this wonderful two-week opera season. The curtain rises in late June and performances spill into July. (p265)

## July

**The month of music: days are hot and sun-filled, and lake shores and Alpine meadows double as perfect summer stages for Swiss yodellers, alpenhorn players and flag throwers.**

### Montreux Jazz

A fortnight of jazz, pop and rock in early July is reason enough to slot Montreux Jazz into your itinerary. Some concerts are free, some ticketed, and dozens are staged alfresco with lake views from heaven. (p76)

### Paléo

A Lake Geneva goodie, this six-day open-air world-music extravaganza – a 1970s child – is billed as the king of summer music fests. Nyon in late July are the details to put in the diary. (p70)

### Verbier Festival

Verbier's high-profile classical-music festival lasts for two weeks from July to early August. There are plenty of free events during the fringe Festival Off, alongside the official fest. (p151)

## August

**It's hot and cloudless, and the sun-baked Alps buzz with hikers, bikers and families on holiday – a pedalo on Lake Geneva is a cool spot to watch fireworks on 1 August, Switzerland's national day.**

### Swiss National Day

Fireworks light up lakes, mountains, towns and cities countrywide on this national holiday celebrating Switzerland's very creation. Some of the most impressive illuminations light up the Rheinfall. (p65)

### Schwingen

This high-entertainment festival in Davos sees thick-set men with invariably large tummies battle it out in sawdust for the title of *Schwingen* (Swiss Alpine wrestling) champion. (p290)

### Street Parade

Mid-August brings with it Europe's largest street party in the form of Zürich's famous Street Parade, around since 1992. (p240)

## September

**Golden autumn days and grape harvests make this a great month for backcountry rambles. In the Alps, the cows come home in spectacular style.**

### La Désalpe de Charmey

The cows descend from their summer grazing pastures in folksy style, adorned with elaborate floral headdresses and accompanied by costumed locals. (p88)

## October

**As the last sun-plump grapes are harvested and the first bottles of new wine are cracked open, sweet chestnuts drop from dew-strung trees. It's nippy now, especially at altitude, where the first snow closes mountain passes.**

### Foire du Valais

Cows battle for the title of bovine queen on the last day of the cow-fighting season at this 10-day regional fair in Martigny in the lower Valais. Everyone rocks up for it, and it's a great excuse to drink and feast. (p145)

## December

**Days are short and it's cold everywhere. But there are Christmas markets and festive celebrations, not to mention the first winter Alpine skiing from mid-December on.**

### L'Escalade

Torch-lit processions in the Old Town, fires, a run around town for kids and adults alike, and some serious chocolate-cauldron smashing and scoffing make Geneva's biggest festival on 11 December a riot of fun. (p50)

# Itineraries

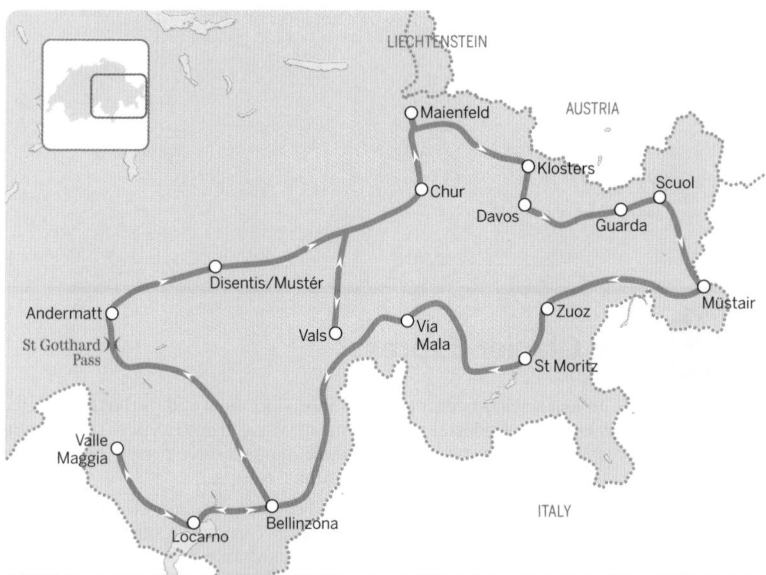

## Lost in Graubünden & Ticino

Swinging through the rugged Alpine landscapes of Graubünden and the sunnier climes and lakeside towns of Italian-speaking Ticino, this circular route of Switzerland's southeast can be picked up at any point.

From **Chur**, head north for a detour to pretty **Maienfeld** and its vineyards. Spin east to ski queens **Klosters** and **Davos**, then surge into the Engadine Valley, with pretty towns like **Guarda** and **Scuol** (and its tempting thermal baths). The road then ribbons southeast to the Austrian border, which you cross to head south through a slice of Austria and Italy before veering back into Switzerland to contemplate frescos at **Müstair**. Continue southwest through picture-postcard **Zuoz** to chic **St Moritz**. Climb the Julier Pass mountain road and drop down the **Via Mala** gorges.

The southbound road crosses into Ticino and **Bellinzona**. Steam on past lakeside **Locarno** and up the enchanting **Valle Maggia**. Backtracking to Bellinzona, the main route takes you along the Valle Leventina before crossing the **St Gotthard Pass** to **Andermatt**. Nip into the monastery of **Disentis/Mustér** before plunging into designer spa waters in highly recommended **Vals**, the last stop before you arrive back in Chur.

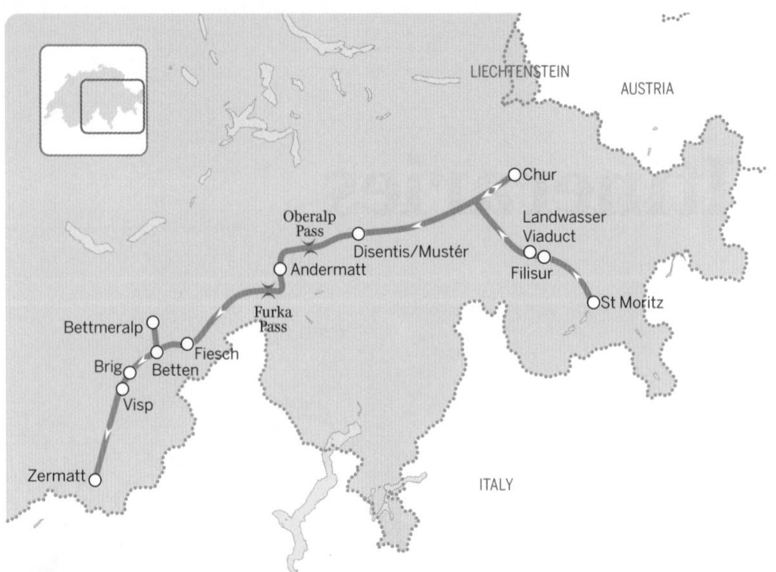

## The Glacier Express

This 290km train journey has been a traveller must since 1930 and the birth of winter tourism in the Swiss Alps. Undertake it any time of year – in one relentless eight-hour stretch or, perhaps more enjoyably, as several sweet nuggets interspersed with overnight stays in some of Switzerland's most glamorous Alpine resorts.

This trip is spectacular in either direction, but boarding the cherry-red train in **St Moritz** (grab a seat on the left, or southern, side of the carriage) in the Upper Engadine Valley makes for a gradual build-up to the journey's inevitable climax: the iconic Matterhorn. About an hour from St Moritz, just after **Filisur**, the narrow-gauge train plunges dramatically out of a tunnel onto the six dark limestone arches of the emblematic **Landwasser Viaduct** (1901–02), built 65m above the Landwasser River in a considerate, photographer-friendly curve. Switzerland's oldest city and Graubünden's capital, **Chur**, about 2½ hours from St Moritz, makes a lovely overnight stop with its quaint old town, historic hotels and busy cafe and bar scene.

From Chur the track snakes along the Rhine Valley, through the spectacular Rhine Gorge (Ruinaulta in Romansch) with its bizarre limestone formations – the gorge is known as Switzerland's Grand Canyon. Next it's a gradual climb to **Disentis/Mustér**, home to an 18th-century Benedictine monastery, and then a stiff ascent to the **Oberalp Pass** (2044m), the literal high point of the journey, snow covered from November to April. Next stop is ski resort **Andermatt**, another perfect place to stretch cramped legs and overnight. The roller-coaster journey continues with a descent then a steady climb to the **Furka Pass**, enabled by Switzerland's highest Alpine tunnel (and, at 15.4km, the longest of the 91 tunnels on this journey). Next port of call is **Betten**, cable-car station for the drop-dead gorgeous, car-free village and ski resort of **Bettmeralp**. Hop off here or in neighbouring **Fiesch** and spend a day hiking or skiing and staring open-mouthed at the gargantuan icy tongue of the Aletsch Glacier.

From here the Glacier Express swings southwest along the Rhône Valley into Valais, stopping at **Brig**, its eclectic *schloss* (castle) topped with exotic onion domes; wine-producing **Visp**; and – drum roll – final destination **Zermatt**, where that first glimpse of the Matterhorn makes a fitting finale.

## Switzerland's Greatest Hits

This is the big one, bringing you the best of Switzerland in one epic, month-long, circular tour – from lakes to vineyards, mountains to meringues.

Start in **Geneva** with its vibrant museums and signature pencil fountain. Then take the slow road east along the southern shore of the lake in France – stop for lunch in **Yvoire** – or the fast road (A1) shadowing the Swiss northern shore (possible lunch stops are **Lausanne**, **Vevey** or **Montreux**). The next port of call is art-rich **Martigny** and châteaux-crowned **Sion**, worth lingering in for its wealth of vineyards, wines and memorable Valaisian dining. Continue east along the Rhône Valley, nipping up to **Leukerbad** to drift in thermal waters beneath soaring mountain peaks. In **Visp**, head south to obsessively stare at the iconic Matterhorn from the hip streets, slopes and trails of stylish, car-free **Zermatt**.

In the second week, get a taste of the Glacier Express with a train trip to Oberwald. Stop off in **Betten** for a cable-car side trip up to picture-book **Bettmeralp**, with its car-free streets and amazing vistas of the 23km-long Aletsch Glacier from atop Bettmerhorn. From **Oberwald**, drive north over the Grimsel Pass (2165m) to **Meiringen** (eat meringues!) and west into the magnificent Jungfrau Region with its once-in-a-lifetime train journey up to Europe's highest station; base yourself in **Interlaken** or **Grindelwald**. If you have a penchant for Italian passion rather than hardcore Alpine extremes, stay on the *Glacier Express* as far as **Andermatt** instead, then motor south into Italianate Ticino for shimmering lake life in the glitzy and gorgeous towns of **Lugano** and **Locarno**.

The third week unveils a trip north to **Lucerne**, where you can cruise on a boat to lovely Lake Lucerne resorts like **Weggis** and **Brunnen**. Feast on *Kirschtorte* (cherry cake) in rich medieval **Zug**, then hit big-city **Zürich** to the north for a taste of urban Switzerland at its best (five days in all). Should you fancy some border-hopping, **Vaduz**, the tiny capital of tiny Liechtenstein, is very close by. Unesco-listed **St Gallen** is the next stop, from where you can spend a week lapping up Switzerland's north.

Ending up in the Jura, it's a quick and easy flit south to **Neuchâtel** on the northern shore of Lac de Neuchâtel, from where the motorway speeds to Lausanne on Lake Geneva and, eventually, Geneva.

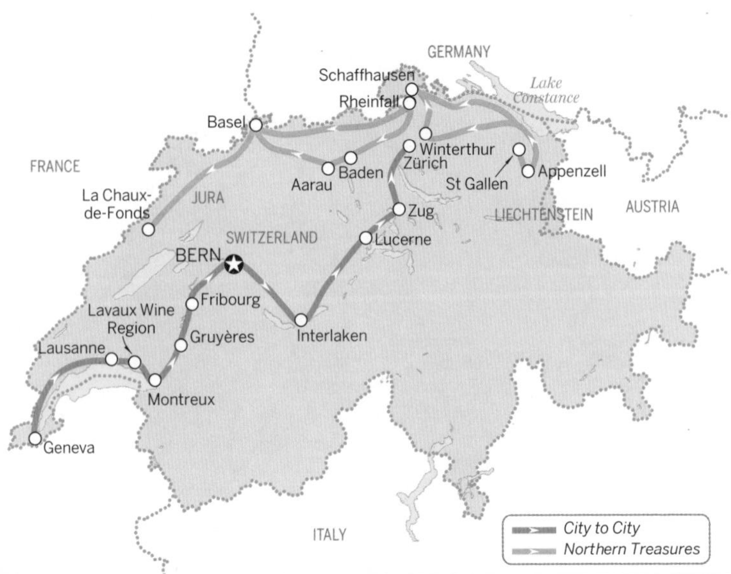

## City to City

This Geneva-to-Zürich, 385km trip is for urbanites keen to mix metropolitan fire with small-town charm. It's eminently doable by car or public transport. Fly into one city and out of the other, or zip back to point A by train in 2¾ hours.

Landing in **Geneva**, explore Switzerland's most cosmopolitan big city, then trundle along the shore of Europe's largest Alpine lake to bustling **Lausanne**, a hilly lakeside town with a lively bar and cafe scene and a sweet old town. Continue along the same glorious route, aptly dubbed the Swiss Riviera, to the **Lavaux wine region** and beyond, past lakeside Château de Chinon, to **Montreux**. Head north next to **Gruyères**, land of chateaux, cheese, cream and pearly white meringues. Further north, you arrive in **Fribourg** on the French–German language frontier – cross it to pretty Swiss capital **Bern**. Later, drop down to the lakeside towns around **Interlaken** (there are plenty of top skiing, hiking and other outdoor options around here), then swing north to another bewitching lake lady, **Lucerne**. Rolling onwards, via tycoon magnet **Zug**, to Switzerland's most hip 'n' happening city, **Zürich**, the atmosphere changes completely.

## Northern Treasures

Artistic, architectural and natural wonders are in the spotlight on this week-long spin through the country's oft-overlooked north.

In spite of all its natural wonders, Switzerland boasts overwhelming human-made beauty too, and there's no finer spot to appreciate this than in **St Gallen**, the seat of a grand abbey and church complex safeguarding one of the world's oldest libraries (hence its privileged Unesco World Heritage Site status). Say cheese in **Appenzell**, a 50-minute journey from St Gallen on a narrow-gauge railway, then bear west along the southern shore of Lake Constance (with great summer outdoor action) or to **Winterthur** (with art museums and a kid-friendly science centre). Both routes end up in **Schaffhausen**, a quaint medieval town that could easily be German. Don't miss standing in the middle of **Rheinfall**, Europe's largest waterfall.

Next, continue further west to art-rich **Basel**, either direct or via a pretty southwestern detour through **Baden** and **Aarau**. From Basel, it's an easy drive west again into the depths of Switzerland's unexplored Jura. Push west to **La Chaux-de-Fonds** to discover several early works by architect Le Corbusier, who was born here.

Climbing a rock face over Aletsch Glacier (p172), Valais

## Plan Your Trip

# Switzerland Outdoors

In a country where a half-day hike over a 2500m mountain pass is a Sunday stroll and three-year-olds ski rings around you, it would be an understatement to call the Swiss 'sporty'. They're hyperactive. Why? Just look at their phenomenal backyard, with colossal peaks, raging rivers and slopes that beg outdoor adventure.

## Best Outdoor Adventures

### Best Skiing

**St Moritz** (p294) Excellent varied terrain, a whopping 350km of pistes, glacier descents and freeride opportunities.

### Best Hiking

**Faulhornweg** (p124) A classic high-Alpine hike, with photogenic views of the glacier-capped Jungfrau massif and Lakes Thun and Brienz.

### Best Climbing

**Zermatt** (p162) A holy grail of mountaineering where rock climbers can get to grips with the 4000ers and measure up to the Matterhorn.

### Best Rafting

**Swissraft** (p283) Roll along the fast-flowing Vorderrhein and past bizarre limestone formations in the Rhine Gorge.

### Best Mountain Biking

**Klosters & Davos** (p287 & p289) Freeride heaven with 600km of mountain-bike tracks, including some challenging descents and single tracks.

## Planning Your Outdoor Experience

Your outdoor experiences in Switzerland are far more likely to run smoothly with a little planning. Bear in mind that you'll need to book hiking huts well in advance (particularly during the peak summer months). Or pick a central base and plan day hikes from there. Other activities in popular adventure destinations also get booked up well ahead, so arrange these before you go to avoid disappointment. You can often beat the queues and save money by purchasing ski passes and organising ski hire online.

### When to Go

Alpine weather is notoriously fickle. Even in August it can feel like four seasons in a day, with sun, fog, storms and snow; so check the forecast on www.meteoschweiz.ch before you head out.

**December to April** The slopes buzz with skiers and boarders until Easter. Prices skyrocket during school holidays.

**May and June** Crowds are thin and the weather is often fine. Snow patches linger above 2000m. Many huts remain closed and mountain transport is limited.

**July and August** A conga line of high-altitude hikers and cyclists makes its way through the Swiss Alps. All lifts and mountain huts are open (book ahead).

**September to early October** Pot luck: can be delightful or drab. Accommodation prices drop, as do the crowds, but many hotels and lifts close.

**Mid-October to November** Days get shorter and the weather is unpredictable. Expect rain, fog and snow above 1500m. Most resorts go into hibernation.

## Skiing & Snowboarding

In a land where every 10-person, 50-cow hamlet has a ski lift, the question is not where you can ski but how. Ritzy or remote, party mad or picture perfect, virgin or veteran, black run or blue – whatever your taste and ability, Switzerland has a resort to suit.

### Ski Run Classifications

Ski runs are colour coded according to difficulty:

**Blue** Easy, well-groomed runs that are suitable for beginners.

**Red** Intermediate runs that are groomed but often steeper and narrower than blue runs.

**Black** For expert skiers with polished technique and skills. They are mostly steep and not always groomed, and they may have moguls and vertical drops.

### Safety on the Slopes

➡ Avalanche warnings should be heeded and local advice sought before detouring from prepared runs.

- Never go off-piste alone. Take an avalanche pole, a transceiver or a shovel and, most importantly, a professional guide.
- Check the day's avalanche bulletin online at www.slf.ch or by calling 187.
- The sun in the Alps is intensified by snow glare. Wear ski goggles and high-factor sunscreen.
- Layers help you adapt to the constant change in body temperature. Your head, wrists and knees should be protected.
- Black run looks tempting? Make sure you're properly insured first; sky-high mountain-rescue and medical costs can add insult to injury.

## Passes, Hire & Tuition

Yes, Switzerland is expensive and no, skiing is not an exception. That said, costs can be cut by avoiding school-holiday times and choosing low-key villages over upscale resorts. Ski passes are a hefty chunk out of your budget and will set you back around Sfr70 per day or Sfr350 for six days. Factor in around Sfr40 to Sfr70 per day for ski hire and Sfr20 for boot hire, which can be reserved online at www.intersportrent.com. Equipment for kids is roughly half price.

All major resorts have ski schools, with half-day group lessons typically costing Sfr50 to Sfr80. **Schweizer Skischule** (www.swiss-ski-school.ch) has a clickable map of 170 ski schools across the country.

### TOP SLOPES FOR...

**Snowboarding** Saas Fee, Laax or Davos.

**Families** Arosa, Lenzerheide, Bettmeralp or Klosters.

**Off-piste** Engelberg, Andermatt, Verbier or Davos.

**Glacier skiing** Glacier 3000 near Gstaad, Mt Titlis in Engelberg or Saas Fee.

**Scenic skiing** Zermatt or Männlichen.

**Scary-as-hell descents** The Swiss Wall in Champéry or the Inferno from Schilthorn to Lauterbrunnen.

**Cross-country skiing** Davos, Arosa or Kandersteg.

**Non-skiers** Gstaad or Grindelwald.

Skiing near the Matterhorn (p162), Zermatt

A good deal for keen skiers is the **Magic Pass** (www.magicpass.ch; adult/child Sfr1299/799), which aims to attract more skiers to the country's lesser-known resorts. It covers 25 resorts and is valid for an entire winter season (November to April). Promotional rates are sometimes available online.

## Regions

Switzerland has scores of fantastic resorts – the following ski regions are just a glimpse of what is up in the Alps.

### Graubünden

Rugged Graubünden has some truly legendary slopes. First up is super-chic St Moritz (p294), with 350km of groomed slopes, glacier descents and freeride opportunities. The twin resorts of (pretty) Klosters (p287) and (popular) Davos (p288) share 320km of runs; the latter has excellent parks and half-pipes. Boarders also rave about the terrain parks, freeriding and après-ski scene in Laax (p282). Family-oriented Arosa (p280) and Lenzerheide (p279) in the next valley are scenic picks for

Ice climber on a frozen waterfall

beginners, intermediates and cross-country fans. Want to give the crowds the slip? Glide across to the uncrowded slopes of Pizol (p286), Scuol (p291), Samnaun (p292) or Pontresina (p300).

### Valais & Vaud

Nothing beats skiing in the shadow of the Matterhorn, soaring 4478m above Zermatt (p162). Snowboarders, intermediates and off-pisters all rave about the car-free resort's 360km of scenic runs. Almost as gorgeous is Crans-Montana (p158), a great beginners' choice with gentle, sunny slopes, and Matterhorn and Mont Blanc puncturing the skyline. Verbier (p150) has some terrifically challenging off-piste for experts. Hard-core boarders favour snow-sure, glacier-licked Saas Fee (p169). Snuggling up to France's mammoth Portes du Soleil ski arena, Champéry (p149) has access to 650km of slopes. Queues are few and families welcome in lovely, lesser-known Bettmeralp (p173) in a quiet corner of Valais.

### Bernese Oberland

At its winter-wonderland heart is the Jungfrau Region, an unspoilt Alpine beauty criss-crossed with 214km of well-maintained slopes, ranging from easy-peasy to hair-raising, that grant fleeting views of the 'Big Three': Eiger, Mönch and Jungfrau. Grindelwald (p120), Wengen (p130) and Mürren (p131) all offer varied skiing and have a relaxed, family-friendly vibe. For more glitz, swing west to Gstaad (p141), which has fine downhill on 220km of slopes and pre- and post-season glacier skiing at nearby Glacier 3000 (p143).

### Central & Northeastern Switzerland

Surprisingly little known given its snow-sure slopes and staggering mountain backdrop, Engelberg (p213) is dominated by glacier-capped Mt Titlis (p217). The real treasures here are off-piste, including Galtiberg, a 2000m vertical descent from the glacier to the valley. Wonderfully wild Andermatt (p218) is another backcountry ski-touring and boarder favourite.

Hiking near the Matterhorn (p162), Zermatt

## Resources

### Books

➡ *Which Ski Resort – Europe* (Pat Sharples and Vanessa Webb) This well-researched guide covers the top 50 resorts in Europe.

➡ *Where to Ski and Snowboard* (Chris Gill and Dave Watts) Bang-up-to-date guide to the slopes, covering all aspects of skiing.

### Websites

**Bergfex** (www.bergfex.com/schweiz) Comprehensive website with piste maps, snow forecasts and details of 226 ski resorts in Switzerland.

**On the Snow** (www.onthesnow.co.uk) Reviews of Switzerland's ski resorts, plus snow reports, webcams and lift-pass details.

**If You Ski** (www.ifyouski.com) Resort guides, ski deals and info on ski hire and schools.

**MadDogSki** (www.maddogski.com) Entertaining ski guides and insider tips on everything from accommodation to après-ski.

**World Snowboard Guide** (www.worldsnowboardguide.com) Snowboarder central. Has the low-down on most Swiss resorts.

**Where to Ski & Snowboard** (www.wheretoskiandsnowboard.com) Resort overviews and reviews, news and weather.

# Walking & Hiking

It's only by slinging on a backpack and hitting the trail that you can begin to appreciate just how big this tiny country really is: it's criss-crossed by more than 60,000km of marked paths.

## Walk Descriptions

➡ Times and distances for walks are provided only as a guide.

➡ Times are based on the actual walking time and do not include stops for snacks, taking photos or rests, or side trips.

➡ Distances should be read in conjunction with altitudes – significant elevation can make a greater difference to your walking time than lateral distance.

## Safe & Responsible Hiking

To help preserve the ecology and beauty of Switzerland, consider the following tips when hiking.

➡ Pay any fees required and obtain reliable information about environmental conditions (eg from park authorities).

➡ Walk only in regions, and on trails, within your realm of experience. Increase length and elevation gradually.

### ONLINE SKI DEALS

➡ For last-minute ski deals and packages, check out websites like www.igluski.com, www.j2ski.com, www.snowfinders.co.uk and www.myswitzerland.com.

➡ Speed to the slopes by prebooking discounted ski and snowboard hire at Ski Set (www.skiset.co.uk) or Snowbrainer (www.snowbrainer.com).

➡ If you want to skip to the front of the queue, consider ordering your ski pass online, too. Swiss Passes (www.swisspasses.com) gives reductions of up to 30% on standard ski-pass prices.

**KID MAGNETS**

➡ Cow trekking along the Rhine in Hemishofen (p260)

➡ Zipping above Grindelwald on the First Flyer (p126)

➡ Taking a husky-drawn sleigh ride at Glacier 3000 (p143) near Gstaad

➡ Dashing through the snow on the 15km toboggan run from Faulhorn (p126)

➡ Racing helter-skelter down the mountain on trotti-bikes (scooters), jumbo scooters or dirt bikes at resorts up and down the country (p126)

➡ Swinging above the treetops at the Rheinfall's Adventure Park (p260)

➡ Catapulting down the super-speedy Feeblitz (p170) luge track in Saas Fee

➡ Stick to the marked route to prevent erosion and for your own safety.

➡ Where possible, don't walk in the mountains alone. Two is considered the minimum number for safe walking.

➡ Take all your rubbish with you.

## Walk Designations

As locals delight in telling you, Switzerland's 62,500km of trails would be enough to stretch around the globe 1.5 times. And with (stereo)typical Swiss precision, these footpaths are remarkably well signposted and maintained. That said, a decent topographical map and compass are still recommended for Alpine hikes. Like ski runs, trails are colour coded according to difficulty:

**Yellow** Easy. No previous experience necessary.

**White-red-white** Mountain trails. You should be sure-footed, as routes may involve some exposure.

**White-blue-white** High Alpine routes. Only for the physically fit; some climbing and/or glacier travel may be required.

**Pink** Prepared winter walking trails.

## Regions

Alpine hikers invariably have their sights set high on the trails in the Bernese Oberland, Valais and Graubünden, which offer challenging walking and magnificent scenery. Lowland areas such as the vine-strewn Lavaux wine region and the bucolic dairy country around Appenzell can be just as atmospheric and are accessible virtually year-round.

In summer some tourist offices, including Lugano's, run guided hikes – free with a local guest card. Other resorts, such as Davos-Klosters and Arosa, give you a head start with free mountain transport when you stay overnight in summer.

## Best Hikes

**High-Alpine day hike** Strike out on the Faulhornweg for spellbinding views of Lakes Thun and Brienz, Eiger, Mönch and Jungfrau.

**Epic mountain trek** Gasp at mighty Matterhorn on the Matterhorn Glacier Trail, a hike taking in wild glaciers and 4000m peaks. Or get close-ups of Eiger and the other Jungfrau giants on the Eiger Trail from Kleine Scheidegg.

**Glacier hike** Be blown away by the Aletsch Glacier and keep an eye out for black-nosed sheep.

**Family hike** Please the kids on the action-packed Globi Trail in Lenzerheide, the marmot-filled Felixweg at Männlichen or by walking a St Bernard at the high mountain pass of the same name.

**Vineyard walk** Take a family-friendly stroll through the vine-strewn Rhône Valley on the Sentier Viticole from Sierre to Salgesch. It's never lovelier than on a golden September day during the grape harvest.

**Off-the-beaten-track hike** Admire the pristine beauty of the Swiss National Park on the challenging Lakes of Macun hike.

**Summer stroll** Amble through rustic hamlets and along old mule trails on the Cima della Trosa walk, with bird's-eye–Lago Maggiore views.

**Pushchair hike** Walking with tots is a breeze on the buggy-friendly trails in Zermatt and Verbier.

## Accommodation

One of the hiker's greatest pleasures in the Swiss Alps is staying in a mountain hut, and the **SAC** (SAC; www.sac-cas.ch; per person non-members Sfr20-40, members up to Sfr28) runs 152 of them. Bookings are essential. Annual membership, costing between Sfr80 and Sfr175, entitles you to discounts on SAC huts, climbing halls, tours, maps and guides.

DR.SEM/SHUTTERSTOCK ©

Paragliding in the Swiss Alps



If you are walking in the lowlands and fancy going back to nature, consider spending the night at a farmstay. Explore your options with **Agrotourismus Schweiz** (031 359 50 30; www.agrotourismus.ch) and **Swiss Holiday Farms** (031 329 66 99; www.bauernhof-ferien.ch).

## Resources

### Books

**Rother** (www.rother.de) and **Cicerone** (www.cicerone.co.uk) publish regional walking guides to Switzerland.

- *Walking Easy in the Swiss & Austrian Alps* (Chet Lipton) Gentle two- to six-hour hikes in the most popular areas.
- *100 Hut Walks in the Alps* (Kev Reynolds) Lists 100 hut-to-hut trails in the Alps for all levels of ability.
- *Trekking in the Alps* (Kev Reynolds) Covers 20 Alpine treks and includes maps and route profiles.

### Websites

Get planning with the routes, maps and GPS downloads on the following websites:

**Switzerland Tourism** (www.myswitzerland.com) Excellent information on walking in Switzerland, from themed day hikes to guided treks and family-friendly walks. An app covering 32 walks is available for download.

**Wanderland** (www.wanderland.ch) The definitive Switzerland hiking website, with walks and accommodation searchable by region and theme, plus information on events, guides, maps and packages.

### Maps

A great overview map of Switzerland is Michelin's 1:400,000 national map No 729 *Switzerland*. For an interactive walking map, see http://map.wanderland.ch. Or visit www.myswitzerland.com/map for a zoomable country map.

To purchase high-quality walking maps online, try these:

**Kümmerly + Frey** (www.swisstravelcenter.com) Has the entire country mapped. Most are scaled at 1:60,000 and are accurate enough for serious navigation.

**Swiss Alpine Club** (www.sac-cas.ch) Highly detailed and reliable walking maps at a scale of 1:25,000.

Gletscherschlucht (Glacier Gorge; p120)

# Cycling & Mountain Biking

## Routes

Switzerland is an efficiently run paradise for the ardent cyclist, laced with 9000km of cycling trails and 4500km of mountain-biking routes.

Andermatt makes a terrific base if you're keen to test your stamina on mountainous passes such as Furka, Oberalp and St Gotthard. Two striking national routes begin here: a 320km pedal to Geneva via the Rhône glacier and pastoral Goms, and a heart-pounding 430km stretch along the Rhine to Basel. Serious bikers craving back-breaking inclines and arresting views flock to Lenzerheide, and Klosters and Davos.

Mountain and downhill bikers whizz across to Alpine resorts like Arosa. To hone your skills on obstacles, check out the terrain parks in Davos and Verbier.

## Bike Hire

Reliable wheels are available in all major towns, and many cities now offer free bike hire from April to October as part of the ecofriendly initiative **Schweiz Rollt** (Suisse Roule; www.schweizrollt.ch), including Bern, Zürich, Geneva, Martigny, Sion and Neuchâtel.

Available at all major train stations, **SBB Rent a Bike** (☎041 925 11 70; www.rentabike.ch; half/full day from Sfr27/35), has city/mountain/e-bikes/tandem bikes for Sfr35/43/54/80 per day. For Sfr8 more, you can pick up your bike at one station and drop it off at another. Bikes can be reserved online. A one-day bike pass for SBB trains costs Sfr20.

If you're sticking around awhile, it's worth registering for public bike-sharing scheme **PubliBike** (www.publibike.ch/en), with almost 100 'pick-up and return' stations dotted around Switzerland and a low yearly membership fee. You can also purchase a QuickBike option (24 hours). Use the website to order and check sales and station locations.

## Resources

**Veloland** (www.veloland.ch) Info on cycling in Switzerland – from national routes to bike rental, events and family tours.

**Mountainbikeland** (www.mountainbikeland.ch) The low-down on national, regional and local routes.

**GPS Tour** (www.gps-tour.info) Hundreds of GPS cycling and mountain-bike tours in Switzerland available for download.

# Adventure & Water Sports

## Rock Climbing

Switzerland has been the fabled land for mountaineers ever since Edward Whymper made the first successful ascent of the Matterhorn in 1865, albeit a triumph marred by rope-breaking tragedy. Within reach for hard-core Alpinists are some of Europe's most gruelling climbs: Monte Rosa (4634m), the Matterhorn (4478m), Mont Blanc (4807m), and Eiger (3970m).

If you're eager to tackle the biggies, Zermatt's Alpin Center arranges some first-class climbs to surrounding 4000ers. Wildly scenic Kandersteg hooks proficient ice climbers with its frozen waterfalls, while glaciated monoliths, such as Piz Bernina, draw climbers to Pontresina.

### SOS SIX

The standard Alpine distress signal is six whistles, six calls, six smoke puffs – that is, six of whatever sign or sound you can make – repeated every 10 seconds for one minute.

The climbing halls in Chur and Interlaken are perfect for limbering up.

## Resources

**SAC** (www.sac-cas.ch) Browse for information on countrywide climbing halls, tours and courses.

**Schweizer Bergführerverband** (www.4000plus.ch) The official site of the Swiss Mountain Guide Association.

**Rock Climbing** (www.rockclimbing.com) Gives details on hundreds of climbing tours in Switzerland, many with climbing grades and photos.

**Verband Bergsportschulen Schweiz** (www.bergsportschulen.ch) The leading mountain-sports schools in Switzerland.

## Vie Ferrate

For the buzz of mountaineering but with the security of being attached to the rock face, clip onto a *via ferrata* (*Klettersteig* in German). These head-spinning fixed-rope routes are all the rage in Switzerland. Some favourites include those in Andermatt and Mürren for scenery, and Leukerbad and Kandersteg for more of a challenge.

**Via Ferrata** (www.viaferrata.org) provides maps and routes graded according to difficulty.

## Paragliding & Hang-Gliding

Where there's a beautiful breeze and a mountain, there's tandem paragliding and hang-gliding in Switzerland.

In the glacial realms of the Unesco-listed Aletsch Glacier, Fiescheralp is a prime spot to catch thermals, as is First for spirit-soaring vistas to mighty Jungfrau. If lake scenery is more your style, glide like a bird over glittering Lake Lucerne and Lago di Lugano.

## Bungee Jumping

Regional tourist offices have details of bungee-jumping specialists. Great leaps include Grindelwald's glacier-gouged Gletscherschlucht (p120) and the 134m jump from Stockhorn near Interlaken. If you fancy yourself a bit of a Bond, head to the Verzasca Dam (p194), the world's second-highest bungee jump at 220m, which starred in the opening scene of *GoldenEye*.

## Skydiving & BASE Jumping

Extreme-sports-mecca Interlaken is the place for heart-stopping skydiving moments. Free fall past the vertical face of Eiger, then drink in the scenery in glorious slow motion.

Even more nerve-wracking is BASE jumping, the decidedly risky pursuit of leaping off fixed objects and opening the parachute just before you splat. While this is exhilarating to watch in Lauterbrunnen (p129), this is one sport best left to the experts.

## Rafting & Hydrospeeding

In summer, the raging Saane, Rhine, Inn and Rhône rivers create a dramatic backdrop for rafting and hydrospeeding. Memorable splashes include the thundering Vorderrhein through the limestone Ruinaulta gorge and rivers near Interlaken.

**Swissraft** (p283) has bases all over the country. Expect to pay around Sfr115 for a half-day rafting/hydrospeeding tour, including transport and equipment.

## Kayaking & Canoeing

Lazy summer afternoons are best spent absorbing the slow, natural rhythm of Switzerland's crystal-clear lakes and rivers. Consult **Kanuland** (http://kanuland.myswitzerland.com) for routes and paddle-friendly accommodation tips. A half-day canoeing tour costs between Sfr85 and Sfr120.

## Windsurfing & Waterskiing

Excellent wind sweeps down from the heights in Silvaplana, where you can take kitesurfing and windsurfing lessons on two wind-buffeted cobalt lakes.

The rugged mountains rearing up around Lake Thun make fascinating viewing while you're windsurfing and wakeboarding. Pretty little Estavayer-le-Lac also attracts waterskiers and wakeboarders.

See www.windsurf.ch for windsurfing clubs and schools across Switzerland and www.wannakitesurf.com for an interactive map of kitesurfing hot spots.

# Regions at a Glance

No place inspires exploration quite like this tiny country whose four languages and cultural diversity create curiosity and beg discovery. The French-speaking wedge – Suisse Romande – embraces Switzerland's western fringe from Geneva and Lake Geneva to the remote Jura in the north and Valais in the east. Moving east into 'middle-ground' Mittelland with Swiss capital Bern as its heart, Germanic Switzerland kicks in – and makes itself heard across the Alps in the country's main outdoor-action playgrounds: the Bernese Oberland, Graubünden and the Engadine Valley. Then there is Ticino, a charismatic pocket of Italian-speaking passion and exuberance.

## Geneva

**Museums**
**Shopping**
**Boats & Lakes**

Close to 150 nationalities jostle for a stool at the bar in this cosmopolitan city of luxury watchmakers and chocolate gods serenaded by Mont Blanc – all at the western tip of Europe's largest lake.

p42

## Lake Geneva & Vaud

**Wine**
**Castles**
**Pretty Villages**

Its southern shore belongs to France, but the Swiss dress up Lake Geneva's northern shore with emerald terraced vineyards, fairy-tale châteaux, flower paths and quaint old villages made for meandering – pure, utter Riviera seduction, *ma chère*.

p59

## Fribourg, Drei-Seen-Land & the Jura

**Cheese**
**Wine**
**Rural Life**

Gourmets and outdoor-lovers swoon over this peaceful, green corner of Switzerland, spilling down to the shores of the Three Lakes Region (Drei-Seen-Land). Here fruits of the farmland are king – Gruyère cheese, thick cream and pea-green absinthe.

p80

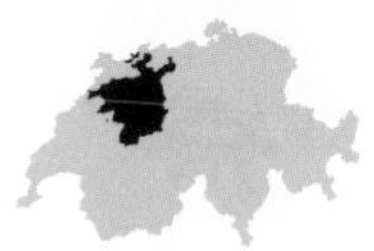

## Mittelland

**Art & Architecture**
**Old Towns**
**Curiosities**

Capital Bern, with its world-class art museums and bear pit, draws crowds, but its fairy-tale Old Town and counterculture fun are the real surprises – as are hip sleeps in old-world Solothurn.

**p100**

## Bernese Oberland

**Adventure Sports**
**Stunning Scenery**
**Hiking**

It doesn't get more extreme than this. Be it skydiving, ice climbing or glacial bungee-jumping, the adrenalin rush burns. Ritzy film-set resorts, spellbinding glaciers, cinematic peaks: this is the great outdoors on a blockbuster scale.

**p113**

## Valais

**Wine**
**Alpine Action**
**Local Tradition**

Eccentric, earthy, as melt-in-your-mouth as the Matterhorn's chocolate-box angles: Valais is a rare and traditional breed no one dares mess with. Zermatt, Verbier, the Glacier Express, Switzerland's finest wine – it's home to the crème de la crème.

**p144**

## Ticino

**Lakes & Mountains**
**Food**
**Hilltop Villages**

Italian weather, Italian style…this Italian-speaking canton is a different side of Switzerland: picture-postcard villages in wild valleys, petrol-blue lakes with palm-fringed shores, alfresco dining beneath chestnut trees. Buon appetito!

**p176**

## Central Switzerland

**Views**
**Great Outdoors**
**Culture**

More Swiss than Swiss, the country's heartland is built from picture-book, William Tell legend: bucket-list sunsets, legendary mountains (off-piste perfection) and shimmering cobalt-blue waters.

**p197**

## Northwestern Switzerland

**Art**
**Castles**
**Nightlife**

The urbanite ticket of northwestern Switzerland, big-city Basel woos with explosive art, avant-garde architecture and a mighty giant of a river that sticks its tongue out eastwards to lick fairy-tale castles and medieval villages.

**p220**

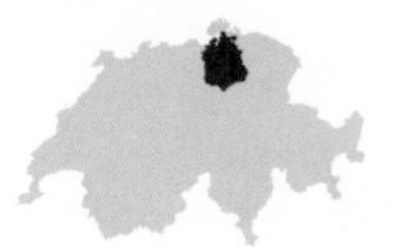

## Zürich

Nightlife
Dining Out
Culture

The party never stops in edgy Züri-West, flipside of Zürich the banker. Throw nocturnal baths, fine art and international cuisine into the urban mix to get one hell of a potent cocktail.

p234

## Northeastern Switzerland

Nature
Culture
Food

Exploring this backwater – a deeply Germanic, rural land of Alpine dairy farms and half-timbered villages – opens the door on a fantastical world of enchanting castles, secret libraries, thunderous waterfalls and cows you can ride.

p254

## Graubünden

Winter Sports
Walking
Train Journeys

Skiing mecca of Davos and St Moritz fame, this glamorous region is where winter tourism began. Dodge paparazzi at a quartzite spa, hike the Swiss National Park and gaze at the mountains aboard the iconic Glacier Express.

p273

## Liechtenstein

Smallness
Nature
Castle

Thanks to a monarchy that refuses entreaties from neighbours, this pea-sized principality remains staunchly independent. It's got pretty hikes, a royal castle and a booming business in false teeth and passport stamps.

p302

Lugano (p182), Ticino

# On the Road

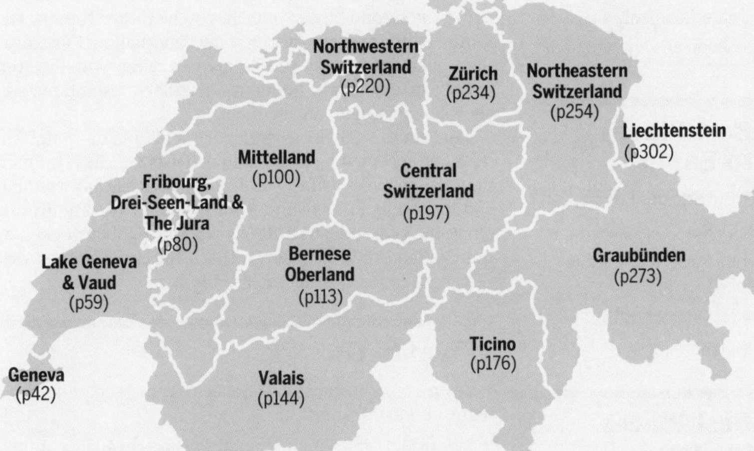

Northwestern Switzerland (p220)
Zürich (p234)
Northeastern Switzerland (p254)
Liechtenstein (p302)
Mittelland (p100)
Central Switzerland (p197)
Fribourg, Drei-Seen-Land & The Jura (p80)
Lake Geneva & Vaud (p59)
Bernese Oberland (p113)
Graubünden (p273)
Ticino (p176)
Geneva (p42)
Valais (p144)

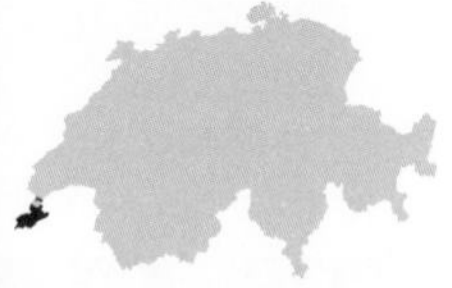

# Geneva

POP 198,072 / AREA 375M

**Includes ➡**



## Best Places to Eat

- ➡ Buvette des Bains (p52)
- ➡ Le Petit Lac (p55)
- ➡ Le Relais d'Entrecôte (p54)
- ➡ La Finestra (p53)
- ➡ Manora (p53)

## Best Places to Stay

- ➡ Hôtel Beau-Rivage (p52)
- ➡ Mandarin Oriental (p52)
- ➡ Hôtel Les Armures (p52)
- ➡ La Cour des Augustins (p51)
- ➡ Starling Residence (p51)

## Why Go?

Like the swans that frolic on its eponymous Alpine lake (Europe's largest), Geneva (Genève) is a rare bird. Slick, cosmopolitan and constantly perceived as the Swiss capital (it isn't), the people of Switzerland's second-largest city chatter in almost every language among streets paved by gold.

The headquarters of the World Trade Organization, World Health Organization, International Committee of the Red Cross, the second-largest branches of the United Nations and World Bank (among some 200-odd international organisations, including not-for-profits) are here, along with the overload of luxury hotels, boutiques, jewellers, restaurants and chocolatiers accompanying them.

Beneath this flawless exterior, lies a fascinating rough-cut diamond, peopled by artists and activists educated in international schools, drifters and denizens. Geneva's counterculture dwells in Les Grottes, the Quartier des Pâquis and along the post-industrial Rhône where neighbourhood bars hum with attitude and energy. This is the Geneva of the 'real' *Genevois*...or as close as you'll get to it.

## When to Go

- ➡ Being a busy business city, Geneva has markedly cheaper hotel rates at weekends.
- ➡ Surprisingly, the summer months of June to August are the best times to visit, when temperatures rise and conference season cools down: room rates drop, the city comes alive with parties, picnics, fetes and festivals...and everyone jumps in the lake.
- ➡ From March to May and September to November, Geneva is a hotbed of global conferences and trade shows – hotels fill up and prices soar.
- ➡ If you can find an off-weekend with reasonable room rates, the months of April and May are a lovely time to visit.
- ➡ Winter, with its December festivals and nearby skiing, is a real charmer, but room rates are unexpectedly high.

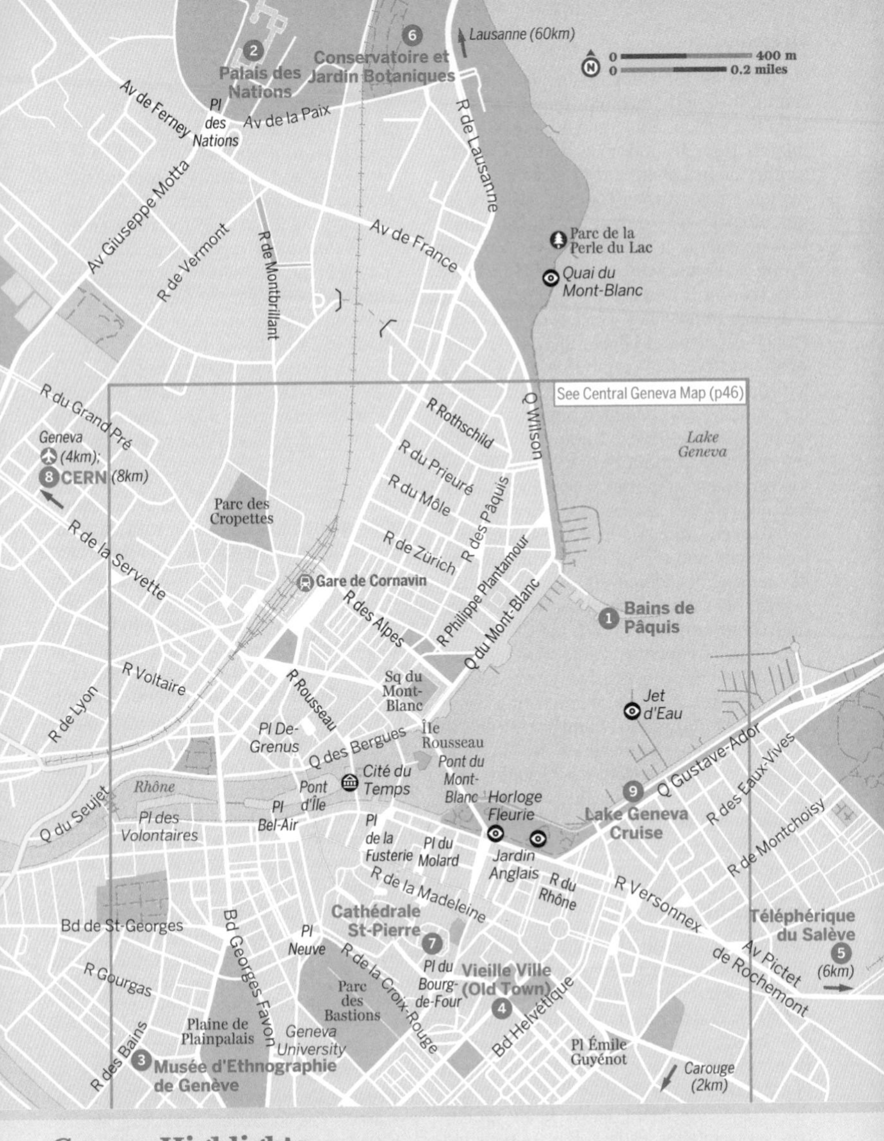


## Geneva Highlights

**1 Bains des Pâquis** (p50) Swimming in the lake or drooling over fondue at the *très genevois* Bains des Pâquis.

**2 Palais des Nations** (p49) Getting a crash course in international affairs at the Palace of Nations.

**3 Musée d'Ethnographie de Genève** (p45) Broadening your global horizons at the Museum of Ethnography.

**4 Vieille Ville** (p44) Lounging on a cafe terrace in Geneva's stunning Old Town.

**5 Téléphérique du Salève** (p58) Riding a vintage cable-car for astounding views in Étrembières, France.

**6 Conservatoire et Jardin Botaniques** (p49) Taking a stroll among rose beds at the Botanic Gardens.

**7 Cathédrale St-Pierre** (p44) Climbing the tower of Gothic St Peter's Cathedral.

**8 CERN** (p49) Boning up on the Big Bang during a scientist-led tour.

**9 Lac Léman** (p45) Sailing, cruising, or riding a *mouette* on Lake Geneva.

## History

Occupied by the Romans and later a 5th-century bishopric, rich old Geneva has long been the envy of all. Its medieval fairs drew interest from far and wide, and in the 16th century John Calvin and his zealous Reformation efforts turned the city into 'Protestant Rome'. Savoy duke Charles Emmanuel took a swipe at it in 1602, but was repelled by the Genevans, who celebrate their victory each year on 11 December.

French troops made Geneva capital of the French department Léman in 1798 but they were chucked out in June 1814 and Geneva joined the Swiss Confederation. Watchmaking, banking and commerce prospered. Local businessman Henry Durant founded the International Committee of the Red Cross in 1863 and Geneva's future as an international melting pot was secured as other international organisations adopted the strategically located city and birthplace of humanitarian law as their headquarters. After WWI the League of Nations strived for world peace from Geneva and after WWII the UN arrived.

Geneva frequently ranks among the world's 10 most expensive cities, relying heavily on international workers and world markets for its wealth. Immigrants (people of 184 different nationalities, not born in Switzerland) comprise 42% of Geneva's population, and when you include 'naturalized' immigrants, that figure jumps to a whopping 61%, making Geneva one of the most multicultural cities in Western Europe.

## Sights

Geneva's major sights are split by the Rhône, which flows through the city to create its greatest attraction (the lake), and several distinct neighbourhoods. On the *rive gauche* (left bank), mainstream shopping districts Rive and Eaux-Vives climb from the water to Plainpalais and **Vieille Ville** (Old Town), while the *rive droite* (right bank) holds grungy bar- and club-hot Pâquis, the train-station area and the international quarter with most world organisations.

Many museums are free on the first Sunday of the month.

### Old Town

**★Cathédrale St-Pierre** CATHEDRAL

(www.cathedrale-geneve.ch; Cour de St-Pierre; towers adult/child Sfr5/2; ⏲9.30am-6.30pm Mon-Sat, noon-6.30pm Sun Jun-Sep, 10am-5.30pm Mon-Sat, noon-5.30pm Sun Oct-May) Geneva's cathedral is predominantly Gothic with an 18th-century neoclassical facade. Between 1536 and 1564 Protestant John Calvin preached here; see his seat in the north aisle. Inside the cathedral, 96 steps spiral up to the **northern tower** offering a fascinating glimpse at the cathedral's architectural construction. From here, another 60 steps climb into the **southern tower**, revealing close-up views of the bells and panoramic city vistas. From Jun-Sep, daily free carillon (5pm) and organ (6pm) concerts are a bonus.

In the basement, the **Site Archéologique de la Cathédrale St-Pierre** (☎022 310 29 29; www.site-archeologique.ch; Cour de St-Pierre; adult/child Sfr8/4; ⏲10am-5pm) features 4th-century floor mosaics and an eerie tomb.

A combined ticket covering Cathédrale St-Pierre, Site Archéologique de la Cathédrale St-Pierre and Musée International de la Réforme is Sfr18/10 per adult/child.

**★Musée International de la Réforme** MUSEUM

(Museum of the Reformation; ☎022 310 24 31; www.mir.ch; Rue du Cloître 4; adult/child Sfr13/6; ⏲10am-5pm Tue-Sun) This modern museum in an 18th-century mansion zooms in on the Reformation. State-of-the-art exhibits and audiovisuals bring to life everything from the earliest printed bibles to the emergence of Geneva as 'Protestant Rome' in the 16th century, and from John Calvin all the way to Protestantism in the 21st century.

A combined ticket covering the museum, Cathédrale St-Pierre and Site Archéologique de la Cathédrale St-Pierre is Sfr18/10 per adult/child.

### DISCOUNT CARDS

The **Geneva Pass** (24/48/72 hours Sfr26/37/45) yields a bounty of savings: free public transport, admission to city museums, and discounts on everything from city tours and speedboat rental to theatre tickets and lake cruises. Buy it at the **tourist office** (p57), participating hotels or online (www.geneve.com/en/see-do/geneva-pass).

When checking in at your accommodation, you should be offered a free **Public Transport Card**, which provides unlimited local bus and tram travel for the duration of your stay. Don't be afraid to ask for one if your host forgets.

**★Jet d'Eau** FOUNTAIN

(Quai Gustave-Ador) When landing by plane, this lakeside fountain is your first dramatic glimpse of Geneva. The 140m-tall structure shoots up water with incredible force – 200km/h, 1360 horsepower – to create the sky-high plume, kissed by a rainbow on sunny days. At any one time, 7 tonnes of water are in the air, much of which sprays spectators on the pier beneath. Two or three times a year it is illuminated pink, blue or another colour to mark a humanitarian occasion.

The Jet d'Eau is Geneva's third pencil fountain. The first shot water into the sky for 15 minutes each Sunday between 1886 and 1890, to release pressure at the city's water station, and the second spurted 90m high from the Jetée des Eaux-Vives on Sundays and public holidays from 1891 onward. The current one was born in 1951.

**Jardin Anglais** GARDENS

(The English Garden; Quai du Général-Guisan) Before finding your way into the Vieille Ville, join the crowds taking selfies in front of the Horloge Fleurie, the *pièce de résistance* of this, Geneva's flowery waterfront garden, landscaped in 1854 on the site of an old lumber-handling port and merchant yard.

**Horloge Fleurie** LANDMARK

(Flower Clock; Quai du Général-Guisan) In the Jardin Anglais you'll find Geneva's most photographed clock, crafted from 6500 living flowers. It's been ticking since 1955 and boasts the world's longest second hand (2.5m).

**Musée d'Art et d'Histoire** GALLERY

(Museum of Art and History; ☎022 418 26 00; www.mah-geneve.ch; Rue Charles-Galland 2; ⏰11am-6pm Tue-Sun) FREE Built between 1903 and 1910, this elegant museum holds masterpieces such as Konrad Witz' *La pêche miraculeuse* (c 1440–44), portraying Christ walking on water on Lake Geneva, in its treasure chest. There are excellent temporary exhibitions (Sfr15/free per adult/child). In an interesting twist, plans for a Sfr127-million renovation of the museum by world-class architect Jean Nouvel were shelved after Geneva's citizens voted against the project in a mid-2016 referendum.

**Maison de Rousseau et de la Literature** MUSEUM

(☎022 310 10 28; www.m-r-l.ch; Grand-Rue 40; adult/child Sfr5/3; ⏰11am-5.30pm Tue-Sun) A 25-minute audiovisual display traces the troubled life of Geneva's greatest thinker, Jean-Jacques Rousseau. He was born in this house in 1712.

**Musée Barbier-Mueller** GALLERY

(☎022 312 02 70; www.barbier-mueller.ch; Rue Jean Calvin 10; adult/child Sfr8/5; ⏰11am-5pm) This refined private gallery space, opened in 1977, is filled with objects from ancient societies – think pre-Columbian South American art treasures, Pacific Island statues and African weaponry. As an interesting aside, revolutionary protestant John Calvin lived in the house opposite.

## Pleinpalais

Wedged between the Rhône and Arve rivers, this fairly nondescript district is home to the University of Geneva and a bevy of museums.

**★Musée d'Ethnographie de Genève** MUSEUM

(Geneva Museum of Ethnography; ☎022 418 45 50; www.ville-ge.ch/meg; Bd de Carl-Vogt 65-67; ⏰11am-6pm Tue-Sun) FREE Admission is free to the permanent collection of this excellent

### THE LAKE OR LE LAC?

**Lake Geneva** is known by the locals as 'Lac Léman'. In fact, calling it by any other name in the presence of a *Genevois* will be met with a furrowed brow (at the very least) and seal your fate as 'just another tourist'. It's a bit likereal San Franciscans never calling their home 'San Fran' – didn't you know? Respecting the local lingo will earn you brownie points in this city where appearance is everything!

The lake, shared by Switzerland and France, occupies an area of 580 sq km at a maximum depth of 310m. No known monsters occupy its cool, crystal clear waters, which in summer, lure bathers by the thousands. On a clear day, from the lake's shoreline in Geneva, you can see Mont Blanc (4808m), which is the tallest mountain in the Alps and the highest in Western Europe – it's a common misconception that the massif is Swiss, but although a portion of the mountain extends into Switzerland, its summit belongs to France. So now you know.

## Central Geneva

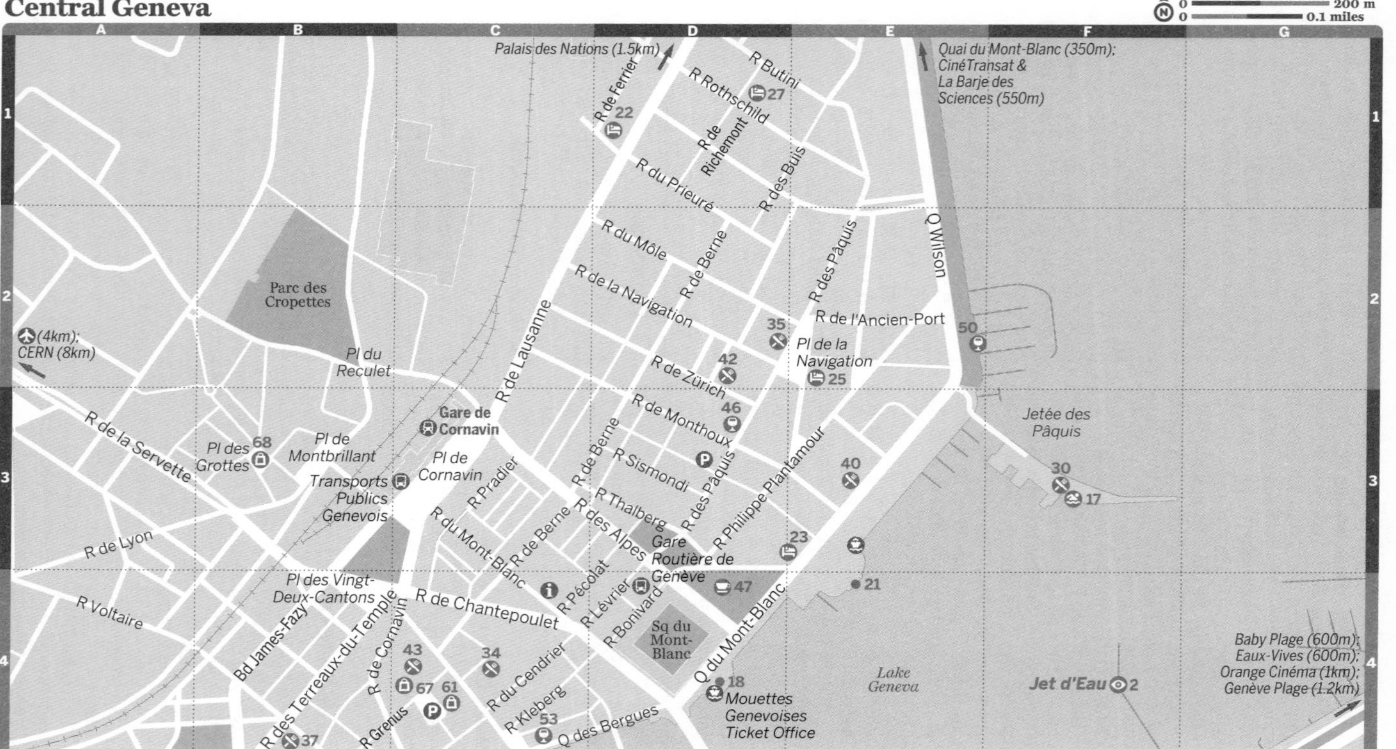

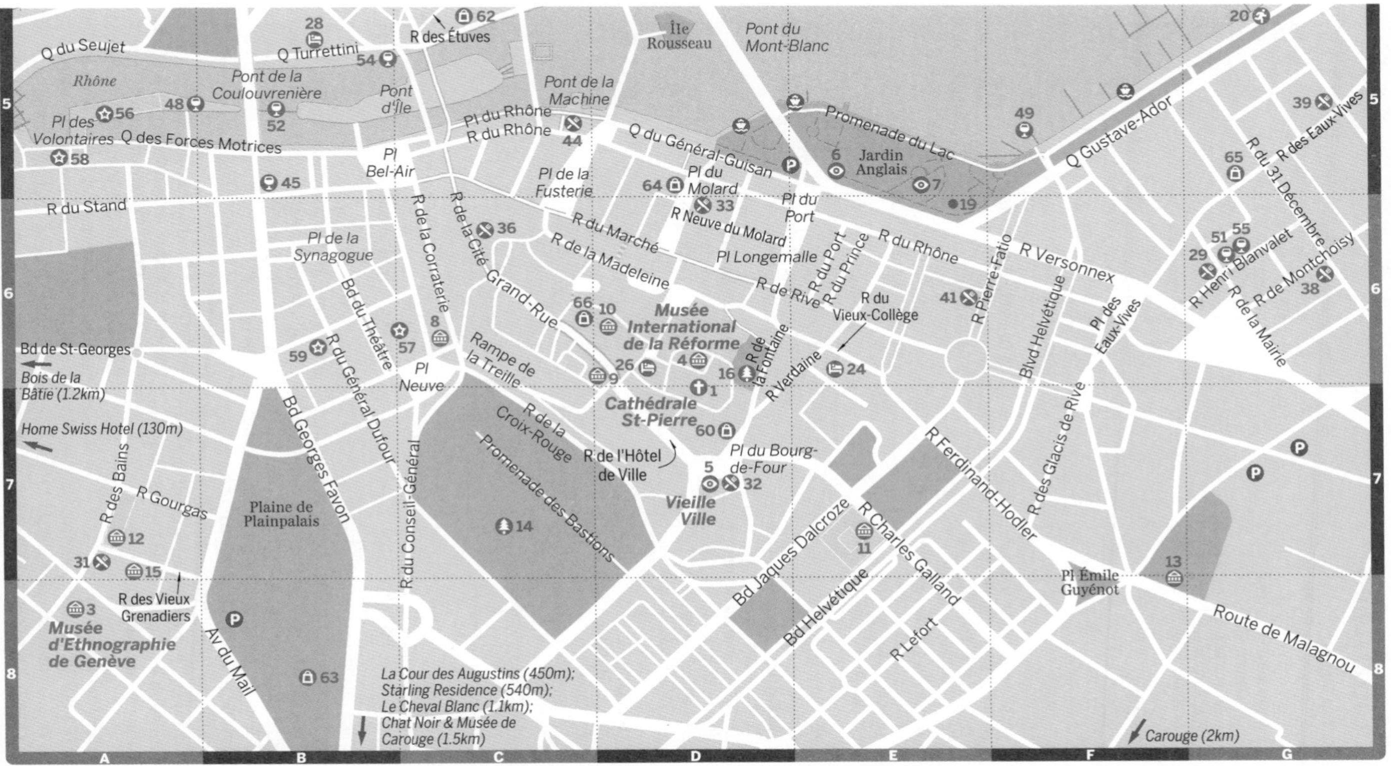

Q du Seujet
Rhône
Pl des Volontaires
Q des Forces Motrices
R du Stand
Q Turrettini
Pont de la Coulouvrenière
Pont d'Île
R des Étuves
Pl Bel-Air
Pl du Rhône
R du Rhône
Pont de la Machine
Île Rousseau
Pont du Mont-Blanc
Q du Général-Guisan
Pl de la Fusterie
Pl du Molard
R Neuve du Molard
Pl du Port
Promenade du Lac
Jardin Anglais
Q Gustave-Ador
R des Eaux-Vives
R du 31 Décembre
R Henri Blanvalet
R de Montchoisy
R de la Mairie
R du Marché
R de la Madeleine
Pl Longemalle
R du Port
R du Prince
R du Rhône
R Pierre-Fatio
R Versonnex
R de Rive
R du Vieux-Collège
Blvd Helvétique
Pl des Eaux-Vives
Pl de la Synagogue
Bd du Théâtre
R de la Corraterie
R de la Cité
Grand-Rue
Musée International de la Réforme
R de la Fontaine
R Verdaine
Bd de St-Georges
Bois de la Bâtie (1.2km)
R du Général Dufour
Pl Neuve
Rampe de la Treille
Cathédrale St-Pierre
Home Swiss Hotel (130m)
Bd Georges Favon
R du Conseil-Général
R de la Croix-Rouge
Promenade des Bastions
R de l'Hôtel de Ville
Pl du Bourg-de-Four
Vieille Ville
R Ferdinand-Hodler
R des Glacis de Rive
R des Bains
R Gourgas
Plaine de Plainpalais
Bd Jaques Dalcroze
R Charles Galland
Pl Émile Guyénot
R des Vieux Grenadiers
Musée d'Ethnographie de Genève
Av du Mail
Bd Helvétique
R Lefort
Route de Malagnou
La Cour des Augustins (450m); Starling Residence (540m); Le Cheval Blanc (1.1km); Chat Noir & Musée de Carouge (1.5km)
Carouge (2km)
A
B
C
D
E
F
G
5
6
7
8

## Central Geneva

**Top Sights**
1 Cathédrale St-Pierre ............ D7
2 Jet d'Eau ............ F4
3 Musée d'Ethnographie de Genève ............ A8
4 Musée International de la Réforme ............ D6
5 Vieille Ville ............ D7

**Sights**
6 Horloge Fleurie ............ E5
7 Jardin Anglais ............ E5
8 Le Rath ............ C6
9 Maison de Rousseau et de la Literature ............ D6
10 Musée Barbier-Mueller ............ D6
11 Musée d'Art et d'Histoire ............ E7
12 Musée d'Art Moderne et Contemporain ............ A7
13 Musée d'Histoire Naturelle ............ F8
14 Parc des Bastions ............ C7
15 Patek Philippe Museum ............ A7
Site Archéologique de la Cathédrale St-Pierre ............ (see 1)
16 Terrasse Agrippa d'Abigné ............ D6

**Activities, Courses & Tours**
17 Bains des Pâquis ............ F3
18 CGN Ferries & Cruises ............ D4
19 Le Petit Train ............ E6
20 Les Corsaires ............ G5
21 Swissboat ............ E4

**Sleeping**
22 City Hostel ............ D1
23 Hôtel Beau-Rivage ............ E3
24 Hôtel Bel'Esperance ............ E6
25 Hotel Edelweiss ............ E2
26 Hôtel Les Armures ............ D6
27 Hôtel N'vY ............ D1
28 Mandarin Oriental ............ B5

**Eating**
29 ALMA ............ G6
30 Buvette des Bains ............ F3
31 Café des Bains ............ A7
32 Café du Bourg-de-Four ............ D7
33 Café du Centre ............ D6
34 Chez Ma Cousine ............ C4
35 Gelatomania ............ D2
36 La Finestra ............ C6
37 La Réplique ............ B4
38 L'Adresse ............ G6
39 Le Décanteur ............ G5
40 Le Grill ............ E3
41 Le Relais d'Entrecôte ............ E6
42 Les 5 Portes ............ D2
43 Manora ............ C4
44 Mövenpick ............ C5

**Drinking & Nightlife**
45 Boulevard du Vin ............ B5
46 Café Art's ............ D3
47 Cottage Café ............ D4
48 La Barje des Lavandières ............ A5
49 La Buvette du Bateau ............ F5
50 La Terrasse ............ E2
51 L'Atelier Cocktail Club ............ G6
52 Le Bateau Lavoir ............ B5
53 Le Rouge et Le Blanc ............ C4
54 Terrasse Le Paradis ............ B5
55 Yvette de Marseille ............ G6

**Entertainment**
56 Bâtiment des Forces Motrices ............ A5
57 Grand Théâtre de Genève ............ C6
58 L'Usine ............ A5
59 Victoria Hall ............ B6

**Shopping**
60 Caran d'Ache - Maison de Haute Écriture ............ D7
61 Collection Privée ............ C4
62 Favarger ............ C5
63 Flea Market ............ B8
64 Globus ............ D5
65 Le Verre en Cave ............ G5
66 Librairie-Galerie Bernard Letu ............ C6
67 Manor ............ C4
68 Marché des Grottes ............ B3

hands-on museum, 'The Archives of Human Diversity', which examines the similarities and differences of our planet's myriad of cultures. It showcases around 1000 artefacts from the museum's 80,000-strong collection. In 2017, the 'MEG' was awarded the prestigious title of European Museum of the Year. Admission fees (adult/child Sfr 9/6) apply to visiting temporary exhibits.

**Patek Philippe Museum** MUSEUM
(☎022 807 09 10; www.patekmuseum.com; Rue des Vieux-Grenadiers 7; adult/child Sfr10/free; ⏲2-6pm Tue-Fri, 10am-6pm Sat) This elegant museum by one of Switzerland's leading luxury watchmakers displays exquisite timepieces and enamels from the 16th century to the present.

**Musée d'Art Moderne et Contemporain** GALLERY
(Museum of Modern and Contemporary Art (MAMCO); ☎022 320 61 22; www.mamco.ch; Rue des Vieux-Grenadiers 10; adult/child Sfr8/free; ⏲noon-6pm Tue-Fri, 11am-6pm Sat & Sun; 🚋Musée d'Art Moderne) Set in an industrial 1950s factory, the Modern and Contemporary Art Museum plays cutting-edge host to young,

international and cross-media exhibitions. It's free on the first Sunday of the month and between 6pm and 9pm the first Wednesday of every month.

**Parc des Bastions** PARK

It's all statues – not to mention a giant chess board – in this green city park where a laid-back stroll uncovers Red Cross cofounder Henri Dufour (who drew the first map of Switzerland in 1865) and the 4.5m-tall figures of Bèze, Calvin, Farel and Knox (in their nightgowns ready for bed). Depending on what's on, end with an art-driven exhibition across the square at Le Rath.

**Le Rath** GALLERY

(☎022 418 33 40; http://institutions.ville-geneve.ch/fr/mah/lieux-dexposition/musee-rath; Pl Neuve; adult Sfr10-20, child/free; ⏲11am-6pm when hosting temporary exhibitions) Across the traffic-busy square from the green city park, Parc des Bastions, is this historic building – Switzerland's oldest purpose-built museum dating to 1826. Worth a look for its iconic Roman facade, you can only enter the gallery when it is hosting a visiting exhibition: click on the Expositions & Événements link on the homepage for details.

## Right Bank

Cross the water aboard a canary-yellow *mouette* (seagull) boat, on the Pont du Mont-Blanc (notorious for traffic jams) or on foot across pedestrian Pont de la Machine. It's here, in the newer part of town that you'll find Gare CFF de Cornavin (p57), the Pâquis neighbourhood and the Palais des Nations.

**★CERN** RESEARCH CENTRE

(☎022 767 84 84; www.cern.ch; Meyrin; ⏲guided tours in English 11am & 1pm Mon-Sat) FREE Founded in 1954, the European Organisation for Nuclear Research, 8km west of Geneva, is a laboratory for research into particle physics. It accelerates protons down a 27km circular tube (the Large Hadron Collider, the world's biggest machine) and the resulting collisions create new matter. Come anytime to see the permanent exhibitions shedding light on its work, but for two-hour guided tours in English reserve online up to 15 days ahead and bring photo ID.

Tours often fill up months ahead – access the online booking portal here: http://visit.cern/tours/guided-tours-individuals. To get here take tram 18 from Gare CFF de Cornavin (p57; Sfr3, 20 minutes).

**★Conservatoire et Jardin Botaniques** GARDENS

(Conservatory & Botanical Gardens; ☎022 418 51 00; www.ville-ge.ch/cjb/index_en.php; Chemin de l'Impératrice 1; ⏲8am-5pm Nov-Apr, to 7.30pm Apr-Nov) FREE Geneva's premier botanical park – renowned for its Botanical Conservatory – boasts over 12,000 species of plants from around the world, meticulously arranged in a series of beautiful themed gardens. Highlights include a spectacular collection of roses and the loved-by-everyone **Animal Park** protecting ancient species of indigenous and often endangered animals as well as everyday chickens, goats and sheep and the more exotic peacocks, flamingos and deer.

**Quai du Mont-Blanc** WATERFRONT

Flowers, statues, outdoor art exhibitions and views of Mont Blanc (on clear days only) abound on this picturesque northern lakeshore promenade, which leads past the Bains des Pâquis (p50), where the *Genevois* have frolicked in the sun since 1872, to **Parc de la Perle du Lac**, a city park where Romans built ornate thermal baths. Further north, the peacock-studded lawns of **Parc de l'Ariana** ensnare the UN and Geneva's pretty Conservatoire et Jardin Botaniques.

**Palais des Nations** HISTORIC BUILDING

(Palace of Nations; ☎022 917 48 96; www.unog.ch; Av de la Paix 14; adult/child Sfr12/7; ⏲10am-noon & 2-4pm Mon-Sat Apr-Aug, Mon-Fri Sep-Mar; guided tours 10.30am, noon, 2.30pm & 4pm) Home to the UN since 1966, the Palais des Nations was built between 1929 and 1936 to house the now-defunct League of Nations. Visits are by guided tour (bring photo ID; no reservation required for groups of less than 15 people) and include a one-hour tour of the building and entry to the surrounding 46-hectare park, generously peppered with century-old trees and peacocks. Spot the grey monument coated with heat-resistant titanium, donated by the USSR to commemorate the conquest of space.

**Musée International de la Croix-Rouge et du Croissant-Rouge** MUSEUM

(International Red Cross & Red Crescent Museum; ☎022 748 95 11; www.redcrossmuseum.ch; Av de la Paix 17; adult/child Sfr15/7; ⏲10am-6pm Tue-Sun Apr-Oct, to 5pm Nov-Mar) Compelling multimedia exhibits at Geneva's fascinating International Red Cross and Red Crescent Museum trawl through atrocities perpetuated by humanity. The litany of war

### GENEVA FOR CHILDREN

Parents will find that Geneva's modern infrastructure, efficient transport system and ubiquitous amenities such as baby-changing facilities make the city easy to navigate with children in tow.

Geneva offers an abundance of family-friendly activities. Predictably, the lake is an endless source of family entertainment: feed the ducks and swans; rent a nippy speedboat or sleek sailing boat from **Les Corsaires** (☎022 735 43 00; www.lescorsaires.ch; Quai Gustave-Ador 33; ⏰10.30am-8.30pm Apr-Oct); fly down the waterslide at 1930s lakeside swimming-pool complex **Genève Plage** (☎022 736 24 82; www.geneve-plage.ch; Quai de Cologny 5, Port Noir; adult/child Sfr7/3.50; ⏰10am-8pm mid-May–mid-Sep); or dive into the lake-water pools at historic and uberhip Bains des Pâquis, around since 1872.

Other amusing options include an electric-train tour, the Tarzan-inspired tree park with rubber-tyre swings at lakeside **Baby Plage** (Quai Gustave-Ador; 👪), and the well-equipped playgrounds for toddlers in lakeside Parc de la Perle du Lac and Bois de la Bâtie where peacocks, goats and deer roam in woods. Every kid adores the stuffed bears, tigers and giraffes, Swiss fauna and hands-on Wednesday-afternoon workshops at the **Musée d'Histoire Naturelle** (Natural History Museum; www.ville-ge.ch/mhng; Rte de Malagnou 1; ⏰10am-5pm Tue-Sun; 👪) FREE.

For technology-mad older kids, CERN (p49) is just the ticket.

and nastiness, documented in films, photos, sculptures and soundtracks, is set against the noble aims of the organisation founded by Geneva businessmen Henry Dunant in 1863. Excellent temporary exhibitions command an additional entrance fee.

Take bus 8 from Gare CFF de Cornavin (p57) to the Appia stop.

## Activities

**★Bains des Pâquis** SWIMMING

(☎022 732 29 74; www.bains-des-paquis.ch; Quai du Mont-Blanc 30; pools adult/child Sfr2/1, sauna, hammam & Turkish bath Sfr20; ⏰9am-9.30pm Mon-Sat, from 8pm Sun) This hip and trendy pool in Pâquis, with its waterfront bar and restaurant, is a Real McCoy vintage child – it dates to 1872. From May to September it's abuzz with swimmers enjoying a refreshing dip in Lake Geneva. The rest of the year, the focus shifts to the on-site sauna, hammam and Turkish baths – open to the general public Wednesday through Monday, women only on Tuesday.

## Tours

The one-stop shop for boat, bus and electric-train tours is Ticket Point (p57), a waterfront kiosk on Quai du Mont-Blanc.

**★CGN Ferries & Cruises** BOATING

(Compagnie Générale de Navigation; ☎0900 929 929; www.cgn.ch; Quai du Mont-Blanc; 👪) Lake Geneva's biggest ferry operator runs regular scheduled ferry services and a variety of themed lake cruises aboard beautiful belle époque steamers. Check the website for full details.

**Swissboat** BOATING

(☎022 732 47 47; www.swissboat.com; Quai du Mont-Blanc 4; 45 min cruises from adult/child Sfr13/8; ⏰Apr-Oct) This operator runs a variety of thematic cruises on Lake Geneva and along the Rhône River. Check the homepage for full details.

**Le Petit Train** ECOTOUR

(☎022 735 43 00; www.petit-train-geneve.ch; Jardin Anglais; adult/child Sfr8/5; ⏰10.15am-6.30pm Apr & May, to 8pm Jun & Sep, to 9.30pm Jul & Aug, reduced hours Feb, Mar, Oct & Nov) Adults and kids alike enjoy the 30-minute circuit on this dinky red solar-powered train along the Left Bank between Jardin Anglais and Parc des Eaux-Vives. 'Trains' depart at 90-minute intervals from February to November.

## Festivals & Events

**L'Escalade** CARNIVAL

Smashing sweet marzipan-filled *marmites en chocolat* (chocolate cauldrons) and gorging on the broken pieces makes Geneva's biggest festival (second weekend of December) loads of fun. Torch-lit processions enliven the Vieille Ville and a bonfire is lit in the cathedral square to celebrate the defeat of Savoy troops in 1602.

## Sleeping

**★Starling Residence** APARTMENT €
(☎022 304 03 00; www.shresidence.ch; Rte des Acacias 4; r/apt from Sfr109/220; ❄📶) For something different, this low-cost option operated by Geneva's hotel-management school offers excellent value. Service levels are exceptional (and if they're not, dob on the students!) and the spacious rooms (many with kitchenette), studios and fully-fledged apartments are modern and spotlessly clean. To get here, take tram 15 from the station – it'll take you less than 15 minutes.

**Home Swiss Hotel** HOTEL €
(☎022 322 95 50; www.homeswisshotel.ch/en; Av de Ste-Clotilde 7; d/ste/apt from Sfr107/159/277; P❄📶) This smart business and leisure hotel about 15-minutes walk from downtown Geneva offers excellent value in an expensive city, with bright rooms (some with kitchenettes and balconies) decorated with Swiss flair in the national colours.

**City Hostel** HOSTEL €
(☎022 901 15 00; www.cityhostel.ch; Rue de Ferrier 2; dm Sfr33-36, s Sfr65-73, tw Sfr79-95; ⏲reception 7.30am-noon & 1pm-midnight; P@📶) This clean, well-organised hostel near the train station feels more like a hotel than a hostel. With a variety of different options for rooms, breakfast (Sfr6) is served in a nearby cafe and parking costs Sfr12 to Sfr15 per night.

**★La Cour des Augustins** HOTEL €€
(☎022 322 21 00; www.lacourdesaugustins.com/en/; Rue Jean-Violette 15; s/d/ste from Sfr156/168/380; P❄📶) With a selection of bright, playful guest rooms, chic suites and spacious long-stay apartments, this funky design hotel on the fringe of the Old Town is popular with repeat visitors to Geneva, and for good reason. Parquetry floors, quirky furnishings, luxe linens and stark, white walls accented with bright splashes of colour along a variety of design themes keep things fresh and interesting.

**Hôtel Bel'Esperance** HOTEL €€
(☎022 818 37 37; www.hotel-bel-esperance.ch; Rue de la Vallée 1; s/d/tr/q from Sfr150/170/210/250; ⏲reception 7am-10pm; @📶) This midrange hotel offers good year-round value in the otherwise expensive Geneva. Rooms are quiet and well cared for, those on the 1st floor share a kitchen, and there are fridges for guests to store picnic supplies – or sausages – in. Ride the lift to the 5th floor to flop on its uniquely wonderful flower-filled rooftop terrace, complete with barbecue after a long day's sightseeing.

**Hôtel N'vY** HOTEL €€
(☎022 544 66 66; www.hotelnvygeneva.com; Rue de Richemont 18; r weekend/weekday from Sfr175/260; ❄@📶) Contemporary flair abounds at this modish four-star northeast of the train station, from the purple-lit bar downstairs to in-room amenities like international power outlets, Bluetooth connectivity and chromotherapy lighting. Among the five room categories, all but the standards come with big-screen TV, espresso machine and parquet wood floor. Upper-floor executive rooms have views of Lake Geneva and the Alps.

### A DETOUR INTO BOHEMIA

Bohemia strikes in **Carouge**, where the lack of any real sights – bar fashionable 18th-century houses overlooking courtyard gardens and tiny **Musée de Carouge** (www.carouge.ch/musee; Pl de la Sardaigne 2; ⏲2-6pm Tue-Sun) FREE displaying 19th-century ceramics – is part of the charm.

Carouge, today a neighbourhood 3½km south of Gare CFF de Cornavin (p57), was refashioned by Vittorio Amedeo III, king of Sardinia and duke of Savoy, in an 18th century in a bid to rival Geneva as a centre of commerce. In 1816 the Treaty of Turin handed it to Geneva and today its narrow streets are filled with bars, boutiques and artists' workshops.

Trams 12 and 18 link central Geneva with Carouge's plane-tree-studded central square, **Place du Marché**, which is abuzz with market stalls on Wednesday and Saturday mornings. Horses can be seen trotting along the streets during April's Fête du Cheval, and horse-drawn carriages line up on Place de l'Octroi in December to take Christmas shoppers for a ride.

DON'T MISS

## TOP PICNIC SPOTS

With mountains of fine views to pick from, Geneva is prime picnicking terrain for those reluctant to pay too much to eat. Shop for supplies at downtown *boulangeries* and delis, or at the takeaway food hall in the Globus (p57) department store, and head for one of these classic picnic spots:

➡ In the contemplative shade of Henry Moore's voluptuous sculpture *Reclining Figure Arch Leg* (1973) in the park opposite the Musée d'Art et d'Histoire (p45).

➡ Behind the cathedral on **Terrasse Agrippa d'Abigné** (Rue de l'Evêché 7), a tree-shaded park with benches, a sandpit and a seesaw for kids, and a fine rooftop and cathedral view.

➡ On a bench on Quai du Mont-Blanc (p49) with Mont Blanc view (sunny days only).

➡ On the world's longest bench (126m) on chestnut-tree-lined Promenade de la Treille in Parc des Bastions (p49).

**Hotel Edelweiss** HOTEL €€
(☎022 544 51 51; www.hoteledelweissgeneva.com; Pl de la Navigation 2; d Sfr150-330; ) Plunge yourself into the heart of the Swiss Alps with this Heidi-style hideout, very much the Swiss Alps *en ville* with its fireplace, wildflower-painted pine bedheads and big, cuddly St Bernard lolling over the banister. Its chalet-styled restaurant is a key address for traditional cheese fondue.

★**Mandarin Oriental** HOTEL €€€
(☎022 909 00 00; www.mandarinoriental.com/geneva; Quai Turrettini 1; d/ste from Sfr655/1350; ) Occupying a prime waterfront position, the striking Mandarin Oriental Geneva does not fail to live up to the exceptionally high bar set by the sister properties of this internationally recognised brand. Superior rooms are classically furnished and slightly larger than River View rooms, spacious Mandarin rooms are all out plum and purple and the suites, well, can you afford one?

★**Hôtel Beau-Rivage** HISTORIC HOTEL €€€
(☎022 716 66 66; www.beau-rivage.ch; Quai du Mont-Blanc 13; d weekend/weekday from Sfr550/670; ) If only the walls of this lavish, historic hotel, run by the esteemed Mayer family for five generations, could talk! Boasting an evocative setting where the Rhône meets Lake Geneva and offering exceptional views across the lake to the Swiss Alps, the Beau-Rivage is a 19th-century jewel. You'll certainly remember spending a night in one of its luxe, 'grand European' rooms.

★**Hôtel Les Armures** HISTORIC HOTEL €€€
(☎022 310 91 72; www.hotel-les-armures.ch; Rue du Puits St-Pierre 1; s/d from Sfr450/695; ) This intimate, refined 17th-century beauty slumbers against the quiet nocturnal heartbeat of the Old Town. Its 28 rooms and four junior suites are refurbished in a luxe, modern style with downy beds, Nespresso machines, painted ceilings, stone feature walls and exposed wooden beams. Service levels are as you'd expect for a hotel accustomed to hosting distinguished international guests.

## Eating

Geneva flaunts ethnic cuisines galore. If it's local and traditional you're after, dip into a cheese fondue or platter of pan-fried *filets de perche* (perch fillets), a simple Lake Geneva speciality.

### Pâquis & Right Bank

There's a tasty line-up of more affordable restaurants on Place de la Navigation and the streets surrounding the train station. For Asian-cuisine lovers without a fortune to blow, try one of the quick-eat joints on Rue de Fribourg, Rue de Neuchâtel, Rue de Berne or the northern end of Rue des Alpes. Hungry students can be found devouring half-chickens at the Pâquis branch of the Vieille Ville institution, **Chez Ma Cousine** (Rue Lissignol 5; mains Sfr14-19; ⏲11am-3pm & 5.45-11.30pm Mon-Fri, 11am-11.30pm Sat; ).

★**Buvette des Bains** CAFETERIA €
(☎022 738 16 16; www.bains-des-paquis.ch; Quai du Mont-Blanc 30, Bains des Pâquis; mains Sfr14-23; ⏲7am-10.30pm; ) Meet Genevans at this earthy beach bar – rough and hip around the edges – at the Bains des Pâquis lakeside pool and sauna complex. Grab breakfast, a salad or the *plat du jour* (dish of the day), or dip

into a *fondue au crémant* (sparkling-wine fondue). Dining is self-service on trays and alfresco in summer.

In summer you'll need to pay Sfr2/1 per adult/child to enter the pool area where the canteen is located.

**★Manora** CAFETERIA €
(022 909 44 80; www.manor.ch/fr/u/manora; Centre Commercial Manor, Rue de Cornavin 6; small plates Sfr4-14; ) The cafeteria in the Manor (p57) shopping centre by Gare CFF de Cornavin (p57) is one of the best spots in town to get a reasonably priced lunch and everybody knows it – you won't be dining alone. The food is fresh and keeps on coming. There's a veritable smorgasbord of choice from salads to sandwiches, seafood, soups, meats, pasta and pastries.

**La Réplique** INTERNATIONAL €
(022 731 11 21; www.saintgervais.ch/pages/caferestau; Rue du Temple 6; mains Sfr18-22; 8.30am-5pm Mon, to 11.30pm Tue-Thu, to 1am Fri, 5pm-1am Sat) Secreted away on the ground floor of the Théâtre St-Gervais, this welcoming eatery serves delicious, reasonably priced *plats du jour* all day long. Choose your main course and watch in delight as they fill your plate brimful with a noteworthy profusion of fresh vegetable side dishes. Light eaters can opt for the *soupe du jour* (Sfr8).

**Les 5 Portes** BISTRO €€
(022 731 84 38; www.les5portes.com; Rue de Zürich 8; lunch set menu Sfr18, dinner mains Sfr28-44; noon-11pm Mon-Fri, 6-11pm Sat, 11am-5pm & 6-10pm Sun) The Five Doors – with, indeed, five doors – is a fashionable Pâquis port of call that successfully embraces the gamut of moods and moments for eating and drinking. Its Sunday brunch is a particularly buzzing affair.

**Le Grill** INTERNATIONAL €€€
(022 908 92 20; www.kempinski.com/en/geneva/grand-hotel-geneva/dining/le-grill; Quai du Mont-Blanc 19; 2-/3-course lunch menu Sfr38/45, dinner mains Sfr39-89; bar terrace noon-2pm & 7.30-11pm Jun-Sep) For one of the finest city views of the lake and snow-capped Mont Blanc beyond, head up to this smart-casual terrace restaurant with water-facing balconies, on the 2nd floor of the Grand Hôtel Kempinksi. Evening dining is pricier, but stick with the excellent-value Express lunch menu served on the FloorTwo bar terrace and you'll leave feeling very smug (and full).

## Vieille Ville

**Café du Bourg-de-Four** CAFE €€
(022 311 90 76; www.cafedubourgdefour.ch; Pl du Bourg-de-Four 13; mains Sfr22-34; 7am-midnight Mon-Fri, noon-midnight Sat, noon-6pm Sun; ) There's a great pedestrian vibe to this classic cafe-bar on the fringe of the Old Town, with daily *plat du jour* menus offering excellent value. In summer, the action spills out onto a street-side terrace where business-folk and tourists dine casually, side-by-side, on stodgy French and Swiss delights like steak *tartares* and unspeakably good *rösti*.

**★La Finestra** ITALIAN €€€
(022 312 23 22; www.restaurant-lafinestra.ch/fr; Rue de la Cité 11; mains Sfr29-52, set menu Sfr85; noon-2.30 & 7-10.30pm Mon-Fri, 7-10.30pm Sat) Since 2006 this handsome little restaurant nestled in the heart of the Old Town has been serving authentic haute-Italian cuisine in a casual, yet refined setting. The low ceilings and tiny tables wedged into the basement level of this historic building make for an intimate, if not slightly claustrophobic sitting, but the presentation, flavour and service make up for it.

### WE ALL SCREAM FOR...

Ice cream! On a warm day, nothing beats a lakeside stroll and a sweet treat from one of these Geneva staples.

**Gelatomania** (Rue des Pâquis 25; 11.30am-11pm Sun-Thu, to midnight Fri & Sat May-Sep, noon-7pm Oct-Apr; ) There's a reason why there's a constant queue at this gelateria with quirky flavours like organic carrot and such combinations as orange and lemon, cucumber and mint, and lime and basil, as well as caramel, pistachio and all your old-school faves.

**Mövenpick** (022 311 14 00; Rue du Rhône 19; 1/2/3 scoops in cornet Sfr5/9/12; noon-11pm daily Apr-Oct, to 8pm Wed-Sun Nov-Mar; ) The luxe address to sit down riverside and drool over the creamiest of Swiss ice cream topped with whipped cream, hot chocolate sauce and other decadent treats.

DON'T MISS

## WATERFRONT DINING

Summer life in Geneva is pretty fabulous, with often-perfect weather and the backdrop of the Alps drawing constant throngs to the lakeshore to hang out in pop-up terrace bars like **La Terrasse** (☎078 691 13 78; www.laterrasse.ch; Quai Wilson 31a; ⌚8am-midnight Apr-Sep), to see and be seen. Further afield of Quai du Mont-Blanc you'll find some special summertime shacks on the water for alfresco dining, drinking and living the good life.

➡ For casual Right Bank eats, pop in to Rhône-side **Terrasse Le Paradis** (☎076 715 83 70; www.terrasse-paradis.ch; Quai Turrettini; ⌚9am-9pm Jun-Sep), where you can recline on a deck chair and while away civil hours in the sunshine eating sandwiches and sipping beakers of homemade lemonade or pots of mint tea.

➡ **Le Bateau Lavoir** (☎022 321 38 78; www.bateaulavoir.ch; Passerelle des Lavandières; ⌚11am-midnight Mon-Thu, 11am-2am Fri, 5pm-2am Sat May-Sep) is an eye-catching boat with a rooftop terracek moored between the old market hall and Pont de la Coulouvrenière. Its cabin-size dining area cooks fondue and other basic local dishes, the crowd is hip, and there are 360 degrees of lake view. Its very design and name evokes the washhouse boats – yes, where undies etc were washed – that floated here in the 17th century.

➡ **La Barje des Lavandières** (☎022 344 83 56; www.labarje.ch; Promenade des Lavandières; ⌚11am-midnight Mon-Fri, noon-midnight Sat, noon-11pm Sun May-Sep) is not a barge but a vintage caravan parked on the banks of the Rhône near the Bâtiment des Forces Motrices. Part proceeds from the sale of food, booze (which, in summer, flows) and the variety of concerts and performances hosted here goes towards providing training programs for disadvantaged young people.

➡ Where to find the best *filets de perche* (perch fillets) is a bone of contention for many locals, but we think you can't go past the ferry ride to get to, and the vibe when you get there, of Le Petit Lac (p55). Oh, and the fish is divine.

## Rive & Eaux-Vives

**★Le Relais d'Entrecôte** STEAK €€

(☎022 310 60 04; www.relaisentrecote.fr; Rue Pierre-Fatio 6; steak, salad & chips Sfr42, desserts SFr 9-14; ⌚noon-2.30pm & 7-11pm) Key vocabulary at this timeless classic, where everyone eats the same dish, is *à point* (medium), *bien cuit* (well done) and *saignant* (rare). It doesn't even bother with menus; just sit down, say how you like your steak cooked and wait for it to arrive – two handsome servings pre-empted by a green salad and accompanied by perfectly crisp, skinny fries.

**ALMA** PERUVIAN €€

(☎022 736 31 48; www.alma-geneve.com; Rue Henri-Blanvalet 6; mains Sfr26-39; ⌚noon-3pm & 5.30pm-midnight Tue-Wed, to 2am Thu-Fri, 5.30pm-2am Sat; ❄✎) Healthy Peruvian food is all the rage in Geneva and ALMA is one of the better places to dine on what has been hailed as one of the world's 'most important' cuisines, for its long multicultural history. Sample dishes like *tiradito apaltado* (akin to spicy sashimi) and *pulpo anticuchero* (spiced grilled octopus) artfully presented in fabulously chic, casual surrounds.

**Café du Centre** SEAFOOD €€

(☎022 311 85 86; www.cafeducentre.ch; Place du Molard 5; mains Sfr29-44; ⌚6.30am-midnight Mon-Fri, 9am-midnight Sat & Sun) Beloved for its fresh seafood since 1933, Café du Centre has a charming old-school brasserie feel, with crisply dressed waiters bustling among linen-clad tables carrying plates of fish, lobster, mussels and oysters. There's plenty of meat on the menu, too, especially in the more modestly priced *plats du jour* (Sfr19).

**L'Adresse** INTERNATIONAL €€

(☎022 736 32 32; www.ladress.ch; Rue du 31 Décembre 32; mains Sfr24-49; ⌚11am-midnight Tue-Sat) The Address is an urban loft with a fabulous rooftop terrace, at home in a hybrid fashion–lifestyle boutique and contemporary bistro fashioned out of old artists' workshops. It's the Genevan address for lunch (great value at Sfr19/26 for one/two courses), brunch or Saturday slunch – a 'tea-dinner' meal of cold and warm nibbles, sweet and savoury, shared over a drink around 5pm.

**Le Décanteur** ITALIAN €€

(☎022 700 67 38; www.ledecanteur.ch; Rue des Eaux-Vives 63; charcuterie Sfr3-7, mains Sfr20-25; ⏱11am-3pm & 6-11pm Mon-Wed, 11am-3pm & 6pm-midnight Thu & Fri, 6pm-midnight Sat) No address is lovelier for fresh homemade *pâtes* (pasta), copious salads laced with fresh mozzarella, wafer-thin carpaccio and other true Italian dishes. The daily menu is written with a flamboyant hand on the blackboard wall and seating is in the faintly industrial-styled interior or on the busy pavement terrace outside. After work, it transforms from a stylish restaurant into a first-rate wine bar.

## Pleinpalais

**Café des Bains** MODERN EUROPEAN €€€

(☎022 320 21 22; www.cafedesbains.com; Rue des Bains 26; mains Sfr28-62; ⏱noon-2pm Mon-Fri, 7-10pm Mon-Sat) Beautiful objects and an eye for design, *sans* garish brand-name dropping, are the trademarks of this fusion restaurant opposite the contemporary-art museum, for whom the preparation and presentation of dishes mirrors the process of making art. Dining on the summer terrace beneath a canopy of trees and parasols is a worthwhile experience.

## Beyond the City Centre

★**Le Petit Lac** SEAFOOD €€€

(☎022 751 11 44; www.lepetitlac.ch; Quai de Corsier 14, Corsier; 3-course set menu Sfr 52, mains Sfr27-43; ⏱noon-2pm & 7-10pm; P) Take an afternoon boat with CGN (p50) from Jardin-Anglais or Genève-Pâquis to Corsier for an early dinner at this superb lakefront seafood restaurant, which serves a mean rendition of the local speciality *filets de perche*. Located near the French border, those with their own wheels would be able to combine a meal here with a visit to **Yvoire** or a ride on the Téléphérique du Salève (p58).

## Drinking & Nightlife

★**Cottage Café** CAFE

(☎022 731 60 16; www.cottagecafe.ch; Rue Adhémar-Fabri 7; ⏱7am-midnight Mon-Fri, from 9am Sat; 🚸) This charming little cafe in the **Square des Alpes**, near the waterfront, is a great spot to dip into for a chat with friends. Whether you're looking for coffee and cake or a glass of wine any time of the day, they serve tapas from 6pm and light breakfasts daily. On clearer days, the views of Mont Blanc from its garden are swoon-worthy, and lunching or lounging inside is akin to hanging out in your grandmother's book-lined living room.

★**Yvette de Marseille** BAR

(☎022 735 15 55; www.yvettedemarseille.ch; Rue Henri Blanvalet 13; ⏱3.30pm-midnight Mon & Tue, to 1am Wed & Thu, to 2am Fri & Sat) No bar begs the question 'what's in the name?' more than this buzzy drinking hole. With an urban and edgy feel, it occupies a mechanic's workshop once owned by the eponymous Yvette. Take note of the the garage door, the trap door in the floor where cars were repaired, and the building number 13 (aka the departmental number of the Bouches-du-Rhône department, home to Marseille).

★**La Buvette du Bateau** BAR

(☎022 508 56 89; www.bateaugeneve.ch; Quai Gustave-Ador 1; ⏱noon-midnight Tue-Thu, noon-2am Fri, 5pm-2am Sat, 11am-10pm Sun mid-May–mid-Sep) Few terraces are as quite so dreamy as this. Moored permanently by the quay near Jet d'Eau, this fabulous belle époque paddle steamer sailed Lake Geneva's waters from 1896 until its eventual retirement in 1974, and is now one of the busiest lounge bars in town during the summer. Flower boxes festoon its decks and the cabin kitchen cooks tapas, bruschetta and other drink-friendly snacks.

★**Village du Soir** CLUB

(☎022 301 12 69; www.villagedusoir.com; Rte des Jeunes 24, Carouge; ⏱8pm-5am Fri-Sun) Get in quick to enjoy the 'Village of the Night', which was granted a five- year lease to repurpose an industrial site by Geneva Stadium. Until they're turfed out, it's the place to be for a regularly packed calendar of events including DJ nights and gigs by local and visiting bands, exhibitions, pop-up restaurants, food trucks, fun and frivolity. The lease is set to expire in 2022 so check the situation closer to your visit.

**★Chat Noir** BAR
(☎022 307 10 40; www.chatnoir.ch; Rue Vauthier 13; ⏲6pm-4am Tue-Thu, to 5am Fri & Sat) One of the busiest night spots in Carouge, the Black Cat is usually packed thanks to its all-rounder vibe: arrive after work for an aperitif with a selection of tapas to nibble on, and stay until dawn for dancing, live music and DJ sets.

**L'Atelier Cocktail Club** COCKTAIL BAR
(☎022 735 22 47; www.ateliercocktailclub.ch; Rue Henri Blanvalet 11; ⏲5pm-2am Tue-Sat) Reputed to mix the best mojitos in town, this cocktail bar in Eaux-Vives is one of the city's hottest 'after work' spots. Its interior decor mixes classic bistro features with upcycled vintage, complete with leather armchairs to sink into and a piano to tinkle on between cocktails.

**Bar du Nord** BAR
(☎022 342 38 20; www.bardunord.ch; Rue Ancienne 66; ⏲5pm-2am Mon-Fri, 9am-2am Sat) One of Carouge's oldest drinking holes (around since the 1970s), this trendy bar is stuffed with Bauhaus-inspired furniture, the best whisky selection in town and a small courtyard terrace out back. The best nights are Thursdays and Fridays with good music and DJs.

**Café Art's** BAR
(☎022 738 07 97; www.cafe-arts.ch; Rue des Pâquis 17; ⏲11am-2am Mon-Fri, 8am-2am Sat & Sun) As much a place to drink as a daytime cafe, this Pâquis hang-out lures a local crowd with its Parisian-style terrace and arty interior. Food-wise, think meal-size salads, designer sandwiches and a great-value lunchtime *plat du jour*.

**Le Cheval Blanc** BAR, CLUB
(☎022 343 61 61; www.lechevalblanc.ch; Pl de l'Octroi 15; ⏲5pm-late Mon-Fri, from 11am Sat, from 10.30am Sun) The White Horse is a real Carouge favourite. Quaff cocktails and tapas – some of Geneva's best – at the pink neon-lit bar upstairs, then head downstairs to its club and concert space.

**Boulevard du Vin** WINE BAR
(☎022 310 91 90; www.boulevard-du-vin.ch; Bd Georges Favon 3; ⏲5pm-midnight Mon-Sat; 📶) Wine sluggers will enjoy this excellent wine shop that doubles as a wine bar with weekly *dégustation* (tasting) sessions. Food platters add a gastronomic dimension.

**La Barje des Sciences** BAR
(☎022 344 83 56; www.labarje.ch; Parc Moynier; ⏲11am-1am Mon-Sat, to 9pm Sun mid-May–Sep) At this dreamy summertime sister-venue of La Barje des Lavandières (p54) near the lakefront in Parc Moynier, just above Parc de la Perle du Lac, you can nibble on tapas and sip drinks until sundown, then dance the evening away to the sound of DJs or live music on the outdoor terrace; with part-proceeds creating projects helping young people in need.

**Le Rouge et Le Blanc** WINE BAR
(☎022 731 15 50; www.lerougeblanc.ch; Quai des Bergues 27; ⏲5pm-midnight Mon-Sat) Enviably perched across from the water, The Red and The White is one of the city's most popular after-work addresses. Its wine list – Swiss and world vintages – is outstanding and the food gets rave reviews, too.

## ☆ Entertainment

**★L'Usine** PERFORMING ARTS
(www.usine.ch; Pl des Volontaires 4) At the gritty heart of Geneva's alternative culture scene, this nonprofit collection of 18 arts-related initiatives is housed beside the Rhône in a former gold-processing factory. On any given night, expect to see cutting-edge theatre at **TU** (www.theatredelusine.ch), live music at **Le Zoo** (www.lezoo.ch) or up-and-coming VJ artists at **Kalvingrad** (www.kalvingrad.com).

**CinéTransat** CINEMA
(www.cinetransat.ch; Parc de La Perle du Lac, Rue de Lausanne; ⏲lounge-chair rental from 7pm, films start at sunset) FREE Free summer movie series, held under the stars in Parc de la Perle du Lac. For more comfortable viewing, arrive early and rent a *transat* (lounge chair, Sfr5).

**Victoria Hall** LIVE MUSIC
(☎022 418 35 00; www.ville-ge.ch/culture/victoria_hall; Rue du Général Dufour 14) Concert hall for the Orchestre de la Suisse Romande and Orchestre de Chambre de Genève.

**Grand Théâtre de Genève** OPERA
(☎022 322 50 50; www.gtg.ch; Bd du Théâtre 11) Geneva's stunning Grand Théâtre underwent a major transformation between 2016 and 2019. As well as receiving an all round facelift, technological upgrades make it now one of Europe's premier opera houses.

**Bâtiment des Forces Motrices** PERFORMING ARTS
(☎022 322 12 20; www.bfm.ch; Pl des Volontaires 2) Geneva's one-time riverside pumping station (1886) is now a striking space for classical-music concerts, dance and other performing arts.

## Shopping

Designer shopping is wedged between Rue du Rhône and Rue de Rive. **Globus** (www.globus.ch/fr/store/116/globus-geneve; Rue du Rhône 48; 9am-7pm Mon-Wed, to 9pm Thu, to 7.30pm Fri, to 6pm Sat; food hall 7.30am-10pm Mon-Fri, 8.30am-10pm Sat) and **Manor** (022 909 46 99; www.manor.ch; Rue de Cornavin 6; 9am-7pm Mon-Wed, to 9pm Thu, to 7.30pm Fri, 8.30am-6pm Sat), both with fabulous food halls, are the main department stores. The Carouge district and Grand-Rue in the Vieille Ville (p44) are peppered with art and antique galleries; or try Geneva's twice-weekly **flea market** (Plaine de Plainpalais; Wed & Sat) or the Thursday evening **Marché des Grottes** (www.ville-geneve.ch/plan-ville/marches/marche-grottes; Place des Grottes 1; Thu 4-8.30pm) for food, wine and cheese.

**Caran d'Ache - Maison de Haute Écriture** ARTS & CRAFTS
(022 310 90 00; www.carandache.com; Pl du Bourg-de-Four 8; 10am-6pm Mon-Sat) Beautifully designed boutique packed with a rainbow of pencils, pastels, paints and crayons crafted by Swiss colour maker Caran d'Ache in Geneva since 1915.

**Favarger** CHOCOLATE
(022 738 18 26; www.favarger.com; Quai des Bergues 19; 10am-6pm Mon-Fri, 9am-5pm Sat) A veteran on the Swiss chocolate scene, this respected chocolatier has a stylish lake-facing boutique near the spot where its first factory opened in 1826. A favourite for its vintage and contemporary design packaging, its speciality is Avelines, a supersmooth cocktail of milk chocolate, almonds and hazelnuts bundled into glorious melt-in-the-mouth bites.

**Librairie-Galerie Bernard Letu** BOOKS
(022 310 47 57; www.letubooks.com; Rue Calvin 2; 11.30am-6.30pm Tue-Fri, 11am-5pm Sat) Distinguished Old Town bookseller with a superb collection of large-format art books and other treasures.

**Le Verre en Cave** WINE
(022 736 51 00; www.verreencave.ch; Rue des Eaux-Vives 27; 10am-7pm Mon-Wed & Fri, to 8pm Thu, to 6pm Sat) A great resource for wine lovers, with dozens of vintages from Switzerland and 10 other countries, and a 'try-before-you-buy' selection of 32 wines available for free tasting.

**Collection Privée** HOMEWARES
(076 323 71 94; Pl De-Grenus 8; 2-6pm Tue-Fri, to 5pm Sat) Art-deco lamps, furniture and other 19th- and 20th-century objets d'art and curiosities.

## Information

The helpful, well-stocked **Geneva Tourist Information Office** (022 909 70 00; www.geneve.com; Rue du Mont-Blanc 18; 10am-6pm Mon, 9am-6pm Tue-Sat, 10am-4pm Sun) is just downhill from **Gare CFF de Cornavin** (www.sbb.ch; Pl de Cornavin) train station. The office produces a variety of local maps and guides, including a variety of themed walking maps in several languages with selected itineraries chosen to suit the tastes and sensibilities of speakers of that language.

**Ticket Point** (022 781 04 04; www.sttp.ch; Quai du Mont Blanc) is a one-stop shop for boat, bus and electric-train tours.

## Getting There & Away

### AIR

**Geneva (Cointrin) Airport** (GVA; Aéroport International de Genève; www.gva.ch), 4km northwest of the town centre, is served by a wide variety of Swiss and international airlines.

### BOAT

**CGN** (p50) runs up to four steamers per day from Jardin Anglais and Pâquis to other Lake Geneva villages, including Nyon (adult return Sfr39, 1¼ hours) and Lausanne (Sfr66, 3½ hours).

### BUS

**Gare Routière de Genève** (022 732 02 30; www.coach-station.com; Pl Dorcière) Operates buses across the border into neighbouring France.

### TRAIN

More-or-less-hourly connections run from Geneva's central train station, Gare CFF de Cornavin (p57), to most Swiss towns and cities. Left-luggage lockers in the main hall cost Sfr4/6/8/10 per six hours for a small/medium/large/extra-large locker.

**Geneva Airport** (Sfr3, six minutes)
**Lausanne** (Sfr22.40, 35 to 50 minutes)
**Bern** (Sfr50, 1¾ hours)
**Zürich** (Sfr87, 2¾ hours)

## Getting Around

### TO/FROM THE AIRPORT

The quickest way to/from Geneva airport is by train (Sfr3, six minutes, several hourly); otherwise take bus 10 from the Rive stop (Sfr3,

WORTH A TRIP

## VIVE LA FRANCE!

Geneva's proximity to France makes for some lovely day trips and the opportunity to save some money when dining (in euros)!

Oh-so-pretty French **Yvoire** (population 840), a medieval walled village 27km northeast of Geneva on the lake's southern shore, is the spot for everybody from diplomats to rubbish collectors to dust off the urban cobwebs on weekend afternoons. The postcard village with fishing port and fairy-tale château (closed to visitors) has cobbled pedestrian streets to stroll, flowers galore to admire and a restored medieval vegetable garden to visit: **Jardin des Cinq Sens**. Main street Grand-Rue is lined with souvenir shops, touristy boutiques and several restaurants including recommended **Le Bateau Ivre** (☎33 450 72 81 84; www.restaurant-lebateauivre.com; Grande Rue, Yvoire; menus €19-34; ⊙noon-3pm & 7-10pm). The CGN (p50) boat ride from Geneva's Jardin Anglais or Pâquis (adult return Sfr50, 1¾ hours) is very much part of the trip.

Quaint Swiss **Hermance**, 16km northeast of Geneva on the French–Swiss border, lures a chic crowd with its narrow streets lined with medieval houses, the odd pricey art gallery and the legendary **Auberge d'Hermance** (☎022 751 13 68; www.hotel-hermance.ch; Rue du Midi 12, Hermance; menu without wine Sfr70-88, with wine Sfr89-128, mains Sfr45-92; ⊙noon-2pm Thu-Sat, 7-10pm Wed-Sat, noon-4pm Sun; P), a prestigious culinary address where chickens are baked whole and served in a magical herbal salt crust. TPG bus E (Sfr3, 30 minutes, at least hourly) links Hermance with Rue de Pierre Fatio in Rive on Geneva's left bank. Or take a seasonal CGN (p50) steamer (adult return Sfr32, one hour).

In good traffic it will take you less than 20 minutes to travel the 9km from Geneva to the departure point of the **Téléphérique du Salève** (☎+33 04 50 39 86 86; www.telepherique-du-saleve.com; Rte du Téléphérique, Étrembières; round-trip adult/student/child €11.80/8.60/6.50; ⊙9.30am-7pm Sun-Wed, to 11pm Thu-Sat; 👪) cable car. Going up to the peak of **Mont Salève** (1100m) will take less than five minutes and you'll be rewarded with breathtaking views of Geneva, Lake Geneva, the Jura Mountains and to the southeast, The Alps, with (if the weather's fine) a clear view of the iconic Mont Blanc.

30 minutes, four to nine hourly). When arriving at the airport, before leaving the luggage hall, grab a free public transport ticket from the machine next to the information desk.

A metered taxi into town costs Sfr35 to Sfr50 and takes about 15 minutes.

### BICYCLE

From May to October, free bikes are available for up to four hours at **Genèveroule** (☎022 740 13 43; www.geneveroule.ch; Pl de Montbrillant 17; 4hr free, then per hour Sfr2; ⊙8am-9pm May-Oct, to 6pm Nov-Apr), just outside the train station; simply show your photo ID and leave a Sfr20 cash deposit. The rest of the year Genèveroule rents out bikes from Sfr12 per day. A second office, known as Terrassière, is located at Ruelle des Templiers 4 in the Eaux-Vives neighbourhood (left bank).

### BOAT

Yellow shuttle boats called **Les Mouettes** (☎022 732 29 44; www.mouettesgenevoises.ch; Quai du Mont-Blanc 8; single/60min ticket Sfr2/3; ⊙7.30am-7.30pm Mon-Fri, 10am-2pm Sat, 3-6pm Sun Sep-May, until 9pm May-Sep) – the name means 'seagulls' – cross the lake every 10 minutes between 7.30am and 6pm. Buy single-ride tickets from machines on the dock, or use any valid TPG bus ticket.

### CAR & MOTORCYCLE

Much of the Vieille Ville is off limits to cars and street parking is a challenge; use the public car park **Parking du Mont Blanc** (☎022 310 01 30; www.parkgest.ch; Quai du Général-Guisan; per 25min Sfr1; ⊙24hr). Before leaving, validate your parking ticket in an orange TPG machine to get 90 minutes of free travel for two people on city buses, trams and boats.

### PUBLIC TRANSPORT

Tickets for buses, trolley buses and trams run by **TPG** (TPG; www.tpg.ch; Rue de Montbrillant; ⊙7am-7pm Mon-Fri, 9am-6pm Sat) are sold at dispensers at stops. TPG's main ticket office is inside Geneva's train station. A one-hour ticket for multiple rides in the city costs Sfr3; a *saut-de-puce* ticket valid for three stops in 30 minutes is Sfr2. A day pass offering unlimited rides costs Sfr10, or Sfr8 if purchased after 9am.

### TAXI

Either hop in one at the train station, book online (www.taxi-phone.ch) or call ☎022 331 41 33.

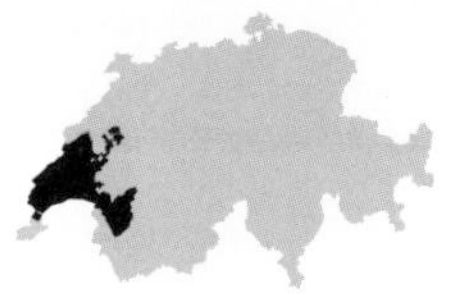

# Lake Geneva & Vaud

**Includes ➡**



## Best Places to Eat

- Denis Martin (p75)
- Hôtel-Restaurant de la Plage (p71)
- Eat Me (p66)
- Holy Cow (p67)
- La Crémerie (p75)

## Best Places to Stay

- Grand Hotel du Lac (p74)
- Fairmont Le Montreux Palace (p77)
- Hôtel Beau-Rivage Palace (p66)
- Hotel Lavaux (p73)
- Hôtel le Rivage (p72)

## Why Go?

Western Europe's largest lake, known by the francophones who people its shores as Lac Léman but the rest of the world as Lake Geneva, is anchored by the city that claims it, wrapping around her southern shore.

Half the lake belongs to France and most of its eastern shoreline, but the rest of it is the pride of the Vaudoise, from where views across the lake onto the Alps are nothing short of spellbinding. Explorations into the Alps reward summer hikers with perfect air and unthinkable vistas. In winter, the region becomes a pricey playground for the world's ski-loving elite.

The shore-hugging rail journey from Geneva to Montreux, past the terraced vineyards of the Lavaux, to Lausanne, home to a boisterous student population and the International Olympic Committee and Vevey (of Nestlé fame), whizzing by fairy-tale châteaux, luxurious lakeside manors and sparkling 'beaches', is one you simply must take.

## When to Go

- Spring and early autumn, with their warm days and riot of beautiful, perfectly manicured flower beds, are perfect seasons to visit.
- The lakeside flower trail from Montreux to Château de Chillon and Morges' tulip festival make the month of May a must.
- July ushers in a twinset of world-renowned fests – the international jazz get-together in Montreux and Nyon's multifaceted Paléo music fest – while more boats than ever zig-zag around the lake.
- Swimming in the lake is most pleasant in July and August, while January and February translate as skiing in the Vaud Alps.

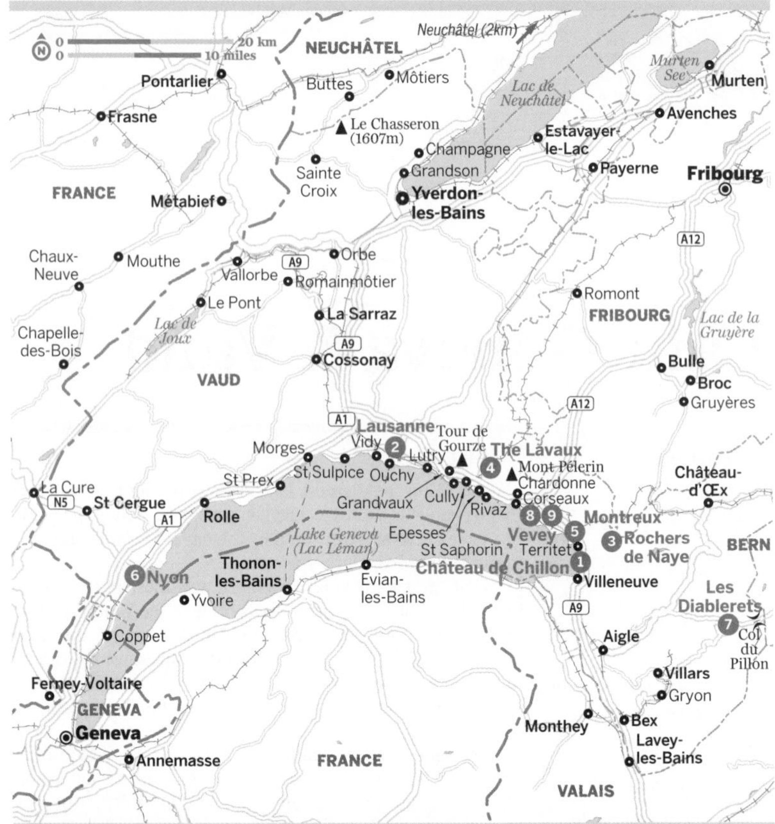


## Lake Geneva & Vaud Highlights

1. **Château de Chillon** (p77) Meandering the Flower Path from this magnificent castle to Montreux.
2. **Olympic Museum** (p61) Celebrating the sporting event that unites the planet in Lausanne.
3. **Rochers de Naye** (p76) Riding a cogwheel railway to an elevation of 2042m to meet the marmots and swoon at the views.
4. **The Lavaux** (p71) Wining, dining and getting giddy over jaw-dropping vistas from the terraced vineyards above Cully.
5. **Montreux Jazz Festival** (p76) Staying classy at the world's premier festival of jazz by the lake.
6. **Paléo Festival** (p70) Getting earthy at the alternative rock, EDM and arts festival, in Nyon.
7. **Peak Walk by Tissot** (p78) Ascending to the pinch-yourself panoramas of this suspension bridge between the peaks of two mountains in Les Diablerets.
8. **Chaplin's World** (p73) Celebrating the great entertainer in Vevey.
9. **Villa Le Lac** (p74) Contemplating the progression of modern architecture, also in Vevey.

## History

As early as 58 BCE Caesar's troops had penetrated what is now southwestern Switzerland. In the following centuries a mix of Celtic tribes and Romans lived a life of peace and prosperity.

By the 4th century CE the Romans had largely pulled out of Switzerland and Germanic tribes stepped into the vacuum. Christianised Burgundians arrived in the southwest in the 5th century and picked up the Vulgar Latin tongue that was the precursor to French. Absorbed by the Franks, Vaud became part of the Holy Roman Empire in 1032.

In the 12th and 13th centuries the dukes of Savoy slowly assumed control of Vaud and embarked on the construction of impressive lakeside castles. The canton of Bern appreciatively took them over when, in 1536, it declared war on Savoy and seized Vaud.

The French Revolution in 1789 had heavy consequences for its neighbours, and by December 1797 the Directorate in Paris placed Vaud under its protection. In 1803 Napoleon imposed the Act of Mediation that created the Swiss Confederation, in which Vaud, with Lausanne as its capital, became one of six separate cantons.

The second half of the 19th century was one of industrial development and comparative prosperity for the canton, but that was later slowed by the turbulence of the two world wars.

# Lausanne

POP 146,372 / ELEVATION 495M

Surrounded by vineyards, rolling down a trio of hillsides to the lakeshore, Switzerland's fourth-largest city, Lausanne, likes to think it gives Geneva a run for its money.

While the busy and gridlocked Geneva seems to focus on the past and its reputation for hosting more international organisations than anywhere in the world, Lausanne choses instead to look to the future. The city is known for its upbeat vibe, perhaps on account of its enviable location (vistas this end of the lake are more dramatic than Geneva's) and its high-brow though party-hearty student population – Lausanne's EPFL Research Institute is considered Europe's version of Boston's MIT. The headquarters of the International Olympic Committee are here, as well as unique museums undergoing exciting transformations and a new aquarium contrasting with the city's Gothic Old Town.

The neighbourhoods of *chichi* lakeside Ouchy and Flon, with its re-imagined warehouses, reflect Lausanne's more modern leaning hip, urban culture; both beckon you to visit.

## History

The Romans first set up camp on the lake at Vidy. At this time it was a key stop on the route from Italy to Gaul that came to be known as Lousonna. In the face of an invasion by the Alemanni in the 4th century CE, inhabitants of Lousonna fled to the hilly inland site that subsequently became the heart of medieval Lausanne.

In 1529 Guillaume Farel, one of John Calvin's followers, arrived in town preaching about the Reformation, but it wasn't until seven years after that, when Bern occupied the city that the Catholics were obliged to take notice.

From the 18th century Lausanne exerted a fascination over writers and freethinkers, attracting such literary giants as Voltaire, Dickens, Byron and TS Eliot (who wrote *The Waste Land* here).

## Sights

Down by the water in **Ouchy**, Lake Geneva (Lac Léman) is the source of many a sporting opportunity in Lausanne. Whether you're interested in spending the day sailing, windsurfing or swimming; the tourist office will be able to provide you with more details. It's impossible to miss the many seasonal stands in front of Château d'Ouchy where you can go to rent pedalos and kayaks for a day on the water, while cycling and rollerblading are popular on the silky-smooth waterfront promenades. West of Ouchy, **Vidy Beach**, backed by thick woods and parklands, is one of Lake Geneva's few sandy beaches.

**★Olympic Museum** MUSEUM

(Musée Olympique; Map p62; ☎021 621 65 11; www.olympic.org/museum; Quai d'Ouchy 1; adult/child Sfr18/10; ⏲9am-6pm daily May–mid-Oct, 10am-6pm Tue-Sun mid-Oct–Apr; P 👪) Musée Olympique is easily Lausanne's most lavish museum and an essential stop for sports buffs of all ages. Several state-of-the-art installations recount the Olympic story from the year 776BC, when the first games were played in Ancient Greece to the present day. Video, interactive displays, memorabilia and temporary themed exhibitions all come together to take you on a journey through the history of the world's most illustrious sporting spectacle. Other attractions include peaceful tiered landscaped gardens, site-specific sculptural works and a fabulous cafe that comes complete with champion lake views from its terrace.

# Lausanne

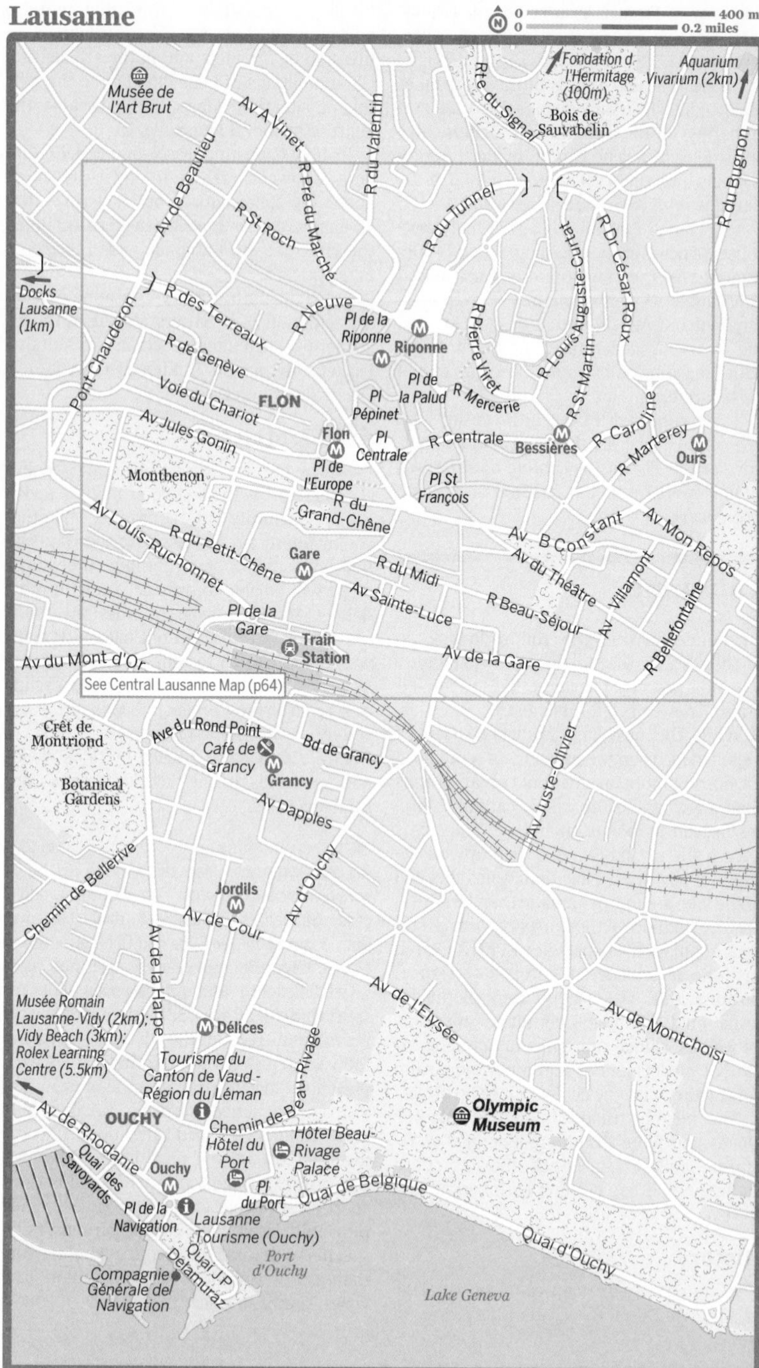
0 400 m
0 0.2 miles
Musée de l'Art Brut
Av A Vinet
R du Valentin
Rte du Signal
Fondation de l'Hermitage (100m)
Aquarium Vivarium (2km)
Bois de Sauvabelin
R du Bugnon
Av de Beaulieu
R Pré du Marché
R St Roch
R du Tunnel
R Louis Auguste-Curtat
R Dr César Roux
Docks Lausanne (1km)
R des Terreaux
Pont Chauderon
R Neuve
Pl de la Riponne
Riponne
R Pierre Viret
R de Genève
Voie du Chariot
FLON
Pl Pépinet
Pl de la Palud
R Mercerie
R St Martin
R Caroline
Av Jules Gonin
Flon
Pl Centrale
R Centrale
Bessières
R Marterey
Ours
Pl de l'Europe
Montbenon
Pl St François
R du Grand-Chêne
Av Louis-Ruchonnet
R du Petit-Chêne
Gare
Av B Constant
Av Mon Repos
R du Midi
Av du Théâtre
Av Villamont
R Bellefontaine
Av Sainte-Luce
R Beau-Séjour
Pl de la Gare
Train Station
Av de la Gare
Av du Mont d'Or
See Central Lausanne Map (p64)
Crêt de Montriond
Ave du Rond Point
Café de Grancy
Grancy
Bd de Grancy
Botanical Gardens
Av Dapples
Av Juste-Olivier
Chemin de Bellerive
Jordils
Av d'Ouchy
Av de Cour
Av de la Harpe
Av de l'Elysée
Av de Montchoisi
Musée Romain Lausanne-Vidy (2km); Vidy Beach (3km); Rolex Learning Centre (5.5km)
Délices
Tourisme du Canton de Vaud - Région du Léman
Chemin de Beau-Rivage
Olympic Museum
OUCHY
Av de Rhodanie
Hôtel du Port
Hôtel Beau-Rivage Palace
Quai des Savoyards
Ouchy
Pl du Port
Quai de Belgique
Pl de la Navigation
Lausanne Tourisme (Ouchy)
Quai J P Delamuraz
Port d'Ouchy
Quai d'Ouchy
Compagnie Générale de Navigation
Lake Geneva

**★Cathédrale de Notre Dame** CATHEDRAL

(Map p64; ☎021 316 71 60; www.cath-vd.ch/cvd_parish/notre-dame; Pl de la Cathédrale; ⏰9am-7pm Apr-Sep, to 5.30pm Oct-Mar) Lausanne's Gothic cathedral, Switzerland's finest, stands proudly at the heart of the Old Town. Raised in the 12th and 13th centuries on the site of earlier, humbler churches, it lacks the lightness of French Gothic buildings but is remarkable nonetheless. Pope Gregory X, in the presence of Rudolph of Habsburg (the Holy Roman Emperor) and an impressive following of European cardinals and bishops, consecrated the church in 1275.

**Place de la Palud** SQUARE

(Map p64) In the heart of the **Vieille Ville** (Old Town), this pretty as a picture 9th-century medieval market square, was once bogland. For five centuries it has been home to the city government, now housed in the 17th-century **Hôtel de Ville**. Opposite, you'll find the **Fontaine de la Justice** (Justice Fountain), from where, atop a brightly painted column, the allegorical figure of Justice herself, clutching scales and dressed in blue, presides over the square.

Bear left along Rue Mercière to pick up **Escaliers du Marché** (Map p64), a timber-canopied staircase with a tiled roof that heads up to Rue Pierre Viret and beyond to the Cathédrale de Notre Dame.

**Musée Historique de Lausanne** MUSEUM

(Map p64; ☎021 315 41 01; www.lausanne.ch/mhl; Pl de la Cathédrale 4; adult/child Sfr8/free, 1st Sat of month free; ⏰11am-6pm Tue-Thu, to 5pm Fri-Sun) Until the 15th century, the city's bishops resided in this lovely manor across from the cathedral (after which it became a jail, then a court, then a hospital). Since 1918 it has devoted itself to evoking Lausanne's heritage through paintings, drawings, stamps, musical instruments, silverware and so on. Don't miss the film featuring Lausanne in 1638.

**Musée de l'Art Brut** MUSEUM

(Map p62; ☎021 315 25 70; www.artbrut.ch; Av des Bergières 11-13; adult/child Sfr10/free; ⏰11am-6pm Tue-Sun) *Brut* means crude or rough, and that's what you get in this extraordinary gallery with its huge collection of works by untrained artists (many from the fringes of society or with a mental illness). The collection was put together by French artist Jean Dubuffet in the 1970s in what was a late-18th-century country mansion. Exhibits offer a striking variety and, at times, surprising technical capacity, and an often inspirational view of the world. Take bus 2, 3 or 21 to the Beaulieu-Jomini stop.

### 10 O'CLOCK & ALL IS WELL!

Some habits die hard. From the height of Lausanne's **cathedral bell tower**, a *guet* (nightwatchman) still calls out the hours into the night, from 10pm to 2am. Four times after the striking of the hour he calls out: '*C'est le guet! Il a sonné dix, il a sonné dix!*' (Here's the nightwatchman! It's 10 o'clock, it's 10 o'clock!). In earlier times this was a more serious business, as the *guet* kept a look-out for fires around the town and other dangers. He was also charged with making sure the townsfolk were well behaved and the streets quiet during the solemn moments of church services.

**Fondation de l'Hermitage** MUSEUM

(☎021 320 50 01; www.fondation-hermitage.ch; Rte du Signal 2; adult/child Sfr19/5; ⏰10am-6pm Tue, Wed & Fri-Sun, to 9pm Thu) High-calibre temporary art expositions grace this beautiful 19th-century residence ensnared in the green peace and tranquillity of the Bois de Sauvabelin on Lausanne's northern fringe. A delight to stroll, the wooded park has a lake and contemporary 35m-tall wooden watchtower with spiral staircase to climb (great views).

Prolong the inspiring cultural foray with a guided visit and Sunday brunch (Sfr62) in the foundation's lovely cafe-bistro **L'Esquisse** or, on Friday or Saturday evening, take the guided visit at 6.45pm followed by dinner (Sfr89). Both require an advance phone reservation.

**Rolex Learning Centre** NOTABLE BUILDING

(☎021 693 11 11; www.rolexlearningcenter.epfl.ch; École polytechnique fédérale de Lausanne, Rte Cantonale; P) This quirky building (which topographically looks like a slice of Emmental cheese) houses the main campus of the **École polytechnique fédérale de Lausanne** (EPFL), hailed as Europe's answer to Boston's MIT. Designed by Japanese architects Kazuyo Sejima and Ryue Nishizawa, it should be considered a 'must-see' (you can go

## Central Lausanne

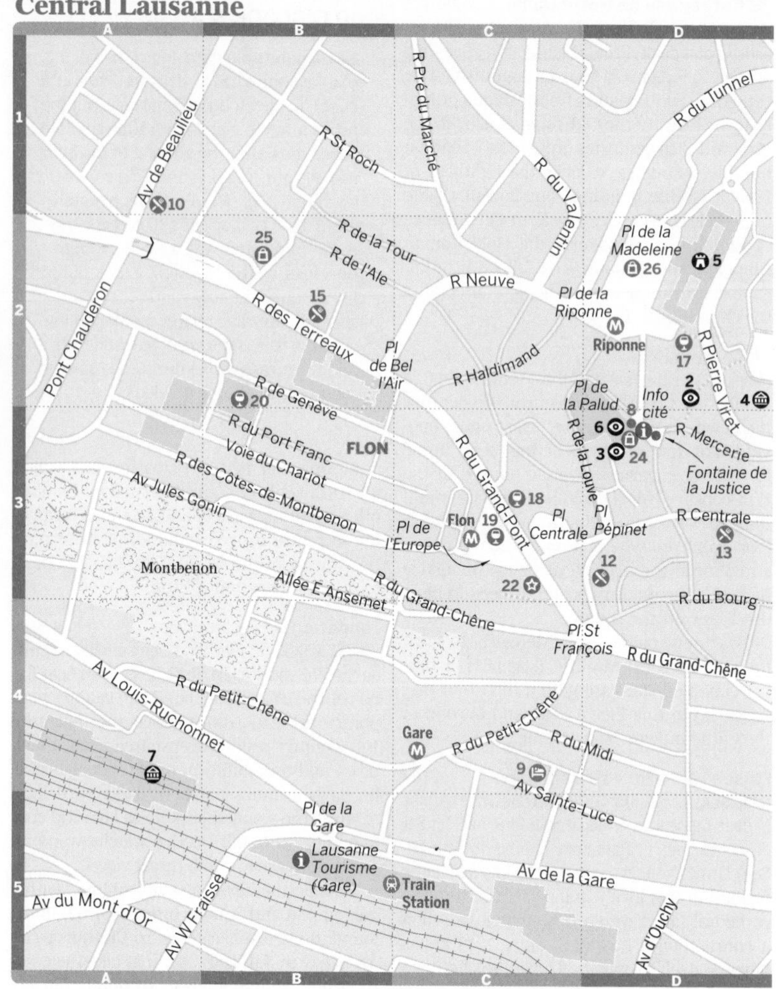


inside and stroll around) for students of architecture and fans of ultra-modern design.

## Activities

**Guides d'Accueil MdA** WALKING

(Map p64; ☎021 320 12 61; www.lausanne-a-pied.ch; Pl de la Palud; adult/child Sfr10/free; ⏱May-Sep) Walking tours of the Old Town, departing from in front of the Hôtel de Ville (town hall) on Place de la Palud. Themed tours for up to five people on demand. English-language tours are held daily and no reservations are required. Check the homepage for specifics.

## Festivals & Events

**Festival de la Cité** CULTURAL

(www.festivalcite.ch) This week-long festival in the first week of July sets the city's streets and squares humming with visual arts and open-air performances of dance, theatre and circus.

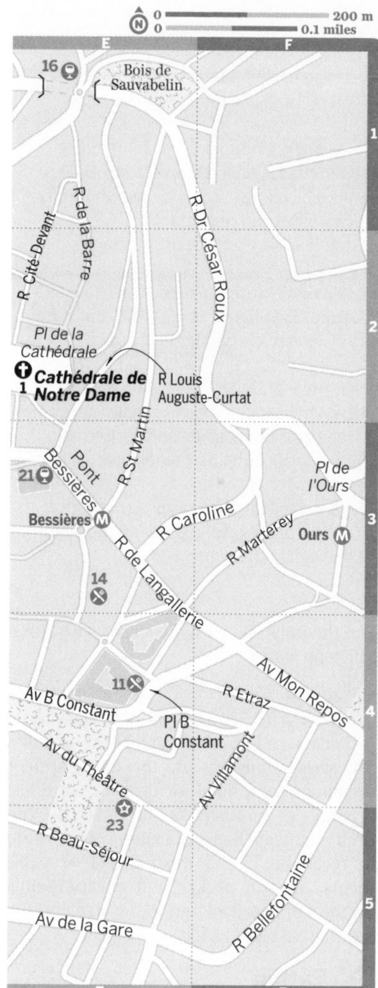


## Central Lausanne

**Top Sights**
1 Cathédrale de Notre Dame ................ E2

**Sights**
2 Escaliers du Marché ................ D2
3 Hôtel de Ville ................ D3
4 Musée Historique de Lausanne ................ D2
5 Palais de Rumine ................ D2
6 Place de la Palud ................ D3
7 Plateforme 10 ................ A4

**Activities, Courses & Tours**
8 Guides d'Accueil MdA ................ D3

**Sleeping**
9 Hôtel Elite ................ C4

**Eating**
10 Au Canard Pekinois ................ A1
11 Café St-Pierre ................ E4
12 Eat Me ................ D3
13 Eligo ................ D3
14 Holy Cow ................ E3
15 Holy Cow ................ B2

**Drinking & Nightlife**
16 Caffè Bellini ................ E1
17 Great Escape ................ D2
18 Le D! Club ................ C3
19 Les Arches ................ C3
20 MAD ................ B2
21 Terrasse des Grandes Roches ................ E3

**Entertainment**
22 Le Romandie ................ C3
23 Opéra de Lausanne ................ E5

**Shopping**
24 Marché à la Place de la Palud ................ D3
25 Marché de Chauderon ................ B2
26 Marché du Centre-ville ................ D2



**Swiss National Day** FIREWORKS
On 1 August hire a pedalo early evening and sit back to enjoy fireworks on the lake at around 10pm.

## Sleeping

Lausanne offers everything from hostels to high-end hotels. When checking in at your accommodation, be sure to pick up a **Lausanne Transport Card**, which gives you unlimited use of public transport for the duration of your stay.

**SYHA Lausanne Jeunotel** HOSTEL €
(021 626 02 22; www.youthhostel.ch/lausanne; Chemin du Bois-de-Vaux 36; 4-bed dm Sfr43, s/d from Sfr43/105/130; P) A stone's throw from Lake Geneva, near the offices of the International Olympic Committee, this Swiss YHA (SYHA) is classed as a 'top' level hostel for its smartly renovated rooms, 24-hour reception and pleasant location nestled among parkland a stone's throw from the lake. A breakfast buffet is included in the rate and daily lunches and dinners are available (Sfr17.50).

## PLATEFORME 10

If you take a moment from being awestruck by the magnificent Alpine views and turn your head to look out the left side of the train as you pull into Lausanne from Geneva, you'll see the so-named Plateforme 10.

Scheduled to be open by June of 2022, Plateforme 10 is a new supermuseum being built as its own self contained art district right next to the Lausanne train station. Built to be more than just the museums, Plateforme 10 will be a cultural centre for the whole city and will include libraries, bookshops, meeting places, cafes and restaurants.

The new museum's main draw will be the fact that it will bring three of Lausanne's finest museums together under one roof.

The collection of the **Musée Cantonal des Beaux-Arts** (https://mcba.ch/) houses works by Swiss and foregn artists, ranginf from Ancient Egyptian art to Cubism, but the core of the collection is made up of various works by landscape painter Louis Ducros (1748-1810)

Set to reopen at its new Plateforme 10 location in June of 2022, the **Musée de Design et d'Arts Appliqués Contemporains** (https://mudac.ch/) has five major collections spaning a range of artistic disciplines. This ode to modern design and applied arts hosts six intriguing temporary exhibitions each year, as well as its permanent collection of ceramics, jewellry, glassware, design and graphic arts.

The **Musée de l'Elysée** (https://elysee.ch/) is an excellent photography museum hosting a permanent collection of more than 1,200,000 photographs covering the history of the art, from the tintypes of the 1850s right through to the digital age,

**Starling Hotel** HOTEL €€
(☎021 694 85 85; www.shlausanne.com; Rte Cantonale 31, St Sulpice; d/ste from Sfr150/260; P ❄ ᯤ) Located opposite the striking Rolex Learning Centre (p63) building on the outskirts of town, this bright new hotel has fresh, smartly designed rooms, new bedding, lots of natural light, opening windows and plenty of plugs and ports for your high-tech gadgets. Many rooms even have views over the lake.

**Hôtel du Port** HOTEL €€
(Map p62; ☎021 612 04 44; www.hotel-du-port.ch; Pl du Port 5; s/d from Sfr160/190; P ᯤ) A perfect location in Ouchy, just back from the lake, makes this a good choice. The better doubles look out across the lake (Sfr20 extra) and are spacious (23 sq m). Some very good junior suites are situated on the 3rd floor.

★**Hôtel Beau-Rivage Palace** HISTORIC HOTEL €€€
(Map p62; ☎021 613 33 33; www.brp.ch; Pl du Port 17-19; r from Sfr520; P ❄ ᯤ ≋) Easily the most stunningly located hotel in town, this luxury lakeside address is sumptuous. A beautifully maintained early-19th-century mansion set in immaculate grounds, it tempts with magnificent lake and Alp views, a grand spa, and a number of bars and upmarket restaurants (including a superb gastronomic temple headed by Anne-Sophie Pic, the only French female chef with three Michelin stars).

**Hôtel Elite** BOUTIQUE HOTEL €€€
(Map p64; ☎021 320 23 61; www.elite-lausanne.ch; Av Sainte Luce 1; s/d from Sfr210/290; P ❄ ᯤ) The same family has run this lovely apricot townhouse of a hotel for three generations. A couple of sunloungers and tables dot the pretty handkerchief-sized garden, and inside at reception it's all fresh flower arrangements and soft background music. Rooms on the 4th floor look out to the lake and the best have a balcony, too.

## Eating

Lausanne's dining scene is laid-back, but meal prices aren't, though a healthy student population in such a compact city means it's relatively easy to find lower-cost options if you're travelling on a budget.

★**Eat Me** TAPAS €
(Map p64; ☎021 311 76 59; www.eat-me.ch; Rue Pépinet 3; small plates Sfr10-20; ⏲noon-2pm & 5pm-midnight Tue-Sat; ᯤ ✍) Eat Me's tagline of 'The world on small plates' will give you an idea of what this fun, immensely popular and downright delicious resto-bar is all about: global tapas, basically, with everything from baby burgers (sliders) to electric sashimiviche (Sichuan sashimi à la

*ceviche*!) and shrimp lollipops. Everything is well priced and it's just downright fun. Bring your friends!

★**Holy Cow** BURGERS €
(Map p64; ☎021 312 24 04; www.holycow.ch; Rue Cheneau-de-Bourg 17; burger with chips & drink Sfr14-26; ⏰11am-11pm; 🚹) A Lausanne success story, with branches in Geneva, Zürich and France, burgers (beef, chicken or veggie) feature local ingredients, creative toppings and witty names. Grab an artisanal beer, sit at a shared wooden table, and wait for your burger and fab fries to arrive in a straw basket. A second outlet can be found at **Rue des Terreaux** (Map p64; Rue des Terreaux 10).

**Au Canard Pekinois** CHINESE €
(Map p64; ☎021 329 03 23; www.au-canard-pekinois.ch; Pl Chauderon 16; mains Sfr16-48; ⏰noon-2.30pm & 7-10.30pm) Authentic Hong Kong–style Cantonese cuisine is order of the day at this restaurant named after their eponymous speciality 'Peking Duck': if you're a fan of that dish, you'd better make your way here fast. Other favourites, like ma po tofu, and a variety of dim sum options make the cut, presented in a stylish, formal setting.

**Eligo** MODERN EUROPEAN €€
(Map p64; ☎021 320 00 03; www.eligo-restaurant.ch; Rue du Flon 8; mains Sfr25-68, 4-/6-course dinner Sfr90/150; ⏰noon-2pm & 7-10pm Tue-Sat) With a name from the Latin meaning 'to choose', this glamorous establishment replete with chic concrete-and-wood interior and Chef Guillaume Raineix at the helm, keeps it simple with a judicious menu grounded in local, market-fresh ingredients and technical prowess. Raineix's reputation precedes him, having honed his craft in Paris' toughest kitchens, including Four Seasons at Hotel George V. Reservations recommended.

**Café de Grancy** MODERN EUROPEAN €€
(Map p62; ☎021 616 86 66; www.cafedegrancy.ch; Av du Rond Point 1; mains Sfr19-44; ⏰8am-midnight Mon-Fri, 10am-midnight Sat & Sun; 📶) This place just to the south of the train station has sink-into-me lounges at the front for drinking, and creative cuisine for hip dining further back. An unbeatable value *pâte du jour* (pasta of the day) served with salad or soup is a lunchtime winner. Wednesday evening fondues, first-Tuesday-of-the-month themed dinners and great weekend brunches draw the crowds.

**Café St-Pierre** MODERN EUROPEAN €€
(Map p64; ☎021 326 36 36; www.cafesaintpierre.ch; Pl B Constant 1; meals Sfr18-36; ⏰7.30am-midnight Tue & Wed, to 1am Thu, to 2am Fri, 11am-2am Sat, 11am-6pm Sun; 📶) The fact that every table is snapped up by noon while friendly waiters zip between tables and that the telephone is constantly ringing says it all – this hip cafe-bar buzzes! Its interior is contemporary and relaxed, and the cuisine is modern European – think pasta, big salads and fish at lunchtime, creative tapas from 7pm, and brunch on weekends. Reserve in advance.

## Drinking & Nightlife

Lausanne has a reputation for enjoying the good life and knowing how to party (in Swiss terms) in locations as diverse as edgy student digs, smart city cafes and refined waterfront bars. The re-imagined warehouse quarter **Le Flon** is the heart of the city's nightlife scene, with bars, clubs and cafes pulling big crowds for a city of this size, especially on Thursdays and weekends.

### BRIDGE BARS

Where there's a bridge, there's a bar. At least that's how it works in artsy Lausanne where the monumental arches of its bridges shelter the city's most happening summertime bars.

**Les Arches** (Map p64; www.lesarches.ch; Pl de l'Europe; ⏰11am-midnight Mon-Wed, to 1am Thu, to 2am Fri & Sat, 1pm-midnight Sun) Occupying four arches of Lausanne's magnificent Grand Pont (built between 1839 and 1940) above Place de l'Europe, this is the perfect port of call for that all-essential, after-work drink in the warm evening sun or that final drink before bed.

**Terrasse des Grandes Roches** (Map p64; ☎021 312 34 18; http://lesgrandesroches.ch; Escaliers des Grandes-Roches; ⏰2pm-midnight Apr-Sep) Mid-evening, Lausanne's hipsters move to this fabulous terrace replete with pool table, table football, palm trees and deckchairs beneath an arch of the Bessières Bridge, built between 1908 and 1910. Steps lead up to it from Rue Centrale and down to it from opposite MUDAC on Rue Pierre Veret.

Come dusk, many of the city's stylish cafe-bars and bistros morph into great places for lively tapas bars.

**★Great Escape** PUB
(Map p64; 021 312 31 94; www.the-great.ch; Rue de la Madeleine 18; 11.30am-late Mon-Fri, from 10am Sat, from noon Sun) Everyone knows the Great Escape, a busy student pub with pub grub (great burgers) and an enviable terrace with a view over Place de la Riponne. From the aforementioned square, walk up staircase Escaliers de l'Université and turn right.

**Caffè Bellini** BAR
(Map p64; 021 351 24 40; www.caffebellini.ch; Rue de la Barre 5; 10am-1am Mon-Thu, to 2am Fri & Sat) Lausanne's most charming terrace is tucked away in the Old Town and is the spot for summertime drinks, with fairy lights, a cool crowd and a retro-influenced interior. Antipasto platters and pizzas are good, and the service is chipper but occasionally forgetful. Call to reserve your spot.

**MAD** CLUB
(Map p64; 021 340 69 69; www.madclub.ch; Rue de Genève 23; 11pm-4am Thu-Sun) With five floors of entertainment, four dance floors and a restaurant called Bedroom, MAD (Moulin á Danse de Lausanne) is a mad sort of place, going strong since 1985 in the Flon area. Music can be anything (reggaeton, mashup, hardcore), the dress code is snappy, and 3rd-floor Jetlag Club is only for partygoers aged over 26. Sunday is gay night.

**Le D! Club** CLUB
(Map p64; 021 351 51 40; www.dclub.ch; Pl Centrale; 11pm-5am Wed-Sat) DJs spin house in all its latest sub-forms at this heaving club. Take the stairs down from Rue du Grand-Pont and turn right before descending all the way into Place Centrale.

## ☆ Entertainment

A patron of the arts, Lausanne has a vibrant theatre, classical music (including opera) and performing arts (including dance) scene. For listings, check out local paper *24 Heures*, online at www.24heures.ch.

**Le Romandie** LIVE MUSIC
(Map p64; 021 311 17 19; www.leromandie.ch; Pl de l'Europe 1a; 10pm-4am Tue & Thu-Sat) Lausanne's premier rock club resides in a post-industrial location within the great stone arches of the Grand-Pont. Expect live rock, garage and even punk.

**Docks Lausanne** CONCERT VENUE
(021 623 44 44; www.lesdocks.ch; Av de Sévelin 34; 7pm-2am Tue-Sun) Gigs embracing every sound, be it hip-hop, heavy metal or reggae.

**Opéra de Lausanne** OPERA
(Map p64; 021 315 40 20; www.opera-lausanne.ch; Av du Théâtre 12; box office noon-6pm Mon-Fri) Opera and classical music concerts presented in a recently refurbished building.

## Shopping

**★Marché du Centre-ville** MARKET
(Lausanne Market; Map p64; Place de la Riponne; Wed & Sat 8am-2pm) The pedestrianised streets of the Old Town around the Place de la Riponne, in the foreground of the Palais de Rumine (p59), come to life every Wednesday and Saturday with purveyors of quality regional produce such as fruit, vegetables, cheeses and meats. It's a great spot to stock up on picnic-hamper provisions or to try local snacks such as *taillé aux greubons* (flaky pastry cooked with pork fat). From early November to Christmas Eve it's also the location of Lausanne's bustling **Christmas market**.

There's also a flea market, **Marché de Chauderon** (Place Chauderon Flea Market; Map p64; Place Chauderon; 9am-7pm Tue & Thu) FREE, and a craft market **Marché à la Place de la Palud** (Place de la Palud Crafts Market; Map p64; Place de la Palud; 10.30am-7pm first Fri of the month).

## Information

Lausanne has tourist information coming out of its ears:

**Lausanne Tourisme – Gare** (Map p64; 021 613 73 73; www.lausanne-tourisme.ch; Pl de la Gare 9; 9am-7pm) At the station.

**Lausanne Tourisme – Ouchy** (Map p62; 021 613 73 21; www.lausanne-tourisme.ch; Av de Rhodanie 2; 9am-7pm Apr-Sep, to 6pm Oct-Mar) By the water.

**Info cité** (Map p64; 021 315 25 55; www.lausanne.ch/infocite; Pl de la Palud 2; 8am-noon & 1-5pm) A government office in the Old Town with some tourist links.

**Tourisme du Canton de Vaud – Région du Léman** (Map p62; 021 613 26 26; www.lake-geneva-region.ch; Av d'Ouchy 60; 8am-noon & 1-5.30pm Mon-Fri) Focusing on Lake Geneva.

## Getting There & Away

Lausanne is 66 km from Geneva to the south-west via the A1 motorway and 30km northwest of Montreux along the A9.

> **SAVVY TRAVEL**
>
> The seven-day **Lake Geneva-Alps Regional Pass** (adult/child Sfr130/65) provides free bus and train travel in the Lake Geneva region for three days in seven, and half-price travel on the other four days. It also gives 50% off CGN boat services and 25% off some cable cars, including Glacier 3000 (p78).
>
> A cheaper five-day version (adult/child Sfr105/50) is also available. Holders of one of the various Swiss rail passes receive a 20% discount off the Regional Pass. Order online at www.swissrailways.com/en/products/regionalalpspass.

#### BOAT

**CGN** (Map p62; www.cgn.ch; Quai Jean-Pascal Delamuraz; leisure cruises from Sfr25) runs passenger boats (no car ferries) from Ouchy to destinations around Lake Geneva (including France). To hop on and off as you please, buy a one-day pass (adult/child Sfr64/32) covering unlimited lake travel. Family passes are available.

Destinations include Montreux (Sfr27, 1½ hours, up to six daily), Vevey (Sfr21, one hour, up to seven daily), Nyon (Sfr35, 2¼ hours, up to four daily) and Geneva (Sfr45, 3½ to four hours, up to five daily).

#### TRAIN

You can travel by train to and from Geneva (Sfr22.40, 35 to 50 minutes, up to six hourly), Geneva Airport (Sfr27, 45 to 50 minutes, up to four hourly) and Bern (Sfr33, 65 to 70 minutes, one or two hourly).

### Getting Around

Remember to collect your free **Lausanne Transport Card** for unlimited use of public transport during your stay.

#### CAR & MOTORCYCLE

Parking in central Lausanne is a headache. In blue zones you can park for free (one-hour limit) with a time disk, which you'll find in your rental car. Most white zones are meter parking. Costs vary, but max out around Sfr3 an hour with a strict two-hour limit.

#### PUBLIC TRANSPORT

Lausanne is the smallest city in the world to have its own fully fledged metro system, and its 28 stations make it a cinch to get around.

Buses and trolley buses service most destinations; the m2 Métro line (single short trip Sfr2.10, day pass Sfr9) connects the lake (Ouchy) with the train station (Gare) and the Flon district.

# AROUND LAUSANNE

## Morges

POP 15,250

The pretty wine-growing village of Morges feels a bit like an extension of ever-expanding Lausanne, some 12km to the east. Dominating its bijou port is the squat château, but the real highlight here is the town's famous tulip festival held from mid-April to mid-May, which turns lakeside Parc de l'Indépendence into a vivid sea of colour.

Views across the lake from the park to the snowy hulk of Mont Blanc on the other side of the water are equally impressive, especially when the tulips are in bloom.

### Sights

**Château de Morges** CHATEAU

(☎021 316 09 90; www.chateau-morges.ch; Pl du Port; adult/child Sfr10/3; ⏰10am-5pm Jul & Aug, 10am-noon & 1.30-5pm Tue-Fri, 1.30-7pm Sat & Sun Mar-Jun & Sep-Nov) Dominating Morge's port is the squat, four-turreted 13th-century Château de Morges. Built by Savoy duke Louis in 1286, it is home to four military-inspired museums and 10,000 toy soldiers on parade housed in the **Musée de la Figurine Historique**.

### Sleeping & Eating

**TCS Camping Morges** CAMPGROUND €

(☎021 801 12 70; Promenade du Petit-Bois 15; campsite from Sfr12; P ❄) You can't beat this almost-lakefront campground for being one of the cheapest places to sleep by Lake Geneva.

★**La Maison d'Igor** BOUTIQUE HOTEL €€

(☎021 803 06 06; www.maison-igor.ch; Rue St-Domingue 2; s/d from Sfr170/190; P 📶) Igor Stravinsky's elegant old digs have been reborn as Morges' most charming boutique hotel, with eight individually and stylishly themed rooms (some with lake and Alp views). The hotel combines period features with contemporary details, a charming **restaurant** with a Mediterranean-influenced menu (mains Sfr28 to Sfr42), manicured grounds, a vegetable garden and a generous dollop of charm throughout.

**Balzac** CAFE €

(☎021 811 02 32; www.balzac.ch; Rue de Louis de Savoie 37; plat du jour Sfr24, mains Sfr26-39; ⏰8am-6.30pm Tue-Fri, 9am-5.30pm Sat, 11am-5.30pm Sun) Lovers of exotic hot chocolate, teas and dishes with an Asian twist should make a pilgrimage to this old-fashioned cafe, one block back from the lakeside promenade in the heart of Morges's old centre.

**Buvette du Mont Tendre** SWISS €€
(☎078 739 59 47; www.buvette-mont-tendre.ch; Rte du Mont-Tendre, Montricher; mains Sfr16-28; May-Sep; P) Claude Crottaz and his team prepare traditional Swiss cuisine in this breathtakingly located mountain hut atop Mont Tendre (1679m), the highest peak in the Jura, some 44km northwest of Morges. You'll need wheels to get here.

### Getting There & Around

Morges is 15km west of Lausanne via the A1 motorway.

Frequent regional trains between Geneva (Sfr18.80, 30 minutes) and Lausanne (Sfr7.40, 12min) stop in Morges.

Morges is one of the towns that have adopted the PubliBike (p335) system. You can purchase a **QuickBike option** (24 hours) from the Town Hall (located at Place de l'Hôtel-de-Ville 1).

## Nyon

POP 18,269

Of Roman origin, but with a partly Celtic name (the 'on' comes from *dunon,* which means fortified enclosure), Nyon is Lake Geneva's middle child, a pretty lakeside town, half-way between Geneva and Lausanne. There is a selection of good museums here, festivals galore and the pièce de résistance, a gleaming, white-turreted fairy-tale château.

Surrounded by vineyards and sloping casually downhill to the edge of Lake Geneva, Nyon makes a lovely, quieter alternative base to its bigger siblings on either side.

### Sights & Activities

**Château de Nyon** CHATEAU
(☎022 316 42 73; www.chateaudenyon.ch; Pl du Château; adult/child Sfr8/free; 2-5pm Tue-Sun Nov-Mar, from 10am Mar-Nov; P) Nyon's castle was started in the 12th century, modified 400 years later and now houses the town's historical museum and a rare collection of fine porcelain. Beneath the castle in its ancient cellars, you'll find **Le Caveau de Nyon** (☎022 361 95 25; www.caveaudenyon.ch; Pl du Château 5; 2-9pm Fri & Sat, 11am-8pm Sun), where you can taste different Nyon wines by local producers. Don't miss the sweeping view of Lake Geneva from the château terrace.

**Château de Coppet** CHATEAU
(☎022 776 10 28; www.chateaudecoppet.ch; Rue de la Gare 2, Coppet; adult/child Sfr8/6; 2-6pm Apr-Oct; P) This is the former home of Jacques Necker, Louis XVI's banker and minister of finance, before it was handed down to his daughter after she was exiled from Paris by Napoleon. It remains the little town of Coppet's crowning glory. Visitors can tour the rooms, sumptuously furnished in Louis XVI style, where de Staël entertained the likes of Edward Gibbon and Lord Byron.

**Musée du Léman** MUSEUM
(Lake Geneva Museum; ☎022 361 92 20; www.museeduleman.ch; Quai Louis Bonnard 8; adult/child Sfr 8/free; 10am-5pm Tue-Sun Apr-Oct, 2-5pm Tue-Sun Nov-Mar; P) Since 1954, this nautically themed museum on the waterfront has documented the history of all things Lac Léman, or as most know it, Lake Geneva.

**Château de Prangins** MUSEUM
(☎058 469 38 90; www.chateaudeprangins.ch; Av du Général Guiguer 3, Prangins; adult/child Sfr10/free; 10am-5pm Tue-Sun; P) About 2km north of Nyon, this 18th-century mansion houses a branch of the **Musée National Suisse** covering Swiss history from 1730 to 1920. Or simply opt for a stroll through the château's perfect French-style gardens with its *potager* (vegetable garden) and historical trail.

**Musée Romain de Nyon** MUSEUM
(Roman Museum; ☎022 361 75 91; www.mrn.ch; Rue Maupertuis 9; adult/child Sfr 8/6; 10am-5pm Tue-Sun Apr-Oct, 2-5pm Tue-Sun Nov-Mar; P) In the foundations of what was a 1st-century basilica, the multimedia display of the Musée Romain lends insight into Nyon's Roman beginnings as Colonia Iulia Equestris.

### Festivals & Events

★**Paléo Festival** MUSIC
(www.paleo.ch; Rte de Saint-Cergue; Jul) Nyon's six-day Paléo Festival, now in its fourth decade, is a key date in Europe's summer festival diary. Switzerland's biggest outdoor international music extravaganza, it lures rock, pop, jazz and folk-music lovers from far and wide.

**Visions du Réel** FILM
(www.visionsdureel.ch/en; Apr) This important festival on the international documentary-film festival circuit showcases the works of cutting-edge filmmakers from around the world. Screenings take place at a number of permanent and pop-up venues throughout town.

## Sleeping & Eating

**★Nyon Hostel** HOSTEL €
(☎022 888 12 60; www.nyonhostel.ch; Chemin des Plantaz 47; 6-bed dm Sfr33, s/d from 88/116; ) There's a bus stop at the front door of this hostel in the suburbs above Nyon, providing quick, easy access to the station. With a simple included breakfast, helpful, friendly staff, a large kitchen, outdoor terrace and airy balconies off each room, it's a smart choice for value and comfort in an otherwise expensive neck of the woods.

**La Barcarolle** HOTEL €€
(☎022 365 78 78; www.labarcarolle.ch; Rte de Promenthoux, Prangins; d from Sfr220; ) Rooms at this lovely lakeside property about 3km from Nyon, are spacious, comfortable and stylish, but it's the magnificent views of Lake Geneva, the Alps and Mont Blanc that you can enjoy from many balconied rooms and from the bar, from the restaurant or when wandering the manicured grounds, that make this place extra special.

**★La Plage de Nyon** SWISS €
(☎022 362 61 01; www.laplagedenyon.ch; Rte de Genève 12; small plates Sfr5-18, mains Sfr18-38; ) In the warmer months you'll love the refreshingly chilled-out vibe of this casual 'beachfront' kitchen. It uses seasonal ingredients and lake-fresh fish to produce healthy, seafood-centric small and share plates that taste great, plus heartier choices like fondue.

**★Hôtel-Restaurant de la Plage** SWISS €€
(☎022 364 10 35; www.hoteldelaplage.info; Chemin de la Falaise, Gland; mains Sfr34-86; noon-2pm & 7-9.30pm Tue-Sun Feb–mid-Dec; ) This low-key lakeside hotel in Gland, 7km northeast of Nyon, gets packed on account of its rendition of Lake Geneva's ubiquitous *filets de perche* (perch fillets), pan-fried in a divinely buttery, herbed secret-recipe sauce; fries and green salad included. Unless you specify otherwise, you automatically get two (very large) servings per person.

**Gelateria Venezia** ICE CREAM €
(☎022 362 09 89; Rue de Rive 44; gelato from Sfr3.50; 11am-7pm) The Italian-style ice cream at this legendary gelateria attracts punters from near and far (even from across the lake in France). Daniele Dona of Venetian descent is the culinary force behind this flavour revelation. From Nyon's CGN boat jetty on the lakefront, walk one block inland and look for the line outside the door.

## Information

The office of **Nyon Région Tourisme** (☎022 365 66 00; www.lacote-tourisme.ch; Ave Viollier 8; 9am-noon & 2-5pm) is just downhill from the station. It stocks a discount Nyon Museums Pass.

## Getting There & Away

Nyon is 26km north of Geneva along the A1 motorway. If you follow the A1 for another 42km, you'll reach Lausanne.

Regular express rail services from Geneva (Sfr9, 15 minutes) and Lausanne (Sfr18.60, 30 minutes) stop in Nyon.

# The Lavaux

East of Lausanne, the mesmerising serried ranks of lush, pea-green vineyards that stagger up the steep terraced slopes above Lake Geneva form the Lavaux wine region – sufficiently magnificent to be a Unesco World Heritage Site. One-fifth of the Canton de Vaud's wine is produced on these steep, gravity-defying slopes.

Hike up them for astonishing vistas of the Lavaux's unique terraced vineyards tumbling down the hillside into the lake, against the breathtaking backdrop of the Central Alps.

Walking between vines, and wine tasting on weekends in local *caveaux* (wine cellars), are key reasons to explore the string of 14 villages beaded along this 40km stretch of fertile and wealthy shore.

## Lutry

POP 9097

This captivating medieval village, just 4km east of Lausanne, was founded in the 11th century by French monks. Lutry celebrates its annual wine harvest with parades and tastings during the last weekend in September.

Stroll along the pretty waterfront and the main street lined with little galleries and shops, and the occasional cafe and wine cellar.

### Sights & Activities

Lutry's central **Église de St Martin et St Clément** (Rte de Taillepied) was built in the early 13th century, and there's a modest, medieval **château** (☎021 796 21 70; Rue du Château) a short way north. It's not open to the public, but you're more than welcome to walk around the building and take a quick peek inside.

DON'T MISS

### VINEYARD VISTAS

Climb to these prime vantage points for astonishing, 360-degree bird's-eye vistas of Lavaux' unique terraced vineyards tumbling down the hillside into the lake.

**Mont Pélerin** Ride the **GoldenPass** (☎021 989 81 90; www.goldenpass.ch/en/) funicular from Vevey (Sfr14, 11 minutes, every 20 minutes) through vineyards to the village of Chardonne, and onwards to the foot of this, the Lavaux's highest mountain (1080m). View not yet good enough? From the top funicular station, hike to the satellite-dish-encrusted communication tower near the top of Mont Pélerin and hop in the **Ascenseur Plein Ciel** (www.mob.ch; Mont Pélerin; adult/child Sfr5/3; ⏱8am-6pm Apr-Oct) for even more elevation and even better views.

**La Tour de Gourze** (www.gourze.ch; Rte de la Tour-de-Gourze) Built in the 12th century as a defence tower, this old stone structure peers out over Lavaux vines, Lake Geneva, the Vaud and the Jura beyond from its hilltop perch at 924m. Hike or take the narrow lane that twists up to the tower from Chexbres.

★**Domaine du Daley** WINE
(☎021 791 15 94; www.daley.ch; Chemin des Moines; 3-wine tasting from Sfr20; ⏱tasting with appointment, minimum 4 people 9am-8pm) Vines have been cultivated here since 1392, making it the region's oldest wine-producing estate – and a lovely spot for a memorable *dégustation* (tasting).

★**Plage de Curtinaux** BEACH
(Lutry Beach; Buvette de la Plage) In summer, there's a pebble-and-grass beach at the eastern end of Lutry town with *buvette* (snack bar and tables), stand-up paddle hire and pontoons. It's popular with locals and visitors from Lausanne.

**Lavaux Express** RAIL
(☎0848 848 791; www.lavauxexpress.ch; Quai Gustave Doret 1, Lutry; adult/child Sfr15/12; ⏱Tue-Sun Apr-Oct) A fun and easy way to lose yourself in green vines and blue lake views is aboard the Lavaux Express – a tractor-pulled tourist train that chugs through the Lavaux's vineyards and villages. Pick from two routes: Lutry CGN boat pier up to the wine-growing villages of Aran and Grandvaux (one hour return trip); or Cully pier to Riex, Epesses and Dézaley (1¼ hours).

**Caveau des Vignerons** WINE
(☎078 661 26 25; Grand Rue 23; ⏱5-9pm Tue-Fri, 11am-2pm & 5-9pm Sat) The traditional charms (low ceiling, barrel tables) of this low-key cellar attract locals and tourists alike. Well-priced wines and meat-and-cheese plates keep everyone happy. The two main wine types available in the area are Calamin and Dézaley, and most of the whites (about three-quarters of all production) are made with the Chasselas grape.

**Grandvaux Walking Trail** WALKING
A beautiful 5.5km walking trail winds east through vines and the tiny hamlets of Le Châtelard and Aran to the larger wine-making villages of Grandvaux and Riex. For staggering vine and lake views, hike up to La Conversion (3.8km) above Lutry and continue on the high trail to Grandvaux (4km).

## Sleeping & Eating

★**Hôtel le Rivage** HOTEL €€
(☎021 796 72 72; www.rivagelutry.ch; Rue du Rivage 1; s/d from Sfr135/150; P 📶) The three room types at this wonderful lakefront hotel, immediately in front of Lutry Port, have been recently renovated to a high standard of style and comfort. The priciest room is a Deluxe, which features oversized top-floor rooms with balconies overlooking the lake.

**Café de la Poste** SWISS €€
(☎021 791 18 72; Grand Rue 48; mains Sfr22-49; ⏱10.30am-11pm) This little cafe has a wonderful lakefront terrace with beautiful views across the lake to the Alps and serves traditional Swiss fare, including the Lake Geneva speciality, *filets de perche*.

## Getting There & Away

Lutry is 5km southeast of Lausanne along Rte 9.

The easiest way to get here is by frequent local train from Lausanne (Sfr3.70, five minutes), or catch bus 9 from Place St François (Sfr3.70, 14 minutes).

You could even walk if you were feeling active, but remember, what goes down, must come up.

## Cully

POP 1766

Lakeside Cully, 5km east of Lutry, is a lovely village for a waterfront meander and early-evening mingle with *vignerons* (winegrowers) in its numerous vineyards.

Many visitors will choose to hike along the well-signposted walking trail uphill (be warned, it's a hard slog) to the inland villages of Riex and Epesses and have a tipple in a wine cellar there instead, before looping back to Cully.

### Sights & Activities

**★Lavaux Vinorama** WINE

(☎021 946 31 31; www.lavaux-vinorama.ch; Rte du Lac 2, Rivaz; ⏰10.30am-8.30pm Mon-Sat, to 7pm Sun, closed Mon & Tue Nov-Jun) FREE This thoroughly modern tasting and discovery centre, 5km east of Cully in Rivaz, sits in a designer bunker at the foot of a terraced vineyard by the lake and is fronted by a shimmering 15m-long bay window decorated with 6000 metallic pixels inspired by the veins of a vine leaf. Inside, a film evokes a year in the life of a wine-growing family and, in the state-of-the-art Espace Dégustation, you can sample dozens of different wines.

### Festivals & Events

**Lavaux Classic** MUSIC

(www.lavauxclassic.ch; ⏰late Jun/early Jul) For over a decade, this festival, held in Cully and at venues around the Lavaux, has been bringing music to the vines in a series of outdoor concerts.

### Sleeping & Eating

**★Hotel Lavaux** HOTEL €€

(☎021 799 93 93; www.hotellavaux.ch; Rte Cantonal; s/d with lake view from Sfr174/220; P📶) Perfectly placed to take in views across the lake or of the famous Lavaux vineyards, the region's nattiest hotel has sleekly simple and contemporary rooms and a summer terrace perfect for sundowners.

If arriving by train, alight at Cully and head east on foot for about 1.5km, or catch a (less-frequent) train to Epesses.

**Auberge du Raisin** HOTEL €€

(☎021 799 21 31; www.aubergeduraisin.ch; Pl de l'Hôtel de Ville 1; r from Sfr160; P📶) This grand old hotel-restaurant started taking in weary travellers in the 15th century. One of the Lavaux's finest dining establishments, it has a rotisserie that cooks up a lavish meaty meal and offers a creative take on fish dishes (mains Sfr35 to Sfr52). In summer, head to the terrace for superb views over the lake to France. Advance reservations are essential.

### Getting There & Away

Cully is 9km southeast of Lausanne and 17km northwest of Montreux along Rte 9.

Local trains between Lausanne and (Sfr5.60, 10 minutes) and Montreux (Sfr9.20, 20 minutes) stop in Cully.

## Vevey

POP 17,676

There's something very special about Vevey that's hard to put your finger on, and that only those in the know would understand. Perhaps that's what gives the place its charm; a certain understated swankiness that's a little bit stuck in the 1970s and a little bit chic and cutting edge. It's not as over-the-top as fussy, fancy Montreux and it's just the place for Lausanne's brainy rebels to go when they graduate from university and decide they'd rather be *vignerons* (winegrowers) than scientists. It's just that kind of place: a little bit different. In a very good way.

However you look at Vevey, one thing is for sure: its position is perhaps the best on Lake Geneva, looking deep into the crux of the Alps across the shore. Vevey's Old Town is tiny but delightful, with a lakeside central square and promenade, some great museums, secret beaches, one hell-of-a-hotel, and did we mention Nestlé?

### Sights

**★Chaplin's World** MUSEUM

(www.chaplinsworld.com; Rte de Fenil 2, Corsier-sur-Vevey; adult/child Sfr23/17; ⏰10am-6pm) Opened in 2016, this engaging museum celebrates the life and work of iconic London-born film star Charlie Chaplin. Split between the neoclassical Manoir de Ban – the Corsier-sur-Vevey mansion where Chaplin spent his last quarter century – and a purpose-built interactive studio, the exhibits include multimedia displays, excerpts from Chaplin's films, recreations of film sets, family photos and other evocative memorabilia, right down to Chaplin's trademark hat and cane. A tour of the mansion's splendid gardens rounds out the visit.

Chaplin's World is about 3km north of Vevey, by the A9 motorway. Bus 212, departing Vevey station every 30 minutes from 5.30am to 7pm in the direction of **Fenil-sur-Corsier**, will get you to the 'Corsier-sur-Vevey, Chaplin' stop (Sfr3.70), in less than 15 minutes.

Allow at least a couple of hours to do this place justice; better yet, make an entire day of it with visits to the on-site restaurant and gift shop.

**★Alimentarium** MUSEUM
(☎021 924 41 11; www.alimentarium.ch; Quai Perdonnet; adult/child Sfr12/free; ⏲10am-5pm Tue-Fri, to 6pm Sat & Sun) Nestlé's headquarters have been in Vevey since 1814, hence its presence in the form of this museum dedicated to nutrition and all things edible, past and present. Boring it is not. Its displays are clearly meant to entertain as well as inform, starting with the gigantic silver fork that sticks out of the water in front of the lakeside mansion (a great picnic spot, thanks to the handful of wooden chairs screwed into the rocks here on the lakeshore).

Particularly fun are the Alimentarium's **cooking workshops** for both adults and kids, guided tours for families, and gardening workshops. Finish up with a healthy lunch in the museum restaurant.

**★Villa Le Lac** HISTORIC SITE
(www.villalelac.ch; Route de Lavaux 21; adult/child Sfr12/6; ⏲10am-5pm Fri-Sun Jun-Sep) Declared a World Heritage Site in 2016, Villa Le Lac, built by world-renowned Swiss architect Le Corbusier between 1923 and 1924, is a must for architecture buffs. The little white lakefront house, with its functional rooftop sun deck and ribbon windows, is the perfect overture to the great modern architect's better-known concrete building theme. His mother lived here from 1924 until 1960, followed by his brother until 1973. Visiting exhibitions are hosted each summer.

**Musée Jenisch** MUSEUM
(☎021 925 35 20; www.museejenisch.ch; Av de la Gare 2; adult/child Sfr12/free; ⏲10am-6pm Tue, Wed & Fri-Sun, to 8pm Thu) This museum exhibits Swiss art from the 19th and 20th centuries, as well as a broad collection of works on paper by international artists. Check out the special section on Oskar Kokoschka, the Viennese expressionist. Another section is dedicated to prints and engravings by artists ranging from Dürer and Rembrandt to Canaletto and Corot.

**Musée Suisse du Jeu** MUSEUM
(Swiss Museum of Games; ☎021 977 23 00; www.museedujeu.com; Rue du Château 11, Château de La Tour-de-Peilz; adult/child Sfr9/3; ⏲11am-5.30pm Tue-Sun; 👪) An amusing spot for kids, the Swiss Game Museum has games arranged by theme – educational, strategic, simulation, skill and chance – and there are several you can play, including outdoor ones in the elegant waterfront grounds. The museum is in a château on the lakeshore.

**Musée Suisse de l'Appareil Photographique** MUSEUM
(☎021 925 34 80; www.cameramuseum.ch; Grande Place 99; adult/child Sfr8/free; ⏲11am-5.30pm Tue-Sun) Focussing on the instrument rather than the image, this photography museum explores inventors, techniques and equipment and is a must for gear nuts.

**Chemin de Fer – Musée Blonay-Chamby** MUSEUM
(Blonay-Chamby Railway Museum; ☎021 943 21 21; www.blonay-chamby.ch; Pl de la Gare 3; adult/child Sfr20/15; ⏲9am-5pm Sat & Sun May-Oct; P 👪) This fun-for-the-whole-family steam-railway museum 6km east of Vevey has a fabulous permanent collection of locomotives and rolling stock, plus regular opportunities to take a ride.

## Sleeping

**Vevey Hotel & Guesthouse** HOSTEL €
(☎021 922 35 32; www.veveyhotel.com; Grande Place 5; dm from Sfr32; ⏲reception 7am-10.30am & 3-8pm) Housed in a 19th-century building with excellent facilities, this new addition to the Riviera's budget scene is a standout. Dorms are mixed or single sex, communal spaces are light and bright, plus there are rooms for singles, doubles and small groups, along with a few free bikes to borrow.

**Astra Hotel** HOTEL €€
(☎021 925 04 04; www.astra-hotel.ch; Pl de la Gare; s/d from Sfr109/138) Directly opposite Vevey station, the modern Astra gets top points for convenience. Unusual features, like a sunny rooftop terrace and hot tub, up the ante a little more. Rooms are large by European standards and are furnished to a high level of comfort and practicality in a clean, modern style.

**★Grand Hotel du Lac** HOTEL €€€
(☎021 925 06 06; www.hoteldulac-vevey.ch; Rue d'Italie 1; d/ste from Sfr297/513; P ❄ 📶 🏊) One of Switzerland's finest hotels, the 1868 Grand

WORTH A TRIP

## FONDUE MOITIÉ-MOITIÉ

The township of Châtel-St-Denis, 13km northeast of Vevey, warrants a visit solely to sample its legendary fondue *moitié-moitié* (made from a combination of Gruyére and Vacherin Fribourgeois cheeses).

Indulge at the well-known, family-run and very traditional **Café Tivoli** (021 948 70 39; www.cafetivoli.ch; Pl d'Armes 18, Châtel-St-Denis; fondue per person Sfr25; 11.30am-2pm & 6-9.30pm Mon-Fri, 11.30am-9.30pm Sat, 11.30am-9pm Sun), where you pay a per-person fee for your share of the bounty of the *caquelon* (fondue pot), or across the street at the quaint, cafeteria-style **La Crémerie** (021 948 71 87; www.lacremerie.ch; Pl d'Armes 21, Châtel-Saint-Denis; mains Sfr18-32; 7am-11pm Mon-Sat, to 8pm Sun; P) with its wonderful staff and adjacent *laiterie* (dairy) – basically a cheese shop selling every dairy product you can think of.

Hotel du Lac, still fresh from a stunning renovation by Pierre-Yves Rochon, impresses at every level. You'll adore the sumptuous oversized rooms that beckon you to stay in. Marvel at the prime lakeside position with inspiring views over Lake Geneva into the heart of the Alps. Is there any need to go on?

**Hôtel des Trois Couronnes** HISTORIC HOTEL €€€
(021 923 32 00; www.hoteldestroiscouronnes.ch; Rue d'Italie 49; d/ste from Sfr310/460; P@) The Three Crowns – an elegant, soft-cream-and-taupe mansion lavishly strung with white flower boxes on the waterfront – is among Lake Geneva's best. Its trio of floors open onto interior galleries, the period decor pays perfect homage to its mid-19th-century origins, and its luxury spa is divine.

### Eating & Drinking

★**Denis Martin** SWISS €€€
(021 921 12 10; www.denismartin.ch; Rue du Château 2; tasting menu from Sfr320; from 7pm Tue-Sat, closed 3 weeks Jul & Aug & 2 weeks Dec & Jan) Charismatic and engaging, chef Denis Martin is one of the country's biggest names in Swiss contemporary cooking and molecular cuisine. His tasting menu is a thrilling succession of 20-odd different bite-sized taste sensations, served in a traditional 17th-century mansion a block from the lake. Reservations essential.

★**Le Non-Stop** PUB
(021 922 35 68; Rue du Simplon 33; 11am-11pm) This bar-and-burger joint looks more like a British pub than anything else, and the crowd that mills around it smiling all day certainly adds to that impression, but it's actually a hot spot for some pretty serious American-style burgers to go with your beer.

**Le Littéraire** CAFE
(021 922 42 00; Quai Perdonnet 33; 9am-9pm; ) Take the local town library, add a trendy cafe with ceiling-to-floor windows facing the lake and a summertime terrace, and you get this local favourite. Check the blackboard outside for the good-value *plat du jour*.

### Information

**Montreux-Vevey Tourisme** (084 886 84 84; www.montreux-vevey.com; Grande Place 29; 9am-6pm Mon-Fri, to 3pm Sat, to 1pm Sun May-Sep, 9am-noon & 1-5.30pm Mon-Fri, 9am-1pm Sat Oct-Apr) On the square in the former market building.

### Getting There & Away

Vevey has an idyllic position tucked away in the corner of Lake Geneva between Montreux, 7km to the east along Rte 9, and Lausanne, 18km to the west, also via Rte 9. You can also take the A9 motorway to Lausanne: it ups the distance to 26km, but, depending on how you drive, it might shave a few minutes off the trip.

Vevey is linked by frequent regular trains to Lausanne (Sfr11.20, 15 minutes) and Montreux (Sfr3.70, 10 minutes).

## Montreux

POP 26,433

In the 19th century, writers, artists and musicians (Lord Byron and the Shelleys among them) flocked to magical Montreux, what was then a pleasing lakeside resort. It's been a visitor-magnet for the rich, famous and everyone in-between ever since.

Montreux's main draws include peaceful walks along a lakeshore blessed with 19th-century hotels, a mild microclimate, a hilltop Old Town, one of the world's premier jazz festivals, Friday-morning lakeside markets and a fabulous 13th-century fortress.

Rock-trivia buffs love the story of British hard rockers Deep Purple recording an album at the town's casino in 1971 and commemorating a fire that broke out during a Frank Zappa and the Mothers of Invention gig (also held at the casino). The pall of smoke cast over Lake Geneva inspired Deep Purple to pen their heavy-chorded classic, 'Smoke on the Water'.

From 1979 until his premature death in 1991, the lead vocalist came to Montreux with rock band Queen to record hit after hit at the Mountain Studios in Montreux Casino – he had an apartment in town and a lakeside chalet in nearby Clarens.

## Sights

**★Queen: The Studio Experience** MUSEUM
(www.mercuryphoenixtrust.com/studioexperience; Rue du Théâtre 9, Casino Barrière de Montreux; 10.30am-10pm) FREE Queen recorded seven albums in this lovingly preserved studio (they also owned the joint from 1979 to 1993), and a visit here will give you a strong sense of their oeuvre and relationship with the town. Charming paraphernalia (handwritten lyric notes and the like) means this shrine of sorts definitely has a kind of magic. Best of all, it's free!

The experience offers the possibility of mixing tracks and signing the wall outside the studio's door, making it a hands-on affair. Other luminaries who have used the hallowed space include David Bowie, Iggy Pop and the Rolling Stones.

**Freddie Mercury Statue** MONUMENT
(Pl du Marché) Year round, fresh flowers adorn the feet of this 3m-tall statue of Freddie Mercury in front of Montreux's old covered market on the waterfront. Created by Czech sculptor Irena Sedlecká, it's lovingly dedicated to Mercury as a 'lover of life, singer of songs'.

**Musée de Montreux** MUSEUM
(021 963 13 53; www.museemontreux.ch; Rue de la Gare 40; adult/child Sfr6/free; 10am-noon & 2-5pm Easter-Oct) Displays range from Roman finds and period furniture to thimbles and street signs at Montreux's local history museum, situated inside an old winegrower's house.

## Festivals & Events

**Montreux Jazz Festival** MUSIC
(www.montreuxjazzfestival.com) Montreux's bestknown festival, established in 1967, takes over the town for two weeks in July. Free concerts take place daily (tickets for bigger-name gigs cost anything from Sfr60 to Sfr450), and the music is not just jazz: The Strokes, Cat Power, Van Morrison, BB King, Paul Simon, and Sharon Jones and the Dap-Kings have all played here.

## Sleeping & Eating

**★Tralala Hôtel** BOUTIQUE HOTEL €€
(021 963 49 73; www.tralalahotel.ch; Rue du Temple 2; s/d/ste from Sfr130/190/250; ) This Old Town boutique hotel references Montreux's extraordinary musical heritage. The 35 stylish rooms come in three sizes – S ('Small and Sexy'), L or XL – and each pays homage to a different artist, from David Bowie to Aretha Franklin.

WORTH A TRIP

### ROCHERS DE NAYE

From Montreux station, a splendid **cogwheel railway** (adult/child return Sfr70/35, 55 minutes, hourly) hauls itself up the mountain to Rochers de Naye, a natural platform at 2042m that has particular appeal for kids with its native marmots, **Mongolian yurts** (www.goldenpass.ch; Rochers de Naye; 8-person yurt Sfr300, adult/child compulsory package incl breakfast, dinner & return train fare Sfr80/50) and, in December, the magical **Maison du Père Noël** (Santa Claus House; www.montreuxnoel.com; Village du Père Noël, Rochers de Naye; adult/child Sfr39/19; 11am-10pm late Nov–24 Dec; ).

The journey getting there is almost as impressive as the experience at the top, where incredible lake and mountain views and the lovely **Rambertia** (Jun–mid-Oct) gardens await.

Tickets for the train and the range of experiences available can be booked online (www.goldenpass.ch) or at the GoldenPass Center (p77) in Montreux station.

DON'T MISS

## LAKE GENEVA'S MOST FAMOUS CASTLE

From the Montreux waterfront, fairy-tale Chemin Fleuri (Floral Path) – a silky smooth promenade framed by flowerbeds positively tropical in colour and vivacity – snakes dreamily along the lake for 4km to the magnificent stone hulk of lakeside **Château de Chillon** (021 966 89 10; www.chillon.ch; Av de Chillon 21; adult/child Sfr12.50/6; 9am-7pm Apr-Sep, 9.30am-6pm Mar & Oct, 10am-5pm Nov-Feb, last entry 1hr before close). Occupying a stunning position on Lake Geneva, this oval-shaped 13th-century fortress is a maze of courtyards, towers and halls filled with arms, period furniture and artwork. The landward side is heavily fortified, but lakeside it presents a gentler face.

Chillon was largely built by the House of Savoy and taken over by Bern's governors after Vaud fell to Bern. Don't miss the medieval frescos in the Chapelle St Georges and the spooky Gothic dungeons. The fortress gained fame in 1816 when Byron wrote 'The Prisoner of Chillon', a poem about François Bonivard, who was thrown into the dungeon for his seditious ideas and freed by Bernese forces in 1536. Byron carved his name into the pillar to which Bonivard was supposedly chained. Painters William Turner and Gustave Courbet subsequently immortalised the castle's silhouette on canvas, and Jean-Jacques Rousseau, Alexandre Dumas, père and Mary Shelley all wrote about it.

It's about a 3km easy walk around the lakeshore from Montreux to Chillon, or take bus 201 (10 minutes). CGN (p50) boats and steamers – a wonderful way to arrive – call at Château de Chillon from Lausanne (1¾ hours), Vevey (50 minutes) and Montreux (15 minutes).



**Hôtel Masson** HISTORIC HOTEL €€
(021 966 00 44; www.hotelmasson.ch; Rue Bonivard 5, Veytaux; s/d from Sfr130/240; closed mid-Dec–early Mar; P ) In 1829 this vintner's mansion was converted into a hotel. The old charm has remained intact and the property, set in magnificent grounds, is on the Swiss Heritage list of the country's most beautiful hotels. It lies back in the hills southeast of Montreux, best reached by taxi.

**Hôtel La Rouvenaz** HOTEL €€
(021 963 27 36; www.rouvenaz.ch; Rue du Marché 1; s/d/ste from Sfr190/270/430; @ ) You cannot get any closer to the lake or the heart of the action than this newly renovated, family-run spot with its own tasty Italian **restaurant** downstairs and **wine bar** next door. Its 18 rooms are simple but pleasant, and five have lake views. Low season prices plummet.

★**Fairmont Le Montreux Palace** HISTORIC HOTEL €€€
(021 962 12 12; www.fairmont.com/Montreux; Av Claude Nobs 2; d/ste from Sfr359/750) Built in a record 18 months in 1906, this stunning example of belle époque architecture maintains a traditional and elegant atmosphere: today it's managed by the luxury Fairmont brand. Entry-level Fairmont rooms are gaudy and cramped for the price: it's worth paying extra for the renovated Deluxe rooms or splurging on a Deluxe Lake View room with balcony (from Sfr479).

**Restaurant le 45** EUROPEAN €€€
(021 966 33 33; www.suisse-majestic.ch; Grand Hôtel Suisse-Majestic, Av des Alpes 45; mains Sfr22-56; noon-2pm & 7-10pm; P ) Although the presentation of a fairly standard European and international hotel menu can be a little hit and miss, the panoramic view and expansive terrace combined make dining at this restaurant of the Grand Hôtel Suisse-Majestic worth consideration.

## Information

The staff at **Montreux-Vevey Tourisme** (021 962 84 84; www.montreuxriviera.com; Pl de l'Eurovision; 9am-6pm Mon-Fri, to 5pm Sat & Sun May-Sep, reduced hours Oct-Apr) can assist with hotel recommendations and bookings and will help you try and find a bed during festival time.

Stop in at the **GoldenPass Centre** (021 989 81 90; www.goldenpass.ch; Montreux train station; 8am-6pm) for information about the **GoldenPass** (p72) trains and funiculars that operate out of Montreux and Vevey.

## Getting There & Away

Montreux is 30km southeast of Lausanne along the A9 motorway, from where it's a further 66km via the A1 to Geneva.

Montreux has regular direct train services to Geneva (Sfr31, 1¼ hours) and Lausanne (Sfr13, 20 to 35 minutes) where you'll transfer if you're travelling onwards to Zürich (Sfr81, 2½ hours).

Montreux is also a stop on the scenic GoldenPass (p72) route into the Bernese Oberland.

## The Vaud Alps

The 'High Country' rises in the northeast corner of Vaud about midway between Aigle and Gruyères. In winter it could almost be considered the francophone extension of the swank Gstaad ski scene.

Tucked in a captivating Alpine nook, this area is essentially ski-bunny country, but in recent years, new attractions and improved trails have drawn visitors to the peaks in green season, when hiking and biking your way around this relatively unknown part of the Swiss Alps might induce rapture.

The medieval wine-making village of Aigle is the gateway town for the region with enough to keep you occupied for a few hours to a day, but the region's real allure lies in the mountains themselves. If you're looking for a scenic day trip from Montreux, or find yourself in Aigle with your own wheels, you're in luck – even if you don't ski or hike.

### Les Diablerets

ELEV 1150M

The mountain village and ski resort of Les Diablerets is overshadowed by its eponymous massif (3209m). Of the village's three main ski areas, Isenau and Glacier 3000 are the most popular, with the latter boasting the area's highest peaks.

Glacier 3000, so named for its position atop the 3.5km-long Glacier de Tsanfleuron, has had a surge in popularity since the 2014 opening of the incredible Peak Walk by Tissot suspension bridge. It's largely responsible for the village's growth as a green-season destination: should you be so inclined, it's possible to go canyoning, hydrospeeding, paragliding, dirt monster-biking, or just exhaust yourself among the almost 250km of walking and hiking trails.

Whether you plan to ski, bike or hike (or not), Les Diablerets's alpine vistas are top-of-the-world class, and it's a cinch to get here from Montreux if you just need to get up high for some pure mountain air.

#### Sights & Activities

**★Peak Walk by Tissot** BRIDGE

(Les Diablerets; 9am-4.30pm; closed 2 weeks mid-Oct) FREE On clear days the views from this world-first peak-to-peak footbridge are heaven-sent; think legendary Mont Blanc and the Matterhorn, plus Eiger, Mönch and Jungfrau. The 107m-long walk, between View Point Peak (2965m) and Scex Rouge (2971m), culminates with a spacious viewing platform and viewfinders complete with mountain names and altitudes, making it a must for lovers of the high life and not for those with vertigo or a fear of heights!

Take the cable car from Col du Pillon in Les Diablerets up to **Glacier 3000** (www.glacier3000.ch; Les Diablerets; 1-day lift pass adult/child Sfr63/42).

**Col de Bretaye Hikes** HIKING

In green season, a popular hike starts at the Col de Bretaye pass, taking you past the pretty Lac de Chavonnes and on through verdant mountain country to Les Diablerets, taking about four hours. Views from the pass are magnificent.

WORTH A TRIP

#### AIGLE

A must for anyone with a passion for wine, Aigle, at the southeast end of Lake Geneva, is the capital of the Chablais wine-producing region in southeast Vaud.

Two thousand years of wine making are evoked in the compelling **Musée de la Vigne et du Vin** (Wine and Vine Museum; www.museeduvin.ch; Pl du Château 1; adult/child Sfr11/5; 10am-6pm Jul & Aug, closed Mon Apr-Jun, Sep & Oct, 10am-4pm Tue-Sun Jan-Mar, Nov & Dec), a thoroughly modern and interactive wine museum inside Aigle's fairy-tale castle. The six hands-on digital experiments make wine etc – in the 'lab' are particularly fun.

Afterwards cross the castle courtyard to the 13th-century **Maison de la Dîme** (Pl du Château 1) and peek at whatever temporary exhibition is on upstairs (entry included in the museum ticket).

Aigle's **tourist office** (024 466 30 00; www.aigle-tourisme.ch; Rue Colomb 5; 8.30am-noon & 1.30-6pm Mon-Fri, 8.30am-noon Sat Apr-Oct) is in the new town, a 700m walk from the château. Trains run frequently to Aigle from Geneva (Sfr34, 1¼ hours), Lausanne (Sfr18.60, 30 minutes) and Montreux (Sfr7.40, 10 minutes).

DON'T MISS

## SKIING IN THE VAUD ALPS

The region's star performer is the village of Les Diablerets, whose **Isenau** (www.myisenau.ch; 1-day lift pass adult/child Sfr54/36, includes Villars-Gyron; ) and Glacier 3000 ski areas get top billing. The former is marginally easier to reach while the latter, perched atop a 3.5km-long glacier, has the highest peaks and a wider range of accommodations, facilities and amenities.

The amalgamated **Villars-Gryon** (www.villars-diablerets.ch/Z4031; 1-day lift pass adult/child Sfr54/36, includes Isenau) ski area, centred on the village of **Villars-sur-Ollon**, offers combined access to Les Diablerets's three ski areas, effectively linking five alpine areas into a gargantuan ski field of over 100 sq km, with at least 34 lifts. It offers breathtaking scenery and covers all levels of difficulty.

Lastly, little by name but not by size or nature, **Leysin** (www.leysin.ch; 1-day lift pass adult/child Sfr35/25), at 1350m, started out as a tuberculosis centre, but has healed into life to become a sprawling ski resort catering to all levels and boasting a whopping 60km of runs.

To get to the pass, take a local train from Villars-sur-Ollon to Col de Bretaye (Sfr17.80, 20 minutes).

## Eating

**★Botta 3000** SWISS €€
(024 492 09 31; www.glacier3000.ch; Les Diablarets; mains Sfr22-52; 10am-4.30pm) The striking white-cube-design of this high-altitude restaurant atop the Glacier de Tsanfleuron is the contemporary handiwork of Swiss starchitect Mario Botta, with gastronomic dining on the top floor and a self-service terrace and picnic area below.

From here, the ski back down to Reusch (1350m) is an exhilarating 2000m descent over 14km.

## Information

The **Office du Tourisme Les Diablerets** (024 492 00 10; www.villars-diablerets.ch; Chemin du Collège 2; 9am-6pm) is the best place to make sense of the somewhat confusing selection of pass and transport options for the area's numerous ski resorts.

## Getting There & Around

Aigle is the gateway town for the Les Diablerets region. It's an easy 20km drive along Rte 11 from Aigle to the village.

Alternatively, local trains run between Les Diablerets and Aigle (Sfr11.40, 50 minutes).

Each ski area is reached by separate cable cars, which are linked to the village by bus.

# Château d'Œx

POP 3168

Château-d'Œx is an attractive mountain village resort whose moderate ski runs are popular with local families. In the green season, it's a pretty town among gorgeous surrounds, best known for its hot-air ballooning and seemingly endless kilometres of hiking and mountain biking trails.

Best of all, Château-d'Œx's location and convenient access make it equally worthy as a scenic day-trip from Montreux, or overnight stop.

For one week in the second half of January, Château-d'Œx hosts **Semaine Internationale de Ballons à Air Chaud** (www.ballonchateaudoex.ch), an annual festival involving around 100 hot-air balloons, ranging from the standard floater to odd creatures such as a massive Scottish bagpipe player.

Another great reason to hang out in Château-d'Œx is to see cheese being made and scoff sugary-sweet homemade meringues smothered in far more cream than the doctor ordered at **Le Chalet** (026 924 66 77; www.lechalet-fromagerie.ch; Rte de la Gare 2; mains Sfr18-38; 9am-6pm Mon-Thu, Sat & Sun, to midnight Fri, cheesemaking 10am-noon Wed-Sun). This *fromagerie* is in a sizeable chalet strung with flower boxes in spring and summer, and surrounded by snow in winter.

## Information

The **Château-d'Œx Tourist Office** (026 924 25 25; www.chateau-doex.ch; Pl du Village 6; 9am-12pm & 2-5pm Mon-Fri, 9am-12:30pm & 1-5pm Sat & Sun) is in the centre of the village.

## Getting There & Away

Château-d'Œx is a scenic, though winding, 50km drive up into the Alps from Montreux and takes almost bang-on an hour each way. It's not a great drive if you're easily car-sick. In that event, it's much easier to catch a regional train from Montreux (Sfr20.40, one hour).

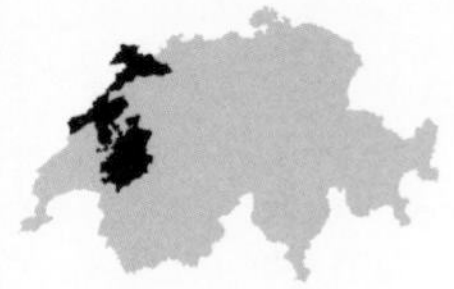

# Fribourg, Drei-Seen-Land & the Jura

**Includes ➡**



## Best Places to Eat

- Georges Wenger (p98)
- Le Mondial (p85)
- Chez Boudji (p87)

## Best Places to Stay

- Hotel Cailler (p88)
- Auberge aux 4 Vents (p83)
- Hotel Alpha (p83)
- Auberge du Mouton (p98)

## Why Go?

A far cry from the dramatic, heavily touristed Alpine landscapes most readily associated with 'la Suisse', this gentle western corner comprising the Canton of Fribourg, the Jura Mountains and the three lakes of Drei-Seen-Land is where you go to 'get away'.

Fribourg's eponymous, evocative capital boasts medieval riverside streetscapes and a wealth of historical attractions down dale from the fields of Gruyères, where the cheesemakers are. In the rolling hills, thick forests and pretty villages of the Jura, you'll find the delightful Val de Travers and mind-boggling Creux du Van, while Drei-Seen-Land is a veritable watery wonderland.

The region offers the chance to delight in world-renowned cheeses, meet absinthe's green fairy and savour resist-if-you-can meringues smothered in double cream, then work off the calories as you explore Fribourg's cultural cache, amble among the Jura's verdant countryside or up the pace with more vigorous hiking, mountain biking, sailing and cross-country skiing.

## When to Go

- Summer is the perfect time to discover Fribourg's fields of green, the Jura's mountain streams and the occasional sea of yellow sunflowers. In Fribourg town, festivals, fetes and alfresco dining are de rigueur.
- In the shoulder seasons and cooler climes of spring and autumn – great for hiking – you'll be delighted by nature's scenic show of blooming buds and falling leaves. You'll feel like you have the hills to yourself.
- In winter the gentle slopes of the Jura's handful of ski resorts are less crowded than the Alps and much cheaper: perfect for beginners. The region is known as a centre for cross-country skiing.

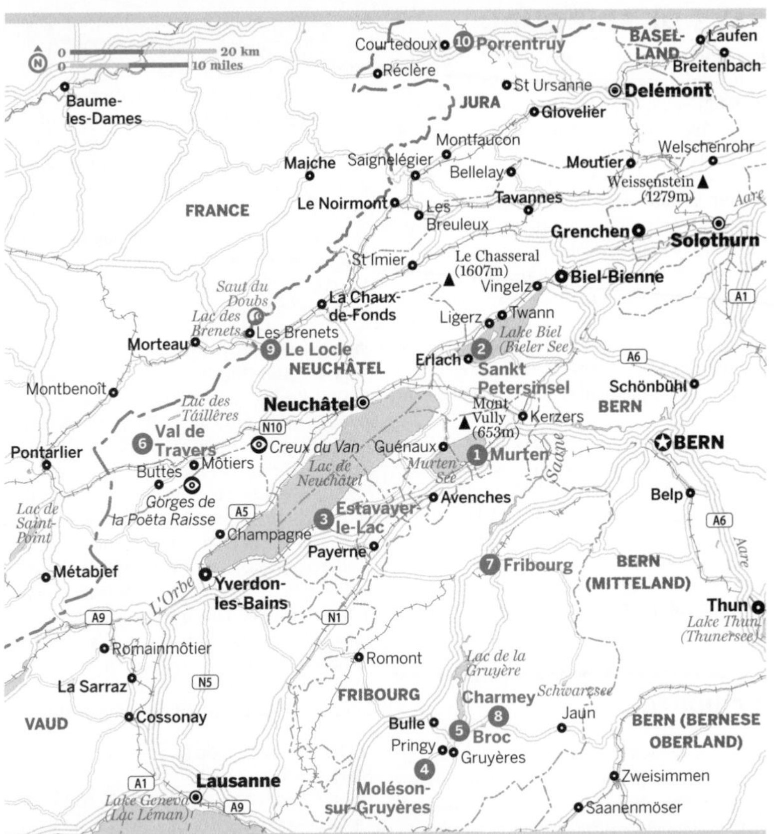


# Fribourg, Drei-Seen-Land & the Jura Highlights

❶ **Murten Festival of Lights** (p92) Lighting up on the inside in response to the incredible illuminations against the backdrop of medieval Murten.

❷ **Sankt Petersinsel** (p89) Cruising the Bielersee to St Peter's Island from Biel-Bienne for a picnic and a swim.

❸ **Estavayer-le-Lac** (p97) Turning back the clock as you stroll the streets of this beautiful medieval village on the Murtensee.

❹ **Fromagerie d'Alpage de Moléson** (p87) Falling into a food coma after fulfilling your every cheese fantasy.

❺ **Maison Cailler** (p87) Buzzing with a sweet, chocolate rush in this Swiss chocolate factory in Broc.

❻ **Maison de l'Absinthe** (p99) Ambling around medieval lanes, giddy on absinthe in the delightful Val de Travers.

❼ **Cathédrale St Nicolas de Fribourg** (p82) Climbing the 368 steps to the top of the cathedral tower for amazing views over medieval Fribourg.

❽ **Les Bains de la Gruyère** (p88) Soaking in the thermal waters against the backdrop of the pre-Alps in Charmey.

❾ **Musée de l'Horlogerie du Locle** (p96) Learning what makes clocks tick-tock in this impressive Le Locle tribute to Swiss precision and ingenuity.

❿ **Musée de l'Hôtel Dieu** (p98) Taking a trip back in time in this beautiful baroque museum of antiquities in Porrentruy.

# PAYS DE FRIBOURG

Pre-Alpine foothills surround the picturesque Fribourg region (Pays de Fribourg, population 307,461) at the heart of which you'll find the handsome, medieval city of Fribourg, wrapped around a lazy bend in the otherwise-rushing Rhine. Here, historical buildings and attractions, a well-preserved Old Town and a selection of top restaurants and quality hotels beckon you to linger.

Gourmands will be lured by nearby Gruyères, not so much for its sprinkling of pleasant rural villages, but for the eponymous, world-renowned Appellation d'Origine Contrôllée (AOC) cheese and the opportunity to see first-hand how it's been made for centuries.

Tie up your visit with a soak in the thermal waters and outdoor activities of charming Charmey, and Pays de Fribourg presents a tempting package indeed. Just be sure to brush up on your French and your German – the region's unique *Röstigraben* (linguistic divide) means that the region's western towns speak French, while the eastern speak German.

## Fribourg

POP 34,897 / ELEV 629M

Nowhere is Switzerland's socio-linguistic divide felt more keenly than in Fribourg (Freiburg or 'Free Town'), a handsome medieval city built upon a dramatic gorge carved by the Sarine River, which cleaves the city in two. Inhabitants on the river's west bank, where the Old Town, university and train station are, speak French, and those on the east, German! Naturally, it's a pretty multilingual place.

With a high concentration of excellent museums and some knockout viewpoints from which to appreciate the enchanting historic architecture that seems to crawl up out of the gorge, Fribourg oozes visual appeal.

Throw a healthy dose of Catholicism and a sizeable student population into the cultural cocktail and you get a fascinating town with sometimes feisty nightlife and a healthy waft of originality.

### Sights

**★Cathédrale St Nicolas de Fribourg** CATHEDRAL

(St Nicolas Cathedral; ☎026 347 10 40; www.cathedrale-fribourg.ch; Rue des Chanoines 3; tower adult/child Sfr3.50/1; ⏲9.30am-6pm Mon-Fri, 9am-4pm Sat, 2-5pm Sun, tower 10am-noon & 2-5pm Mon-Fri, 10am-4pm Sat, 2-5pm Sun Apr-Oct) Before entering this brooding 13th-century Gothic cathedral, contemplate the main portal with its 15th-century sculptured portrayal of the *Last Judgment*. On your right upon entering, inside the Chapelle du Saint Sépulcre, is an exceptionally lifelike sculptural group (1433) depicting Christ's burial. Unless you suffer vertigo, or are of poor health, a 368-step climb of the cathedral's 74m-tall tower for remarkable views over the medieval town should be considered a must-do.

**★Espace Jean Tinguely – Niki de Saint Phalle** MUSEUM

(☎026 305 51 40; www.mahf.ch; Rue de Morat 2; adult/child Sfr6/free; ⏲11am-8pm Wed-Sun) Jump on the button to watch the *Retable de l'Abondance Occidentale et du Mercantilisme Totalitaire* (1989–90) make its allegorical comment on Western opulence. This museum, created in memory of Fribourg's modern artistic prodigy, Jean Tinguely (1925–91), is located in a tramway depot dating to 1900. The nifty space showcases his machines alongside the boldly out-there creations of French-American artist Niki de Saint Phalle (1930–2002), who worked with Tinguely from the 1950s until his death.

**★Musée Suisse de la Marionnette** MUSEUM

(Swiss Puppetry Museum; ☎026 322 85 13; www.marionnette.ch; Derrière-les-Jardins 2; adult/child Sfr5/3; ⏲10am-5pm Wed-Sun) In an age where technology is everything, it's refreshing to see that some unique, age-old crafts that have brought joy to children and adults alike throughout the ages are being kept alive and well at this fabulous little museum.

#### THE LEGEND OF FRIBOURG'S LINDEN TREE

Legend has it that in 1476 a messenger sprinted from Murten to Fribourg to relay the joyous news that the Swiss had defeated Charles the Bold...only to drop dead with exhaustion on arrival. Onlookers, saddened by this tragic twist, took the linden twig from the messenger's hat, planted it and cared for it – the tree you see today, **Tilleul de Morat** (Morat Linden Tree; Place de l'Hôtel de Ville 1), over half a millennium later, is born of that very twig.

In addition to the museum's collection of handmade and historical puppetry, there are regular marionette shows and puppetry workshops and the views from the bridge out front are fabulous.

**Old Town** AREA

The 12th-century Old Town was laid out in simple fashion, with Grand-Rue as the main street and parallel Rue des Chanoines and Rue des Bouchers devoted to markets, church and civic buildings. The settlement later spread downhill to the river: the bridges here – stone **Pont du Milieu** (Middle Bridge; 1720) and covered **Pont du Berne** (1250) – offer great views.

**Musée d'Art et d'Histoire** MUSEUM

(Museum of Art & History; ☎026 305 51 40; www.mahf.ch; Rue de Morat 12; adult/child Sfr8/5; ⊙11am-6pm Tue, Wed & Fri-Sun, to 8pm Thu) FREE Fribourg's art and history museum, with an excellent collection of late Gothic sculpture and painting, is housed in the Renaissance Hôtel Ratzé. Gothic meets Goth in the underground chamber, where religious statues are juxtaposed with some of Jean Tinguely's sculptural creations. Don't miss the museum's walled, bench-clad garden, pierced by a Niki de St Phalle sculpture – it's a beautiful picnic spot.

**Basilique de Notre-Dame de Fribourg** CHURCH

(☎026 323 20 31; www.basilique-fribourg.ch; Rue de Morat 1; ⊙8.30am-6pm Mon, Wed & Fri, 9.30am-7.30pm Tue & Thu) The highlight of this church is an 18th-century Crèche Napolitaine featuring 75 figurines re-enacting the nativity, annunciation and scenes from daily life. Push your way through the heavy grey drapes and drop a one/two-franc coin into the slot to view the crib for four/eight minutes.

**Musée Gutenberg** MUSEUM

(Gutenberg Museum; ☎026 347 38 28; www.gutenbergmuseum.ch; Place de Notre-Dame 16; adult/child/family Sfr10/6/22; ⊙11am-6pm Wed, Fri & Sat, to 8pm Thu, 10am-5pm Sun) Embark on a voyage of the printed word in this printing and communication museum, housed in a 16th-century granary and with a multimedia show to bring the historical exhibition up to 21st-century speed. To create a completely different perspective on print and visuals, the museum hosts blind dinners (four courses Sfr60); reserve in advance.

DON'T MISS

### THE PORT

No address better reflects Fribourg's creative spirit than **Le Port** (☎026 321 22 26; www.leport.ch; Planche-Inférieure 5; ⊙10am-11pm Tue-Sun May-Oct). Squirrelled away in a former gas warehouse on the banks of the River Sarine, the Port bursts with energy. On summer days Fribourgeois hang out on its tree-shaded terrace on the riverbanks between tai chi classes, visits to pop-up *ateliers* (workshops) and dining on seasonal lunchtime platters (Sfr20) of locally cured meats and homegrown veg.

Come dark – once the last tango class has left the dance floor – live bands, film screenings, dance nights and discos move in.

**Fri Art** GALLERY

(☎026 323 23 51; www.fri-art.ch; Petites Rames 22; adult/child Sfr8/5; ⊙noon-6pm Wed & Fri, to 10pm Thu, 2-5pm Sat & Sun) For an inspiring dose of contemporary art, head to this old red-brick seminary for some excellent temporary exhibitions. Late-night opening on Thursday includes free admission from 6pm and a bar serving drinks.

## Sleeping

★**Hotel Alpha** BOUTIQUE HOTEL €

(☎026 322 72 72; www.alpha-hotel.ch; Rue du Simplon 13; s/d from Sfr90/114; P 📶) There's something wonderful about this simple boutique hotel that's hard to put your finger on. The compact, modern rooms may lack air-conditioning but design smarts and incredible staff have made excellent use of the building's good bones to make it a quiet, cosy haven – with enormous pillows, muted tones and sensible pricing. Love.

★**Auberge aux 4 Vents** BOUTIQUE HOTEL €€

(☎026 347 36 00; www.aux4vents.ch; Res Balzli Grandfrey 124; s Sfr130-170, d Sfr180-260, s/d/tr/q with shared bathroom Sfr65/130/170/200; P 🏊) 'Stylish' scarcely does justice to this eight-room country inn, 2km north of town, where offbeat design rules. Its four-bedded *dortoir* is Switzerland's most luxurious dorm, and the dreamy Blue Room sports a bathtub that rolls out on rails through the window for a soak beneath the stars.

# Fribourg

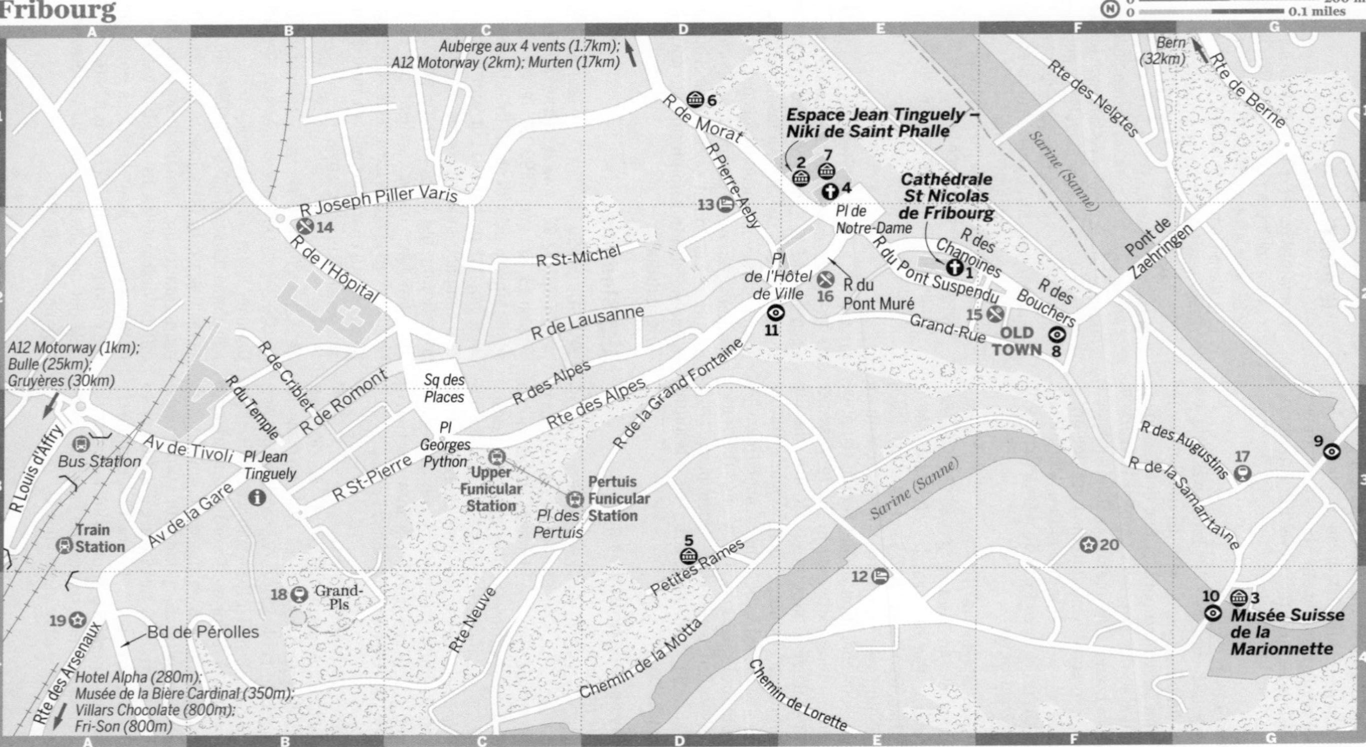

0 200 m
0 0.1 miles
Auberge aux 4 vents (1.7km); A12 Motorway (2km); Murten (17km)
Bern (32km)
Rte de Berne
Rte des Neigtes
Sarine (Sanne)
R de Morat
R Pierre-Aeby
Espace Jean Tinguely – Niki de Saint Phalle
Cathédrale St Nicolas de Fribourg
Pl de Notre-Dame
R des Chanoines
R du Pont Suspendu
R des Bouchers
Pont de Zaehringen
Pl de l'Hôtel de Ville
R du Pont Muré
Grand-Rue
OLD TOWN
R Joseph Piller Varis
R de l'Hôpital
R St-Michel
R de Lausanne
A12 Motorway (1km); Bulle (25km); Gruyères (30km)
R de Criblet
R du Temple
R de Romont
Sq des Places
R des Alpes
Rte des Alpes
R de la Grand Fontaine
Pl Georges Python
Upper Funicular Station
Pertuis Funicular Station
Pl des Pertuis
R Louis d'Affry
Bus Station
Av de Tivoli
Pl Jean Tinguely
R St-Pierre
Av de la Gare
Train Station
Petites Rames
Sarine (Sanne)
R des Augustins
R de la Samaritaine
Musée Suisse de la Marionnette
Grand-Pls
Bd de Pérolles
Rte Neuve
Chemin de la Motta
Chemin de Lorette
Rte des Arsenaux
Hotel Alpha (280m); Musée de la Bière Cardinal (350m); Villars Chocolate (800m); Fri-Son (800m)

## Fribourg

**Top Sights**
1 Cathédrale St Nicolas de Fribourg ........ E2
2 Espace Jean Tinguely – Niki de Saint Phalle ........ E1
3 Musée Suisse de la Marionnette ........ G4

**Sights**
4 Basilique de Notre-Dame de Fribourg ........ E1
5 Fri Art ........ D3
6 Musée d'Art et d'Histoire ........ D1
7 Musée Gutenberg ........ E1
8 Old Town ........ F2
9 Pont de Berne ........ G3
10 Pont du Milieu ........ G4
11 Tilleul de Morat ........ D2

**Sleeping**
12 Au Sauvage ........ E4
13 Hine Adon ........ D2

**Eating**
14 Le Mondial ........ B2
15 Restaurant du Cygne ........ F2
16 Restaurant du Gothard ........ E2

**Drinking & Nightlife**
17 Banshee's Lodge ........ G3
18 Fribourg Plage ........ B4

**Entertainment**
19 Café Culturel de l'Ancienne Gare ........ A4
20 Le Port ........ F3

**Hine Adon** APARTMENT €€
(026 322 37 77; www.hineadon.ch; Rue Pierre-Aeby 11; apt Sfr120-280; @) If you decide that a little bit of space is what you're after, these nifty Old Town apartments (one to 2½ bedrooms, with full kitchen facilities) are an appealing option. The decor mixes old and new design details, break fast is available (Sfr7.50) and service is sterling.

**Au Sauvage** HISTORIC HOTEL €€
(026 347 30 60; www.hotel-sauvage.ch; Planche Supérieure 12; s/d from Sfr170/240; ) Filled with medieval character, this Old Town hotel comes complete with 16 charming rooms above a restaurant in a twinset of 16th-century houses. Find it steps from the river, flagged with a medieval sign featuring a savage caveman and his club.

## Eating

**★Le Mondial** CAFE €
(026 321 27 72; www.cafelemondial.ch; Rue de l'Hôpital 39; mains Sfr18-29; 8am-11pm Mon-Thu, to midnight Fri, 9am-midnight Sat) This airy cafe-restaurant – a stylish mix of modern and vintage – gets packed at lunchtime and after work when students and suited business people tuck into its house specialities, warm tartines and moreish *ballons* (burger-style creations). Not to be missed between meals are its feisty homemade cakes.

**Restaurant du Gothard** BISTRO €€
(026 322 32 85; Rue du Pont Muré 16; mains Sfr22-38; 9am-11.30pm Mon, Tue, Thu & Fri, 8am-11.30pm Sat & Sun) Tinguely's old eating haunt is a kitsch mix of 19th-century furnishings, Niki de Saint Phalle drawings and nostalgia-tinged bric-a-brac. Pick from the day's specials chalked on blackboards; fondues and horse steaks are firm favourites.

**Restaurant du Cygne** EUROPEAN €€€
(026 322 32 04; www.restaurantducygne.ch; Rue des Bouchers 2; set menu Sfr65, mains Sfr30-40; 9am-11pm Wed-Sun, to 2pm Tue) Follow your nose to this always-humming local institution. Restaurant du Cygne is somewhere in between a high-end brasserie or gastropub, serving consistently good fare in a smart, yet casual environment, at reasonable prices. The menu is simple: steak and seafood done a few ways (perhaps with fricasseed mushrooms, or drizzled with *beurre café de Paris*) and a selection of small plates to start.

## Drinking & Nightlife

Rte de la Fonderie is the place to go if you're looking for a night out on the town. Here you'll be treated to the buzziest DJ clubs and band venues in Fribourg. You'll find it right next to the university in the industrial zone west of the train station.

**Fribourg Plage** BEER GARDEN
(www.fribourgplage.ch; Parc des Grand-Places; ⌚11am-11.30pm daily mid-Jun–Aug) When the sun shines there's no lovelier spot for hanging out in a pink or lime-green deckchair than at this urban beach, complete with golden sand and beach volley court, on the lawns of a city park. 'Protection anti-stress' is its strapline.

**Banshee's Lodge** IRISH PUB
(☎026 322 53 94; Rue d'Or 5; ⌚4pm-1am Wed-Sun) In the heart of the Old Town, this cosy Irish pub is a great place to meet other travellers and have some good craic.

## ☆ Entertainment

**★Café Culturel de l'Ancienne Gare** ARTS CENTRE
(CCAG; ☎026 322 57 72; www.cafeanciennegare.ch; Esplanade de l'Ancienne-Gare 3; ⌚9am-11.30pm Mon-Thu, to 3am Fri, 1pm-3am Sat, 11am-midnight Sun) In the old train station's 19th-century hall, this hip and easy hang-out also doubles as a nerve centre of sorts for arty happenings involving film, performance and fashion. The hybrid cafe and cultural centre serves decent meals and snacks. To find it, head down Rte des Arsenaux and spot the cafe by the railway tracks on your right.

**Fri-Son** LIVE MUSIC
(☎026 424 36 25; www.fri-son.ch; Rte de la Fonderie 13; cover varies; ⌚9pm-5am Wed-Sun) DJs spin various sounds inside this graffiti-covered warehouse, one of western Switzerland's biggest stages for live concerts. Themed dance nights – deep bass, house, Swiss rock – are often free. Tickets for concerts are sold online.

## Shopping

**★Villars Chocolate** CHOCOLATE
(☎026 426 65 49; www.villars.com; Rte de la Fonderie 2; ⌚8.30am-5.30pm Mon-Sat) The adjacent burnt-red and caramel brick factory of this chocolatier, in business since 1901, churns out slabs of Alpine-rich Gruyère milk chocolate, and loved-by-kids *têtes au choco* (chocolate-covered marshmallow heads). You can't go inside, but you can stock up on choc at factory prices in this cafe-outlet while savouring hot chocolate topped with whipped cream and chocolate shavings.

DON'T MISS

### FRIBOURG FUNICULAR

The **Funiculaire de Fribourg** (Sfr3; ⌚7am-8pm Mon-Sat, 9.30am-8pm Sun Jul & Aug, 9.30am-7pm Sep-Jun), built in 1899 by the Cardinal Brewery, which managed it until the city of Fribourg took over in 1965, is unique in that it uses waste water for propulsion.

The funicular ferries passengers faithfully every six minutes up and down Fribourg's steep hillside from the riverside Old Town Pertuis station to the Upper station, an ascent of roughly 500m in just two minutes.

Even if you don't ride the funicular, it's an easy walk from the train station to the Upper station, for fantastic views over the river and the Old Town.

## ℹ Information

**Fribourg Tourisme** (☎026 350 11 11; www.fribourgtourisme.ch/en; Place Jean Tinguely 1, Equilibre; ⌚9am-6pm Mon-Fri year-round, 9am-3pm Sat May-Sep, 9am-12.30pm Sat Oct-Apr) Mountains of information on Fribourg town and region, planted on the ground floor of Fribourg's most striking contemporary building (have no fear – it won't fall on your head). The tourist office also runs an information desk in the cathedral (p82), also open weekends.

## ℹ Getting There & Away

The A12 motorway linking Geneva with Bern (via Lausanne) whizzes past the outskirts of the city.

**TPF** (☎026 913 05 11; www.tpf.ch/en) buses depart from behind the bus station, accessible from the train station, for Avenches (Sfr10, 25 minutes) and Bulle (Sfr16.80, 45 minutes), from where you can get connections to Charmey (Sfr7.60, 25 minutes) and Gruyères (Sfr5.20, 10 minutes).

Fribourg has regular rail connections to Geneva (from Sfr42, 1¼ hours), Neuchâtel (Sfr22, 55 minutes) and Bern (from Sfr14.20, 20 minutes) onwards to Zurich (from Sfr59, 1½ hours).

## ℹ Getting Around

Fribourg is one of the towns that have adopted the PubliBike (p335) system. You can purchase a QuickBike pass (24 hours) from the Fribourg Tourisme office.

# Gruyères

POP 1789 / ELEV 830M

Named after the emblematic *gru* (crane) brandished by its medieval counts, the village of Gruyères is a riot of 15th- to 17th-century houses tumbling down a hillock. Crowned by a picturesque castle, its cobbled streets are surrounded by Alpine pastures where nutty, semi-hard AOC Gruyère cheese (spelled without the town's final 's') has been produced for centuries.

Most visitors come here for the cheese, but the region's verdant, undulating landscapes make for some pleasant walking, and the nearby villages of Broc and Bulle also hold some worthwhile attractions.

## Sights & Activities

**★Château de Gruyères** CASTLE

(☎026 921 21 02; www.chateau-gruyeres.ch; Rue du Château 8; adult/student/child Sfr12/8/free; ⏲9am-6pm Apr-Oct, 10am-5pm Nov-Mar) This bewitching turreted castle, home to 19 different counts of Gruyères, who controlled the Sarine Valley from the 11th to 16th centuries, was rebuilt after a fire in 1493. Inside you can view period furniture, tapestries and modern 'fantasy art', plus watch a 20-minute multimedia film about Gruyères' history. Don't miss the short footpath that weaves its way around the castle. Combined tickets covering the chateau and other area attractions are available.

**★Fromagerie d'Alpage de Moléson** FARM

(☎026 921 10 44; www.fromagerie-alpage.ch; Place de l'Aigle 12, Moléson-sur-Gruyères; adult/child Sfr5/2; ⏲9am-7pm May-Sep) At this 17th-century *fromagerie d'alpage* (mountain dairy), 5km southwest of Gruyères in Moléson-sur-Gruyères, cheese is made in summer using old-fashioned methods – at 10am daily you can watch how they do it. The Alpine chalet also sells cheese and serves fondue, *soupe du chalet* (a thick and hearty vegetable and potato soup topped with Gruyère double cream and cheese) and other typical mountain dishes in its restaurant.

**La Maison du Gruyère** FARM

(☎026 921 84 00; www.lamaisondugruyere.ch; Place de la Gare 3, Pringy-Gruyères; adult/child Sfr7/6; ⏲9am-6.30pm Jun-Sep, to 6pm Oct-May) The secret behind Gruyère cheese is revealed in Pringy, directly opposite Gruyères train station (1.5km below town). Cheesemaking takes place three to four times daily between 9am and 11am, and 12.30pm and 2.30pm. A combined ticket for the dairy and Château de Gruyères costs Sfr16 (no child combo).

**HR Giger Museum** MUSEUM

(☎026 921 22 00; www.hrgigermuseum.com; Château St Germain; adult/student/child Sfr12.50/8/4; ⏲10am-6pm daily Apr-Oct, 1-5pm Wed-Fri, 10am-6pm Sat & Sun Nov-Mar) Biomechanical art fills this space, dedicated to the man behind the alien in the *Alien* films – Chur-born,



### BROC & BULLE

One of Switzerland's oldest chocolate makers, **Maison Cailler** (☎026 921 59 60; www.cailler.ch; Rue Jules Bellet 7; adult/student/child Sfr12/9/free; ⏲10am-6pm Apr-Oct, to 5pm Nov-Mar), can be found in Broc, 2km north of Gruyères. It's been in business since 1825, and you can enjoy a factory tour with a sweet chance to taste and buy chocolate in the factory shop. Don't miss the fabulous chocolate workshops – some designed for children.

If you don't overdo the choc, you'll want to pop in to **Chez Boudji** (☎026 921 90 50; www.boudji.ch; Gite d'Avau 1; mains Sfr16-38; ⏲11.30am-2.30pm & 5.30-9.30pm May-Nov) for a cheesy meal and wonderful views.

Around 4km northwest of Broc you'll find Bulle, the area's main transport hub, well worth a whistle-stop tour for a glimpse of its 13th-century **chateau** (now administrative offices) and the **Musée gruérien et Bibliothèque de Bulle** (Gruyères Museum & Bulle Library; ☎026 916 10 10; www.musee-gruerien.ch; Rue de la Condémine 25; adult/student/child Sfr12/9/free; ⏲10am-5pm Tue-Sat Jun-Sep, 10am-noon & 1.30-5pm Tue-Fri, 10am-5pm Sat Oct-May) to teach yourself some local history. It's also the meeting point for free guided walking tours of the town; enquire within.

Zürich-based Giger (b 1940). The museum bar opposite, **Bar HR Giger** (☎026 921 08 00; www.hrgiger.com/barmuseum.htm; Rue du Château St Germain 3; ⏰10am-8.30pm), is kitted out in the same surrealist style. Neither is suitable for young children. A combined museum and Château de Gruyères (p87) ticket costs Sfr19.

★**Sentier des Fromageries** WALKING
(Cheese Dairy Path) Cheese is still produced in a few mountain chalets with traditional shingle roofs along this 7.3km trail that takes walkers through cow-specked high-country pastures. Ask at the Maison du Gruyère (p87) for the brochure outlining the walk. It can be done as a four-hour loop, or a two-hour one-way walk, with return transport on bus 263 from Moléson at the trail's midpoint.

## Sleeping & Eating

Gruyères' restaurants, which you'll find attached to local hotels and/or clustered around the main square, are mostly rustic, informal affairs. Cheese fondue is the natural star of every menu: *moitié-moitié* is a mix of Gruyère and soft local Vacherin. There is no sweeter end to a meal than pearly piped meringues smothered in thick double Gruyère cream.

★**Hotel de Gruyères** INN €
(☎026 921 80 30; www.gruyereshotels.ch; Rlle des Chevaliers 1; s/d Sfr120-160; P 📶) This 37-room traditionally styled hotel with lots of wood and rustic design elements, has wonderful views of the surrounding mountains, especially from balcony rooms. Even if your room doesn't have a view, the communal terrace is a lovely place to sit and enjoy the vista.

**La Ferme du Bourgoz** B&B €
(☎026 921 26 23; www.lafermedubourgoz.ch; Chemin du Bourgo 14; s/d Sfr80/100; P) Authentic cheese dreams are guaranteed at the cheesemaking Murith family's home. Simple, cosy rooms come with unbeatable farm-fresh breakfasts, plus chunks of the family's Gruyère for sale.

## Information

**La Gruyère Tourisme** (☎084 842 44 24; www.la-gruyere.ch; Rue du Bourg 1; ⏰9.30am-5.30pm Jul & Aug, shorter hours rest of the year) If there was a 'Bachelor of Fine Cheese' degree, the staff here would have earned it – they'll field any questions you have about the area and its eponymous world export.

## Getting There & Away

Gruyères can be reached by hourly bus or train from Fribourg (Sfr16.80, 55 minutes, via Bulle) or Montreux (Sfr19.80, 1¼ hours, via Montbovon). Gruyères town is a 10-minute walk uphill from the train station.

# Charmey

POP 1772 / ELEV 876M

The charming, sometimes, cloud-shrouded, baroque village of Charmey, located in Pays de Fribourg's pre-Alps region, is a local centre for family-friendly skiing, with 30km of downhill slopes; in summer, it's a haven for hikers and mountain bikers.

The town's thermal baths, **Les Bains de la Gruyère** (☎026 927 67 67; www.les-bains-de-charmey.ch; Gros-Plan 30; 3/5hr Sfr26/37; ⏰9am-9pm Mon-Thu, to 10pm Fri & Sat, to 8pm Sun), boast first-class new facilities and provide ample relaxation opportunities, from simple swimming to massages and beauty treatments.

## Festivals & Events

★**La Désalpe de Charmey** PARADE
(www.desalpe.ch) Every fourth Sunday in September thousands of spectators gather to celebrate the tradition of 'Rindyà', when herds of cattle, adorned with head-dresses of flowers, are brought down from their summer Alpine pastures to the warmer plains for winter. There's much clanging of bells, musical celebrations and the sale and consumption of a lot of really good cheese.

## Sleeping

★**Hotel Cailler** HOTEL €€
(www.hotel-cailler.ch/en; d/ste from Sfr250/390) The charming, externally retro, internally modern, Swiss-chic Hotel Cailler has a secret underground passage (OK, it's not a secret...) linking the hotel to Les Bains de la Gruyère opposite. Sexy chalet-style rooms and suites feature lots of exposed alpine wood, chocolate leather accents and some have balconies and/or spa tubs. Bring someone special or you'll feel like a loner.

## Information

**Charmey Tourisme** (☎026 927 55 80; www.charmey.ch; ⏰8am-noon & 1.30-6pm Mon-Fri, to 4.30pm Sat, 9am-noon Sun) can provide maps and suggestions for local walks and hikes.

OFF THE BEATEN TRACK

### MONKS' HEADS: THE ABBEY OF BELLELAY

For over 800 years, villagers from around the hamlet of **Bellelay** and its eponymous **abbey**, located midway between Biel-Bienne and Porrentruy, have produced a semi-hard cheese with a nutty flavour (similar to Gruyère), originally churned by the monks of the abbey.

As legend has it, the cheese was given the name Tête de Moine (Monk's Head) by soldiers of the French Revolution who annexed the region (and the abbey) in the last decade of the 17th century. To serve the cheese, the rind is removed and shavings are scraped off the top in a circular motion, in the style of peeling an apple. The soldiers, as the story goes, compared the practice to the custom of shaving monks' heads (not scalping, we hope!) and the moniker stuck.

Nowadays, a nifty device called a *girolle* (an indispensable tool of the Swiss kitchen) makes getting at the cheesy goodness so much easier.

You can visit the grounds of the impressive abbey, although most of it now operates as a psychiatric hospital. To learn about the history of little Bellelay and to sample the merchandise, head uphill to the gallery-museum at **Maison de la Tête de Moine** (☎032 484 03 16; www.maisondelatetedemoine.ch/en/maison; Bellelay; adult/child Sfr6/free; ⏰11am-6pm Wed-Sun).



### Getting There & Away

Charmey is 13km northeast of Gruyéres and 43km south of Fribourg. Public transport is limited; you're better off with your own wheels.

## DREI-SEEN-LAND

Comprising the pristine jewels of the Bielersee, Murtensee and Lac de Neuchâtel, each linked by artificial canals, this heavily forested area is a summer playground and a wonderful place to chill out. On a clear day, views to the Alps from along the western shores of each lake are nothing short of spectacular.

Even though it takes its official name from the German, the predominant language of the beautiful Drei-Seen-Land (Pays de Trois Lacs, in French; 'Three Lakes Region', in English), is French – just to confuse!

With an enviable position on the northwestern shore of Lac de Neuchâtel, the city of Neuchâtel, abutted by the gentle Jura Mountains, which rise to its west and north, is the area's most populous. Lovely Biel-Bienne is the crowning jewel of the Bielersee, as Murten is to the Murtensee, with charming medieval, baroque and renaissance villages surrounding them.

## Biel-Bienne

POP 50,013 / ELEV 429M

Slap bang on the *Röstigraben,* Switzerland's French–German divide, double-barrelled Biel-Bienne is the country's most bilingual town. Locals are prone to switching language mid-conversation; indeed it's often a tad tricky to know which one to use.

For many Swiss, Biel-Bienne is simply a place to change trains, but for visitors it's a beautiful, compact, lakefront town offering distant views of the Alps and a delightfully slow pace away from the tourist crowds. It's worth a visit to perhaps take a swim in the Bielersee, have a tipple in the surrounding vineyards and explore the 'Ring', its well-preserved Old Town with its many fascinating stories.

If you're planning to explore Drei-Seen-Land and the Jura, Biel-Bienne makes a great central base.

### Sights

**Old Town** AREA

Biel-Bienne's beautiful Old Town huddles around the 'Ring', a plaza whose name harks back to bygone days when community bigwigs sat here in a semicircle passing judgement on unfortunate miscreants brought before them. Leading from the Ring is Burggasse, home to the stepped-gabled town hall, theatre and several shuttered houses. The Old Town also features an assortment of gilded fountains, including the Fountain of Justice (1744).

★**Sankt Petersinsel** ISLAND

(St Peter's Island) Political theorist Jean-Jacques Rousseau said he spent the happiest time of his life on this lovely island in the middle of the Bielersee, actually joined to the

## Biel-Bienne

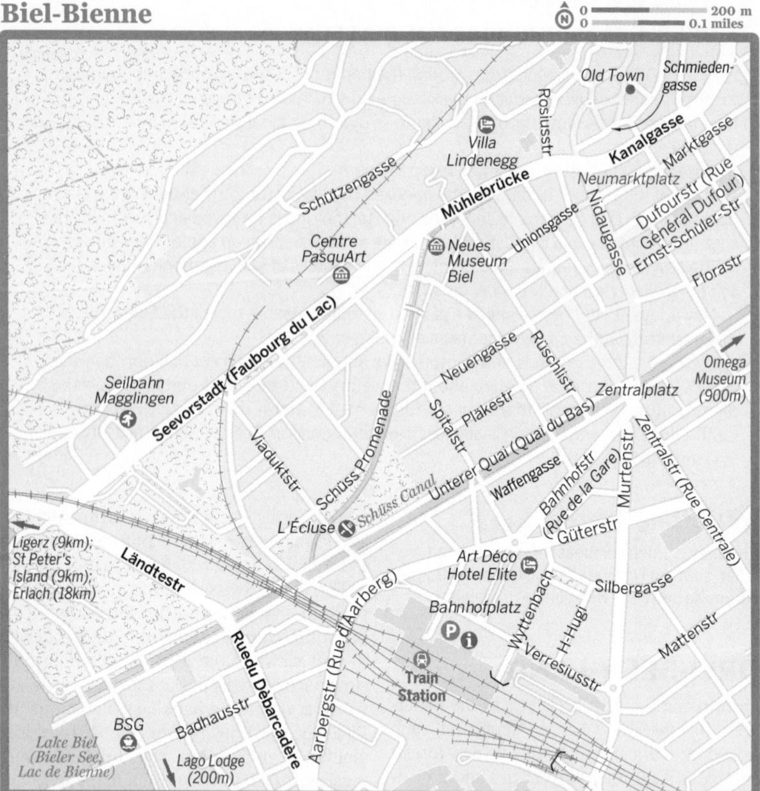




mainland by a long natural promontory. You can walk along it from the village of Erlach, or get here by catching a boat.

**Neues Museum Biel** MUSEUM

(NMB; ☎032 328 70 30; www.nmbiel.ch; Schüsspromenade 24-28; adult/child Sfr10/free; ⏲11am-5pm Tue-Sun) FREE The Neues Museum features an extensive and fascinating collection of art, history and archaeological exhibits from Biel and beyond. Highlights include a section on Biel's clock-making history and the reconstructed 19th-century apartments of museum benefactor Dora Neuhaus.

**Centre PasquArt** MUSEUM

(☎032 322 55 86; www.pasquart.ch; Seevorstadt 71-73; adult/child Sfr11/free; ⏲2-6pm Wed-Fri, 11am-6pm Sat & Sun) With a determinedly modern annex bolted onto an imposing 1886 hospital building, this place displays intriguing contemporary art exhibitions with a strong focus on photography and film.

**Omega Museum** MUSEUM

(☎032 343 91 31; www.omegamuseum.com; Stämpflistrasse 96; ⏲10am-6pm Tue-Fri, 11am-5pm Sat) FREE For watch buffs. This well-done museum also has English-language tours on demand.

### Activities

★ **Seilbahn Magglingen** FUNICULAR

(Magglingen Funicular; www.vb-tpb.ch; Seevorstadt; adult/child Sfr7/3.70) Outside town, the funicular scales Magglingen hill, which is riddled with hiking trails and photogenic views. The tourist office has leaflets outlining short walks.

### Sleeping & Eating

★ **Villa Lindenegg** GUESTHOUSE €€

(☎032 322 94 66; www.lindenegg.ch; Lindenegg 5; s/d from Sfr100/160; P ☎) Minutes from the centre, this gorgeous 19th-century country villa with a garden offers elegance and personal service at a very affordable price. Its eight rooms mix modern with historic, some have balconies and there's a friendly bistro for dining or early evening aperitifs.

★**Art Déco Hotel Elite** BOUTIQUE HOTEL €€
(☎032 328 77 77; www.elite-biel.com; Bahnhofstrasse 14; s/d from Sfr180/220; ❄📶) This beautiful art deco hotel in the centre of town has been a Biel icon since its construction. Fresh from loving restoration and renovation in 2016, the property now offers large, wonderfully appointed rooms that honour the building's traditional style while adding a touch of modernity.

★**L'Écluse** INTERNATIONAL €€
(☎032 322 18 40; www.restaurant-lecluse.ch; Schüsspromenade 14d; mains Sfr27-60; ⏲10am-11.30pm Tue-Sat) Set in pretty parkland between two canals, this iron-columned former watch factory houses one of Biel-Bienne's most charming restaurants. Meat, seafood and pasta dishes come accompanied by fresh vegetables and excellent *pommes frites*. On summer evenings head for the outdoor terrace, overhung with trees and globe lamps and buzzing with multilingual chatter.

## Information

The office of **Tourismus Biel Seeland** (☎032 329 84 84; www.biel-seeland.ch; Bahnhofplatz 12; ⏲8am-6pm Mon-Wed & Fri, to 7pm Thu, 9am-4pm Sat) is just outside the train station.

## Getting There & Away

Trains run to Bern (Sfr15.60, 25 to 35 minutes), Solothurn (Sfr11.40, 15 to 30 minutes) and Neuchâtel (Sfr12.60, 15 to 30 minutes).

**BSG** (☎032 329 88 11; www.bielersee.ch; Badhausstrasse 1a, Biel-Bienne) operates intra- and interlake ferries and a variety of themed cruises, including boats along the Aare River to Solothurn (one way/return Sf61/122, 2¾ hours).

Neighbouring Lac de Neuchâtel and Lac de Morat (Lake Murten) are connected to Bielersee by canal, and ferry services from Biel to each are operated by **Navigation Lacs de Neuchâtel et Morat** (☎032 729 96 00; www.navig.ch) in Neuchâtel.

# Ligerz

POP 522

The lush green vines that stagger down the steep hillside towards Lake Biel's northern shore are spectacular and there's no better spot to savour this viticultural magnificence, especially when heavy with grapes before the autumnal harvest, than this quaint lakefront hamlet. On clear days the views across the vines and the Bielersee to the snowcapped Bernese Alps, which seem almost close enough to touch, are breathtaking.

## Sights & Activities

★**Ligerz Wine Museum** MUSEUM
(Rebbaumuseum am Bielersee 'Hof'; ☎032 315 21 32; www.rebbaumuseum.ch; Bielstrasse 66, La Neuveville; adult/child Sfr6/free; ⏲1.30-5pm Sat & Sun May-Oct; P) Learn about the wines of the Bielersee region on a guided tour of this small museum and the delightful 16th-century noble's home in which it is housed. A minimum of ten people are required for the tour to proceed, so be sure to phone in advance to make a reservation. Some French or German language ability is helpful but not essential. Tastings are available, but this should be considered more of a museum tour than a cellar door.

**Vinothek Viniterra Bielersee** WINE
(☎032 315 77 47; www.viniterra-bielersee.ch; Im Moos 4, Twann-Tüscherz; ⏲5-9pm Tue-Fri, 2-8pm Sat, 2-7pm Sun) Taste and buy 300-odd vintages by Lake Biel winegrowers in this popular cellar door outlet in the village of Twann-Tüscherz, 2km north of Ligerz.

**Vinifuni Funicular** RAIL
(☎032 315 12 24; www.vinifuni.ch; adult one way Sfr6.40) The Vinifuni funicular climbs through vines for six minutes, from German-speaking Ligerz to hilltop French-speaking Prêles. Once at the top, you'll be spoiled for scenic walks and wonderful views across the vineyards and Bielersee to the Alps. Enquire at the station for local walking maps.

## Sleeping & Eating

**Restaurant Aux Trois Amis** SWISS €€
(☎032 315 11 44; www.aux3amis.ch; Untergasse 17; mains Sfr28-54; ⏲11am-11pm Mon, Tue & Thu-Sat, to 8pm Sun) A quintessential village bistro with a beautiful vine-covered facade that's centuries old. The place is particularly worthy of a visit during the hotter summer months, when its cool, tree-shaded terrace heaves with punters purring contentedly as they spend their day eating, drinking and gazing

at the tumbling vines, just centimetres away, and the slate-blue water rippling towards St Peter's Island below.

## Getting There & Away

Regular local trains connect Ligerz with Neuchâtel (Sfr17.60, 20 minutes) and Biel-Bienne (Sfr7, 15 minutes).

# Murten

POP 6024 / ELEV 450M

On the eastern shore of Murtensee (Lac de Morat) German-speaking Murten is unique and delightful. Its name, derived from the Celtic word *moriduno,* mean 'fortress on the lake', and the enclosed Old Town of this little village is exactly that.

In May 1476 the Burgundy duke Charles the Bold set off from Lausanne to besiege Murten, only to have 8000 of his men butchered or drowned in Murtensee during the Battle of Murten. Contemplate that as you swim! Today Murten is a popular domestic summer-holiday destination and a hub for the arts. It's the host city of the unique and delightful Festival of Light.

Canals link Murtensee with Lac de Neuchâtel (west) and Bielersee (north) to complete the nautical trinity that is the Drei-Seen-Land, making it possible to travel by boat, canoe or kayak from Murten, as far north as Biel-Bienne.

## Sights

**Old Town** AREA

Murten is a cobblestone three-street town crammed with arcaded houses. A string of hotel-restaurants, culminating in a 13th-century castle (closed to visitors), line Rathausgasse. Shops and eateries stud parallel Hauptgasse, capped by the medieval Berntor city gate at its eastern end. Parallel Deutsche Kirchgasse and its western continuation, Schulgasse, hug the **Ringmauer** (Rampart Walls).

**Papiliorama** MUSEUM

(031 756 04 60; www.papiliorama.ch; Moosmatte 1, Kerzers; adult/child Sfr18/9; 9am-6pm Apr-Oct, 10am-5pm Nov-Mar) Tropical butterflies flutter alongside hummingbirds and other exotic birds 11km northeast of Murten at Papiliorama. Indigenous butterflies flit about in the Swiss Butterfly Garden, tarantulas creep and crawl in Arthropodarium, night creatures from Latin America hide in Nocturama, and in Jungle Trek – a re-creation of a Belize nature reserve complete with mangroves, tropical dry forest and a 7m-high panorama bridge – intrepid explorers do just that. Papiliorama is 80m from Kerzers train station, and linked to Murten (Sfr4.60, nine minutes) by train.

## Festivals & Events

★ **Murten Festival of Lights** LIGHT SHOW

(Murten Licht Festival; www.murtenlichtfestival.ch; Jan) After enjoying phenomenal success in its first year (2016), drawing crowds of up to 80,000, Murten's one-of-a-kind 10-day winter festival, featuring all manner of projections and installations, has secured its place on the Swiss art and culture circuit. Take a look at the website to get a sense of how impressive the whimsical, wide-scale illumination of this beautiful medieval village really is.

## Sleeping & Eating

**Hotel Murtenhof & Krone** HOTEL €€

(026 672 90 30; www.murtenhof.ch; Rathausgasse 1-5; s/d from Sfr124/168; ) The Murtenhof, in a 16th-century patrician's house, is a spacious space to sleep. Its terrace restaurant (mains Sfr26 to Sfr42, open 11am to 10pm) cooks up dreamy lake views and traditional cuisine; local perch fillets and fera are highlights.

★ **La Pinte du Vieux Manoir** BOUTIQUE HOTEL €€€

(026 678 61 61; www.vieuxmanoir.ch; Rue de Lausanne 18, Meyrier; s/d from Sfr290/440; ) This unabashedly luxurious timber Normandy house, built as a whim on the lakeside in the early 1900s, is the ultimate splurge. To ensure your loved one says 'yes!', opt to dine at the solitary table for two at the end of the jetty at sunset. Find the Old Lake Manor 1km south of Murten.

**Chesery** MEDITERRANEAN €

(026 670 65 77; www.chesery-murten.ch; Rathausgasse 28; mains Sfr18-26; 11am-10pm) This cosy eating and drinking hybrid fuses a tasty choice of well-topped bruschetta and other lunchtime munchies with a dazzling display of *brocante* (secondhand and antique homewares), atmospherically arranged the length of a covered passage linking Rathausgasse with Hauptgasse.

WORTH A TRIP

### AVENCHES (AVENTICUM)

The Roman stronghold of Aventicum grew on the site of the former capital of the Celtic Helvetii tribe. In the late 3rd century its almost 6km of defensive ramparts failed to withstand attacks by the Germanic Alemanni tribe and by the 5th century the settlement had tumbled into obscurity.

In the town of Avenches, 8km southwest of Murten, much of the ruins of **Aventicum** have been unearthed and are today inseparable from Avenches' cultural identity and streetscape. In particular, the surprising **Roman Amphitheatre** – like a mini-Colosseum – is unmissable, abutting the northern end of the village's medieval Old Town. It's amazing to think that so many centuries later it continues to host crowds of thousands for various performances around the year, the most notable being the **Avenches Opera Festival** (www.avenchesopera.ch; Aug-Sep).

Learn about the fascinating history of this place in the simple but engaging **Römermuseum Avenches** (Roman Museum; www.aventicum.org; Av Jomini, Avenches; adult/child Sfr4/free; 10am-5pm Tue-Sun May-Oct, Wed-Sun Nov-Apr) and then, if you want to explore further, you can rent bikes at the excellent **SYHA Avenches** (026 675 27 17; www.youthhostel.ch/avenches; Rue de Lavoir 5; dm Sfr33-37) hostel, where you might even wish to spend a night. Unless **camping** (026 675 17 50; www.avenches.ch/camping; Camping Port-Plage; per person Sfr8.30; Apr-Sep) by the beach is more your style?

Hourly trains to/from Murten (Sfr5.20, 20 minutes) stop at Avenches.

★**Restaurant des Bains** MODERN EUROPEAN €€€
(026 670 23 38; www.desbains-murten.ch; Ryf 35; mains Sfr32-60; 11am-11.30pm Mon-Thu, to midnight Fri & Sat, to 10pm Sun) This lakefront smart-casual restaurant, serving modern Swiss locavore cuisine, flouts a green lawn tumbling down to the Murtensee where you can dine alfresco on fresh, locally caught seafood accompanied by seasonal vegetables sourced from nearby farms. In winter, warm your cockles over Gruyère fondue in the winter garden. It's magical at sunset, year-round.

## Information

**Murten Tourismus** (026 670 51 12; www.regionmurtensee.ch; Französische Kirchgasse 6; 9am-noon & 1-6pm Mon-Fri, 10am-noon & 1-5pm Sat & Sun)

## Getting There & Away

From the train station, 300m south of the Old Town's city walls, hourly trains run to/from Fribourg (Sfr12.40, 30 minutes), Bern (Sfr14.20, 35 minutes) and Neuchâtel (Sfr14.20, 25 minutes).

**Navigation Lacs de Neuchâtel et Morat** (p91) runs seasonal boats to/from Neuchâtel.

# Neuchâtel

POP 32,819

Snuggled up against the foothills of the Jura Mountains, Neuchâtel is the jewel in the crown of its eponymous lake – an attractive medieval waterfront city with a rich history and a delightful Old Town.

Neuchâtel is a key base for explorations into the Fribourg and Jura region, including the pretty Val-de-Travers. The sandstone elegance of its compact Old Town, with a score of interesting galleries, museums and attractive period architecture, can be easily explored on foot, although be warned: Neuchâtel's hills will give your calves a workout.

A diverse student population ensures that Neuchâtel isn't just about the past – the town has a youthful, relaxed vibe.

## Sights & Activities

★**Musée d'Art et d'Histoire** MUSEUM
(www.mahn.ch; Esplanade Léopold Robert 1; adult/child Sfr8/free, Wed free; 11am-6pm Tue-Sun) The museum is notable for three clockwork androids made between 1764 and 1774 by watchmaker Jaquet Droz. The Writer can be programmed to dip his pen in an ink pot and write up to 40 characters, while the Musician plays up to five tunes on a real organ. The Draughtsman is the simplest, with a repertoire of six drawings. The androids are activated on the first Sunday of the month at 2pm, 3pm and 4pm.

★**Laténium** MUSEUM
(032 889 69 17; www.latenium.ch; Espace Paul Vouga, Hauterive; museum entry adult/child Sfr9/4, free 10am-noon 1st Sun of month; 10am-5pm Tue-Sun; P) This impressive modern museum and

## Neuchâtel

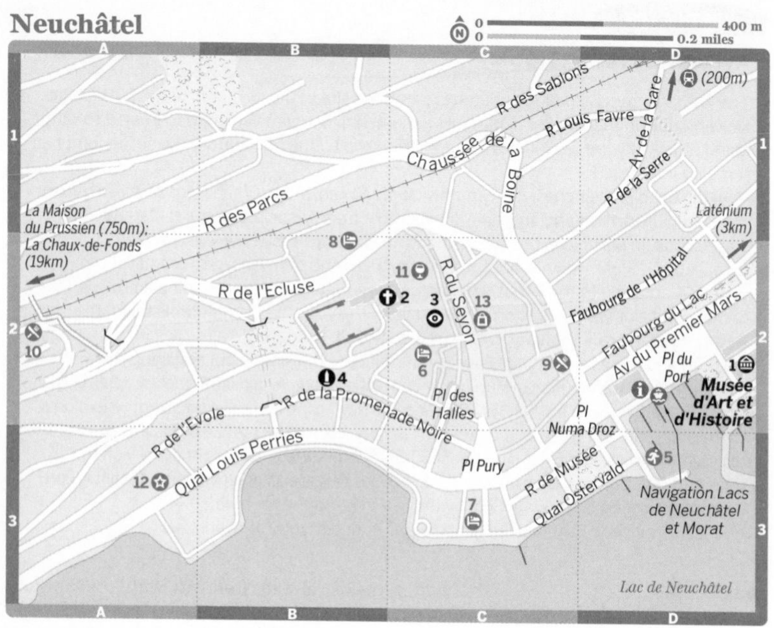


### Neuchâtel

**Top Sights**
1 Musée d'Art et d'Histoire ........ D2

**Sights**
2 Église Collégiale ........ B2
3 Old Town ........ C2
4 Prison Tower ........ B2

**Activities, Courses & Tours**
5 Marine Service Loisirs ........ D3

**Sleeping**
6 Auberg'Inn ........ C2
7 Hôtel Beau Rivage ........ C3
8 Hôtel de l'Ecluse ........ B2

**Eating**
9 Bistrot du Concert ........ C2
10 Famiglia Leccese ........ A2

**Drinking & Nightlife**
11 Chauffage Compris ........ C2

**Entertainment**
12 La Case à Chocs ........ A3

**Shopping**
13 Chocolaterie Walder ........ C2

adjacent archaeological park, 3km northeast of Neuchâtel on the waterfront in Hauterive, is the largest of its kind in Switzerland. It's an atmospheric trip back in time, from local prehistory to the Renaissance. Its permanent collection is an exploration of human evolution in Europe from Neanderthal to modern times and spans eight rooms or zones filled with artefacts, human skeletons, models and hands-on educational stations.

**Old Town** AREA

The Old Town streets are peppered with 18th-century mansions and decorative fountains. Heading uphill along Rue du Château, walk through the medieval city gate to the **Prison Tower** (Tour des Prisons; Rue Jehanne de Hochberg 5; Sfr2; 8am-6pm Apr-Sep). Scale the tower for views over the town below and its lake and Alpine backdrop. Inside the largely Gothic **Église Collégiale**, a mix of Romanesque elements (notably the triple apse) looms large.

**Mt Chaumont** MOUNTAIN

Soak up views across the three lakes to the Alps from Mt Chaumont (1160m), a ride on bus 7 from Neuchâtel to La Coudre then a 12-minute **funicular** (www.transn.ch; adult/child 4.20/2.20) ride up the mountain.

**Marine Service Loisirs** WATER SPORTS
(032 724 61 82; www.msloisirs.ch; Port de la Ville; Apr-Oct) The port buzzes with summer fun: hire motor boats, pedalos and two- or four-seated pedal-powered buggies to navigate the lake waters.

## Sleeping

**Auberg'Inn** GUESTHOUSE €€
(032 721 44 20; www.auberginn.ch; Rue Fleury 1; s/d from Sfr120/180; ) A hostel-style place to stay next to a chivalrous fountain, this trend-setting inn flaunts five design-driven rooms on the upper floors (no lift) of a late-Renaissance townhouse. Find reception around the back at Café du Cerf.

**Hôtel de l'Ecluse** HOTEL €€
(032 729 93 10; www.hoteldelecluse.ch; Rue de l'Ecluse 24; s/d from Sfr150/200; ) Stride down Rue de l'Ecluse to find the entrance of this house with blue wooden shutters. Rooms are modern with kitchenettes, and the stone-clad courtyard out back is a breath of fresh air. Weekend rates are lower and guests who don't want breakfast pay Sfr15 less.

★**Hôtel Beau Rivage** BOUTIQUE HOTEL €€€
(032 723 15 15; www.beau-rivage-hotel.ch; Esplanade du Mont Blanc 1; s/d from Sfr340/410; P ) Overlooking the lake and sculpture-studded gardens, this majestic hotel is five-star magic – as is its spa, verandah bar and the culinary wonders of its restaurant team.

## Eating & Drinking

★**Famiglia Leccese** ITALIAN €
(032 724 41 10; www.famiglia-leccese-ne.ch; Rue de l'Ecluse 49; mains Sfr16-28; 7-11pm Tue-Sat, noon-2pm Sun) Never was there a slice of Italy – Lecce in southern Italy to be precise – outside of the country as authentic as this earthy, friendly, brilliant and *bellissimo* Italian-run joint. It's tucked out of the way: look for the fairy lights behind Claude Cordey Motos.

★**Bistrot du Concert** BISTRO €€
(032 724 62 16; www.bistrotduconcert.ch; Rue de l'Hôtel de Ville 4; mains Sfr20-29; 8am-midnight Mon-Thu, to 1am Fri & Sat) A solid all-round address (and probably the most popular in town, to boot), this charismatic industrial-styled bar has a soulful spirit, vintage zinc bar, packed-out pavement terrace, and tasty menu chalked on the blackboard.

★**La Maison du Prussien** GASTRONOMY €€€
(032 730 54 54; www.hotel-prussien.ch; Rue des Tunnels 11; bistro dinner set menus Sfr58, restaurant Sfr125-175; 11.30am-2pm Mon-Fri, 6.30pm-midnight Mon-Sat) This hotel-restaurant is enclosed by woods and is in earshot of the impetuous babbling of a nearby brook. Dining is a grand affair in both its smart-casual bistro and fine-dining restaurant. At the helm of each is chef Jean-Yves Drevet whose gastronomic presentations vary according to the seasons.

**Chauffage Compris** WINE BAR
(032 721 43 96; www.chauffagecompris.ch; Rue des Moulins 37; 11am-1am Mon-Thu, to 2am Fri & Sat) Despite its name – Heating Included – this retro bar, with a decorative tiled entrance, is one cool place to loiter, be it for morning coffee, evening aperitif, night-owl drink or simple snacks.

## Entertainment

**La Case à Chocs** CLUB
(032 544 35 84; www.case-a-chocs.ch; Quai Philippe Godet 20; 10pm-4am Fri-Sun) Alternative venue in a converted brewery with live music, DJ sets, and a free-spirited vibe.

## Shopping

★**Chocolaterie Walder** CHOCOLATE
(032 725 20 49; www.walder-confiserie.ch; Grand-Rue 1; 7.30am-6.30pm Tue-Fri, 7am-5pm Sat) This third-generation chocolate maker, in the biz since 1919, creates dozens of different chocolates, including *les éclats* (Sfr9.80 per 100g) – square tablets of milk or dark chocolate studded with caramelised pumpkin seeds or roasted hazelnuts perhaps, or unusually flavoured with coriander, lemongrass and dill, saffron, cinnamon or absinthe.

## Information

The office of **Neuchâtel Tourism** (032 889 68 90; www.neuchateltourism.ch; Place du Port 2; 9am-noon & 1.30-5.30pm Mon-Fri, 9am-noon Sat) is located down by the water at Place de Port. Be sure to pick up a free copy of the worthwhile walking-tour *Neuchâtel on foot* brochure.

## Getting There & Around

### BICYCLE

In the warmer months you can pick up a rental bike (free for the first four hours) from the seasonal port-side kiosk run by **Neuchâtel Roule** (www.neuchatelroule.ch; Esplanade Léopold Robert; 7.30am-9.30pm Apr-Sep).

#### BOAT

From late April to mid-October, Navigation Lacs de Neuchâtel et Morat (p91) operates regular ferry services to/from Estavayer-le-Lac (Sfr20, 1¾ hours), Yverdon-les-Bains (Sfr20, 2½ hours), Murten (Sfr25, 1¾ hours) and Biel-Bienne (Sfr30, 2½ hours).

Buy tickets on board; return fares are simply double the one-way fares quoted.

#### TRAIN

Neuchâtel station is on Av de la Gare, a 10-minute walk northeast of the Old Town or two-minute ride on bus 6 (to Place Pury).

Frequent trains connect the city with Geneva (Sfr42, 1¼ hours), Bern (Sfr20.40, 30 minutes) and Biel-Bienne (Sfr13.20, 15 minutes).

## Yverdon-les-Bains

POP 29,400 / ELEV 437M

The Romans were the first to discover the reputedly healing properties of Yverdon-les-Bains' thermal springs and since that time there have been baths here. Yverdon has a pretty Old Town and castle dating back to around the 13th century. From here it's a pleasant, almost-2km walk down to the shores of Lake Neuchâtel and the town's beach.

While some of Yverdon's luxury resorts remain, the central thermal baths facility is dated. Even so, there are plenty of other attractions in the surrounding area to keep you occupied.

### Sights & Activities

**Plage d'Yverdon-les-Bains** BEACH

Yverdon's beach is a wonderful spot to sunbake and bathe in the warmer months.

**Centre Thermal** SPA

(☎024 423 02 32; www.cty.ch; Av des Bains 22; 3hr ticket adult/child Sfr19/11.50; ⏲8am-10pm Mon-Sat, to 8pm Sun) You don't need a reason to languish in the toasty-warm indoor and outdoor pools (temperatures between 28°C and 34°C) at these baths with water sourced from a 14,000-year-old mineral spring 500m below ground. By the time the water hits the surface it has picked up all sorts of salubrious properties from the layers of rock, and is particularly soothing for rheumatism and respiratory ailments.

### Information

Yverdon-les-Bain's **tourist information office** (☎024 423 61 01; www.yverdonlesbainsregion.ch; Av de la Gare 2; ⏲9am-6pm Mon-Fri, 9.30am-3.30pm Sat & Sun) is by the train station.

### Getting There & Away

Regular trains run to and from Lausanne (Sfr18.60, 30 minutes), Neuchâtel (Sfr15.40, 20 minutes) and Estavayer-le-Lac (Sfr11.20, 15 minutes).

# THE JURA MOUNTAINS

Welcome to Switzerland's not-so-wild west, where there are plenty of cows, fewer cowboys and it's quite possible that a gun has never been slung. It's incredibly peaceful up here. This low-mountainous peripheral region, little known by overseas visitors, is known throughout Switzerland as a nice place to visit, but not a place where anybody wants to live. For those reasons, the Jura is often unfairly overlooked – but that just makes it all the more appealing.

If walks among sleepy medieval hamlets that rarely see a tour bus, strolls among undulating fields of verdant green, and hikes through ancient forests to rocky outcrops overlooking a trio of lakes against an Alpine backdrop sounds like your Swiss fantasy come true, then the Jura is for you.

Highlights include the scenic villages of St Ursanne and Porrentruy; the Val de Travers, where you might spy a green absinthe fairy; and the unmissable Creux du Van.

## La Chaux-de-Fonds

POP 37,582 / ELEV 1018M

The Jura's largest city and Switzerland's highest, La Chaux-de-Fonds is a pretty town of steep, sloping streets, which, along with its smaller neighbour Le Locle, was awarded World Heritage status in 2009 for its historic value as a centre of precision watchmaking. Many of Switzerland's finest timepiece manufacturers are here.

La Chaux is also the birthplace of the great modern architect Le Corbusier (1887–1965), a key player in Germany's – and then the world's – Bauhaus movement. A number of his early, pre-Bauhaus buildings remain here today. The city also has a healthy collection of attractive art nouveau architecture (not of Le Corbusier's design).

### Sights & Activities

★ **Musée de l'Horlogerie du Locle** MUSEUM

(Watchmaking Museum; ☎032 933 89 80; www.mhl-monts.ch; Rte des Monts 65, Le Locle; adult/child Sfr10/5; ⏲10am-5pm Tue-Sun May-Oct,

WORTH A TRIP

## DAY TRIPS FROM YVERDON-LES-BAINS

### Charles the Bold & Greta Garbo

The imposing fortress of **Château de Grandson** (www.chateau-grandson.ch; Place du Château; adult/child Sfr12/5; ⊙8am-6pm Apr-Oct, to 5pm Nov-Mar) lies 5km along the lakefront from Yverdon. Its thick stone walls hide a smattering of small museums; the history museum evokes the fate of Charles the Bold, who in early 1476, in his battle against Swiss Confederate troops, found some of his routed Burgundian troops strung from apple trees in the castle orchard. The prize exhibit in the château's car museum is Greta Garbo's white Rolls Royce.

### Music in the Mountains

Music boxes have been made in Sainte-Croix, high in the Jura mountains 20km northwest of Yverdon, since the mid-19th century. The town's **Centre International de la Mécanique d'Art** (CIMA; www.musees.ch; Rue de l'Industrie 2, Sainte-Croix; adult/child Sfr18/12; ⊙1¼hr guided tour 2pm & 3.30pm Tue-Sun May-Oct, plus 10.30am Jul-Sep, 3pm Tue-Fri, 2pm & 3.30pm Sat & Sun Nov-Apr) documents the art of making them. Music boxes contain a rotating spiked cylinder that bends and releases metal prongs, causing them to vibrate and hum melodiously.

### Roman Gods & Romanesque Sundays

Sunday is the day to take a road trip southwest to **Orbe** (where Nescafé was invented in 1938) and its **Mosaïques Romaines d'Orbe-Boscéaz** (Boscéaz; adult/child Sfr6/5; ⊙10am-6pm Sat & Sun Jun-Sep), a series of pavilions containing spectacular mosaics on the site of a 3rd-century Gallo-Roman villa. Continuing 8km southwest, the little village of Romainmôtier is wholly dominated by the Cluny order's **Abbatiale de Romainmôtier** (www.concerts-romainmotier.ch; ⊙7am-8pm), a remarkable sandstone church whose origins reach back to the 6th century.

### Swiss Army Life

At **Fort de Pre-Giroud 39-45** (www.pre-giroud.ch; adult/child Sfr15/7; ⊙11.15am-5.30pm Wed-Sun Jul & Aug, 11.45am-5pm Sat & Sun mid-May–Jun & Sep–mid-Oct), high in the hills 31km southwest of Yverdon-les-Bains, what appears to be a stereotypical Swiss chalet is the front for a Swiss Army bunker where troops were mobilised underground during WWII. Guided tours and a museum give an idea of what life was like for Swiss troops during the war that surrounded them, but which left Switzerland (relatively) untouched. Wear solid shoes and warm clothing as it's chilly inside.

### Stuffed Frogs & Medieval Ramparts

On the Lac Neuchâtel shoreline 20km northeast of Yverdon-les-Bains, **Estavayer-le-Lac** has a charming medieval core featuring Switzerland's only fully accessible fortified ramparts. Wander the warren of shops and homes within the fortified walls, and pop into the quirky **Musée des Grenouilles** (www.museedesgrenouilles.ch; Rue du Musée 13, Estavayer-le-Lac), with its unique collection of stuffed frogs posed in scenes from 19th-century life. Afterwards, if it's a sunny day, head down to the waterfront for a swim.

2-5pm Tue-Sun Nov-Apr; P) In Le Locle, 8km west of La Chaux-de-Fonds, grand 18th-century rooms filled with all manner of clocks make this museum tick. The manor house, Château des Monts, was built for an 18th-century watchmaker atop a hill 3km from the town centre.

**★Vue-des-Alpes** MOUNTAIN

(P) About 8km south of La Chaux-de-Fonds, just off Rte N20, Vue-des-Alpes (1283m) is a mountain pass popular for its two 7.3km and 11km mountain-bike loop trails and for its 700m luge, **Toboggan Géant** (☎079 349 51 78; www.toboggans.ch; Fontaines; adult/child Sfr4/3, three descents Sfr11/8; ⊙1-6pm Mon-Fri, 10am-6pm Sat & Sun; ♿). In winter locals sledge, snowshoe and ski down the gentle slopes (three drag lifts) or along 53km of cross-country trails. Year-round it offers jaw-dropping views of the distant Alps over the thee lakes of Drei-Seen-Land.

★**Saut du Doubs** WATERFALL

(Le Saut-du-Doubs 227, Les Brenets; ) The River Doubs, which forms part of the Swiss–French border, widens out at the peaceful village of Les Brenets, 15km southwest of La Chaux-de-Fonds. It takes a little over an hour to walk from the village along Lac des Brenets to the Saut du Doubs (no vehicular access), a splendid crashing waterfall where the river cascades 27m into a natural pool. If walking poses challenges, boats operated by **Navigation sur le Lac des Brenets** (032 932 04 14; www.nlb.ch; Les Brenets; one way adult/child Sfr15/8) will get you there.

**La Maison Blanche** NOTABLE BUILDING

(The White House; 032 910 90 30; www.maisonblanche.ch; Chemin de Pouillerel 12; adult/child Sfr10/7; 10am-5pm Fri-Sun; P) This neoclassical house with a white facade and shiny roof is prized as Le Corbusier's first independent piece of work – and a notable break from the regional art nouveau. Architecturally unrecognisable as Le Corbusier to anyone familiar with his later work, it sat derelict in the leafy hilltop neighbourhood above La Chaux until 2004, when the modern-architecture treasure was renovated and refurnished (with some original furnishings).

★**Train à Vapeur Franches Montagnes** RAILWAY

(Franches Montagnes Steam Trains; 032 952 42 90; www.les-cj.ch; adult/child from Sfr38/22) From June to September local rail company **Chemins de fer du Jura** operates up to 12 themed steam-train tours from La Chaux-de-Fonds to Saignelégier and Glovelier.

## Eating

★**Georges Wenger** GASTRONOMY €€€

(032 957 66 33; www.georges-wenger.ch; Rue de la Gare 2, Le Noirmont; tasting menus per person Sfr94-250, mains Sfr69-74; P) It's worth the 19km journey from La Chaux-de-Fonds to dine on the two-Michelin-starred magnificence of master-chef Georges Wenger, opposite little Le Noirmont station. Since 1981, the team here has expertly transformed seasonal ingredients from trusted local suppliers into delicate, beautifully presented dishes that show off the rich gastronomic heritage of the region.

## Information

Pick up the Le Corbusier pamphlet at **Jura Tourisme** (032 889 68 95; www.chaux-de-fonds.ch; Place Le Corbusier, Espacité 1; 9am-6.30pm Mon-Fri, 10am-4pm Sat Jul & Aug, shorter hours rest of the year) for a DIY walking tour of his designs around town.

## Getting There & Away

Half-hourly trains run from Neuchâtel to La Chaux-de-Fonds (Sfr10.40, 30 minutes).

# Porrentruy

POP 6637 / ELEV 425M

Pretty Porrentruy is almost the northernmost town in the Jura Mountains. Only smaller Boncourt lies 12km further north, from where it's a short hop across the border (3km) into the French township of Delle.

Fine old buildings line the main street, Grand Rue, set against the backdrop of the town's bulky and impressive 13th-century **Château de Porrentruy** (Chemin du Château; P), with its 44m-tall Tour de Réfous. The castle is now occupied by offices, so you can't go in, but you're free to walk around the inner courtyard for a closer look.

Everything from books and clocks to pharmaceutical objects are displayed in **Musée de l'Hôtel Dieu** (032 466 72 72; www.museehoteldieu.ch; Grand Rue 5; adult/child Sfr6/4; 2-5pm Tue-Sun Easter–mid-Nov), Porrentruy's former hospital, worth a meander for its gorgeous baroque building with cobbled courtyard and home to the **tourist office** (032 466 59 59; www.porrentruy.ch; Grand Rue 5; 9am-noon Mon-Sat & 2-5.30pm Mon-Fri).

The **Auberge du Mouton** (032 535 83 57; www.dumouton.ch; Rue du Cygne 1; s/d/ste from Sfr110/130/150), dating to 1715, makes a pleasant place to overnight in the heart of Porrentruy's Old Town.

## Getting There & Away

Regular regional trains link Porrentruy with St Ursanne (Sfr5.20, 10 minutes), and Delémont (Sfr11.40, 30 minutes) onwards to Biel-Bienne (Sfr28, one hour).

From Porrentruy it's a 30-minute drive across the border into France, where you can pick up a TGV from Belfort-Montbéliard and be whisked away to Paris (from €61, 2½ hours).

# Val de Travers

Wander awhile in the forests of the Val de Travers (whether or not you've been downing the potent green liquid from the region's distilleries), and it's easy to see why this

WORTH A TRIP

## ST URSANNE

One of the Jura's most enchanting villages is medieval, riverside St Ursanne. As early as the 7th century a centre of worship existed on the site of 12th-century **Église Collégiale**, a grand Gothic church with a splendid Romanesque portal on its southern flank and an intriguing crypt.

Ancient houses, the 16th-century town gates, a stone bridge and a bevy of eating options on the miniature central square, Place Roger Schaffter, tumble towards the Doubs River from the church. The thin crisp apple *tartes flambées* are to die for at the 10-room **Hôtel de la Demi Lune** (032 461 35 31; www.demi-lune.ch; Rue Basse 2; mains Sfr22-45), with riverside terrace.

The **Jura Tourisme** (032 420 47 73; Place Roger Schaffter; 10am-noon & 2-5pm Mon-Fri, 10am-4pm Sat & Sun) office has information on river kayaking, canoeing and walking. St Ursanne train station, in the hills above town, has frequent direct services to Porrentruy (Sfr5.20, 10 minutes).

place has been dubbed Pays des Fées (Fairyland). As sunlight sparkles off the surface of a brook, or streams through chinks in the lime-green canopy, you can almost see them dancing. The fairies, that is... Today, walking and hiking trails dot the valley, which is also a popular region for cycling due to its scenic vistas and relatively flat terrain.

If time permits, a visit to the area's main villages – fabulous Fleurier (the larger of the two), or the magical Môtiers with its pretty castle, distilleries and a sprinkling of galleries and cafe-bars with absinthe on the menu (even in the soufflé) – is recommended.

## Sights

**★Creux du Van** NATURAL FEATURE
(www.creuxduvan.com; Couvet) About 14km east of Môtiers, a short walk leads to the enormous abyss known as the Creux du Van (Rocky Hole) – *van* is a word of Celtic origin meaning 'rock'. Created by glacial erosion, the spectacular crescent-moon wall interrupts the habitually green rolling countryside in startling fashion: imagine an enormous gulf 1km long and 440m deep. The way the vast canyon seemingly appears out of nowhere as you approach it from the field above is mind-blowing.

**★Maison de l'Absinthe** MUSEUM
(032 860 10 00; www.maison-absinthe.ch; Grande Rue 10, Môtiers; adult/child Sfr10/8; 10am-6pm Tue-Sat, to 5pm Sun) Learn all about absinthe (and sample the hard stuff in the bar afterwards) in this chic museum that annotates the history of the potent liqueur (with, some say, hallucinogenic properties), its influence on some of the more revolutionary artists and writers of the 18th century and its prohibition around the world.

## Sleeping

**★Ecohotel L'Aubier** FARMSTAY €€
(032 732 22 11; www.aubier.ch; Les Murailles 5, Rochefort; s/d from Sfr140/180; P) This spirit-soothing, green sleep is squirrelled away on a biodynamic farm in Montezillion, a hamlet 8km southwest of Neuchâtel. Contemporary, light-flooded rooms overlook fields of grazing cows, whose milk is mixed with carrot juice to make carrot cheese.

## Information

**Tourist Information Office** (032 886 43 00; www.val-de-travers.ch; Place de la Gare 1, Noiraigue; 8am-6pm) The tourist information office for the Val de Travers is located in the village of Noiraigue.

## Getting There & Away

Local trains run from Neuchâtel into Val de Travers. Stops of interest are Môtiers (Sfr8.20, 40 minutes) and Fleurier (Sfr8.40, 45 minutes).

It's a nice idea to have your own wheels (two or four) to explore the many far-flung delights of this wonderful valley and the Jura mountains beyond.

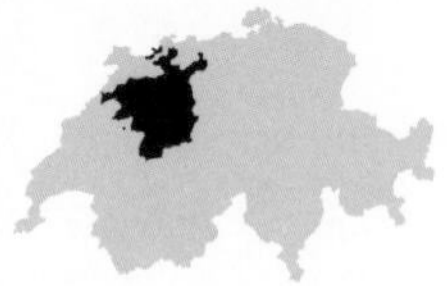

# Mittelland

**Includes ➡**



## Best Places to Eat

- Terrasse & Casa (p107)
- Kornhauskeller (p108)
- Cantinetta Bindella (p112)
- Landgasthof Sommerhaus (p110)

## Best Places to Stay

- Bellevue Palace (p107)
- Hotel Schweizerhof (p107)
- Hotel Möschberg (p110)
- Holiday Inn Bern West (p106)
- SYHA Hostel Solothurn (p112)

## Why Go?

At the heart of this central region lies Bern, the laid-back city that few realise is Switzerland's capital. Most mistakenly assume that title belongs to Geneva or Zürich. Incorrect.

When in 1848 politicians had to settle on a capital for the troubled Swiss Confederation, little Bern-in-the-middle seemed the obvious choice – Geneva was too French, Zürich too German. Bern was just right. It still is, with its fairy-tale 15th-century, World Heritage–listed Old Town of terraced stone buildings, covered arcades, clock towers, cobbled streets and a remarkably easygoing vibe.

If you can tear yourself away from Bern's wealth of historical and cultural attractions, you'll find the surrounding countryside to be as beautiful as the capital is charming, from the villages and farms of Emmental, producing the cheese that couldn't be more Swiss if it tried, to Solothurn, Switzerland's most alluring baroque town. Plan to linger.

## When to Go

- The summer guarantees warm to hot days, frequently blue skies and kilometres of lush green meadows dotted with cows.
- In autumn, foliage is particularly dazzling, especially against the backdrop of Emmental's ruddy farmhouses.
- Winter brings the opportunity to sample Bern's two fabulous Christmas markets along with mulled wine and Treberwurst, the local sausage with a definite boozy kick.

## Mittelland Highlights

1. **Berner Altstadt** (p103) Wandering the cobblestone streets of Bern's beautifully preserved Old Town.
2. **Museum für Kommunikation** (p104) Reminiscing in Bern about a time not so long ago when smartphones didn't rule the world.
3. **Historisches Museum Bern** (p104) Contemplating the mind of Einstein in this educational museum.
4. **Emmentaler Schaukäserei** (p110) Eating your weight in cheese then watching how it's made (in that order) in Emmental.
5. **St Ursen-Kathedrale** (p111) Taking a moment to contemplate spirituality, whatever your religion, in Solothurn's stunning cathedral.
6. **Kunstmuseum** (p111) Practising your art appreciation skills at this well presented art museum in Solothurn.

# Bern

POP 141,762 / ELEV 540M

Wandering through the picture-postcard, Unesco World Heritage–listed Old Town, with its provincial, laid-back air, it's hard to believe that Bern (Berne in French) is the capital of Switzerland.

Bern's flag-festooned, cobbled centre, rebuilt in distinctive grey-green sandstone after a devastating 1405 fire, is an aesthetic delight, with 6km of covered arcades, cellar shops and bars, and fantastical folk figures frolicking on 16th-century fountains. From the surrounding hills, you're presented with an equally captivating picture of red roofs

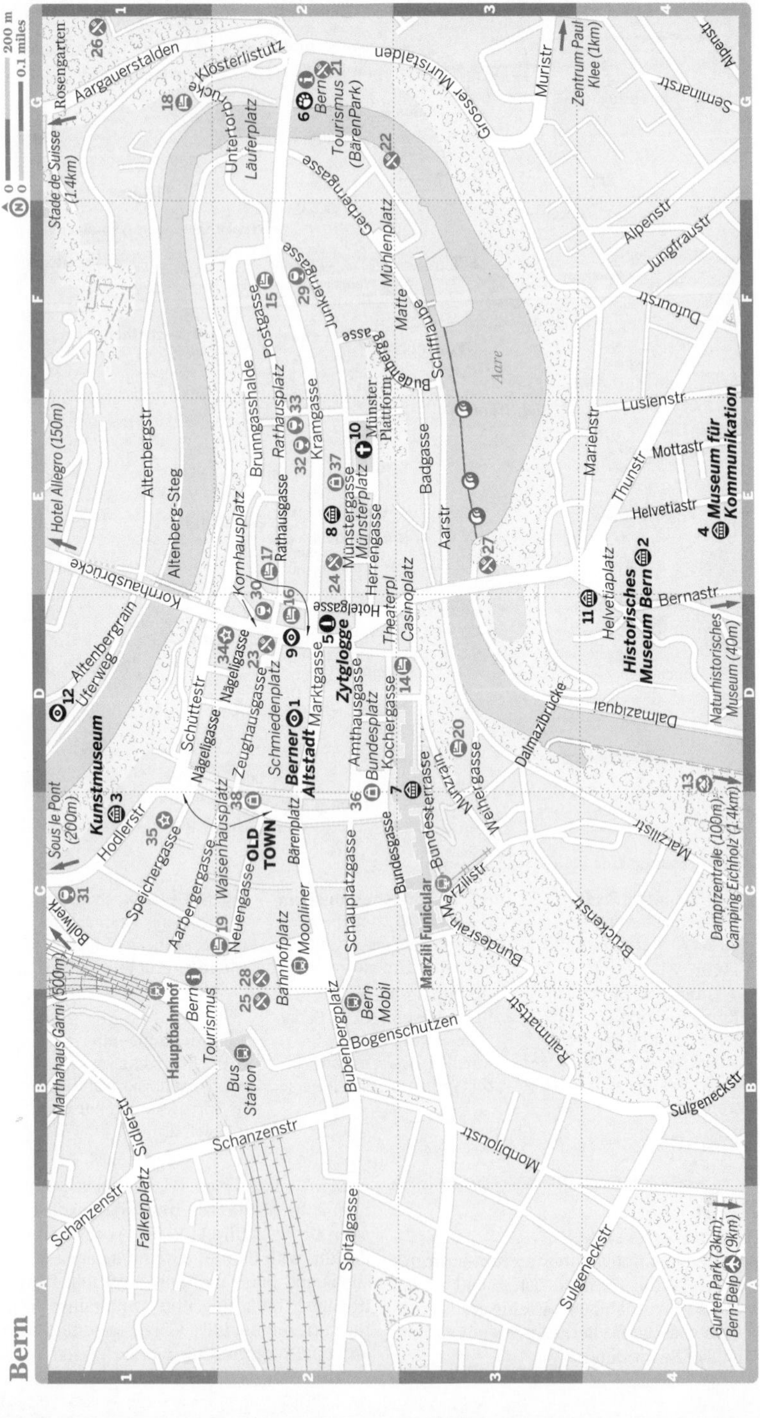

# Bern

0 200 m
0 0.1 miles

Marthahaus Garni (500m)
Bollwerk
31
Sous le Pont (200m)
12 Altenbergrain
Uferweg
Hotel Allegro (150m)
Stade de Suisse (1.4km)
Rosengarten
Aargauerstalden
26
Schanzenstr
Kunstmuseum
3
Hodlerstr
Falkenplatz
Sidlerstr
Speichergasse
35
Altenbergstr
Kornhausbrücke
Altenberg-Steg
18
Hauptbahnhof
Bern Tourismus
Aarbergergasse
Schüttestr
Nägeligasse
Klösterlistutz
Untertorbrücke
Schanzenstr
19
Waisenhausplatz
34
Nägeligasse
Läuferplatz
Bus Station
25
28
Neuengasse
38
OLD TOWN
Zeughausgasse
23
Kornhausplatz
30
17
Brunngasshalde
Postgasse
15
Schmiedenplatz
Rathausgasse
Rathausplatz
Bahnhofplatz
Bärenplatz
Berner Altstadt
1
9
16
32
33
29
6
Bern Tourismus
21
(BärenPark)
Moonliner
Marktgasse
Kramgasse
Junkerngasse
5
Zytglogge
Hotelgasse
24
8
37
Spitalgasse
Bubenbergplatz
Schauplatzgasse
Münstergasse
Gerberngasse
Bern Mobil
36
Amthausgasse
Bundesplatz
Münsterplatz
10
Münster Plattform
Herrengasse
Bogenschutzen
Bundesgasse
7
Kochergasse
Theaterpl
Badenberggasse
Mühlenplatz
22
14
Casinoplatz
Matte
Marzili Funicular
Bundesterrasse
Badgasse
Schifflaube
Aarstr
Munzrain
20
Marzilistr
Weihergasse
Grosser Muristalden
Monbijoustr
Bundesrain
27
Aare
Rainmattstr
Dalmazibrücke
Muristr
Sulgeneckstr
Zentrum Paul Klee (1km)
11
Helvetiaplatz
Marienstr
Brückenstr
Thunstr
Historisches Museum Bern
2
Alpenstr
Dalmaziquai
Helvetiastr
Mottastr
Lusienstr
Dufourstr
Jungfraustr
Marzilistr
Bernastr
Seminarstr
13
Sulgeneckstr
4
Museum für Kommunikation
Alpenstr
Gurten Park (3km);
Bern-Belp (9km)
Dampfzentrale (100m);
Camping Eichholz (1.4km)
Naturhistorisches Museum (40m)

## Bern

**Top Sights**

1 Berner Altstadt ... D2
2 Historisches Museum Bern ... E4
3 Kunstmuseum ... C1
4 Museum für Kommunikation ... E4
5 Zytglogge ... D2

**Sights**

6 BärenPark ... G2
7 Bundeshaus ... D3
8 Einstein-Haus Bern ... E2
9 Kindlifresserbrunnen ... D2
10 Münster ... E2
11 Schweizerisches Alpines Museum ... D4
12 University Botanical Garden ... D1

**Activities, Courses & Tours**

Hammam & Spa ... (see 20)
13 Marzili Pools ... D4

**Sleeping**

14 Bellevue Palace ... D3
15 Hotel Belle Epoque ... F2
16 Hotel Glocke Backpackers Bern ... D2
17 Hotel Goldener Schlüssel ... E2
18 Hotel Landhaus ... G1
19 Hotel Schweizerhof ... C2
20 SYHA Hostel ... D3

**Eating**

21 Altes Tramdepot ... G2
22 Cinématte Restaurant ... G2
Fugu Nydegg ... (see 15)
23 Kornhauskeller ... D2
24 Metzgerstübli ... E2
25 Namamen ... B2
26 Restaurant Rosengarten ... G1
27 Terrasse & Casa ... E3
28 Tibits ... C2

**Drinking & Nightlife**

29 Alpin ... F2
30 Café des Pyrénées ... D2
31 Kapitel Bollwerk ... C1
32 Marta ... E2
33 Volver ... E2

**Entertainment**

Bern Ticket ... (see 34)
Cinématte ... (see 22)
34 Konzerttheater Bern ... D2
35 Turnhalle ... C1

**Shopping**

36 Berner Wochenmärkte ... C2
37 Holz Art ... E2
38 Markt Bern ... C2



arrayed on a spit of land within a bend of the Aare River.

In a nutshell, Bern seduces and surprises at every turn. Its museums are excellent, its drinking scene dynamic and its locals happy to switch from their famously lilting dialect to textbook French, High German or English – which all goes to show that there's more to Bern than bureaucracy.

## Sights

### ★Berner Altstadt — AREA

(Bern Old Town) Bern's flag-bedecked medieval centre has 6km of covered arcades and cellar shops and bars descending from the streets. After a devastating fire in 1405, the wooden city was rebuilt in today's sandstone. Bern's clock tower, Zytglogge, is a focal point; crowds congregate to watch its revolving figures twirl at four minutes before the hour, after which the actual chimes begin. Tours enter the tower to see the clock mechanism from May to October; contact the tourist office for details.

Equally enchanting are the 11 decorative fountains (1545) depicting historical and folkloric characters. Most are along Marktgasse as it becomes Kramgasse and Gerechtigkeitsgasse, but the most famous – the Kindlifresserbrunnen (p105), a giant snacking on children – lies in Kornhausplatz. Inside the 15th-century Gothic Münster (p105), a 344-step hike up the lofty spire – Switzerland's tallest – is worth the climb for its impressive views over the Aare river and the terraced rooftops of the medieval town.

### ★Zytglogge — TOWER

(Marktgasse) Bern's most famous Old Town sight, this ornate clock tower once formed part of the city's western gate (1191–1256). Crowds congregate to watch its revolving figures twirl at four minutes before the hour, after which the chimes begin. Tours enter the tower to see the clock mechanism from May to October; contact the tourist office for details. The clock tower supposedly helped Albert Einstein hone his special theory of relativity, developed while working as a patent clerk in Bern.

**★Museum für Kommunikation** MUSEUM
(Museum of Communication; ☎031 357 55 55; www.mfk.ch; Helvetiastrasse 16; adult/child Sfr15/5; ⏲10am-5pm Tue-Sun) Fresh from extensive renovation and expansion, Bern's Museum of Communication opened its doors in August 2017. Occupying almost 2000 sq metres of exhibition space, it has cutting-edge interactive stations that explore the hows and whys of human communications with a focus on the role technology plays in our interactions with each other. Expect engaging, hands-on, high-tech interactive exhibits complemented by the museum's fabulous original collection of retro phones and computers.

**★Zentrum Paul Klee** MUSEUM
(☎031 359 01 01; www.zpk.org; Monument im Fruchtland 3; adult/child Sfr20/7; ⏲10am-5pm Tue-Sun) Bern's answer to the Guggenheim, Renzo Piano's architecturally bold, 150m-long wave-like edifice houses an exhibition space that showcases rotating works from Paul Klee's prodigious and often playful career. Interactive computer displays and audio guides help interpret the Swiss-born artist's work. Next door, the fun-packed **Kindermuseum Creaviva** (☎031 359 01 61; www.creaviva-zpk.org; Monument im Fruchtland 3; ⏲10am-5pm Tue-Sun; 👪) FREE lets kids experiment with hands-on art exhibits or create original artwork with the atelier's materials during the weekend **Five Franc Studio** (www.creaviva-zpk.org/5-franc-studio; Zentrum Paul Klee; Sfr5; ⏲10am-4.30pm Sat & Sun; 👪). Bus 12 runs from Bubenbergplatz direct to the museum.

**★Historisches Museum Bern** MUSEUM
(Bern Historical Museum; ☎031 350 77 11; www.bhm.ch; Helvetiaplatz 5; adult/child Sfr13/4, incl Einstein-Haus Bern Sfr18/8; ⏲10am-5pm Tue-Sun) Tapestries, diptychs and other treasures vividly illustrate Bernese history from the Stone Age to the 20th century in this marvellous

## BÄRENPARK

A popular etymological theory is that Bern got its name from the bear (Bär in German), when the city's founder, Berthold V, duke of Zähringen, snagged one here on a hunting spree. To the dismay of some, there was still a 3.5m-deep cramped bear pit in the city until 2009, when it was replaced by today's spacious 6000-sq-metre open-air riverside park dotted with trees and terraces, in which three bears now roam relatively freely.

You'll find the **BärenPark** (Bear Park; ☎031 357 15 25; www.baerenpark-bern.ch; Grosser Muristalden 6; ⏲9.30am-5pm) FREE at the eastern end of the Nydeggbrücke. With any luck you'll spot three adult bears – Finn, Björk, Ursina – as they frolic, swim, eat and poop in the woods, as nature (almost) intended. Obviously, things are quieter in the winter, when hibernation is the name of the game. An inclined elevator provides barrier-free access between the riverside walkway on the banks of the Aare to the top of the steep enclosure.

Bern and bears had gone paw in paw for centuries: the city's seal has featured a black bear as its heraldic beast since 1224 and Eurasian browns have been kept in *bärengraben* (bear pits) around the Swiss capital since 1513. But despite being the city's star attraction for over 500 years, it wasn't until the late 20th century that campaigners like the Swiss Animal Protection society began to condemn the conditions of the city's last remaining bear pit, which had been in use since 1857. Criticism of the cramped, 3.5m-deep enclosure forced Bern to face an inevitable dilemma: balancing the bear's historical importance with their humane treatment. In an effort to improve the bears' living conditions, new pools, caves and shaded areas were added to the pit, but the euthanasia of Pedro (the final bear to live in the enclosure) in 2009 seemed to serve as a metaphor for the historic *bärengraben*–their time was up too.

As Switzerland passed new legislation to protect animals in captivity, work began on the vast, 6000-sq-metre BärenPark. The modern SFr24.5 million enclosure, replete with swimming pool, now gives Finn, Björk and Ursina an environment that's as close to their typical habitat as is possible here (camera-wielding visitors notwithstanding). The old bear pit still remains at the entrance to the park.

Visitors can't feed the bears; instead seasonal food is hidden around the wooded areas, bushes and grottos of the park for them to find. While it might not be the great beech-wood forests of central Switzerland that wild bears would've experienced in the Middle Ages, the specialists from Tierpark Dählhölzli zoo who helped plan the park have finally given Bern's most famous residents a little dignity.

castle-like edifice, the best of several museums surrounding Helvetiaplatz. The highlight for many is the 2nd floor, devoted to a superb permanent exhibition on Einstein.

**★Kunstmuseum** MUSEUM

(Museum of Fine Arts; ☎031 328 09 44; www.kunstmuseumbern.ch; Hodlerstrasse 8-12; adult/child Sfr7/free; ⏲10am-9pm Tue, to 5pm Wed-Sun) Bern's Museum of Fine Arts houses Switzerland's oldest permanent collection, ranging from an exquisite early Renaissance *Madonna and Child* by Fra Angelico to 19th- and 20th-century works by the likes of Hodler, Monet and Picasso.

**Einstein-Haus Bern** MUSEUM

(☎031 312 00 91; www.einstein-bern.ch; Kramgasse 49; adult/student Sfr6/4.50; ⏲10am-5pm Mon-Sat mid-Feb–Mar, 10am-5pm daily Apr–mid-Dec) Housed in the humble apartment that Einstein shared with his young family while working at the Bern patent office, this small museum includes a 20-minute biographical film telling Einstein's life story. Displays trace the development of Einstein's general equation $E=mc^2$ and the sometimes poignant trajectory of his family life.

**Münster** CATHEDRAL

(www.bernermuenster.ch; Münsterplatz 1; tower adult/child Sfr5/2; ⏲10am-5pm Mon-Sat, 11.30am-5pm Sun Apr–mid-Oct, noon-4pm Mon-Fri, 10am-5pm Sat, 11.30am-4pm Sun mid-Oct–Mar) Bern's 15th-century Gothic cathedral boasts Switzerland's loftiest spire (100m); climb the 344-step spiral staircase for vertiginous views. Coming down, stop by the **Upper Bells** (1356), rung at 11am, noon and 3pm daily, and the three 10-tonne **Lower Bells** (Switzerland's largest). Don't miss the main portal's **Last Judgement**, which portrays Bern's mayor going to heaven, while his Zürich counterpart is shown into hell. Afterwards wander through the adjacent **Münsterplattform**, a bijou clifftop park with a sunny pavilion cafe.

**Naturhistorisches Museum** MUSEUM

(☎031 350 71 11; www.nmbe.ch; Bernastrasse 15; adult/child Sfr8/free; ⏲2-5pm Mon, 9am-5pm Tue-Fri, 10am-5pm Sat & Sun) The Natural History Museum near Helvetiaplatz features the famous moth-eaten and taxidermied remains of Barry, a 19th-century St Bernard rescue dog. Its best-loved exhibit traces the history of St Bernard dogs in the Swiss Alps and recounts some of Barry's legendary (ie not necessarily factual!) accomplishments.

**Schweizerisches Alpines Museum** MUSEUM

(☎031 350 04 40; www.alpinesmuseum.ch; Helvetiaplatz 4; adult/child Sfr14/6; ⏲10am-5pm Tue-Sun) The Swiss Alpine Museum hosts special exhibitions; its permanent collection of relief maps and Alpine mountaineering exhibits are kept under wraps.

**Kindlifresserbrunnen** FOUNTAIN

(Kornhausplatz) Bern is home to 11 decorative 16th-century fountains depicting historic and folkloric characters. The most famous is Kindlifresserbrunnen (Ogre Fountain), which depicts a giant snacking on children. The other fountains are located along Marktgasse, as it becomes Kramgasse and Gerechtigkeitsgasse.

**Bundeshaus** HISTORIC BUILDING

(☎031 322 85 22; www.parliament.ch; Bundesplatz; ⏲tours 11.30am & 3pm Mon-Fri, 11.30am, 2pm & 3pm Sat) FREE Home of the Swiss Federal Assembly, the Florentine-style Bundeshaus (1902) contains statues of the nation's founding fathers, a stained-glass dome adorned with cantonal emblems and a 214-bulb chandelier. When parliament is in recess, there are 45-minute tours (in English at 2pm every other Saturday; reserve ahead). During parliamentary sessions, bring official ID to watch from the public gallery. The adjacent Bundesplatz features a fountain comprising 26 illuminated water jets, representing every Swiss canton; it's the perfect summertime playground for kids.

**Gurten Park** PARK

(☎031 961 23 23; www.gurtenpark.ch; Gurten; Gurten funicular one way/return adult Sfr6/10.50, child Sfr3/5.50; ⏲Gurten funicular 7am-11.30pm Mon-Sat, to 8pm Sun) A great outdoorsy escape only 3km south of town, this small peak boasts a couple of restaurants, a miniature railway, cycling trails, a summer circus, winter sledge runs, an adventure playground and more. Enjoy fine views as you hike down the mountain (about one hour), following the clearly marked paths. To get there, take tram 9 towards Wabern, alight at Gurtenbahn and ride the **Gurten funicular** to the top.

**University Botanical Garden** GARDENS

(☎031 631 49 45; www.botanischergarten.ch; Altenbergrain 21; ⏲8am-5.30pm Mar-Sep, to 5pm Oct-Feb) FREE A flight of steps leads from the northern end of Lorrainebrücke to the University Botanical Garden, a riverside garden with plenty of green specimens to admire and a couple of greenhouses.

## Activities

**Marzili Pools** SWIMMING
(www.aaremarzili.ch; 8.30am-8pm Jun-Aug, to 7pm May & Sep) FREE In summer this open-air 25m swimming pool beside the Aare River is the perfect place to get a tan and kick back with locals among the expansive lawns, foosball tables and sunbathing racks.

**Hammam & Spa** HAMMAM
(www.hammam-bern.ch; Weihergasse 3; admission Sfr45, treatments extra; 9am-9.30pm Mon, Tue, Thu & Fri, 1-9.30pm Wed, 10am-8pm Sat & Sun) Housed in an eye-catching octagonal building, Bern's hammam is a lovely place to decompress in a 1001-Nights atmosphere. Tuesday is ladies only.

## Festivals & Events

★ **Berner Weihnachtsmarkt** CHRISTMAS MARKET
(Christmas Markets; Waisenhausplatz & Münsterplatz) Bern's Christmas Markets, held over the month of December in Waisenhausplatz and Münsterplatz, are a real treat, offering beautiful hand-made goods and the chance to warm your cockles over a glühwein or two.

**Buskers Bern** MUSIC
(www.buskersbern.ch; early Aug) International performers flood Bern's Old Town during this three-day street-music festival.

**Gurten Rock Festival** MUSIC
(www.gurtenfestival.ch; Gurtenkulm; mid-Jul) A solid indie line-up makes this one of Bern's biggest summertime events. Buy tickets early.

**Jazz Festival Bern** MUSIC
(www.jazzfestivalbern.ch; mid-Mar–May) Local and international jazz, blues and soul acts.

## Sleeping

**Holiday Inn Bern West** HOTEL €
(031 985 24 00; www.holidayinn.com; Riedbachstrasse 96; d from Sfr149; P) This above-average Holiday Inn is located adjacent a shopping complex and water park, making it a great option if you're travelling with kids. It's about 7km outside town, but the Bern Brünnen Westside train station is directly opposite and you'll get a free travel card on arrival for the duration of your stay.

**Marthahaus Garni** HOTEL €
(031 332 41 35; www.marthahaus.ch; Wyttenbachstrasse 22a; s/d from Sfr125/160, without bathroom from Sfr78/125; @) In a leafy residential location, this five-storey building feels like a friendly boarding house. Clean, simple rooms have lots of white and a smattering of modern art, and guests enjoy access to kitchen facilities.

**Camping Eichholz** CAMPGROUND €
(031 961 26 02; www.campingeichholz.ch; Strandweg 49, Wabern; campsite per adult/child/tent Sfr12/7.50/10; ) With big grassy sites adjoining one of Bern's most popular swimming spots, this campground is an appealing warm-weather option. Take tram 9 to Wabern, then walk 10 minutes towards the river.

**SYHA Hostel** HOSTEL €
(031 326 11 11; www.youthhostel.ch/bern; Weihergasse 4; dm Sfr38-42, s/d Sfr67/111; reception 7am-noon & 2pm-midnight; @) In a lovely riverside location, this well-organised hostel sports spotless dorms and a leafy terrace. An excellent breakfast is included, and good-value lunches and dinners (Sfr17.50) are also available. It's an easy 10-minute trip from the train station; walk downhill from the parliament building or ride the funicular.

**Hotel Glocke Backpackers Bern** HOSTEL €
(031 311 37 71; www.bernbackpackers.com; Rathausgasse 75; dm/d from Sfr37/144, s/d without bathroom Sfr76/120; reception 8-11am & 3-10pm; @) Modern bedrooms with maximum of six beds, clean bathrooms, nice kitchen and laundry facilities and a sociable lounge, all in a prime Old Town location, make this many backpackers' first choice, although street noise might irritate light sleepers.

**Max Aviation Apartments** APARTMENT €
(031 901 32 28; www.maxav.immobilien; Alleeweg 15; apt from Sfr109; P) This selection of popular, self-contained apartments offers great value and more space in expensive Bern. They're furnished to a good standard with tasteful decor and all the comforts of home. Parking is an additional Sfr16 per night.

**Hotel Landhaus** HOTEL €
(031 348 03 05; www.landhausbern.ch; Altenbergstrasse 4; dm/s/d from Sfr38/115/160; P @) Fronted by the river and Old Town spires, this well-run boho hotel offers a mix of stylish six-bed dorms, family rooms and doubles. Its buzzing ground-floor cafe and terrace attracts a cheery crowd. Breakfast (included with private rooms) costs Sfr10 extra for dorm-dwellers.

**Hotel Belle Epoque** HOTEL €€
(031 311 43 36; www.belle-epoque.ch; Gerechtigkeitsgasse 18; s/d from Sfr180/250; ) Conveniently situated along Bern's main arcaded thoroughfare is this romantic Old Town hotel with opulent art nouveau furnishings. TVs are tucked away into steamer-trunk-style cupboards to preserve the belle-époque design ethos.

**Hotel Goldener Schlüssel** HOTEL €€
(031 311 02 16; www.goldener-schluessel.ch; Rathausgasse 72; s/d from Sfr148/190; ) Going strong for 500 years, this hotel boasts comfy, updated rooms in the heart of the Old Town.

**Hotel Allegro** BUSINESS HOTEL €€
(031 339 55 00; www.kursaal-bern.ch; Kornhausstrasse 3; s/d from Sfr189/278; ) Cool and modern, this curved sliver of a building across the river from the Old Town offers excellent views from its front rooms, along with multiple fine dining and drinking spaces. The 7th-floor penthouse suite is an ode to Paul Klee.

★**Bellevue Palace** LUXURY HOTEL €€€
(031 320 45 45; www.bellevue-palace.ch; Kochergasse 3-5; s/d from Sfr329/440; P) For many years this was Bern's only five-star hotel and the guest list has included bigwigs from Nelson Mandela down. It's gilded, polished, sashed and swathed, and suitably discreet, with classic period antiques and service that will make you feel like royalty. Don't turn up looking shabby unless its shabby-chic.

★**Hotel Schweizerhof** BOUTIQUE HOTEL €€€
(031 326 80 80; www.schweizerhof-bern.ch; Bahnhofplatz 11; s/d from Sfr289/329; P) This classy five-star offers lavish accommodation with excellent amenities and service. A hop, skip and a jump from the train station, it's geared for both business and pleasure.

## Eating

★**Namamen** RAMEN €
(031 311 83 03; www.namamen.ch; Schanzenstrasse 4; ramen from Sfr16; 11am-10.30pm) Authentic Japanese ramen with a European twist in funky surrounds. Cheap and tasty – what more could you ask for?

**Tibits** VEGETARIAN €
(031 312 91 11; www.tibits.ch; Gurtengasse 3; per 100g from Sfr3.50; 6.30am-11.30pm Mon-Wed, to midnight Thu-Sat, 8am-11pm Sun) This vegetarian buffet restaurant inside the train station is perfect for a quick healthy meal any time of day. Serve yourself, weigh and pay. Takeaway costs slightly less than eating on-site.

★**Terrasse & Casa** SWISS €€
(031 350 50 01; www.schwellenmaetteli.ch; Dalmaziquai 11; mains Sfr20-64; Terrasse 9am-12.30am Mon-Sat, 10am-11.30pm Sun, Casa noon-2.30pm & 6-11.30pm Mon-Fri, 6-11.30pm Sat, noon-11pm Sun) Dubbed 'Bern's Riviera', this twinset of eateries enjoys a blissful Aare-side setting. Terrasse is a glass shoebox with wooden decking over the water, sunloungers overlooking a weir (illuminated at night) and comfy sofa seating, perfect for lingering over Sunday brunch, a drink, or midweek two-course lunch specials. Next door, Casa serves Italian delicacies in a cosy, country-style house.

**Altes Tramdepot** SWISS €€
(031 368 14 15; www.altestramdepot.ch; Grosser Muristalden 6, Am Bärengraben; mains Sfr18-46; 11am-12.30am Mon-Fri, from 10am Sat & Sun) At this cavernous microbrewery, Swiss specialities compete against wok-cooked stir-fries for your affection, and the microbrews go down a treat – sample three different varieties for Sfr10.90, four for Sfr14.60, or five for Sfr18.20.

**Cinématte Restaurant** SWISS €€
(031 312 21 22; www.cinematte.ch; Wasserwerkgasse 7; mains Sfr31-47; 6-9pm Thu-Mon) This chic eatery with a delightful wooden deck overlooking the Aare serves an ever-changing menu of Swiss specialities.

**Fugu Nydegg** ASIAN €€
(031 311 51 25; www.fugu-nydegg.ch; Gerechtigkeitsgasse 16; mains Sfr26-44; 11.30am-2pm & 5-11pm Mon-Fri, 11.30am-midnight Sat, to 10pm Sun; ) If it's Bangkok-style pad thai, Japanese noodles or Thai fish you're craving, then Fugu will hit the spot. Choose between the crisp, cool interior or the seating out front.

**Metzgerstübli** EUROPEAN €€
(031 311 00 45; www.metzgerstübli.ch; Münstergasse 60; 3-course dinner Sfr85, mains Sfr15-49; 10am-11pm Tue-Fri, 7am-noon & 5-11.30pm Sat & Sun) This homely restaurant in the Old Town has convivial staff serving a well-executed menu of standard European fare: meat, fish, pasta. Dinner set menus are great value for money.

**Restaurant Rosengarten** EUROPEAN €€
(031 331 32 06; www.rosengarten.be; Alter Aargauerstalden 31b; mains Sfr20-46; 9am-midnight) Panoramically perched on a hilltop adjacent to Bern's rose garden, this restaurant is nicest in warm weather, when you can enjoy the

DON'T MISS

### BERN'S ONION MARKET

Market traders take over Bern on the fourth Monday in November during the legendary **onion market** (Onion Market; ⏲Nov), a riot of 600-odd market stalls selling delicately woven onion plaits, wreaths, ropes, pies and sculptures alongside other tasty regional produce. Folklore says the market dates back to the great fire of 1405 when farmers from Fribourg canton helped the Bernese recover – they were allowed to sell their produce in Bern as a reward.

In reality the market probably began as part of Martinmas, the medieval festival celebrating winter's start. Whatever the tale the onion market is a fabulous excuse for pure, often-crazy revelry as street performers surge forth in the carnival atmosphere and people walk around throwing confetti and hitting each other on the head with squeaky plastic hammers.

terrace seating. From grilled Provençal-style pork cutlets to marinated lamb with tzatziki, the menu spans multiple culinary worlds.

**★Kornhauskeller** MEDITERRANEAN €€€
(☎031 327 72 72; www.bindella.ch; Kornhausplatz 18; mains Sfr24-58; ⏲11.45am-2.30pm & 6pm-12.30am) Fine dining takes place beneath vaulted frescoed arches at Bern's ornate former granary, now a stunning cellar restaurant serving Mediterranean cuisine. Beautiful people sip cocktails alongside historic stained-glass windows on the mezzanine, while in its neighbouring cafe, punters lunch in the sun on the busy pavement terrace.



## Drinking & Nightlife

**★Kapitel Bollwerk** BAR
(☎031 311 60 90; www.kapitel.ch; Bollwerk 41; ⏲11am-11.30pm Tue & Wed, to 3.30am Thu, to 5am Fri, 4pm-6am Sat) Starting as a restaurant where businesspeople come for light, healthy lunches, this award-winning venue morphs by evening into a bar recognised around town for its savvy bartenders and unparalleled choice of cocktails. Come 11pm it transforms again into one of Bern's hippest clubs, with international DJs spinning electronic music.

**Sous le Pont** BAR
(☎031 306 69 55; www.souslepont-roessli.ch; Neubrückstrasse 8; ⏲11.30am-midnight Tue-Thu, to 2am Fri, 6pm-2am Sat) Delve into Bern's grungy underground scene at this alternative-arts centre in the Reitschule, a graffiti-covered former riding school built in 1897. It's behind the station, by the railway bridge.

**Volver** BAR
(☎031 312 04 04; www.barvolver.ch; Rathausplatz 8; ⏲5-11.30pm Mon, 8am-11.30pm Tue & Wed, to 12.30am Thu-Sat) This corner bar with a chalkboard tapas menu is a hip spot for cocktails and coffees from morning to night.

**Alpin** WINE BAR
(☎031 311 25 75; www.alpinbern.ch; Gerechtigkeitsgasse 19; ⏲11am-6.30pm Tue-Fri, 9.30am-4pm Sat) Alpin specialises in Swiss wine and has an attached cafe, making it perfect for a try-before-you-buy session.

**Marta** BAR
(☎031 331 14 14; www.cafemarta.ch; Kramgasse 8; ⏲1-11.30pm Tue, Wed & Sun, to 12.30am Thu & Fri, 9am-12.30am Sat) In the afternoon street-level tables under Bern's Old Town arcades make a pleasant spot to enjoy cream tea with scones and homemade jam. Come evening the action moves downstairs into the cellar, where you'll find occasional live music and DJ sets.

**Café des Pyrénées** BAR
(☎031 311 30 63; www.pyri.ch; Kornhausplatz 17; ⏲9am-11.30pm Mon-Wed, to 12.30am Thu-Sat, noon-9pm Sun) This Bohemian corner joint remains a beloved Bern institution for its traditional Parisian cafe-bar vibe. Its central location near the tram tracks makes for good people-watching.

## Entertainment

**★Turnhalle** PERFORMING ARTS
(☎031 311 15 51; www.turnhalle.ch; Speichergasse 4; ⏲cafeteria 11.45am-2pm Mon-Fri, bar-cafe 9am-12.30am Mon-Wed, to 2am Thu, to 3.30am Fri & Sat) Part bar, part nightspot, part community arts centre that hosts frequent evening performances, Turnhalle also serves an excellent-value weekday lunch (dishes Sfr6 to Sfr8). The cafeteria-style offerings include mains (with one daily veggie option), salads, vegetables and desserts. Choose up to six items, then grab a seat on the spacious sunny patio out front.

**★ Dampfzentrale** CULTURAL CENTRE
(☎031 310 05 40; www.dampfzentrale.ch; Marzilistrasse 47; ⊙club 11pm-late Sat, other events variable hours) Host to an action-packed Saturday-night club, this industrial brick riverside building also stages concerts, festivals and contemporary dance; check the website for details.

**Konzerttheater Bern** PERFORMING ARTS
(☎031 329 51 11; www.konzerttheaterbern.ch; Kornhausplatz 20) Built in 1903, Bern's neoclassical theatre stages opera, dance, classical music and plays (in German). Check the website for the latest programming.

**Stade de Suisse** STADIUM
(www.stadedesuisse.ch; Papiermühlestrasse 71; tours adult/child Sfr20/15; ⊙tours 3-4.15pm Sat) Home to the local Young Boys team, Bern's 32,000-seat stadium was built over the demolished Wankdorf Stadium, which hosted the 1954 World Cup final.

**Cinématte** CINEMA
(☎031 312 21 22; www.cinematte.ch; Wasserwerkgasse 7; ⊙6-11.30pm Thu-Mon) This riverside venue has a varied line-up of art-house and cult films, plus a wooden-decked terrace restaurant (p107).

**Bern Ticket** PERFORMING ARTS
(☎031 329 52 52; www.bernbillett.ch; Nägeligasse 1a; ⊙10am-6.30pm Mon-Fri, to 2pm Sat) Buy theatre and music concert tickets here, near the theatre.

## Shopping

**Markt Bern** MARKET
(Bern Market; www.marktbern.ch; Waisenhausplatz; ⊙8am-6pm Tue, to 4pm Sat Jan-Nov, also 9am-8pm Thu Apr-Oct) Leather, jewellery, shoes, clothing, kitchenware and gifts are among the many items on offer at this large market in the heart of the Old Town.

**Holz Art** ARTS & CRAFTS
(☎031 312 66 66; www.holz-art-bern.ch; Münstergasse 36; ⊙10am-12.30pm & 2-6.30pm Tue-Fri, 9.30am-4pm Sat) Holz Art sells exquisite hand-carved wooden toys, ornamental chalets and clocks.

**Berner Wochenmärkte** MARKET
(www.bernerwochenmarkt.ch; Bundesplatz; ⊙8am-12.30pm Tue & Sat) Bursting with fresh produce and flowers, this colourful bi-weekly market fills the large square in front of Bern's parliament building.

## Information

The **Bern Tourismus** (☎031 328 12 12; www.bern.com; Bahnhoftplatz 10a; ⊙9am-7pm Mon-Sat, to 6pm Sun) office at the train station is fully stocked with all you need to know about the capital and its neighbouring cantons, including walking maps and an excellent iPod audio tour.

There's another desk at **BärenPark** (☎031 328 12 12; www.bern.com; Grosser Muristalden 6, Bärengraben; ⊙9am-6pm Jun-Sep, 10am-4pm Mar-May & Oct, 11am-4pm Nov-Feb) with helpful staff, but not a lot of materials on-hand.

## Getting There & Away

The A12 motorway links Geneva with Bern (via Lausanne).

### AIR

Tiny Bern-Belp Airport (BRN; ☎031 960 21 11; www.flughafenbern.ch) with, 9km southeast of the centre, offers direct flights to London and other European cities with Bern-based SkyWork (www.flyskywork.com) and other budget airlines.

### TRAIN

Trains run at least hourly to Geneva (Sfr51, 1¾ hours), Basel (Sfr41, 55 minutes), Interlaken Ost (Sfr29, 55 minutes) and Zürich (Sfr51, 55 minutes to 1½ hours).

## Getting Around

### TO/FROM THE AIRPORT

Airport Bus Bern 334 (www.bernmobil.ch) links Bern-Belp Airport with Belp train station, where frequent S-Bahn trains connect into Bern. Single tickets covering the entire 30-minute journey (adult/child Sfr7/3.70) can be purchased at machines or on board.

### BICYCLE & SCOOTER

Borrow a free bike from **Bern Rollt** (☎031 318 93 50; www.bernrollt.ch; Milchgässli; first 4hr free, per additional hour Sfr1; ⊙8am-9.30pm), adjacent to the train station. You'll need ID and Sfr20 as a deposit.

Bern is also rolling out the PubliBike (p335) bike-sharing scheme. Pick up a 'QuickBike' pass for 24 hours from the offices of Bern Tourismus.

### BUS, TRAM & FUNICULAR

**Bern Mobil** (www.bernmobil.ch; tickets 30min/1hr/day Sfr2.60/4.60/13) operates an excellent bus and tram network. Tickets are available from machines at all stops. Local hotel guests receive a Bern Ticket, offering free use of public transport throughout the city. The ticket covers all Bern Mobil services – including the Marzili and Gurten funiculars – within zones 100 and 101 (city centre and immediate surroundings). It does not cover Moonliner buses or services beyond zones 100 and 101.

**Moonliner** (☎031 321 88 12; www.moonliner.ch; tickets from Sfr6) night buses transport night owls from Bahnhofplatz two or three times between midnight and 4am on Friday and Saturday nights. Discount passes are invalid.

Postal buses depart from the bus station on the western side of Bahnhofplatz.

# Emmental

POP 26,541

One of Switzerland's most famous dairy products – holey Emmental cheese, from where the simplified term 'Swiss cheese' comes – has its very origins in this rural idyll northeast of Bern. The gateway towns of Burgdorf and Langnau preside over these verdant lowlands – a mellow patchwork of rustic chalets, thatch-roofed storehouses and grazing cows plonked among fields of gold and green.

As lovely as all that is, the charm of the farm is not likely to be the reason you'll want to come here. Let's face it, it's all about the cheese.

If you're a lover of the soft, nutty, stringy, melty, gooey stuff, you're in for a real treat of tastings, opportunities to learn about the long history of the 'brand', demonstrations, shopping from the farm door, and did we mention eating lots of cheese already?

## Sights

**★Emmentaler Schaukäserei** DAIRY

(Emmental Open Cheese Dairy; ☎034 435 16 11; www.showdairy.ch; Schaukäsereistrasse 6, Affoltern; ⏲9am-6.30pm Apr-Oct, to 5pm Nov-Mar) FREE Watch Emmental cheese being made into 95kg wheels and taste it at the Emmental Open Cheese Dairy in Affoltern. Short videos explain the modern production process and how Emmental gets its famous holes, while traditional cheesemaking happens once a day over an open fire in the 18th-century herdsman's cottage.

From Bern take the S-Bahn to Hasle-Rüegsau, then bus 471 to Affoltern (total journey Sfr17, one hour).

**Museum Schloss Burgdorf** CASTLE

(Burgdorf Castle Museum; ☎034 423 02 14; www.museumschlossburgdorf.ch) This robust 12th-century castle could be straight out of a book with its drawbridge, thick stone walls and trio of museums focusing on castle history, Swiss gold and ethnology.

## Sleeping & Eating

**★Hotel Möschberg** FARMSTAY €

(☎031 710 22 22; www.hotelmoeschberg.ch; Grosshöchstetten; s/d without bathroom Sfr100/138; ) Situated between fields of cows and gentle walking trails, 4km west of Langnau above the dairy-farming hamlet of Grosshöchstetten, this ecofriendly hotel and retreat centre (a women's agricultural school in the 1930s) is a quintessential slice of the Emmental. Rooms are simple but stylish; dinner is a vibrant homemade affair with organic wine (dinner/full board Sfr25/55).

**Emme Lodge** HOSTEL €

(☎034 402 45 26; www.emmelodge.ch; Mooseggstrasse 32, Langnau; dm/s/d from Sfr22/58/90) This off-the-beaten-track hostel, a 10-minute walk from Langnau station, is a farmhouse-style chalet built in 1768 with a huge overhanging roof, basic rooms and a notably cheery, convivial atmosphere.

**★Landgasthof Sommerhaus** SWISS €€

(☎034 422 50 40; www.sommerhaus-burgdorf.ch; Sommerhaus 1, Burgdorf; mains Sfr22-58; ⏲9am-11.30pm Mon, Tue, Fri & Sat, to 9pm Sun) At this country-style farmhouse just outside Burgdorf, hearty Swiss meat-and-potatoes staples (including wild game in season) are accompanied by locally grown vegetables. It's especially appealing in warm weather, with its spacious outdoor terrace, grassy lawn, kids' play area and lovely rural vistas.

### HOLEY MOLY: AOC EMMENTALER CHEESE

Named for its birthplace in the Emme River valley, Switzerland's incomparable Emmentaler cheese has a proud history dating to the Middle Ages. Copycat cheesemakers around the world have appropriated the Emmental name, but only authentic Emmentaler Switzerland AOC conforms to the original production technique, using raw milk from grass-fed cows, cellar ripened in giant wheels for at least 120 days.

Emmentaler's famous holes, known as 'eyes', result from the release of carbon-dioxide bubbles by bacteria during the ageing process. Once seen as an imperfection, they're now worn with pride: the larger the holes, the longer the cheese has matured, and the more pronounced its flavour.

## Information

The **tourist office** (☎034 402 42 52; www.emmental.ch; Bahnhofstrasse 44, Burgdorf; ⏲9am-noon & 1.30-6pm Mon-Fri, plus 8am-noon Sat May-Sep) for the Emmental region is located in Burgdorf.

## Getting There & Away

Frequent trains link Burgdorf (Sfr11.60, 15 minutes) and Langnau (Sfr18.40, 30 minutes) with Bern.

## Getting Around

The area's low terrain makes it perfect for cycling – discover fun facts along the Emmental Cheese Route (www.kaeseroute.ch/en), a cycling loop through the heart of the Emme Valley.

# Solothurn

POP 16,163 / ELEV 440M

Surprising Solothurn (*Soleure* in French) is something special. It looks and feels different to the rest of Switzerland in a way that's hard to pin down. The beautiful baroque Old Town, with its grey cobblestone streets, feels distinctly more European than Swiss, with definite Germanic and Italianate influences and a little less of the French and Roman flavours more commonly seen in this part of the country.

The imposing, 66m-tall facade of the magnificent St Ursus Cathedral, standing majestically among fountains, piazzas, churches and city gates, gives weight to Solothurn's claim to be Switzerland's most beautiful baroque town.

Solothurn is often overlooked, but it's well worth spending a day or a night here, if you're looking for a beautiful, historic location that's by the water at the foot of the mountains and retains a sleepy, rural vibe, especially after dark when the few day-trippers leave.

## Sights

**★St Ursen-Kathedrale** CATHEDRAL
(Hauptgasse; ⏲8am-6.30pm) Architect Gaetano Matteo Pisoni restrained himself with the classical Italianate facade of Solothurn's monolithic 18th-century cathedral, but went wild inside with a white-and-gilt trip of wedding-cake baroque.

**★Kunstmuseum** GALLERY
(☎032 624 40 00; www.kunstmuseum-so.ch; Werkhofstrasse 30; ⏲11am-5pm Tue-Fri, from 10am Sat & Sun) FREE The centrepiece of Solothurn's Fine Arts Museum is Ferdinand Hodler's famous portrait of William Tell (looking a bit like a red-haired, bearded Goliath in a white hippy top and short trousers). The *Madonna of Solothurn* (1522), by Holbein the Younger, is among a small number of other major works.

**Zeitglockenturm** LANDMARK
(Marktplatz) A knight, a king and a Grim Reaper jig on the hour atop this 12th-century astronomical clock with its hands reversed so the smaller one shows the minutes. It's on Marktplatz, which springs to life during the Wednesday morning market.

**Jesuitenkirche** CHURCH
(Jesuit Church; Hauptgasse 75) The unprepossessing facade of this church (1680–89) disguises an interior of baroque embellishments and stucco work. All the 'marble' in here is fake – mere spruced-up wood and plaster.

**Gerechtigkeits-Brunnen** FOUNTAIN
(Fountain of Justice; Hauptgasse) West of the clock tower, this fountain (1561) portrays a blindfolded Justice, holding aloft a sword, while the four most important contemporary figures in Europe sit at her feet: the Holy Roman Emperor, the Pope, the Turkish Sultan and…the mayor of Solothurn!

**Museum Altes Zeughaus** MUSEUM
(☎032 627 60 70; www.museum-alteszeughaus.ch; Zeughausplatz 1; adult/child Sfr6/4; ⏲1-5pm Tue-Sat, 10am-5pm Sun) Fresh from extensive renovations completed in late 2016, the early 17th-century rust-coloured facade of this vast, multi-windowed arsenal museum is a reminder that Solothurn was once a centre for mercenaries, many of whom fought for French kings. Inside you'll find an impressive collection of displays and artefacts that date from the Middle Ages and chronicle the history of this beautiful baroque town.

**Baseltor** GATE
Just east of the cathedral, this is Solothurn's most attractive city gate. Nearby, the city's former bastion makes a decent picnic spot.

## Festivals & Events

**Solothurner Filmtage** FILM
(Solothurn Film Days; www.solothurnerfilmtage.ch; ⏲late Jan-early Feb) The most prestigious celebration of the Swiss film industry takes place over eight days at a variety of venues in town. Book accommodation well in advance.

## Sleeping

**★SYHA Hostel Solothurn** HOSTEL €
(☎032 623 17 06; www.youthhostel.ch/solothurn; Landhausquai 23; dm/s/d from Sfr33/80/104; ⊙Mar-Nov; @☜) In an enviable Old Town location along the Aare River bike path, this wheelchair-accessible, renovated 17th-century customs house is a striking mix of glass, stainless steel and raw concrete. Dorms – some with nice riverfront views – sport three to 10 beds. Breakfast is included and lunch and dinner are available (Sfr17.50).

**Gasthaus Kreuz** GUESTHOUSE €
(☎032 622 20 20; www.kreuz-solothurn.ch; Kreuzgasse 4; s/d without bathroom from Sfr60/100) This riverside guesthouse and cultural centre exudes a hipster ethos, with its cherry-red shared shower block, big creaky-floored rooms and spartan furnishings. Its street-level cafe-bar hosts bands, concerts and cultural happenings.

**Baseltor** BOUTIQUE HOTEL €€
(☎032 622 34 22; www.baseltor.ch; Hauptgasse 79; s/d from Sfr130/200; ☜) Charmingly set in the shade of the cathedral, this atmospheric inn with steel-grey wooden shutters and an attractive minimalist interior is flanked by an excellent slow-food restaurant (mains Sfr29 to Sfr42).

## Eating & Drinking

**Pittaria** MIDDLE EASTERN €
(☎032 621 22 69; www.pittaria.ch; Theatergasse 12; mains Sfr12-24; ⊙10.30am-3pm & 5.30-9pm Tue-Fri, 10.30am-6pm Sat) Gregarious owner Sami Daher serves heavenly mint tea and bargain-priced Palestinian cuisine (home-made mango chutney, creamy hummus, crunchy falafel) at this laid-back eatery featuring bench seating adorned with Persian rugs and plush camels.

**★Cantinetta Bindella** ITALIAN €€
(☎032 623 16 85; www.bindella.ch; Ritterquai 3; mains Sfr22-54; ⊙11.30am-2pm & 6-10pm Mon-Sat) This refined Italian eatery attracts a devoted crowd with its candlelit interior and leafy walled garden where linen tablecloths spread beneath the trees. The menu embraces all things Tuscan.

**Solheure** BAR
(☎032 637 03 03; www.solheure.ch; Ritterquai 10; ⊙5-11.30pm Mon, noon-midnight Tue-Thu, from 2pm Sun, from 5pm Mon; ☜) Old stone walls, kitsch-meets-cool chairs and a sun-flooded riverfront terrace ensure that half of Solothurn can be found at this trendy riverside bar in a former warehouse.

## Information

The helpful staff of the **Region Solothurn Tourismus** (☎032 626 46 46; www.solothurn-city.ch; Hauptgasse 69; ⊙9am-6pm Mon-Fri, to 1pm Sat) office, located just in front of the cathedral and to the right, can provide you with English-language walking tours and maps of the town.

## Getting There & Away

Trains run at least twice hourly to Bern (Sfr17.20, 45 minutes), Biel (Sfr14, 30 minutes), Zurich (Sfr38, 55 minutes).

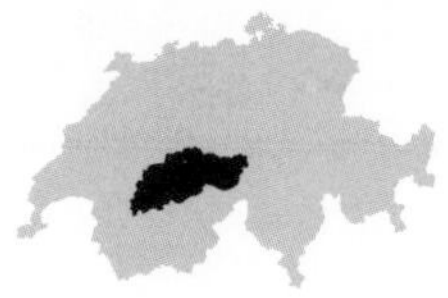

# Bernese Oberland

POP 207,652

**Includes ➡**



## Best Places to Eat

➡ Beau-Rivage da Domenico (p136)

➡ Nico's (p141)

➡ Chesery (p143)

➡ The Verandah (p118)

➡ Cafe 3692 (p125)

## Best Places to Stay

➡ Victoria-Jungfrau Grand Hotel & Spa (p118)

➡ Gletschergarten (p122)

➡ Hotel Eiger (p132)

➡ Esther's Guest House (p133)

➡ The Hayloft (p141)

## Why Go?

Nature works on an epic scale here. Whether you're hiking in the shadow of the fearsome north face of Eiger, carving powder on a crisp winter's morning in Gstaad, or gawping at the misty Staubbach Falls, the Swiss Alps don't get more in-your-face beautiful than this. Nowhere are the resorts quainter, the peaks higher, the glaciers grander. Fittingly watched over by Mönch (Monk), Jungfrau (Virgin) and Eiger (Ogre), the Bernese Oberland sends spirits soaring to heaven.

The region's cinematic looks haven't gone unnoticed. Mark Twain wrote that no opiate compared to walking here (and he should know), Arthur Conan Doyle thought Meiringen a pretty spot for a Sherlock Holmes whodunnit, while Ian Fleming brought the icy wilderness of Schilthorn to screens in 007 films. Yet try as they might, few photographers manage to do the Bernese Oberland justice. Listen for tutting tourists at postcard carousels trying – and failing – to find something to match their memories.

## When to Go

➡ Winter brings prime skiing, downhill races and ringing in the New Year ogre-style at Interlaken's Harder Potschete.

➡ Summer is the time for feasts of music, folk, theatre and street-art festivals, plus excellent Alpine hiking.

➡ Room rates plunge in autumn, the cows come home from their summer pastures, and Spiez hosts its wine festival.

# Bernese Oberland Highlights

1 **Klettersteig** (p132) Getting dizzy with with zip-wires, hanging bridges and Eiger views on Mürren's *via ferrata*.

2 **Faulhornweg** (p124) Enjoying Alpine highs on this day hike from Schynige Platte to First, above Grindelwald.

3 **Junfraujoch** (p127) Being spellbound by 4000m peaks and the glinting Aletsch Glacier.

4 **Meiringen** (p139) Doing some Sherlock Holmes–style detective work to find glorious waterfalls and meringues.

5 **Interlaken** (p115) Testing your limits canyoning, skydiving and ice climbing in Switzerland's adventure-sports mecca.

6 **Lauterbrunnen** (p129) Marvelling at the 72 waterfalls cascading down the cliffs in the Lauterbrunnen Valley.

7 **Gstaad** (p141) Slaloming on the glitzy slopes of this super-chic ski resort.

8 **Thun** (p133) Mooching around lakeside parks, castles and a medieval Old Town with a youthful buzz.

## Getting There & Around

The Bernese Oberland is easily accessible by road and train from major Swiss airports, including Basel, Bern, Geneva and Zürich, as well as from Lucerne.

Note that a Swiss or Eurail Pass alone will take you only so far into the area.

Getting around the region by train and mountain railway is a breeze but it's worth bearing in mind that summit journeys are only really worth making on clear days. Check the webcams on www.jungfraubahn.ch and www.swisspanorama.com before you leave.

Frequent trains link cities, including Zürich (Sfr70, two hours), Lucerne (Sfr32, 1¾ to two hours) and Bern (Sfr29, one hour), to Interlaken, the gateway to the Bernese Oberland.

DON'T MISS

### INTERLAKEN FREE WALKING TOUR

Want to see Interlaken like a local? Guides show visitors their home turf on fun and insightful two-hour guided walking tours, which begin at 6pm every day from April to September, and at 11am on Monday, Wednesday and Saturday from October to March. The meeting point is Backpackers Villa Sonnenhof (p117). The tour is free, but tips are, of course, appreciated. For more details, consult www.interlakenfreetour.com.

# INTERLAKEN

POP 5692 / ELEV 570M

Once Interlaken made the Victorians swoon with mountain vistas from the chandelier-lit confines of grand hotels; today it makes daredevils scream with adrenaline-loaded activities. Straddling the glacier-fed Lakes Thun and Brienz and capped by the pearly white peaks of Eiger, Mönch and Jungfrau, the town is the gateway to Switzerland's fabled Jungfrau region and the country's hottest adventure destination bar none. If the touristy town itself leaves you cold, the mountains on its doorstep will blow your mind, particularly if you're abseiling waterfalls, thrashing white water or gliding soundlessly above 4000m summits.

## Sights

Cross the turquoise Aare River for a mooch around Interlaken's compact and quiet old quarter, Unterseen.

**Harder Kulm** MOUNTAIN

(www.jungfrau.ch/harderkulm; adult/child Sfr16/8) For far-reaching views to the 4000m giants, take the eight-minute funicular ride to 1322m Harder Kulm. Many hiking paths begin here, and the vertigo-free can enjoy the panorama from the Zweiseensteg (Two Lake Bridge) jutting out above the valley. The wildlife park near the valley station is home to Alpine critters, including marmots and ibex.

**Bernatone Alphornbau** WORKSHOP

(☎079 840 38 10; www.bernatone.ch; Im Holz, Habkern; ⊙10am-noon & 1.30-5pm Mon-Fri; 👪) It doesn't get more Swiss than the alphorn, that fabulous-looking instrument often played by bearded Alpine men with ruddy cheeks and a good set of lungs at summer folk festivals. Call ahead and you can visit the workshop of master alphorn craftsman maker Heinz Tschiemer. A genuine alphorn, which takes around 60 days to make, will set you back around Sfr3000 but smaller instruments are also available for purchase. From Interlaken West, take bus 106 to Haberkern.

**Heimwehfluh** MOUNTAIN

(www.heimwehfluh.ch; funicular adult/child return Sfr16/8, toboggan Sfr9/7; ⊙10am-5pm Apr-late Oct; 👪) A nostalgic funicular trundles up to family-friendly Heimwehfluh for long views across Interlaken. Kids love the bob run down the hill – lay off the brakes to pick up speed.

**St Beatus Caves** CAVE

(www.beatushoehlen.ch; adult/child Sfr18/10; ⊙9.45am-5pm late Mar-late Oct) Sculpted over millennia, the St Beatus Caves are great for a wander through caverns of dramatically lit stalagmites, stalactites and underground lakes. Lore has it that in the 6th century the caves sheltered St Beatus, monk, hermit and first apostle of Switzerland, who apparently did battle with a dragon here. They are a half-hour boat or bus ride from Interlaken West.

## Activities

Switzerland is the world's second-biggest adventure-sports centre and Interlaken is its busiest hub. Almost every heart-quickening pursuit you can think of is offered around Interlaken. You can white-water raft on the Lütschine, Simme and Saane Rivers, canyon the Saxetet, Grimsel or Chli Schliere gorges, and canyon jump at the Gletscherschlucht

## Interlaken

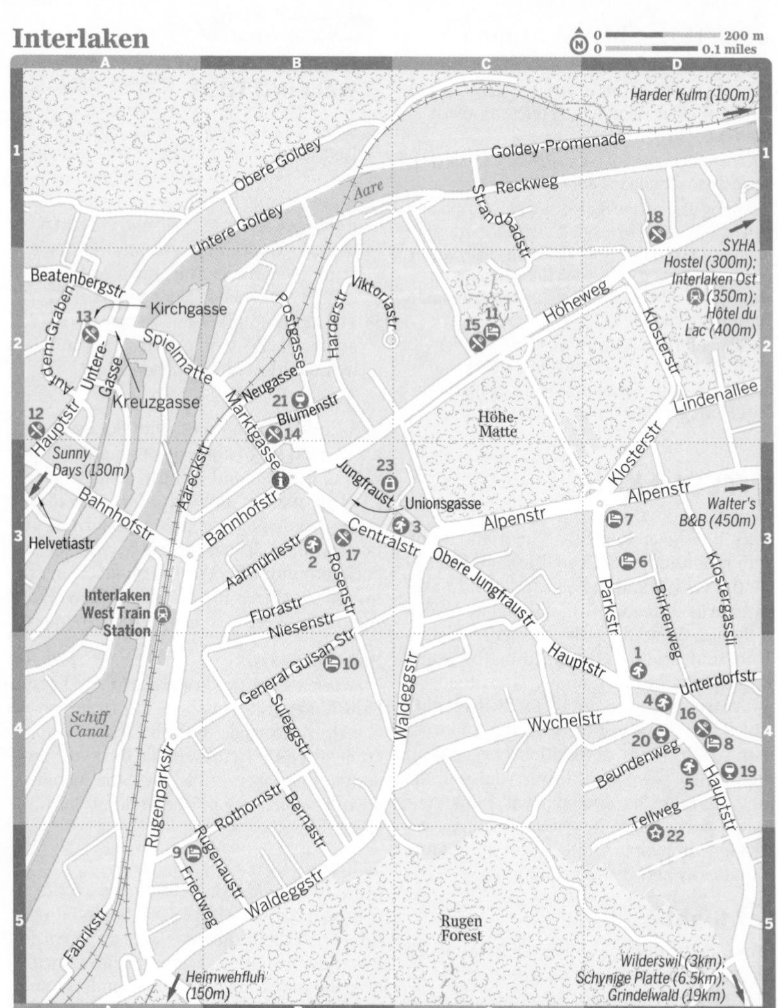


near Grindelwald. If that doesn't grab you, there's paragliding, glacier bungee jumping, skydiving, ice climbing, hydrospeeding and, phew, much more.

Sample prices are around Sfr120 for rafting or canyoning, Sfr140 for hydrospeeding, Sfr130 to Sfr180 for bungee or canyon jumping, Sfr170 for tandem paragliding, Sfr180 for ice climbing, Sfr220 for hang-gliding, and Sfr430 for skydiving. A half-day mountain-bike tour will set you back around Sfr25.

Most excursions are without incident, but there's always a small risk, so it's wise to ask about safety records and procedures.

**Outdoor Interlaken** ADVENTURE SPORTS

(☎033 826 77 19; www.outdoor-interlaken.ch; Hauptstrasse 15; ⏲8am-7pm) This is a one-stop adventure-sports shop for rafting, canyoning, skydiving, paragliding and just about any other buzz-inducing activity you care to mention.

**Skydive Switzerland – Scenic Air** SCENIC FLIGHTS

(☎033 821 00 11; www.skydiveswitzerland.ch; Hauptstrasse 26; skydiving Sfr395-450; ⏲7.30am-8pm) Arranges scenic flights, skydiving and other activities.

## Interlaken

**Activities, Courses & Tours**
1 Alpinraft ... D4
2 Hang Gliding Interlaken ... B3
3 K44 ... C3
4 Outdoor Interlaken ... D4
5 Skydive Switzerland – Scenic Air ... D4

**Sleeping**
6 Arnold's B&B ... D3
7 Backpackers Villa Sonnenhof ... D3
8 Balmer's Herberge ... D4
9 Hotel Alphorn ... A5
10 Swiss Inn ... B4
11 Victoria-Jungfrau Grand Hotel & Spa ... C2

**Eating**
12 Arcobaleno ... A2
13 Benacus ... A2
14 Café de Paris ... B2
15 La Terrasse ... C2
16 Little Thai ... D4
17 Sandwich Bar ... B3
18 The Verandah ... D1

**Drinking & Nightlife**
19 3 Tells ... D4
20 Barracuda Bar ... D4
21 Hüsi Bierhaus ... B2

**Entertainment**
22 Tellspiele ... D5

**Shopping**
23 Funky Chocolate Club ... B3
Vertical Sport ... (see 3)

**Alpinraft** ADVENTURE SPORTS
(☎033 823 41 00; www.alpinraft.com; Hauptstrasse 7; ⏲8am-6pm) Can arrange most sports, including canyoning, bungee jumping, rafting and ice climbing.

**Hang Gliding Interlaken** SCENIC FLIGHTS
(☎079 770 07 04; www.hangglidinginterlaken.com; Aarmuehlestrasse 3; flight Sfr235; ⏲7.30am-10pm) Organises hang-gliding above Interlaken. Call ahead for bookings and meeting-point details.

**K44** CLIMBING
(www.k44.ch; Jungfraustrasse 44; adult/child Sfr21/14; ⏲9am-10pm) Not ready to climb Eiger just yet? Squeeze in some practice at this climbing hall. There are 70 routes from 4a to 8a to test out.

## Festivals & Events

**Harder Potschete** CULTURAL
(www.harderpotschete.ch) Cackling, clanging bells and causing mischief, the ogre-like Potschen dash through Interlaken on 2 January. The revelry spills into the night with upbeat folk music and fiendish merrymaking.

**Jungfrau Marathon** SPORTS
(www.jungfrau-marathon.ch) Eiger, Mönch and Jungfrau are always breathtaking, but never more so than for runners competing in September's Jungfrau Marathon to Kleine Scheidegg. Even if you're not quite up to the challenge, it's impressive to see the Alpine athletes who are.

## Sleeping

Interlaken runs the whole gamut: from party-hard backpacker digs to family-run B&Bs and grand hotels with spas, gourmet restaurants and mountain views. Call ahead during the low season, as some places close.

**Backpackers Villa Sonnenhof** HOSTEL €
(☎033 826 71 71; www.villa.ch; Alpenstrasse 16; dm Sfr40-47, d Sfr110-148; P 📶) Repeatedly voted one of Europe's best hostels, Sonnenhof is a slick, ecofriendly combination of ultramodern chalet and elegant art nouveau villa. Dorms are immaculate, and some have balconies with Jungfrau views. There's also a relaxed lounge, a well-equipped kitchen, a kids' playroom and a vast backyard for mountain gazing. Special family rates are available.

**Sunny Days** B&B €
(☎077 456 23 38; www.sunnydays.ch; Helvetiastrasse 29; d Sfr132-223; P 📶) A little ray of sunshine indeed, this chalet-style B&B set in pretty gardens has sweet, simple rooms, the pick of which have balconies facing the Jungfrau.

**Arnold's B&B** B&B €
(☎033 823 64 21; www.arnolds.ch; Parkstrasse 3; d Sfr100-150; P 📶) Frills are few, but the welcome from Beatrice and Armin is warm at this family-run B&B. The light, home-style rooms are housed in a converted 1930s villa.

**Walter's B&B** B&B €
(☎033 822 76 88; www.walters.ch; Oelestrasse 35; d/tr Sfr76/114; 📶) Walter is a real star with his quick smile, culinary skills and invaluable tips. The rooms are a blast from the 1970s, but they are super-clean and you'd be hard pushed to find better value in Interlaken.

**SYHA Hostel** HOSTEL €
(☎033 826 10 90; www.youthhostel.ch; Untere Bönigstrasse 3, Am Bahnhof Ost; dm Sfr39-45, s Sfr127, d Sfr138-147, f Sfr210; P @ ) Slick, modern and incredibly central, this is a cut above your average SYHA hostel. The riverside digs offer spotless, wood-floored dorms with mountain and park views. Facilities include bike rental, a snack bar and a lounge with a pool table.

**Balmer's Herberge** HOSTEL €
(☎033 822 19 61; www.balmers.com; Hauptstrasse 23; dm/s/d/tr/q Sfr36/60/113/120/152; @ ) Adrenaline junkies hail Balmer's for its fun frat-house vibe. These party-mad digs offer beer-garden happy hours, wrapped lunches, a pumping bar with DJs, and chill-out hammocks for nursing your hangover.

**Hotel Alphorn** HOTEL €€
(☎033 822 30 51; www.hotel-alphorn.ch; Rothornstrasse 29a; s Sfr140-160, d Sfr160-180, tr Sfr225-240; P ) Super-central yet peaceful, the Alphorn is a five-minute toddle from Interlaken West station. Decorated in cool blues and whites, the rooms are spotlessly clean.

**Hôtel du Lac** HOTEL €€
(☎033 822 29 22; www.dulac-interlaken.ch; Höheweg 225; s/d Sfr160/240; P ) Smiley old-fashioned service and a riverfront location near Interlaken Ost make this 19th-century hotel a solid choice. It has been in the same family for generations and, despite the mishmash of styles, has kept enough belle-époque glory to remain charming.

**Swiss Inn** B&B €€
(☎033 822 36 26; www.swiss-inn.ch; General Guisan Strasse 23; d/apt Sfr180/270; P ) A tranquil retreat set in rose-strewn gardens, this handsome villa extends a warm welcome. Opt for a bright, spacious double or a family-sized apartment complete with kitchenette and balcony.

**★Victoria-Jungfrau Grand Hotel & Spa** LUXURY HOTEL €€€
(☎033 828 28 28; www.victoria-jungfrau.ch; Höheweg 41; d Sfr479-749, junior ste from Sfr539, ste from Sfr950; P @ ) The reverent hush and impeccable service here (as well as the prices) evoke an era when only royalty and the seriously wealthy travelled. A perfect melding of well-preserved art nouveau features and modern luxury make this Interlaken's answer to Raffles – with plum views of Jungfrau, three first-class restaurants and a gorgeous spa.

## Eating

**Little Thai** THAI €
(☎033 821 10 17; www.mylittlethai.ch; Hauptstrasse 19; mains Sfr18-27; 11am-2pm & 5-10pm Wed-Mon) This hole-in-the-wall den is authentically Thai, festooned with pics of the King of Thailand, kitschy fairy lights and lucky cats. Snag a table to chomp on Eddie's freshly prepared spring rolls, homemade curries and spicy papaya salads.

**Sandwich Bar** SANDWICHES €
(www.sandwichbar.ch; Rosenstrasse 5; sandwiches Sfr6-9.50; 7.30am-7pm Mon-Fri, 8am-5pm Sat) Choose your bread and get creative with fillings such as air-dried ham with sun-dried tomatoes and brie with walnuts. Or try the soups, salads, toasties and locally made ice cream. Efficient service and a location near Interlaken West train station.

**Café de Paris** CAFE €
(www.cafe-de-paris-interlaken.ch; Am Marktplatz, Marktgasse 14; 7am-12.30am; ) Right in the heart of town, this bright, modern cafe rustles up inexpensive snacks and mains, from wraps, club sandwiches and salads through to numerous takes on rösti.

**★The Verandah** SWISS €€
(☎033 822 75 75; Höheweg 139, Hotel Royal-St Georges; mains Sfr21-38; 6-10pm) This restaurant at Hotel Royal-St Georges is a winning combination of old-school elegance and contemporary style, with its stucco trimmings and slick bistro seating. The menu has riffs on Swiss food, with classics such as fondue and rösti, grilled fish and meats.

**Benacus** INTERNATIONAL €€
(☎033 821 20 20; www.benacus.ch; Kirchgasse 15; mains Sfr34-48; 11.30am-1.30pm & 5pm-12.30am Tue-Fri, 5pm-12.30am Sat) Super-cool Benacus is a breath of urban air with its glass walls, wine-red sofas, lounge music and street-facing terrace. The menu swings from creative tapas to Med-style flavours.

**Arcobaleno** ITALIAN €€
(☎033 823 12 43; www.ristorante-pizzeria-arcobaleno.ch; Hauptstrasse 18; pizza Sfr12.50-23.50, mains Sfr23.50-27.50; ) Italian in the best of traditions, with smiley service and generous home cooking, Arcobaleno is a find in Interlaken's Unterseen district. The antipasti, pasta and risotto dishes and pizzas are the real deal. A kids' menu is also available.

DON'T MISS

## SCHYNIGE PLATTE

The must-do day trip from Interlaken is the Schynige Platte plateau (1967m), which provides a natural balcony on the Bernese Alps and Lakes Thun and Brienz, glinting far below. A relic from a bygone era of slow travel, the **cog-wheel summit train** (www.schynigeplatte.ch; one way/return Sfr40/64; 7.25am-4.45pm late May-late Oct; ) allows the views to unfold little by little. Up top, the colourful **Alpengarten** (www.alpengarten.ch; 8.30am-6pm late May-Oct) FREE nurtures 600 types of Alpine blooms, including snowbells, arnicas, gentians, anemones and edelweiss. Hiking trails teeter along the ridge and through meadows chiming with cowbells, while paragliders launch themselves from the plateau in summer.

For astounding views of first light caressing the summits of Eiger, Mönch and Jungfrau, consider an overnight stay at the charmingly old fashioned **Hotel Schynige Platte** (033 828 73 73; http://hotelschynigeplatte.ch; s/d/tr Sfr165/240/330; late May-late Oct), which also hosts free **alphorn concerts** (11am-2pm) in peak summer season.

The cog-wheel train to the summit departs from Wilderswil, a four-minute bus ride south of Interlaken Ost station (Sfr3.60). If you're driving, it's five minutes south of town via Gsteigstrasse.

**La Terrasse** FRENCH €€€
(033 828 28 28; www.victoria-jungfrau.ch; Höheweg 41; mains Sfr38-65; 7-10pm Tue-Sat) Housed in Interlaken's plushest belle époque hotel, La Terrasse is a class act, with a season-driven menu and a sumptuous setting redolent of a French orangery. The cuisine plays up French-Swiss flavours.

## Drinking & Nightlife

**Hüsi Bierhaus** PUB
(www.huesi-interlaken.ch; Postgasse 3; 1.30pm-12.30am Mon-Thu, to 1.30am Fri, 11.30am-1.30am Sat, 11.30am-12.30am Sun) Some 50 different craft beers from around the world – Trappist brews to Swiss IPAs – keep the punters happy at Hüsi's. It also rolls out tasty pub grub from schnitzel to beer-laced bratwurst. Cover band Uptown Lights plays Saturday nights.

**Barracuda Bar** LOUNGE
(Hauptstrasse 16; 4pm-12.30am Wed & Thu, 9am-midnight Fri-Sun; ) Taking you through from coffee to cocktails, this cafe-lounge is a nicely chilled spot, with occasional live music.

**3 Tells** PUB
(www.the3tells.com; Hauptstrasse 49; 4pm-midnight Tue & Wed, 2pm-midnight Thu & Fri, 10am-midnight Sat & Sun; ) A pub in the relaxed Irish mould, 3 Tells has live sports, free wi-fi and Guinness on tap.

## Entertainment

**Tellspiele** THEATRE
(0338223722; www.tellspiele.ch; Tellweg 5; tickets Sfr58-349; box office 9am-noon & 2-5pm Mon-Fri) There are twice-weekly performances of Schiller's *Wilhelm Tell* (William Tell) between mid-June and early September, staged in the open-air theatre in Rugen Forest. The play is in German, but an English synopsis is available.

## Shopping

★**Funky Chocolate Club** CHOCOLATE
(078 606 35 48; https://funkychocolateclub.com; Jungfraustrasse 35; 10am-6.30pm; ) 'Chocolate today, broccoli tomorrow' is the strapline of this venture. Run by two passionate chocoholics, Tatiana and Vladimir, the Funky Chocolate promises you will get 'chocolate wasted'. It delivers with a shop brimming with fair-trade and organic chocolate (vegan, dairy, nut and gluten-free varieties available).

**Vertical Sport** SPORTS & OUTDOORS
(http://verticalsport.ch; Jungfraustrasse 44; 9am-noon & 1.30-6pm Mon-Fri, 9am-4pm Sat) Located at the K44 climbing hall, this store sells and rents top-quality climbing gear and is run by expert mountaineers who can give sound advice.

## Information

**Tourist Office** (033 826 53 00; www.interlakentourism.ch; Marktgasse 1; 8am-7pm Mon-Fri, to 5pm Sat, 10am-4pm Sun Jul & Aug, shorter hours Sep-Jun) Interlaken's well-stocked, well-staffed tourist office also provides hotel booking services.

### DISCOUNT TRAVEL PASSES

You can save francs as you get around the Bernese Oberland with the **Berner Oberland Regional Pass** (www.regiopass-berneroberland.ch; 4-/6-/8-/10-day pass Sfr250/310/350/390; ⏲May-Oct), which allows unlimited travel on most trains, buses, boats, mountain railways and cable cars, as well as discounts on local sights and attractions (for instance, a 50% reduction on tickets to Jungfraujoch). The Junior Card (Sfr30) allows kids to travel free with their parents; unaccompanied, they pay half-price.

A good alternative is the **Jungfrau Travel Pass** (www.jungfrau.ch; 3-/4-/5-/6-day pass Sfr180/205/230/255), which provides three to six days of unlimited regional travel, though you still have to pay Sfr61 from Eigergletscher to Jungfraujoch.

Staying in local accommodation entitles you to a *Gästekarte* (Guest Card), good for discounts throughout the entire region. Ask your hotel for the card if one isn't forthcoming.

## Getting There & Away

Interlaken has two train stations: Interlaken West and Interlaken Ost; each has bike rental, money-changing facilities and an adjacent ferry landing stage for boats headed for Lake Thun and Lake Brienz.

Trains to Lucerne (Sfr32, 1¾ to two hours), Brig (Sfr45, one to 1¾ hours, via Spiez) and Montreux (Sfr71, 2¼ to 2¾ hours, via Spiez/Visp or Bern/Lausanne) depart frequently from Interlaken Ost train station.

The A8 motorway heads northeast to Lucerne and the A6 northwest to Bern, but the only way south for vehicles without a big detour round the mountains is to take the car-carrying train from Kandersteg, south of Spiez.

Should you wish to hire a car in Interlaken for trips further into Switzerland, big-name rental companies, including **Hertz** (☎033 822 61 72; www.hertz.ch; Hauptstrasse 4), are reasonably central.

## Getting Around

You can easily get around Interlaken on foot, but taxis and buses are found at each train station. Alternatively, pick up road bikes, tandems, all-terrain bikes and e-bikes at **Flying Wheels** (☎033 557 88 38; www.flyingwheels.ch; Höheweg 133) or other rental agencies around town.

# JUNGFRAU REGION

## Grindelwald

POP 3740 / ELEV 1034M

Grindelwald's sublime natural assets are film-set stuff – the chiselled features of the Eiger's north face, the glinting tongues of Oberer and Unterer Glaciers and the crown-like peak of Wetterhorn will make you stare, swoon and lunge for your camera. Skiers and hikers cottoned onto its charms in the late 19th century, which makes it one of Switzerland's oldest resorts, and it has lost none of its appeal over the decades, with geranium-studded Alpine chalets and verdant pastures set against an Oscar-worthy backdrop.

## Activities

### Summer Activities

Grindelwald is outstanding hiking territory, veined with trails that command arresting views to massive mountain faces, crevassed glaciers and snowcapped peaks.

High-altitude walks – around Männlichen, First and Pfingstegg – can be reached by taking cable cars up from the village. Anyone craving a challenge can tackle the Schwarzhorn *via ferrata* (mountain hiking route with cables), a giddying 5½-hour scramble from First to Grosse Scheidegg.

**Gletscherschlucht** GORGE

(Glacier Gorge; www.grindelwaldsports.ch; adult/child Sfr19/10; ⏲9.30am-6pm Sat-Thu, to 10pm Fri) Turbulent waters carve a path through this craggy glacier gorge. A footpath weaves through tunnels hacked into cliffs veined with pink and green marble. It's justifiably a popular spot for canyon and bungee-jumping expeditions. The gorge is a half-hour walk south from Grindelwald or take bus 2 from the train station.

**★Kleine Scheidegg Walk** HIKING

One of the region's most stunning day hikes is the 15km trek from Grindelwald Grund to Wengen via Kleine Scheidegg, which heads up through wildflower-freckled meadows to skirt below the Eiger's north face and reach Kleine Scheidegg, granting arresting views of the 'Big Three': Eiger (3970m), Mönch (4107m) and Jungfrau (4158m). Allow around 5½ to six hours.

**Pfingstegg** HIKING

A **cable car** (www.pfingstegg.ch; one way/return Sfr12.60/18.80; ⌚8am-7pm, to 5.30pm in low season, closed Nov-Apr) rises up to Pfingstegg, where short hiking trails lead to Stieregg, near the deeply crevassed Unterer Gletscher. Check to see whether the trail skirting the base of the Oberer Gletscher (1½ hours) via the Restaurant Milchbach is open. Along this, you pass the Breitlouwina, a geologically fascinating rock terrace scarred with potholes caused by moving ice.

**Grindelwald Sports** ADVENTURE SPORTS

(☎033 854 12 80; www.grindelwaldsports.ch; Dorfstrasse 103; ⌚8.30am-7pm) Opposite the tourist office, this outfit arranges mountain climbing, ski and snowboard instruction and the heart-stopping canyon swing and bungee in the Gletscherschlucht. It also houses a cosy cafe and sells walking guides.

**Paragliding Jungfrau** PARAGLIDING

(☎079 779 90 00; www.paragliding-jungfrau.ch) Call ahead to organise your jump from First (from Sfr180) at a height of 2150m. Longer flights (Sfr280) are also available if you want to maximise your air time. Meeting points are provided at the time of booking.

**Bort Scooter Trail** ADVENTURE SPORTS

(rental incl cable car to Bort Sfr32) Midway between First and Grindelwald is Bort, where you can rent scooters to zoom back down to the valley on a 4.5km marked trail. Kids can enjoy free play at Bort's Alpine playground.

**Sportzentrum Grindelwald** HEALTH & FITNESS

(www.sportzentrum-grindelwald.ch; Dorfstrasse 110) If the weather turns gloomy, Grindelwald's sport centre shelters a swimming pool, a mini spa, bouldering and climbing halls, an ice rink and an indoor rope park. See the website for opening times and prices. A guest card yields substantial discounts.

### Winter Activities

Stretching from Oberjoch at 2486m right down to the village, the region of First presents a fine mix of cruisey red and challenging black ski runs. From Kleine Scheidegg or Männlichen there are long, easy runs back to Grindelwald, with the Eiger towering above. For a crowd-free swoosh, check out the 15.5km of well-groomed cross-country skiing trails in the area. Or slip on snowshoes to pad through the winter wonderland in quiet exhilaration on six different trails.



## Jungfrau Region

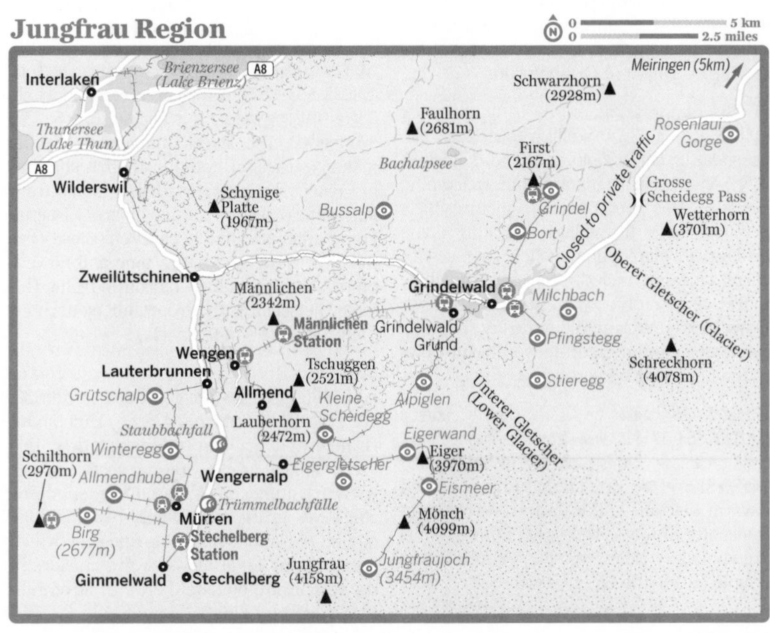

### SKIING THE JUNGFRAU REGION

Whether you want to slalom wide, sunny slopes at the foot of the Eiger or ski the breathtakingly sheer 16km Inferno run from Schilthorn to Lauterbrunnen, there's a piste that suits in the Jungfrau region. Grindelwald, Männlichen, Mürren and Wengen have access to 214km of prepared runs and 44 ski lifts. A one-day ski pass for either Grindelwald-Wengen or Mürren-Schilthorn costs Sfr63/32 per adult/child, while a seven-day ski pass for these regions will set you back Sfr309/155. Comprehensive passes for the entire Jungfrau ski region cost only slightly more (adult per day/week Sfr72/384), but switching between ski areas by train can be slow and crowded.

## Festivals & Events

**World Snow Festival** ART
In late January, artists get chipping at the six-day World Snow Festival to create extraordinary ice sculptures.

**Eiger Bike Challenge** SPORTS
(www.eigerbike.ch) A major fixture in the mountain-biking calendar, the 88km Eiger Bike Challenge races over hill and dale in mid-August.

## Sleeping

Grindelwald brims with characterful B&Bs and holiday chalets. Pick up a list at the tourist office, or log onto www.wir-grindelwalder.ch for a wide selection of holiday apartments.

Local buses, tourist-office guided walks and entry to the sports centre are free with the guest card, which is given to all visitors staying overnight in Grindelwald.

**Naturfreundehaus** HOSTEL €
(☎033 853 13 33; www.nfh.ch/grindelwald; Terrassenweg 18; dm Sfr35-40, s Sfr57-58, d Sfr94-96; P 📶) Vreni and Heinz are your welcoming hosts at this wood chalet, picturesquely perched above the village. Creaking floors lead up to cute pine-panelled rooms with check curtains, including a shoebox single that's apparently Switzerland's smallest. Downstairs there's an old curiosity shop of a cafe and a garden granting wonderful views to the Eiger and Wetterhorn.

**Hotel Tschuggen** HOTEL €
(☎033 853 17 81; www.tschuggen-grindelwald.ch; Dorfstrasse 134; s Sfr85-102, d Sfr135-190, f Sfr230-310; P 📶) Monika and Robert extend a warm welcome at this dark-wood chalet in the centre of town. The light, simple rooms are spotlessly clean; opt for a south-facing double for terrific Eiger views.

**Gletscherdorf** CAMPGROUND €
(☎033 853 14 29; www.gletscherdorf.ch; Locherbodenweg 29; sites per adult/child Sfr8.50/5, tent Sfr10-15; 📶) This riverfront campsite near the Pfingstegg cable car is among Switzerland's most stunning, with awesome views of the Eiger, Wetterhorn and Unterer Gletscher. Be aware that the closer you get to the river, the colder it gets. The excellent facilities include a common room, a laundry and free wi-fi.

**Alpenblick** HOTEL €
(☎033 853 11 05; www.alpenblick.info; Obere Gletscherstrasse 16; dm Sfr35-50, d Sfr100-180; P 📶) In a quiet corner of town, 10 minutes' stroll from the centre, Alpenblick is a great budget find, with squeaky-clean, pine-filled rooms. Basement dorms are jazzed up with bright duvets. There's a diner-style restaurant and a terrace with glacier views.

★ **Gletschergarten** HISTORIC HOTEL €€
(☎033 853 17 21; www.hotel-gletschergarten.ch; Obere Gletscherstrasse 1; s Sfr130-170, d Sfr230-320; P 📶) The sweet Breitenstein family makes you feel at home in their rustic timber chalet, brimming with heirlooms from landscape paintings to snapshots of Elsbeth's grandfather who had 12 children (those were the days...). Decked out in pine and flowery fabrics, the rooms have balconies facing Unterer Gletscher at the front and Wetterhorn (best for sunset) at the back.

**Berghaus Bort** B&B €€
(☎033 853 17 62; www.berghaus-bort.ch; d Sfr132-302, tr Sfr194-383, q Sfr260-476; 📶) High above Grindelwald at First middle station, this lovely chalet grants speedy access to the trails in summer and slopes in winter. Alpine chic rules in the wood-floored rooms done out in red and white, the finest of which have dreamy Eiger views. A fire crackles in the restaurant; outside there's an adventure playground for kids.

**Hotel Bodmi** HOTEL €€

(☎033 853 12 20; www.bodmi.ch; Terrassenweg 104; s Sfr198-218, d Sfr256-312, f Sfr369-435; P 📶) Wake up to memorable Eiger views and creamy goat's cheese – courtesy of the resident herd – at this postcard-perfect chalet. Surrounded by meadows, the hotel sits above First cable-car station and is a great base for summer hiking and winter skiing. Unwind in the spa or in the restaurant (mains Sfr22 to Sfr44) dishing up market-fresh Alpine fare.

**Romantik Hotel Schweizerhof** HISTORIC HOTEL €€€

(☎033 854 58 58; www.hotel-schweizerhof.com; Dorfstrasse; s incl half board Sfr265-370, d incl half board Sfr460-660; P 📶 🏊) The grand dame of Grindelwald, this plush art nouveau hotel

## Grindelwald

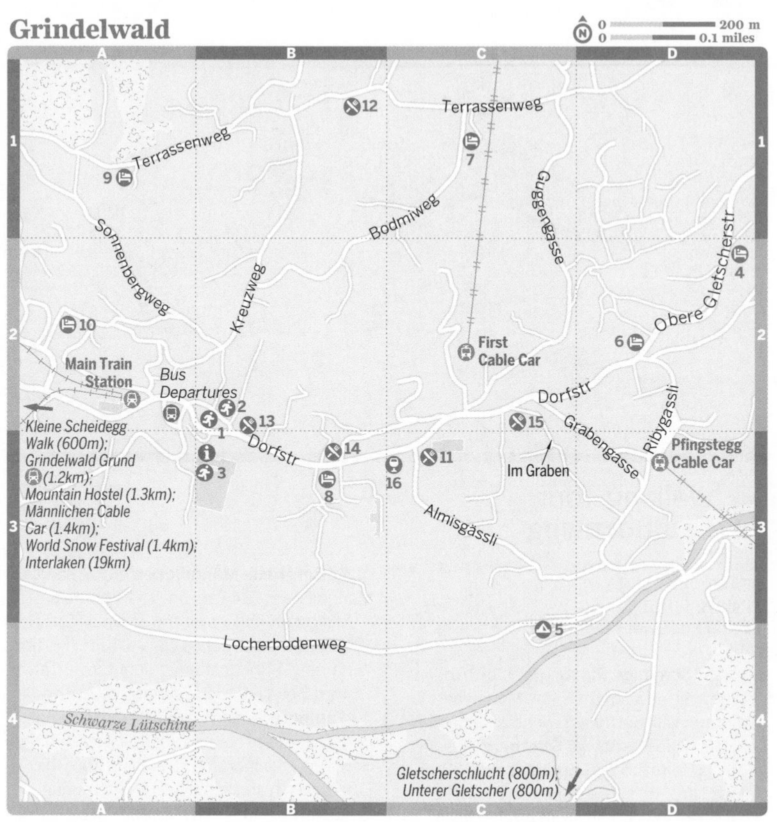


## Grindelwald

**Activities, Courses & Tours**

1 Eiger Bike Challenge ........ B2
2 Grindelwald Sports ........ B2
3 Sportzentrum Grindelwald ........ B3

**Sleeping**

4 Alpenblick ........ D2
5 Gletscherdorf ........ C4
6 Gletschergarten ........ D2
7 Hotel Bodmi ........ C1
8 Hotel Tschuggen ........ B3
9 Naturfreundehaus ........ A1
10 Romantik Hotel Schweizerhof ........ A2

**Eating**

11 C & M ........ C3
12 Cafe 3692 ........ B1
13 Grindel Lounge ........ B2
14 Memory ........ B3
15 Onkel Tom's Hütte ........ C2

**Drinking & Nightlife**

16 Avocado Bar ........ C3

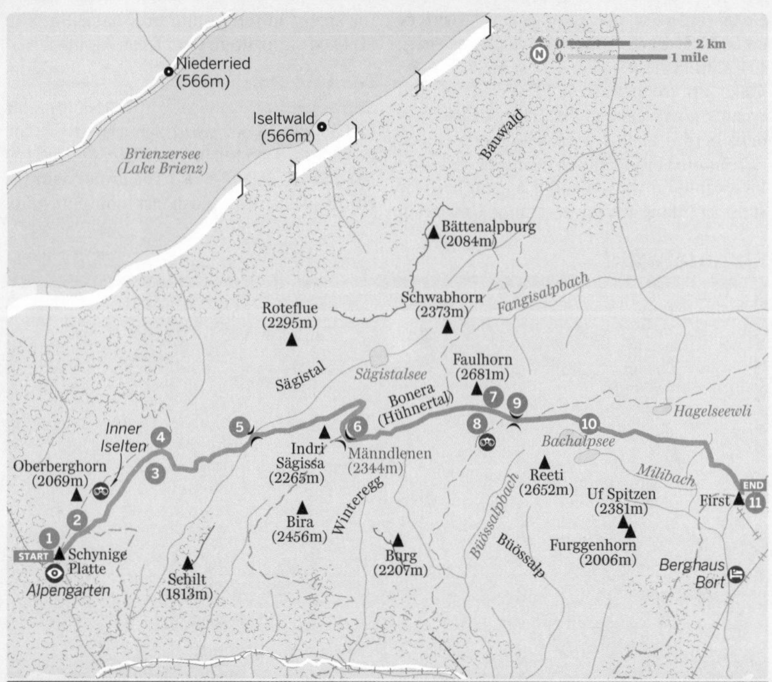


# Walking Tour **Faulhornweg**

**START:** SCHYNIGE PLATTE
**FINISH:** FIRST
**LENGTH:** 15KM; 4½ TO 5½ HOURS

From ① **Schynige Platte** (p119; 1967m) you get the first views of the Eiger, Mönch and Jungfrau. Walk northeast over rolling pastures past the Alpine hut of ② **Oberberg**, heading gently up to reach ③ **Louchera** at 2020m.

Head around scree slopes on the western flank of canyon-like ④ **Loucherhorn** (2230m) to cross a low grassy crest. The way dips and rises before coming to ⑤ **Egg**, a boulder-strewn pass at 2067m, 1¼ to 1½ hours from Schynige Platte.

Egg opens out northeastward into the Sägistal, a moorlike valley completely enclosed by ridges. Filling the lowest point, the aquamarine Sägistalsee (1937m) seeps away subterraneously. Skirt the Sägistal's southern side below Indri Sägissa before swinging around the talus-choked gully of Bonera (or Hühnertal). The route picks through rough karst slabs to the wood-shingled mountain hut of ⑥ **Berghaus Männdlenen** on the saddle of Männdlenen (2344m), one to 1½ hours on.

Make a steeply rising traverse along a broad ledge between stratified cliffs to the ridge of Winteregg. Shortly after a minor turn-off at 2546m, head left to the summit of 2681m ⑦ **Faulhorn**, one to 1¼ hours from Männdlenen. These lofty heights afford a spellbinding 360-degree panorama stretching from the Eiger, Mönch and Jungfrau to shimmering Brienzersee and Thunersee and, on clear days, the Black Forest in Germany and Vosges in France. Just below the summit sits 19th-century ⑧ **Berghotel Faulhorn**, the oldest and highest mountain hotel in the Alps.

Look out for marmots as you descend to ⑨ **Gassenboden** (2553m) then drop eastward into the grassy basin of the ⑩ **Bachalpsee** (2265m). The blue lake contrasts starkly with the ice-shrouded peaks of Wetterhorn (3701m), Schreckhorn (4078m) and Finsteraarhorn (4274m). A well-trodden path descends through pastures to the gondola-lift station at ⑪ **First** (p125; 2167m), 1½ to two hours from Berghotel Faulhorn.

has stylish rooms with gleaming slate-floored bathrooms. The spa is a big draw, with massage jets, treatment rooms, a teeth-chattering ice grotto and a pool with wide-screen mountain vistas. The restaurant uses home-grown vegetables and herbs.

## Eating & Drinking

**★Cafe 3692** CAFE €
(☎033 853 16 54; www.cafe3692.ch; Terrassenweg 61; snacks & light meals Sfr7-25; ⏰8.30am-6pm Sun-Tue, to midnight Fri & Sat) Run by dream duo Myriam and Bruno, Cafe 3692 is a delight. Bruno is a talented carpenter and has let his imagination run riot – a gnarled apple tree is an eye-catching artwork, a mine-cart trolley cleverly transforms into a grill, and the ceiling is a wave of woodwork. Garden herbs and Grindelwald-sourced ingredients are knocked up into tasty specials.

**Onkel Tom's Hütte** PIZZA €
(☎033 853 52 39; Im Graben 4; pizzas Sfr13-33; ⏰noon-10pm Fri-Tue) Tables are at a premium in this incredibly cosy barn-style chalet. Yummy pizzas are prepared fresh in three sizes to suit any appetite. The encyclopedic wine list flicks from Switzerland to South Africa.

**Grindel Lounge** CAFE €
(www.grindellounge.ch; Dorfstrasse 119; snacks Sfr7-24; ⏰9am-8pm Tue-Sun) This lounge-cafe has a nicely laid-back vibe and vintage touch. Nab one of the leather sofas to unwind over a speciality hot chocolate, or snacks such as foccacia, salads, *tarte flambée* and home-made cakes.

**Memory** SWISS €€
(☎033 854 31 31; Dorfstrasse 133; mains Sfr17-36; ⏰9am-11.30pm) Always packed, the Eiger Hotel's unpretentious restaurant rolls out tasty Swiss grub such as rösti, raclette and fondue, as well as – titter ye not – 'horny' chicken with a spicy 'Christian' sauce. Try to bag a table on the street-facing terrace.

**C & M** SWISS €€
(☎033 853 07 10; www.cundm-grindelwald.ch; Almisgässli 1; snacks Sfr7.50-18, mains Sfr29-49; ⏰9am-11pm Wed-Mon; 👪) Just as appetising as the menu are the stupendous views to Unterer Gletscher from this gallery-style cafe's sunny terrace. Enjoy a salad, coffee and cake, or seasonally inspired dishes such as home-smoked salmon and river trout with herb butter. There's a kids' menu for the little 'uns.

**Avocado Bar** BAR
(Dorfstrasse 158; ⏰3pm-12.30am; 📶) This is a young 'n' fun place to kick back on a leather pouffe with a post-ski schnapps or people-watch on the terrace in summer. There's occasional live music on Wednesdays.

## Information

**Tourist Office** (☎033 854 12 12; www.grindelwald.ch; Dorfstrasse 110; ⏰8am-6pm Mon-Fri, 9am-6pm Sat & Sun; 📶) The tourist office in the Sportzentrum hands out brochures and hiking maps, and has a free internet terminal and wi-fi. There's an accommodation board outside or you can ask staff to book rooms for you.

## Getting There & Around

Grindelwald is off the A8 from Interlaken. A smaller road continues from the village over the Grosse Scheidegg Pass (1960m). It's closed to private traffic, but from mid-June to early October postal **buses** (Sfr54, 2¼ hours) travel this scenic route to Meiringen roughly hourly from 8am to 5pm. Cable cars haul you up to the mountains above Grindelwald, including **First** (www.jungfrau.ch; return adult/child Sfr66/33; ⏰8.30am-5pm, to 4.15pm in winter), Männlichen (p130) and Pfingstegg (p121).

# First

ELEV 2167M

A minor summit with a big view deep into the heart of the Jungfrau region, First is a terrific base for striking out on Alpine hikes, with its jewel-like lake, mountain trails and adrenaline-loaded activities. It's popular among families, adventure seekers and peak gazers alike, with a staggering vista of Eiger's fearsome north face and the 4078m fang of Schreckhorn.

## Sights

**Bachalpsee** LAKE
Utterly entrancing in the still of early morning, with its perfect reflection of the white pyramid of Schreckhorn (4078m), this glacial lake is less than an hour's walk from the First cable-car top station, through high meadows brushed with wildflowers and chiming with cowbells.

**First Cliff Walk by Tissot** VIEWPOINT
FREE Next to Berggasthaus First at around 2200m, this lookout platform, jutting out 45m into the void, provides heart-pumping views of the valley and surrounding mountains. If you have vertigo, forget it.

DON'T MISS

### SLIDE & SWING

Not only skiers love the deep powder at First. You can also stomp through the snow on the No 50 trail to Faulhorn in winter. Faulhorn is also the starting point for Europe's longest (15km) **toboggan run** (⏲ Dec-Apr).

Other ways to ramp up the thrill factor include the **First Flyer** (adult/child Sfr29/22, incl cable car Sfr74/45; ⏲ 10am-5.30pm late Jun & Aug, to 4.30pm Sep, to 4pm Oct, noon-3.45pm mid Jan–mid-Apr), a breathtakingly fast flying fox that swings between First and Schreckfeld at speeds of up to 84km/h.

## Activities

First has 60km of well-groomed pistes, which are mostly wide, meandering reds suited to intermediates. The south-facing slopes make for interesting skiing through meadows and forests. Freestylers should check out the kickers and rails at Bärgelegg, or have a go on the superpipe at Schreckfeld station.

**Faulhorn Walk** HIKING
From First, you can trudge up to Faulhorn (2681m; 2½ hours) via the cobalt Bachalpsee. As you march along the ridge, the unfolding views of the Jungfrau massif are entrancing. Stop for lunch and 360-degree views at Faulhorn. From here, you can either continue on to Schynige Platte (another three hours) and return by train, or you can hike to Bussalp (1800m; 1½ hours) and return by bus 126 to Grindelwald (Sfr24, 27 minutes).

**Trottibike** ADVENTURE SPORTS
(adult/child Sfr32/22; ⏲ Apr-Oct) At the First-Bort cable-car station, sturdy trotti-bike (scooters) are available should you wish to tear back downhill to Grindelwald, with the meadows and mountains blurring past. Helmets are included in rental prices.

**First Mountain Cart** ADVENTURE SPORTS
(adult/child Sfr19/15; ⏲ Jul-Oct) A cross between a go-kart and a sled, the First mountain carts are a fun way to bomb downhill on a 3km track from Schreckfeld to Bort.

## Sleeping

**Berggasthaus First** HUT €€
(☎ 033 828 77 88; www.berggasthausfirst.ch; dm with breakfast adult/child Sfr65/47, with half-board Sfr95/68, s/d Sfr135/230; 📶) Early birds can catch a spectacular sunrise by overnighting in a rustic dorm at Berggasthaus First by the First cable-car summit station. The well-kept, pine-clad dorms and rooms are brilliantly located for experiencing the summit before the crowds rock up. It's worth shelling out the extra for half-board.

## Getting There & Away

**Cable cars** (www.jungfrau.ch; return adult/child Sfr66/33; ⏲ 8.30am-5pm, to 4.15pm in winter) run roughly every 10 minutes from Grindelwald to First.

# Kleine Scheidegg

The Eiger, Mönch and Jungfrau soar almost 2000m above you at Kleine Scheidegg (2061m), where restaurants huddle around the train station. Most people only stay for a few minutes while changing trains for Jungfraujoch, but it's worth lingering to appreciate the dazzling views, including those to the fang-shaped peak of Silberhorn, and the stupendous walking trails that thread in all directions.

Kleine Scheidegg is a terrific base for hiking. There are short, undemanding trails (one hour apiece) to Eigergletscher, down to Wengernalp, and up the Lauberhorn behind the village. These areas become intermediate ski runs from December to April. Alternatively, you can walk the spectacular 6km **Eiger Trail** from Eigergletscher to Alpiglen (two hours), which affords close-ups of the mountain's fearsome north face.

## Sleeping & Eating

There's a light scattering of places to stay at Kleine Scheidegg. Most are simple, but the views of the Jungfrau trio are five-star.

**Restaurant Grindelwaldblick** HOSTEL €
(☎ 033 855 13 74; www.grindelwaldblick.ch; dm Sfr43-50, half-board extra Sfr25; ⏲ closed Nov & May) For fine views and belly-filling mountain fare, you could stay the night at Restaurant Grindelwaldblick (2116m).

**Hotel Bellevue des Alpes** HOTEL €€€
(☎ 033 855 12 12; www.scheidegg-hotels.ch; s Sfr230-280, d Sfr380-550) Rambling, creaky and atmospheric, Hotel Bellevue des Alpes is a formerly grand Victorian hotel. It has a world-beating location and a rather macabre

history of people using its telescopes to observe mountaineering accidents on the Eiger.

**Alpiglen** SWISS €€
(☎033 853 11 30; www.alpiglen.ch; mains Sfr21-42; ⊙late May-late Oct; ) Eiger seems close enough to touch from the terrace of this endearingly old-fashioned mountain hut. Platters of cured meats and *Hobelchäs* (Alpine cheese) are just the ticket after a long hike. More substantial options include homemade bratwurst with rösti. Kids are well catered for with their own menu and playground.

### Getting There & Away

Trains to Kleine Scheidegg depart half-hourly from Wengen (Sfr24, 26 minutes) and Grindelwald (Sfr31, 33 minutes). Kleine Scheidegg is the departure point for trains to Jungfraujoch.

## Jungfraujoch

The trip to Jungfraujoch (3454m) has never been easier. Visitors can choose between the classic railway which follows an audacious route right through the heart of the Eiger, or a 15 minute ride on the tri-cable Eiger Express gondola. Either way you're in for some of Europe's most phenomenal Alpine views.

The icy wilderness of swirling glaciers and 4000m turrets that unfolds up top is staggeringly beautiful. Outside there are views of the moraine-streaked 23km-long tongue of the Aletsch Glacier, the longest glacier in the Alps and a Unesco World Heritage Site. The views across rippling peaks stretch as far as the Black Forest in Germany on cloudless days. Inside the adjacent Sphinx weather station you'll find ice sculptures, restaurants, indoor viewpoints and souvenir shops.

### Sights & Activities

**★Jungfraujoch** MOUNTAIN, VIEWPOINT
(www.jungfrau.ch; return Interlaken Ost–Jungfraujoch Sfr210.80, Kleine Scheidegg–Jungfraujoch Sfr128; ⊙trains 8am-6.43pm May-Sep, shorter hours rest of year) Two million people a year make the once-in-a-lifetime trip to Jungfraujoch, Europe's highest train station at 3454m. The train that chugs up from Kleine Scheidegg ramps up the drama as it delves into Eiger's icy heart to emerge at the Sphinx meteorological station. At the summit, sensational views of the Aletsch Glacier and a never-ending ripple of Alpine peaks unfold. Besides the staggering panorama, there's an Ice Palace and Snow Fun Park to explore. Warm clothing and sturdy shoes essential.

**Aletsch Glacier** GLACIER, VIEWPOINT
Jungfraujoch commands a phenomenal view of the largest glacier in the Alps: the 23km Aletsch Glacier, which powers its way through peaks hovering around the 4000m mark. The glacier is the icing on the cake of the Swiss Alps Jungfrau-Aletsch Unesco World Heritage Site. From late June to early October, Grindelwald Sports (p121) offers two-day hikes across the glacier, led by experienced mountain guides.

### Sleeping

**Mönchsjochhütte** HUT
(☎033 971 34 72; www.moenchsjoch.ch; dm Sfr28, incl half-board Sfr64; ⊙late Mar–mid-Oct) At Mönchsjochhütte, 3650m up into the mountains, you'll share your dinner table and dorm with hardcore rock climbers, psyching themselves up to tackle Eiger or Mönch. It's worth tumbling out of your bunk at dawn to catch sunrise.

### Getting There & Away

Trains from Interlaken Ost follow two different routes to Jungfraujoch: one via Lauterbrunnen, Wengen and Kleine Scheidegg, the other via Grindelwald and Kleine Scheidegg. Either way, the journey time is 2¼ to 2½ hours each way and the return fare is Sfr210.80. The last train back from Jungfraujoch leaves at 6.43pm in summer and 4.43pm in winter.

Note that the ordinary return ticket to Jungfraujoch is valid for one month, and you're allowed to break your journey at various stops along the way, so a single ticket can form the backbone of an extended exploration of the Jungfrau region. For example, from Interlaken Ost, you could venture as far as Grindelwald and stop for a few days' hiking, before moving on to Kleine Scheidegg, Jungfraujoch, Wengen and Lauterbrunnen.

From early May to late October you can qualify for a discounted Good Morning Ticket (Sfr145) by taking one of the first two trains from Interlaken Ost (6.35am or 7.05am) and boarding a return train from the summit no later than 1.13pm.

Getting these early trains is easier if your starting place is deeper in the region. For example, if you sleep overnight at Kleine Scheidegg, you'll qualify for a Good Morning discount (Sfr95 return instead of Sfr128) on either of the first two trains leaving Kleine Scheidegg for Jungfraujoch (8am and 8.30am).

Swiss Travel Pass holders travel free as far as Grindelwald or Wengen, and receive a 25% discount on the remainder of the journey to Jungfraujoch summit.

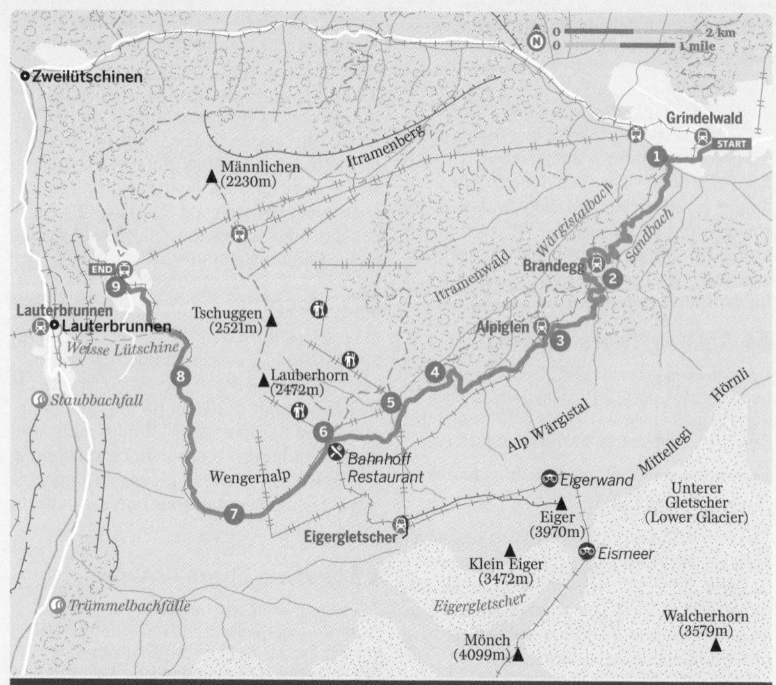


# Walking Tour Kleine Scheidegg

**START:** GRINDELWALD
**FINISH:** WENGEN
**LENGTH:** 15KM; 5½ TO SIX HOURS

Cross the railway tracks at **1 Grindelwald Grund** and head left for Kleine Scheidegg. The views southeast to the limestone crown of Wetterhorn (3701m) and the Unterer Gletscher are breathtaking. Eiger's fearsome north face draws ever closer as you follow the often-steep track shadowing the Sandbach stream, before dipping in and out of forest. Pass under an arched rail bridge to reach **2 Restaurant Brandegg**, about one hour from Grindelwald.

At the road, take the second left, signposted to Alpiglen, and head up a gravel path, which passes through the forest, then follows the Wengernalpbahn railway tracks. The trail weaves through meadows flecked with gentians and thistles in summer, then ducks under a small rail tunnel before reaching the delightfully rustic **3 Alpiglen**, two to 2½ hours from Grindelwald Grund.

The trail climbs gently now, skirting below Eiger's north face, and leading through rolling pastures. Head past clusters of mountain pines and farmhouses in the hollow of **4 Mettla** (1809m).

Make your way to the **5 Arvengarten** ski lifts to contour the mountainsides at roughly 2000m. This minor pass provides a close-range vantage point of Eiger (3970m), Mönch (4099m) and Jungfrau (4158m). Sidling around the slopes below the rail line you arrive at **6 Kleine Scheidegg** (p126), 1¼ to 1¾ hours from Alpiglen.

From Kleine Scheidegg train station, the descent rewards with more dazzling views of the 'Big Three' and the pearly fin of Silberhorn (3695m) before reaching **7 Wengernalp** at 1874m. Wonderful views include the Gspaltenhorn and Schilthorn, beyond which the land plunges into the deep glacial trough of the Lauterbrunnental. A trail leads northward through pockets of Alpine forest to cross the railway lines again, from where a well-formed track skirts the slopes via **8 Allmend** to reach car-free **9 Wengen** (p130), 1½ to two hours from Wengernalp.

# Lauterbrunnen

POP 2452 / ELEV 796M

Lauterbrunnen's wispy Staubbach Falls inspired both Goethe and Lord Byron to pen poems to their ethereal beauty. Today the postcard-perfect village, nestled deep in the valley of 72 waterfalls, attracts a less highfalutin crowd. Laid-back and full of chalet-style lodgings, Lauterbrunnen is a great base for nature lovers wishing to hike or climb, and a magnet for thrill-seeking BASE jumpers.

## Sights & Activities

Hikes heading up into the mountains from the waterfall-laced valley include a 2½-hour uphill trudge to Mürren and a more gentle 1¾-hour walk to Stechelberg. In winter, you can glide past frozen waterfalls on a well-prepared 12km cross-country trail.

For a chance to see BASE jumpers in hair-raising action, head to the base station of Schilthorn.

**★Staubbachfall** WATERFALL

(Staubbach Falls; ⌚8am-8pm Jun-Oct) Especially in the early morning light, you can see how the vaporous, 297m-high Staubbach Falls captivated prominent writers with its threads of spray floating down the cliffs. What appears to be ultra-fine mist from a distance, however, becomes a torrent when you walk behind the falls. Be prepared to get wet. Wear sturdy shoes for the short but steep uphill walk.

**★Trümmelbachfälle** WATERFALL

(Trümmelbach Falls; www.truemmelbachfaelle.ch; adult/child Sfr11/4; ⌚9am-5pm Apr-Nov) These glacier falls are a bang-crash spectacle. Inside the mountain, up to 20,000L of water per second corkscrews through ravines and potholes shaped by the swirling waters. The 10 falls drain from 24 sq km of Alpine glaciers and snow deposits. It's a 45-minute walk to the falls from Lauterbrunnen, or take bus 141 from the train station.

**Doris Hike** HIKING

(☎033 855 42 40; www.doris-hike.ch) Doris' informative guided hikes include glacier, waterfall and high-alpine options.

## Sleeping

Most of the resort sprawls along one street, and not all places have an official address, but there are accommodation signs to orientate you as you enter the village.

**Valley Hostel** HOSTEL €

(☎033 855 20 08; www.valleyhostel.ch; Fuhren; dm Sfr30-36, d Sfr38-43; P 📶) This relaxed, family-run hostel has an open-plan kitchen, a garden with tremendous views of the Staubbach Falls, a laundry and free wi-fi. Most of the spacious, pine-clad dorms have balconies. The friendly team can help organise activities from paragliding to canyoning.

**Chalet im Rohr** GUESTHOUSE €

(☎033 855 21 82; www.chaletimrohr.ch; Im Rohr 424; r per person Sfr33; 📶) Ablaze with scarlet geraniums in summer, this 400-year-old chalet is a bargain. Creaky floorboards and small windows add to its cosy, old-world charm. The 1970s-style rooms are humble but spotless and there's a huge communal balcony overlooking Staubbachfall.

**Camping Jungfrau** CAMPGROUND €

(☎033 856 20 10; www.camping-jungfrau.ch; Weid 406; sites per adult/tent/car Sfr10/13/4, dm Sfr30-35; P 📶) Affording knockout views of the mountains and falls, this campsite also offers cosy dorms and huts for those craving more comfort. The top-notch facilities include a kitchen, a kiosk, bike rental and wi-fi. There's even a dog shower for messy pups!

**Hotel Staubbach** HOTEL €€

(☎033 855 54 54; www.staubbach.com; Im Rohr; d Sfr130-180, tr Sfr220-250, q Sfr250-290; P 📶) The bright rooms with downy duvets are immaculately kept at this grand old hotel; the best have balconies with Staubbach Falls views. There's a sociable vibe in the lounge, with free coffee and a kids' play area.

## Eating & Drinking

**Airtime** CAFE €

(☎033 855 15 15; www.airtime.ch; snacks & light meals Sfr6-15.50; ⌚9am-6pm; 📶) Inspired by their travels in New Zealand, Daniela and Beni have set up this funky cafe, book exchange, laundry service and extreme-sports agency. Munch home-roasted granola, sandwiches, pies and homemade cakes (including a gluten-free chocolate one) as you use the free wi-fi or browse a novel. You can book adrenaline-fuelled pursuits such as ice climbing, canyoning and bungee jumping here.

**Flavours** CAFE €

(☎033 855 36 52; www.flavours.ch; snacks & light meals Sfr8-18; ⌚9am-6pm; 📶) Whether you fancy a slap-up egg-and-bacon breakfast, a burger, salad, homemade cake with locally roasted coffee or freshly pressed juice,

WORTH A TRIP

## MÄNNLICHEN

On the ridge dividing the Grindelwald and Lauterbrunnen Valleys, **Männlichen** (www.maennlichen.ch; cable car Wengen-Männlichen one way/return Sfr23/46; ⏲ every 20min 8.30am-4.50pm), at 2230m, is one of the region's top viewpoints. Europe's longest **cable car** (www.maennlichen.ch; adult/child Sfr30/15; ⏲ 8.15am-5pm) connects Grindelwald Grund to Männlichen. Another cable car comes up from Wengen on the other side of the ridge.

From Männlichen top station, walk up to the crown of the hill to enjoy the view. At the southern end of the ridge are Tschuggen (2520m) and Lauberhorn (2472m), with the 'Big Three' looming behind. From here, you notice the difference between the two valleys – the broad expanse of the Grindelwald Valley to the left, and the glacier-carved, U-shaped Lauterbrunnen Valley to the right. To the north you can see a stretch of Thunersee.

For uplifting views of the glaciated Jungfrau range, it's worth devoting 1½ hours to hiking the **Panoramaweg** to **Kleine Scheidegg** (p126). A more playful alternative for kids is the **Felixweg** (www.felix-weg.ch; 👪), with insights into local wildlife and barbecue areas.

In winter, Männlichen's broad cruising terrain is perfect for skiing in the shadow of the Eiger, Mönch and Jungfrau. A one-day ski pass costs Sfr63/32 per adult/child. An alternative for non-skiers is the speedy 45-minute sled run down to Holenstein, negotiating steep bumps and hairpin bends.

Should you fancy staying the night, you can hike up to the rustic **Berggasthaus Männlichen** (☎ 033 853 10 68; www.berghaus-maennlichen.ch; s Sfr80-95, d Sfr150-180; ⏲ Jun-Oct), with simple digs and sublime mountain views.



Flavours is the go-to place. Housed in the former bakery, the cafe opens onto a terrace with beanbags and a nicely chilled vibe.

**Hotel Oberland** SWISS €€
(☎ 033 855 12 41; pizza Sfr16-24.50, mains Sfr22-40; ⏲ 11.30am-9pm) The street-facing terrace at this traditional haunt is always humming. On the menu are Swiss and international favourites from fondue to pizza, vegetable curry and hybrid dishes such as Indian-style rösti. There are plenty of veggie picks, too.

**Horner Bar** BAR
(☎ 033 855 16 73; Hotel Horner; ⏲ 9.30am-2.30am; 📶) BASE jumpers tell hair-raising parachute tales at this buzzy pub, as they come back to earth over a pint or four. The vibe gets clubbier as the night wears on. Internet access and wi-fi are free when you buy a drink.

### ℹ Information

**Tourist Office** (☎ 033 856 85 68; www.lauterbrunnen.swiss; Stutzli 460; ⏲ 8.30am-noon & 2-6.30pm Jun-Sep, shorter hours rest of year) Opposite the train station.

### ℹ Getting There & Away

Regular trains make the short hop from Interlaken (Sfr7.60, 21 minutes). Situated in the valley of the same name, Lauterbrunnen is a major jumping-off point for reaching Alpine resorts such as Wengen (Sfr6.80, 14 minutes) by train and Mürren (Sfr11.40, 23 minutes) by cable car/train.

### ℹ Getting Around

If you're travelling to the car-free resorts of Wengen or Mürren, there's a multistorey **car park** (☎ 033 828 74 00; www.jungfraubahn.ch; per day/week Sfr14/84) by the station, but it's advisable to book ahead. There is also an open-air car park by the Stechelberg cable-car station, charging Sfr10 for a day.

## Wengen

POP 1300 / ELEV 1274M

Photogenically poised on a mountain ledge, Wengen's celestial views have lured Brits here since Edwardian times. The fact that you can only reach the village by train gives it a romantic appeal. From the bench in front of the church at dusk, the vista takes on watercolour dreaminess, peering over to the misty Staubbach Falls, down to the Lauterbrunnen Valley and up to the glacier-capped giants of the Jungfrau massif. In winter Wengen morphs into a ski resort with a low-key, family-friendly feel.

### Festivals & Events

**Lauberhornrennen** SPORTS
(www.lauberhorn.ch; ⏲ mid-Jan) The highlight in Wengen's calendar is the world-famous Lauberhorn downhill ski race, where pros reach speeds of up to 160km/h.

## Sleeping

**Hotel Bären** HOTEL €€

(☎033 855 14 19; www.baeren-wengen.ch; s Sfr190-280, d Sfr260-310, f Sfr390-490, all incl half-board; 📶) Loop back under the rail track and head down the hill to this snug log chalet with bright, wood-floored rooms and dreamy mountain views. The affable Brunner family serves hearty breakfast and dinners (included in the half-board room rate).

**Hotel Edelweiss** HOTEL €€

(☎033 855 23 88; www.edelweisswengen.ch; Am Acher; s Sfr85-100, d Sfr170-200; 📶) With spectacular Jungfrau views from its many balconies, this family-run, multitiered chalet is only a five-minute walk downhill from the train station. Extra perks include a sauna, a welcoming children's play area and some of Wengen's most moderate room prices.

**Hotel Berghaus** HOTEL €€

(☎033 855 21 51; www.berghaus-wengen.ch; s Sfr105-165, d Sfr210-330; 📶) Sidling up to the forest, this family-run chalet is a five-minute toddle from the village centre. Rooms are light, spacious and pin-drop peaceful – ask for a south-facing one for dreamy Jungfrau views. Call ahead and they'll pick you up from the train station.

## Eating & Drinking

**Restaurant Bären** SWISS €€

(☎033 855 14 19; mains Sfr30-53; ⏲8am-1.30pm & 5-11.30pm Mon-Fri, 5-11.30pm Sat & Sun; 🖊) Mixing tradition with creative flair, this excellent restaurant (attached to the hotel of the same name) prides itself on using regionally raised meats, homegrown herbs, vegetables and edible flowers and locally hunted game. Dishes range from perfectly cooked veal with strawberry risotto to vegetarian *Spätzle* with stewed mushrooms. Wild cards such as chestnut mousse and wasabi-pumpkin-seed parfait for dessert.

★**Restaurant 1903** SWISS €€€

(☎033 855 34 22; www.hotel-schoenegg.ch; mains Sfr35-58; ⏲6.30-10pm, closed May & mid-Oct–mid-Dec) At Hotel Schönegg, chef Sylvain Stefanazzi Ogi serves seasonally inspired dishes. The pine-clad, candlelit dining room is wonderfully cosy in winter and the leafy mountain-facing terrace is perfect for summertime dining.

**Tanne Bar** BAR

(⏲4pm-late) A popular hang-out for Swiss and Scandi skiers, this snug, wood-panelled bar on Wengen's main drag cranks it up during the ski season with après-ski glühwein and cocktails as the night wears on.

## Information

**Tourist Office** (☎033 856 85 85; www.wengen.ch; ⏲9am-6pm, to 9pm Jul & Aug, closed Sat & Sun Nov, Mar & Apr; 📶) Next to the Männlichen cable car.

## Getting There & Away

Trains curl up the mountain twice hourly to Wengen from Lauterbrunnen (Sfr6.80, 14 minutes).

# Stechelberg

POP 260 / ELEV 922M

To witness the drama of the waterfall-gone-mad Lauterbrunnen Valley, where a staggering 72 falls cascade over perpendicular walls of rock, make for Stechelberg. The valley takes its name from *lauter* (clear) and *Brunnen* (spring). To see the cataracts at their thundering best, visit in spring when the snow thaws, or after heavy rain. Though long a bolthole for hikers, this tiny, silent village still feels like a well-kept secret.

The 6.7km **Stechelberg-Lauterbrunnen Walk** affords a glimpse of some of the valley's most impressive waterfalls, including the Trümmelbachfälle (p129). Allow roughly two hours one way. The walk begins at the Hotel Stechelberg bus stop.

Blissfully rural **Alpenhof Stechelberg** (☎033 855 12 02; www.alpenhof-stechelberg.ch; s/d Sfr30/60, tr Sfr60-100; 🅿) harbours light-filled, neat-and-tidy rooms that offer fantastic value for your franc. A hearty breakfast with local dairy products is served for Sfr12.

Bus 141 runs regularly between Stechelberg and Lauterbrunnen (Sfr4.40, 19 minutes), where there are plenty of onward connections to Interlaken and the surrounding resorts.

# Mürren

POP 450 / ELEV 1650M

Arriving on a clear evening, as the train from Grütschalp floats along the horizontal ridge towards Mürren, the peaks across the valley feel so close that you could reach out and touch them. And that's when you'll think you've died and gone to Heidi heaven. With its low-slung wooden chalets and spellbinding views of Eiger, Mönch and Jungfrau, car-free Mürren is the Swiss Alps in a nutshell.

## Sights & Activities

**Allmendhubel** MOUNTAIN
() In summer the Allmendhubel **funicular** (www.schilthorn.ch; return adult/child Sfr14/7; every 20min 9am-5pm) takes you above Mürren to a panoramic restaurant and the Skyline Chill relaxation area where funky wave-shaped loungers grant wraparound mountain views. Kids love the giant butterflies, marmot burrows and alpine flowers at the adventure playground.

**North Face Trail** HIKING
From the top station of Allmendhubel funicular, you can set out on many walks, including the spectacular North Face Trail (1½ hours), via Schiltalp to the west, leading through wildflower-strewn meadows with big views to the glaciers and waterfalls of the Lauterbrunnen Valley and the monstrous Eiger north face – bring binoculars to spy intrepid climbers.

**Swiss Ski School** SKIING
(033 855 12 47; www.swiss-snowsports-muerren.ch; Haus Finel, Inder Gruben; 9am-12.30pm & 1.30-5pm) Mürren's ski school has private and group ski and snowboarding lessons, including tuition for children.

## Festivals & Events

**Inferno Run** SPORTS
(www.inferno-muerren.ch) Mürren is famous for its hell-for-leather Inferno Run down from Schilthorn in mid- to late Januar)y. Daredevils have been competing in the 16km race since 1928 and today the course attracts 1800 intrepid amateur skiers. It's also the reason for all the devilish souvenirs.

## Sleeping

Hotels are sprinkled throughout town along the streets between the train and cable-car stations. In summer, rates are up to 30% cheaper than the high-season winter prices. Not everywhere has an official address, but everything is easy to find in tiny Mürren.

**Eiger Guesthouse** GUESTHOUSE €€
(033 856 54 60; www.eigerguesthouse.com; s Sfr95-140, d Sfr120-200, q Sfr180-250; ) Run by a fun-loving, on-the-ball team, this central pick offers great value. Besides clean, spruced-up rooms (the best have Eiger views), there's a downstairs pub serving tasty grub (mains Sfr21 to Sfr41) and a good selection of draught beers.

DON'T MISS

### CLIFFHANGER

Feel like an adventure? Little beats Mürren's vertigo-inducing **Klettersteig** (033 856 86 86; www.klettersteig-muerren.ch; mid-Jun–Oct). This high-altitude, 2.2km *via ferrata* (hiking route with cables) is one of Switzerland's most astonishing, wriggling across breathtakingly steep limestone cliffs to Gimmelwald.

Equipped with harness, helmet and karabiner, you can flirt with mountaineering on ladders that snake across the precipices and bring you to a zip-line – whoa, there goes the Eiger! – and an 80m-long suspension bridge. Equipment can be rented for Sfr28 per day from **Intersport** (033 855 23 55; www.staegersport.ch/muerren; Chalet Enzian; 9am-noon & 1-6pm), near the Klettersteig's entrance.

**Hotel Alpenruh** HOTEL €€
(033 856 88 00; www.alpenruh-muerren.ch; s Sfr140-220, d Sfr200-280; ) Lots of loving detail has gone into this much-lauded chalet. Grimacing masks to ward off evil spirits and assorted knick-knacks enliven the place, while the light-flooded rooms feature lots of chunky pine. Guests praise the service, food (mains Sfr19 to Sfr45) and unbeatable views to the Jungfrau massif.

★**Hotel Eiger** HOTEL €€€
(033 856 54 54; www.hoteleiger.com; s Sfr183-228, d Sfr275-370, ste Sfr420-1250; ) This huge wooden chalet harbours sleek and contemporary rooms. The service is first-rate, as are the views from the swimming pool, with picture windows perfectly framing the Eiger, Mönch and Jungfrau. The restaurant is one of Mürren's best.

## Eating

**Tham's** ASIAN €
(033 856 01 10; mains Sfr15-30; 11.30am-9pm) Tham's serves Chinese, Thai and other Asian dishes cooked by a former five-star chef who's taken to the hills to escape the rat race.

**Stägerstübli** SWISS €€
(☎033 855 13 16; www.staegerstuebli.ch; mains Sfr21-38; ⊙11am-11.30pm) The kind of heart-warmingly cosy chalet where you just pray for the flakes to fall, Stägerstübli is a real locals' haunt. With a nod to the seasons, the menu makes the most of regional produce in dishes such as veal stew with spring onions and homemade wild garlic *Spätzli* (egg noodles).

**Restaurant La Grotte** SWISS €€
(☎033 855 18 26; Hotel Blumental; mains Sfr15-45; ⊙11am-2pm & 5-9pm) Brimming with cowbells, cauldrons and Alpine props, this kitsch-meets-rustic mock cave of a restaurant is touristy but fun. Fondues and flambés are good bets.

## Information

The **tourist office** (☎033 856 86 86; www.mymuerren.ch; ⊙8.30am-noon & 1-5.15pm; 📶) is in the sports centre.

## Getting There & Away

The quickest and easiest way to reach Mürren from Lauterbrunnen is to take the cable car to Grutschalp (four minutes) then transfer to a Mürren-bound train (14 minutes, total one-way fare Sfr11.40).

# Gimmelwald

POP 130 / ELEV 1367M

This pipsqueak of a village has long been a hideaway for hikers and adventurers tiptoeing away from the crowds. The secret is out, though, and Gimmelwald continues to lure a steady stream of new admirers each year with its drop-dead-gorgeous scenery, rural authenticity and sense of calm.

The surrounding hiking trails include one down from Mürren (30 to 40 minutes) and one up from Stechelberg (1¼ hours).

## Sleeping

Gimmelwald's small handful of cosy, rustic accommodation options are all located within a five-minute walk of the cable-car station.

★**Esther's Guest House** GUESTHOUSE €
(☎033 855 54 88; www.esthersguesthouse.ch; Kirchstatt; s Sfr60-90, d Sfr120-180, apt Sfr240-250; 📶) In 2017 this charming family-run B&B passed from Esther and André to son Uri and his wife Dana, who have maintained the same welcoming ambience and loving attention to guests' comfort. Drenched with piny light, the rooms are spotless, while the apartments are ideal for families. The attic room, with its slanted roof and star-gazing window, is a favourite.

**Mountain Hostel** HOSTEL €
(☎033 855 17 04; www.mountainhostel.com; dm Sfr45; 📶) A backpacking legend, this basic, low-ceilinged hostel just above Gimmelwald's cable-car station has a sociable vibe. After a sweaty day's hiking, you can kick back in a hammock in the mountain-facing garden, play pool or grab pizza and draught beer in the on-site bar (Gimmelwald's lone eating and drinking venue).

**Hotel Mittaghorn** GUESTHOUSE €
(☎033 855 16 58; mittaghorn@gmail.com; Poeschenried 39; d Sfr100-120, tr Sfr140-150, q Sfr180; ⊙May-Oct; 📶) Staring in wonder at the mountains is the main pursuit at this stunningly situated wooden chalet, run by the irrepressible Walter and his sidekick, Tim. Creaking floors and doors lead to simple, cosy rooms and shared bathrooms with pay-as-you-go showers.

## Getting There & Away

Aside from walking, cable cars are the only way to reach Gimmelwald; the five-minute ride down from Mürren or up from Stechelberg costs Sfr6.20. Bus 141 links the Stechelberg cable-car station with Lauterbrunnen's train station (14 minutes).

# THE LAKES

Anyone who travels to Interlaken for the first time from Bern will never forget the moment they clap eyes on **Thunersee (Lake Thun)**. Some people literally gasp at the sight of the Alps rearing above the startlingly turquoise waters. Bordering Interlaken to the east, **Brienzersee (Lake Brienz)** has just as many cameras snapping with its unbelievably aquamarine waters and rugged mountain backdrop.

# Thun

POP 43,500 / ELEV 559M

Ringed by mountains, hugging the banks of the startlingly aquamarine Aare River and topped by a turreted castle, medieval Thun is every inch the picture-book Swiss town. History aside, the town is infused with a young spirit, with lively crowds sunning themselves at riverside cafes and one-of-a-kind boutiques taking shelter under the unusual arcades.

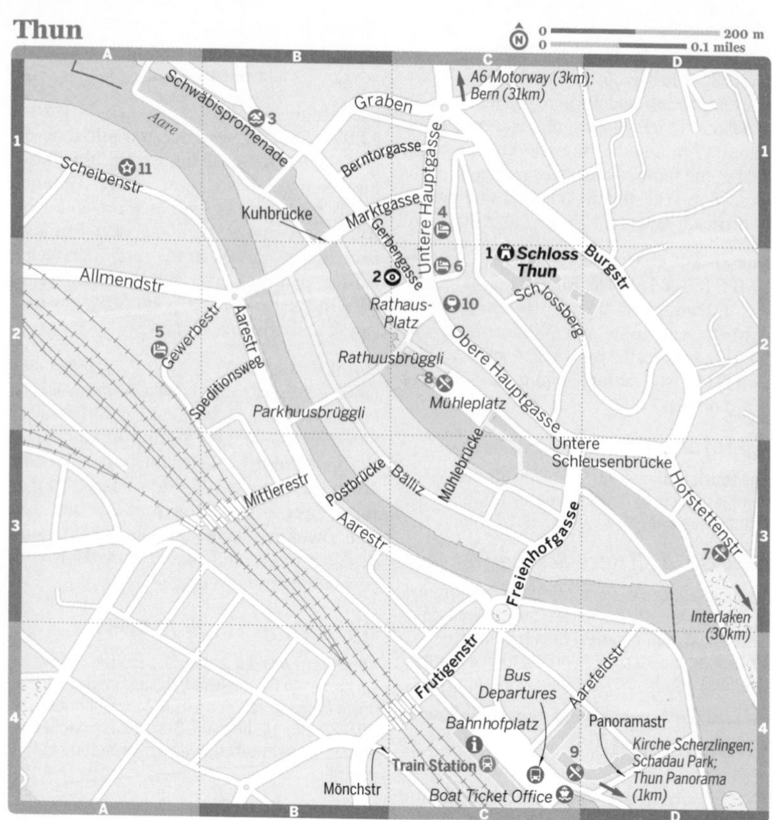




## Sights

The tourist office's 1½-hour guided tours (Sfr15 per person) run every Saturday from May to November and every Wednesday from July to August, taking in the Altstadt and castle. For a magical 360-degree view of Thun, the lake and the glaciated Jungfrau mountains, walk 20 minutes south of the centre to Jakobshübeli viewpoint.

**★Schloss Thun** CASTLE

(www.schlossthun.ch; Schlossberg 1; adult/child Sfr10/free; ⏲10am-5pm) Sitting on a hilltop and looking proudly back on 900 years of history, Schloss Thun is the castle of your wildest fairy-tale dreams, crowned by a riot of turrets and affording tremendous views of the lake and Alps. It once belonged to Duke Berchtold V of the powerful Zähringen family. Today, it houses a museum, showcasing prehistoric and Roman relics, tapestries, majolica and plenty of shining armour.

**Thun Altstadt** OLD TOWN

It's a pleasure to wander Thun's attractive riverfront Old Town, where plazas and lanes are punctuated by 15th- and 16th-century townhouses. A stroll takes in the 300-year-old **Untere Schleusenbrücke**, a covered wooden bridge that is a mass of pink and purple flowers in summer. Nearby is the split-level, flag-bedecked **Obere Hauptgasse**, with its arcades concealing boutiques and galleries. At the street's northern tip is cobblestone **Rathausplatz**, centred on a fountain and framed by arcaded buildings.

**Schadau Park** GARDENS

FREE These beautiful botanical gardens spread along the shores of Lake Thun, with sublime views to the snowcapped Jungfrau range on clear days. The grounds bristle with tulips and crocuses in spring, rhododendrons in summer and golden beech trees in autumn. In the park you'll find the mid-19th-century, candyfloss-pink Schloss Schadau

**Thun**

**Top Sights**
1 Schloss Thun ........ C2

**Sights**
2 Thun Altstadt ........ C2

**Activities, Courses & Tours**
3 Flussbad Schwäbis ........ B1

**Sleeping**
4 Schwert ........ C1
5 Spedition Thun ........ A2
6 Zunfthaus zu Metzgern ........ C2

**Eating**
7 Beau-Rivage da Domenico ........ D3
8 Genuss am Fluss ........ C2
9 Mani's Coffee & Bagels ........ C4

**Drinking & Nightlife**
10 Atelier Classic Bar ........ C2

**Entertainment**
11 Konzepthalle6 ........ A1

(now a restaurant), 1250-year-old **Kirche Scherzlingen** (www.scherzligen.ch; ⏲10am-6pm Apr-Oct), and the early-19th-century **Thun Panorama** (Schadau Park; adult/child Sfr9/free; ⏲11am-5pm Tue-Sun), one of the world's oldest panoramic paintings.

**Schloss Oberhofen** CASTLE
(www.schlossoberhofen.ch; adult/child Sfr10/2; ⏲11am-5pm Tue-Sun mid-May–late Oct) Scenically perched on the lake, turreted Schloss Oberhofen was wrested from Habsburg control after the Battle of Sempach (1386) and now traces Bernese life from the 16th to the 19th centuries. A spin takes in the frescoed chapel, ornate Napoleonic drawing room and Turkish smoking room. The manicured English landscaped **gardens** command arresting views of the Bernese Alps. Oberhofen is 25 minutes by boat from Thun (one way/return Sfr13/22). Alternatively, it's a 20-minute ride on bus 21 (Sfr3).

**Schloss Hünegg** CASTLE
(www.schlosshuenegg.ch; Staatstrasse 52, Hilterfingen; adult/child Sfr9/3; ⏲2-5pm Mon-Sat & 11am-5pm Sun mid-May–mid-Oct) The plaything of a wealthy Prussian baron and modelled on the chateaux in the Loire region of France, silver-turreted Schloss Hünegg is a feast of art nouveau and neo-Renaissance styles, featuring fabulous 19th-century stuccoed salons.

## Activities

**Flussbad Schwäbis** SWIMMING
(Grabenstrasse 40; adult/child Sfr4.50/2.50; ⏲9am-7pm May-Aug, to 6pm Sep) Cool off in the turquoise Aare River at this open-air pool, with a splash area, slides and sandpit for kids.

**Thunersee** WATER SPORTS
(Lake Thun) In summer you can cool off on and around the lake with activities ranging from swimming and messing around in boats to scuba diving, windsurfing, waterskiing, wakeboarding, stand-up paddle boarding and sailing. Thun tourist office has a complete list of centres and schools in its Thunersee brochure, or see the website.

## Festivals & Events

**Schlosskonzerte** MUSIC
(www.schlosskonzerte-thun.ch; ⏲Jun) Held against the backdrop of Schloss Thun (and at a number of other cultural venues), this series of concerts swings from classical to jazz.

## Sleeping

**Zunfthaus zu Metzgern** HISTORIC HOTEL €
(☎033 222 21 41; www.zumetzgern.ch; Untere Hauptgasse 2; s/d/tr without bathroom Sfr71/139/200) Sitting on Thun's prettiest square is this 700-year-old guild house. Bold artworks glam up the well-kept rooms. Downstairs the chef uses local organic ingredients to prepare dishes such as lamb with caramelised apricots and poached rainbow trout with fig-vanilla sauce.

**Spedition Thun** DESIGN HOTEL €€
(☎033 550 59 09; www.speditionthun.ch; Gewerbestrasse 4; s Sfr145, d Sfr190-254; P 📶) A breath of fresh air to Thun's hotel scene, the Spedition has been designed with a razor-sharp eye for detail – for which it snapped up the Unesco Prix Versailles for Europe's best hotel interior in 2017. The 15 rooms seamlessly fuse the character of a century-old-listed building with rich, earthy colours, luxurious textures, vintage furnishings and ultra-modern bathrooms.

**Schwert** HISTORIC HOTEL €€
(☎033 221 55 88; www.schwert-thun.ch; Untere Hauptgasse 8; s Sfr75-100, d Sfr145-230; 📶) Nestled at the foot of the castle is this graceful 18th-century hotel with an inviting restaurant. Hardwood floors, high ceilings and the occasional antique lend the individually decorated rooms old-world flair.

WORTH A TRIP

## SCHILTHORN

On a clear day, nothing compares to the 360-degree, 200-peak panorama from the top of 2970m Schilthorn, where vistas extend all the way from Titlis to Mont Blanc to the German Black Forest.

Despite the stellar views, some visitors seem more preoccupied with practising their delivery of the line, 'The name's Bond, James Bond', because several scenes from *On Her Majesty's Secret Service* were shot here in 1968–69. Embrace your own inner Bond while soaking up trivia about stunt skiing and other aspects of the film's production at the interactive exhibition of **Bond World 007** (www.schilthorn.ch; free with cable-car ticket; ⌚8am-6pm) up top, or savour the views over lunch at the revolving mountaintop restaurant, **Piz Gloria** (☎033 856 21 50; www.schilthorn.ch; Höheweg 2; mains Sfr21-45; ⌚8am-5pm).

En route from Mürren to Schilthorn, you'll change cable cars at Birg station (2677m), where you can contemplate more spine-tingling views from the sun terrace and eyrie-like **Skyline Walk** (www.schilthorn.ch; Birg; 👪) viewpoint, or test your nerves on the aptly named **Thrill Walk** (www.schilthorn.ch; Birg), a sequence of see-through plexiglass platforms anchored to the cliff face.

From Interlaken, the grand round-trip excursion to Schilthorn involves a train ride from Interlaken Ost to Lauterbrunnen, followed by a cable car to Grütschalp, a train to Mürren and another pair of cable cars to Schilthorn via Birg. On the return journey, retrace your route from Schilthorn to Mürren, then enjoy alternative mountain and valley perspectives by taking a cable car to Stechelberg, bus 141 to Lauterbrunnen and a train back to Interlaken.

Sound complicated? No worries! In classic Swiss fashion, all connections are perfectly synchronised. Round trip fares are Sfr131.80 from Interlaken (82 minutes), Sfr114.20 from Lauterbrunnen (54 minutes), or Sfr82.80 from Mürren (17 minutes). Swiss Travel Pass holders only pay for the Mürren–Schilthorn section (Sfr41.10 return, including 50% discount).

## Eating & Drinking

**Mani's Coffee & Bagels** BAGELS €

(☎033 221 60 65; www.manis.ch; Panoramastrasse 1A; bagels Sfr2.50-10.50, lunch Sfr13; ⌚7am-10pm Mon-Fri, 8am-6pm Sat, 9am-6pm Sun) With its slick, monochrome, wood-floored interior, this industro-cool cafe and wine bar wouldn't look out of place in NYC. On the drinks menu you'll find aromatic plantation coffees, cacao-rich hot chocolate, matcha teas, carefully selected wines and craft beers. These marry well with antipasti, freshly made bagels, creative salads and Alsatian *tarte flambée*.

★**Beau-Rivage da Domenico** ITALIAN €€

(☎033 221 41 10; https://beau-rivage-thun.ch; Hofstettenstrasse 6; pizza Sfr11-24, mains Sfr26-45; ⌚9am-midnight Mon-Thu, to 1am Fri & Sat, to 11.30pm Sun) Beau-Rivage da Domenico serves Italian food with the warmth and generosity of the *Bel Paese* in a graceful old-world building. High-quality, seasonal ingredients shine in simple dishes cooked well – from homemade pasta and pizza to grilled king prawns with lemon risotto and entrecôte steak with pepper sauce. Dotted with lemon and olive trees, the terrace is a summer boon.

**Genuss am Fluss** FUSION €€

(☎033 223 88 99; http://am-fluss.ch; Mühleplatz 9; mains Sfr33-42; ⌚9am-11pm Wed-Mon) Right on the banks of the Aare River, this contemporary glass-walled lounge restaurant attracts a young crowd who come for the relaxed vibe, *pinchos* (light bites) with wine, and Mediterranean-inspired mains. The olive-tree-dotted waterfront deck is perfect for sundowners and people-watching.

**Atelier Classic Bar** COCKTAIL BAR

(www.bar-atelier.ch; Rathausplatz 3; ⌚5pm-midnight Tue & Wed, to 1am Thu, to 2am Fri & Sat, to midnight Sun) There's a pinch of magic in the mixology at this award-winning cocktail bar, which is way up there with Switzerland's best. Antique furnishings, low lighting and brick vaults create a decadent, urban-chic backdrop for cocktails mixed with flair – whether you're in the mood for an Erotica (vodka, passion fruit and Champagne), a Gin Sour or a classic Negroni. Perfect date-night material.

## Entertainment

**Konzepthalle6** ARTS CENTRE

(www.konzepthalle6.ch; Scheibenstrasse 6) A Cutting-edge design space and cultural centre, Konzepthalle6 hosts events from concerts to poetry slams and urban art exhibitions in a converted factory.

## Information

**Tourist Office** (033 225 90 00; www.thunersee.ch; Bahnhofplatz; 9am-12.30pm & 1.30-6pm Mon-Fri, 10am-3pm Sat) Pick up information on Thun and its lakeside surrounds at the tourist office at the station. For a free audio guide for your smartphone, visit the website.

## Getting There & Away

Thun is on the main north–south train route from Frankfurt to Milan and beyond. Frequent trains run to Interlaken West (Sfr16.60, 37 minutes) and Bern (Sfr16.60, 21 minutes). The bus station is in front of the train station. Boats glide across the lake to Interlaken West (Sfr45) and Spiez (Sfr22).

Thun is on the A6 motorway, which runs from Spiez north to Bern.

# Spiez

POP 12,477 / ELEV 628M

Hunched around a horseshoe-shaped bay on Lake Thun, with a medieval castle rising above emerald vineyards, the oft-overlooked town of Spiez makes a great escape. The vibe is low-key but the setting magical, with views to conical Niesen (2362m) and a fjord-like slither of the lake.

## Sights & Activities

**Schloss Spiez** CASTLE

(www.schloss-spiez.ch; Schlossstrasse 16; adult/child Sfr10/2; 2-5pm Mon, 10am-5pm Tue-Sun Easter–mid-Oct) This turreted medieval castle is smothered in oil paintings of its former masters, the influential von Bubenburg and von Erlach families. But it's the view that will grab you, whether from the lofty tower (which also sports 13th-century graffiti) or the banqueting hall.

**Freibad Spiez** SWIMMING

(www.freibadspiez.ch; adult/child Sfr6.60/3.30; 7.30am-8pm mid-May–early Sep) Spiez' lido attracts sun-worshipping locals and families who come to frolic in the lake or swim laps in the Olympic-sized swimming pool. It has volleyball and tennis courts, minigolf and the longest water slide in the Bernese Oberland.

## Festivals & Events

**Läset-Sunntig** WINE

(www.laeset-spiez.ch) Spiez uncorks its finest wines at this festival in mid-September. Traditional parades and markets accompany much drinking and merrymaking.

## Sleeping & Eating

You'll find many, rather ordinary, pizza and pasta places located around the boat station. The best places to eat are the hotel restaurants.

**Seegarten Marina** HOTEL €€

(033 655 67 67; www.seegarten-marina.ch; Schachenstrasse 3; s Sfr120-140, d Sfr180-240; P) Sitting prettily on the banks of Lake Thun, this hotel has simple, somewhat-dated



WORTH A TRIP

### BUNKER MENTALITY

Ever wondered why the radio keeps playing on deep in the heart of a tunnel? Riddled with more holes than Emmental cheese, Switzerland is full of subterranean surprises, including the formerly top-secret WWII bunkers at **Faulensee** (033 654 25 07; www.artilleriewerk-faulensee.ch; adult/child Sfr10/5; 10am-3pm 1st Sat of month Apr-Nov), built to house troops defending Thun, Spiez and the Lötschberg railway. During summer, they're open to the public once a month.

Cleverly disguised as farmhouses, the entrances to the bunkers are guarded by cannons and connected by underground tunnels in which you'll find offices, laboratories, kitchens and cramped sleeping quarters. Tours last 1½ to two hours, and you'll need to be wearing warm clothing and sturdy shoes. To ask about English explanations, call or email ahead.

Faulensee can be reached by bus from Spiez train station and from Interlaken West by boat (one way/return Sfr12.80/21.60).

rooms that are nevertheless large and spotless. Friendly service adds to the appeal, as does the waterfront restaurant, dishing up Swiss classics.

**Strandhotel Belvédère** HISTORIC HOTEL €€€
(033 655 66 66; www.belvedere-spiez.ch; Schachenstrasse 39; s Sfr245-340, d Sfr345-480, ste Sfr490-750; P) Whisking you back 100 years, the chandelier-lit public areas at this genteel hotel exude art nouveau flair. Some rooms overdo the Laura Ashley–style pastels and florals, but they are comfy, especially those with lake-facing balconies. There's a spa and a Gault Millau–rated restaurant.

## Information

The **tourist office** (033 655 90 00; www.thunersee.ch; Am Bahnhof; 8am-noon & 1.30-5.30pm Mon-Fri, 9am-noon Sat) is outside the train station. It's open shorter hours in the shoulder seasons.

## Getting There & Away

From Interlaken West, trains run frequently to Spiez (Sfr10.60, 17 minutes). By boat it's Sfr11.20 from Thun and Sfr15.20 from Interlaken West. Seestrasse, the main street, is down to the left as you exit the train station, and leads to the castle (15 minutes' walk).

Spiez is just off the A8 between Interlaken, 20km east, and Thun, 14km northwest.



# Brienz

POP 2996 / ELEV 566M

If a child had to draw a picture of a fantasy Alpine village, Brienz would probably be it, with its collection of dark-timber chalets sprouting red geraniums, tooting steam train and views across the startlingly turquoise waters of its namesake lake to high mountains and thick forests beyond. The deeply traditional village has a stuck-in-time feel with woodcarving workshops and a lakefront promenade.

## Sights & Activities

Kids can splash around in the water playground on the tree-fringed lake promenade.

**Rothorn Bahn** RAILWAY
(www.brienz-rothorn-bahn.ch; one way/return Sfr57/88; hourly 7.30am-4.30pm Jun-late Oct; ) This is the only steam-powered cogwheel train still operating in Switzerland, climbing up to Rothorn at 2350m, from where you can set out on hikes or enjoy the long views over Brienzersee to snow-dusted 4000m peaks. Walking up from Brienz takes around five hours.

**Giessbachfälle** WATERFALL
(Giessbach Falls; funicular one way/return Sfr5/10) Illuminating the fir forest like a spotlight in the dark, the Giessbachfälle plummet 500m over 14 rocky ridges. Europe's oldest funicular, dating to 1879, creaks up from the boat station, but it's only a 15-minute walk up to the most striking section of the falls. Giessbach is easily reached by boat from Brienz (Sfr11.20) or take bus 152 (Sfr3.60, 22 minutes).

**Ballenberg Open-Air Museum** MUSEUM
(www.ballenberg.ch; adult/child Sfr24/12; 10am-5pm mid-Apr–Oct; ) For a fascinating insight into the rural Switzerland of yore, visit this open-air museum, set across 80 hectares east of Brienz. Authentically reconstructed farming hamlets take you on an architectural stroll around Switzerland, with 100 century-old buildings from humble wooden huts in Valais to hip-roofed farmhouses in the Bernese Oberland.

**Brunngasse** AREA
In town, mosey down postcard-perfect Brunngasse, a curving lane dotted with stout wooden chalets, each seemingly trying to outdo its neighbour with window displays of vines, kitsch gnomes and billowing geraniums.

## Sleeping & Eating

**Camping Aaregg** CAMPGROUND €
(033 951 18 43; www.aaregg.ch; Seestrasse 22; sites per adult Sfr13, car & tent Sfr20; Apr-Oct) Set on a little peninsula, this is a peaceful lakeside campsite with excellent facilities, including a restaurant and playground. It's a 10-minute walk east of the train station.

**Hotel Steinbock** HISTORIC HOTEL €€
(033 951 40 55; www.steinbock-brienz.ch; Hauptstrasse 123; s Sfr140-160, d Sfr180-230, f Sfr240-280; P) Guarded by a namesake *Steinbock* (ibex), this beautiful pine chalet dates to 1787. The plush, warm-hued rooms have organic mattresses, flat-screen TVs and slick bathrooms with pebble-floored showers for a spot of DIY reflexology. There's a cosy restaurant and wine cellar downstairs.

**Grand Hotel Giessbach** LUXURY HOTEL €€€
(033 952 25 25; www.giessbach.ch; s Sfr169-249, d Sfr325-626) Overlooking Brienzersee and the thundering Giessbach Falls from its hilltop perch, this lavish 19th-century hotel is a

romantic retreat with antique-filled rooms, polished service and a restaurant with far-reaching views from its terrace.

**Seehotel Bären** SWISS €€

(033 951 24 12; www.seehotel-baeren-brienz.ch; Hauptstrasse 72; mains Sfr24-39.50; noon-10pm; ) In a prime spot right on the lakefront, the Bären is a top pick for alfresco dining. The chef makes the most of regionally sourced ingredients, from pike perch and Lake Thun whitefish to lamb marinated in hay.

### Information

The train station, boat station, Rothorn Bahn and post office all huddle in the compact centre. The **tourist office** (033 952 80 80; www.brienz-tourismus.ch; Hauptstrasse 143; 8am-6pm Mon-Fri, 9am-1pm & 2.30-6pm Sat, 10am-1pm & 3-5pm Sun mid-Jun–Oct, closed Sat & Sun in winter) is in the train station.

### Getting There & Away

Brienz is accessible by train (Sfr8.40, 17 minutes) and boat (Sfr32) from Interlaken Ost. The Brünig Pass (1008m) is the road route to Lucerne. The A8 and A6 take you west to Interlaken and Thun.

# EAST BERNESE OBERLAND

## Meiringen

POP 4737 / ELEV 595M

When the writer Arthur Conan Doyle left his fictional detective Sherlock Holmes for dead at the base of the Reichenbach Falls near Meiringen, he ensured that a corner of Switzerland would forever remain English eccentric. Every 4 May, fans in tweed deerstalker hats and capes gather here for the anniversary of Holmes' 'death'.

Espionage aside, Meiringen's claim to fame is as the birthplace of those airy egg-white marvels that grace sweet trolleys from Boston to Brighton – meringues.

### Sights & Activities

The Haslital is an outdoorsy wonderland, laced with 300km of marked hiking and cycling trails that lead to wild valleys, waterfalls and high-alpine moors. The 2.7km marmot trail is a kid favourite. Mountain bikes and e-bikes can be rented at the train station.

When the flakes fall, beginners and intermediates whizz down the region's 60km of slopes; a day ski pass costs Sfr57/28 per adult/child. Families can stomp along glittering winter walking trails and race on sled runs such as the 5.5km one to Grosse Scheidegg.

**★Reichenbachfälle** WATERFALL

Gazing over the mighty Reichenbach Falls, where the cataract plunges 250m to the ground with a deafening roar, you can see how Arthur Conan Doyle thought them perfect for dispatching his burdensome hero, Sherlock Holmes. In 1891, in *The Final Problem,* Conan Doyle acted like one of his own villains and pushed both Holmes and Dr Moriarty over the precipice here. To reach the falls, take the **funicular** (www.reichenbachfall.ch; one way/return adult Sfr7/10, child Sfr6/8; 9am-5.30pm May–mid-Oct) from Willigen, south of the Aare River, to the top.

It takes an hour to wander back down to Meiringen. Alternatively, take the steep path up the side of the falls to the village of Zwirgi. At Gasthaus Zwirgi, you can rent trottibikes (adult/child Sfr17/15) to scoot back down to Meiringen.

**Triftbrücke** BRIDGE

(Trift Bridge; cable car one way/return Sfr12/24; cable car 9am-4pm Jun, Sep & Oct, to 5pm Jul & Aug) The Hasli Valley is laced with 300km of signposted walking trails. A huge hit is this 170m-long, 100m-high suspension bridge, Europe's longest and highest. To reach the bridge from Meiringen, take a train to Innertkirchen, then a bus to Nessental, Triftbahn. Here a cable car takes you up to 1022m, from where it's a 1½- to two-hour walk to the bridge (1870m).

**Aareschlucht** GORGE

(www.aareschlucht.ch; adult/child Sfr8.50/5; 8.30am-6.30pm Jul & Aug, 8.30am-5.30pm Apr-Jun, Sep & Oct) Less than 2km from Meiringen is the narrow, 1.4km-long Aare Gorge, where tunnels and galleries lead past milky-blue torrents and limestone overhangs. The canyon is spectacularly illuminated on Thursday, Friday and Saturday evenings in summer. To make your way here, take the **Meiringen-Innertkirchen-Bahn** (one way/return Sfr3.60/7.20; 6am-10.45pm) train.

**Sherlock Holmes Museum** MUSEUM

(www.sherlockholmes.ch; Bahnhofstrasse 26; adult/child Sfr4/3, combined with Reichenbachfälle funicular Sfr11/8; 1.30-6pm Tue-Sun May-Sep, 4.30-6pm Wed-Sun rest of year) Sherlock fans won't want to miss this museum in the basement of the English church in Meiringen. The highlight is a re-created sitting room of

221b Baker St. Multilingual audioguides are available.

**Gletscherschlucht Rosenlaui** GORGE
(www.rosenlauischlucht.ch; adult/child Sfr8/4; 9am-6pm Jun-Sep, 10am-5pm May & Oct) A round trail takes in waterfalls and 80m-high cliffs at this dramatic glacier gorge. The walk back to Meiringen takes at least two hours, but hourly buses also ply the route from June to September.

## Sleeping & Eating

★**Hotel Victoria** BOUTIQUE HOTEL €€
(033 972 10 40; www.victoria-meiringen.ch; Bahnhofplatz 9; s Sfr155-240, d Sfr195-290; P) It's the little touches that count at this boutique-chic hotel, from the designer furnishings in your room to the mountain views and room service. Simon puts an imaginative spin on market-fresh flavours in the Gault Millau-rated restaurant.

**Hotel Alpbach** HOTEL €€
(033 971 18 31; www.alpbach.ch; Kirchgasse 17; s Sfr95-130, d Sfr190-270; P) Friendly service is a lucky dip, but we can't fault the charming pine-clad quarters at this central hotel. Up the romance by opting for a four-poster bed. There's a small sauna and steam room, as well as a rustic restaurant.

**Park Hotel du Sauvage** HISTORIC HOTEL €€
(033 972 18 80; www.sauvage.ch; Bahnhofstrasse 30; s Sfr105-125, d Sfr180-280; P) Arthur Conan Doyle once stayed in this art nouveau classic, but today it's pensioners on whodunnit weekends who spy on the breakfast buffet. After the old-fashioned grandeur in the lobby, the rooms are something of an anticlimax.

**Frutal** CAFE €
(Bahnhofstrasse 18; cakes Sfr3-6; 7am-6.30pm) A kitsch plastic meringue licks its lips in the window of this old-fashioned tearoom. You'll do likewise when you taste the feather-light meringues here.

**Molki Meiringen** CHEESE €
(Lenggasse 1; 8am-12.15pm & 2-6.30pm Mon-Fri, 7.30am-5pm Sat) Stop by this dairy for tangy Haslital cheeses and homemade ice cream.

## Information

As you exit the train station (bike rental available), you'll see the post office, bus station and **tourist office** (033 972 50 50; www.haslital.ch; Bahnhofplatz 12; 8am-noon & 1.30-6pm Mon-Fri; ) opposite.

## Getting There & Away

Frequent trains go to Lucerne (Sfr24, 1¼ hours) and Interlaken Ost (Sfr6.60, 33 minutes). In summer, buses and cars can take the pass southeast (to Andermatt), but the road southwest over Grosse Scheidegg (to Grindelwald) is closed to private vehicles.

Meiringen is just off the A6, which swings south to the Valais border and heads west to skirt the northern shore of Lake Brienz to reach Interlaken.

# WEST BERNESE OBERLAND

## Kandersteg

POP 1314 / ELEV 1176M

Turn up in Kandersteg wearing anything but muddy boots and you'll attract a few odd looks. Hiking is this town's raison d'être, with 550km of surrounding trails. An amphitheatre of spiky peaks studded with glaciers and jewel-coloured lakes creates a sublime natural backdrop to the rustic village of dark-timber chalets.

### Sights & Activities

In winter there are more than 50km of cross-country ski trails, including the iced-over Oeschinensee. The limited 15km of downhill skiing is suited to beginners, and day passes cost Sfr39. Kandersteg's frozen waterfalls attract ice climbers to the village.

**Oeschinensee** LAKE
(www.oeschinensee.ch; cable-car one way/return Sfr18/26; 9am-5pm; ) Mountains rise like natural ramparts above the impossibly turquoise Oeschinensee, where you can fish, stroll, swim or hire a row boat. A cable car takes you to within 20 minutes' walk of the lake. Once there it takes an hour to hike back down to Kandersteg. Kids will have a blast on the summer bob run (adult/child Sfr5/4) next to the top station. In winter you can hike across the frozen lake on the circular, 1½-hour Unesco Ice Walk.

**Blausee** LAKE
(www.blausee.ch) From Kandersteg it's a scenic 5km hike up to the Blausee – named after its startling shade of blue – and its nature park. The restaurant on its shore serves the organic trout caught here. Bus 230 also runs here hourly from the station (Sfr6.80, 11 minutes)

**Gemmi Pass** HIKING

Kandersteg has some first-rate hiking in its wild backyard on the cantonal border with Valais. A superb trek is the high-level Gemmi Pass (2314m) to Leukerbad, involving a steep descent. Allow six to seven hours for this moderately challenging trek, best tackled from July to September. The trailhead is **Sunnbüel cable car** (one way/return Sfr26/36; 8.30am-6pm Jun-Oct) top station. To reach the base station, take bus 241 from the station.

**Klettersteig Allmenalp** VIA FERRATA

(www.allmenalp.ch) For a challenge, you could tackle the tough, 3½-hour *via ferrata* at Allmenalp. Equipment can be hired at the valley station for Sfr25. A **cable car** (8am-6pm late Jun-mid-Oct) whisks you up to the starting point at Allmenalp.

**Alpine Centre Kandersteg** CLIMBING

(033 675 01 01; http://alpine-center.ch; Bahnhofstrasse 15; 9am-noon & 1.30-6pm Mon, Tue, Wed & Fri, 9am-noon & 1.30-4pm Sat) This sport rental shop and climbing hall offers guided *via ferrata* tours in summer and ice climbing in winter. Visit the website for times and prices.

## Sleeping & Eating

★ **The Hayloft** B&B €

(033 675 03 50; www.thehayloft.ch; Altes Bütschels Hus; s/d/tr Sfr60/120/180) Picture a dark-wood, 500-year-old chalet snuggled against the hillside, flower-strewn meadows where cows graze placidly, views of waterfalls and glaciers – ahhh…this place sure is idyllic! The farm-turned-B&B is in the capable hands of Peter and Kerry, who welcome guests like members of the family and serve delicious breakfasts and dinners (Sfr30).

**Ruedihus** HISTORIC HOTEL €€

(033 675 81 81; www.doldenhorn-ruedihus.ch; s Sfr110-150, d Sfr240-390; P) Oozing 250 years of history from every creaking beam, this archetypal Alpine chalet is a stunner. Romantic and warm, the cottage-style rooms feature low ceilings, antique painted furniture and four-poster beds. Home-grown herbs are used to flavour dishes served in the cosy restaurant.

**Berghotel Oeschinensee** HOTEL €€

(033 675 11 19; www.oeschinensee.ch; s Sfr90-110, d Sfr150-200) Both the food and staggering lake and mountain views are worth writing home about at this late-19th-century mountain chalet, lovingly run by the fifth generation of the Wandfluh family. Fitted out with pine furnishings, rooms are simple and silent.

★ **Nico's** SWISS €€

(033 675 84 84; http://alfasoleil.ch; Äussere Dorfstrasse 99; mains Sfr29-58; 6-11.30pm Wed, 8.30am-11.30pm Thu-Mon) The chef takes pride in using locally sourced, organic and foraged ingredients at this refined restaurant in Alfa Soleil hotel.

**Bernerhof** SWISS €€

(033 675 88 75; www.bernerhof.ch; Hotel Bernerhof, Äussere Dorfstrasse 26; mains Sfr21-46, 5-course menu Sfr56; 8am-10pm Fri-Sun, 3-10pm Mon-Thu) Locals sing the praises of this cosy tavern snuggled away in the chalet-style Hotel Bernerhof. It's a good choice if you're in the mood for some hearty Swiss grub. The seasonal menu is the way to go, making best use of the ingredients available. There are always some vegan and veggie options.

## Information

The **tourist office** (033 675 80 80; www.kandersteg.ch; Äussere Dorfstrasse 26; 8am-noon & 1.30-6pm Mon-Fri, 8.30am-noon & 3-6pm Sat Jun-Sep, shorter hours rest of year) can suggest hiking routes and other activities in the area.

## Getting There & Away

Kandersteg is at the northern end of the **Lötschberg Tunnel** (www.bls.ch), through which trains trundle to Goppenstein (30km from Brig) and onwards to Iselle in Italy. Hourly trains to Interlaken Ost (Sfr15.10, 70 minutes) involve a change at Spiez (Sfr9.40, 31 minutes).

If you're driving, Kandersteg is 26km south of Spiez, which connects up with the A8 heading east to Interlaken and the A6 west to Thun.

# Gstaad

POP 3600 / ELEV 1100M

Gstaad might have the glitz and glamour of its French twin, Cannes, but with its timber-lined village heart and cow-grazed pastures, it appears smaller than its reputation – too tiny for its designer ski boots, as it were. George Clooney, Valentino, Madonna, Paris Hilton and even Margaret Thatcher have flexed platinum cards to let their hair down here. While the principal competitive sports are celebrity-spotting and gazing wistfully into Gucci-filled boutiques, others might enjoy the outstanding hiking, mountain biking and skiing on slopes as smooth as silk.

## Activities

### Winter Activities

Non skiers and families are in their element in Gstaad, with off-piste fun including ice skating, curling, horse-drawn trap rides, winter hiking on 30 trails, snowshoeing, airboarding at Saanenmöser and snow golf at Wispile. See www.gstaad.ch for the low-down.

**Gstaad Mountain Rides** SKIING

These 220km of ski slopes cover a good mix of blues, reds and blacks, and include neighbouring resorts such as Saanen, Saanenmöser, St Stephan and Zweisimmen. A two-day ski pass costs Sfr124/62 per adult/child.

Beginners can test out the snow on gentle, tree-lined runs at Wispile and Eggli, while more proficient skiers can cruise challenging reds at Les Diablerets. Snowboarders tackle the curves, bowls and jumps at the ski-cross slope at Riedenberg.

### Summer Activities

Hiking is the main summer pursuit and the opportunities are boundless, with 300km of marked trails threading through the region. Stop by the tourist office for details on *via ferrate* and mountaineering in the surrounding limestone peaks.

Cyclists and mountain bikers are in their element with 280km of marked trails and 500km of GPS routes in the area. The tourist office (p143) website has details on bike rental, hotels and routes. For route suggestions and services, see www.veloland.ch and for GPS downloads, www.gps-tracks.com. Bikes can be transported for free on seven lifts, including Wispile and Eggli. Advance bookings are required for many activities.

**Wispile** HIKING

A scenic three-hour hike takes you from Wispile to Launensee, a crystalline Alpine lake, with views of the craggy Wildhorn massif en route. Wispile is also the best bet for families, with a dairy trail, a petting zoo and a downhill scooter trail from its middle station.

**Swiss Adventures** ADVENTURE SPORTS

(☎033 748 41 61; www.swissadventures.ch; Alpinzentrum Gstaad) Organises guided climbs and *via ferrate*, rafting, canyoning and, in winter, snowshoe trekking, ice climbing and airboarding.

**Paragliding Gstaad** PARAGLIDING

(☎079 224 42 70; www.paragstaad.com) Reputable outfit offering tandem flights at Wispile, Videmanette and Glacier 3000.

**Llama & Co** HIKING

(☎078 718 90 43; www.lama-und-co.ch; Schindelweg 2, Zweisimmen) A sure-fire hit with the kids are these guided llama and goat hikes, from two-hour walks to full-day treks.

## Festivals & Events

**Suisse Open** SPORTS

(www.creditagricolesuisseopengstaad.ch; ⏱late Jul) Gstaad hosts this famous tennis tournament at the Roy Emerson Arena in late July.

**Menuhin Festival** MUSIC

(www.gstaadmenuhinfestival.ch; ⏱mid-Jul–early Sep) Top-drawer classical-music festival with 50 concerts over seven weeks.

## Sleeping

There's no denying that Gstaad comes with its price tag, but though palatial five-star pads abound, there are humbler, cheaper picks with plenty of Alpine flair. Rates go through the roof during winter high season; expect discounts of 30% to 50% in summer. The tourist office has a list of self-catering chalets.

**SYHA Hostel** HOSTEL €

(☎033 744 13 43; www.youthhostel.ch/saanen; Spitzhornweg 25, Saanen; dm Sfr38.50-44.50; 📶) Situated in Saanen, this is a peaceful chalet hostel with bright, clean dorms and a games room.

**Le Grand Chalet** HERITAGE HOTEL €€

(☎033 748 76 76; www.grandchalet.ch; Neueretstrasse 43; d Sfr280-700; P 📶 🏊) In a serene setting with views deep into the snowcapped Alps, this family-run, chalet-style hotel is utterly charming. Done out in warm pine and with traditional fabrics, the rooms are restful and the best come with mountain-facing balconies. A fitness area, outdoor swimming pool and gourmet restaurant playing up regional produce sweeten the deal.

**Iglu-Dorf** IGLOO €€

(☎041 612 27 28; www.iglu-dorf.com; Saanenmöser; per person Sfr159-479; late Dec-Easter) Fondue and mulled wine pave the way to subzero slumber land at this 'igloo village', situated at 2000m and affording magical views to 3000m peaks. Night-time snowshoeing is part of the fun. Up the price for a little Eskimo-style romance in an igloo complete with its own whirlpool.

**Gstaad Palace** LUXURY HOTEL €€€

(☎033 748 50 00; www.palace.ch; Palacestrasse 28; s Sfr440-660, d Sfr710-1140, ste Sfr1560-4330; P ❄ @ 🏊) Opulent, exclusive and – in case

WORTH A TRIP

## GLACIER 3000

One of Switzerland's biggest year-round outdoor playgrounds is **Glacier 3000** (www.glacier3000.ch), situated high above the pass road between Gstaad and Les Diablerets and affording sensational views of 24 4000m peaks. The glacier has the longest ski season in the Bernese Alps, running from late October through early May. A day ski pass, covering 30km of runs between 1350m and 3000m, costs Sfr63 for adults and Sfr42 for children. Boarders can practice on the rails, kickers and boxes at the snow park.

In summer, hikers can negotiate the glacier trail from Scex Rouge to Sanetsch Pass, tackle the high-altitude hike to the arrow-shaped Oldenhorn at 3123m, or get giddy crossing the suspension bridge linking two mountains on the Peak Walk by Tissot. For those up for more of a challenge, there is the Gemskopf *via ferrata*. There's plenty up here to entertain the little ones, too, from a loop-the-loop **Alpine Coaster** (Sfr9) to short and scenic **husky rides** (Sfr15); call ☎079 933 65 33 to book ahead for the latter.

To reach it from Gstaad, take a bus from the station to Col du Pillon (Sfr11.40, 39 minutes), where a cable car (return adult/child Sfr79/40) runs to the summit.

you happen to be wondering – accessible by helicopter, this hilltop fairy-tale palace has attracted celebrity royalty such as Michael Jackson, Robbie Williams and Liza Minnelli. Lavish quarters, a luxurious spa, several gourmet restaurants and an Olympic pool justify the price tag.

## Eating

If Gstaad's ritzy restaurants aren't for you, head for the mountain-chalet restaurants at the summit stations of the cable cars.

**Michel's Stallbeizli** SWISS €

(☎033 744 43 37, 033 744 16 83; www.stallbeizli.ch; Gsteigstrasse 41; snacks & fondue Sfr16-22; ⏲10am-6pm Tue & Wed, to 10pm Thu, to 11.30pm Fri & Sat, to 8pm Sun mid-Dec–Mar; 👪) Dining doesn't get more back-to-nature than at this converted barn. In winter you can feast away on fondue, drink Alpine herbal tea, or munch home-cured meat and cheese, with truly moo-ving views (pardon the pun) of the cud-chewing cows and goats in the adjacent stable.

**16 Art** INTERNATIONAL €€

(☎033 748 16 16; www.16eme.ch; Mittelgässli 16, Saanen; mains Sfr24-36; ⏲5pm-1am Thu-Mon) Huddled away down a pretty backstreet, this former bell factory now chimes with a season-driven, largely regionally sourced menu. The art-slung, timber-lined interior is wonderfully cosy, the welcome warm and the flower-swathed terrace appealing when the sun's out. Bus 180 from Gstaad stops close by.

**Wasserngrat** SWISS €€

(☎033 744 96 22; mains Sfr20-50; ⏲9.30am-4.30pm Thu-Sun Aug & mid-Dec–Mar) Marvel at views of Les Diablerets glacier and Gstaad from the slope-side perch of Wasserngrat, where a fire crackles in the rustic-chic restaurant and skiers warm up over fondue on the sunny terrace. Top ingredients such as truffles and foie gras flavour classic Alpine dishes.

★ **Chesery** FRENCH €€€

(☎033 744 24 51; Alte Lauenenstrasse 6; lunch menus Sfr78-94, dinner menus Sfr165-178; ⏲11am-2.30pm & 6-11pm Tue-Sun) Founded by the Aga Khan in the 1960s, this dairy-turned-Michelin-starred-restaurant is the pinnacle of fine dining in Gstaad. Taste sensations play up seasonality and are served with full-bodied wines and French finesse.

## Information

The **tourist office** (☎033 748 81 81; www.gstaad.ch; Promenade 41; ⏲8.30am-6.30pm Mon-Fri, 9am-noon & 1.30-5pm Sat & Sun; 📶) has stacks of info on the area.

## Getting There & Away

Gstaad is on the Golden Pass route between Montreux (Sfr27, 1½ hours) and Spiez (Sfr28, 1½ hours; change at Zweisimmen). There's an hourly service to Geneva airport (Sfr53, three hours) via Montreux. A postal bus goes to Les Diablerets (Sfr13.60, 50 minutes) about five times daily.

N11 is the principal road connecting Aigle and Spiez, and it passes close to Gstaad at Saanen.

# Valais

POP 335,700

**Includes ➡**



## Best Places to Eat

- ➡ Le Namasté (p152)
- ➡ Restaurant Château de la Bâtiaz (p149)
- ➡ Whymper Stube (p167)
- ➡ Gletscher Grotte (p171)
- ➡ Chüestall (p175)

## Best Places to Stay

- ➡ Kulmhotel Gornergrat (p167)
- ➡ Berghotel Riederfurka (p173)
- ➡ WellnessHostel 4000 (p171)
- ➡ Martigny Boutique-Hôtel (p148)

## Why Go?

Natural beauty Valais has a tale of rags to riches, of changing seasons and celebrities, of an outdoors so fantastic it's always fashionable. Wedged in a remote corner of southern Switzerland, this is where farmers were so poor they didn't have two francs to rub together a century ago and where luminaries flock today to sip Champagne cocktails in posh Verbier nightclubs.

Landscapes here leave you dumbstruck: from the unfathomable Matterhorn (4478m) that defies trigonometry, photography and many a carabiner, to the Rhône Valley's vineyard tapestry; and the shimmering 23km Aletsch Glacier. With such backdrops, how can any hike, bike or ski tour be anything but great?

As earthy as a vintner's boots in September, as clean as the aesthetic in Zermatt's lounge bars, this canton is fickle. The west speaks French and the east German, but both are united in matters of cantonal pride by fine wine and glorious cheese.

## When to Go

- ➡ December to early April, ski and snowboard enthusiasts flock here to enjoy world-class winter sports.
- ➡ The China-blue-sky days of July and August lure hikers, bikers and adventure-sport lovers for a dose of adrenaline.
- ➡ Summer sees the curtain rise on music festivals in Verbier and Sion, and Combats de Reines, which sees bulls lock horns and try to push each other backwards.
- ➡ In late September and October leaves turn gold on vines, grapes and chestnuts are harvested, and the autumnal feast of La Brisolée is laid out on the table for all to celebrate.

## History

As in neighbouring Vaud, Julius Caesar was an early 'tourist' in these parts. The Roman leader brought an army to conquer the Celtic community living in the valley, penetrating as far as Sierre. Once under Roman domination, the four Celtic tribes of Valais were peaceably integrated into the Roman system.

Sion became a key centre in the valley when the Bishop of Valais settled here from AD 580. By 1000 the bishop's power stretched from Martigny to the Furka Pass. But a succession of Dukes of Savoy encroached on the bishop's territory and a Savoyard army besieged Sion in 1475. With the help of the Swiss Confederation, the city was freed at the Battle of Planta. Internal opposition was equally intense and Valais' independently minded communes stripped the bishops of their secular power in the 1630s, shifting control to a regional parliament.

Valais joined the Swiss Confederation in 1815.

# LOWER VALAIS

Stone-walled vineyards, tumbledown castle ruins and brooding mountains create an arresting backdrop to the meandering Rhône valley in western Valais. Intriguing towns dot the valley, such as Roman-rooted Martigny and vine-strewn Sion and Sierre, where the French influence shows not only in the lingo, but also in the locals' passion for art, wine and pavement cafes.

Glitzy resorts like Verbier and Crans-Montana have carved out reputations for sunny cruising, big panoramas and celebrity style, but there's more. Narrow lanes wriggle up to forgotten side-valleys such as Val d'Anniviers, packed with rural charm and crowd-free skiing in the shadow of ice-capped mountains.

## Martigny

POP 17,215 / ELEV 476M

Once the stomping ground of Romans in search of wine and sunshine en route to Italy, small-town Martigny is Valais's oldest town. Look beyond its concrete high-rises to enjoy a world-class art gallery, Roman amphitheatre and a posse of droopy St Bernard dogs to romp with in the surrounding mountains.

### Sights

**★Fondation Pierre Gianadda** GALLERY

(☎027 722 39 78; www.gianadda.ch; Rue du Forum; adult/10-25yr Sfr18/10; ⏲9am-7pm) This renowned gallery harbours a stunning art collection with works by Picasso, Cézanne and Van Gogh. The sculpture garden (with cafe and picnic area) features Henry Moore's organic sculptures, Niki de Saint Phalle's buxom *Bathers* and César's *Le Sein* (The Breast). Admission includes the collection of Roman milestones, the **Musée Archéologique Gallo-Romain**, and the classic cars from vintage Fords to Swiss Martinis (the type you drive, not drink) in the **Musée de l'Auto**. The Fondation also hosts classical-music recitals.

**★Château de la Bâtiaz** CHATEAU

(☎027 722 31 21; www.batiaz.ch; Chemin du Château; ⏲11am-midnight Wed-Sat, to 6pm Sun Jul & Aug, 11am-6pm Wed, Sun & 11am-midnight Thu, Fri May, Jun, Sep & Oct) FREE Clinging to a crag above town, 800-year-old Bâtiaz Castle is worth the 15-minute uphill climb. Once there, add another 120 steps to the top of castle for far-reaching views over the surrounding vineyards and Rhône Valley. Slightly less appealing is the gruesome collection of medieval torture instruments inside. The château's medieval restaurant (p149) is now a highlight with its medieval menu. Although opening times are set, look for the blue flag flying to confirm it's open.

**Musée et Chiens du Saint-Bernard** MUSEUM

(☎027 722 65 42; www.museesaintbernard.ch; Rte du Levant 34; museum adult/child Sfr12/7; ⏲10am-6pm) A tribute to the lovably dopey St Bernard, this museum next to Martigny's Roman amphitheatre includes real-life fluff bundles in the kennels. You can join the dogs for walks at various locations year-round; check the website for details and reserve in advance. Upstairs an exhibition traces the role of St Bernards in hospice life, on canvas and in film. There are puppy- and dog-feeding sessions and hourly times for petting and taking photographs.

### Festivals & Events

**Foire du Valais** CULTURAL

(www.foireduvalais.ch; ⏲Oct) Pigs don't fly in Martigny, but cows fight: this 10-day regional fair climaxes with a bovine bash-about of epic proportions.

# Valais Highlights

❶ **Gornergrat** (p163) Staring across the valley with fascination at the incomparable Matterhorn.

❷ **Eggishorn** (p172) Feasting your eyes on the 23km-long Aletsch Glacier.

❸ **Saas Fee** (p169) Riding the underground Mittelallin funicular to an icy 3500m.

❹ **Martigny** (p145) Feasting on medieval fare inside Château de la Bâtiaz.

❺ **Col du Grand St Bernard** (p150) Walking a big-eyed St Bernard on a high mountain pass.

❻ **Leukerbad** (p160) Lounging in a bubbly whirlpool

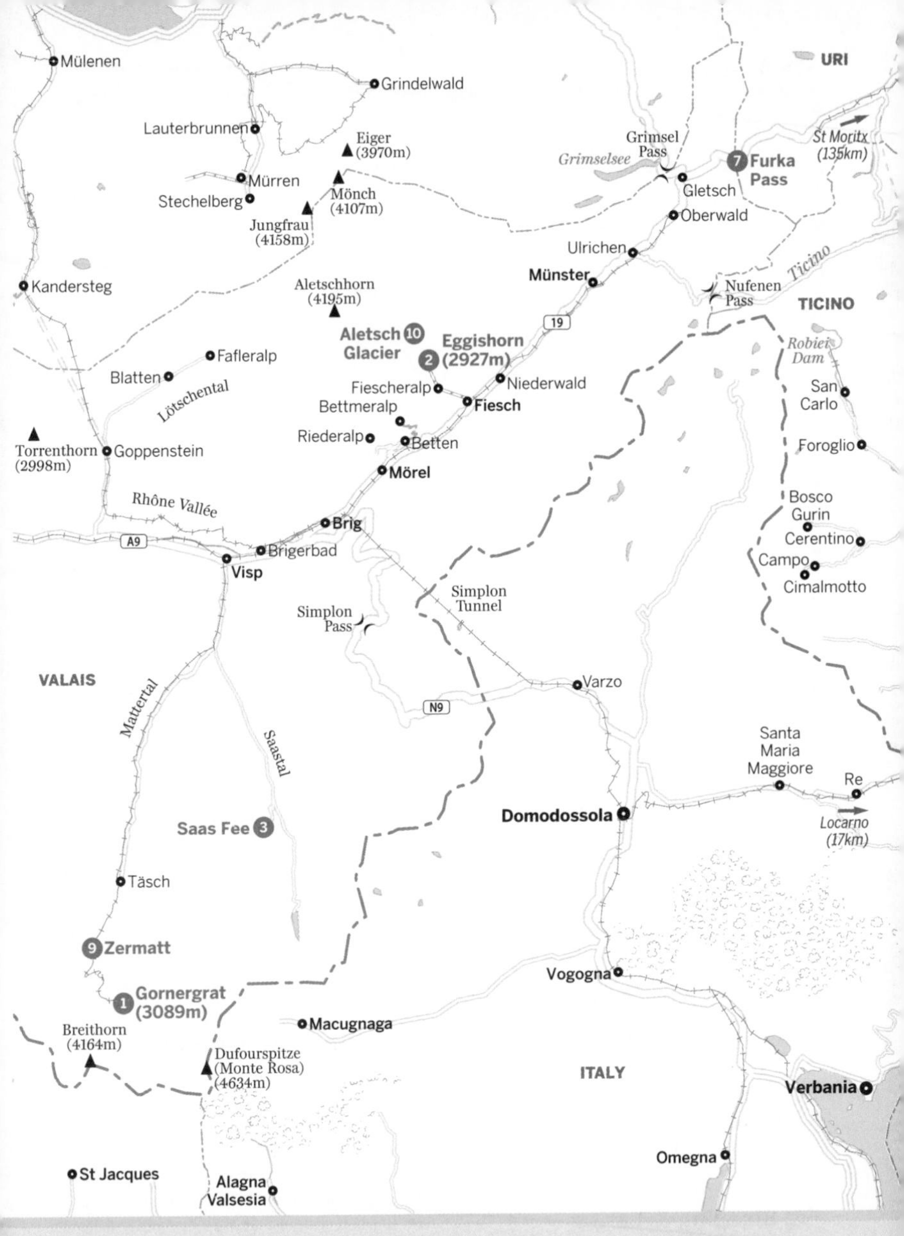


as snow falls on surrounding peaks.

**7 Furka Pass** (p175)
Pretending to be James Bond as you drive the hairpin curves.

**8 Sentier Viticole** (p157)
Walking the Vineyards Trail from Salgesch to Sierre.

**9 Glacier Express** (p163)
Boarding the train in Zermatt for an eight-hour extravaganza to St Moritz.

**10 Aletschji–Grünsee Suspension Bridge** (p171)
Conquering your fears on this 80m-high suspension bridge.

## Martigny

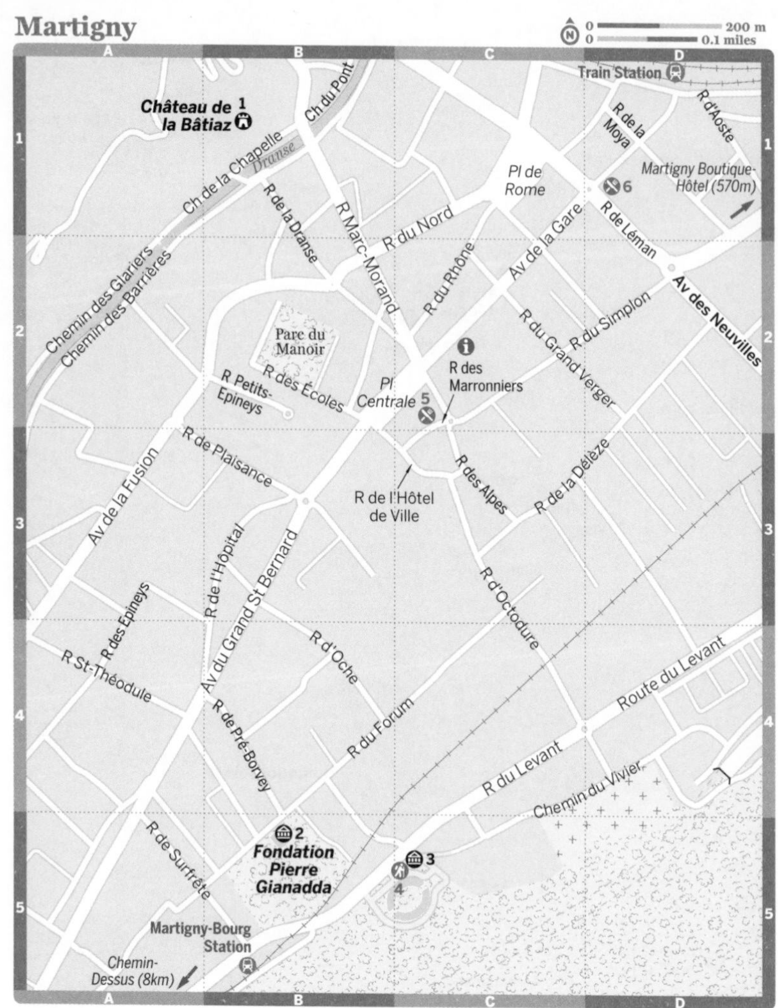


**Foire au Lard** FOOD & DRINK
(www.foireaulard.ch; ⌚Dec) There's sizzling action at Martigny's Bacon Fair, celebrated since 1801.

## Sleeping & Eating

Everything happens on Place Centrale, abuzz with pavement cafes and bistros, and on parallel Rue des Marronniers.

**Hôtel Beau Site** HOTEL €
(☎027 722 81 64; www.chemin.ch; Chemin-Dessus; s/d/q Sfr110/150/190; ⌚Jun-Aug, rest of year advance reservation only; P 📶) 🍃 High above Martigny at 1211m, this ecofriendly art nouveau house from 1912 is an oasis of peace. Rooms are simple with shared bathroom, there's a library and piano, and the restaurant's vegetarian meals are sourced locally. You'll need wheels. From Martigny, follow signs for Col des Planches, driving uphill for 7km through Le Bourg and Chemin-Dessous to the hamlet of Chemin-Dessus.

★**Martigny Boutique-Hôtel** BOUTIQUE HOTEL €€
(☎027 552 10 00; www.martigny-hotel.ch; Rue des Vorziers 7; rooms from Sfr150; P 📶)

## Martigny

**Top Sights**



**Sights**



**Activities, Courses & Tours**



**Eating**



This 52-room hotel sits a three-minute walk back from Martigny's train station and is modern and chic. Part of a social integration project, the hotel employs 30 people with disabilities and is strongly linked to Martigny's love of the arts. Reception features arts and crafts for sale, plus there's a superb bar and a restaurant uniquely featuring Peruvian-Swiss cuisine.

★**Restaurant Château de la Bâtiaz** MEDIEVAL €
(☎027 722 31 21; www.batiaz.ch/taverne; Chemin du Château; mains from Sfr16; ⏱11am-midnight Wed-Sat, to 6pm Sun Jul & Aug, 11am-6pm Wed, Sun & 11am-midnight Thu, Fri May, Jun, Sep & Oct) There aren't many places you can tuck into a 'medieval menu' in an 800-year-old medieval castle. The restaurant is proving popular inside Château de la Bâtiaz (p145). There's a roaring fire, local beers and wines, plus a menu that includes tasty specials such as lentil salad with mustard sauce and pork ragoût with cannelle beans.

**Crêperie Le Rustique** CRÊPES €
(☎027 722 88 33; Av de la Gare 44; crêpes Sfr10-17; ⏱11.30am-10.15pm Mon-Sat) Locals love the Rustic, handily placed between the train station and town, and known for its wholly affordable dining at any time of day. Kick off with one of 30-odd types of savoury pancakes, ranging from Mexican, Madras and Milanese to traditional *jambon-fromage* (ham and cheese). Then move onto the sweet crêpe menu: Black Forest gateau, tiramisu or banana-chocolate anyone?

### Information

**Tourist Office** (☎027 720 49 49; www.martigny.com; Av de la Gare 6; ⏱9am-6.30pm Mon-Fri, to 5pm Sat, 10am-3pm Sun Jul & Aug, reduced hours Sep-Jun) Ask about vineyard walks and cycling trails in Martigny's terraced, green surrounds.

### Getting There & Away

Martigny is on the E62, 134km east of Geneva, 41km south of Montreux and 28km west of Sion. By a very winding mountain road, it is 44km to Chamonix, France.

Martigny is on the main train line between Lausanne (Sfr23, 50 minutes) and Brig (Sfr25, 55 minutes); alight at Martigny Gare for Place Centrale, and Martigny Bourg for the Fondation Pierre Gianadda.

From Martigny the panoramic **Mont Blanc Express** (www.mont-blanc-express.com) goes to Chamonix (Sfr31, 1½ hours) in France, and the *St Bernard Express* to Le Châble (Sfr11.40, 30 minutes; ski lift or bus connection for Verbier) and Orsières (Sfr11.40, 30 minutes) via Sembrancher.

### Getting Around

**Valaisroule** (☎079 127 50 25; www.valaisroule.ch; Pl de la Gare; 4 hours free, 5th hour Sfr10; ⏱9am-12.15pm & 1-6pm Wed-Sun Jun-Oct) Borrow a bike for free (four hours) to pedal around town from this stand by Martigny Gare. It also rents out mountain bikes and electric bikes (both Sfr15 for the first hour, then Sfr5 per hour).

# AROUND MARTIGNY

## Champéry

Some 20km up its own valley and close to the French border, Champéry is stuck between the pointy jaws of Dents du Midi and Dents Blanches. This cutesy alpine resort (1055m) is one of 12 resort villages in the vast **Portes du Soleil** (www.portesdusoleil.com) recreational area, with eight in France and four in Switzerland – it's heaven for backcountry skiers and snowboarders in winter, with 650km of downhill runs and the French ski resorts of Morzine and Avoriaz only a lift-ride away. It is also a mecca for hikers, mountain bikers and paragliders in summer.

There's lots of history here too. The Hotel Dent-du-Midi opened in 1857, and In 1969 Champéry became one of the founding villages of the Portes du Soleil ski area and resort. It's a joy to wander the old main street of the village.

With great views out over the valley and mountains, **Hotel Suisse** (☎024 479 07 07; http://hotel-champery.ch; Rue du Village 55; s/d incl breakfast from Sfr190/260; P 📶) features comfortable rooms in a gorgeous old building on Rue du Village, the old road through town. The location is as good as it gets, 'tea time' (with cake) is included in winter, and the hotel's Bar des Guides is a top spot to knock back a brew.

The Champéry **tourist office** (☎024 479 20 20; www.champery.ch; Rue du Village 54; ⏰8am-6pm) is on the old village main street, up from the station.

# Col du Grand St Bernard

This is where the legend of the St Bernard dog was born, at 2473m on the Great St Bernard pass between Switzerland and Italy. So perilous was this transalpine crossing that monks had already established a hospice on the pass in the 11th century to provide spiritual succour and to rescue travellers lost in the snow. The dogs uncovered and rescued lost souls until the 1950s when helicopters were introduced.

Nowadays, few visitors make it as far as this spectacular alpine pass, which is well worth a visit if you love walking with big dogs (you can go for a stroll with a St Bernard in summer!), remote border crossings, rugged mountains, hiking and the outdoors. Most whizz over the Swiss–Italian border far below in the 5.8km-long **Tunnel du Grand St Bernard**, which opened in 1964 and took virtually all the cross-border traffic away.

## Sights

**Grand St Bernard Museum** MUSEUM
(www.gsbernard.net; Col du Grand St Bernard; adult/child Sfr10/6; ⏰10am-6pm Jun-Oct) The exhibition at this museum, in the same building as the Auberge de l'Hospice on the Col du Grand St Bernard, tells the complete story of this remote mountain pass, inaccessible by vehicle for half the year. Open in summer, tickets are valid for both the museum and dog kennels, with plenty of St Bernard dogs to see.

> **DON'T MISS**
>
> **HIKE WITH A DOG**
>
> Everyone loves a St Bernard, so **Fondation Barry** (☎027 722 65 42; www.fondation-barry.ch; Rue du Levant 34; adult/child Sfr48/10) has come up with a clever plan. From mid-July to mid-September you can accompany the doe-eyed woofers on a 1½-hour walk on the Col du Grand St Bernard. These walks have been so successful that there are now autumn, winter and spring walking tours, too – check out details on the website.

## Sleeping

**Auberge de l'Hospice** HOTEL €
(☎027 565 11 53; www.aubergehospice.ch; s/d/tr Sfr78/116/144, breakfast/half-board Sfr12/42; ⏰June–mid-Oct; P 📶) This is the modern version of the hospice over the road. Families are warmly welcomed at this hotel, with 30 rooms, a cafe-restaurant and shop, plus a wonderful restaurant terrace looking out on the Col du Grand St Bernard and Italian Alps beyond. Expect some comforts here, but it's only open in summer.

**Hospice du Grand St Bernard** HOSTEL €
(☎027 787 12 36; www.gsbernard.net; dm incl breakfast/half-board/full board Sfr30/48/64, d Sfr86/122/148; P) Overlooking the lake, the hospice has a 1000-year history of hospitality. In winter, the only way here is on foot (snowshoes or skis) from the entrance to the tunnel 6km downhill. Dorms are spartan, but the monks are welcoming and the setting is magical. Advance reservations obligatory.

## Getting There & Away

The Grand St Bernard pass is generally open from the start of June until late September. The easiest way to get there is with your own wheels. Make sure you take the clearly marked sign for Col du Grand St Bernard pointing right, just before the Tunnel du Grand St Bernard. The road climbs 6km up to the pass from there.

The only access once the road is closed (late September to June) is by foot, with snowshoes or skis.

In summer, you can take the *St Bernard Express* train from Martigny to Orsières (Sfr11.40, 30 minutes, hourly) then a **TMR** (☎027 721 68 40; www.tmrsa.ch) bus from the Orsières station (Sfr16.60, 45 minutes, two to three daily in summer).

# Verbier

POP 3000 / ELEV 1500M

Ritzy Verbier is the diamond of the Valaisian Alps: small, stratospherically expensive and cut at all the right angles to make it sparkle in the eyes of accomplished skiers and piste-bashing stars. Yet despite its ritzy packaging, Verbier is that rare beast of a resort – all things to all people. It swings from schnapps-fuelled debauchery to VIP lounges, bunker hostels to design-oriented hotels, burgers to Michelin stars. Here ski bums and celebs slalom in harmony on powder that is legendary.

Unlike smaller resorts, Verbier scarcely shuts between seasons. Bar a couple of weeks in May and October, there's always something happening.

## Activities

A recreation mecca, there's an activity to suit every urge. For an overview and on-the-ground guidance hook up with a local mountain guide at **Les Guides de Verbier** (☎027 775 33 70; www.guideverbier.com; Rue de Médran 41). For a one-stop shop online go to www.verbierbooking.com.

### Skiing

Verbier's skiing is among Europe's finest, with exciting and varied terrain suitable for skiers and boarders of all levels. The resort sits at the heart of the **Quatre Vallées** (Four Valleys), comprising 412km of pistes and 94 ski lifts. A regional ski pass costs Sfr67/322 per one/five days.

### Hiking

The walking here is superb, with 500km of signposted trails. The tourist office (p153) has a detailed map with explanations for 29 different hiking trails. There's something for everyone, including families. Notable shorter strolls include the **Sentier des Sculptures**, a sculpture path with works of art sculpted in wood with a chainsaw by ex-Valaisian ski champ William Besse; the art-endowed **Verbier 3D Parc de Sculptures** between Les Ruinettes and La Chaux; and the two-hour trail from Les Ruinettes along the irrigation channel **Bisse du Levron**. Grander hikes include the 5½ hour **Sentier des Chamois**, a trail popular with wildlife lovers keen to spot chamois, marmots and eagles.

### Adventure Sports

Verbier is becoming known as an adventure-sports centre and there's plenty to choose from. Check in at the tourist office for information on everything from year-round dog-sledding to climbing to *via ferrata*.

**Fly Verbier** PARAGLIDING
(☎027 771 68 18; www.flyverbier.ch; Rte de Verbier Station 23; tandem flight Sfr190; ⏰May-Oct) Want to try tandem paragliding in the Swiss Alps? These guys claim that Verbier's microclimate makes it one of the top five places in the world to fly. Book online or call on the day.

DON'T MISS

**MONT FORT AT SUNRISE**

Nothing stirs the soul quite like seeing the sun rise from the top of **Mont Fort** (adult/child Sfr61/38), at a panoramic 3329m. The Médran **cable car** offers departures on Thursdays in July at 4.45am and in August at 5am. The trip cost covers unlimited travel on cable cars for the rest of the day, and includes an early-bird breakfast in the giant igloo-shaped Les Gentianes **restaurant** (2950m) on the Col des Gentianes. Reserve at least 24 hours in advance at the Médran ticket office on Place de Médran

**Verbier-La Tzoumaz Bike Park** MOUNTAIN BIKING
(☎027 775 25 11; www.verbierbikepark.ch; adult/child day pass Sfr35/18; ⏰8am-5.30pm Jul-Sep, 9am-12.30pm & 1.30-4.30pm Mon-Fri, 9am-4.30pm Sat & Sun Jun & Oct) Ride the Médran cable car from Verbier up to Les Ruinettes to pick up dozens of downhill trails between trees in Verbier's first-class bike park. Trails range from dead easy to super-hard with 2m jumps, and three are equipped with a timing system. There is also a mountain-bike school.

**Trottinettes** SCOOTER RENTAL
(☎027 775 25 11; www.verbier.ch/en/fppoi-trottinettes-les-ruinettes-verbier-19066.html; lift up & scooter down Sfr22; ⏰8am-5pm Jul & Aug, reduced hours Jun, Sep & Oct) Hugely popular with families, *trottinettes* (downhill scooters) are one way of getting down the mountain from Les Ruinettes. Buy your ticket at the ticket office on Place de Médran then ride the Médran cable car up to Les Ruinettes to collect your scooter and helmet. Children under eight years must ride with an adult. Allow one hour for the descent.

## Festivals & Events

**Verbier Festival** MUSIC
(www.verbierfestival.com; ⏰Jul-Aug) Summer's high-profile classical-music festival lasts for two weeks from July to early August. There are plenty of free events during the fringe Festival Off, alongside the official fest.

## Sleeping

There's plenty of top-notch options here, but Verbier is also doable for ski bums on a budget with pre-planning. Rates nosedive by 30% to 50% in July and August.

**Cabane du Mont-Fort** HUT €
(☎027 778 13 84; www.cabanemontfort.ch; dm winter/summer incl breakfast Sfr52/37, incl half-board Sfr92/75; ⊙Dec–mid-May & Jul–mid-Sep; 📶) Above the clouds with mesmerising vistas to the Massif des Combins, this 2457m-high Alpine hut is brilliant for walkers in summer and skiers in winter, with direct access to La Chaux. Expect cosy slumber in pine-panelled dorms and a busy restaurant serving tasty mountain grub. There's 58 beds in 15 rooms.

**Les Touristes** HOTEL €
(☎027 771 21 47; www.hoteltouristes-verbier.ch; Rte de Verbier; s/d from Sfr75/150; P 📶) An authentic original, Les Touristes opened to summer tourists in 1933, well before skiing took off. Today, it is a one-kilometre walk downhill from the hip hub of modern Verbier, next to a fourth-generation bakery in the old village of Verbier. Its 16 rooms are basic with pine trappings, floral bedding, washbasins and shared showers in the corridor.

**Dzardy's Bar & Backpacker** HOSTEL €
(☎027 565 25 31; www.backpacker-verbier.ch; Rte de Verbier 13, Le Châble; dm Sfr39; ⊙bar & hostel reception 4-10pm; 📶) This former bunker has a new raison d'être with its seven no-frills dorms above a busy bar (the hostel reception), 200m from the Le Châble cable-car station. But with Verbier a cable-car ride away, it's a gift. Bring your own sleeping bag, bathroom towel and locker padlock.

★**W Hotel** DESIGN HOTEL €€€
(☎027 472 88 88; www.wverbier.com; Rue de Médran 70, Pl Blanche; d from Sfr300; P 📶) From the coffee tables on each balcony, fashioned from cut-off tree trunks on wheels, to the five-star spa, this sophisticated hotel near the Médran cable car is sensational. At home in four contemporary chalet-style buildings linked by glass corridors, design is the driver here. Choose from the Cozy Room, Wonderful Room, Spectacular Room and WOW Suite collection.

**Hotel Farinet** HOTEL €€€
(☎076 575 23 94; www.hotelfarinet.com; Pl Centrale; rooms from Sfr420; ⊙mid-Dec–Apr; P 📶) The Farinet, above the Xtreme sports shop on Verbier's central square, is legendary. Known as much for its celebrity-studded bars, DJs and clubs as its stylish accommodation, it is *the* address for all-nighters. Rooms range from standard twins to two-bedroom suites to the penthouse suite.

## Eating

★**Le Namasté** SWISS €
(☎027 771 57 73; www.namaste-verbier.ch; Les Planards; mains from Sfr15; ⊙daily mid-Dec–Easter & mid-Jul–Aug, Tue-Sun mid-May–Jun, Sep & Oct) Its name means 'Welcome' in Hindi and it's always packed. Jean-Louis – a metal sculptor who creates fantastical beasts from old tools – and his wife Annick are the creative energy behind this cosy mountain cabin at 1937m with traditional Swiss kitchen. Ski to it from Savoleyres or, come nightfall, skidoo up and sledge down. Drive up in summer.

**Fer à Cheval** PIZZA €
(☎027 771 26 69; http://feracheval.ch; Rue de Médran; pizza from Sfr18, mains from Sfr25; ⊙11am-11pm) Thank goodness for the Horseshoe, an affordable, down-to-earth pizzeria with sunny terrace, electric atmosphere and fabulous food any hour. Find it footsteps from Place Centrale, towards the Médran cable-car station. Our favourite 'table': the wooden cart.

**Chez Dany** SWISS €€
(☎027 771 25 24; www.facebook.com/Chez-Dany-Verbier-1690409104608455; Hameau de Clambin 10; mains Sfr15-30; ⊙9am-midnight Dec-Apr & Jul-Sep) On a sunny plateau at 1720m, high above Verbier village between Les Ruinettes and Médran, this buzzy chalet is a celebrity favourite for juicy steaks on the slopes. The terrace affords sweeping views to the Massif des Combins. Skidoo or ski up and sledge down, or call for a snow taxi.

## Drinking & Nightlife

**Pub Mont Fort** PUB
(☎027 771 90 62; www.pubmontfort.com; Chemin de la Tinte 10; ⊙3pm-2am) In winter, this après-ski heavyweight near the Médran cable car station apparently sells the most beer in Switzerland. Its shots and shakers are equally popular. Enough said.

**Farm Club** CLUB
(☎079 257 78 83; www.hotelnevai.com/farm-club; Rte de Verbier Station 55; ⊙Dec-Apr) A legend in its own right, this swanky club beneath the Nevaï hotel has rocked since 1971. Look gorgeous to slip past the velvet rope and mingle

with socialites out spending daddy's (or sugar daddy's) pension on Moët magnums.

**Off Piste** BAR
(www.wverbier.com/off-piste; Pl Blanche; ⏲11am-8pm) With its comfy sofa seating, cocktails, music and light bites – not to mention the summertime sandy beach with potted palm and olive trees – this outdoor bar run by the W Verbier hotel is a must-visit during the warmer months Watch for live concerts and summertime barbecues.

**Milk Bar** CAFE
(☎027 771 67 77; Rue de Médran 2; ⏲10am-7.30pm) Old but gold, this mythical hut which has been in business since 1936 is justifiably famous for its *grands crus de cacao* (hot chocolate), thick fruity milkshakes, homemade tarts and crêpes dripping in homemade caramel. The atmosphere in the wooden interior is winter toasty and mellow; on the flowery terrace out back, it's laid-back and refreshingly low-key.

## Information

**Tourist Office** (☎027 775 38 88; www.verbier.ch; Pl Centrale; ⏲8.30am-7pm Dec-Apr, to 6pm May-Nov) Extremely efficient set up right on Place Centrale with maps, brochures and English-speaking staff.

## Getting There & Away

Swish *St Bernard Express* trains from Martigny run year-round to Le Châble (Sfr11.40, 30 minutes) from where you can board a Verbier-bound bus (Sfr6.20, 30 minutes) or – in season – the **Le Châble-Verbier** (☎027 775 25 11; www.televerbier.ch; adult single/return Sfr10/15, child Sfr5/8; ⏲7am-4.45pm Nov, to 7.30pm Dec-Apr, Jul & Aug) cable car, across from the train station.

# Sion

POP 32,170 / ELEV 490M

French-speaking Sion is bewitching. Deceptively modern and industrial from afar, this small town that rises abruptly out of the built-up floor of the Rhône valley is deliciously gourmet, with excellent dining options and a surrounding ring of vine-terraced hills criss-crossed with ancient irrigation channels known as *bisses*. The Rhône River bisects Sion and a twinset of 13th-century hilltop châteaux play guard atop a pair of craggy rock hills above the old town.

Sion moves to a relaxed beat, with winemaking (and tasting) playing an essential role in the town's mantra and pavement cafes lining the helter-skelter of quaint lanes that thread sharply downhill from its castles to its medieval Old Town. Market day (Friday) and summertime's high-drama *son et lumière* show – visible from anywhere in town – are Sion musts.

## Sights & Activities

★**Château de Valère** CHATEAU
(Rue des Châteaux; adult/child Sfr8/4; ⏲11am-6pm Jun-Sep, to 5pm Oct-May) Slung on a hillock opposite Château de Tourbillon is this 11th- to 13th-century château that sprouted up around a fortified basilica. The church interior reveals beautifully carved choir stalls, a frescoed apse and the world's oldest playable organ that dates from 1440; summertime concerts on Saturday (4pm) are magical. The château also hosts the **Musée Cantonal d'Histoire** (☎027 606 47 15; adult/child Sfr8/4; ⏲11am-6pm Jun-Sep, to 5pm Tue-Sun Oct-May) and nestles a lunchtime cafe with view within its walls.

### COW FIGHTS

Serious stuff in Val d'Hérens, the tributary valley to the south of Sion, **Combats de Reines** (Cow Fights; Kuhkämpfe in German) are organised to decide which beast is most suited to lead the herd to summer pastures. Contests take place on selected Sundays from March to May and August to September.

Bulls are fed oats concentrate (believed to act as a stimulant) before they charge and lock horns, then try to force each other backwards. The winner, or herd's 'queen', can be worth Sfr20,000. Combatants rarely get hurt so visitors shouldn't find the competition distressing. There is a grand final in Aproz (a 10-minute postal-bus ride west of Sion) in May on Ascension Day, and the last meeting of the season is held at Martigny's Foire du Valais (p145) in October.

## Sion

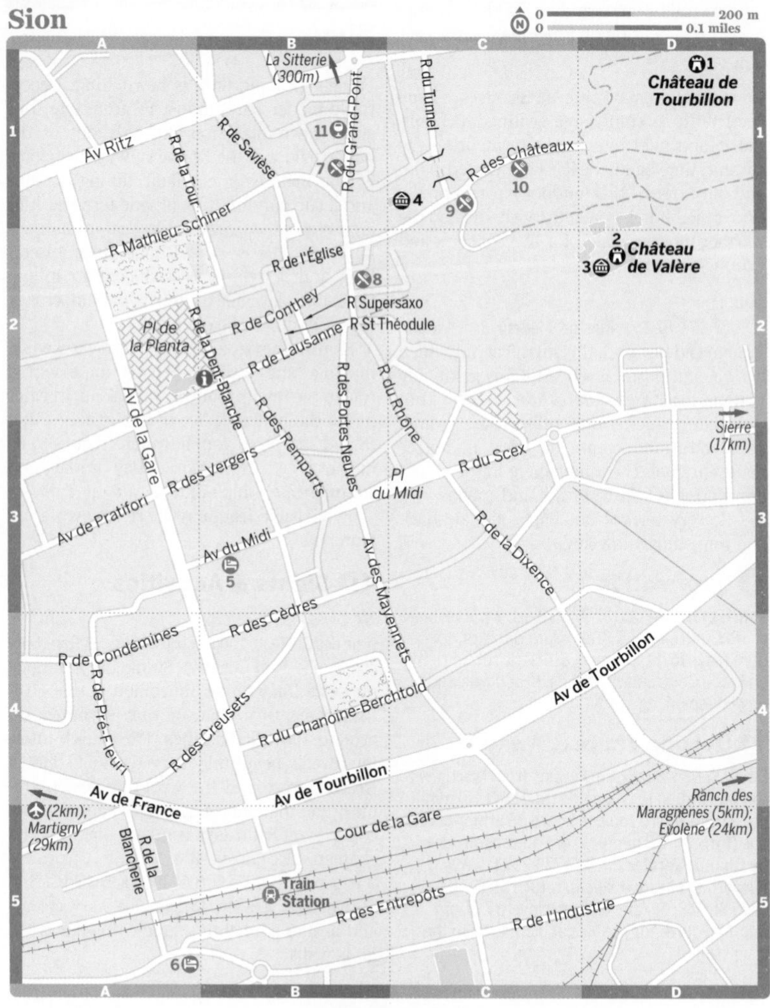


**★Château de Tourbillon** CHATEAU
(Rue des Châteaux; ⏱10am-6pm May-Sep, 11am-5pm mid-Mar–Apr & Oct–mid-Nov) FREE Lording it over the fertile Rhône Valley from its hilltop perch above Sion, the crumbling remains of this medieval stronghold, destroyed by fire in 1788, are worth the stiff trudge for the postcard views alone; wear solid shoes as the rocky path is hairy in places.

**Musée d'Art** GALLERY
(☎027 606 46 90; www.musees-valais.ch; Pl de la Marjorie 15; adult/child Sfr8/4; ⏱11am-6pm Tue-Sun Jun-Sep, to 5pm Oct-May) Lodged in a small château, this well-curated fine-arts museum showcases works by Swiss artists including Ernest Bieler and Caspar Wolf, alongside star pieces by Austrian expressionist Oskar Kokoschka.

**Bisse de Clavau** WALKING
There is far more to hiking around Sion than seductive strolling between grape-heavy vines. What makes trails in this part of the Rhône Valley unique is the *bisses* – miniature canals built from the 13th century to irrigate the steeply terraced vineyards and fields. Best known is the Bisse de Clavau, a 550-year-old

## Sion

**Top Sights**

1 Château de Tourbillon ........ D1
2 Château de Valère ........ D2

**Sights**

3 Musée Cantonal d'Histoire ........ D2
4 Musée d'Art ........ C1

**Sleeping**

5 Hôtel Elite ........ B3
6 Sion Youth Hostel ........ A5

**Eating**

7 Au Cheval Blanc ........ B1
8 Brasserie du Grand-Pont ........ B2
9 La Cave de Tous Vents ........ C1
10 L'Enclos de Valère ........ C1

**Drinking & Nightlife**

11 Le Verre à Pied ........ B1

irrigation channel that carries water to the thirsty, sun-drenched vineyards between Sion and St Léonard.

Vines, planted on narrow terraces supported by drystone retaining walls, are devoted to the production of highly quaffable Valaisian dôle (red) and Fendant (white) wines. Taste them alone or with lunch at **Le Cube Varone** (☎079 566 95 63; www.facebook.com/cube.varone; mains from Sfr20; ⏰11am-9pm Sat, to 6pm Sun May-Oct), an old winegrower's hut on the Bisse de Clavau footpath (7.5km, 2½ hours). Every dish on the tempting menu is paired with an appropriate wine and the vista is out of this world.

## Festivals & Events

**Festival de Sion** MUSIC
(www.sion-festival.ch; ⏰mid-Aug–early Sep) This three-week-long international music festival stages some extraordinary classical concerts (piano, violin), a violin competition, and an accompanying fringe Festival Off with free concerts.

## Sleeping

In-town options are few and disappointingly cookie-cutter; Sion's vine-clad surrounds are more appealing.

**Sion Youth Hostel** HOSTEL €
(☎027 323 74 70; www.youthhostel.ch; Rue de l'Industrie 2; dm/s/d incl breakfast Sfr33/69/98; ⏰Apr-Oct; P 📶) Only 100m from the south exit of Sion train station, the youth hostel offers reasonable rates for single and double rooms, or two-bed/four-bed dorm rooms. A buffet breakfast is included and an evening meal costs Sfr17. There's a lovely garden terrace and spacious dining and lounge areas.

**Hôtel Elite** HOTEL €€
(☎027 322 03 27; www.hotelelite-sion.ch; Av du Midi 6; s/d Sfr120/170; P 📶) Aptly named, this bright, modern, two-star address just off the main street is the best place to stay in town. Rates include a buffet breakfast, the rooms are comfortable, and the location is excellent for exploring Sion.

## Eating

Rue du Grand-Pont, so-called because of the river that runs beneath its entire length, is peppered with tasty places to eat well and drink fine Valais wine. For a coffee or glass of chilled local Fendant, try a cafe terrace on the northern side of Place du Midi or beneath leafy steel pergolas on pedestrian Rue des Remparts.

**Brasserie du Grand-Pont** BISTRO €
(☎027 322 20 96; http://grand-pont.ch; Rue du Grand-Pont 6; mains from Sfr20; ⏰9am-midnight Mon-Sat) On sunny days every table is snagged by noon at this buzzing bistro with art-slung walls and bubbly staff. The 'please everyone' menu takes taste buds around the globe. Note the fabulous Titanic of an old building with rust-coloured shutters and rusty wrought-iron balconies.

★**Au Cheval Blanc** SWISS €€
(☎027 322 18 67; www.au-cheval-blanc.ch; Rue du Grand-Pont 23; mains from Sfr30; ⏰10am-midnight Tue-Fri, 11am-midnight Sat) A local institution known for its great food and convivial vibe, this traditional bistro with leafy pavement terrace on Rue du Grand-Pont uses the best local produce. The icing on the cake is its Val d'Hérens beef prepared just as you like it – as tartare, carpaccio, with vinaigrette, as a *tagliata di filetto* or *en rossini*.

**Au Vieux Mazot** SWISS €€
(☎027 283 11 25; Rue Centrale, Evolène; mains from Sfr20; ⏰10am-midnight Tue-Sat) Don't even consider stepping foot in Evolène in Val d'Hérens, 24km south of Sion by road, without sampling the famed local beef at this legendary spot, also known as Chez Raymonde. Meat lovers melt over the Val d'Hérens beef cooked in a traditional wood-fuelled oven. Otherwise, there's typical raclettes, röstis and so on.

WORTH A TRIP

### SUBTERRANEAN SAILING

Tiny St Léonard, 5.5km northeast of Sion, hides Europe's biggest underground lake, **Lac Souterrain St Léonard** (027 203 22 66; www.lac-souterrain.com; Rue du Lac 21; adult/child Sfr10/6; 10am-5pm mid-Mar–Oct, to 5.30pm Jul-Aug). To see the emerald waters shimmer, join a 30-minute guided tour by boat. Trains link Sion and St Léonard (Sfr3.60, three minutes, hourly).

**Buffet de la Gare de St Léonard** SWISS €€
(027 203 43 43; www.buffet-gare.ch; Av de la Gare 35, St Léonard; mains from Sfr20; 10am-3pm & 6pm-midnight Wed-Sun) This tiny restaurant in St Léonard has cooked up great-value dining courtesy of the same family since 1918 and is well worth the effort to get to. Trains link Sion and St Léonard (Sfr3.60, three minutes, hourly).

**La Sitterie** SWISS €€
(027 203 22 12; www.lasitterie.ch; Rte du Rawil 41; mains from Sfr28, lunch menu Sfr48, dinner menu from Sfr75; 11am-3pm & 6pm-midnight Tue-Sun) An 800m walk north from the old town, chef Jacques Bovier works with seasonal local products to create a dining experience that thrills every time (ever had Chasselas grape sorbet?). Lime green and slate grey dominate the contemporary interior, and summer dining is in a dreamy flower garden with terraced vineyard view.

**L'Enclos de Valère** SWISS €€
(027 323 32 30; www.enclosdevalere.ch; Rue des Châteaux 18; mains from Sfr35, 3-course menu Sfr58; 9am-midnight Tue-Sat, noon-3pm Sun May-Sep, 10am-2pm & 6pm-midnight Tue-Sat Oct-Apr) Midway up the steep cobbled lane leading to Sion's château twinset is this cottagey restaurant with a garden that's bristling with vines and fruit trees (spot the kiwis). Game (goat, chamois, venison) dominates autumn's *ardoise* (blackboard menu).

## Drinking & Nightlife

**Le Verre à Pied** WINE BAR
(027 321 13 80; www.facebook.com/leverreapiedsion; Rue du Grand-Pont 29; 10.30am-1pm & 4.30-8.30pm Mon-Sat, 10.30am-2pm & 5-8pm Sun) To get under the skin of Sion you have to taste its wine and this no-frills *oenothèque* (wine shop) and *caveau* (wine cellar) is the perfect place. Sit in the industrial interior or around an oak barrel outside, and sip your pick of 150-odd Valaisian wines. Cheese and meat platters, oysters and so on, prepared by neighbouring restaurants, quell hunger pangs.

## Information

**Tourist Office** (027 327 77 27; http://siontourisme.ch; Pl de la Planta; 9am-6pm Mon-Fri, to 12.30pm Sat; ) At Place de la Planta, 600m north of the station.

## Getting There & Around

**Aéroport de Sion** (027 329 06 00; www.sionairport.ch; Rte des Aviateurs) Sion airport is 2km west of the train station.

**Valaisroule** (079 127 50 22; https://wallisrollt.ch; Pl de la Planta; 9am-12.15pm & 1-6pm Wed-Sun late May–mid-Oct) Pick up a free bike (four hours) to explore Sion's riverbanks and vineyards.

All trains on the express route between Lausanne (Sfr32, 50 to 80 minutes, half-hourly) and Brig (Sfr20.40, 35 to 45 minutes, half-hourly) stop in Sion.

# Sierre

POP 16,700 / ELEV 533M

One of Switzerland's sunniest towns, Sierre is the last French-speaking town in Valais. The residents of neighbouring Salgesch to the east speak German, as do those further east. Château-dotted vines rise high above the town centre and the local Pinot noir helps keep everyone happy. If you're aiming for Crans-Montana using public transport, Sierre is where Switzerland's longest funicular departs and slices through vineyards and beyond on its uphill climb to Montana Gare.

## Sights

**Sierre Musée Valaisan de la Vigne et du Vin** MUSEUM
(027 456 35 25; www.museeduvin-valais.ch; Rue Ste Catherine 4; adult/child Sfr6/free, free with Salgesch Weinmuseum ticket; 2-6pm Wed-Fri & 11am-6pm Sat-Sun Mar-Nov) This enchanting wine museum with old presses and other wine-related curios sits inside the 17th-century turreted manor of **Château de Villa**. Taste afterwards in the **Oenothèque** (www.chateaudevilla.ch; 10.30am-1.30pm & 4.30-8.30pm Mon-Fri, 10.30am-9pm Sat & Sun), a bulging cellar with 630 Valais wines to try and buy. The museum is a one-kilometre walk from the train station; pick up a map from

the tourist office (p158). This is also the start (or end) of the Sentier Viticole (Vineyards Trail).

**Salgesch Weinmuseum** MUSEUM
(Wine Museum; ☎027 456 45 25; www.museeduvin-valais.ch; adult/child Sfr6/free, free with Sierre Musée Valaisan de la Vigne et du Vin ticket; ⏰2-6pm Mon-Fri, 11am-6pm Sat-Sun Apr-Nov) This gabled wine museum turns the spotlight on wine growing around Salgesch with the focus on education. This is also the start (or end) of the Sentier Viticole (Vineyards Trail). It's a one-kilometre walk from Salgesch station, so easy to use as your start or finishing point.

## Activities

**★Sentier Viticole (Vineyards Trail)** WALKING
(☎027 456 35 25; www.museeduvin-valais.ch) Ask at the Sierre Salgesch Tourist Office for a map to the Sentier Viticole (Vineyards Trail) that links two wine museums, the Musée Valaisan de la Vigne et du Vin de in Sierre with the Weinmuseum in Salgesch. The 6km trail has 80 educational panels about the vines, countryside and local people along the way. Allow two to three hours for the walk and half a day total including the museums.

You can do the walk in either direction and get back to where you started by train.

## Festivals & Events

**Marché des Cépages** WINE, MUSIC
(www.marchedescepages.ch; ⏰early Sep) Sierre's Marché des Cépages is not to be missed. Glass in hand, it is a wonderful walk through vineyards with music, 40 or so local winegrowers to mingle with, and much wine to taste and be merry on. It kicks off between vines on the Salgesch-bound Sentier Viticole behind Château de Villa.

## Sleeping & Eating

**Hotel Arkanum** BOUTIQUE HOTEL €€
(☎027 451 21 00; www.hotelarkanum.ch; Unterdorfstrasse 1, Salgesch; s/d from Sfr110/190; P 📶) If you've ever dreamed of sleeping in a wine barrel or press, make for this quirky hotel in Salgesch where each of the beamed rooms has a different wine-related theme. Its restaurant serves delicious Valaisian specialities and Salgesch wines.

**Hotel Terminus** HOTEL €€
(☎027 455 13 51; www.hotel-terminus.ch; Rue du Bourg 1; s/d Sfr145/230; P 📶) Hotel Terminus has four floors of top-quality rooms within a few hundred metres of Sierre's railway station. Continental breakfast is included to set you up for your day of wine touring. There are superb suites on the upper floors and cuisine by chef **Didier de Courten** (mains Sfr84, tasting menus Sfr190; ⏰noon-1pm & 7-9pm Tue-Sat) if your pockets are deep.

**★Château de Villa** SWISS €€
(☎027 455 18 96; www.chateaudevilla.ch; Rue Ste-Catherine 4; fondue Sfr23-26, mains Sfr25-40; ⏰11.30am-2pm & 6-10.30pm) All turreted towers and centuries-old beams, Sierre's showpiece château rolls out a royal banquet of a raclette – taste five different types of raclette cheese (Sfr35) from the Valais, washed down



### LA BRISOLÉE: A TRADITIONAL AUTUMN FEAST

Come the gold-leaf days of autumn, the last of the grape harvests ushers in the first of the season's sweet chestnuts. And so begins La Brisolée, an autumnal banquet of local produce traditionally shared among family and close friends. Ordering it out is not quite the same, but to savour what is as close as you'll get to the real McCoy try one of these two addresses, highly recommended year-round:

**La Cave de Tous Vents** (☎027 322 46 84; www.cave-tous-vents.ch; Rue des Châteaux 16; mains from Sfr22; ⏰5pm-midnight Sep-Jun) Flickering candles illuminate the brick vaults of this medieval wine bar where couples dine in cosy nooks. Just as gooey is the fondue, including varieties with saffron or chanterelles. Late September to October, its brisolée royale is a magnificent, help-yourself-to-as-much-as-you-can-eat feast of six different Valais cheeses, hot roast chestnuts, apples, pears and dried meats.

**La Grande Maison** (☎027 565 35 70; www.lagrandemaison.ch; Route du Santesch 13, Chandolin-près-Savièse; 4-course meal Sfr78; ⏰5pm-midnight Mon-Fri, 11am-midnight Sat & Sun) Up in the hills 6.5km from Sion is this old house with atmospheric, wood-beamed rooms (double Sfr134 to Sfr160) and a top-notch restaurant to feast on autumnal game and fruits of the local forest – a rare and real treat.

WORTH A TRIP

### FONDATION PIERRE ARNAUD

Don't miss **Fondation Pierre Arnaud** (☎027 483 46 10; www.fondationpierre arnaud.ch; Rte de Crans 1, Lens; adult/child Sfr18/free; ⊙10am-6pm Wed-Sun), a stunning art gallery with mountain peaks looming large on its dazzling mirrored facade and silver-leafed edelweiss in the Alpine rooftop garden. Inside is equally brilliant, with the gallery hosting two contemporary art exhibitions each year. End with lunch in **L'Indigo**, the museum bistro with wooden-decking terrace looking across the serene water of Lac du Louché to the mountains beyond. Take bus 353 from La Poste bus stop in Crans-Montana to Lens (Sfr4.40, 20 minutes).

with perfectly matched local wines. September ushers in that fabulous old Valaisian chestnut, La Brisolée (p157).

## Information

**Sierre Salgesch Tourist Office** (☎027 455 85 35; www.sierre-salgesch.ch; Pl de la Gare 10; ⊙8.30am-6pm Mon-Fri, 9am-5pm Sat, to 1pm Sun) At Sierre station, you'll find friendly staff, plus excellent maps, brochures and advice in English.

## Getting There & Away

By the E62, Sierre is 175km east of Geneva, 45km east of Martigny and 38km west of Brig.

There are two trains per hour heading west to Geneva (Sfr54, two hours) and east to Brig (Sfr15.40, 30 minutes). Hourly trains link Salgesch and Sierre (Sfr3, three minutes).

The town is the leaping-off point for Crans-Montana.

# Crans-Montana

POP 6500 / ELEV 1500M

Crans-Montana has been on the map ever since Dr Théodore Stéphani took a lungful of crisp Alpine air in 1896 and declared it splendid for his tuberculosis patients. Full of sparkling cheer in winter, the modern sprawling resort embracing a string of lakes is now the much-loved haunt of celebrities and the nouveaux riches.

## Activities

Skiing is intermediate paradise, with cruising on sunny, almost exclusively south-facing slopes and 360-degree vistas reaching from the Matterhorn to Mont Blanc. Downhill runs tot up to 160km, boarders play daredevils in the Aminona terrain park and there's 50km of cross-country trails.

Hiking and mountain biking are big in summer.

**Crans-Montana Bike Park** MOUNTAIN BIKING
(www.mycma.ch; Route des Téléphériques 32; half/full day adult Sfr25/30, child Sfr14/15; ⊙Jun-Oct) Downhill speed freaks are well catered for with marked trails and obstacles graded according to difficulty at this mountain-bike park at the base station of the Crans Cry d'Er cable car. There are lots of options here, so check it all out online.

**Alex Sports** SKIING, MOUNTAIN BIKING
(☎027 481 40 61; www.alexsports.ch; Rte des Télépheriques; ⊙9am-5.30pm Dec-Apr, Jul & Aug) This sports shop, next to the Crans Cry d'Er cable car and across the road from the Crans-Montana Bike park, rents out all the gear for summertime mountain biking and winter skiing.

## Festivals & Events

**Caprice Music Festival** MUSIC
(www.caprices.ch; ⊙early Apr) This is considered one of the top snow-music festivals in Europe. A serious party at altitude with stupendous views.

## Sleeping & Eating

**Crans-Montana Youth Hostel** HOSTEL €
(☎027 481 31 14; www.youthhostel.ch; Rte du Zotzet 8; dm/s/d incl breakfast Sfr29/68/78; ⊙Dec-Mar & May-Oct; P 📶) Just opened as a hostel in 2017, this place is the latest use for Bella Lui house, which was built in 1930 and is listed as a historic place. The hostel is centrally located, incredibly reasonable, with fantastic views and breakfast included. The building spent time as a sanatorium, spa and hotel before becoming Switzerland's newest youth hostel.

**Lago Lodge** HOTEL €€
(☎027 481 34 14; www.auberge-lagolodge.ch; Lac Grenon; d/tr/q from Sfr180/234/300; P 📶) A hit with families, this contemporary space on the shore of Lake Grenon is brilliant value. Decor is bright and colourful. The room

for 10 – imagine two doubles and a single topped by an enormous mezzanine covered in mattresses – must be the best 'dorm' in Switzerland.

**★Chetzeron** SWISS €€
(☎027 488 08 09; www.chetzeron.ch; Chetzeron 2112; mains from Sfr25; ⊙Jul-Oct & Dec-Apr; 📶) Laze on chaises longues at 2112m and congratulate yourself on snagging a spot at one of Swiss Alps' hippest mountain hangouts – a restyled 1960s cable-car station. Walk (about 1km) or order a 4WD in summer; or ski in winter, down a blue piste from the top of the **Cry d'Er cable car** (adult single/return Sfr15/20); come dusk, call for a snowmobile ride.

Spacious hotel rooms (double from Sfr320) have stunning views and the kitchen cooks first-class grilled meats, homemade sausages and vegetarian plates.

## Information

**Tourist Office** (☎027 485 04 04; www.crans-montana.ch; Rue Centrale, Crans; ⊙8.30am-6.30pm Mon-Sat) In Rue Centrale, a 300m walk west from Montana Gare at the top of the funicular.



OFF THE BEATEN TRACK

### VAL D'ANNIVIERS

Brushed with pine and larch, scattered with dark-timber chalets and postcard villages set against 4000m peaks, this peaceful valley beckons skiers eager to slalom away from the crowds for fresh powder and hikers seeking big nature.

The road south from Sierre corkscrews precipitously past postage-stamp orchards and vineyards, arriving after 13km in medieval **Vissoie** (www.valdanniviers.ch/tourism/from-niouc-vissoie.html), a valley crossroads for five ski stations. About 11km along a narrow road winding back north towards Sierre is **Vercorin** (www.valdanniviers.ch/tourisme/vercorin.html), geared up for families with gentle skiing on 35km of pistes.

More enticing for skiers are the combined villages of **St Luc** (www.valdanniviers.ch/tourism/saint-luc.html) and **Chandolin** (www.valdanniviers.ch/tourism/chandolin.html), with 75km of broad, sunny runs and fairy-tale panoramas. Chandolin is the more attractive of the two, a huddle of timber houses hanging on for dear life to steep slopes at around 2000m. While here, visit **Espace Ella Maillart** (☎027 476 17 15; www.ellamaillart.ch; Chemin des Tsavonnés) FREE, dedicated to the remarkable Swiss adventurer who lived in Chandolin when she wasn't exploring remote Afghanistan and Tibet, or winning ski races and regattas.

Solar-system models punctuate the **Chemin des Planètes** (Planets Trail; 👪), an uphill amble from Tignousa (above St Luc) to the **Weisshorn Hotel** (☎027 475 11 06; www.weisshorn.ch; s/d with half-board Sfr150/280; ⊙Jun–mid-Oct & late Dec–mid-Apr; 📶). Sitting at 2337m,this grand 19th-century hotel is accessible on foot or by mountain bike only (or on skis in winter, when luggage is transported for you from St Luc). Equally pretty is storybook **Grimentz** (www.valdanniviers.ch/tourism/grimentz-saint-jean.html) with its Valaisian granaries (built on stilts to keep out thieving mice), burnt-timber, geranium-bedecked chalets and ultra-modern cable car linking it to the ski slopes of neighbouring **Zinal** (www.valdanniviers.ch/tourism/zinal-ayer.html).

From Zinal, climbers can approach several 4000m+ peaks, including Dent Blanche (4357m), Obergabelhorn (4063m), Zinalrothorn (4221m), Weisshorn (4506m) and Bishorn (4153m). For climbing and hiking guides, check with **Guides Anniviers** (www.valdanniviers.ch/tourism/guides.html).

About 12km south of Grimentz, the road ends at a sizeable car park, where a network of good hiking trails leads to viewpoints over the impressive **Moiry Glacier**.

Each village has its own small tourist office, but they all come under the umbrella of **Val d'Anniviers Tourism** (www.valdanniviers.ch). Each can tell you about the whole valley as well as their village. All have standard opening hours of 8.30am to noon & 1.30 to 5pm, seven days per week.

PostBuses make the 13km run from Sierre to Vissoie, the valley's transport hub (Sfr10.60, 30 minutes), then branch off for other parts of the valley, including Moiry Glacier. However, the best way to explore the area is with your own wheels.

## Getting There & Away

It's 20km up a very winding road from Sierre to Crans-Montana.

From Sierre train station, a short walk will take you to the station for Switzerland's longest **funicular** (027 481 23 48; www.cie-smc.ch; Gare SMC de Montana; ticket Sfr13.20) that slices through vineyards and beyond on its uphill climb to Montana Gare. Journey time is 12 minutes and a funicular runs every half-hour. Less novel buses also link the two (Sfr13.20, 40 minutes, hourly).

# UPPER VALAIS

Bijou villages of wood chalets stand in collective awe of the drum-roll setting of vertiginous ravines, spiky 4000m pinnacles and monstrous glaciers in the east of Valais. The effervescent thermal waters of Leukerbad, the dazzling 23km Aletsch Glacier, the bubbling resorts of Zermatt and Saas Fee and the soaring pyramid of the Matterhorn attract visitors from far and wide.

## Leukerbad

POP 1600 / ELEV 1411M

Some 14km and 700 vertical metres up a zig zag road from the Rhône Valley town of Leuk is the gorgeous mountain village of Leukerbad. Gazing up to an amphitheatre of towering rock turrets and canyon-like spires, Europe's largest thermal spa resort is pure drama. Beauty-conscious Romans once took to Leukerbad's steamy thermal waters, where today visitors soak after clambering up the Gemmi Pass, braving Switzerland's longest *via ferrata* or carving powder on Torrenthorn.

### Sights

**Torrent-Bahnen** CABLE CAR

(027 472 81 10; www.torrent.ch; Promenade; single/return Sfr11.50/23; 8.45am-12.15pm & 1.15-5.15pm Jul–mid-Oct & late Dec-early Apr) The Torrent cable car carries winter skiers up to **Rinderhütte** (2350m) from where a chair-lift continues to 2610m. Downhill skiing is intermediate. In summer, tearing down the mountain on a **monster scooter** (adult/child Sfr15/12) is the way to go; count one hour for the steep, at times rocky, descent.

### Activities

**Gemmi Pass Hike** HIKING

(www.myswitzerland.com/en-us/the-classic-among-classics.html; Jun-Oct) This classic hike takes walkers from Leukerbad over the Gemmi Pass to Kandersteg in the Bernese Oberland. From Leukerbad, take the **Gemmibahn** (027 470 18 39; www.gemmi.ch; Gemminbahnen; single/return Sfr23/34; 8.30am-noon & 1-5.30pm

DON'T MISS

### FLOATING IN THERMAL SPAS

Somehow it feels downright decadent to float alfresco in toasty-warm 35°C thermal water when the Alpine air is so cold and crisp. Throw in a china-blue sky, a chaise longue in a whirlpool and a snowy-mountain vista and you're dangerously close to heaven on earth. Leukerbad in Upper Valais is a hot choice, in addition to the following:

**Les Bains de Lavey** (www.lavey-les-bains.ch; Rte des Bains 48; adult 3hr Sfr27/18; 9am-9pm Sun-Thu, to 10pm Fri & Sat; ) The thermal water at this tiny spa, just inside the cantonal frontier of neighbouring Vaud and an easy exit off the motorway (follow signs for 'Lavey'), flows from Switzerland's hottest source. There are also hotel, restaurant and 'wellness' facilities here.

**Les Bains d'Ovronnaz** (027 305 11 11; www.thermalp.ch; Rte des Bains 93; adult/child Sfr22/13; 8am-8.30pm or 9pm; ) Combine ski slopes with bath time at this three-pool spa in Ovronnaz, an attractive, family-friendly ski resort a 10km zigzag uphill from Riddes (15km northeast of Martigny). Accommodation and massages are also an option here.

**Thermalbad Brigerbad** (027 948 48 48; www.thermalbad-wallis.ch; Thermalbad 1, Brigerbad; 3hr adult/child Sfr24/15; 9am-9pm; ) In the Upper Valais, open-air Thermalbad Brigerbad, halfway between Visp and Brig, tempts with 12 different indoor and outdoor pools. Children love the curly-wurly water slide down the mountain and there's a campground next door.

Jun-Oct) cable car up to the pass, then follow the well-marked trail for two to three hours to Sunnbüel, before taking the cable car down and bus into Kandersteg. It's spectacular mountain scenery, but be prepared as the weather can change quickly.

This hike is only of medium difficulty unless you decide to not use the cable cars at both ends – you can do both the climb and the descent on foot. Check the website and weather forecast before heading out.

**Adventure Trail Gemmi** VIA FERRATA
(https://sites.google.com/site/viaferratae; ⌚Jul-Sep) Sitting just below the top Gemmi cable car station at 2300m, this *via ferrata* is an unusual 800m horizontal course, with features such as a 65m-long rope bridge and a 20m-high ladder that turns through 540 degrees. Lots of excitement to be had here! Talk to the tourist office (p162) or Alpincenter Leukerbad (p162).

**Klettersteig Gemmi-Daubenhorn** VIA FERRATA
(https://sites.google.com/site/viaferratae; ⌚Jul-Sep) Check out the website if you're interested in Switzerland's longest *via ferrata*. It's only for the adventurous and best tackled with a guide. 216 metres of ladders and 2,000 metres of steel cable have been installed in the rock face of the Dauberhorn, which towers above Leukerbad. Ask about equipment rental and guides at the tourist office or directly to Alpincenter Leukerbad.

**Walliser Alpentherme & Spa Leukerbad** SPA
(☎027 472 10 10; www.alpentherme.ch; Dorfplatz; thermal baths 3hr/day Sfr23/28, with Valaisan Sauna Village Sfr39/53, Roman-Irish bath with/without soap-brush massage Sfr74/54; ⌚pools 9am-8pm, sauna village & baths 10am-8pm) These luxurious baths comprise outside and inside pools with whirlpools, jets, Jacuzzi and dramatic mountain view. There's the Valaisan Sauna Village (lots of rustic wood), the Roman-Irish Bath and the Mountain Spring Spa, with everything from hot-stones to massages to scrubs.

**Leukerbad Therme** SWIMMING
(☎027 472 20 20; www.burgerbad.ch; Rathausstrasse 32; adult/child day ticket Sfr30/16.50, 3hr ticket Sfr25/14; ⌚8am-8pm; 👪) At the bottom of the village near the tourist office, this brash complex sports 10 different indoor and outdoor pools with water ranging in temperature from 28° to 43°C. Throw in whirlpools, massage jets, steam grottoes and a brightly coloured curly-wurly waterslide and the crowds love it. Kids aged under eight years swim for free.

DON'T MISS

### BATHING BY MOONLIGHT

There is possibly nothing closer to heaven on earth than a moonlit dip – or rather a long and lazy, languid lounge – in Leukerbad's invigorating thermal waters. Indulge the last Saturday of the month or 31 July (the eve of Swiss National Day) at Walliser Alpentherme & Spa Leukerbad , which exceptionally opens its pools from 8.30pm until 11.30pm (admission Sfr27 including Valaisan Sauna Village).

## Sleeping & Eating

**Hotel Wildstubel** HOTEL €
(☎027 470 12 01; www.gemmi.ch; Gemmi Pass; d per person from Sfr90; ⌚mid-Dec–late Apr & Jun-Oct; 📶) Ride the Gemmi cable car to this functional high-altitude hotel with a mix of bunk beds and regular doubles, all pine-clad and squeaky clean. Bathrooms are shared and childen under four years sleep for free. Rates are per person, go down with increased numbers and include half-board and return cable car from Leukerbad. All in all, an adventurous place to hang out!

**Hôtel de la Croix Fédérale** HOTEL €€
(☎027 472 79 79; www.croix-federale.ch; Kirchstrasse 43; d/q from Sfr160/289; P📶) The welcome is heartfelt at this flowery chalet wedged between boutiques on main street Leukerbad. Snug rooms are all-pine and the downstairs restaurant serves one of the best feasts in town.

**Thermal Hotels Leukerbad** HOTEL €€
(☎027 472 10 00; http://thermalhotels.ch; Dorfplatz; s/d from Sfr150/250; P📶🏊) Practically filling the central square, this elegant hotel squirrels away the equally delicious Maison Blanche (White House) restaurant in the 'old building' constructed in 1645. Guests want for nothing, including fluffy white bathrobes and matching slippers to stylishly slip into the neighbouring thermal spa and baths run by the hotel.

**Hotel Escher** HOTEL €€

(☎027 470 14 31; www.hotel-escher.ch; Tuftstrasse 7; s/d from Sfr90/170; P 📶) The perfect mix of value-for-money and comfort, rooms at the family-run Escher are cosy modern with feather duvets and crisp white bathrooms. But the real thrill is the spectacular view from the breakfast room – no snoozing over your muesli here!

**La Ferme Gemmet** DELI €

(☎027 470 41 40; www.lafermegemmet.ch; Dorfstrasse 18; ⏰9am-12.15pm & 3-8pm Mon, Tue & Thu-Sat) The Gemmet Farm is no ordinary delicatessen. The stylish shop with shelves of Valais wine on the walls and a glass-covered counter safeguarding carefully aged *alpkäse* (Alpine cheese only produced in summer) and fresh milk (bring your own bottle) is a showcase for produce from the Gemmet family farm, some 50km east towards Brig.

★ **Walliserkanne** SWISS €€

(☎027 472 79 79; www.facebook.com/croixfederale; Kirchstrasse 43; mains from Sfr20; ⏰9.30am-11pm Mon-Sat, 5-11pm Sun) Fondues, perfectly crisp wood-fired rösti and game dishes make this cosy address run by the Grichtling family since 1931 a Valaisian highlight. But the real treat is the house speciality – gargantuan meat steaks sizzling on a hot slate, served on a hefty wooden platter with fries or rösti and dipping sauces – and a big paper bib.

## Information

**Tourist Office** (☎027 472 71 71; www.leukerbad.ch; Ratplatz; ⏰9am-noon & 1.15-pm Mon-Sat) At the bus station building and has everything you could need.

**Alpincenter Leukerbad** (Bergführer Leukerbad; ☎079 754 00 52; www.bergführer-leukerbad.ch) Guiding and equipment rental for Leukerbad's *via ferrata*.

## Getting There & Away

It's a 14km drive up to Leukerbad from Leuk. Hourly postal buses link Leukerbad with Leuk (Sfr12, 30 minutes) and Visp (Sfr20.40, one hour); the bus station adjoins the tourist office.

# Zermatt

POP 5760 / ELEV 1605M

You can sense the anticipation on the train from Täsch: couples gaze wistfully out of the window, kids fidget and stuff in Toblerone, folk rummage for their cameras. And then, as they arrive in Zermatt, all give little whoops of joy at the pop-up-book effect of the **Matterhorn** (4478m), the hypnotically beautiful, one-of-a-kind peak that rises like a shark's fin above town.

Since the mid-19th century, Zermatt has starred among Switzerland's glitziest resorts. British climber Edward Whymper reached the Matterhorn's summit in 1865 and plucky souls have come here ever since to climb: Theodore Roosevelt climbed the Matterhorn in 1881 and a 20-year-old Winston Churchill scaled Monte Rosa (4634m) in 1894. Today skiers cruise along well-kept pistes, spellbound by the scenery, while style-conscious darlings flash designer threads in the town's swish lounge bars. But all are smitten with the Matterhorn, an unfathomable monolith you can't quite stop looking at.

## Sights

Meander main-strip **Bahnhofstrasse** with its flashy boutiques and the stream of horse-drawn sleds or carriages and electric taxis, then head downhill towards the noisy Vispa river along **Hinterdorfstrasse**. This old-world street is crammed with 16th-century pig stalls and archetypal Valaisian timber granaries propped up on stone discs and stilts to keep out pesky rats; look for the

### CLIMBING THE MATTERHORN

Some 3000 alpinists summit Europe's most photographed, 4478m-high peak each year. You don't need to be super-human to do it, but you do need to be a skilled climber (with crampons), be in tip-top physical shape (12-hours-endurance performance) and have a week in hand to acclimatise beforehand to make the iconic ascent up sheer rock and ice.

No one attempts the Matterhorn without local know-how: mountain guides at the Snow & Alpine Center (p164) charge Sfr1600 per person for the eight-hour return climb, including the cable car from Zermatt to Schwarzee and half-board accommodation in a mountain hut. Client:guide ratios are 1:1. Mid-July to mid-September is the best time of year to attempt the ascent. You'll probably be required to do training climbs first, just to prove you really are 100% up to it. The Matterhorn claims more than a few lives each year.

WORTH A TRIP

## GLACIER EXPRESS: THE NUTS & BOLTS

Marketed as the world's slowest express train, the **Glacier Express** (www.glacierexpress.ch; adult/child 1-way St Moritz–Zermatt Sfr153/76.50, obligatory seat reservation summer/winter Sfr33/13, on-board 3-course lunch Sfr45; ⊙3 trains daily May-Oct, 1 daily mid-Dec–Feb) is one of Europe's legendary train journeys. It starts and ends in two of Switzerland's oldest, glitziest mountain resorts – Zermatt and St Moritz – and the Alpine scenery is truly magnificent in parts. But a ticket is not cheap, and to avoid disappointment it pays to know the nuts and bolts of this long mountain train ride, 290km in distance.

➡ Check the weather forecast: ride the *Glacier Express* on a grey, cloudy day and you'll definitely feel you've been taken for a ride. Beneath a clear blue sky is the *only* way to do it.

➡ Don't assume it is hard-core mountain porn for the duration of the journey: the views in the 191 tunnels the train passes through are not particularly wonderful, for starters.

➡ The complete trip takes almost eight hours. If you're travelling with children or can't bear the thought of sitting all day watching mountain scenery that risks becoming monotonous, opt for just a section of the journey: the best bit is the one-hour ride from Disentis to Andermatt, across the **Oberalp Pass** (2033m) – the highest point of the journey in every way. The celebrity six-arch, 65m-high **Landwasser Viaduct**, pictured on almost every feature advertising the *Glacier Express*, dazzles passengers during the 50km leg between Chur and Filisur.

➡ Windows in the stylish panoramic carriages are sealed and can't be opened, making it tricky to take good photographs or film. If photography/video is the reason you're aboard, ditch the direct glamour train for regional express SBB trains along the same route – cheaper, no reservations required, with windows that open, opportunities to mingle with locals and time to stretch your legs when changing trains.

**fountain** commemorating Ulrich Inderbinen (1900–2004), a Zermatt-born mountaineer who climbed the Matterhorn 370 times, the last time at age 90. Nicknamed the King of the Alps, he was the oldest active mountain guide in the world when he retired at the ripe old age of 95.

★**Matterhorn Glacier Paradise** CABLE CAR
(www.matterhornparadise.ch; Schluhmattstrasse; adult/child return Sfr100/50; ⊙8.30am-4.20pm) Views from Zermatt's cable cars are all remarkable, but the Matterhorn Glacier Paradise is the icing on the cake. Ride Europe's highest-altitude cable car to 3883m and gawp at 14 glaciers and 38 mountain peaks over 4000m from the **Panoramic Platform** (only open in good weather). Don't miss the **Glacier Palace**, an ice palace complete with glittering ice sculptures and an ice slide. End with some exhilarating **snow tubing** outside in the snowy surrounds.

★**Gornergratbahn** RAILWAY
(www.gornergrat.ch; Bahnhofplatz 7; adult/child round trip Sfr94/47; ⊙7am-7.15pm) Europe's highest cogwheel railway has climbed through picture-postcard scenery to **Gornergrat** (3089m) – a 30-minute journey – since 1898. On the way up, sit on the right-hand side of the train to gaze at the Matterhorn. Tickets allow you to get on and off en route; there are restaurants at Riffelalp (2211m) and Riffelberg (2582m). In summer an extra train runs once a week at sunrise and sunset – the most spectacular trips of all.

★**Matterhorn Museum** MUSEUM
(☎027 967 41 00; www.zermatt.ch/museum; Kirchplatz; adult/child Sfr10/5; ⊙11am-6pm Jul-Sep, 3-6pm Oct–mid-Dec, 3-7pm mid-Dec–Mar, 2-6pm Apr-Jun) This crystalline, state-of-the-art museum provides fascinating insight into Valaisian village life, mountaineering, the dawn of tourism in Zermatt and the lives the Matterhorn has claimed. Short films portray the first successful ascent of the Matterhorn on 14 July 1865 led by Edward Whymper, a feat marred by tragedy on the descent when four team members crashed to their deaths in a 1200m fall. The infamous rope that broke is exhibited.

**Sunnegga** VIEWPOINT
(www.matterhornparadise.ch; adult/child one way Sfr12/6 return 24/12; 👪) Take a ride on the Sunnegga Express 'tunnel funicular' up to Sunnegga (2288m) for amazing views of the

## Zermatt

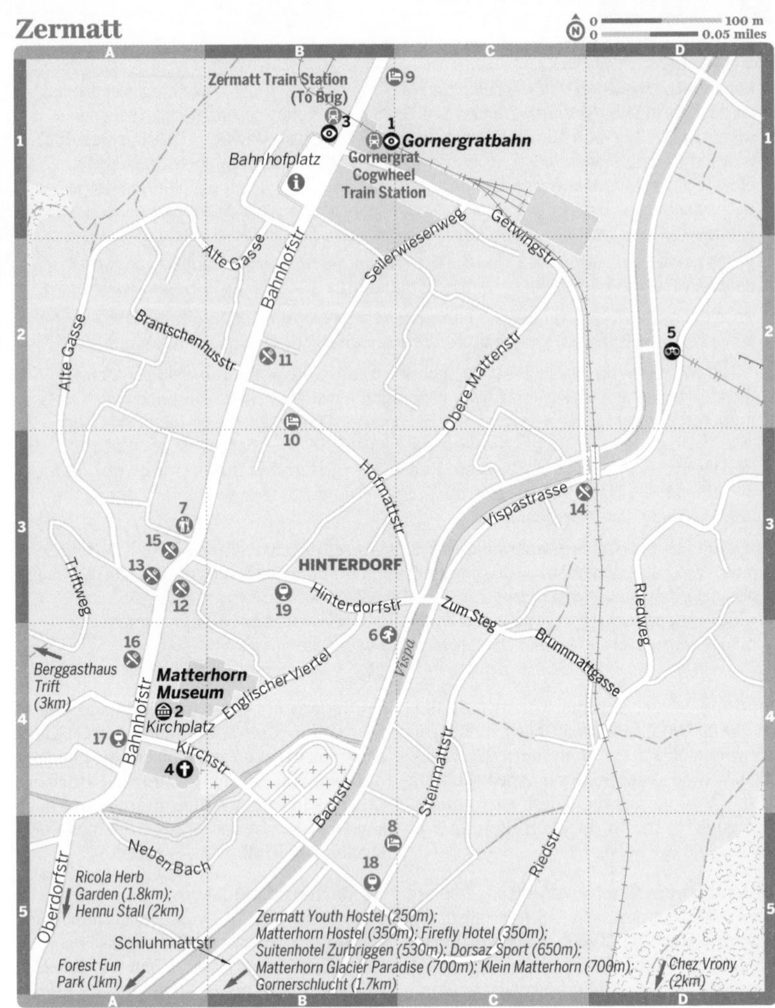


Matterhorn. This is a top spot for families – take the Leisee Shuttle (free) down to the lake for beginner ski slopes at Wolli's Park in winter, and a children's playground plus splashing around in the lake in summer. A marmot-watching station is a few minutes' walk from Sunnegga. It's a relatively easy downhill walk back to Zermatt (via Findeln) in about 1½ hours.

**Mountaineers' Cemetery** CEMETERY
(Kirchstrasse) A walk in Zermatt's pair of cemeteries – the Mountaineers' Cemetery in the garden of Zermatt's **St Mauritius Church** (Kirchplatz) and the main cemetery across the road – is a sobering experience. Numerous gravestones tell of untimely deaths on Monte Rosa, the Matterhorn and Breithorn.

## Activities

An essential stop in activity planning is the **Snow & Alpine Center** (027 966 24 60; www.alpincenter-zermatt.ch; Bahnhofstrasse 58; 9am-noon & 3-7pm Mon-Fri, 4-7pm Sat & Sun Dec-Apr, 9am-noon & 3-7pm Jul-Sep), home to Zermatt's ski school and mountain guides. In winter buy **lift passes** here (Sfr79/430 for a one-day/one-week pass excluding Cervinia, Sfr92/494 including Cervinia).

## Zermatt

**Top Sights**
1 Gornergratbahn ... B1
2 Matterhorn Museum ... A4

**Sights**
3 Glacier Express ... B1
Mountaineers' Cemetery ... (see 4)
4 St Mauritius Church ... A4
5 Sunnegga ... D2

**Activities, Courses & Tours**
6 Air-Taxi ... B4
7 Snow & Alpine Center ... A3

**Sleeping**
8 Chesa Valese ... B5
9 Hotel Bahnhof ... C1
10 Vernissage Backstage Hotel ... B2

**Eating**
11 Bayard Metzgerei ... B2
12 Brown Cow Pub ... A3
13 Le Gitan – Zermatterstübli ... A3
14 Snowboat Bar & Yacht Club ... C3
15 Stefanie's Crêperie ... A3
16 Whymper Stube ... A4

**Drinking & Nightlife**
17 Elsie Bar ... A4
18 Papperla Pub ... B5
19 Z'alt Hischi ... B3



### Skiing

Zermatt is cruising heaven, with mostly long, scenic red runs, plus a smattering of blues for ski virgins and knuckle-whitening blacks for experts. The main skiing areas in winter are **Rothorn**, **Stockhorn** and **Klein Matterhorn** – 52 lifts, 360km of ski runs in all with a link from Klein Matterhorn to the Italian resort of **Cervinia** and a freestyle park with half-pipe for snowboarders.

Summer skiing (20km of runs) and boarding (gravity park at Plateau Rosa on the Theodul glacier) is Europe's most extensive. Count Sfr84/125 for a one-/two-day summer ski pass.

### Hiking

Zermatt is a hiker's paradise, with 400km of summer trails through some of the most incredible scenery in the Alps – the tourist office has trail maps. For Matterhorn close-ups, nothing beats the highly dramatic **Matterhorn Glacier Trail** (two hours, 6.5km) from Trockener Steg to Schwarzsee; 23 information panels en route tell you everything you could possibly need to know about glaciers and glacial life.

For those doing lots of walking, local excursion passes offer a convenient way to get into the high country. A **Peak Pass**, offering unlimited use of the Schwarzsee, Rothorn and Matterhorn Glacier Paradise cable cars plus the Gornergratbahn cog railway, costs Sfr220 for three days or Sfr315 for a week. To find your perfect walk, search by duration, distance and difficulty on the hiking page of the excellent tourist-office website (www.zermatt.ch).

### Adventure Sports

**Air-Taxi** PARAGLIDING
(☎027 967 67 44; www.paragliding-zermatt.ch; Bachstrasse 8; flights from Sfr170) For sky-high mountain views to make you swoon, ride warm thermals alone or in tandem (both summer and winter flights) with Zermatt's paragliding school.

**Forest Fun Park** ADVENTURE SPORTS
(☎027 968 10 10; www.zermatt-fun.ch; Zen Steckenstrasse 110; adult/child Sfr33/23; ⏲10am-7pm Jun-Oct; 👪) Let rip Tarzan-style in the forest with zip-lines, river traverses, bridges and platforms all graded according to difficulty. The easiest of the three trails is for children from age four.

## Sleeping

Book well ahead in winter, and bear in mind that nearly everywhere closes from May to mid- or late June and mid-October to November or early December. With advanced warning, many places will pick you and your bags up at the station in an electro-shuttle. Check when you book.

★ **Hotel Bahnhof** HOTEL €
(☎027 967 24 06; www.hotelbahnhof.com; Bahnhofstrasse; dm Sfr35-50, s/d from Sfr80/120; ⏲closed May–mid-Jun & mid-Oct–Nov; 📶) Opposite the train station, these budget digs have comfy beds, spotless bathrooms and family-perfect rooms for four. Dorms are cosy and there's a stylish lounge with armchairs to flop in and books to read. No breakfast, but feel free to prepare your own in the snazzy, open-plan kitchen. Ski storage room, lockers and laundry available.

## HIKING ZERMATT WITH KIDS

Try out these short-walk favourites for families with younger children:

➡ Take the *Sunnegga Express* up to Sunnegga then the Leisee Shuttle (or walk the 10 minutes) downhill to **Leisee**, a lake made for bracing summer dips with bijou pebble beach and old-fashioned wooden raft for children to tug themselves across the water pirate-style.

➡ In town, embark on the 20-minute walk along the river to the **Gornerschlucht** (☎027 967 20 96; www.gornergorge.ch; adult/child Sfr5/2.50; ⏲9.15am-5.45pm Jun–mid-Oct; 👪), a dramatic gorge carved out of green serpentinite rock and accessed by a series of wooden staircases and walkways.

➡ The easy circular walk around the **Ricola Herb Garden** (www.ricola.com; Blatten; ⏲Jun-Sep; 👪) FREE, in the pretty mountain hamlet of Blatten (signposted from Gornergratschlucht), bristles with aromatic herbs that end up in Ricola sweets and there's a family-fun 'touch and smell' quiz to do.

➡ The 1¼-hour circular walk (2.9km) in Füri takes in the **Gletschergarten Dossen** (Dossen Glacier Garden) with its bizarre glacial-rock formations, a picnic area with stone-built barbecues to cook up lunch, and the dizzying 90m-high, 100m-long steel suspension bridge above the Gornerschlucht Gorge.

**Zermatt Youth Hostel** HOSTEL €
(☎027 967 23 20; www.youthostel.ch/zermatt; Staldenweg 5; dm Sfr42-45, d with shared/private bathroom Sfr130/150; ⏲reception 7am-10pm; 📶) From the sheets stacked at reception to the children's playroom rammed with toys and the line-up of recycling bins in the corridor, every detail has been thought of at this impeccably clean HI hostel. Rooms split across two houses are bright and modern, and the four-course evening meal (Sfr17.50) served in the airy canteen is unbeatable value.

**Chesa Valese** CHALET €€
(☎027 966 80 80; www.chesa-valese.ch; Steinmattstrasse 2; s/d incl breakfast from Sfr180/290; 📶) This traditional burnt-red wood chalet with slate-roof conservatory and flowery garden is romantic, charming and ablaze with red geraniums in summer. Cosy rooms are country-style and the very best stare brazenly at the Matterhorn. Rates include access to the Wellness Centre with sauna, steam bath and Jacuzzi.

**Suitenhotel Zurbriggen** BOUTIQUE HOTEL €€
(☎027 966 38 38; www.zurbriggen.ch; Schluhmattstrasse 68; high season d/ste/apt from Sfr290/420/490; 📶) Owned by Swiss Alpine-skiing legend Pirmin Zurbriggen, this modern hotel with double rooms, suites and apartments has a handy position near the cable-car station for Matterhorn Glacier Paradise. The decor includes picture windows and local larch. Suites have south-facing balconies, allowing you to revel in the Matterhorn's magic, plus there's a smart wellness area with Matterhorn views.

★ **Firefly Hotel** BOUTIQUE HOTEL €€€
(☎027 967 76 76; www.firefly-zermatt.com; Schluhmattstrasse 55; d/q from Sfr595/1590; 📶) From the chopped wood neatly stacked outside to the cowhide chairs, this exquisite Alpine hotel – named after a bar on a paradise island where the owners holidayed – enchants. Earthy design reflects the elements, each kitchen-equipped room venerating fire, water, earth or air. Thankfully, stylish ground-floor **Bar 55** is open to non-guests, too (5pm to 1am).

**Vernissage Backstage Hotel** DESIGN HOTEL €€€
(☎027 966 69 70; www.backstagehotel.ch; Hofmattstrasse 4; s/d from Sfr180/250; 📶) Crafted from wood, glass and the trademark creativity of local artist Heinz Julen, this 19-room lifestyle hotel is effortlessly cool. Cube loft rooms are just that: a loft room with a giant glass cube in their centre with bed on top, and bathroom and kitchenette inside. Check out photos on the website. Rates include use of the Backstage Spa.

## Eating

★ **Bayard Metzgerei** SWISS €
(☎027 967 22 66; www.metzgerei-bayard.ch; Bahnhofstrasse 9; sausage Sfr6; ⏲noon-6.30pm Jul-Sep, 4-6.30pm Dec-Mar) Join the line for

a street-grilled sausage (pork, veal or beef) and chunk of bread to down with a beer on the hop – or at a bar stool with the sparrows in the alley – of this first-class butcher's shop.

**★Snowboat Bar & Yacht Club** INTERNATIONAL €
(☎027 967 43 33; www.zermattsnowboat.com; Vispastrasse 20; mains Sfr22-39; ⏰noon-midnight) This hybrid eating-drinking, riverside address with deckchairs sprawled across its rooftop sun terrace, is a blessing. When fondue tires, head here for barbecue-sizzled burgers (not just beef, but crab and veggie burgers, too), super-power creative salads (the Omega 3 buster is a favourite) and great cocktails. The vibe? Completely friendly, fun and funky.

**Brown Cow Pub** PUB FOOD €
(☎027 967 19 31; www.hotelpost.ch; Bahnhofstrasse 41; ⏰9am-2am, kitchen 9am-10.30pm) Dozens of dining joints line Bahnhofstrasse, including this busier-than-busy pub, one of several eating spots inside the legendary **Hotel Post**. The Brown Cow serves pub grub (hot dogs from Sfr9, burgers from Sfr16) all day.

**Stefanie's Crêperie** CRÊPES €
(Bahnhofstrasse 60; crêpes sweet Sfr5-10, savoury Sfr11-14; ⏰1-10pm) Perfectly thin, light crêpes – topped with a good choice of sweet or savoury toppings – served to go on the main street. Just up from the Snow & Alpine Center.

**★Chez Vrony** SWISS €€
(☎027 967 25 52; www.chezvrony.ch; Findeln; breakfast Sfr15-28, mains Sfr25-45; ⏰9.15am-5pm Dec-Apr & mid-Jun–mid-Oct) Ride the *Sunnegga Express* funicular to 2288m, then ski down or summer-hike 15 minutes to Zermatt's tastiest slope-side address in the Findeln hamlet. Delicious dried meats, homemade cheese and sausage come from Vrony's own cows that graze away the summer on the high Alpine pastures (2100m) surrounding it, and the Vrony burger (Sfr31) is legendary. Advance reservations essential in winter.

**Whymper Stube** SWISS €€
(☎027 967 22 96; www.whymper-stube.ch; Bahnhofstrasse 80; raclette Sfr9, fondue from Sfr25; ⏰11am-11pm Nov-Apr & Jun–mid-Oct) This cosy bistro, attached to the **Monte Rosa Hotel** that Whymper left from to climb the Matterhorn in 1865, is legendary for its excellent raclette and fondues. The icing on the cake is a segmented pot bubbling with three different cheese fondues. Service is relaxed and friendly, tables are packed together, and the place – all inside – buzzes come dusk.

**Le Gitan – Zermatterstübli** SWISS €€
(☎027 968 19 40; www.legitan.ch; Bahnhofstrasse 64; mains from Sfr23; ⏰noon-3pm & 7-10pm) Le Gitan stands out for its elegant chalet-style interior and extra-tasty cuisine. Plump for a feisty pork or veal sausage with onion sauce and rösti, or dip into a cheese fondue – with

## TOP THREE SKY-HIGH SLEEPS

Zermatt is all about big views and there's no finer means of getting to the heart of its trademark mountain panorama than to sleep above the clouds.

**Kulmhotel Gornergrat** (☎027 966 64 00; www.gornergrat-kulm.ch; d incl half-board from Sfr295/335; ⏰mid-May–mid-Oct & mid-Dec–Apr; 📶) At 3100m, Switzerland's highest hotel, at the top of the Gornergrat cogwheel railway, appeals to those who like the atmosphere and views of an Alpine hut, but shiver at the thought of thin mattresses and icy water. The sleek rooms offer downy duvets and picture-perfect views. When the crowds leave, the solitude and panoramas of this century-old hotel are magical.

**Berggasthaus Trift** (☎079 408 70 20; www.zermatt.net/trift; dm/d incl half-board Sfr70/16; ⏰Jul-Sep) It's a long way up to this 2337m-high mountain hut, but the two-hour hike from Zermatt is outstanding. At the foot of Triftgletscher, this haven offers simple, cosy rooms and a great terrace to kick back on to stare out at the mesmeric glacial landscape. Call in advance to ensure a bed and a friendly welcome at this family-run place.

**Monte Rose Hütte** (☎027 967 21 15; www.section-monte-rosa.ch; dm Sfr45, incl half-board Sfr85) 🍃 Hardcore climbers adore Monte Rose Hütte, perched on the edge of the Monte Rose glacier at 2883m and accessible only on foot via a four-hour glacial trail (only for serious mountaineers with a guide). Nonclimbers can admire the solar-powered, crystalline hut deemed the height of state-of-the-art Alpine self-sufficiency from the viewing platform at the top of the Gornergrat railway.

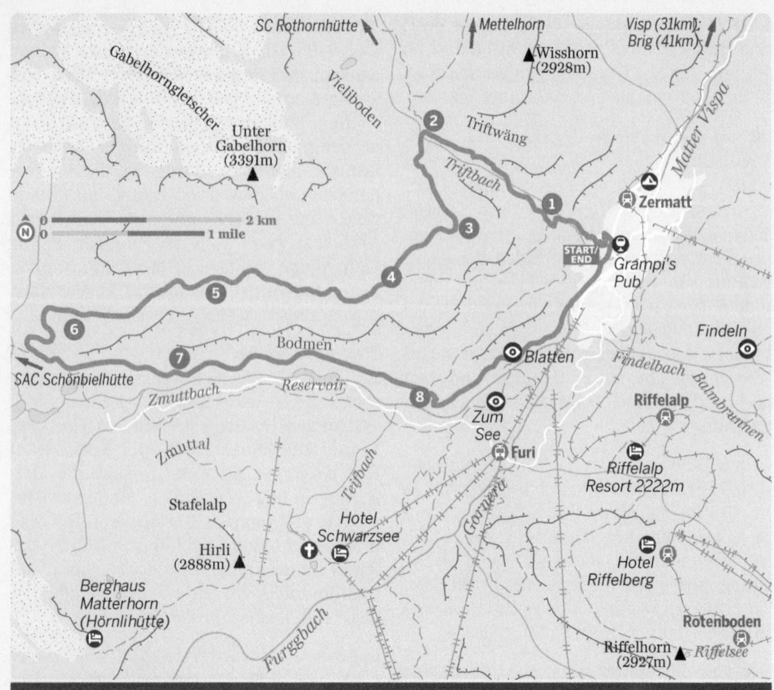


# Walking Tour
# Höhenweg Höhbalmen

**START/FINISH:** ZERMATT
**DISTANCE:** 18KM
**DURATION:** 6½ TO 7½ HOURS

This circular hike embodies all that is unique about the Swiss Alps, leading you into another world of glittering streams, crevassed glaciers and the entrancing angles of Matterhorn and two dozen other 4000er peaks. Depending on the weather, this route can normally be done June to October.

From Zermatt train station walk along Bahnhofstrasse and turn right at Grampi's Pub onto a footpath that climbs above town. Cross the Triftbach and climb through larch forest to 1 **Pension Edelweiss** (1961m). The path rises gently to recross the stream near a hydroelectricity diversion tunnel, then makes several broad switchbacks above the Triftbach Gorge. Continue uphill to 2 **Berggasthaus Trift** (p167; 2337m), a great base if you want to split the hike into two days.

Cross the Triftbach a final time, cutting southward over the tiny Alpine meadow, and begin a zigzagging ascent up the grassy slopes. As you climb onto the high balcony of the 3 **Höhbalmenstaffel**, a sensational panorama unfolds. The trail contours the rolling fields of 4 **Höhbalmen**, where the rare purple-yellow Haller's pasque flower grows, to reach a signpost at 2665m, 40 to 50 minutes from Berggasthaus Trift. Head west: the route traverses narrowing ledges opposite the fearsome north face of Matterhorn, reaching 5 **Schwarzläger** (2741m), the highest point of the walk, after 40 to 50 minutes.

Make a steady, sidling descent over the sparse mountainsides of 6 **Arben**. The path snakes down to meet a more prominent walking track alongside the high lateral moraine wall left by the receding Zmuttgletscher. Follow this down left in zigzags through glacial rubble and continue along gentler terraces above the icy cold Zmuttbach, past a waterfall, to 7 **Kalbermatten** (2105m), one to 1¼ hours from Schwarzläger.

Head on down above a reservoir, bearing right at a junction by the dam wall, to 8 **Zmutt** (1936m), a photogenic hamlet. From here a footpath descends through hay fields, then along the edge of the valley to Zermatt, 1¼ to 1½ hours from Kalbermatten.

Champagne (yes!), or, if you're feeling outrageously indulgent, Champagne and fresh truffles. End with coffee ice-cream doused in kirsch, or apricot sorbet with *abricotine* (local Valais apricot liqueur).

## Drinking & Nightlife

Still fizzing with energy after schussing down the slopes? Zermatt pulses in party-mad après-ski huts, suave lounge bars and Brit-style pubs. Most close (and some melt) in low season.

**Hennu Stall** BAR
(027 966 35 10; www.facebook.com/Hennustall Zermatt; Klein Matterhorn; 2-10pm Dec-Apr) Last one down to this snowbound 'chicken run' is a rotten egg. Hennu is the wildest après-ski shack on Klein Matterhorn, located below Fri on the way to Zermatt. Order a caramel vodka and take your ski boots grooving to live music on the terrace. A metre-long 'ski' of shots will make you cluck all the way down to Zermatt.

**Elsie Bar** WINE BAR
(027 967 24 31; www.elsiebar.ch; Kirchplatz 16; 4pm-1am) In a building originally erected in 1879, this elegant, old-world wine bar with wood-panelled walls, across from the church, has been known as Elsie's since 1961. Oysters, caviar and snails are on the winter menu, along with a top selection of wine and whisky.

**Papperla Pub** PUB
(www.julen.ch; Steinmattstrasse 34; 2pm-2am; ) Rammed with sloshed skiers in winter and happy hikers in summer, this buzzing pub with red director chairs on its pavement terrace blends pulsating music with lethal Jägermeister bombs, good vibes and pub grub (from 5pm). Its downstairs **Schneewittli club** rocks until dawn in season.

**Z'alt Hischi** BAR
(027 967 42 62; www.hischibar.ch; Hinterdorfstrasse 44; 9.30pm-2am Fri & Sat) Squirrelled away in an old wooden chalet, wedged between 17th-century granaries and pig stalls on Zermatt's most photographed street, this bijou watering hole demands at least one late-night drink.

## Information

**Tourist Office** (027 966 81 00; www.zermatt.ch; Bahnhofplatz 5; 8.30am-6pm; ) A wealth of information here, iPads to surf on and free wi-fi.

## Getting There & Away

Zermatt is car-free. Motorists have to park in the **Matterhorn Terminal Täsch** (027 967 12 14; www.matterhornterminal.ch; Täsch; per 24hr Sfr15.50) and ride the Zermatt Shuttle train (return adult/child Sfr16.80/8.40, 12 minutes, every 20 minutes from 6am to 9.40pm) the last 5km up to Zermatt. Täsch is 31km south of Visp.

Dinky electro-taxis zip around town transporting goods and the weary (and noiselessly taking pedestrians by surprise – watch out!). Pick one up at the main rank in front of the train station on Bahnhofstrasse.

Direct trains to Zermatt depart hourly from Brig (Sfr38, 1½ hours), stopping at Visp en route. Zermatt is also the start/end point of the Glacier Express (p163) to/from St Moritz.

# Saas Fee

POP 1760 / ELEV 1800M

Hemmed in by a magnificent amphitheatre of 13 implacable peaks over 4000m and backed by the threatening tongues of nine glaciers, the village of Saas Fee looks somewhat tiny in the revealing light of summer. Until 1951 only a mule trail from Saas Grund in the valley below led to this isolated outpost and locals scraped a living from farming.

Nowadays, the benefits of the popularity of winter sports and a worldwide tourism boom are clear to see. Saas Fee is an affluent, car-free resort where every well-to-do skier and hiker wants to be. Modern chalets surround the village, but its commercial heart, well endowed with old timber chalets and 19th-century granaries built on stilts to keep the rats out, retains a definite old-world charm.

You'll have to drive or hop on a bus to get here. Unlike neighbouring Zermatt, one valley over, Saas Fee is not accessible by train.

## Sights

**Allalin** GLACIER
(Saas Fee–Allalin single/return Sfr53/72) Year-round, the underground Mittelallin funicular climbs to an icy 3500m where the world's highest **revolving restaurant** on the Allalin glacier basks in glorious 360-degree views of Saas Fee's 4000m glacial giants. Wrap up warm to visit the subzero **Eispavillion** (ice cave), hollowed out 10m below the ice surface, or soar down Feegletscher's 20km of summer ski slopes. To reach the glacier, ride the Alpin Express cable car to Felskinn (3000m), then the funicular.

## FAMILY FAVE: MARMOT SPOTTING

They may spend nine-tenths of their lives underground (sleeping, hiding from predators and in hibernation), but come the warm sunny days of July, marmots pop out of their painstakingly dug tunnels and burrows beneath the slopes to stretch their legs, take in the air and unwittingly entertain walkers.

The rocky slopes above the tree line in **Spielboden** (2443m) shelter colonies of the small alpine mammal known for its shrill whistle. Unusually, these Valaisian marmots are not fearful of humans and will happily eat carrots, peanuts and bread from your hand.

To see marmots close-up, ride the **Spielbodenbahn cable car** from Talstation Längflue to mid-station Spielboden (single/return Sfr24/34) and buy some *marmeltierfutter* (marmot food, aka small plastic bags of chopped carrot, bread chunks and peanuts in shells, which the marmots shell themselves) for Sfr4.50 from the Spielboden restaurant across from the cable-car station. Then amble downhill along the steep path keeping your eyes peeled. It takes 2½ hours to walk down to Saas Fee village.

**Hohsaas** CABLE CAR
(www.hohsaas.info) There's a lot of fun to be had from Saas Grund, down in the valley below Saas Fee. The Kreuzboden and Hohsaas gondolas are ready to whisk you up to 3145m on the east side of the Saastal for stupendous views of the Mischabel chain, including Alphubel and Allalinhorn. Put on your skis in winter or hiking boots in summer. There are also **monster scooters** for downhill descents to Saas-Grund. Postbuses to Saas-Grund from Saas-Fee (Sfr3.60, 10 minutes) depart regularly.

**Saaser Museum** MUSEUM
(Dorfstrasse 6; adult/child Sfr5/2.50; ⌚10-11.30am & 2-5pm Tue-Sun mid-Dec–Apr, 10-11.30am & 1.30-5.30pm Jul & Aug) Meander along the main street, past the church, to this old wooden Valaisian house where village life in the 19th century is evoked through traditional embroidered costumes, household items and other ethnographic exhibits.

## Activities

### Skiing & Snowboarding

Saas Fee's slopes are snow-sure, with most skiing taking place above 2500m on 145km of pistes, suited to beginners and intermediates. Boarders gravitate towards the kickers, half-pipe and chill-out zone at the glacial freestyle park on Allalin (p169) in summer and lower down the slopes at **Morenia** (2550m) in winter. Ski-mountaineering is possible along the famous **Haute Route to Chamonix**. A one-/six-day lift pass costs Sfr71/376. For lessons get in touch with the **Swiss Ski & Snowboard School** (☎027 957 23 48; www.skischule-saas-fee.ch; Dorfplatz 1; ⌚9am-noon & 3-6pm Mon-Fri, 3-6pm Sat & Sun), also home to Saas Fee's mountain guides.

### Hiking

The tourist office (p172) has bags of information on 350km of summer trails ranging from kid-easy to jaw-droppingly challenging. Walkers can buy individual one-way tickets for cable cars.

### Adventure Sports

★ **Abenteuerwald** ADVENTURE SPORTS
(Adventure World; ☎027 958 18 58; www.saas-fee.ch/en/seilpark; Hochseilgarten; adult/child Sfr31/26; ⌚10am-7pm Mon-Sat Jul & Aug, noon-6pm Tue-Sat Jun & Sep–mid-Oct; 👪) Known far and wide among local outdoor types, this tree-climbing course is spectacular. Wannabe Janes and Tarzans can across suspension bridges, monkey nets and various other obstacles strung up high between trees. It is the zip wires that cross the Fee Gorge, however, that really stun. Not for the vertigo-prone or children under 115cm in height.

**Feeblitz** LUGE
(www.feeblitz.ch; Panoramastrasse; 1/6/10 descents adult Sfr6.70/37.70/61, child Sfr4.70/26/42; ⌚Jun-Oct & mid-Dec–Apr; 👪) Cross the bridge over the river and turn along Mischistrasse to reach Saas Fee's speed-fiend luge track, next to the Alpin Express cable car.

**Hannig** SCOOTER RENTAL
(☎027 957 26 15; www.saas-fee.ch/en/adventure; scooter 1 descent Sfr10; ⌚8.45am-4.45pm; 👪) In summer take the family up to Hannig (2350m) to devour a ravishing glacial panorama while the kids run riot on a woodcrafted playground with 14m tube slide. Hire

a mountain scooter and helmet from Hannigbahn top station and fly down the mountain on a bone-rattling, 5.5km-long dirt track. The less adventurous can walk (1½ hours).

## Sleeping

During the winter ski season (December to April) many hotels only offer half-board. Most close in May and November. Irrespective of season, hotel guests and those staying in self-catering chalets get a free **Visitor's Card**, which yields a bonanza of savings, including reduced car-parking fees, cable-car tickets and so on.

**★WellnessHostel 4000** HOSTEL €
(027 958 50 50; www.wellnesshostel4000.ch; Panoramastrasse 1; dm/s/d incl breakfast from Sfr43/106/127; reception 7am-10pm Jun-Apr; ) This striking, modern building next to 17th-century granaries on stilts is possibly Switzerland's loveliest hostel. It adjoins a pool and spa with gym, various saunas and steam baths, and tea station. Sharp and stylish rooms range from six-bed dorms to swanky family rooms and doubles, and standard rates include the pool. 'Experience-4000plus' rates throw in the gym and spa.

**Hotel Metropol Saas Fee** HOTEL €€
(0279585858; www.metropol-saas-fee.ch; Untere Dorfstrasse 35; d incl breakfast from Sfr220; ) The original Metropol Grand Hotel, built in 1893, indicated the first signs of tourism in Saas Fee, and the modern refurnished Metropol certainly lives up to expectations. Comfortable rooms, delicious meals, a spa and indoor pool, huge sun terrace and popular bar are features here.

**Sunstar Boutique Hotel Beau-Site** BOUTIQUE HOTEL €€
(027 958 15 60; www.saasfee.sunstar.ch; Obere Dorfstrasse 30; r from Sfr280; mid-Dec–mid-Apr & mid-Jun–mid-Oct; ) Right in the village heart on the main drag, Beau-Site is as beautiful as its name suggests. Service is polished, rooms are classically elegant with antique furnishings, and on winter days nothing beats the fireplace bar or the spa's steam baths, grotto-like pool and saunas.

## Eating

**Gletscher Grotte** SWISS €
(027 957 21 60; www.gletschergrotte.ch; mains from Sfr15; 9am-4pm Dec-Apr & Jun-Oct) Follow the hip crowd to this historic wooden chalet out in the middle of nowhere, where you can snuggle up in sheepskin and feast on raclette, rösti and other heart-warming winter fodder.

**★Spielboden** SWISS €€
(027 957 22 12; www.spielboden-saasfee.ch; Spielboden; mains from Sfr20, 3-course menu Sfr65; 10am-4pm mid-Dec–Apr & Jul–Sep) This stylish *bergrestaurant*, next to the cable-car station of the same name at 2450m, is a real treat. Its unassuming exterior hides a striking 'mountain chic' interior with contemporary wooden furnishings, appealing bar area and bijou terrace with chaises longues to take in coffee and staggering mountain panoramas. Cuisine is contemporary and delicious.

**La Gorge** SWISS €€
(027 958 16 80; www.lagorge.ch; Blomattenweg 2; mains Sfr15-39; 8am-11.30pm Jul-Apr; ) Head to the Gorge to feast on incredible aerial views of glacial white water racing in the Fee Gorge far below; a second terrace offers views to the Allalin glacier. Two stone knight-in-shining-armour turrets complete the setting. Cuisine is predictable Swiss.

**Fletschhorn** FRENCH €€€
(027 957 21 31; www.fletschhorn.ch; Eggen; mains Sfr25-55, lunch menu Sfr90; mid-Dec–Apr & Jul–mid-Oct) Tucked in a forest glade, this Michelin-starred hotel-restaurant with dramatic views is among Switzerland's top addresses. Chef Markus Neff interprets French cuisine with finesse, with signatures such as crispy, rosemary-infused suckling pig and roast pigeon with black truffles. The sommelier will help you choose a bottle of wine from the 30,000 on the list. You'll need help to pick one.

## Drinking & Nightlife

**Black Bull Snowbar** BAR
(079 301 09 00; www.facebook.com/BlackBullSnowbar; Dorfstrasse 53; 3.30pm-2am) Near the river, this wooden hut with bar stools to squat on outside is high-energy people-watching terrain. Full-on après-ski fun.

**Popcorn!** BAR, CLUB
(027 958 19 14; www.popcorn.ch; Obere Dorfstrasse 6; 8pm-4am) A hip, long-standing favourite that never seems to lose its street-cred, this party bar is as wild as the party gets in Saas Fee. Its hotel rooms (dorm Sfr35, doubles from Sfr100) are strictly for party lovers; ask for the highest floor possible if you're keen to sleep.

### Information

**Tourist Office** (☎ 027 958 18 58; www.saas-fee.ch; Obere Dorfstrasse 2; ⏰ 8.30am-noon & 2-6pm Mon-Fri, 8am-6pm Sat, 9am-noon & 3-6pm Sun) At the entrance to the village.

### Getting There & Away

Buses depart half-hourly from Brig (Sfr19.60, 1¼ hours) and Visp (Sfr16.60, 45 minutes). If coming from Zermatt, get off the train at Stalden and hop on the bus there.

By road, Saas Fee is 28km south of Visp and 38km from Zermatt. Saas Fee is car-free; park at the village entrance (Sfr19/14 per day winter/summer) and walk in, or pay for an **electric taxi** (☎ 079 220 21 37) to take you to your hotel.

## Brig

POP 13,000 / ELEV 688M

Close to the Italian border and bisected by the Rhône and Saltina rivers, lively Brig has been an important crossroads since Roman times. It's worth lingering to see the cobbled Stadtplatz, framed by al fresco cafes and candy-hued townhouses. Cafe terraces, restaurants and hotels abound on central square Hauptplatz and Alte Simplonstrasse. For a lovely drive, head 22km south of town to **Simplon Pass**, which links Brig with Domodossola, Italy.

Kaspar von Stockalper (1609–91), a shrewd businessman who dominated the Simplon Pass trade routes, built **Stockalper Palace** (☎ 027 921 60 30; www.facebook.com/stockalperschloss; Alte Simplonstrasse 28; adult/child Sfr8/free; ⏰ 9.30am-4.30pm Tue-Sun) and dubbed himself the 'Great Stockalper'. Locals didn't like his bloated ego and sent him packing to Italy. Wander for free the main court and beautiful baroque gardens with quintessential parterres, fountains and clipped hedges.

### Information

**Tourist Office** (☎ 027 921 60 30; www.brig-tourismus.ch; Bahnhofplatz 2; ⏰ 8am-noon & 1.30-5pm Mon-Fri) Over the road from the train station.

### Getting There & Away

Brig is 211km east of Geneva and 80km east of Martigny on the E62. It's 68km further east to Andermatt.

Brig is a stop for the Glacier Express (p163) from Zermatt to St Moritz.

Brig is also on the main line between Italy (Milan via Domodossola) and Geneva (Sfr60, 2½ hours, hourly).

## Aletsch Glacier

The mighty Aletsch Glacier, at 23km, is the longest glacier in the European Alps and a Unesco World Heritage Site. Streaming down in a broad curve around the Aletschhorn (4195m), the glacier looks just like a frozen three-lane superhighway and is breathtaking.

While most view the glacier from its head at Jungfraujoch in the Bernese Oberland, the best views are from Eggishorn (2927m), Bettmerhorn (2647m) and Moosfluh (2333m) in Valais. These viewpoints sit at the top of cable cars and lifts climbing from Fiesch, Bettmeralp (1950m) and Riederalp (1925m). There are superb hikes (p174) above the glacier.

Depending where you are viewing from, if the weather is good you may see the jewels of the Bernese Oberland – the Eiger, Mönch and the Jungfrau – more or less directly to the north, at the head of the glacier.

### Getting There & Away

You'll want to get to Eggishorn, Bettmerhorn or Moosfluh via cable cars and lifts climbing from Fiesch, Bettmeralp and Riederalp.

Fiesch is on the railway line between Brig (40 minutes, Sfr10.60, hourly) and Andermatt (1½ hours, Sfr26, hourly). By car it's 18km northeast of Brig. There's a huge car-park area at the base of the cable car.

The base train stations Mörel (for Riederalp) and Betten (for Bettmeralp) are also on the train route between Brig and Andermatt. Cable-car departures are linked to train arrivals. Mörel is 8km and Betten is 15km northeast of Brig. There are large car-park areas at the valley base of each of the cable-car stations.

### Fiesch

POP 1000

Fiesch sits in the Rhône Valley at 1049m, 18km northeast of Brig. It's a ski village in winter and a hiking, paragliding and 'viewpoint' village in summer. While many come to play in the magnificent surrounding alpine landscape, many more turn up to take the cable cars up to Eggishorn for one of the most thrilling natural highs around: a view of the spectacular Aletsch Glacier.

The **Fiesch & Eggishorn Cable Car** (www.eggishorn.ch; Furkastrasse; adult/child return from Fiesch Sfr45/22.50) climbs to the Eggishorn lookout in two stages. The first ascends from Fiesch to Fiescheralp (2212m), where you'll find ski lifts, hiking trails and places to stay and refuel. The second cable car then continues up to Eggishorn.

Nothing can prepare you for what awaits on arrival – the full 23km length of the Aletsch Glacier, plus, in the distance, the glistening summits of Jungfrau (4158m), Mönch (4107m), Eiger (3970m) and Finsteraarhorn (4274m).

Fiesch is also a paragliding hot spot. **Flug Taxi** (027 971 53 21; www.flug-taxi.ch; Fieschertalstrasse 57; flights from Sfr130) offers some great tandem-flight options and a paragliding school.

## Information

**Fiesch Tourist Office** (027 970 60 70; www.fiesch.ch; Furkastrasse; 8.30am-noon & 1.30-5pm Mon-Fri, 9am-4pm Sat) In the middle of Fiesch village (not at the train station).

## Getting There & Away

Fiesch is on the railway line between Brig (40 minutes, Sfr10.60, hourly) and Andermatt (1½ hours, Sfr26, hourly). By car, it's 18km northeast of Brig.

# Bettmeralp & Riederalp

POP 990

This twinset of family-friendly car-free hamlets, up high at over 1900m, is accessible only by cable car from the Rhône Valley floor far below. It's like going up to a different world; this is the stuff of Swiss Alpine dreams. Paved with snow December to March, kids are pulled around on traditional wooden sledges and skis are the best way to go to the local supermarket at the top of the cable car.

## Sights

**Centre Pro Natura d'Aletsch** MUSEUM

(www.pronatura-aletsch.ch; Riederfurka; 9am-6pm mid-Jun–mid-Oct) A summer-must in Riederfurka (2065m), a chairlift ride or 20-minute walk uphill from Riederalp, is this Alpine garden and exhibition on local flora and fauna. It's at Villa Cassel, an exquisite villa built as a summer residence on the slopes for a rich Englishman in 1902. There's also a top nature walk that rounds the nearby Riederhorn.

## Activities

### Winter Sports

With the run at the top of the Bettmerhorn cable car skirting the edge of the Aletsch Glacier, skiing is sensationally picturesque – 250km of easy or intermediate ski runs lie in the so-called **Aletsch Arena** (www.aletscharena.ch) ski area, with a one-day ski pass costing Sfr55 (Sfr60 with cable car up from the valley).

DON'T MISS

### ULTIMATE GLACIER VIEW

If you've got a head for heights, the ultimate panoramic platform is the 124m-long **Aletschji–Grünsee Suspension Bridge** (late Jun–mid-Oct) across the terrifyingly untamed, 80m-deep **Massa Gorge** at the foot of the Aletsch Glacier. Glacial views are unparalleled. Pick up the trail, accessible June to October, behind Berghotel Riederfurka and allow five hours for the complete hike from Riederalp to Belalp.

This trail can also be walked in the opposite direction from Belalp to Riederalp. Belalp is accessed by Postbus from Brig.

### Hiking

Hiking in the summer is as mind-blowing as the winter sports. From Bettmeralp take the cable car to Bettmerhorn for a bird's-eye glacier view. Exit the station and follow the wooden walkway through oversized boulders to the so-called Eis Terrasse (Ice Terrace), where information panels tell you about the glacier and several marked footpaths start.

From Riederalp, the Moosfluh cable car runs in summer, taking you up to Moosfluh, from where there are tracks leading alongside and above the Aletsch Glacier.

## Sleeping & Eating

★**Berghotel Riederfurka** HOTEL €

(027 929 21 31; www.artfurrer.ch; Riederfurka; dm incl breakfast Sfr65, d Sfr130-150; ) Planted firmly on the *alpages* (pasture) up high in Riederfurka, this oasis of peace, tranquillity and Alpine tradition has been around with the cows since the mid-19th century. Rooms are cosy, with lots of wood, and the restaurant is one of the best on the slopes.

**Villa Cassel** HISTORIC HOTEL €€

(027 928 62 20; www.pronatura-aletsch.ch/vacations; Riederfurka; dm incl breakfast/half-board Sfr50/70, d Sfr170/210; mid-Jun–mid-Oct; ) Short but sweet is the season at this fabulous mountainside villa, the stunning summer pad of wealthy Englishman Ernest Cassel who – so the story goes – had to pay local farmers to stuff the bells of their cows with hay after their incessant ringing upset one of his house guests – a young Winston Churchill no less. Rooms today are simple pine with shared bathrooms.

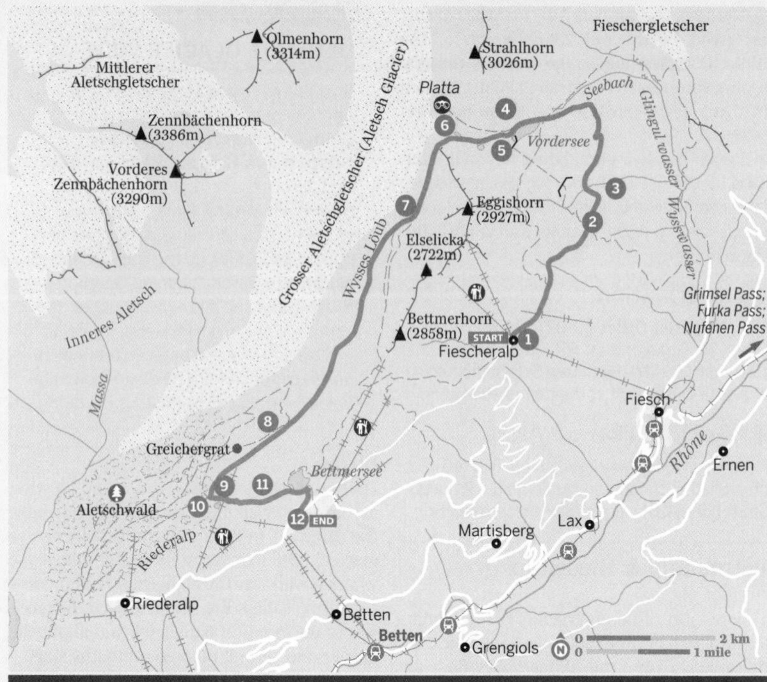


# Walking Tour
# Aletsch Glacier

**START** FIESCHERALP
**FINISH** BETTMERALP
**LENGTH** 17KM; FIVE TO SIX HOURS

This high-Alpine walk is a nature-gone-wild spectacle of moors, jagged mountains and deeply crevassed glaciers. From **1 Fiescheralp cable-car station** (2212m), views are immediately spectacular as you walk northeast along the flat dirt trail. Bear right past the path going up to Eggishorn and the turn-off to Märjela via the small **2 Tälli tunnel** – to shorten the route by an hour you can walk through the dimly lit tunnel.

The route soon becomes a broad well-graded foot track, lined with bilberry bushes and tantalising glimpses of Fieschergletscher's icy tongue. Wind your way around the slopes high above the Fieschertal, up through the grassy, rock-strewn gully of **3 Unners Tälli**. Begin a steeper climb in several switchbacks to a small wooden cross erected on a rock platform.

Follow white-red-white markings westward across rocky ledges to the tiny valley of the **4 Märjela**; a signpost marks the junction of trails coming from the Fieschertal and the Tälligrat. Around two hours from Fiescheralp, you reach the **5 Gletscherstube mountain hut** (2363m), a cosy wooden hut.

Head down past several little tarns, crossing the stream at a cairn before making your way to the **6 Märjelensee** (2300m) after 30 minutes. Bordered by the icy edge of the Aletsch Glacier, this lake presents a dramatic picture. Climb southward around a rocky ridge and sidle up to a signposted path fork at **7 Roti Chumma** (2369m). Take the lower right-hand way along a magnificent route high above what seems like an endless sweep of ice. After **8 Biel**, a saddle on the Greichergrat at 2292m where a path turns down right to the Aletschwald, head southwest along a tarn-speckled ridge. Continue along the grassy slopes to **9 Moosfluh** (2333m).

The route continues along the ridge on a short section of marked foot track (not on some walking maps), cutting down leftward to the inky-blue **10 Blausee** (2204m). Duck under the chairlift and drop eastward to **11 Bettmersee** for a refreshing dip. From here a dirt road leads to **12 Bettmeralp**.

**Chüestall** SWISS €€
(☎027 927 15 91; www.chuestall-blausee.ch; Riederalp; mains from Sfr20; ⏰10am-4.45pm Jun-Oct & Dec-Apr) 'Cowshed' is what its name means and that is exactly what this thoroughly modern address on the slopes at 2207m was until 1961. Walk or ski to it from the top of the Moosfluh cable car in Riederalp or Bettmeralp's Blausee (Blue Lake) chairlift.

## Getting There & Away

The cable-car base stations for these resorts – Mörel (for Riederalp) and Betten (for Bettmeralp) – are on the train route between Brig and Andermatt.

From Mörel, east to Andermatt (Sfr30, 1¾ hours, hourly) and west to Brig (Sfr5.20, 15 minutes, hourly).

From Betten, east to Andermatt (Sfr29, 1½ hours, hourly) and west to Brig (Sfr6.80, 25 minutes, hourly).

Mörel is 8km and Betten is 15km northeast of Brig. There are large car-park areas at the valley base of each of the cable-car stations.

## Getting Around

It's an easy 2km amble between trees from Bettmeralp to Riederalp; electric shuttle buses (Sfr6, 10 minutes, hourly June to October) and snowmobile taxis (winter) also link the two.

# Furka Pass

Marking the cantonal frontier between Valais and Uri, the **Furka Pass** (2431m) is the gateway into southeast Switzerland. The run up to the pass offers superlative views over the fissured Rhône glacier. From the tiny Valais village of Gletsch (1762m), it's a nearly continuous 10km climb to the pass, followed by a jaw-dropping 21km descent to Andermatt.

Driving or riding a motorbike over the pass is a popular activity – immortalised in the car chase in the 1964 James Bond classic, *Goldfinger*. You'll want to take great care on the countless hairpin corners of this curly mountain road, first opened in 1867.

The Furka is not the only pass in these parts. Crossing the **Grimsel Pass** (2164m) will take you north to Meiringen, while the **Nufenen Pass** (2478m) leads east into Ticino. All of these alpine passes are only open in summer, generally from 1 June (depending on snowfall and weather conditions). You can still get your vehicle from Valais to Andermatt in winter, though – car trains from Oberwald head through the 15km-long **Furka Base Tunnel**, re-surfacing at Realp near Andermatt.

## Sights & Activities

★**Rhône Glacier** GLACIER
Coming from Valais, the mesmerising Rhône Glacier is first seen from the tiny hamlet of Gletsch. This glacier is the source of the Rhône River, which flows the length of Valais, into Lake Geneva, then south to the Mediterranean. Still 8km long, the glacier has lost 1.4km of its length since 1870. Recent frightening calculations estimate it will lose 50% of its ice volume by 2050 and be down to 10% of the present volume by 2100.

★**Rhône Glacier Ice Grotto** WALKING
(☎027 973 11 29; www.gletscher.ch; Furkastrasse; adult/child Sfr9/6; ⏰8am-6pm, to 7pm midsummer) Head up the Furka Pass road, park next to the closed Hotel Belvédère close to the summit, and take the one-kilometre walk to the Rhone Glacier Ice Grotto. The walk reveals stupendous views, while strolling inside the glacier is enthralling. The Ice Grotto opens up when the pass road does each year.

**Steam Trains** RAIL
(Dampfbahn Furka-Bergstrecke; www.dfb.ch; one way/return Sfr73/121; ⏰Fri-Sun late Jun-early Oct, daily early Jul–mid-Aug) Historic steam trains run on the old tracks that were superseded by the Furka Base Tunnel when it opened in 1982. Trains run between Realp (west of Andermatt) to Oberalp in Valais, stopping at Tiefenbach, Furka, Muttbach-Belvédère and Gletsch. Note: they do not go over the Furka Pass but below it in a tunnel.

## Sleeping

**Grand Hotel Glacier du Rhône** HISTORIC HOTEL €€
(☎027 973 15 15; www.glacier-du-rhone.ch; Gletsch; s/d shared bathroom Sfr85/145, d Sfr170, suite Sfr240; ⏰Jun-Oct; P 📶) This is something special – a historic hotel, originally built in 1835, being carefully renovated and refurnished at Gletsch (1762m). Back when it was first built, the Rhône Glacier was in front of the hotel, but not these days. The restaurant is open for breakfast, lunch and dinner.

## Getting There & Away

To make the most of this amazing alpine scenery you'll want your own wheels. From the Furka Pass it is only 21km by road to Andermatt in Central Switzerland. Heading back into Valais, it is 41km by road to Fiesch.

Yellow PostBuses head over the pass from the end of June until October, linking Oberwald in Valais and Andermatt.

# Ticino

POP 351,946

**Includes ➡**



## Best Places to Eat

- ➡ Ristorante Castelgrande (p182)
- ➡ Arté al Lago (p186)
- ➡ Locanda Locarnese (p193)
- ➡ Ecco (p195)
- ➡ Ristorante le Bucce di Gandria (p188)

## Best Places to Stay

- ➡ Villa del Gusto (p181)
- ➡ Guesthouse Castagnola (p185)
- ➡ Villa Principe Leopoldo Hotel & Spa (p186)
- ➡ The View (p186)
- ➡ Villa Sempreverde (p193)

## Why Go?

The summer air is rich and hot in Ticino. Vespas scoot along palm-fringed promenades. A baroque campanile chimes. Kids play in piazzas flanked by pastel-coloured mansions. Italian weather. Italian style. And that's not to mention the Italian gelato, Italian pasta, Italian architecture, Italian language.

The Alps are every bit as magnificent as elsewhere in Switzerland, but here you can admire them while sipping a full-bodied merlot at a pavement cafe, enjoying a hearty lunch at a chestnut-shaded *grotto* (rustic Ticino-style inn or restaurant), or floating in the mirror-like lakes of Lugano and Locarno. Ticino tempers its classic Alpine looks with Italian good living.

To the north, the stunning medieval fortress town of Bellinzona keeps watch over valleys speckled with homely hamlets and Romanesque chapels. Rearing above them are wild, forested peaks with endless hiking options past lakes and roaring mountain streams.

## When to Go

- ➡ Get into the carnival swing with feasting, parading and merrymaking at the pre-Lenten Rabadan in Bellinzona.
- ➡ Spring brings hikers to the wildflower-cloaked Alps and classical music fans to the Lugano Festival.
- ➡ Lugano stages open-air concerts in July, while Locarno zooms in on cinematic talent at its much-lauded film festival in August.
- ➡ Vintners in Mendrisio and Bellinzona toast the wine harvest in September.
- ➡ On a golden autumn day, nothing beats slow-cooked game and new wine in one of Ticino's rustic *grotti*.

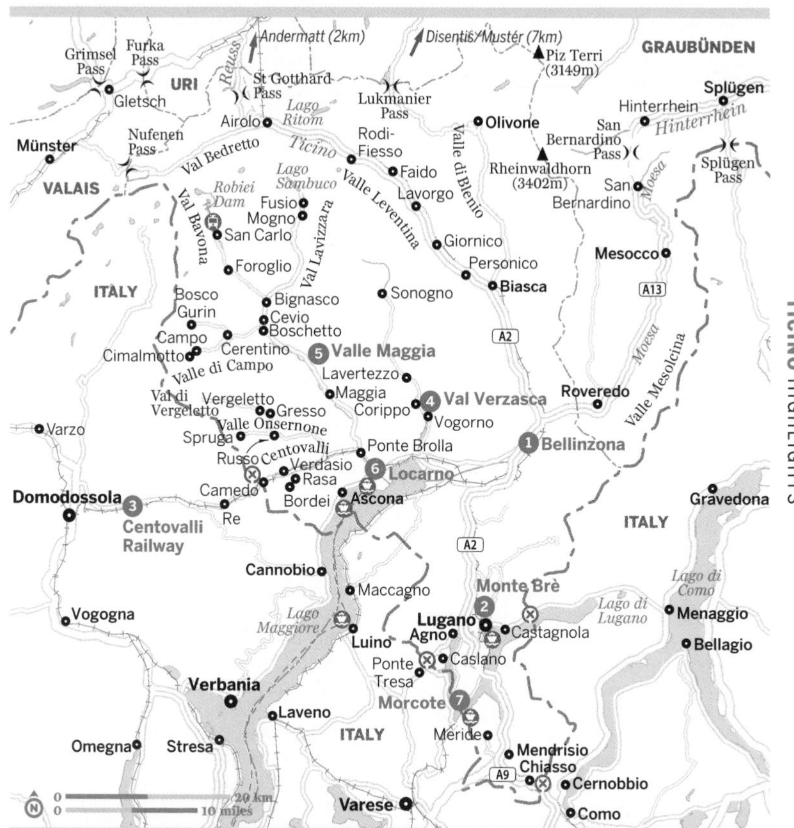


## Ticino Highlights

**1 Bellinzona** (p178) Roaming the trio of medieval forts for top-of-the-beanstalk views of the Old Town and the Alps.

**2 Monte Brè** (p183) Seeing rippling mountains and Lago di Lugano reflecting like a great mirror from this summit.

**3 Centovalli Railway** (p196) Chugging along a long valley, bounded by mountain beyond snow-dusted mountain, to Italy via spectacular tunnels, gorges and viaducts.

**4 Val Verzasca** (p194) Marvelling at cute-as-a-button Corippo, Switzerland's tiniest village, or gasping as you bungee Bond-style from the 220m-high Verzasca Dam.

**5 Valle Maggia** (p195) Hiking and cycling to misty waterfalls, Italianate granite villages and authentic *grotti* in the 'Magic Valley'.

**6 Locarno** (p190) Lounging in lakefront botanical gardens and historic cafe-rimmed piazzas in one of Switzerland's sunniest cities.

**7 Morcote** (p188) Wandering in wonder in this pretty-beyond-belief village that clings precariously to the slopes of Lago di Lugano.

## History

Ticino, long a poor, rural buffer between the Swiss-German cantons north of the Alps and Italy to the south, was absorbed by the Swiss in the late 15th century after centuries of ping-ponging between the lords of Como and the dukes of Milan.

The founding cantons of the Swiss Confederation – Uri, Scwhyz and Unterwalden – defeated a superior Milanese force at Giornico in the Valle Levantina in 1478 and took Bellinzona in 1503, thus securing the confederation's vulnerable underbelly. In 1803 Ticino entered the new Swiss Confederation, concocted by Napoleon, as a free and equal canton.

Closer to Milan than Bern, Ticino reveals a dual identity: the Ticinese share the same language, food, art and architecture as neighbouring Italy, yet they appreciate the political and institutional autonomy within the framework of the Federal Constitution that being part of Switzerland affords them.

In September 2016 Ticino made headline news once again when the Ticinese voted overwhelmingly against the free movement of EU workers within Switzerland and in favour of giving preference Swiss locals if they were equally qualified – a move that reportedly enraged Italian commuters. Opposing agreements with the EU over the free movement of labour, the campaign, entitled 'Ours first', was spearheaded by the ultra-conservative Swiss People's Party (SVP) and won 58% of the vote. The SVP argued that the cross-border worker situation has spiralled out of control, with many jobs being filled by Italians, which in turn has been cited as reducing wages and causing ongoing congestion on the roads.

The **Gotthard Base Tunnel**, the world's longest at 57km, opened fully in December 2016, slashing travel times between Ticino and Italy and the rest of Switzerland. The first flat-track route through the Alps, it links Erstfeld (Uri) with Bodio (Ticino) in just 17 minutes.

## Information

Your first port of call for up-to-date information on the region should be **Ticino Tourism** (www.ticino.ch). This website gives the inside scoop on regional attractions, activities, itineraries, transport, accommodation, food and events. Brochures can be downloaded online and you can search by region and/or theme.

Ask about the 31 mountain huts run by the **Federazione Alpinistica Ticinese** (www.fat-ti.ch) along hiking trails. They and other huts (often unstaffed) are listed at www.capanneti.ch (in Italian and German).

## Getting There & Around

Ticino's nearest international airport is **Milan Malpensa** (☎ +39 02 23 23 23; www.milanomalpensa-airport.com; Ferno, Italy), 80km south of Lugano, which is served by a raft of airlines including budget ones like Ryanair and easyJet. There are regular airport buses to Lugano (Sfr25, 70 minutes) and Bellinzona (Sfr40, two hours). The opening of the Gotthard Base Tunnel in late 2016 has also sped things up between Bellinzona and **Zürich Airport** (ZRH; ☎ 043 816 22 11; www.zurich-airport.com; Sfr64, two hours), making this also a viable option. Trains between Bellinzona and Zurich also stop en route in Lucerne (Sfr54, 1½ hours).

The A2 motorway links Como in the south of the canton to the Gotthard Tunnel in the north; the latter is notorious for traffic jams, so check www.gotthard-strassentunnel.ch before heading out. Helter-skelter pass roads link Ticino to the rest of Switzerland, including the San Bernadino Pass to Graubünden, the St Gotthard Pass to Central Switzerland and the Nufenenpass to Valais.

Ticino is criss-crossed with well-marked cycling trails. Bikes can be hired from major train stations, including Bellinzona, Lugano, Locarno and Ascona. One-day bike hire costs Sfr54 for an e-bike, Sfr35 for a country/city bike and Sfr43 for a mountain bike. See **Rent a Bike** (www.rentabike.ch) for rental details and locations.

# BELLINZONA

POP 18,700 / ELEV 230M

Rearing up at the convergence of several valleys amid lovely Alpine scenery, Bellinzona is Ticino's head-turning capital. Its three hulking medieval fortresses have enthralled artists and poets for centuries, including that greatest of Romantic painters, William Turner. Yet Bellinzona keeps a surprisingly low profile considering that its hat-trick of castles form one of only 12 Unesco World Heritage Sites in Switzerland.

The main castle, Castelgrande, stands high upon a rocky hill, which was a Roman frontier post and Lombard defensive tower, and was later developed as a heavily fortified town controlled by Milan. Though staunchly Swiss today, it is nevertheless infused with a hefty dose of Italian dolce vita.

Beyond the city's medieval mystique and knockout views of oft snow-capped mountains, you'll fall for its historic centre, woven with flower-draped alleys, Renaissance churches and cafe-rimmed piazzas, always brimming with life, laughter, chinking glasses and the out-of-tune toll of countless campaniles.

## Sights & Activities

Guided **walking tours** (www.bellinzonaturismo.ch; Sfr10) of Bellinzona depart from the tourist office at 11am on Saturdays. Worthwhile sights include cobblestoned **Piazza Collegiata**, framed by graceful patrician houses

## Bellinzona

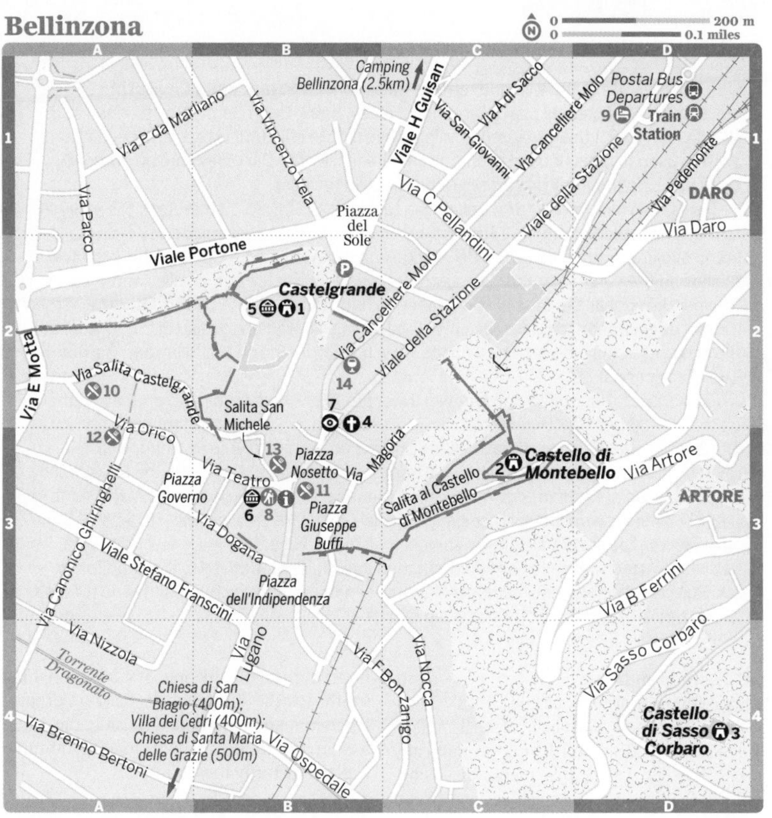




### Bellinzona

**Top Sights**
1 Castelgrande ........ B2
2 Castello di Montebello ........ C3
3 Castello di Sasso Corbaro ........ D4

**Sights**
4 Chiesa Collegiata dei SS Pietro e Stefano ........ B2
5 Museo di Castelgrande ........ B2
6 Palazzo del Comune ........ B3
7 Piazza Collegiata ........ B2

**Activities, Courses & Tours**
8 City Walks ........ B3

**Sleeping**
9 Hotel Internazionale ........ D1

**Eating**
10 Locanda Orico ........ A2
11 Mercato di Bellinzona ........ B3
12 Osteria Mistral ........ A3
Ristorante Castelgrande ........ (see 5)
13 Trattoria Cantinin dal Gatt ........ B3

**Drinking & Nightlife**
14 Il Fermento ........ B2

and wrought-iron balconies; the Renaissance **Palazzo del Comune** (Piazza Nosetto) with its beautiful three-storey inner courtyard; the palm-studded gardens and Italian artworks of **Villa dei Cedri** (www.villacedri.ch; Via San Biagio 9; adult/child Sfr10/7; 2-6pm Wed-Fri, 11am-6pm Sat & Sun); and the churches of **San Biagio** (Piazza San Biagio; 7am-noon & 2-5pm), **Santa Maria delle Grazie** (Via Convento; 7am-6pm) and **SS Pietro e Stefano** (Piazza Collegiata; 8am-1pm & 4-6pm).

OFF THE BEATEN TRACK

## SLOW TOURING TICINO'S NORTHERN VALLEYS

North of Bellinzona, the wild and remote **Valle di Blenio** and **Valle Leventina** spread out at the foot of piebald peaks forming a natural barrier with Central Switzerland and Graubünden. With their grey-stone villages nestling in chestnut woods and centuries-old *grotti* (rustic taverns housed in cool, rock-carved cellars), the valleys are an authentic taste of Ticino mountain life and perfect road trip territory.

Trains run twice hourly from Bellinzona to **Biasca** (Sfr8.80, 13 minutes), the gateway to the Valle di Blenio, with its 13th-century church and *grotti* serving hearty Ticinese home cooking. From Biasca, the barren-looking valley cuts north to majestic, brooding peaks and the Lukmanier Pass. Footpaths thread through the entire valley and there is modest skiing near the pass. If you're keen to hit the trail, a great base is **Olivone** at the base of dagger-shaped Sosto (2221m). Fine hikes also lead up to Lago di Luzzone and the pristine Greina plateau. The website www.bleniotourismo.ch (in Italian and German) lists accommodation.

From Biasca, the freeway powers northwest to **Airolo** in the Valle Leventina and then on to the mighty St Gotthard Pass. High above it is strung a series of mountain hamlets offering superlative views, great walking and the occasional fine feed. Shadowing the railway line, the Gottardo trail (www.gottardo-wanderweg.ch) runs from the Reuss valley in Uri (starting at Erstfeld) down the Valle Leventina. At traditional **Grotto Val d'Ambra** (☎091 864 18 29; www.grottovaldambra.ch; Via dei Grotti 2, Personico; mains Sfr15-28; ⏲10am-11pm Tue-Sun Easter-early Oct) in Personico, try *brasato* (beef braised in red wine) with home-produced wine in the chestnut-shaded garden. **Giornico** is worth a stop for its two Romanesque bridges, the finest example of a Romanesque church in Ticino (Chiesa di San Nicolao) and the picturesque old centre.

**★Castelgrande** CASTLE
(www.bellinzonese-altoticino.ch; Via Salita Castelgrande; ⏲grounds 10am-6pm Mon, 9am-10pm Tue-Sun; Murata 10am-7pm) Rising dramatically above the Old Town, this medieval stronghold is Bellinzona's most visible icon. Head up Salita San Michele from Piazza Collegiata, or take the lift, buried deep in the rocky hill in an extraordinary concrete bunker-style construction, from Piazza del Sole. After wandering the grounds and the museum, stroll west along the Murata, the castle's snaking ramparts, with photogenic views of vine-streaked mountains and castle-studded hills.

**★Castello di Montebello** CASTLE
(www.bellinzonese-altoticino.ch; Salita al Castello di Montebello; castle free, museum adult/child Sfr5/2; ⏲10am-6pm Apr-Oct, 10.30am-4pm Nov-Mar) FREE On cloudless days, you can see Lake Maggiore from this 13th-century hilltop fortification. The fortress is one of Bellinzona's most impressive with its drawbridges, ramparts and small museum catapulting you back to medieval times.

**★Castello di Sasso Corbaro** CASTLE
(www.bellinzonese-altoticino.ch; Via Sasso Corbaro; castle free, museum & tower adult/child Sfr5/2; ⏲10am-6pm Apr-Oct, 10.30am-4pm Nov-Mar) From central Bellinzona, it's a 3.5km hike south to the Castello di Sasso Corbaro. Perched high on a wooded hillside, the castle has an austere beauty with its impenetrable walls and sturdy towers.

**Museo di Castelgrande** MUSEUM
(Castelgrande; adult/child Sfr5/2; ⏲10am-6pm Apr-Oct, 10am-5pm Nov-Mar) This museum has a modest collection of finds from Castelgrande's hill dating to prehistoric times. More engaging are the 15th-century ceiling decorations of a former noble house in central Bellinzona. The pictures range from weird animals to a humorous 'world upside down' series that includes an ox driving a human-pulled plough and a sex-crazed woman chasing a chaste man!

## Festivals & Events

**Rabadan** CARNIVAL
(www.rabadan.ch; ⏲late Feb) Costumed parades, street theatre, jangling jesters and marching bands infuse Bellinzona with carnival fever seven-and-a-half weeks before Easter Sunday.

**La Bacchica** CULTURAL
(www.labacchica.ch) A traditional vintners' festival in September, with wine-tasting, folk processions, plays and music aplenty.

## Sleeping

Characterful digs in Bellinzona are weirdly few and far between. Many functional hotels are strung out along Viale della Stazione.

**Villa del Gusto** B&B €
(091 234 03 35; Via Pratocarasso 56; s Sfr80, d Sfr100-150; ) One of the sweetest options in Bellinzona, this lemon-fronted B&B is run like a tight ship by Michela and Massimo, who lovingly tend their garden with its views to the mountains and bring homemade cakes to the table at breakfast. Splurge on the deluxe double for extra space, style and a free-standing bathtub. Dinners can be prebooked on request.

**Camping Bellinzona** CAMPGROUND €
(091 829 11 18; www.campingbellinzona.ch; Via San Gottardo 131; sites per adult/child/tent Sfr11.50/5.50/20; ) Situated 2.5km north of central Bellinzona, this leafy site is well equipped with a laundry, shop, snack bar, playground and children's activities. From the station, take bus 1 or 191 to Arbedo.

**Hotel Internazionale** HOTEL €€
(091 825 43 33; www.hotel-internazionale.ch; Viale della Stazione 35; s Sfr145-185, d Sfr200-260, tr Sfr285-315; P) Sitting opposite the train station, this candyfloss-pink hotel seamlessly blends turn-of-the-20th-century features like wrought iron and stained glass with streamlined 21st-century design. A slick makeover in 2014 has brought the light, contemporary rooms bang up to date, and the new spa invites relaxation with its sauna, steam room, hydro-massage and salt inhalation room.

## Eating & Drinking

**Mercato di Bellinzona** MARKET
(Piazza Nosetto; 8am-1pm Sat) Fresh produce from Alpine cheeses to fresh bread, *salumi* and fruit is sold at the Saturday morning market in the lanes of the historic centre on and around Piazza Nosetto. Take the lead of locals and turn it into an event following a shop with coffee or lunch at one of the cafe terraces.

**Trattoria Cantinin dal Gatt** ITALIAN €€
(091 825 27 71; www.cantinindalgatt.ch; Vicolo al Sasso 4; lunch menus Sfr18-28, mains Sfr25-36; 11am-3pm & 6pm-midnight Tue-Fri, 9am-3pm & 6pm-midnight Sat; ) Slip up a cobblestone side street to find this cracking little trattoria, brimming with warmth and bonhomie. The brick-vaulted interior is an inviting spot for digging into big Italian flavours courtesy of Tuscan chef Luca. Begin, say, with homemade gnocchi with lobster bisque, shrimp and black olive tapenade, followed perhaps by mains such as roasted rabbit with sweet pepper salsa.

**Osteria Mistral** ITALIAN €€
(091 825 60 12; www.osteriamistral.ch; Via Orico 2; 2-/3-course lunch menu Sfr33/40, 3-/4-/6-course dinner menu Sfr68/82/115; 11.45am-3pm Mon-Fri & 6.45pm-midnight Mon-Sat) Luca Braghelli takes pride in local sourcing and makes the most of whatever is in season at this smart, intimate osteria. Be it homemade pasta or autumn venison, everything is cooked to a T and expertly matched with regional wines.



### WHAT'S COOKING IN TICINO?

Switzerland meets Italy in Ticino's kitchen and some of your most satisfying eating experiences in Ticino will happen in *grotti* – rustic, out-of-the-way restaurants, with granite tables set up under the cool chestnut trees in summer. The trilingual *Guida a Grotti e Osterie* gives a great overview (available from http://www.editore.ch, Sfr26).

Want to eat like a local? Get stuck into these classic Ticinese specialities:

**Polenta** Creamy, savoury cornmeal dish

**Brasato** Beef braised in red wine

**Capretto in umido alla Mesolcinese** Tangy kid-meat stew with a touch of cinnamon, and cooked in red wine

**Cazzöla** A hearty meat casserole served with cabbage and potatoes

**Mazza casalinga** A mixed selection of delicatessen cuts

**Cicitt** Long, thin sausages made from goat's meat and often grilled

**Robiola** Soft and creamy cow's-milk cheese that comes in small discs

**Ristorante Castelgrande** ITALIAN €€
(☎091 814 87 81; www.ristorantecastelgrande.ch; Castelgrande; mains Sfr29-42, menus Sfr72; ⏲6.30pm-midnight Tue-Sat) It's not often you get the chance to eat inside a Unesco World Heritage Site. The medieval castle setting alone is enough to bewitch. Seasonal specialities like pike perch fillets with vanilla-cauliflower puree are married with top-notch wines.

**Locanda Orico** ITALIAN €€€
(☎091 825 15 18; www.locandaorico.ch; Via Orico 13; mains Sfr40-65, lunch menu Sfr48, dinner menus Sfr110-125; ⏲11.45am-2pm & 6.45pm-midnight Tue-Sat) Seasonality is the name of the game at this Michelin-starred temple to good food, housed in a slickly converted *palazzo* in the old town. Creations such as pumpkin gnocchi in jugged chamois meat, and wild turbot with fettuccine and basil butter are served with finesse.

**Il Fermento** BREWERY
(www.ilfermento.ch; Via Codeborgo 12; ⏲11am-9pm Mon-Wed, to 1pm Thu-Fri, to 9pm Sat) For one of the top craft beers in town, swing across to this hip new urban microbrewery. Sip hoppy amber ales, zesty IPAs and malty bitters in the industro-cool interior or out on the pavement terrace if the sun's out.

## Information

The **tourist office** (☎091 825 21 31; www.bellinzonaturismo.ch; Piazza Nosetto; ⏲9am-6.30pm Mon-Fri, 9am-2pm Sat, 10am-2pm Sun Apr-Oct, shorter hours rest of year), in Bellinzona's town hall, sells the Bellinzona Pass (adult/child/family Sfr15/7.50/25), which grants access to several local attractions.

## Getting There & Away

The gateway to Ticino, Bellinzona is a major transport hub. The A2 motorway blazes through, linking it to Lugano in the south and running all the way north to Basel. The A13 motorway connects up to Chur, capital of Graubünden, 116km north.

Bellinzona has frequent **train connections** (Viale della Stazione) to Locarno (Sfr8.80, 27 minutes) and Lugano (Sfr10.20, 30 minutes). It is also on the Zürich–Milan route.

Bus 171 runs roughly hourly northeast to Chur (Sfr59.40, 2¼ to three hours), departing from beside the train station. There is an underground car park on **Piazza del Sole** (Piazza del Sole; per hour Sfr2).

# LUGANO

POP 63,583 / ELEV 270M

Ticino's lush, mountain-rimmed lake isn't its only liquid asset. The largest city in the canton is also the country's third-most-important banking centre. Suits aside, Lugano is a vivacious city, with posh designer boutiques, bars and pavement cafes huddling in the spaghetti maze of steep cobblestone streets that untangle at the edge of the lake and along the flowery promenade. The recent opening of its LAC arts centre has bumped it up in the cultural stakes, too.

Popping up above the lake are the twin peaks of Monte Brè and Monte San Salvatore, both commanding astonishing views deep into the Alps and attracting hikers and mountain bikers in the warmer months.

## Sights

Take the stairs or the **funicular** (Piazzale della Stazione; Sfr1.30; ⏲5am-midnight) from Lugano's train station down to the centre, a patchwork of interlocking *piazze*.

**MASI – Museo d'Arte della Svizzera Italiana** GALLERY
(www.masilugano.ch; LAC Lugano Arte e Cultura, Piazza Bernardino Luini 6; adult/child Sfr15/free; ⏲10am-6pm Tue-Sun, to 8pm Thu) The showpiece of Lugano's striking new LAC (p186) cultural centre, the MASI zooms in predominantly on 20th-century and contemporary art – from the abstract to the highly experimental, with exhibitions spread across three spaces. There is no permanent collection on display at present, but there is a high-calibre roster of rotating exhibitions. Recent focuses have included the work of Swiss surrealist Meret Oppenheim and the epic, thought-provoking work of British photographer Craigie Horsfield.

**Chiesa di Santa Maria degli Angioli** CHURCH
(St Mary of the Angel; Piazza Luini; ⏲7am-6pm) This simple Romanesque church contains two frescos by Bernardino Luini dating from 1529. Covering the entire wall that divides the church in two is a grand didactic illustration of the crucifixion of Christ. The power and vivacity of the colours are astounding.

**Parco Ciani** GARDENS
(Viale Carlo Cattaneo; ⏲6am-11pm) FREE This lakefront promenade necklaces the shore of glassy Lago di Lugano, set against a backdrop

WORTH A TRIP

## LAKE ESCAPES

For a bird's-eye view of Lugano and its namesake lake (Lago di Lugano), head for the hills. A funicular from Cassarate (walk or take bus 2 from central Lugano) hauls you up to the summit of **Monte Brè** (www.montebre.ch; funicular one way/return Sfr16/25; ⌚9.10am-6.45pm) from March to December. The peak is the trailhead for hiking and mountain-biking trails that grant expansive views of the lake and reach deep into the Alps.

From Paradiso, the **funicular** (www.montesansalvatore.ch; funicular one way/return Sfr23/30; ⌚9am-6pm) to Monte San Salvatore operates from mid-March to early November. Aside from the views, the walk down to Paradiso or Melide is an hour well spent.

A lovely place to stay the night is the **Locanda del Giglio** (☎091 930 09 33; www.locandadelgiglio.ch; Roveredo, Capriasca; dm Sfr40-45, s/d Sfr95/150; P 📶) in Roveredo, 12km north of Lugano. Backing onto forest, the eco-focused, solar-powered lodge houses rooms with balconies offering mountain views and even lake glimpses. Take a bus from **Lugano train station** (www.flpsa.ch/en.htm; Piazzale della Stazzione; tickets Sfr2.50-6/60; ⌚every 15min 5.25am-1.20am) to Tesserete (Sfr6.60, 27 minutes) and change for another to Roveredo (Sfr6.40, 11 minutes).

of rugged mountains. Notice the distinctive profiles of cone-shaped twin peaks Monte Brè and Monte San Salvatore. Linden and chestnut trees provide welcome shade in summer, while tulips, camellias and magnolias bloom in spring.

**Piazza della Riforma** SQUARE

Porticoed lanes weave around Lugano's busy main square, which is presided over by the 1844 neoclassical **Municipio** (town hall) and is even more lively when the Tuesday and Friday morning **markets** are held.

**Cattedrale di San Lorenzo** CATHEDRAL

(St Lawrence Cathedral; Via San Lorenzo; ⌚6.30am-6pm) Freshly renovated in 2016, Lugano's early-16th-century cathedral conceals some fine frescos and ornate baroque statues behind its Renaissance facade. Out front are far-reaching views over the Old Town's jumble of terracotta rooftops to the lake and mountains.

**Swissminiatur** AMUSEMENT PARK

(www.swissminiatur.ch; Via Cantonale; adult/child Sfr19/12; ⌚9am-6pm mid-Mar–Oct; 👪) At Swissminiatur you'll find 1:25 scale models of more than 120 national attractions. It's the quick way to see Switzerland in a day. Trains run twice hourly from Lugano.

**Museo Hermann Hesse** MUSEUM

(www.hessemontagnola.ch; Torre Camuzzi, Montagnola; adult/child Sfr8.50/free; ⌚10am-5.30pm daily Mar-Oct, 10.30am-5.30pm Sat & Sun Nov-Feb) This museum showcases German-born Swiss poet, novelist and painter Herman Hesse's personal objects, including some of the thousands of watercolours he painted in Ticino, plus books and other odds and ends that help recreate something of his life.

From Lugano, take bus 436 (direction Agra, Roncone) to Montagnola, Bellevue (Sfr6.40, 19 minutes).

**Parco Botanico San Grato** GARDENS

(www.parcosangrato.ch; Carona; ⌚24hr) FREE Footpaths thread through these hilltop botanical gardens, which afford sensational lake and mountain views. In May the park is ablaze with the colour of azaleas and rhododendrons in bloom.

To reach the park, take bus 434 from Lugano to Carona (Sfr6.40, 25 minutes).

**Schokoland** MUSEUM

(www.alprose.ch; Via Rompada 36, Caslano; adult/child Sfr3/1; ⌚9am-5.30pm Mon-Fri, to 4.30pm Sat & Sun; 👪) Chomp into some cocoa culture at the Alprose chocolate museum, Schokoland – a sure-fire hit with kids. Whiz through chocolate history, watch the sugary substance being made and enjoy a free tasting. The shop, cunningly, stays open half an hour longer. Take the train to Caslano.

## Activities

Popular summer pursuits include swimming, sailing, wakeboarding and rowing on the Lago di Lugano, as well as hiking and mountain biking in the surrounding mountains and valleys; see www.luganotourism.ch for route maps and GPS downloads. **Società Navigazione del Lago di Lugano** (☎091 971 52 23; www.lakelugano.ch; Riva Vela; ⌚Apr-Oct) offers a variety of scenic lake cruises. You can

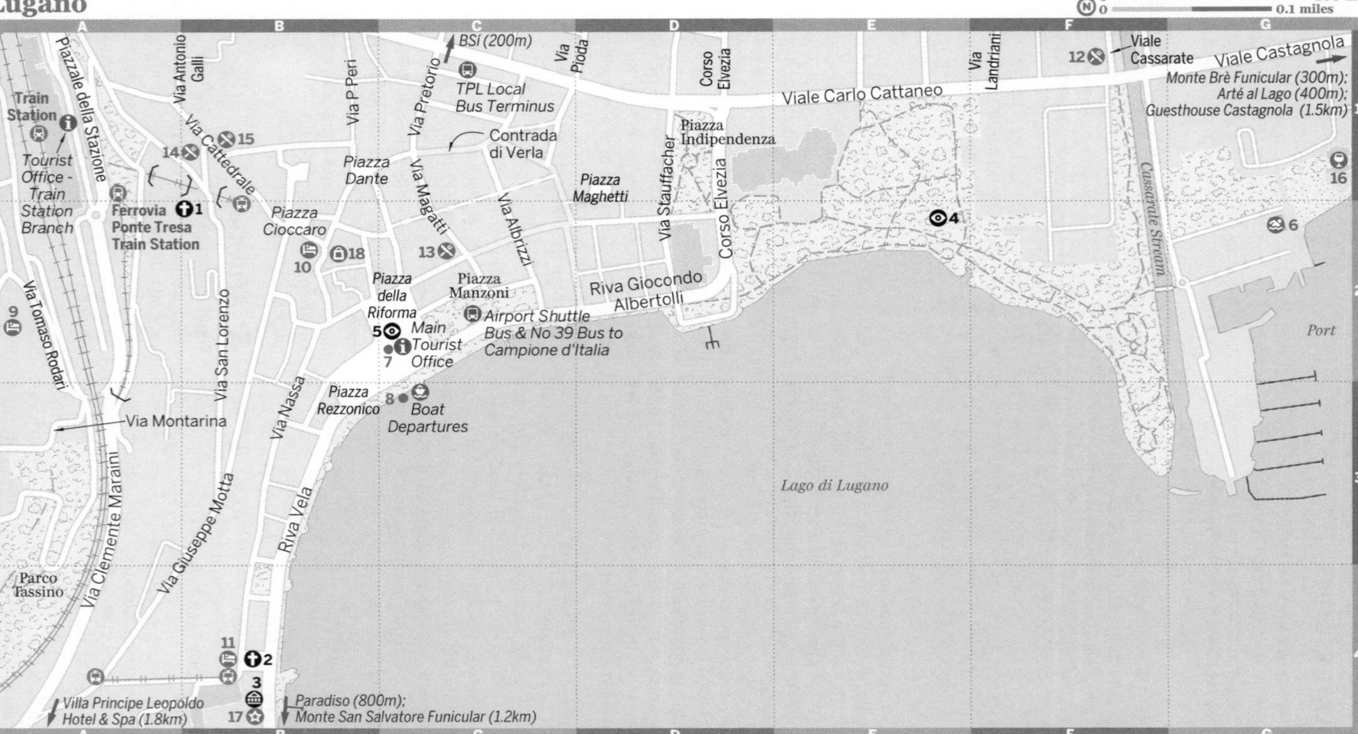
Lugano
0 200 m
0 0.1 miles
Train Station
Tourist Office - Train Station Branch
Piazzale della Stazione
Via Antonio Galli
Via Cattedrale
14
15
Ferrovia Ponte Tresa Train Station
1
Piazza Cioccaro
10
18
Via P Peri
Piazza Dante
Via Pretorio
BSI (200m)
TPL Local Bus Terminus
Contrada di Verla
Via Magatti
13
Via Albrizzi
Via Pioda
Piazza Maghetti
Piazza della Riforma
Piazza Manzoni
5
Main Tourist Office
7
Airport Shuttle Bus & No 39 Bus to Campione d'Italia
Riva Giocondo Albertolli
Piazza Rezzonico
8
Boat Departures
Via Stauffacher
Corso Elvezia
Piazza Indipendenza
Viale Carlo Cattaneo
Via Landriani
4
12
Viale Cassarate
Viale Castagnola
Monte Brè Funicular (300m); Arté al Lago (400m); Guesthouse Castagnola (1.5km)
Cassarate Stream
16
6
Port
Lago di Lugano
9
Via Tomaso Rodari
Via San Lorenzo
Via Montarina
Via Nassa
Via Clemente Maraini
Via Giuseppe Motta
Riva Vela
Parco Tassino
11
2
3
17
Villa Principe Leopoldo Hotel & Spa (1.8km)
Paradiso (800m); Monte San Salvatore Funicular (1.2km)

## Lugano

**Sights**

1 Cattedrale di San Lorenzo ... B2
2 Chiesa di Santa Maria degli Angioli ... B4
3 MASI - Museo d'Arte della Svizzera Italiana ... B4
4 Parco Ciani ... E2
5 Piazza della Riforma ... C2

**Activities, Courses & Tours**

6 Lido ... G2
7 Lugano Guided Tours ... C2
8 Società Navigazione del Lago di Lugano ... C3

**Sleeping**

9 Hotel & Hostel Montarina ... A2
10 Hotel Gabbani ... B2
11 Hotel International au Lac ... B4

**Eating**

12 Al Portone ... F1
13 Bottegone del Vino ... C2
14 Pasta e Pesto ... B1
15 Trani ... B1

**Drinking & Nightlife**

16 Al Lido ... G1

**Entertainment**

17 LAC - Lugano Arte e Cultura ... B4

**Shopping**

18 Gabbani ... B2



also hire pedalos by the **boat landing** (091 222 11 11; www.lakelugano.ch; Lugano-Centrale, Riva Vela; 8.30am-8.30pm).

**Lido** SWIMMING
(Viale Castagnola; adult/child Sfr11/6; 9am-7pm May & Sep, to 7.30pm Jun-Aug; ) Right on the lake and with glorious views across to the mountains, this lidohas beaches, volleyball, splash areas for kids and an Olympic-size swimming pool.

### Festivals & Events

**LuganoMusica** MUSIC
(www.luganomusica.ch) Lugano takes in some classical tunes during this festival from mid-April to June in the Palazzo dei Congressi.

**National Day** CULTURAL
Lago di Lugano explodes in a display of pyrotechnical wizardry around midnight on 1 August to celebrate Switzerland's national day.

### Sleeping

Many Lugano hotels close for at least part of the winter. In summer book well in advance as decent (and decently priced) rooms are like gold dust and sell out in a flash.

**Hotel & Hostel Montarina** HOTEL, HOSTEL €
(091 966 72 72; www.montarina.ch; Via Montarina 1; dm/s/d Sfr29/105/140; ) Occupying a pastel-pink villa dating 1860, this hotel/hostel duo extends a heartfelt welcome. Mosaic floors, high ceilings and wrought-iron balustrades are lingering traces of old-world grandeur. There's a shared kitchen-lounge, toys to amuse the kids, a swimming pool set in palm-dotted gardens and even a tiny vineyard. Breakfast costs an extra Sfr15.

★ **Guesthouse Castagnola** GUESTHOUSE €€
(078 632 67 47; www.gh-castagnola.com; Salita degli Olivi 2; apt Sfr125-180; ) Kristina and Maurizio bend over backwards to please at their B&B, lodged in a beautifully restored 16th-century townhouse. Exposed stone, natural fabrics and earthy colours dominate in three rooms kitted out with Nespresso coffee machines and flat-screen TVs. There's also a family-friendly apartment with washing machine and full kitchen. Take bus 2 to Posta Castagnola, 2km east of the centre.

**Hotel International au Lac** HOTEL €€
(091 922 75 41; www.hotel-international.ch; Via Nassa 68; s Sfr150-190, d Sfr180-330; ) Rooms are comfortable, with some antique furniture, at this lakefront pick. From the balconies of the front rooms you look straight out over Lago di Lugano. The garden with ping pong, a pool and kids' play area, bumps up the family appeal.

**Hotel Gabbani** BOUTIQUE HOTEL €€€
(091 921 34 70; www.hotel-gabbani.ch; Piazza Cioccaro 1; s Sfr190-320, d Sfr220-370; ) Run by the respected local Gabbani food family and within sight of their signature **shop** (www.gabbani.com; Via Pessina 12; 8am-6.30pm Mon-Fri, to 5pm Sat), this enticing place has slickly styled rooms with pops of bright colour, lots of oak, marble and Danish-design chairs. Fittings are ultra-modern and the service excellent.

**Villa Principe Leopoldo Hotel & Spa** LUXURY HOTEL €€€
(☎091 985 88 55; www.leopoldohotel.com; Via Montalbano 5; s Sfr300-2000, d Sfr360-2500; P❄📶🏊) This red-tiled residence set in sculptured gardens was built in 1926 for Prince Leopold von Hohenzollern, of the exiled German royal family. It oozes a regal, nostalgic atmosphere. The gardens and many of the splendid rooms offer lake views. Prices reach for the stars but so does the luxury – gourmet restaurants, tennis courts, a spa, heated pools, personal trainers, you name it.

**The View** DESIGN HOTEL €€€
(☎091 210 00 00; www.theviewlugano.com; Via Guidino 29; ste Sfr700-2150; P❄📶🏊) If you're going to blow the budget, do it in boutique style at this new five-star design hotel in Lugano-Paradiso. The lake views from its 18 suites are astounding and the decor is super-slick, with polished teak, leather and floor-to-ceiling glass. A spa, gourmet restaurant and free e-bike and smart car use are other luxuries that come with the price tag.

## Eating & Drinking

**Pasta e Pesto** ITALIAN €
(☎091 922 66 11; Via Cattedrale 16; pasta Sfr10.50-15, menus Sfr15-19.50; ⏰9.30am-5.30pm Mon-Sat) Doing pretty much what it says on the tin, this cute little place near the cathedral has a pocket-size terrace for digging into fresh homemade pasta with a variety of toppings.

**Trani** ITALIAN €
(☎091 922 05 05; www.trani.ch; Via Cattedrale 12; mains Sfr29-43) Follow the cobbled steps down from Via Cattedrale to this enticing little osteria. The candlelit, brick-vaulted interior is a wonderfully intimate setting for antipasti, homemade pasta bursting with flavour, and grilled fish and meats.

**Bottegone del Vino** ITALIAN €€
(☎091 922 76 89; Via Magatti 3; mains Sfr20-42; ⏰11.30am-midnight Mon-Sat) Favoured by Lugano's downtown banking brigade, this place has a season-driven menu, with ever-changing lunch and dinner options scrawled on the blackboard daily. Expect specialities such as ravioli stuffed with fine Tuscan Chianina beef, accompanied by a wide selection of local wines. Knowledgeable waiters fuss around the tables and are only too happy to suggest the perfect Ticino tipple.

**Arté al Lago** SEAFOOD €€€
(☎091 973 48 00; www.villacastagnola.com; Piazza Emilio Bossi 7; mains Sfr51-56, menus Sfr110-120; ⏰noon-2pm & 7-9.30pm Tue-Sat) This Michelin-starred restaurant at the exclusive lakefront Villa Castagnola is Lugano's culinary star. Chef Frank Oerthle does remarkable things with fish and seafood, with ingredient-focused, deceptively simple-sounding specialities. Gaze out across the lake through the picture windows or up to the contemporary artworks gracing the walls.

**Metamorphosis** MEDITERRANEAN €€€
(☎091 994 68 68; http://metaworld.ch; Riva Paradiso 2; mains Sfr45-52, tasting menus Sfr85-120; ⏰9am-3pm Mon-Tue, 9am-midnight Wed-Fri, 10.30am-midnight Sat) One for special occasions, Metamorphosis is housed in Lugano's futuristic Palazzo Mantegazza, right by the lake shore. Chef Luca Bellanca walks the culinary high-wire, bringing simple, natural Mediterranean flavours to life with imagination and flair.

**Al Portone** GASTRONOMY €€€
(☎078 722 93 24; www.ristorante-alportone.ch; Viale Cassarate 3; mains Sfr44-57, tasting menu Sfr120; ⏰6.30-9.30pm Tue-Sat) Bold artworks grace this contemporary gourmet haunt, while Francis plies you with such season-infused taste sensations as scallops and caviar on a bed of seaweed with passion vinaigrette, pumpkin ravioli with sage sauce, and freshly made *parpadelle* with wild-boar ragout.

**Al Lido** LOUNGE
(http://allidobar.com; Viale Castagnola 6; ⏰9am-9.30pm Mar-Dec, shorter hours in winter) Partygoers flock to this cool summertime beach lounge for DJ beats, drinks, snacks and flirting by the lakefront. It's right next to Lugano's lido (p185) if you fancy a dip before or after.

## Entertainment

**LAC – Lugano Arte e Cultura** ARTS CENTRE
(☎058 866 42 22; www.luganolac.ch; Piazza Bernardino Luini 6) Lugano is justifiably proud of its cutting-edge new cultural centre, which has given the city its artistic mojo back. It brings together contemporary art (at the MASI; p182), music, theatre, poetry recitals, workshops and more. For listings and tickets, visit the website.

## Shopping

Lugano's pedestrian-friendly Via Nassa is a catwalk for designers like Bulgari, Louis Vuitton and Versace. Its graceful arcades also harbour jewellery stores, cafes and gelaterias. For one-off gifts, explore steep, curving Via Cattedrale, where boutiques and galleries sell antiques, vintage clothing, crafts and handcrafted jewellery.

## Information

Lugano's centrally located **main tourist office** (☎058 866 66 00; www.lugano-tourism.ch; Piazza Riforma, Palazzo Civico; ⏰9am-6pm Mon-Fri, 9am-5pm Sat, 10am-4pm Sun) is the starting point for excellent **guided tours** (⏰mid-Mar–Oct) of the city and its surroundings. There's another **branch** (☎091 923 51 20; Piazzale della Stazione; ⏰9am-7pm Mon-Fri, 9am-1pm Sat) at the train station.

## Getting There & Away

### AIR

**Lugano airport** (☎091 610 12 82; www.lugano-airport.ch) is served by a handful of Swiss-Italian carriers.

### BUS

The easiest way to reach St Moritz from Lugano is to take the train to Bellinzona and switch to a postal bus via Thusis (Sfr84, four hours, hourly).

### CAR & MOTORCYCLE

The main artery running north–south through Ticino is the A2 motorway, which links Lugano to Bellinzona, 37km north, and Chiasso on the Italian border, 26km south.

### TRAIN

Lugano has very frequent **train connections** (Piazzale della Stazione) to Bellinzona (Sfr11, 30 minutes), with onward connections to destinations further north. Getting to Locarno (Sfr15.20, one hour) involves a change at Giubiasco. Note that the train station can be reached by foot or funicular (p182).

## Getting Around

A shuttle bus runs to Lugano's airport from **Piazza Manzoni** (one way/return Sfr10/18) and the **train station** (Sfr8/15, 20 minutes). See timetables on www.shuttle-bus.com. A taxi to the airport costs around Sfr30 (20 minutes).

Local buses depart from the **TPL Terminus** (☎058 866 72 24; www.tplsa.ch; Corso Pestalozzi; ⏰8am-6.30pm Mon-Fri, 9am-noon Sat).

Bus 1 runs from Castagnola in the east through the centre to Paradiso, while bus 2 runs from central Lugano to Paradiso via the train station. A single trip costs Sfr2.50 or it's Sfr7.50 for a one-day pass.

# LAGO DI LUGANO

Spilling over into northern Italy, Lago di Lugano is a sparkling blue expanse at Ticino's southernmost tip, with a real holiday flavour as soon as the weather warms. Less overrun than many of the lakes over the border, it is nevertheless bewitching, whether glimpsed from one of the many trails that wriggle along its shores, from a mountain peak or from the deck of the boats that glide across it.

On clear days, the views are nothing short of riveting, with the pleats of sheer, wooded peaks fading into hazy distance – among them the highest of the high, 1704m Monte Generoso. The villages that cling tightly to its shores and tumble haphazardly down its slopes, such as Gandria, Meride and Morcote, are among Switzerland's most beguiling, with hidden back alleys, pastel-painted houses and botanical gardens to explore.

## Gandria

POP 275 / ELEV 327M

Looking as though it will topple off its terraced hillside with the merest puff of breath, lakeside Gandria is ludicrously pretty, with pastel-coloured houses stacked on top of one another like children's building blocks, narrow stairwells, arcades, courtyards and terraced gardens. At the foot of Monte Brè, it is the last Swiss village before reaching Italy on the SS340, and it was once renowned for its production of olive oil (notice the traditional press in front of the town hall). It's perfect for an aimless amble, with hidden corners aplenty and 16th- and 17th-century houses decorated with frescos.

Across the lake from Gandria is the **Museo delle Dogane Svizzere** (Swiss Customs Museum; www.zollmuseum.ch; Riva delle Cantine; adult/child Sfr3/1.50; ⏰1.30-5.30pm Apr–mid-Oct) FREE, accessible by boat. It tells the history of customs (and, more interestingly, smuggling) in this border area. On display are confiscated smugglers' boats that once operated on the lake.

The 5km, one-and-a-half hour **Sentiero di Gandria** (Gandria Trail) hugs the shore of Lago di Lugano, taking you from Gandria to Lugano, or vice versa, and passing through glorious gardens where century-old olive trees and Mediterranean flowers grow. The views out across the lake and up to the slopes of Monte Brè and Monte San Salvatore are outstanding.

## Lago di Lugano

Climb the steps of Gandria's old town and you'll be rewarded with gorgeous lake views from **Ristorante le Bucce di Gandria** (Via Cantonale; mains Sfr22-32; ⏲7pm-midnight Wed-Thu, noon-3pm & 7pm-midnight Fri-Sun), a hillside restaurant. The menu keeps things regional and seasonal, adding a dash of creativity in dishes such as ravioli of salt cod with onion-cardamom cream and venison fillet with fondant potatoes and cinnamon pear. It's all delicious and served with a smile.

Gandria is an hour-and-a-half walk from Lugano on the Sentiero di Gandria, or you can reach the village by boat.

# Campione d'Italia

POP 2067 / ELEV 273M

It's hard to tell, but Campione d'Italia really is part of Italy surrounded by Switzerland. Sitting on the southern shores of Lago di Lugano, it has an appealing old town with a medieval church, a piazza lined with alfresco cafes and a Michelin-starred restaurant, **Da Candida** (☎091 649 75 41; www.dacandida.net; Viale Marco da Campione 4; menus Sfr45-105; ⏲7-11pm Tue, noon-2pm & 7-11pm Wed-Sun). Forested slopes fling up spectacularly above the town. The town's biggest draw is its casino, designed by Ticino's most feted architect, Mario Botta.

There are no border formalities (but take your passport anyway). Many cars in the village have Swiss number plates, and the area uses Swiss telephones and Swiss francs.

The A2 links Lugano to Campione d'Italia, 12km south. **Buses** (Corso Italia) run roughly hourly between Lugano and Campione d'Italia (Sfr6.60, 25 minutes), or you can take the **boat** (Piazza Roma; Sfr13, 21 minutes).

# Morcote

POP 769 / ELEV 272M

Spilling photogenically down a hillside, the one-time fishing village of Morcote, huddling below Monte Abostora, is a joy to explore on foot, with its botanical gardens and dazzling lake and mountain views. It was voted Switzerland's most beautiful village in 2016 and lives up to the hype with its adorable maze of narrow cobbled lanes, passageways, arcaded patrician houses and hilltop church.

Set in subtropical parkland, **Parco Scherrer** (Riva di Pilastri 20; adult/child Sfr7/2; ⏲10am-5pm Mar-Jun, Sep & Oct, 10am-6pm Jul-Aug), 400m west of the boat stop in Morcote, is the dream come true of textile merchant and art enthusiast Hermann Arthur Scherrer, who bought the land sloping down to the lake in 1930. Inspired by his travels, the gardens have a dash of the exotic, bristling with palms and oleanders, camellias and azaleas, cypresses and bamboo. Hidden among the foliage are replicas of grand buildings – from the Temple of Nefertiti to a Siamese teahouse.

Morcote's **tourist office** (☎058 866 49 60; Riva dal Garavell 20; ⏲8.30am-12.30pm & 1.30-5.30 Mon-Fri, 10am-noon & 1-5pm Sat & Sun late Mar–mid-Oct) is on the lakefront just north of the centre of town.

Bus 431 runs between Lugano and Morcote (Sfr6.60, 39 minutes). A minor road swings south to Morcote from the A2 motorway leading to Lugano, a 14km (25-minute) drive away.

# Mendrisio & Around

POP 14,938 / ELEV 354M

Sidling up to Italy in Ticino's southern corner, Mendrisio conceals a well-preserved historic centre, where narrow alleys lead to inner courtyards, terracotta-roofed houses and atmospheric *grotti*, and bells ring out from medieval and baroque churches. The town really springs to life for the Maundy Thursday Procession and the Wine Harvest in September, where you can sample the

WORTH A TRIP

### MONTE GENEROSO

Popping up between Italy and Switzerland, the 1704m peak of **Monte Generoso** (www.montegeneroso.ch; cog railway one way/return Sfr36/54; ⏲9am-4.45pm) has far-reaching views across a patchwork of lakes and mountains. The rack-and-pinion railway that departs from Capolago roughly hourly has been trundling to the top since 1890. Some 51km of marked footpaths fan out from the summit, among them an hour-long nature trail that gives you a handle on local wildlife, which includes a sizeable chamois colony. The mountain also attracts climbers, mountain bikers and paragliders.

Driving from Lugano, take the A2 south to Capolago, 15km away. Trains run frequently between Lugano and Capolago (Sfr6.60, 23 minutes), where you can catch to the rack-and-pinion train to the summit.



region's best merlot. Its surrounds – easily explored on foot or by bicycle – are sprinkled with vineyards and quaint villages capped by Italianate baroque churches.

Housed in a restored, stone-vaulted 17th-century palazzo, **Atenaeo del Vino** (☎091 630 06 36; www.atenaeodelvino.ch; Via Pontico Virunio 1; mains Sfr36-42; ⏲10am-2.30pm & 5-11pm Mon-Sat) matches seasonal fare (think asparagus, mushrooms, seafood, game) with top regional wines drawn from its cavernous cellar. The ambience is relaxed and homely. See the website for details of upcoming cookery and wine classes.

Mendrisio's centrally located **tourist office** (☎091 641 30 50; www.mendrisiottoturismo.ch; Via Luigi Lavizzari 2; ⏲9am-noon Mon-Fri, 2-6pm Sat) is in the heart of the Old Town. It rents out free multilingual audioguides that take you on a spin of the historic centre.

The A2 motorway runs south of Lugano to Mendrisio, 20km away. **Trains** (Via Stefano Franscini) run twice hourly to Mendrisio from Lugano (Sfr8.80, 19 minutes).

## Meride

POP 314 / ELEV 583M

Rimmed by vineyards and slumbering at the foot of Monte San Giorgio, Meride is a pipsqueak of a village with postcard looks. Its medieval centre is woven with cobbled alleys and lined with stone-built, shuttered houses redolent of neighbouring Italy. Anyone with even a passing interest in paleontology will love its fossil museum, while others will appreciate its quaint, off-the-radar charm.

Rising in a pyramid above Lake Lugano, 1097m **Monte San Giorgio** has become Ticino's mountain of myth thanks to its rich stash of Triassic marine-life fossils, which have won it Unesco World Heritage status. A four-hour, 12km circular trail takes you up from Meride. An old mule track wends through thick forest to the summit, commanding fine lake views, then you'll descend on a path with panels detailing the fossils and their excavation sites.

Revamped and expanded by Ticinese starchitect Mario Botta, Meride's **Museo dei Fossili** (Fossil Museum; www.montesangiorgio.ch; Via Bernardo Peyer 9; adult/child Sfr12/6; ⏲9am-5pm Tue-Sun) showcases vestiges of the first creatures to inhabit the region – reptiles and fish dating back more than 200 million years. You're welcomed by a 2.5m long replica of a *Ticinosuchus*.

If you're driving from Lugano, take the A2 south, then exit 394. Bus 524 runs frequently between Meride and Mendrisio (Sfr6.40, 21 minutes), with onward train connections to Lugano (Sfr8.80, 19 minutes). The Meride/Paese bus stop is in the centre of town.

# LAGO MAGGIORE

Only the northeast corner of Lago Maggiore is in Switzerland – the rest slices into Italy's Lombardy region. The second-largest lake in Italy has cinematic looks, with inky blue waters rippling against a backdrop of lush, rugged mountains where the snow lingers into spring. Necklacing the lake are Italianate villages and towns with piazzas, Renaissance churches and alfresco cafes that remind you just how close Italy really is. As if you need reminding: here the sun often shines, warming botanical gardens ripe with lemon trees, oleanders and magnolias that release their perfume as you walk along the lakefront promenades.

In summer everyone heads down to the lake – to walk, flirt, swim, lick gelato or to cruise out to the islands. Cooler still are the pine-brushed mountains and their walking trails, reached by cable car from Locarno.

# Locarno

POP 15,968 / ELEV 205M

With its palm trees and much-hyped 2300 hours of sunshine a year, visitors have swooned over Locarno's near-Mediterranean setting since the late 19th century. Switzerland's lowest-altitude town is quite special, for sure, with an air of chic insouciance, a promenade strung along its mountain-facing lakefront and botanical gardens bristling with subtropical flowers and foliage. Beyond the lake, there's a pretty Renaissance Old Town to roam, which fans out from the Piazza Grande, host of a renowned music and film festival in summer.

For an eyrie-like view over the lake and an escape from the crowds, hitch a ride up to the forested peaks of Cardada and Cimetta. Or do as centuries of pilgrims have done before you and hike up the many steps to the Santuario della Madonna del Sasso.

## Sights

**★Santuario della Madonna del Sasso** CHURCH

(www.madonnadelsasso.org; Via Santuario 2; ⏲7.30am-6pm) Overlooking the town, this sanctuary was built after the Virgin Mary supposedly appeared in a vision to a monk, Bartolomeo d'Ivrea, in 1480. There's a highly adorned church and several rather rough, near-life-size statue groups (including one of the Last Supper) in niches on the stairway. The best-known painting in the church is *La fuga in egitto* (Flight to Egypt), painted in 1522 by Bramantino.

A **funicular** (one way/return adult Sfr4.80/7.20, child Sfr2.20/3.60; ⏲8am-10pm May, Jun & Sep, to midnight Jul & Aug, to 9pm Apr & Oct, to 7.30pm Nov-Mar) runs every 15 minutes from the town centre past the sanctuary to Orselina, but a more scenic, pilgrim-style approach is the 20-minute walk up the chapel-lined Via Crucis (take Via al Sasso off Via Cappuccini).

**Castello Visconteo** MUSEUM, CASTLE

(Piazza Castello; adult/child Sfr7/free; ⏲10am-noon & 2-5pm Tue-Sun Apr-Oct) Named after the Visconti clan that long ruled Milan, this fortified 15th-century castle's nucleus was raised around the 10th century. It now houses a museum with Roman and Bronze Age exhibits and also hosts a small display (in Italian) on the 1925 Locarno Treaty. Locarno is believed to have been a glass-manufacturing town in Roman times, which accounts for the many glass artefacts in the museum.

**Piazza Grande** AREA

Locarno's Italianate Città Vecchia (Old Town) fans out from Piazza Grande, a photogenic ensemble of arcades and Lombard-style houses. A craft and fresh-produce market takes over the square every Thursday, and regular events are staged here during the warmer months.

**Parco Muralto** GARDENS

(Viale Verbano) Locarno's climate is perfect for lolling about the lake. Bristling with palms and ablaze with flowers in spring and summer, these gardens are a scenic spot for a picnic or swim, and tots can let off steam in the adventure playground.

**Falconeria Locarno** WILDLIFE RESERVE

(www.falconeria.ch; Via delle Scuole 12; adult/child/family Sfr28/18/60; ⏲10am-5pm Tue-Sun; 👪) Time your visit to catch one of the impressive displays of falconry here – they take place at 11am in the morning and 3pm in the afternoon. Birds showing off their skills include eagles, hawks, owls, vultures and storks.

## Activities

Locarno's lakefront is made for aimless ambles. For more action, catch a cable car from the Orselina funicular stop to **Cardada** (1332m), followed by a chairlift to **Cimetta** (1671m), where you can hike, mountain bike, paraglide or ski – depending on your will and the weather.

**Cimetta** CABLE CAR

(www.cardada.ch; return adult one way/return from Orselina Sfr30/36, child Sfr15/18; ⏲9.15am-12.30pm & 1.30-4.50pm daily Mar-Nov) On clear days, the panorama that opens up at the 1671m Cimetta is out of this world – below you is the blue glitter of Lake Maggiore and beyond the Alps seem to ripple into infinity. Look carefully and you might be able to make out Switzerland's highest peak, the 4634m Dufourspitze, with its hat of snow.

The mountain is sliced up by walking trails (paths are marked) that can have you stomping along from 1½ to four or so hours, depending on which you choose. Longer routes lead into the Valle Maggia and Val Verzasca. In winter, skiers carve up the same slopes. A one-day ski pass costs Sfr38/22 for adults/children.

Cimetta is also a popular launch spot for paragliders. If you fancy taking flight, check out the offer of **Mountaingliders** (☎079 761 51 06; www.mountaingliders.com; tandem flights Sfr180).

## Locarno

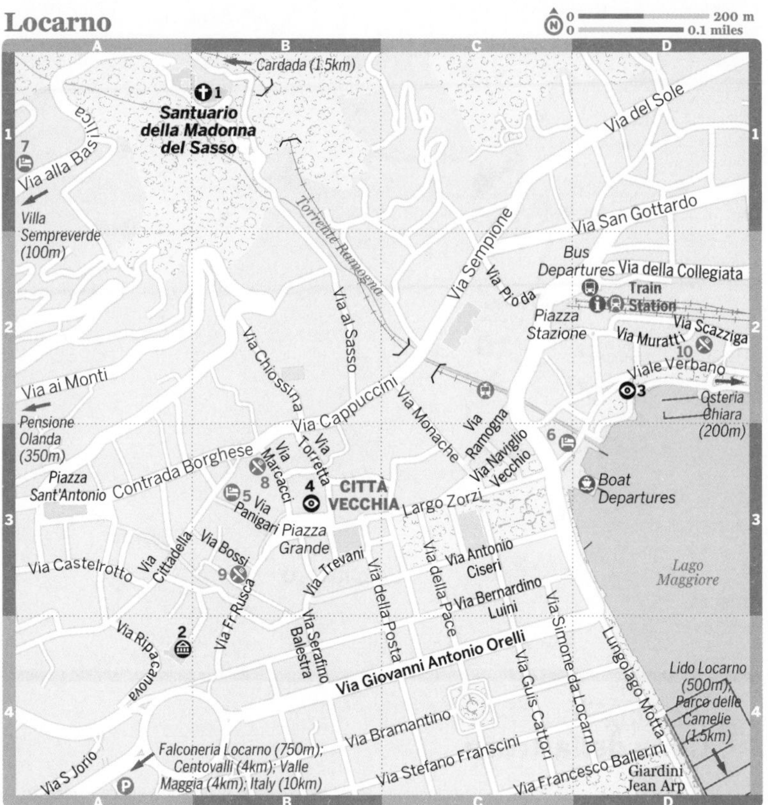


### Locarno

**Top Sights**

1 Santuario della Madonna del Sasso ........ B1

**Sights**

2 Castello Visconteo ........ A4
3 Parco Muralto ........ D2
4 Piazza Grande ........ B3

**Sleeping**

5 Caffè dell'Arte ........ B3
6 Hotel Garni Millenium ........ C3
7 Villa Sempreverde ........ A1

**Eating**

8 L'Archetto ........ B3
9 Locanda Locarnese ........ B3
10 Osteria del Centenario ........ D2

**Lido Locarno** SWIMMING

(www.lidolocarno.ch; Via Respini 11; adult/child Sfr13/7, incl waterslides Sfr18/11; 8.30am-9pm) Locarno's lido has several pools, including an Olympic-size one, children's splash areas and waterslides, and fabulous lake and mountain views. The huge complex uses solar and hydropower.

## Festivals & Events

**Moon and Stars** MUSIC

(https://moonandstars.ch) The stars shine at this open-air music festival in mid-July. Sting, Jamiroquai and Amy Macdonald were among recent headliners. Check the website for the full line-up and tickets.

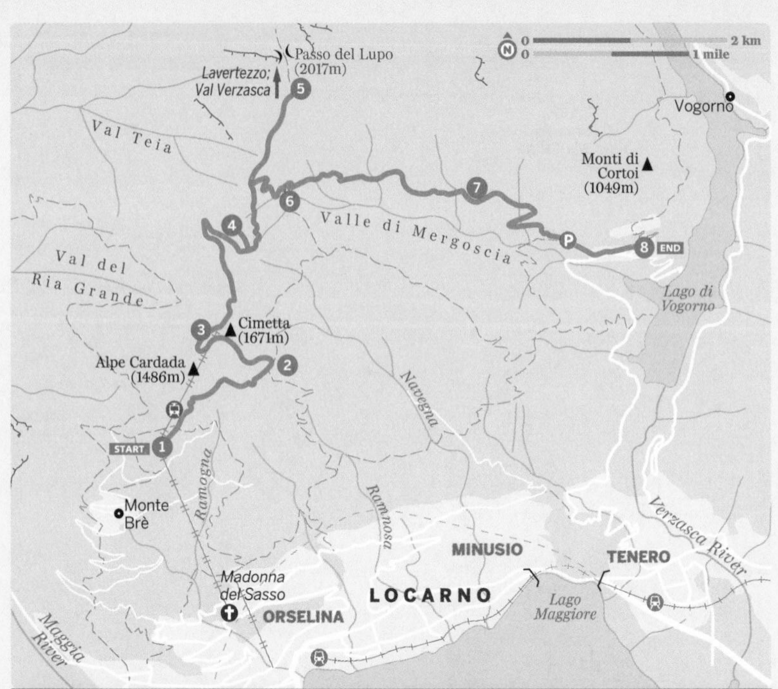


# Walking Tour
# Cima della Trosa

**START** CARDADA, LOCARNO
**FINISH** MERGOSCIA
**LENGTH** 10KM; 3¾ TO FIVE HOURS

This route traverses the rounded mountaintops, affording eagle's-eye perspectives of Lago Maggiore and Alpine peaks, and passing centuries-old hamlets and villages only accessible by foot. The most detailed map is Orell Füssli's 1:25,000 *Locarno/Ascona*.

From the upper cable-car station at 1 **Cardada**, head right, climbing around the open slopes to reach the rustic stone hut of 2 **Capanna Lo Stallone** in the grassy hollow of Alpe Cardada (1486m), after 30 to 40 minutes. The track cuts back left over the bracken-covered mountainsides, then swings right to skirt the forest and arrive at 1671m 3 **Capanna Cimetta**.

Below the upper chairlift station, the left-hand path descends quickly to a saddle (1610m) with a spring-water fountain. Make a rising traverse of the southwestern slopes of 4 **Cima della Trosa**. A short side trail brings you to the cross mounted on the 1869m summit after a further 35 to 45 minutes.

The path soon winds down Cima della Trosa's northeastern flank to a minor col (1657m). From here a side trip to the often snow-dusted peak of 5 **Madone** (2039m) takes 1½ to two hours; the straightforward route follows the ridge, with some harmless rock-scrambling and then arresting views higher up.

Descend in broad zigzags to 6 **Alpe di Bietri** (1499m), stopping for creamy goat's cheese made at the dairy, then continuing on an old mule trail tracing the northern slopes of Valle di Mergoscia. The route descends gently past dilapidated houses and rustic hamlets to reach 7 **Bresciadiga** (1128m), 1¼ to 1¾ hours from Cima della Trosa.

Bear right at a junction, leading past small shrines before coming into a car park. Stroll 600m downhill to intersect with the main road, then follow the sealed road left up steep, vine-clad hillsides to arrive at the square beside the large baroque church of postcard-pretty 8 **Mergoscia**, sitting high above the Val Verzasca, after a final one-to-1¼ hour leg. From Mergoscia, bus 312 runs every two hours back to Locarno (Sfr6.60, 36 minutes).

**Locarno Festival** FILM
(www.pardo.ch) Locarno has hosted this 11-day film festival in August since 1948. At night, films are screened on a giant screen in Piazza Grande (p190).

## Sleeping

During the Locarno Festival in August, room prices soar by 50% to 100% and rooms are like gold dust. Booking ahead in summer is essential. The tourist office has up-to-date listings of B&Bs and holiday lets.

**Pensione Olanda** B&B €
(091 751 47 27; www.pensione-olanda.ch; Via ai Monti 139a; s Sfr65, d Sfr130-160; P) Set in pretty gardens above Locarno, Pensione Olanda keeps it sweet and simple – though the views reaching across the lake to the mountains beyond are priceless. It's a 15-minute uphill walk from the centre, or take bus 32 from the station to 'Olanda' stop.

★ **Villa Sempreverde** B&B €€
(079 322 78 65; www.sempreverde.ch; Via alla Basilica 1; d/tr/q Sfr180/270/360; P) With lake and mountain views to swoon over, this 18th-century house turned B&B reclines in flower-draped gardens on a hill above Locarno. The bright, wood-floored rooms are full of homey touches. Fiorenza's homemade jams and cakes feature at breakfast.

**Caffè dell'Arte** BOUTIQUE HOTEL €€
(091 751 93 33; www.caffedellarte.ch; Via Cittadella 9; d Sfr230-370; ) Designed with a razor-sharp eye for detail, this boutique hotel above a cafe and art gallery has been decorated with flair, originality and lots of unique details. Some rooms have mock frescos, others sport leopard-print sofas and all have Nespresso coffee machines and iPads.

**Hotel Garni Millenium** B&B €€
(091 759 67 67; www.millennium-hotel.ch; Via Dogana Nuova 2; s Sfr90-200, d Sfr150-295; ) Housed in the 19th-century former customs house, this baby-blue B&B has friendly service, dreamy lake views and jazz-themed rooms.

## Eating & Drinking

**L'Archetto** PIZZA €
(076 534 04 82; Via Marcacci 11; pizza Sfr7.50-16; 11.30am-2.30pm & 5-8.30pm Mon-Sat) Even locals rave about the crisp, flavoursome takeaway pizza at this hole-in-the-wall snack spot. *Delizioso*!

**Osteria Chiara** ITALIAN €€
(091 743 32 96; www.osteriachiara.ch; Vicolo dei Chiara 1; mains Sfr34-45; 10am-2.30pm & 6.30-11pm Wed-Sun) Hidden up a flight of steps, Osteria Chiara has all the cosy feel of a *grotto* (rustic Ticino-style inn or restaurant). Sit at granite tables beneath the pergola or at timber tables by the fireplace for homemade pasta and hearty meat dishes such as veal osso buco with saffron-infused risotto. From the lake, follow the signs uphill.

**Locanda Locarnese** ITALIAN €€
(091 756 87 56; www.locandalocarnese.ch; Via Bossi 1; mains Sfr40-45; noon-2.30pm & 7pm-midnight Mon-Sat) Elegant rusticity sums up this smart restaurant, with a beamed ceiling, crisp white tablecloths and an open fire, as well as a smattering of pavement seating. It's a romantic and intimate choice for season-driven dishes.

**Osteria del Centenario** FUSION €€€
(091 743 82 22; Viale Verbano 17; mains Sfr41-62, lunch Sfr25-45, dinner tasting menu Sfr126; 11.30am-3pm & 6.30pm-midnight Tue-Sat) Down by the lake, this is a top culinary address, turning out creative fusion dishes like pigeon served two ways with green curry and lime, and panna cotta with adzuki beans, matcha-tea sauce and vanilla. Service is attentive and the ambience is discreetly elegant.

## Information

**Tourist Office** (084 809 10 91; www.ascona-locarno.com; Piazza Stazione; 9am-6pm Mon-Fri, 10am-6pm Sat, 10am-1.30pm & 2.30-5pm Sun) Conveniently located at Locarno's train station, this tourist office has stacks of information about Locarno and the surrounding region. Ask about the Ticino Discovery Card and the Lago Maggiore Guest Card and its discounts.

## Getting There & Away

If you're driving, Locarno is just off the main A13 road that links to Ascona, 2km southwest, and heads east to Bellinzona, 23km away.

Postal buses to the surrounding valleys leave from outside the train station, and boats from the lakefront. There is cheap street parking along Via della Morettina.

Hourly trains run direct to/from Lucerne (Sfr59, two hours). There's also roughly hourly service to/from Brig (Sfr56, 2¾ hours), passing through Italy (bring your passport, and change trains at Domodossola). Most trains to/from Zürich (Sfr64, 2¼ hours) go via Bellinzona. There are twice-hourly train connections from Lugano (Sfr15.20, 58 minutes).

WORTH A TRIP

### VAL VERZASCA

The startlingly emerald Verzasca River carves a deep 26km path through the forested mountains northeast of Locarno. Tempering the wilderness are tiny hamlets strung along the valley and waiting to be ticked off – each one seemingly more idyllic than the last.

Just beyond the 220m-high **Verzasca Dam**, look to the left and you will see Switzerland's smallest hamlet, **Corippo** (population 13), a cluster of granite-built, slate-roofed houses seemingly pasted on to the thickly wooded mountain flank. Lore has it that in past times locals tied fabric bags to their chickens' tails to stop the eggs rolling down the slope.

About 5km upstream, **Lavertezzo** is known for its narrow, double-humped, Romanesque bridge and the natural pools in the icy stream. Be careful, as storms upstream can turn the river into a raging torrent. Stay at riverside **Osteria Vittoria** (091 746 11 11; www.osteriavittoria.ch; Lavertezzo; d Sfr120-140), a bustling family lodge with its own restaurant and gardens. Most rooms have balconies with views over the Verzasca.

Another 12km takes you to **Sonogno**, a once-abandoned hamlet at the head of the valley, enveloped by chestnut and beech woods.

The two-day, 34km **Sentiero Verzasca** trail takes in all of the above highlights; visit http://wanderland.myswitzerland.com for route maps and details. Bouldering and climbing pros are in their element in this rocky valley.

For still more of a thrill, you could bungee jump from the top of the Verzasca Dam. The experience is five seconds of pure heart-stopping, mind-bending adrenaline. The big jump can be made on weekends between Easter and October for Sfr255. Local bungee experts include **Trekking Outdoor Team** (091 780 78 00; www.trekking.ch) and **Swissraft** (081 911 52 50; www.swissraft.ch). Both companies arrange other active pursuits, including canyoning, climbing, rafting, canoeing, paragliding and skydiving.

Bus 321 operates to Sonogno from Locarno as often as hourly (Sfr11, 1¼ hours).

# Ascona

POP 5439 / ELEV 196M

If ever there was a prize for the 'most perfect lake town', Ascona would surely win hands-down. Palm trees and pristine houses in a fresco painter's palette of pastels line the promenade, overlooking the glassy waters of Lake Maggiore to the rugged green mountains beyond. Michelin-starred restaurants, an 18-hole golf course and the Old Town's boutiques, galleries and antique shops attract a good-living, big-spending crowd.

## Sights & Activities

**Museo Comunale d'Arte Moderna** MUSEUM
(www.museoascona.ch; Via Borgo 34; adult/child Sfr10/free; 10am-noon & 2-5pm Tue-Sat, 10.30am-12.30pm Sun Mar-Dec) Housed in the late-16th-century Palazzo Pancaldi, this museum showcases paintings by artists connected with the town, among them Paul Klee, Ben Nicholson, Alexej von Jawlensky and Hans Arp. But its pride and joy is the Marianne von Werefkin collection, comprising 90 paintings and 170 sketch books by the avant-garde Russian-Swiss Expressionist painter.

**Isole di Brissago** ISLAND
(www.isolebrissago.ch; adult/child Sfr8/2.50; 9am-6pm Apr-late Oct) Marooned in the glimmering waters of Lake Maggiore, this tiny pair of islands is famous for its botanic gardens designed in the 19th century. Magnolias, orchids, yuccas and agaves are among the 1700 species that flourish here.

Navigazione Lago Maggiore **boats** (Sfr16.80, 25 minutes) run regularly between Ascona and Brissago.

**Lido Ascona** SWIMMING
(https://lidoascona.ch; Via Lido 81; adult/child Sfr6/3; lido 8.30am-5.30pm Jun–mid-Sep, bar to 1am) If you are itching to jump into that aqua-blue lake, head to this lido with a beach, diving platform, volleyball court and slides for the kids.

## Sleeping & Eating

**Albergo Antica Posta** GUESTHOUSE €€
(091 791 04 26; www.anticaposta.ch; Contrada Maggiore 4; s Sfr130-280, d Sfr200-300; P) Nestled in the heart of Ascona, this attractively converted 17th-century townhouse has nine bright, parquet-floored rooms. The restaurant serves market-fresh cuisine and opens onto a vine-clad courtyard.

**Castello Seeschloss** HISTORIC HOTEL €€€
(☎091 791 01 61; www.castello-seeschloss.ch; Via Circonvallazione 26; s Sfr205-350, d Sfr230-610; P ❄ 🛜 ≋) This is a 13th-century castle turned romantic waterfront hotel in the southeast corner of Ascona's Old Town, complete with flowery gardens and heated outdoor pool. The most extraordinary rooms, some full of frescos, are in the ivy-covered tower.

★**Ecco** FUSION €€€
(☎091 785 88 88; www.giardino.ch; Via del Segnale 10; tasting menus Sfr180-230; ⏲7pm-midnight Wed-Sun & noon-2pm Sun mid-Apr–late Oct) Super-chic Ecco flaunts two Michelin stars and dining here is an event. Head chef Rolf Fliegauf runs the stove and works wonders with carefully selected seasonal ingredients to create dishes that are richly aromatic, edible works of art.

## Information

**Tourist Office** (☎0848 091 091; www.ascona-locarno.com; Via B Papio 5; ⏲9am-6pm Mon-Fri, 10am-6pm Sat, 10am-2pm Sun)

## Getting There & Away

Ascona is on the main A13 road that leads along Lake Maggiore's northern shore, linking to Locarno, 2km northeast, and runs all the way to Bellinzona, 25km east.

Bus 1 from Locarno's **train station** (Piazza Staggione) and Piazza Grande stops at Ascona's post office with departures every 15 minutes (Sfr2.10, 18 minutes). Boat services on Lake Maggiore stop at Ascona.

# WESTERN VALLEYS

Bounded by mountains and brushed by forests of chestnuts and fragrant pine, the valleys that reach north and west of Locarno into the high Alps are some of the most ravishing in Switzerland. Their little clusters of stone houses with heavy slate roofs, inviting *grotti* (rustic Ticino-style inn or restaurants) and slender campaniles are totally disproportionate to their nature-gone-wild spectacle of gushing mountain rivers that shine unfathomable shades of green, sheer-sided peaks, dams like great mirrors and waterfalls dashed into mist. These are valleys where you can wander, channel your intrepid inner self with all manner of outdoor pursuits or simply kick back and enjoy the most arresting of views.

## Valle Maggia

ELEV 421M

Granite villages cling precariously to steep hillsides and 3000m peaks thrust up above cascading waterfalls in the broad, sunny Valle Maggia northwest of Locarno. The startlingly turquoise Maggia River twists through the valley until it splits at the main town, Cevio, the first of several divisions into smaller valleys. This is a remarkable off-the-radar destination for hiking, cycling, wild swimming, mountain biking and rock climbing.

### Sights & Activities

Hiking trails criss-cross the valley, there's abundant terrain for mountain and downhill bikers, and imposing crags attract experienced climbers in Ponte Brolla, Val Bavona and Bosco Gurin. See www.vallemaggia.ch for maps, suggested routes and accommodation info.

**Cevio** VILLAGE
The centrepiece of Cevio is its vibrant 16th-century **Pretorio** (magistrate's court), covered in the family coats-of-arms of many of the area's rulers, mostly from the 17th century. About 1km away, the heart of the Old Town is graced with 16th-century mansions.

**Val Bavona** VALLEY
A smooth road follows a babbling mountain stream through this valley, where narrow meadows are cradled between steep rocky walls. The impossibly pretty grey-stone hamlet of **Foroglio** is dominated by the wispy spray of its 100m waterfall.

The last village in the valley is San Carlo, where a cable car swings up to **Robiei Dam** (www.robiei.ch; Funivia San Carlo-Robiei; cable car one way/return Sfr19/24; ⏲8am-5pm mid-Jun–early Oct) and its vivid aqua-blue reservoir. It's terrific hiking terrain up here.

**Bosco Gurin** VILLAGE
A road of seemingly endless hairpin bends snakes up to this minor ski centre (with 30km of pistes) and high-pasture village of slate-roofed, whitewashed houses. It is the only village in Ticino where the main language is German, a result of Valais immigrants. This heritage is spelled out in artefacts at the stone-and-wood **Walserhaus** (www.walserhaus.ch; adult/child Sfr5/1; ⏲10-11.30am & 1.30-5pm Tue-Sat, 1.30-5pm Sun mid-Apr–Oct).

**Val di Campo** VALLEY

A winding forest road brings you to this broad, sunny, upland valley. The prettiest of its towns is **Campo**, with scattered houses and Romanesque bell tower. The valley is closed off by **Cimalmotto**, which offers rugged mountain views.

**Via Alta** WALKING

This challenging 52km, six-day hike is one of the region's showcase walks, leading from Locarno to Fusio (or vice versa) through the Valle Maggia and Val Verzasca. The hike takes you to jewel-coloured lakes, mountain refuges and high Alpine peaks.

**Sentiero Cristallina** WALKING

Linking Bignasco in Valle Maggia with Airolo in Val Bedretto, this 41km, two-day hike is a real beauty, taking in stone-built hamlets, Alpine lakes, mountain meadows, forests and high moors.

**Avegno** SWIMMING

If you're tempted to go for a wild swim in the glacially cold Maggia River, Avegno's beaches and natural rock pools are the place to do it.

## Sleeping & Eating

**Casa Moni** B&B €

(091 754 12 86, 079 688 79 91; Via Cantonale, Bosco Gurin; s/d Sfr85/120; P ) Expect a heartfelt *benvenuto* at this extremely peaceful B&B in Bosco Gurin, where the rush of a nearby stream is the backbeat. The colourful rooms have river or mountain views, and there's hiking and skiing right on the doorstep.

**Camping Gordevio** CAMPGROUND €

(091 753 14 44; www.tcs.ch; Gordevio; sites per adult/child/tent Sfr16/8/32; Apr-Oct; P ) Attractively situated near the Maggia River, this well-kept campground has shady pitches, a barbecue area and a solar-powered swimming pool. It's a good base for hiking, canoeing or climbing in the surrounding area.

**Grotto Ca' Rossa** SWISS €€

(091 753 28 32; www.grottocarossa.ch; Via Cantonale 34, Gordevio-Ronchini; mains Sfr25-40; 10am-2.30pm & 5.30pm-midnight Tue-Sun) Spilling onto a flower-strewn garden in summer and with a log fire blazing in winter, this *grotto* is an atmospheric spot for Ticinese specialities.

## Information

**Tourist Office** (091 753 18 85; www.vallemaggia.ch; Maggia; 9am-noon & 2-6pm Mon-Fri, 9am-noon Sat) The valley's tourist office is in Maggia.

## Getting There & Away

The minor Via Cantonale heads north of Locarno into the Valle Maggia. Cevio is a 25km drive north of Locarno. For public transport access, bus 315 runs regularly from Locarno to Cevio and Bignasco (Sfr11, 51 minutes), from where you can make less regular connections into the side valleys. Bus 333 runs three to four times a day from Bignasco to San Carlo (Sfr6.60, 35 minutes) between April and October.

# Centovalli

ELEV 708M

The Centovalli ('hundred valleys') form the westward route from Locarno/Ascona to Domodossola in Italy. From Ponte Brolla, the road winds out in a string of tight curves, high on the north flank of the Melezzo, an Alpine river largely held in check by a dam.

Clinging to the hillsides, a series of grey stone hamlets make serene bases for mountain hikes. Redolent of a more peaceful bygone age, **Rasa** is an utterly charming village. From here, a trail leads 5km to **Intragna**, whose crowning glories are the 65m bell tower of its baroque Chiesa di San Gottardo, and the nearby 80m-high Isorno viaduct.

## Sleeping & Eating

Reached by a cable car from Verdasio or a lovely 8km hike through beech and chestnut woods, the eco-friendly B&B **Alla Capanna** (091 798 18 04; www.montecomino.ch; Monte di Comino, Intragna; r per person with/without half-board Sfr75/50; Apr-Oct; ) in Intragna offers simple, pine furnished dorms and doubles, sublime mountain views and regional culinary favourites. For lodging closer to the river, try **T3e Terre** (091 743 22 22; www.3terre.ch; Via Vecchia Stazione 2, Ponte Brolla; d Sfr185-215, tr Sfr240-270; P ), a petite, green-shuttered hotel in Ponte Brolla, popular with locals for its Mediterranean-infused home cooking.

## Getting There & Away

To see the valley in beautiful slow motion, hop aboard the panoramic **Centovalli Railway** (www.centovalli.ch; one way adult/child Sfr45/22.50). On its route from Locarno to Domodossola (1¾ hours, 11 daily), the train trundles across 83 bridges and burrows through 34 tunnels, offering gasp-inducing views of waterfalls shooting over cliff faces, vineyards, viaducts, church-topped villages, deep ravines, sun-dappled chestnut forests and snow-capped peaks.

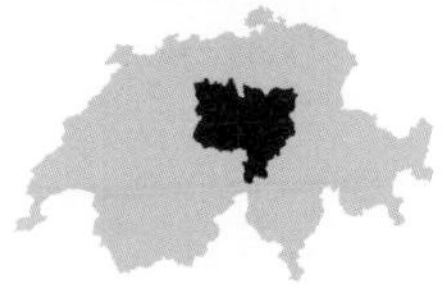

# Central Switzerland

POP 718,400

**Includes ➡**



## Best Places to Eat

- ➡ Wirtshaus Galliker (p204)
- ➡ Das Insel-Restaurant Schwanau (p212)
- ➡ Grottino 1313 (p204)
- ➡ Gasthaus Rathauskeller (p218)
- ➡ Gasthaus Ochsen (p211)

## Best Places to Stay

- ➡ Ski Lodge Engelberg (p215)
- ➡ The Bed & Breakfast (p202)
- ➡ River House Boutique Hotel (p219)
- ➡ Hotel Schmid & Alfa (p211)

## Why Go?

To the Swiss, Central Switzerland – green, mountainous and soothingly beautiful – is the essence of 'Swissness'. It was here that the pact that kick-started a nation was signed in 1291; here that hero William Tell gave a rebel yell against Habsburg rule. Geographically, politically, spiritually, this is the heartland. Nowhere does the flag fly higher.

Locals swell with pride at Lake Lucerne: enigmatic in the cold mist of morning, molten gold in the dusky half-light. The dreamy city of Lucerne is small enough for old-world charm yet big enough to harbour designer hotels and a world-class gallery full of Picassos. From here, cruise to resorts such as Weggis and Brunnen, or hike Mt Pilatus and Mt Rigi. Northeast of Lucerne, Zug has *Kirschtorte* (cherry cake) as rich as its residents and medieval heritage. Come snow time, head to the Alps for Andermatt's austere mountainscapes or Engelberg for powdery off-piste perfection.

## When to Go

- ➡ Any time is a good time to visit Lucerne, although it does get packed in summer and during the Lucerne Festival.
- ➡ Late spring, summer and early autumn are wonderful for walking and hiking in places like Andermatt and Engelberg – and for cruising on Lake Lucerne.
- ➡ Winter presents superb skiing and snowboarding opportunities at countless ski areas in the region. Engelberg, Klewenalp and Andermatt are tops.
- ➡ Zug and Lake Uri are at their best in summer, when swimming in the lakes is heavenly.

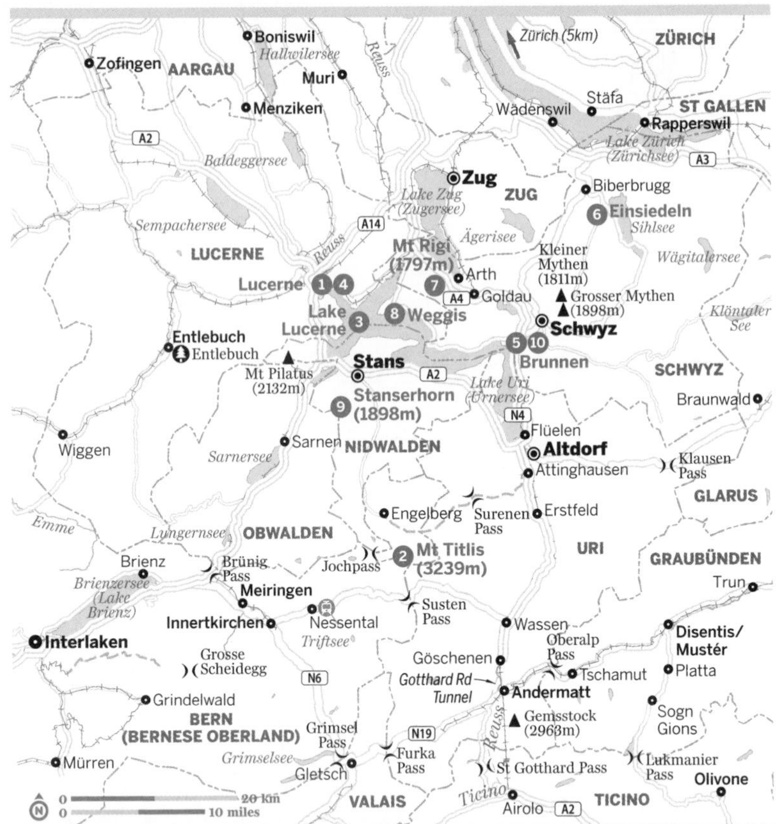


## Central Switzerland Highlights

❶ **Lucerne** (p199) Revelling in the melodious atmosphere of Switzerland's prettiest city.

❷ **Mt Titlis** (p217) Traversing the vertiginous Cliff Walk while trying not to look down.

❸ **Lake Lucerne** (p205) Cruising and witnessing the play of light and shadow, mist and magic.

❹ **Kapellbrücke** (p199) Crossing the Reuss River on Lucerne's legendary covered bridge.

❺ **Swiss Knife Valley Museum** (p210) Sharpening your knife-assembling skills in Brunnen.

❻ **Einsiedeln** (p213) Visiting Klosterkirche along with crowds of pilgrims.

❼ **Mt Rigi** (p207) Enjoying a day trip by ferry, cogwheel railway, cable car and return ferry from Lucerne.

❽ **Weggis** (p208) Relaxing on the waterfront at this genteel Lake Lucerne resort.

❾ **Stanserhorn** (p207) Catching some rays as you ride the open-topped CabriO cable car.

❿ **Swiss Path** (p210) Feeling the spirit of William Tell by walking around fjord-like Lake Uri in Brunnen.

## ℹ Getting There & Around

The nearest major airport is Zürich, and road and rail connections are excellent in all directions.

If you don't have a Swiss Travel Pass (which is valid on lake journeys), consider purchasing the regional **Tell-Pass** (www.tell-pass.ch; adult per 2/3/4/5/10 days Sfr180/210/230/240/300, child up to 10 days Chf30), which is valid from April through October. Sold at Lucerne tourist office and all boat stations, it provides unlimited travel region-wide on trains, boats, buses, cable cars and mountain railways for two to 10 days.

# Lucerne

POP 80,500 / ELEV 435M

Recipe for a gorgeous Swiss city: take a cobalt lake ringed by mountains of myth, add a well-preserved medieval **Altstadt** (Old Town) and a reputation for making beautiful music, then sprinkle with covered bridges, sunny plazas, candy-coloured houses and waterfront promenades. Lucerne is stunning, and deservedly popular since the likes of Goethe, Queen Victoria and Wagner savoured its views in the 19th century. Legend has it that an angel with a light showed the first settlers where to build a chapel in Lucerne, and today it still has amazing grace.

One minute it's nostalgic, the next highbrow. Though the shops are still crammed with what Mark Twain so eloquently described as 'gimcrackery of the souvenir sort', Lucerne doesn't only dwell on the past, with a roster of music gigs keeping the vibe upbeat. Carnival capers at Fasnacht, balmy summers, golden autumns – this 'city of lights' shines in every season.

## Sights

**★Kapellbrücke** BRIDGE

(Chapel Bridge) You haven't really been to Lucerne until you have strolled the creaky 14th-century Kapellbrücke, spanning the Reuss River in the Old Town. The octagonal water tower is original, but its gabled roof is a modern reconstruction, rebuilt after a disastrous fire in 1993. As you cross the bridge, note Heinrich Wägmann's 17th-century triangular roof panels, showing important events from Swiss history and mythology. The icon is at its most photogenic when bathed in soft golden light at dusk.

**★Lion Monument** MONUMENT

(Löwendenkmal; Denkmalstrasse) By far the most touching of the 19th-century sights that lured so many British to Lucerne is the Lion Monument. Lukas Ahorn carved this 10m-long sculpture of a dying lion into the rock face in 1820 to commemorate Swiss soldiers who died defending King Louis XVI during the French Revolution. Mark Twain once called it the 'saddest and most moving piece of rock in the world'. For *Narnia* fans, it often evokes Aslan at the stone table.

### MUSEUM ACCESS

The two-day **Lucerne Museum Card** (www.luzern.com/en/museum-card; 2-day card Sfr36) can save you money if you plan to visit multiple museums.

DON'T MISS

### INSELI PARK

Just a stone's throw from the train station, Inseli is a leafy lakefront park where locals congregate in sunny weather to lounge on the grass, play ping-pong at outdoor tables and drink at the summertime bars **Volière** (☎041 410 00 70; www.facebook.com/voliere.3fach; ⊙11.30am-midnight May–mid-Sep) and **Buvette** (www.facebook.com/buvetteiminseli; ⊙noon-midnight Apr–mid-Sep). From the station, head east past the Kultur und Kongresszentrum (KKL), then turn 100m south along the lakeshore.

**★Museggmauer** FORTRESS

(City Wall; ⊙8am-7pm Apr-Oct) FREE For a bird's-eye view over Lucerne's rooftops to the glittering lake and mountains beyond, wander along the top of the old city walls that date back to 1386. A walkway is open between the **Schirmerturm** (tower), where you enter, and the **Wachturm**, from where you have to retrace your steps. You can also ascend and descend the **Zytturm** or **Männliturm** FREE (the latter is further west and not connected to the ramparts walkway).

**Verkehrshaus** MUSEUM

(Swiss Museum of Transport; ☎0900 333 456; www.verkehrshaus.ch; Lidostrasse 5; adult/child Sfr30/15; ⊙10am-6pm Apr-Oct, to 5pm Nov-Mar; 👪) A great kid-pleaser, the fascinating interactive Verkehrshaus is deservedly Switzerland's most popular museum. Alongside rockets, steam locomotives, aeroplanes, vintage cars and dugout canoes are hands-on activities, such as pedalo boats, flight simulators, broadcasting studios and a walkable 1:20,000-scale map of Switzerland.

The museum also shelters a **planetarium** (adult/child Sfr15/9; ⊙hours vary), Switzerland's largest **3D cinema** (www.filmtheater.ch; adult/child Sfr18/14) and the **Swiss Chocolate Adventure** (adult/child Sfr15/9), a 20-minute ride that whirls visitors through multimedia exhibits on the origins, history, production and distribution of chocolate, from Ghana to Switzerland and beyond.

## Lucerne

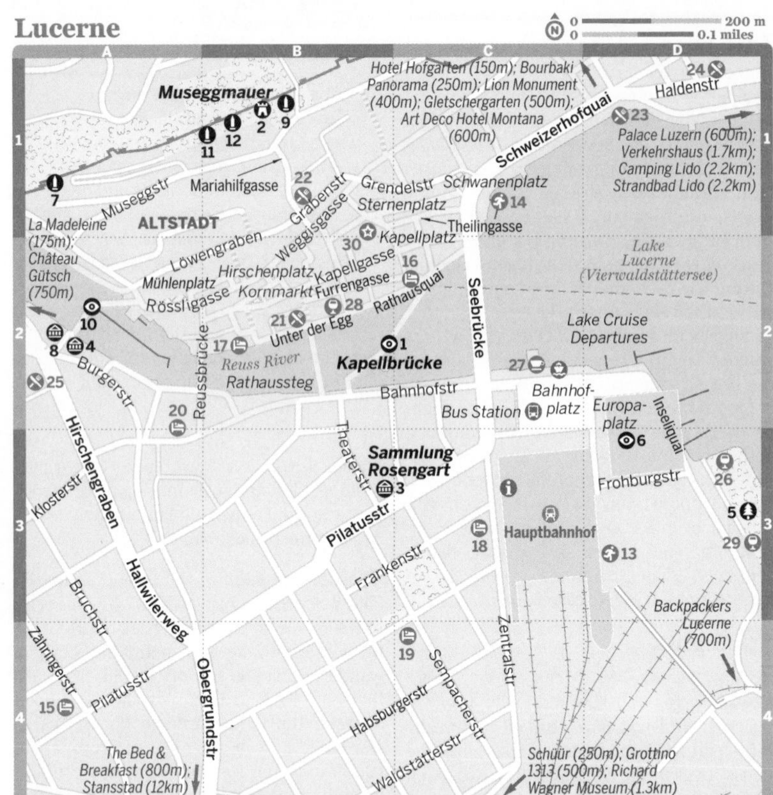


**Kultur und Kongresszentrum** ARTS CENTRE
(KKL; 041 226 79 50; www.kkl-luzern.ch; Europaplatz; guided tour adult/child Sfr15/9; ticket counter 9am-6.30pm Mon-Fri, 10am-4pm Sat) French architect Jean Nouvel's waterfront arts and convention centre is a postmodern jaw-dropper in an otherwise historic city. Inside, the tall, narrow concert hall, partly built below the lake's surface, is surrounded by a reverberation chamber and has an adjustable suspended ceiling, all creating a bubble of silence that results in near perfect acoustics. Countless accolades showered upon the hall have raised the profile of the Lucerne Festival (p202), increasingly one of the highlights on the global music calendar. Check the website for complete opening hours.

**Spreuerbrücke** BRIDGE
(Spreuer Bridge; btwn Kasernenplatz & Mühlenplatz) Downriver from Kapellbrücke, this 1408 structure is dark and small but entirely original. Lore has it that this was the only bridge where Lucerne's medieval villagers were allowed to throw *Spreu* (chaff) and leaves into the river. Here the roof panels consist of artist Caspar Meglinger's movie-storyboard-style sequence of paintings, *The Dance of Death,* showing how the plague affected all levels of society.

**Bourbaki Panorama** LANDMARK
(041 412 30 30; www.bourbakipanorama.ch; Löwenplatz 11; adult/child Sfr12/7; 9am-6pm Apr-Oct, 10am-5pm Nov-Mar) Edouard Castres' painstakingly detailed 1100-sq-metre circular painting depicting the internment of French troops in Switzerland after the Franco-Prussian War of 1870–71 is accompanied by a moving narrative (with written translation in English).

**Gletschergarten** LANDMARK
(Glacier Garden; 041 410 43 40; www.gletschergarten.ch; Denkmalstrasse 4; adult/child Sfr15/8; 9am-6pm Apr-Oct, 10am-5pm Nov-Mar; )

## Lucerne



The Gletschergarten houses a strip of rock bearing the scars (including huge potholes) inflicted on it by the glacier that slid over it some 20 million years ago. Kids of all ages and devotees of kitsch will love getting lost in the *Thousand and One Nights*–style mirror maze inspired by Spain's Alhambra Palace. It's next door to the Lion Monument (p199).

**Kunstmuseum** MUSEUM
(Museum of Art; 041 226 78 00; www.kunstmuseumluzern.ch; Level K, Europaplatz 1; adult/child Sfr15/6; 10am-6pm Tue & Thu-Sun, to 8pm Wed) At this art museum inside the Kultur und Kongresszentrum, the permanent collection garners mixed reviews, but keep an eye out for great temporary exhibitions.

**Historisches Museum** MUSEUM
(History Museum; 041 228 54 24; www.historischesmuseum.lu.ch; Pfistergasse 24; adult/child Sfr10/5; 10am-5pm Tue-Sun) Lucerne's history museum is cleverly organised into a series of attention-grabbing themed sections, each interpreted in German or English with the help of a barcode-reading audioguide.

**Natur-Museum** MUSEUM
(Nature Museum; 041 228 54 11; www.naturmuseum.ch; Kasernenplatz 6; adult/child Sfr8/3; 10am-5pm Tue-Sun) At this hands-on museum full of stuffed critters and creepy crawlies, highlights include a woodland trail with real trees, plus the fabled *Luzerner Drachenstein* (Lucerne Dragon Stone), which legendarily fell from a dragon's mouth as it was flying over Mt Pilatus. (Modern science suggests that the 15th-century stone was probably a meteorite.)

**Richard Wagner Museum** MUSEUM
(041 360 23 70; www.richard-wagner-museum.ch; Richard-Wagner-Weg 27; adult/child Sfr10/free; 10am-noon & 2-5pm Tue-Sun mid-Mar–Nov) Housed in the composer's former residence in Tribschen, on the lake's southern shore, this museum harbours historic musical instruments, including rarities such as a regal (portable organ). Take bus 6, 7 or 8 from the train station to Wartegg.

## Activities

The tourist office (p205) can give details on walks in the area, such as the gentle amble from Schwanenplatz to Sonnmatt.

**Strandbad Lido** SWIMMING
(041 370 38 06; www.lido-luzern.ch; Lidostrasse 6a; adult/child Sfr7/4; 9am-8pm Jun-Aug, 10am-7pm May & Sep) Perfect for a splash or sunbathe is this lakefront beach with a playground, volleyball court and heated outdoor pool near Camping Lido. Alternatively, swim for free on the lake's opposite shore in Seepark, off Alpenquai.

DON'T MISS

## SAMMLUNG ROSENGART

Lucerne's blockbuster cultural attraction is the **Sammlung Rosengart** (041 220 16 60; www.rosengart.ch; Pilatusstrasse 10; adult/child Sfr18/10; 10am-6pm). Occupying a neo-classical building, it showcases the outstanding collection of Angela Rosengart, a Swiss art dealer and close friend of Picasso who, in an act of great civic generosity, made some 200-odd works available to the public. Alongside works by the great Spanish master are paintings and sketches by Klee, Cézanne, Kandinsky, Miró, Matisse and Monet, including the first item ever bought by Rosengart, Swiss artist Paul Klee's childlike *X-chen* (1938).

Complementing this collection are some 200 photographs by David Douglas Duncan of the last 17 years of Picasso's life with his family in their home near Cannes, France. It's a uniquely revealing series that portrays the artist in his roles as an impish craftsman, lover, friend and father.



**SNG** BOATING
(041 368 08 08; www.sng.ch; Alpenquai 11; pedalo/motorboat/pontoon boat per hour from Sfr30/60/90) SNG rents out boats and offers cheap 60-minute lake cruises (adult/child Sfr19/10).

**Next Bike** CYCLING
(041 508 08 00; www.nextbike.ch; Lucerne Bahnhof; bikes per hour/day Sfr2/20) This outfit offers bike rental at the train station; use the app or call the number, provide credit card details and receive a numbered code to open a combination lock. There are several scenic routes along the lakefront, including the easygoing 16km pedal to Winkel via Kastanienbaum.

**SkyGlide** PARAGLIDING
(041 620 20 22; www.skyglide.ch; paragliding from Sfr170) This well-regarded tandem paragliding outfit will send you soaring high over Lake Lucerne.

## Festivals & Events

**Lucerne Festival** MUSIC
(041 226 44 00; www.lucernefestival.ch) This world-class music festival is divided into three separate seasons: Easter, summer and 'at the Piano' (in November). Concerts take place in the KKL (p200) and around town.

## Sleeping

Lucerne is an extremely popular city among visitors to Switzerland and there are lots of options to choose from. Book accommodation well ahead for Fasnacht or the Lucerne Festival. Visit www.luzern-hotels.ch for inspiration.

★ **The Bed & Breakfast** B&B €
(041 310 15 14; www.thebandb.ch; Taubenhausstrasse 34; d from Sfr140, s/d/tr/q without bathroom from Sfr85/130/165/200; P) This friendly B&B feels like home – with stylish, contemporary rooms, crisp white bedding and scatter cushions. Unwind in the garden or with a soak in the old-fashioned tub. Book ahead for the room under the eaves with private bathroom; all others share facilities. Take bus 1 to Eichhof or it's a 15-minute walk from the train station.

★ **Schlössli Hotel & Restaurant** HOTEL €
(041 377 14 72; www.schloesslimeggen.ch; Luzernerstrasse 4, Meggen; s/d Sfr80/100; P) This very friendly hotel in Meggen, 6km east of Lucerne, is a find if you are on a budget. Rooms are simple but spotless, there's free parking and wi-fi, and it's only 10 minutes to Lucerne train station on bus 24 (Sfr4.10). Its **Schlössli** restaurant serves everything from pizzas to salads to Swiss staples.

**Camping Lido** CAMPGROUND €
(041 370 21 46; www.camping-international.ch; Lidostrasse 19; sites per adult/child/Sfr10/5, tent Sfr10-15, dm Sfr25; P) On the lake's northern shore, east of town, this shaded ground also has four- to eight-bed wooden cabins (sleeping bag required). There's a playground, laundry, bike hire and a games room with wi-fi. Take bus 6, 8 or 24 to Verkehrshaus.

**Hotel Alpha** HOTEL €
(041 240 42 80; www.hotelalpha.ch; Zähringerstrasse 24; d Sfr158, s/tw/tr without bathroom Sfr84/126/171; ) Easy on the eyes and wallet, this hotel is in a quiet residential area 10 minutes' walk from the Old Town. Rooms are simple, light and spotlessly clean; cheaper rooms have shared-bathroom facilities.

**Backpackers Lucerne** HOSTEL €
(041 360 04 20; www.backpackerslucerne.ch; Alpenquai 42; dm/tr Sfr33/111, tw Sfr78-84; reception 7.30-10am & 4-11pm; ) Just opposite the lake, a 15-minute walk southeast of the train

station, this is a soulful place to crash, with art-slung walls, bubbly staff and immaculate dorms with balconies. There's no breakfast, but guests have access to a well-equipped kitchen. Blades and mountain bikes for rent.

**Hotel Waldstätterhof** HOTEL €€
(☎041 227 12 71; www.hotel-waldstaetterhof.ch; Zentralstrasse 4; s/d/tr from Sfr110/140/210; P ) Just across from the train station, this hotel with faux-Gothic exterior offers smart, modern rooms with hardwood-style floors and high ceilings, plus excellent service.

**Hotel des Balances** HOTEL €€
(☎041 418 28 28; www.balances.ch; Weinmarkt 4; s/d/ste from Sfr150/220/305; P ) Behind its elaborately frescoed facade, this perfectly positioned Old Town hotel flaunts a light and airy design ethos, with ice-white rooms, gilt mirrors and parquet floors. Suites have river-facing balconies. For the singles and doubles, expect to pay more for river-facing rooms. Breakfast is an additional Sfr32 per person.

**Hotel des Alpes** HOTEL €€
(☎041 417 20 60; www.desalpes-luzern.ch; Furrengasse 3; s/d from Sfr115/175; ) Facing the river and directly overlooking Kapellbrücke, the location is this hotel's biggest draw. Rooms are turn-of-the-21st-century comfy, though light sleepers may find them noisy. You'll pay more for river-facing rooms, though consider the noise factor if you do.

**Art Deco Hotel Montana** DESIGN HOTEL €€
(☎041 419 00 00; www.hotel-montana.ch; Adligenswilerstrasse 22; s/d from Sfr190/260; ) Perched above the lake, this opulent art deco hotel is reached by its own funicular. The handsome rooms reveal attention to detail, from inlaid parquet floors to period lighting. Many have glorious views, as do the terrace and entrance.

**Wilden Mann Hotel** BOUTIQUE HOTEL €€
(☎041 210 16 66; www.wilden-mann.ch; Bahnhofstrasse 30; s/d/ste incl breakfast from Sfr165/270/360; ) Classically elegant rooms adorned with stucco, ruby-red fabrics and antique dressers attract romantics to this 16th-century stunner near the river. The 1st-floor terrace is heaven for alfresco dining.

**Hotel Hofgarten** HOTEL €€
(☎041 410 88 88; www.hofgarten.ch; Stadthofstrasse 14; s/d/tr from Sfr165/240/295; P ) In a building dating from 1670, this hotel has striking, individually decorated rooms, along with a lovely courtyard dining area. Cuisine is based on local produce.

**Château Gütsch** HOTEL €€€
(☎041 289 14 14; www.chateau-guetsch.ch; Kanonenstrasse; d/ste from Sfr330/450; P ) The setting is incomparable at this Russian-owned, fairy-tale hilltop palace. Many rooms and suites enjoy sweeping aerial perspectives over Lake Lucerne, as do the bar and breakfast terrace.

**The Hotel** HOTEL €€€
(☎041 226 86 86; www.the-hotel.ch; Sempacherstrasse 14; r/ste from Sfr255/555; ) This shamelessly hip hotel, bearing the imprint of architect Jean Nouvel, is all streamlined chic, with refined suites featuring stills from movie classics on the ceilings. Downstairs, the hotel boasts one of Lucerne's trendiest restaurants, and the gorgeous green park across the street is a cool place to idle.

**Palace Luzern** HOTEL €€€
(☎041 416 16 16; www.palace-luzern.ch; Haldenstrasse 10; r from Sfr450; ) This luxury belle époque hotel on the lakefront is sure of its place in many a heart. Inside it's all gleaming marble, chandeliers, airy rooms and turn-of-the-20th-century grandeur. You can't go wrong here in the grandest place on the waterfront.

## Eating

**Jazzkantine** CAFE €
(☎041 410 73 73; www.jazzkantine.com; Grabenstrasse 8; pasta from Sfr16, sandwiches from Sfr7; 9am-12.30am Mon-Sat) With its long bar, sturdy wooden tables and chalkboard menus in the back of the Old Town, this arty haunt serves tasty Italian dishes and good coffee. Regular jazz workshops and gigs take place downstairs.

**Takrai** THAI €
(☎041 412 04 04; www.takrai.ch; Haldenstrasse 9; mains from Sfr14.50; 11am-2pm & 5-10pm Mon-Fri, 11am-10pm Sat) This little Thai joint emphasises local organic produce in its generously portioned curries. If you can't nab a table, order takeaway and chow down lakeside.

**Le Piaf** INTERNATIONAL €
(☎041 226 71 00; https://www.lepiaf-luzern.ch/; Europaplatz 1; mains from Sfr17; 9am-8pm) Salads and sandwiches fill the display cases at the KKL's slick bistro-cum-cafeteria; there are also cocottez dishes at lunch and dinner.

★**Wirtshaus Galliker** SWISS €€
(☎041 240 10 02; Schützenstrasse 1; mains from Sfr21; ⏲11.30am-2pm & 6-8.30pm Tue-Sat) Passionately run by the Galliker family for over four generations, this old-style tavern still attracts a lively bunch of regulars. Motherly waitresses dish up Lucerne soul food – rösti, *Chögalipaschtetli* (veal pastry pie) and the like – that is batten-the-hatches filling.

**Brasserie Bodu** FRENCH €€
(☎041 410 01 77; www.brasseriebodu.ch; Kornmarkt 5; mains from Sfr22; ⏲9am-midnight Mon-Sat, from 11am Sun) Banquettes, wood panelling and elbow-to-elbow tables create a warm ambience at this classic French-style bistro, where diners huddle around bottles of Bordeaux and bowls of bouillabaisse (a fish stew) or succulent sirloin steaks.

★**Bam Bou by Thomas** MEDITERRANEAN €€€
(☎041 226 86 86 10; www.bambou-luzern.ch; Sempacherstrasse 14; lunch mains from Sfr23; ⏲11.30am-2pm & 6-10pm Tue-Sat) The Hotel's (p203) below-street-level restaurant has undergone a transformation and is now run by award-winning chefs Corinna and Ralf Thomas, specialising in excellent French-Mediterranean cuisine.

★**Grottino 1313** ITALIAN €€€
(☎041 610 13 13; www.grottino1313.ch; Industriestrasse 7; lunch menus from Sfr20, dinner menu Sfr64; ⏲11.30am-2pm Mon-Fri, 6-11.30pm daily) Offering a welcome escape from Lucerne's tourist throngs, this relaxed yet stylish eatery south of the train station serves 'surprise' menus featuring starters like chestnut soup with figs, creative pasta dishes, meats cooked over an open fire and scrumptious desserts.

**Schiffrestaurant Wilhelm Tell** SWISS €€€
(☎041 410 23 30; https://schiffrestaurant.ch; Landungsbrücke 9; 3-course menu Sfr54; ⏲11am-midnight Tue-Sat, to 11pm Sun) The old paddle steamer *Wilhelm Tell* may have been around for nearly 110 years, but it never gets to leave its dock these days. It now spends its time as a lovely floating restaurant and bar. Come for lunch or dinner, or simply sit out on the deck and enjoy the surroundings with a coffee, cocktail or beer.

## Drinking & Nightlife

**Rathaus Bräuerei** BREWERY
(☎041 410 61 11; www.rathausbrauerei.ch; Unter der Egg 2; ⏲11.30am-midnight Mon-Sat, to 11pm Sun) Sip on some home-brewed beer under the vaulted arches of this buzzy tavern close to Kapellbrücke, or nab a pavement table and watch the river flow. You know this place is good as it's positively brimming with locals.

**Luz Seebistro** CAFE
(☎041 367 68 72; www.luzseebistro.ch; ⏲7.30am-12.30am) On the lakefront just opposite the train station, this fin-de-siècle boathouse makes an atmospheric spot for drinks at sunset or a coffee break any time of day.

## Entertainment

**Schüür** LIVE MUSIC
(www.schuur.ch; Tribschenstrasse 1; ⏲7pm-late) Live gigs are the name of the game here: think everything from metal, garage and pop to electro, Cuban and world, plus theme nights with DJ-spun Britpop and '80s classics. Check its website for what is coming up.

**Stadtkeller** TRADITIONAL MUSIC
(☎041 410 47 33; www.swissfolkloreshow.com; Sternenplatz 3; ⏲shows lunch 12.15pm, dinner 8pm) Alphorns, cowbells, flag throwing, yodelling – name the Swiss cliché and you'll find it at this tourist-oriented club with regular lunch and dinner folklore shows. While it's more than a tad touristy, it's also pretty good fun.

WORTH A TRIP

### ENTLEBUCH

Located southwest of Lucerne, the 39,000-plus sq km **Entlebuch area** (www.biosphaere.ch; a mixed mountain and highland ecosystem) was declared a Unesco Biosphere Reserve in 2001. Far from being a lonely wilderness outpost, the reserve is home to some 17,000 people keen to preserve their traditional dairy-farming lifestyle. The landscape of karst formations, sprawling moors (some 25% of the area), Alpine pastures and mountain streams, which rises from 600m to some 2350m above sea level, makes for some wonderful hiking opportunities. For details pop into the **park office** (☎041 485 88 50; Chlosterbüel 28; ⏲8am-noon & 1.30-5pm Mon-Fri) in Schüpfheim.

**La Madeleine** LIVE MUSIC
(www.lamadeleine.ch; Baselstrasse 15; 8pm-late Wed-Sat) This is a lovely little spot for a low-key gig, with two performance areas and a cosy-glam bar. The monthly schedule is on its website.

## Shopping

Packed with shops, Lucerne is a fun place to browse. Mosey down Haldenstrasse for art and antiques or Löwenstrasse for vintage threads and souvenirs. Fruit and vegetable stalls spring forth along the river quays every Tuesday and Saturday morning. There's also a flea market on Burgerstrasse each Saturday from May to October.

## Information

**Tourist Office** (041 227 17 17; www.luzern.com; Zentralstrasse 5; 8.30am-7pm Mon-Fri, 9am-7pm Sat, 9am-5pm Sun May-Oct, shorter hours Nov-Apr) Reached from Zentralstrasse or platform 3 of the Hauptbahnhof. Day long excursions around Lake Lucerne can be booked here.

## Getting There & Away

Frequent trains connect Lucerne to Interlaken Ost (Sfr33, 1¾ hours), Bern (Sfr40, one to 1½ hours), Lugano (Sfr61, two hours) and Zürich (Sfr26, 45 minutes to one hour).

The A2 freeway connecting Basel and Lugano passes by Lucerne, while the A14/A4 provides the road link to Zürich.

## Getting Around

Walking is a delight in the largely pedestrianised Old Town. For points further afield, catch city **buses** (www.vbl.ch) outside the Hauptbahnhof at Bahnhofplatz. All-day tickets for zone 10, covering the city centre and beyond, cost Sfr8.20; single-ride tickets cost Sfr4.10. Swiss Travel Pass holders travel free. There's an underground car park at the train station.

**Ferries** (www.lakelucerne.ch) shuttle passengers to various points around the lake as well as head out on excursions from the quay in front of the station.

# Lake Lucerne

Majestic peaks hunch conspiratorially around Vierwaldstättersee – which twists and turns as much as the tongue does when pronouncing it. It's little wonder English speakers use the shorthand Lake Lucerne!

To appreciate the views, ride up to Mt Pilatus, Mt Rigi or Stanserhorn. When the clouds peel away, precipitous lookout points reveal a crumpled tapestry of green hillsides and shimmering cobalt below, with glaciated peaks beyond.

Apart from its mountain viewpoints, the lake offers tucked-away resorts, all accessible by boat. The far eastern reach of Lake Lucerne – Lake Uri or Urnersee – is home to the Rütli Meadow, where the country was legendarily born.

The lake's northern and eastern coastlines are easily accessed and if you've got your own wheels, you can drive from Lucerne to Weggis to Brunnen to Flüelen more or less beside the water the whole way.

## Getting Around

Boats operated by **SGV** (www.lakelucerne.ch), including some paddle steamers, criss-cross Lake Lucerne daily throughout the year. Longer trips are relatively cheaper than short ones, and you can alight as often as you want.

From Lucerne, destinations include Alpnachstad (one way/return Sfr27/45, 1¾ hours), Weggis (Sfr19.60/38, 50 minutes), Vitznau (Sfr27/45, 1¼ hours), Brunnen (Sfr39/63, 1¾ hours) and Flüelen (Sfr46/72, 3¼ hours).

An SGV day ticket costs Sfr72/36 per adult/child. The Swiss Travel Pass is valid on scheduled boat trips, while InterRail entitles you to half-price tickets. Passes will also get you discounts on selected mountain railways and cable cars.

Roads closely follow Lake Lucerne's shoreline most of the way around – excluding the stretch from Flüelen to Stansstad. Here the A2 freeway ploughs a fairly straight line, sometimes underground and usually away from the water.

## Mt Pilatus

Rearing above Lucerne from the southwest, and accessed by the world's steepest cog railway, Mt Pilatus (www.pilatus.ch; 9km southwest of Lucerne) makes an unforgettable, scenic day excursion. The mountain rose to fame in the 19th century when Wagner waxed lyrical about its Alpine vistas and Queen Victoria trotted up here on horseback. Legend has it that this 2132m peak was named after Pontius Pilate, whose corpse was thrown into a lake on its summit and whose restless ghost has haunted its heights ever since. It's more likely that the moniker derives from the Latin

## Lake Lucerne

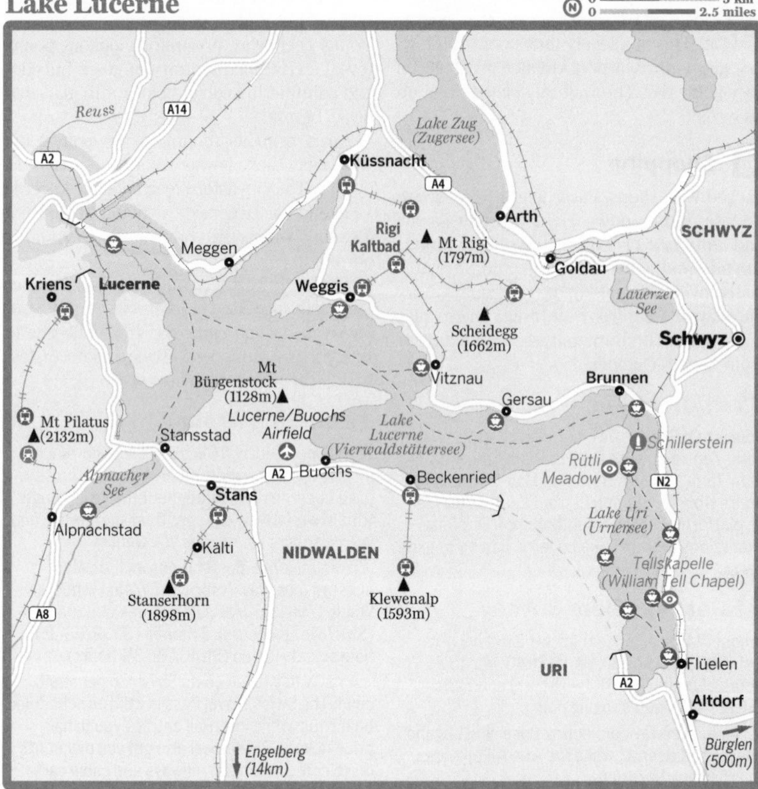


word *pileatus,* meaning cloud covered – as the mountain frequently is.

### Activities

Mt Pilatus is fantastic for walking. Hikes include a steep, partially roped 2.8km scramble (June to September) from Fräkmüntegg to the summit, an easy 3.5km walk through forest and moorland from Krienseregg to Fräkmüntegg, and the 1.5km trudge from Pilatus-Kulm to Tomlishorn, affording views that stretch as far as the Black Forest on a clear day.

**Pilatus Seilpark** ADVENTURE SPORTS
(Rope Park; www.pilatus-seilpark.ch; adult/child Sfr28/21; ⏲10am-5pm May–Oct) For an above-the-treetops adventure in summer, head for Pilatus Seilpark, where 11 head-spinning trails from high-wire bridges to tree climbs are graded according to difficulty. To get here, take the cable car down from Mt Pilatus or up from Krienz to Fräkmüntegg.

In winter, try **sledging** 6km through snowy woodlands from Fräkmüntegg to Kriens. A day-pass ticket between Kriens and Fräkmüntegg by cable car costs Sfr35/17.50 per adult/child. Sledge hire (from Sfr8) is available at Fräkmüntegg station.

### Sleeping

**Pilatus-Kulm** HOTEL €€€
(☎041 329 12 12; www.pilatus.ch/en/hotel-pilatus-kulm; Mt Pilatus; per person from Sfr210; 📶) Dating from 1890 and thoroughly renovated of late, the dramatically perched Pilatus-Kulm hotel offers a swanky mountaintop sleeping experience, with four-course dinner and buffet breakfast included. Discounts are offered in the low season (late November to March).

### Getting There & Away

From May to October, you can reach Mt Pilatus on a classic 'golden round-trip' day excursion. Board a boat from Lucerne to Alpnachstad (one way/return Sfr27/45, 1¾ hours), on the south side of the mountain, then rise with the world's steepest cog railway to Mt Pilatus. From the summit, cable cars bring you down the northern side of the mountain to Kriens (via Fräkmüntegg and Krienseregg), where bus 1 takes you back to Lucerne. The reverse route (Kriens–Pilatus–Alpnachstad–Lucerne) is also possible. The return trip costs Sfr106 (less with valid Swiss, Eurail or InterRail passes). Book at Lucerne's tourist office (p205).

The aerial cableway linking Fräkmüntegg and Pilatus on the northern side of the mountain is proving a real hit. Nicknamed the 'Dragon Ride', because of its design and large windows, it completes the link in 3½ minutes.

## Stanserhorn

Looming above the lake, 1898m Stanserhorn (www.stanserhorn.ch; 13km south of Lucerne) boasts 360-degree vistas of Lake Lucerne, Mt Titlis, Mt Pilatus and other surrounding mountains. Getting to the summit is half the fun. It involves a vintage 1893 funicular followed by a state-of-the-art double-decker cable car with an open upper deck. Once you reach the top, there are 'Stanserhorn Rangers' to point out what is going on, including marmot-viewing, a geo-trail and an earth energy spot to keep you busy.

### Sights

**Stanserhornbahn Funicular** FUNICULAR
(041 618 80 40; www.stanserhorn.ch; funicular & cable-car adult/child return Sfr74/37; mid-Apr–early Nov) From 1893 to 1974, Stanserhorn was accessed from Stans in three sections by funicular trains.

In 1974 the top two sections were replaced by an aerial cable car (which has since been replaced by the CabriO cable car), leaving only the section from Stans to Kälti operated by this lovely historical funicular.

The original 1893 bottom station (450m) is still in use – it's a five-minute walk from Stans train station. Tickets are included with the CabriO cable car to the top.

**CabriO** CABLE CAR
(041 618 80 40; www.cabrio.ch; Stansstaderstrasse 19; funicular & cable-car adult/child return Sfr74/37; mid-Apr–early Nov) This impressive double-decker cable car lets you head up top out into the open air for spectacular views as it whisks you over 1100 vertical metres from its Kälti base station at 711m. The journey takes 6½ minutes. If you're on top and it's windy, hang on to your hat. This is the world's first cable car with a roofless upper deck.

> **LAKE LUCERNE REGION VISITORS CARD**
>
> If you're staying overnight in Lucerne, make sure you ask for your free **Lake Lucerne Region Visitors Card** (Vierwaldstättersee Gästekarte; www.luzern.com/en/festivals-events/visitors-card). Stamped by your hotel, it entitles you to discounts on various museums, sporting facilities, cable cars and lake cruises in Lucerne and the surrounding area.

### Sleeping

**Hotel Engel** HOTEL €€
(041 619 10 10; www.engelstans.ch; Dorfplatz 1; s/d from Sfr120/170; P ) The well-regarded Hotel Engel has very attractive rooms behind its historic facade only a minute or two from Stans train station. There's also a very good on-site restaurant.

### Getting There & Away

Stans is on the Lucerne–Engelberg railway (one way from Lucerne Sfr8.60, 20 minutes). The funicular's base station is a five-minute walk from Stans train station.

Stanserhorn can also be visited on a one-day excursion from Lucerne. Ask at Lucerne's tourist office (p205) for details.

## Mt Rigi

Turner couldn't quite make up his mind about how he preferred 1797m Rigi (www.rigi.ch; 13km east of Lucerne), so in 1842 the genius painted the mountain in three different lights to reflect its changing moods. On a clear day there are impressive views to a jagged spine of peaks including Mt Titlis and the Jungfrau giants. To the north and west, you overlook Arth-Goldau and Zugersee, which curves around until it almost joins Küssnacht and an arm of Lake Lucerne. Sunrises and sunsets viewed from Rigi's summit are the stuff of bucket lists.

### Activities

Rigi is a magnet for hikers; for recommended routes, check the Rigi website. Several easy walks (one to two hours) lead down from Rigi

### MT RIGI FOR FREE

If you have a Swiss Travel Pass, a day excursion to Mt Rigi is likely to be high on your list of activities for Lucerne. The whole trip, including the boat ride to Vitznau, the cogwheel railway to the top, cable car back down to Weggis, then boat ride back to Lucerne, is included with your Swiss Travel Pass.

Kulm to Rigi Kaltbad, with wonderful views. Tourist offices in Lucerne and Weggis can provide information on the Rigi Lehnenweg, a scenic 17.5km trek around the mountain.

Hiking up the mountain is another story. It's at least a 4½-hour climb from Weggis; alternatively, take the **cable car** (www.luftseilbahnseebodenalp.ch; one way/return Sfr13/22) from Küssnacht to Seebodenalp, where a steepish path leads to the summit in just over two hours. While hiking on Rigi, watch out for the Chlyni Lüüt, tiny 'wild folk' with supernatural powers who in mythology once inhabited Rigi!

**Mineralbad & Spa Rigi Kaltbad** SPA
(☎041 397 04 06; www.mineralbad-rigikaltbad.ch; adult/child Sfr37/17; ⏰9am-7pm) After a hard day's hiking, soothe your muscles at the Mineralbad & Spa Rigi Kaltbad, designed by renowned Swiss architect Mario Botta. Basic admission includes unlimited daylight use of the mineral baths; more decadent options include candlelit evening soaks and massage-and-Prosecco packages.

## Sleeping

**Rigi Kulm Hotel** HOTEL €€
(☎041 880 18 88; www.rigikulm.ch; Mt Rigi; per person from Sfr115; 📶) Sunrise is prime-time viewing around here. Since Victorian times, tourists have been staying at the Rigi Kulm Hotel and getting up before the crack of dawn to see the blazing sun light up the sky. Today's hotel, a 20th-century recreation of the original, is the only major establishment at the summit, and has a restaurant and snack kiosk.

## Getting There & Away

Two rival railways carry passengers to the top (one way/return Sfr42/68). One runs from Arth-Goldau (45 minutes), the other from Vitznau (30 minutes). The Vitznau route offers the option of diverting at Rigi Kaltbad on the return trip and taking the cable car down to Weggis. Holders of Eurail and InterRail passes receive a 50% discount on fares, while Swiss Travel Pass holders travel free.

# Weggis

POP 4200 / ELEV 440M

Sheltered from cold northerlies by Mt Rigi, Weggis (9km east of Lucerne) enjoys a mild climate, sprouting a few palm and fig trees by the lakefront. It's hard to believe this genteel lakeside resort with small-town friendliness was the birthplace of the rebellious 'Moderner Bund' art movement, the forerunner of Dada.

With many lakeside hotels and resorts, Weggis makes an excellent place to stay, but most visitors come through while on their day excursion to Mt Rigi from Lucerne.

## Sleeping & Eating

**SeeHotel Gotthard** HOTEL €€
(☎041 390 21 14; www.gotthard-weggis.ch; Gotthardstrasse 11; s/d from Sfr100/160; ⏰closed mid-Oct–mid-Dec; 🅿📶) This friendly waterfront hotel has natty, modern and spotless rooms. The best have lake views and balconies, while others are attractively priced for budget travellers. Guests have access to free bikes and can use the wellness and swimming area at the Hotel Beau-Rivage, across the street.

**Post Hotel Weggis** HOTEL €€
(☎041 392 25 25; www.lh-group.ch; Seestrasse 8; s/d from Sfr160/220; 🅿❄📶) The Post's location opposite Weggis' boat dock is unbeatable. Other pluses include superb rooms, a spa, a 45,000-bottle wine cellar and multiple dining options. You may be in the heart of the action in Weggis, but expect a quiet and peaceful stay.

**Park Weggis** LUXURY HOTEL €€€
(☎041 392 05 05; www.phw.ch; Hertensteinstrasse 34; s/d from Sfr350/550; 🅿📶) This lavish lakefront beauty, west of the ferry quay, has manicured gardens and a great Zen-inspired spa. Understated elegance and smooth service is the order of the day. Revel in the lakefront views, the private beach or the attached **Park Grill** restaurant, specialising in Iberian pork and gourmet steaks from the American Great Plains.

**Grape** AMERICAN €€
(☎041 392 07 07; www.thegrape.ch; Seestrasse 60; pizza/mains from Sfr19/26; ⏰10am-2pm & 6pm-midnight Mon, Tue & Thu, to midnight Fri-Sun) Weggis' California dreamer is this hip haunt

WORTH A TRIP

## KLEWENALP

Up the slopes from Lake Lucerne's southern shore, Klewenalp (www.klewenalp.ch; 15km southeast of Lucerne) is an underrated skiing destination with 40km of well-prepared red and blue runs, which become hiking, climbing and mountain-biking trails in summer. There's also an **Alpine Flower Trail** with over 80 species to check out.

To get here, head first for lakeside Beckenried, accessible by boat from Lucerne (Sfr30, 1¼ hours), by bus from Stans (Sfr6.70, 25 minutes) or 22km by road from Lucerne. Upon disembarking at Beckenried's bus stop-boat dock, walk 200m to the cable car that whisks you up the mountain to Klewenalp (one way/return Sfr25/39, 10 minutes). A trail map at the top outlines your options. Klewenalp can also be visited on a one-day excursion from Lucerne. Ask at Lucerne's tourist office (p205) for details.

with a menu that skips from wood-fired pizza and modern burger combos to steaks and sugary desserts. (Toblerone parfait with cherries and almonds, anyone?)

### Information

**Tourist Office** (☎041 227 18 00; www.wvrt.ch; Seestrasse 5; ⊙8.30am-6pm Mon-Fri, 9am-4pm Sat & Sun) Next to Weggis' boat dock.

### Getting There & Away

Lucerne is a 40-minute boat ride (one way/return Sfr19.60/38; 50 minutes) or 19km drive from Weggis.

A cable car runs from Weggis up to Rigi Kaltbad (one way/return Sfr30/48, 10 minutes), halfway up Mt Rigi.

## Lake Uri

Scything through rugged mountains, the fjord-like Lake Uri (Urnersee) finger of Lake Lucerne mirrors the country's medieval past in its glassy turquoise waters. Road and railway run down its eastern side from Brunnen to Flüelen, but its western side is dominated by steep cliffs and is largely inaccessible unless you are on foot or in a boat. For memorable perspectives on the lake and the legendary events that unfolded here, take SGV's regular ferry service from Brunnen to Flüelen.

Altdorf, 3km south of Flüelen at the southern end of the lake, is where William Tell is reputed to have performed his apple-shooting stunt. A statue of the man himself stands in the main square.

### Sights

**Rütli Meadow** HISTORIC SITE

(Seelisberg) Perched on hillside above Lake Uri's western shore, this meadow is the legendary cradle of Swiss democracy. It was here that the Oath of Eternal Allegiance was allegedly signed by the cantons of Uri, Schwyz and Nidwalden (1291) and where General Guisan gathered the Swiss army during WWII in a show of force against potential invaders. As such, it is the focus of national day celebrations on 1 August.

It is 10 minutes southwest of Brunnen by ferry; the ferry stop is Rütli.

**Tell Museum** MUSEUM

(www.tellmuseum.ch; Postplatz, Bürglen; adult/child Sfr8/2; ⊙10am-5pm Jul & Aug, 10am-11.30am & 1.30-5pm May, Jun, Sep & Oct) Bürglen is believed to be William Tell's birthplace. Here you can visit the Tell Museum, a collection of Tell-related objects, documents and artistic works. The museum is 6km southeast of Flüelen. From Flüelen's boat dock, take bus 408 to the Postplatz stop in Bürglen.

**Tellskapelle** CHAPEL

(William Tell Chapel) On Lake Uri's eastern shore, this chapel is covered in murals depicting four episodes in the Tell legend, including the one that's supposed to have occurred on this spot: his escape from Gessler's boat. There's a huge carillon that chimes behind the chapel. Tellskapelle is 8km south of Brunnen by road.

**Schillerstein** LANDMARK

West across Lake Uri from Brunnen, you'll glimpse a near 30m-high natural obelisk, the Schillerstein, protruding from the water. Its gold inscription pays homage to Friedrich Schiller, the author of the play *Wilhelm Tell*, so instrumental in creating the Tell legend. The monument had a large inauguration ceremony in 1860.

### Getting There & Around

The best way to see Lake Uri is on a boat trip to Flüelen from Lucerne or Brunnen.

Using the A2 freeway, Flüelen, at the southern end of Lake Uri, is 40km southeast of Lucerne.

### SWISS PATH

Equipped with a decent pair of walking boots, you can circumnavigate Lake Uri on foot via the **Swiss Path** (Weg der Schweiz; www.weg-der-schweiz.ch) from Brunnen to Rütli, inaugurated to commemorate the 700th anniversary of Switzerland's 1291 founding pact. As the spectacular views unfold, so too does the symbolism – the trail is divided into 26 sections, each representing a different canton, from the founding trio to Johnny-come-lately Jura (1979). As you stride, bear in mind that 5mm of track represents one Swiss resident, so populous Zürich spans 6.1km and rural Appenzell Innerrhoden a mere 71m.

The 35km, two-day walk over hill and dale takes in some of Central Switzerland's finest scenery, cutting through meadows flecked with orchids and ox-eye daisies, revealing classic Alpine panoramas, shimmying close to the lakeshore and then dipping back into ferny forest. You'll pass historically significant landmarks, such as the Tellskapelle and the obelisk commemorating Schiller. To get a true sense of the area, it's worth completing the entire trail, but it can be broken down into shorter chunks. See the website for maps and distances.

## Brunnen

POP 8600 / ELEV 435M

Tucked into the folds of mountains, where Lake Lucerne and Lake Uri meet at right angles, Brunnen enjoys mesmerising views south and west. A regular guest, Turner was so impressed by the vista that he whipped out his watercolours to paint *The Bay of Uri from Brunnen* (1841). As the local *föhn* wind rushes down from the mountains, it creates perfect conditions for sailing, paragliding, windsurfing and kitesurfing. When the wind is up, brightly coloured sails come out. And don't forget the folkloric hot air of the weekly alpenhorn concerts in summer.

### Sights & Activities

**Swiss Knife Valley Museum** MUSEUM
(041 820 60 10; www.swissknifevalley.ch; Bahnhofstrasse 3; 10am-6.30pm Mon-Fri, to 5pm Sat & Sun; ) FREE This teensy museum displays historical knives from prehistoric, Roman and medieval times, including folding precursors to the Victorinox classic. Touch-screen films in four languages chart the history of knives in general and Victorinox specifically. But the real highlight is the 'build-your-own-knife' section: for Sfr30 staff will help you construct your own souvenir Victorinox (ages six and over; reserve in advance).

**Urmiberg** CABLE CAR
(www.urmiberg.ch; Gersauerstrasse; one way/return Sfr12/20; 9am-6pm Tue-Sun Apr-Oct) Glide over the treetops to Urmiberg for views of the pointy peaks ringing Lake Uri and Lake Lucerne. Kids travel for half-price. The cable-car station is near the lakefront, about 1km west of town.

**Familienstrandbad Hopfräben** SWIMMING
(041 820 21 46; Gersauerstrasse 83; adult/child Sfr5/2.50; 10am-7pm May-Sep) The best of Brunnen's two lakeside beaches, this one has a giant hammock, sun loungers, a lifeguard, a wading pool and pontoons. Find it 1.5km northwest of the town centre, past the river.

**Touch and Go** PARAGLIDING
(041 820 54 31; www.paragliding.ch; Parkstrasse 4; flights from Sfr180) This outfit offers tandem paragliding flights over Lake Lucerne from almost any of the mountains surrounding the lake. It also has a paragliding school.

### Sleeping

There are decent options here from campgrounds to hotels – and between Brunnen and Weggis, a good youth hostel.

**Schlaf im Stroh** FARMSTAY €
(041 820 06 70; www.schlafimstroh-bucheli.ch; Schulstrasse 26a, Ingenbohl-Brunnen; adult/child Sfr27/15, sleeping bag rental Sfr3; May-Oct; P) Kids love meeting the farmyard animals and spending a night in the straw at the Bucheli-Zimmermann family's farmhouse. A hearty breakfast is included. It's only five minutes' walk from Brunnen's train station; cross the bridge, follow signs for Aula/Sporthalle onto Schulstrasse, and look for the big brown barn.

**Gersau Youth Hostel** HOSTEL €
(041 828 12 77; www.youthhostel.ch; Seestrasse 163, Gersau; dm/s/d Sfr35/56/80; P) Smack

on the lakeshore between Vitznau and Gersau, this hostel has an idyllic location, along with kayaks, a swimming platform and a great breakfast. Rooms in the atmospheric old main building have dreamy lake views, low ceilings and thin walls. It's a 15-minute bus ride from Weggis or Brunnen (bus 2; Gersau-Rotschuo stop).

**Camping Hopfreben** CAMPGROUND €
(041 820 18 73; http://camping-hopfraeben.ch; sites per adult/child/tent/car Sfr7.50/3.50/8/5; mid-Apr–mid-Sep; ) Lakefront Camping Hopfreben in west Brunnen is open from Easter to September in an extremely picturesque spot, right by where the Muota River enters the lake.

★**Hotel Schmid & Alfa** HOTEL €€
(041 825 18 18; www.schmidalfa.ch; Axenstrasse 5-7; s/d/apt from Sfr75/140/260; P) Spread across two lakefront buildings, this family-run hotel has inviting rooms with citrusy colour splashes, parquet-style floors and wrought-iron balconies. There are also four spacious, family-friendly apartments with living room and optional kitchen. Budget rooms forgo the best views. The terrace restaurant is renowned for its fresh lake fish.

## Eating & Drinking

★**Gasthaus Ochsen** EUROPEAN €€
(041 820 11 59; www.hotelochsen.ch; Bahnhofstrasse 18; mains Sfr19.50-41; 8am-11pm Mon-Sat, to 10pm Sun May-Sep, shorter hours Oct-Apr) Photos of celebrity Swiss patrons line the walls at Brunnen's oldest haunt, which specialises in *Poulet im Chörbli* (chicken in a basket). There's a great little *apéro* bar under the same ownership just across the way, and decent rooms above the restaurant.

**Weisses Rössli** SWISS €€
(041 825 13 00; www.weisses-roessli-brunnen.ch; Bahnhofstrasse 8; mains from Sfr22; 11am-2pm & 6-9.30pm) Friendly service, hearty Swiss staples accompanied by fresh vegetables, and a front terrace with nice views of Brunnen's main street backed by the lake make this an agreeable spot for lunch or dinner. Weisses Rössli is also a hotel.

**Elvira's Trübli** WINE BAR
(041 820 10 11; Olympstrasse 6; 4pm-midnight Tue-Sat) Affable owner Elvira stocks an impressive array of vintages at this popular wine bar, tucked down a side street just in from the waterfront.

## Information

**Tourist Office** (041 825 00 40; www.brunnentourismus.ch; Bahnhofstrasse 15; 8.30am-6pm Mon-Fri, 9am-1pm Sat Jun-Sep, 8.30am-noon & 1.30-5.30pm Mon-Fri Oct-May) Near the waterfront, the helpful tourist office is a five-minute walk from the train station.

## Getting There & Away

The most pleasant way to reach Brunnen is by boat from Lucerne. The train (Sfr17.60, 45 to 50 minutes) is cheaper and quicker, although a change in Arth-Goldau is sometimes necessary.

There are also road connections from Lucerne, Zug and Flüelen. If you have a car, the drive around the lake from Lucerne (39km) is spectacular.

# Schwyz

POP 14,663 / ELEV 516M

The arrow-shaped Mythen mountains (1898m and 1811m) are the emblem of Schwyz and tower high above the town. They're not the only pointy thing that Schwyz is known for though, for this unassuming little place is also the birthplace of that pocket-sized, multifunctional lifesaver – the Swiss army knife. You can head to the Victorinox factory and check it out for yourself. As if that wasn't enough, Schwyz is also home to the most important document in Swiss history, the 1291 charter of federation.

## Sights

Ask the tourist office about the money-saving **Museumspass** (Sfr10), which grants admission to several of the town's sights.

**Bundesbriefmuseum** MUSEUM
(041 819 20 64; www.bundesbriefmuseum.ch; Bahnhofstrasse 20; adult/child Sfr5/free; 10am-5pm Tue-Sun) This museum is worth a visit just to eyeball the original 1291 charter of federation signed by Nidwalden, Schwyz and Uri cantons. It's accompanied by some academic bickering in German and French about its authenticity, as many historians question the accuracy of Switzerland's founding 'myths'. Pick up an English booklet at the front desk.

**Forum der Schweizer Geschichte** MUSEUM
(Forum of Swiss History; 058 466 80 11; www.forumschwyz.ch; Hofmatt, Zeughausstrasse 5; adult/child Sfr10/free; 10am-5pm Tue-Sun) This cultural hub of the Swiss National Museum offers splendid, engaging multilingual

exhibits focused on the foundation of the Swiss Confederation and the development of Swiss culture and commerce through the centuries.

**Ital Reding-Hofstatt** HISTORIC BUILDING
(041 811 45 05; www.irh.ch; Rickenbachstrasse 24; adult/child Sfr5/free; 2-5pm Tue-Fri, 10am-4pm Sat & Sun May-Oct) Set in baroque gardens, this turreted mansion was once the home of mercenary soldiers. Roam the 17th-century manor's wood-panelled rooms and vaulted cellar and the adjacent 13th-century **Haus Bethlehem** for a taste of the past.

**Hauptplatz** SQUARE
Most action in Schwyz spirals around the gurgling fountain on cobbled Hauptplatz (main square), dominated by the **Rathaus** (town hall), complete with elaborate 19th-century murals depicting the Battle of Morgarten, and the baroque **St Martin's Church**.

**Hölloch Caves** CAVE
These 200km labyrinthine caves, 13km from Schwyz in Muotatal, are Europe's longest and the world's fourth-biggest. Think about it – it's 52km from Zürich to Lucerne, so the cave system is about four times as long! You'll need a guide, sturdy footwear and warm clothing (it's 6°C or 42.8°F in the caves!) to explore them. **Trekking Team** (041 390 40 40; www.trekking.ch) arranges everything from short tours to overnight bivouac expeditions that include the surreal, 'only-in-Switzerland' experience of a fondue feast in the inky cavern darkness.

## Activities

**Adventure Point** ADVENTURE SPORTS
(079 247 74 72; www.adventurepoint.ch) Adventure Point tempts with a range of adrenaline-charged activities, including canyoning (from Sfr125), river tubing (Sfr80 to Sfr125), caving (Sfr95), snowshoeing (from Sfr65), and guided canoe and kayak tours (Sfr80 to Sfr120). Boaters can also go it alone (rental per day from Sfr60).

**Stoos** HIKING
(www.stoos-muotatal.ch) Plenty of hikes begin from Stoos on a plateau above Vierwaldstättersee (Lake Lucerne), affording long views across the Muotatal to Rütli, Rigi and Pilatus. From Schwyz, bus 1 heads to the Stoosbahn stop (15 minutes), where you catch the funicular up to Stoos (10 minutes).

## Sleeping & Eating

**Hirschen Backpacker-Hotel & Pub** HOSTEL €
(041 811 12 76; www.hirschen-schwyz.ch; Hinterdorfstrasse 14; dm Sfr35, s/d Sfr70/120, without bathroom Sfr60/100; P) This cheerful pad makes up for fairly basic digs with a friendly vibe and a welcome drink. There's a kitchen, pub, courtyard and active social calendar. Take bus 1 to Sonnenplätzli or walk five minutes east from Hauptplatz.

**Wysses Rössli** HOTEL €€
(041 811 19 22; www.wrsz.ch; Am Hauptplatz; s/d from Sfr150/210; P@) Goethe once stayed at this centuries-old hotel, right on Haufplatz in central Schwyz, whose spacious rooms have been renovated in generic modern style. The restaurant serves Swiss cuisine with a Mediterranean-style twist.

**Café Laden** CAFE €
(041 55 86 100; www.cafeladen.ch; Schulgasse 7; 8am-7pm Tue-Fri, to 6pm Sat) A cafe with character, come here for coffee, desserts, wine, beer and gluten-free eating options – plus the opportunity to peruse second hand clothing and jewellery. There's a nice outside terrace.

★**Das Insel-Restaurant Schwanau** SWISS €€
(041 811 17 57; www.schwanau.ch; mains from Sfr32, 4-course menu Sfr98; 11am-midnight Wed-Sat, to 6pm Sun Apr-Oct) For delicious nouvelle Swiss cuisine in atmospheric surrounds, don't miss this restaurant atop an island on the Lauerzerzee, flanked by a 17th-century hermit's chapel and the ruins of a castle tower. Ring the bell on the roadside dock and they'll send a boat over.

## Shopping

**Victorinox** SPORTS & OUTDOORS
(041 818 12 99; www.victorinox.ch; Schmiedgasse 57, Ibach; 7.30am-noon & 1.15-6pm Mon-Fri, 8am-3pm Sat) Handy and brilliantly compact, Swiss army knives can be bought at the source at Victorinox's factory shop, 650m southwest of Hauptplatz. Karl Elsener founded the company in 1884 and, after a shaky start, hit pay dirt with the 'Officer's Knife' in 1897.

## Information

**Tourist Office** (041 810 19 91; www.info-schwyz.ch; Zeughausstrasse 10; 8am-6pm Mon-Fri, 9am-2pm Sat) Located down the street from the Forum der Schweizer Geschichte.

### Getting There & Away

Regular trains connect Schwyz with Zug (Sfr9.80, 30 minutes) and Lucerne (Sfr15.40, 40 minutes). To reach the town centre from Schwyz's train station (2km northwest in Seewen), take any bus marked Schwyz Post and alight at Postplatz.

Schwyz is 2km off the A4 freeway, which passes through Brunnen. Buses run frequently from the central Schwyz Post stop to Brunnen's Bahnhof (bus 2, 10 minutes, two to four hourly).

## Einsiedeln

POP 14,600 / ELEV 900M

If you don't know what's there, Einsiedeln can be a bit of a surprise. It's a small town, end of the train line, end of the valley...where is everybody going? They're pilgrims. Pilgrims flock to Einsiedeln, Switzerland's answer to Lourdes. The story goes that in 964 CE the Bishop of Constance tried to consecrate the original monastery but was halted by a heavenly voice, declaring: 'Desist. God Himself has consecrated this building.' A papal order later recognised this as a genuine miracle. Even if you don't believe in miracles, the fabulously over-the-top interior of the abbey church is a must-see.

### Sights

**★Klosterkirche** CHURCH

(Abbey Church; 055 418 61 11; www.kloster-einsiedeln.ch; Benzigerstrasse; 6am-8.30pm) Follow the crowds flowing towards this baroque edifice, the 18th-century handiwork of Caspar Moosbrugger. The interior dances with colourful frescoes, stucco and gold swirls. Yet most pilgrims are oblivious to the marbled opulence, directing their prayers to the holiest of holies, the **Black Madonna**, a tiny statue in a chapel by the entrance.

**Statue of St Benedikt** VIEWPOINT

For a fine view over the abbey complex to the surrounding hills, wander through the monastery stables and continue uphill for 15 minutes to this statue.

### Sleeping

**Hotel Sonne Einsiedeln** HOTEL €

(055 412 28 21; http://hotel-sonne.ch; Hauptstrasse 82; s/d from Sfr80/130; P ) Right on Klosterplatz and as close to the church as you can get, Hotel Sonne is a busy place, also sporting a restaurant and pizzeria. Rooms are simple and clean, and most guests aren't here for the luxury. For church-visiting though, this is the place to stay.

### Drinking & Nightlife

**Doc Holliday's Pub'n Dancing** PUB

(055 412 14 41; www.doc-hollidays.ch; Hauptstrasse 7; hours vary) Stumbling over Doc Holliday's Pub'n Dancing while following a flock of pilgrims to the church may be a bit of a surprise. A picture of the Western gunslinger highlights the logo. Head in here for a beer if pilgrim-ing gets too much.

### Information

**Tourist Office** (055 418 44 88; www.einsiedeln-tourismus.ch; Hauptstrasse 85; 9am-5pm Mon-Fri, 9am-4pm Sat, 10am-1pm Sun) Up near the church, the tourist office is located about 10 minutes' walk from the train station.

### Getting There & Away

Einsiedeln is in a rail cul-de-sac, so getting there usually involves changing trains. Trains to Lucerne (Sfr24, 1¼ hours) require a connection at Biberbrugg and/or Arth-Goldau, while trains to Zürich (Sfr22, 50 minutes), are via Wädenswil.

## Engelberg

POP 4000 / ELEV 1050M

Engelberg (literally 'Angel Mountain') attracts two kinds of pilgrims: those seeking spiritual enlightenment in its Benedictine monastery and those worshipping the virgin powder on its divine slopes. Framed by the glacial bulk of Mt Titlis and frosted peaks, it's a miracle that despite its deep snow, impeccable off-piste credentials and proximity to Lucerne, Engelberg remains lesser known than other resorts of its size. A blessing, some say.

### Sights

**Engelberg Monastery** MONASTERY

(Kloster Engelberg; 041 639 61 19; www.kloster-engelberg.ch; church admission free, tours adult/child Sfr8/free; 1hr tour 10am & 4pm Wed-Sat) The Engelberg valley was once ecclesiastically governed and the Benedictine abbey was the seat of power. Now the resident monks teach instead of rule, but their 12th-century home has kept its grandeur. Rebuilt after a devastating fire in 1729, it contains rooms decorated with incredibly detailed wood inlays, and a baroque monastery church.

**Show Cheese Dairy** DAIRY

(Schaukäserei; 041 638 08 88; www.schaukaeserei-engelberg.ch; cheesemaking 9.30am-4pm, store & restaurant 9am-5pm) FREE Located on the grounds of Engelberg Monastery is a state-of-the-art cheesemaking operation, where you

## Engelberg

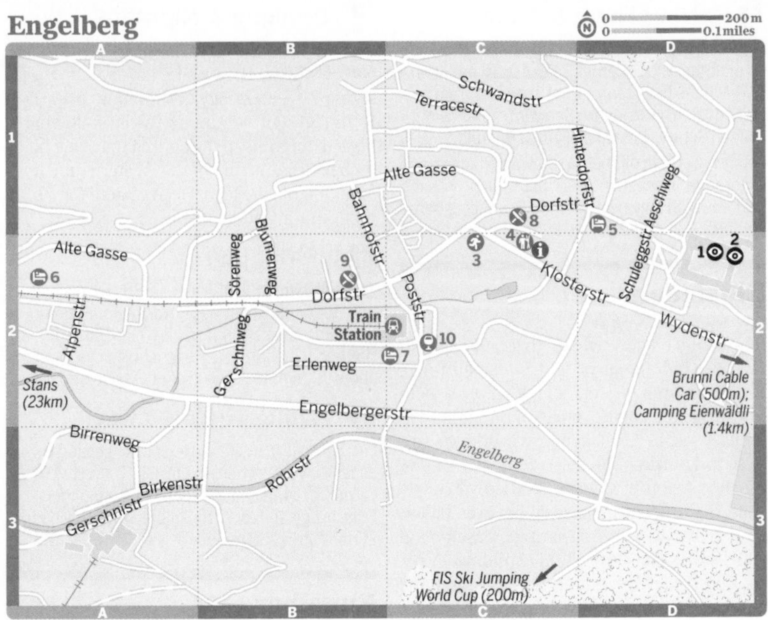


### Engelberg

**Sights**
1 Engelberg Monastery ........ D2
2 Show Cheese Dairy ........ D2

**Activities, Courses & Tours**
3 Bike 'n' Roll ........ C2
Okay Ski Shop ........ (see 10)
4 Ski & Snowboard School ........ C2

**Sleeping**
5 Alpenclub ........ D1
6 Engelberg Youth Hostel ........ A2
7 Ski Lodge Engelberg ........ C2

**Eating**
Alpenclub ........ (see 5)
Brasserie Konrad ........ (see 7)
8 Restaurant-Steakhouse Bierlialp ........ C1
9 Spice Bazaar ........ B2

**Drinking & Nightlife**
Gadä Bar ........ (see 5)
10 Yucatan ........ C2

can watch the cheesemakers, savour dairy goodies in the bistro and buy creamy silo-free cheeses and other Swiss-themed souvenirs.

## Activities

### Hiking

There are some 360km of marked hiking trails in and around Engelberg. For gentle ambles and gorgeous scenery, head for Brunni on the opposite side of the valley. The **Brunni cable car** (www.brunni.ch; cable car one way/return Sfr18/30, incl chairlift Sfr26/42) goes up to Ristis at 1600m, where a chairlift takes you to the Swiss Alpine Club's refurbished **Brunni Hütte** (www.berghuette.ch; dm adult/child Sfr26/14, incl breakfast & dinner Sfr65/41).

More strenuous hikes include the trek over the Surenenpass (2291m) and along to Attinghausen, where you can catch a bus to Altdorf and the southern end of Lake Uri, and the climb over Jochpass (2210m) to Meiringen via Engstlenalp. Pick up a map and check on snow conditions before attempting these more demanding treks.

### Skiing & Snowboarding

Snowboarders catch big air on Titlis, Engstlenalp and the half-pipe at Jochpass, while novice and intermediate skiers slide over to family-friendly Brunni and Gerschnialp for baby blues and cruisy reds. The real thrills for powder hounds, however, lie off-piste. Backcountry legends include Laub, Steinberg and the biggest leg-burner of all, Galtiberg, running from Klein Titlis to the valley 2000m below. A one-day ski pass costs Sfr62.

There's a **Ski & Snowboard School** (☎041 639 54 54; www.skischule-engelberg.ch; Klosterstrasse 3; ⌚8am-5.30pm) inside the tourist office, and places to hire ski/snowboard gear (from about Sfr50 per day) throughout town. Ski Lodge Engelberg is another great source of information, or stop by Dani's **Okay Ski Shop** (☎041 637 07 77; www.okay-shop.com; Hotel Bellevue, Bahnhofplatz), where hardcore riders hang out and exchange tips.

Engelberg also hosts the **FIS Ski Jumping World Cup** (www.weltcup-engelberg.ch).

### Cycling

**Bike 'n' Roll** CYCLING
(☎041 638 02 55; www.bikenroll.ch; Dorfstrasse 31; city/hardtail/full-suspension bike per day Sfr25/30/40; ⌚8.30am-noon & 2-6.30pm Mon-Sat) Rent a mountain bike or join a two-wheeled adventure. Also rents out climbing gear for tackling Engelberg's five *vie ferrate*.

### Adventure Sports

**Outventure** ADVENTURE SPORTS
(☎041 611 14 41; www.outventure.ch; Mühlebachstrasse 5, Stans; ⌚noon-6pm Mon-Fri, 10am-6pm Sat & Sun) This Stans-based outfit offers bungee jumping, tandem paragliding, guided *via ferrata* tours and more.

## Sleeping

**Engelberg Youth Hostel** HOSTEL €
(☎041 637 12 92; www.youthhostel.ch; Dorfstrasse 80; dm/s/d Sfr33/73/96; P 📶) This 112-bed chalet-style hostel is clean and modern, with large dorms and some nice facilities, including a billiards/foosball room and a big garden.

**Camping Eienwäldli** CAMPGROUND €
(☎041 637 19 49; www.eienwaeldli.ch; Wasserfallstrasse 108; sites per adult/child/tent/car from Sfr9/4.50/7/2; P 📶) Attached to the well-regarded Sporthotel Eienwäldli, this deluxe family-run campground has access to its restaurant and spa facilities. Ski and shuttle buses stop less than a minute from the gate. With a restaurant and cafe, it's all here.

★**Ski Lodge Engelberg** HOTEL €€
(☎041 637 35 00; www.skilodgeengelberg.com; Erlenweg 36; s/d/tr/q Sfr150/270/360/450; P 📶) Run by sociable Swedish skiers, this delightful, centrally located lodge fuses art nouveau flair with 21st-century comforts in smart rooms (including family rooms) dotted with black-and-white action shots and vintage skis. Après-ski activities include a sauna, gazing at snowy peaks from an outdoor hot tub, and sharing ski tips over the excellent New Nordic cuisine.

**Alpenclub** BOUTIQUE HOTEL €€
(☎041 637 12 43; www.alpenclub.ch; Dorfstrasse 5; s/d/ste Sfr150/220/480; P 📶) Low wood beams, solid walls and animal-skin rugs echo 200 years of history at this romantic gem in the heart of town. The Steinberg room has stellar Mt Titlis views. The all leather and wood **Gadä Bar** (⌚4pm-late Thu-Sat) is an Engelberg meeting place.

## Eating & Drinking

**Spice Bazaar** INDIAN €
(☎041 639 70 70; www.central-engelberg.ch; Dorfstrasse 48; mains from Sfr18; ⌚11.30am-11pm) This Indian restaurant gets rave reviews from both visitors and locals, and serves up all sorts of favourites, such as Badami Chicken, Tandoori Mix Grill and Swiss-Indian fusion like Spice of Life Fondue.

★**Brasserie Konrad** MODERN EUROPEAN €€
(☎041 637 35 00; www.skilodgeengelberg.com; Erlenweg 36; mains from Sfr29; ⌚5.30-11pm; 📶) At Ski Lodge Engelberg's on-site restaurant, Chef Jonas Bolling conjures up extraordinarily good New Nordic cuisine that's as pretty as a picture and perfect for refuelling after a tough day on the slopes (the three-course skier's menu is a steal at Sfr59). If you're not a hotel guest, be sure to reserve a table.

**Alpenclub** SWISS €€
(☎041 637 12 43; www.alpenclub.ch; Dorfstrasse 5; pizza from Sfr16, mains from Sfr28; ⌚5.30-10pm Mon-Fri, from 11.30am Sat & Sun) This low-ceilinged, candlelit tavern creaks under the weight of its 200-year history at the Alpenclub hotel complex. Feast away on fondue, pizza, Italian staples or the house speciality.

**Restaurant-Steakhouse Bierlialp**
SWISS €€
(☎041 637 17 17; www.restaurant-bierlialp.ch; Dorfstrasse 21; pizza/pasta/meat mains from Sfr15/22/35; ⊙6-11pm) Specialising in meat, pasta and pizza, start at the salad buffet then move on. The pizza and pasta are good, but if you're a meat eater, go for the Irish Black Angus Beef. There's a dessert buffet to top it all off.

**Yucatan** BAR
(☎041 637 13 24; www.bellevue-terminus.ch; Bahnhofplatz; ⊙3pm-midnight) Engelberg's après-ski heavyweight is this lively joint opposite the train station. Mega-burgers, fajitas, quesadillas, Thai curries and caipirinhas fuel parties with DJs, bands and jiving on the bar.

## Information

**Tourist Office** (☎041 639 77 77; www.engelberg.ch; Klosterstrasse 3; ⊙8am-5.30pm Mon-Sat year-round, plus Sun Dec-Easter) A five-minute walk from the train station, this tourist office can help with hotel reservations.

## Getting There & Away

Engelberg is the southern terminus of the Engelberg Express train, which runs hourly to/from Lucerne (Sfr9.20, 45 minutes). Day-trippers should check the Mt Titlis excursion tickets available from the Lucerne tourist office (p205).

A road off the A2 freeway near Stans leads to Engelberg. It's 35km by road from Lucerne to Engelberg.

From late April through October, a free shuttle bus leaves Engelberg's train station roughly every half-hour between 8am and 5pm for all the village's major hotels and attractions. In winter, free ski buses follow multiple routes to and from the slopes.

# Zug

POP 27,600 / ELEV 426M

On the face of it, Zug appears like many other Swiss towns: lapped by a lake and ringed by mountains. However, this is the richest canton in one of the world's richest countries. Figures from 2016 put Zug at the top of the list of well-off cantons, with the purchasing power of residents more than one-and-a-half times the Swiss average. It has a reputation as being tax- and business-friendly, and you're likely to feel things are a tad different just getting off the train, looking around the shops and noticing the cars driving by – this town is affluent. Zug is also known for its legendary local *Kirschtorte* (cherry cake) and the cobblestoned medieval streets of the Old Town.

## Sights

**Zytturm** TOWER
(Kolinplatz) Zug's Old Town is a medieval time capsule. It starts at the town's emblem, the Zytturm, whose distinctive roof is tiled in blue-and-white cantonal colours.

**Kunsthaus Zug** MUSEUM
(☎041 725 33 44; www.kunsthauszug.ch; Dorfstrasse 27; adult/child Sfr8/free; ⊙noon-6pm Tue-Fri, 10am-5pm Sat & Sun) The local art museum holds a superb collection of Viennese modernist works by Klimt, Kokoschka and Schiele. There are also regular high-profile temporary exhibitions.

**Museum Burg Zug** MUSEUM
(☎041 728 29 70; www.burgzug.ch; Kirchenstrasse 11; adult/child Sfr10/free; ⊙2-5pm Tue-Sat, from 10am Sun) Zug's town museum, housed in an 11th-century castle, displays paintings, costumes and a 3D model of the town, plus special themed exhibitions. It's an excellent introduction to Zug – and the town's past tendency to partially sink into the lake.

**Landsgemeindeplatz** SQUARE
This popular waterfront square, surrounded by cafes and restaurants, is historically significant as People's Assemblies took place here from the 14th century until 1847. Markets and festivals are also held here, as well as open-air concerts on Wednesday evenings in summer.

## Activities

**Zugerberg Bahn** CABLE CAR
(www.zbb.ch) This funicular rises to Zugerberg (925m), with impressive views and hiking trails. The Zug day pass (Sfr16.80) is the best deal, as it covers all bus and train rides in the canton and the funicular. From the train station, bus 11 (15 minutes) gets you to the lower funicular station at Schönegg.

**Seebad Seeliken** SWIMMING
(☎041 711 14 56; http://seeliken.ch; Artherstrasse 2; ⊙9am-sunset mid-May–mid-Sep) FREE Shaded by chestnut trees, this locally popular lakefront beach, just south of the Old Town, is perfect for a swim or sunbathe.

**Zuger Veloverleih** CYCLING
(☎076 444 77 35; www.zug-tourismus.ch; Dammstrasse; ⊙9am-7pm May-Oct, to 9pm Jul &

## MT TITLIS

With a name that makes English speakers titter, **Titlis** (www.titlis.ch) is Central Switzerland's tallest mountain, has its only glacier and is reached by the world's first revolving **cable car** (www.titlis.ch/en/tickets/cable-car-ride; adult/child return Sfr89/44.50; ⏲8.30am-5pm), completed in 1992. However, that's the last leg of a breathtaking three-stage journey. First, you glide up to Trübsee (1800m) via Gerschnialp (1300m; don't get off at Gerschnialp if you're continuing to the top). Next, another gondola at Trübsee whisks you up to Stand (2450m), where you board the revolving Rotair for the final head-spinning journey over the dazzling **Titlis Glacier**. As you twirl above the deeply crevassed ice, peaks rise like shark fins ahead, while tarn-speckled pastures, cliffs and waterfalls lie behind.

A glacial blast of air hits you at Titlis station (3020m). Inside is a kind of high-altitude theme park, with a marvellously kitsch **ice cave** where you can watch neon lights make the sculpted ice tunnels sparkle. There's also an overpriced restaurant and a nostalgic **photo studio** on the 4th floor, which specialises in snaps of Bollywood stars in dirndls.

The genuine oohs and ahs come when you step out onto the **terrace**, where the panorama of glacier-capped peaks stretches to Eiger, Mönch and Jungfrau in the Bernese Oberland. For even more thrilling views, step onto the adjacent **Cliff Walk** (www.titlis.ch/en/glacier/cliff-walk; ⏲9.15am-4.45pm) FREE, a 100m-long, 1m-wide, cable-supported swinging walkway that qualified as Europe's highest suspension bridge when opened in 2012. More ambitious hikers can tackle the 45-minute climb to Titlis' 3239m summit (wear sturdy shoes).

For winter sports thrills even in midsummer, take the **Ice Flyer chairlift** (return adult/child Sfr12/6; ⏲9.30am-4.30pm) down to the **Glacier Park** (www.titlis.ch/en/glacier/glacier-park; ⏲9.30am-4.30pm) FREE, where there are free snow tubes, scooters and sledges to test out. The nearby freestyle park has a half-pipe and good summer snowboarding.

The return trip to Titlis (roughly 45 minutes each way) costs Sfr92 from Engelberg. However, in fine weather you can walk some sections. Between Stand and Trübsee, the Geologischer Wanderweg is open from July to September; it takes about two hours up and 1½ hours down. From Trübsee up to Jochpass (2207m) takes about 1½ hours, and down to Engelberg takes around the same time.

If you're hiking, destinations from Engelberg include Gerschnialp (one way/return Sfr9/13), Trübsee (Sfr23/32), Jochpass (Sfr33/46) and Stand (Sfr38/53). Reductions on all fares, including to Titlis, are 50% for Swiss Travel, Eurail and InterRail pass holders.

The last ascent by cable car is at 3.40pm and last descent at 4.50pm; it closes for maintenance for two weeks in early November.

Aug) Provides bikes for free (ID required) just outside the train station (west side).

**Marcello's Bootsvermietung** WATER SPORTS
(www.zuger-see.ch; stand-up paddleboard/pedalo/motorboat per hour Sfr30/40/75) On the waterfront near Landsgemeindeplatz, this place rents out stand-up paddleboards, pedalos and motorboats.

**Strandbad Zug** SWIMMING
(☎041 711 09 82; Chamer Fussweg 13; ⏲9am-7.30pm May-Sep) FREE This lakefront beach, 2km west of the town centre, has shaded areas, picnic tables and its own restaurant.

## Sleeping

With city slickers frequently staying overnight on business, Zug's hotels often have a corporate feel. Many hotels lower their rates on weekends.

**Zug Youth Hostel** HOSTEL €
(☎041 711 53 54; www.youthhostel.ch/zug; Allmendstrasse 8; dm/s/d Sfr35/92/105; ⏲closed Dec–mid-Mar; P 📶) Modern and clean, Zug's hostel is a 10-minute walk west of the train station. It is handy for swimming at Strandbad Zug.

★**Ochsen Zug** HOTEL €€
(☎041 729 32 32; www.ochsen-zug.ch; Kolinplatz 11; r/ste from Sfr195/320; P 📶) Dating from 1543 and claiming to have hosted Goethe, the Ochsen is now a slick business hotel with a historic facade near the Zytturm in the Old Town. Its mix of rooms includes the Japan Room, complete with tatami mats. There are also suites and regular business rooms, plus a restaurant and bar.

**Hotel Löwen am See** HOTEL €€
(☎041 725 22 22; www.loewen-zug.ch; Landsgemeindeplatz 1; s/d from Sfr170/240; P❄☎) Centrally located on Landsgemeindeplatz's cobbled Old Town square facing the lake, this place has simple, comfy rooms. The popular **French Brasserie** is open from 9am to midnight. Book online for weekend discounts.

**Hotel Zugertor** HOTEL €€
(☎041 729 38 38; www.zugertor.ch; Baarerstrasse 97; s/d/tr from Sfr198/238/298; P☎) A five-minute walk north of Zug train station from the east exit, Zugertor is popular with businessmen and meets the required excellent standards. Perhaps not as atmospheric as staying in the Old Town, but still a good option.

## Eating

**Wirtshaus Brandenberg** SWISS €
(☎041 711 95 96; www.brandenberg.ch; Allmendstrasse 3; lunch menus Sfr20.50; ⌚8am-midnight Tue-Sat) For down-to-earth Swiss classics at reasonable prices, locals have been flocking to this beer hall since 1891. It's beloved for its lunch menus and for comfort food like roast chicken, weisswurst and *Hacktätschli* (pan-fried meatballs).

**Confiserie Strickler** BAKERY €
(☎041 711 14 02; www.diezugerkirschtorte.ch; Bundesplatz 4 ; cakes from Sfr4.50; ⌚6.30am-6.30pm Mon-Fri, 7.30am-5pm Sat) With the cheerful (albeit self-serving) motto, 'Keep your curves – enjoy life!', this old-style cafe 5 minutes walk from the train station is a quaint marriage between an English tearoom and an ultra-Swiss bakery. Locals swear by their *Zuger Kirschtorte* (pastry, biscuit, almond paste and butter cream cake, infused with cherry liqueur).

★**Gasthaus Rathauskeller** EUROPEAN €€€
(☎041 711 00 58; http://rathauskeller.ch; Ober-Altstadt 1; mains bistro/Zunftstube from Sfr20/45; ⌚11am-midnight Tue-Sat) You can't miss the late-Gothic Rathauskeller's frescoed facade near the Zytturm. The downstairs bistro serves marvellous high-end takes on classic local ingredients, while the swish upstairs restaurant, **Zunftstube**, has creaky floors, gilt Rosenthal crockery and delicacies such as lobster ragout with summer truffles.

## Information

**Tourist Office** (Reisezentrum Zug; ☎041 723 68 00; www.zugtourismus.ch; ⌚9am-7pm Mon-Fri, 9am-noon & 12.30-4pm Sat, 9-11.30am & noon-3pm Sun) This office is inside the train station.

## Getting There & Away

Zug is on the main north–south train route from Zürich (Sfr17, 25 to 45 minutes) to Lugano. Trains also run regularly to Lucerne (Sfr7.30, 20 to 45 minutes).

For drivers, the north–south N4 runs just west of town, offering good connections north to Zürich, and south towards Lucerne, St Gotthard Pass, Lugano and Italy.

In summer, Zugersee Schifffahrt (www.zugersee-schifffahrt.ch) operates boats from Zug's Schiffsstation, north of Landsgemeindeplatz, to Arth and other destinations around the lake.

# Andermatt

POP 1320 / ELEV 1447M

Blessed with austere mountain appeal, Andermatt contrasts low-key village charm with big wilderness. The town was once an important staging post at a four-way crossroads – the north–south route over the St Gotthard pass (2106m) linking Lucerne with Ticino; the Furka Pass (2431m) corkscrewing west to Valais; and the Oberalp Pass (2044m) looping east to Graubünden. With the opening of the 17km-long Gotthard Road Tunnel in 1980, however, Andermatt found itself bypassed on the all-important north–south route.

Of late there has been some mega-development for Andermatt in the form of hotels and massive expansion of the ski lifts under the name Ski Arena. More hotels are planned, but for now the traditional charm of the town centre remains blissfully intact.

## Sights & Activities

As Andermatt is situated near four major Alpine passes – Susten, Oberalp, St Gotthard and Furka – it's a terrific base for hiking, cycling and bus tours. The tourist office distributes free bilingual (German-English) booklets outlining hiking and cycling opportunities. Check www.postbus.ch for current bus tour offerings.

**Gemsstock** MOUNTAIN
(www.skiarena.ch) This 2961m mountain, reached by cable car, attracts hikers in summer and skiers coming for the snow-sure slopes in winter. The region is also beloved of off-piste skiers seeking fresh powder. This has become part of the Ski Arena conglomeration, so check its website for details. Tobog-

gan runs, well-prepared walking trails and sleigh rides appeal to non-skiers in winter.

**Museo Nazionale San Gottardo** MUSEUM
(☎091 869 15 25; www.passosangottardo.ch/en/musei/museo-nazionale.html; ⏰9am-6pm Jun-Oct) FREE Once at the top of the St Gotthard Pass, visit the Museo Nazionale San Gottardo, which covers the commercial, political and cultural significance of the pass and is housed in a former customs house and hotel. Just 12km south of Andermatt, the pass is in Ticino Canton.

**St Gotthard Pass** SCENIC DRIVE
(Passo San Gottardo; www.passosangottardo.ch/en; ⏰Jun-Oct) An exhilarating drive, this famous mountain pass (2108m) connects cantons Ticino and Uri. Twelve kilometres south of Andermatt by road (in Ticino), the pass can be avoided by using the tunnel below, but for spectacular scenery and a sense of really getting over the Alps, this is the way to go.

Taking the famous cobblestoned Tremola road (on the southern side of the pass, connecting the highest point with the Italian-speaking town of Airolo) via 37 tortuous twists is a must.

**Lai da Tuma Hike** HIKING
This popular hike leads from Oberalp Pass (2044m) to sparkly Lai da Tuma (2344m; Tomasee), the source of the Rhine. Drive or take a train to the pass; the 11km return trip takes three to four hours. The water flowing out of the lake traverses four countries and eventually empties into the North Sea near Rotterdam in the Netherlands.

## Sleeping & Eating

**Base Camp Andermatt** HOSTEL, LODGE €
(☎079 946 47 68; www.basecamp-andermatt.com; Rueti 2; dm/s/d midweek Sfr39/59/115, weekend Sfr49/69/135; P 🛜) Open year-round, this mountain eco-lodge and hostel caters to outdoors enthusiasts. Perks include free wi-fi, a fireplace, guest kitchen and barbecue, a large dining room, a ski/bike service room and a sauna with panoramic views. It's only 350m (but uphill) from the train station, next to the Nätschen chairlift.

★**River House Boutique Hotel** DESIGN HOTEL €€
(☎041 887 00 25; www.theriverhouse.ch; Gotthardstrasse 58; s Sfr150-210, d Sfr200-280; P 🛜) At this stylish eco-hotel in a 250-year-old building, the Swiss-American owners have used local materials to create unique and beautiful rooms with inlaid parquet floors and beams, some with river views. The on-site restaurant features local, eco-friendly produce, plus Swiss wines. Great location in the middle of the village.

**Hotel Sonne** HOTEL €€
(☎041 887 12 26; www.hotelsonneandermatt.ch; Gotthardstrasse 76; s/d from Sfr90/150; P 🛜) You can't miss this main-street hotel, its beautifully weathered wooden facade hung with geranium-filled window boxes and a golden sun emblem. The snug rooms (some with nice views) have comfy beds and loads of pine. The cosy beamed restaurant downstairs serves Swiss specialities.

**Restaurant Zum Dörfli** SWISS €€
(☎041 887 01 32; www.zumdoerfli.ch; Furkastrasse, Zumdorf; mains Sfr26-40) There's little more than a restaurant in Zumdorf, but this place is very good for rösti and meaty mains, plus it hunts its own game meats come autumn. Find it on Furkastrasse, 6km from Andermatt on the way to Realp and the Furka Pass.

## Information

**Tourist Office** (☎041 888 71 00; www.andermatt.ch; Gotthardstrasse 2; ⏰8am-noon & 1.15-5pm Mon-Fri, to 4pm Sat & Sun) The tourist office is 200m east of the train station. It shares the same building as the postal bus ticket office.

## Getting There & Away

If arriving from Zürich (Sfr46, two hours), Locarno (Sfr42.40, 2¼ hours) or other points north and south, you'll need to change trains at Göschenen for the final 10-minute climb to Andermatt. This is because the main line heads through the Gotthard Tunnel and bypasses Andermatt.

Andermatt is on the east–west Glacier Express (www.glacierexpress.ch) route to Zermatt (Sfr74, three hours) and St Moritz (Sfr85, five hours).

Matterhorn Gotthard Bahn (www.mgbahn.ch) can supply details about the car-carrying trains over the Oberalp Pass to Graubünden and through the Furka Tunnel to Valais. Postal buses stop by the train station.

The 17km Gotthard Road Tunnel is one of the busiest north–south routes across the Alps, running from Göschenen to close to Airolo (Ticino), bypassing Andermatt.

The Gotthard Base Tunnel, which opened in 2016, is a 57km railway tunnel designed for high-speed and freight trains, and is said to be the world's longest and deepest traffic tunnel.

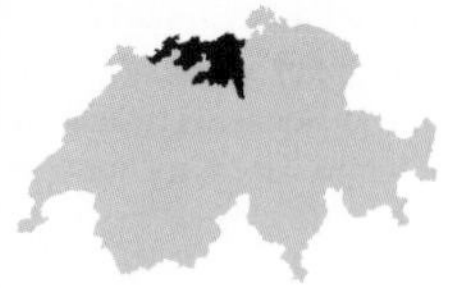

# Northwestern Switzerland

**Includes ➡**



## Best Places to Eat

- Restaurant Stucki (p228)
- Restaurant Schlüsselzunft (p228)
- Markthalle (p227)
- Speck (p231)
- Goldener Schlüssel (p231)

## Best Places to Stay

- Les Trois Rois (p227)
- Hotel Krafft (p227)
- Der Teufelhof (p227)
- Kettenbrücke Hotel (p231)
- SYHA Jugendherberge Baden (p231)

## Why Go?

Tucked in a corner against the French and German borders, northwestern Switzerland, comprising the cantons of Basel and Aargau, boasts an enticing mix of cultural attractions.

Basel, the recommended base for your explorations, has a wealth of avant-garde architecture that juxtaposes with its enchanting Old Town, and is both built for business and deeply cultural. The city itself boasts a diverse collection of almost 40 museums, but a host of lesser-known treasures awaits in the surrounding verdant countryside.

A short excursion outside Basel leads to Switzerland's finest Roman ruins at Augusta Raurica. Further east along the Rhine, the pretty medieval city of Aarau was the original homeland of the Habsburgs, the clan that eventually came to rule over the Austro-Hungarian Empire. Here, a journey around the Aare and Limatt valleys takes in the craggy castles of Habsburg, Wildegg, Lenzburg and Hallwyl, along with a collection of pretty villages and the fetching thermal spa-resort town of Baden.

## When to Go

- In summer, bob down the Rhine and dine al fresco as hot, sunny days draw folks to the banks of the rushing river.
- In December and January, come for magical Christmas markets and January's Vogel Gryff festival.
- February in Basel means only one thing: Fasnacht and the weird, wild and wonderful Morgestraich parade.

## Northwestern Switzerland Highlights

1 **Vitra Design Museum** (p225) Shopping for design-smart souvenirs and ogling the architecture in Weil am Rhein.

2 **Kunstmuseum Basel** (p222) Marvelling at the oldest public art collection in the world at this museum.

3 **Fondation Beyeler** (p225) Appreciating the philanthropy of generous benefactors in this shrine to classic art in Riehen.

4 **Stiftung Langmatt** (p230) Savouring one of Switzerland's sweetest little galleries in Baden.

5 **Fasnacht** (p226) Helping the Swiss smash their stereotypes during Basel's quirky, frenetic festival.

6 **Augusta Raurica** (p225) Contemplating the former Roman empire at Switzerland's most extensive archaeological site.

7 **Schloss Habsburg** (p230) Imagining life in the cradle of a once great empire.

# Basel

POP 176,117 / ELEV 273M

Historically, Basel's position astride the mighty Rhine has contributed to its growth as a key trade and transport hub. Today, it's a global centre for the pharmaceutical industry – titans Roche and Novartis are both headquartered here. But that's of little interest to the many thousands of art and architecture lovers who visit each year for the world-famous ART Basel festival and the city's wealth of galleries, museums and iconic buildings.

Basel's position at the juncture of the French, German and Swiss borders adds to its multicultural appeal, and it's perhaps the place where Switzerland's Franco-Germanic roots are most evident, although the dominant language spoken is Swiss-German.

It's easy to spend a day wandering the cobbled streets of the lofty and beautiful Altstadt in **Grossbasel** (Greater Basel) on the Rhine's south bank before crossing the Mittlere Brücke to **Kleinbasel** (Little Basel) for a more 'everyday' vibe and riverside alfresco dining.

## History

The Romans founded a colony in Raurica, east of Basel, in Celtic territory in 44 BCE. By the time the city (Basileum) was first mentioned in 3rd-century texts, they had established a fort on the heights around what is now the Münster as part of a defence system along the Rhine.

Medieval Basel changed hands repeatedly, passing from the Franks to Burgundy and later to the Habsburgs. In 1501 the city, which had increasingly come to be run by its powerful *Zünfte* (guilds), joined the Swiss Confederation.

By the beginning of the 20th century, Basel was a busy industrial, trade and banking hub, with the chemical and pharmaceutical industries already at the forefront of its burgeoning economy. Basel also has a long tradition as an arts centre. In the 1930s the Kunstmuseum acquired a priceless collection of modern works from Nazi Germany that Hitler and company considered to be 'degenerate art'.

## Sights

Note that most museums are closed on Monday. For brochures on the city's 37 museums and galleries (at last count), make a beeline to Basel Tourismus (p229) or check out www.museenbasel.ch.

### Grossbasel

**★ Kunstmuseum Basel** MUSEUM

(Museum of Fine Arts; ☎061 206 62 62; www.kunstmuseumbasel.ch; St Alban-Graben 16; adult/student/child Sfr16/8/free; ⏰10am-6pm Tue, Wed & Fri-Sun, to 8pm Thu; P) Housing the most comprehensive collection of public art in Switzerland, this superb fine arts museum reopened in mid-2016 after updates to the existing galleries (Hauptbau) and construction of a modernist wing (Neubau). It houses the world's largest collection of Holbeins and a substantial collection of Renaissance and impressionist works among its thousands of pieces. The entrance price includes admission to the permanent collection – surcharges are applicable for visiting exhibits. Guided tours (from Sfr5) are available.

Entry includes admission to the contemporary art exhibitions at **Kunstmuseum Basel | Gegenwart** (Museum of Fine Arts| Contemporary; St Alban-Rheinweg 60; adult/student/child Sfr16/8/free; ⏰11am-6pm Tue-Sun) on the riverfront.

**★ Spielzeug Welten Museum Basel** MUSEUM

(Toy Worlds Museum; ☎061 225 95 95; www.spielzeug-welten-museum-basel.ch; Steinenvorstadt 1; adult/child Sfr7/5; ⏰10am-6pm; P 👪) Adults and kids love this fascinating and lovingly curated fantasy land claiming the world's biggest collection of teddy bears and a slew of extraordinarily detailed doll houses among its 6000 objects displayed over four floors.

**Mittlere Brücke** BRIDGE

It's hard to believe that this bridge, the symbol of Basel, has been spanning the rushing Rhine, connecting lofty Grossbasel with lowly Kleinbasel, since 1226. Strolling across it when in town is an essential activity.

**Marktplatz** SQUARE

(P) Begin exploring Basel's delightful medieval Old Town in the Marktplatz, dominated by the astonishingly vivid red facade of the 16th-century **Rathaus** (Town Hall; ☎061 267 81 81; Marktplatz 9; ⏰8am-5pm Mon-Fri). From here, climb 400m west along Spalenberg through the former artisans' district to the 600-year-old **Spalentor** city gate, one of only three to survive the walls' demolition in 1866. Along the way, linger in captivating lanes such as Spalenberg, Heuberg and Leonhardsberg, lined by impeccably maintained, centuries-old houses.

DON'T MISS

## MODERN ARCHITECTURE IN BASEL

Basel and its environs boast buildings designed by seven winners of architecture's Pritzker Prize. Most of those winners – Frank Gehry, Álvaro Siza, Tadao Ando, Zaha Hadid, Jacques Herzog and Pierre de Meuron – have works over the German border at the Vitra Design Museum (p225).

Several works by local firm Herzog & de Meuron are more central. The Basel-based company is renowned for designing London's Tate Modern gallery, Beijing's Olympic Stadium and Tokyo's Prada Aoyama building. In Basel, along with the **Schaulager** (www.schaulager.org; Ruchfeldstrasse 19) and the stadium at **St Jakob Park**, you'll find less gargantuan projects such as the matt-black **Zentralstellwerk** (Central Signal Box; Münchensteinerstrasse 115) and the surprising glass **Elsässertor** (Viaduktstrasse 3; P) near SBB Basel station and the revamped Volkshaus Basel (p228) on Rebgasse in Kleinbasel.

Another Pritzker laureate, Italian architect Renzo Piano, is responsible for the Fondation Beyeler (p225), while Ticino architect Mario Botta designed the striking Museum Jean Tinguely (p224).

**Münster** CATHEDRAL
(Cathedral; ☎061 272 91 57; www.baslermuenster.ch; Münsterplatz 9; ⏰10am-5pm Mon-Fri, to 4pm Sat, 11.30am-5pm Sun Apr-Oct; P) Blending Gothic exteriors with Romanesque interiors, this 13th-century cathedral was largely rebuilt after an earthquake in 1356. Renaissance humanist Erasmus of Rotterdam (1466–1536), who lived in Basel, lies buried in the northern aisle. Groups of two or more can climb the soaring Gothic towers (Sfr5 per person). Behind the church, leafy **Münster Pfalz** offers sublime Rhine views.

**Schweizerisches Museum für Papier, Schrift und Druck** MUSEUM
(Swiss Museum of Paper, Script & Print; ☎061 225 90 90; www.papiermuseum.ch; St Alban-Tal 37; adult/child Sfr15/9; ⏰11am-5pm Tue-Fri & Sun, 1-5pm Sat) Set in an old paper mill astride a medieval canal and complete with a functioning waterwheel, the Paper Museum evokes centuries past, when a dozen mills operated nearby. This one produced paper for centuries and the museum explores that story. Just to the east stands a stretch of the old city wall.

**Museum für Geschichte** MUSEUM
(Museum of History; ☎061 205 86 00; www.hmb.ch; Barfüsserplatz 4; adult/child Sfr12/7; ⏰10am-5pm Tue-Sun) This flagship of three museums operating under the banner of 'Historisches Museum Basel' (Basel Historical Museum), which opened in 1894, is well worth a look. Its diverse historical collection is one of the largest of its kind in Switzerland, housed under the vaulted ceilings of the former Barfüsserkirche, and showcasing two millennia of applied arts, ceramics, weaponry and more. Highlights include 15th-century 'dance of death' mural fragments and a well-preserved 16th-century choir stall.

**Museum für Wohnkultur** MUSEUM
(Museum of Domestic Life; ☎061 205 86 78; www.hmb.ch; Elisabethenstrasse 27-29; adult/child Sfr10/5; ⏰10am-5pm Tue-Fri & Sun, 2-5pm Sat; 👪) Housed in the beautiful Haus zum Kirschgarten building (1780), this lovely museum features two floors of the house with rooms laid out immaculately in the style of 18th- and 19th-century Basel and showcases a fine Meissen porcelain collection among its many antiques.

**Antikenmuseum Basel** MUSEUM
(Basel Antique Museum; ☎061 201 12 12; www.antikenmuseumbasel.ch/en; St Alban-Graben 5; adult/child Sfr15/free; ⏰10am-5pm Tue, Wed, Sat & Sun, to 10pm Thu & Fri) This multilevel museum contains Switzerland's most comprehensive collection of ancient artefacts, dating from the heyday of the pharaohs in Egypt to Roman times. Entry is free after 7pm on Thursdays and Fridays.

**Museum für Musik** MUSEUM
(Museum of Music; ☎061 264 91 60; www.hmb.ch; Im Lohnhof 9; adult/child Sfr10/5; ⏰2-6pm Wed-Sat, 11am-5pm Sun) This museum, featuring the nation's largest collection of musical instruments focuses on a period spanning five centuries and explores the musical and social context of each instrument.

**Naturhistorisches Museum** MUSEUM
(Natural History Museum; ☎061 266 55 00; www.nmbs.ch; Auginergasse 2; adult/child Sfr7/5; ⏰10am-5pm Tue-Sun) With almost eight million objects and artefacts relating to zoology, anthropology and archaeology in its holdings,

## Basel

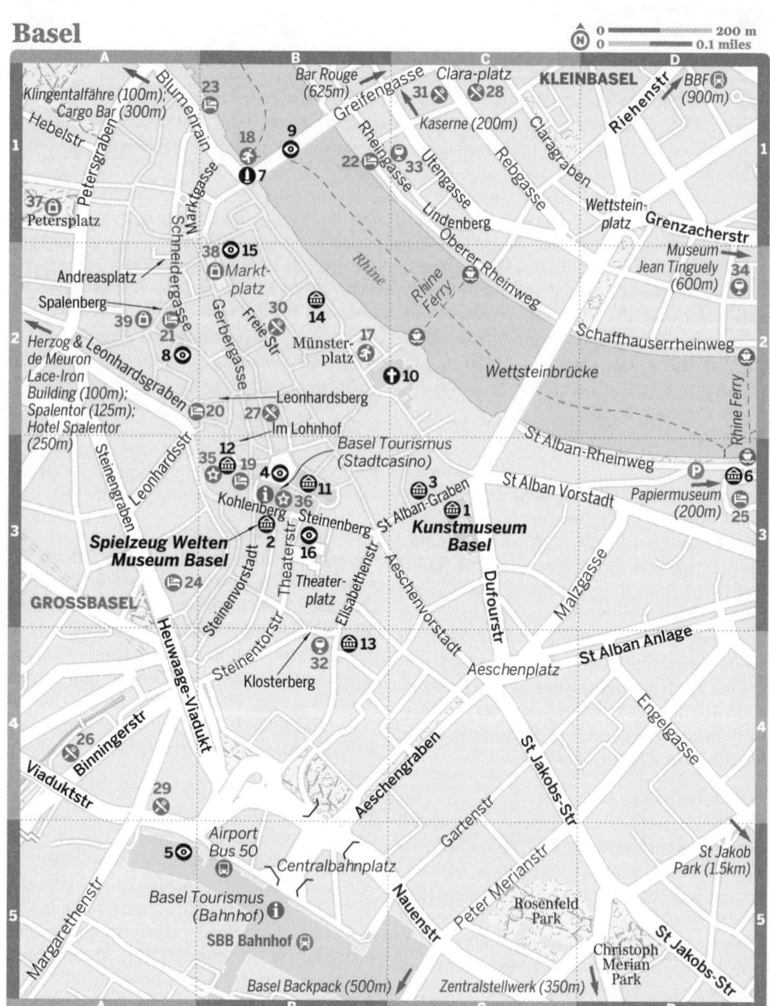


the mission of the Natural History Museum is to maintain an archive of human and animal life in the region. Comprising plenty of life-size and hands-on exhibits, the museum will educate and entertain inquisitive kids and adults alike.

### Kleinbasel

**★Museum Jean Tinguely** MUSEUM

(☎061 681 93 20; www.tinguely.ch; Paul Sacher-Anlage 2; adult/student/child Sfr18/12/free; ⏰11am-6pm Tue-Sun; P) Built by leading Ticino architect Mario Botta, this museum showcases the playful, mischievous and wacky artistic concoctions of sculptor-turned-mad-scientist Jean Tinguely. Buttons next to some of Tinguely's 'kinetic' sculptures allow visitors to set them in motion. It's great fun to watch them rattle, shake and twirl, with springs, feathers and wheels radiating at every angle, or to hear the haunting musical sounds produced by the gigantic *Méta-Harmonies* on the upper floor.

### Outside the Centre

**★Vitra Campus** MUSEUM

(☎+49 7621 702 3500; www.vitra.com/en-hu/campus; Charles-Eames-Strasse 1, Weil am Rhein;

## Basel

**Top Sights**
1 Kunstmuseum Basel .......... C3
2 Spielzeug Welten Museum Basel....... B3

**Sights**
3 Antikenmuseum Basel .......... C3
4 Barfüsserplatz .......... B3
5 Elsässertor .......... A5
6 Kunstmuseum Basel | Gegenwart .......... D3
7 Lällekönig .......... B1
8 Marktplatz .......... A2
9 Mittlere Brücke .......... B1
10 Münster .......... C2
11 Museum für Geschichte .......... B3
12 Museum für Musik .......... B3
13 Museum für Wohnkultur .......... B4
14 Naturhistorisches Museum .......... B2
15 Rathaus .......... B2
16 Tinguely Brunnen .......... B3

**Activities, Courses & Tours**
17 Allianz Cinema Basel .......... B2
18 Basler Personenschiffahrt .......... B1

**Sleeping**
19 Au Violon .......... B3
20 Der Teufelhof .......... A2
21 Hotel Basel .......... A2
22 Hotel Krafft .......... B1
23 Les Trois Rois .......... B1
24 Steinenschanze Stadthotel .......... A3
25 SYHA Youth Hostel Basel .......... D3

**Eating**
26 Acqua .......... A4
Atelier .......... (see 20)
27 Latini .......... B2
28 Lily's Maxim Basel .......... C1
29 Markthalle .......... A4
30 Restaurant Schlüsselzunft .......... B2
31 Volkshaus Basel .......... C1

**Drinking & Nightlife**
32 Atlantis .......... B4
33 Consum .......... C1
34 SUD .......... D2

**Entertainment**
35 Bird's Eye Jazz Club .......... B3
36 Stadtcasino .......... B3

**Shopping**
37 Flohmarkt Petersplatz .......... A1
38 Stadtmarkt .......... B2
39 Weihnachtshaus Johann Wanner .......... A2

Vitra Campus adult/child €17/15, Design Museum only €11/9, 1/2hr tours €7/14; ⏲10am-6pm) Showcasing the works of the adjoining, eponymous high-end furniture manufacturer, Vitra Campus comprises the dazzling **Vitra Design Museum** (of Guggenheim Bilbao architect Frank Gehry fame), the **Vitra Haus** and **Vitra Schaudepot** (both by Herzog & De Meuron) and an ever-expanding bevy of installations by cutting-edge architects and designers, including Carsten Höller's whimsical, corkscrewing 30m-high Vitra Slide. Visiting is a must for serious lovers of architecture and industrial and interior design.

The campus is located just across the German border, in Weil am Rhein.

**★Fondation Beyeler** MUSEUM
(☎061 645 97 00; www.fondationbeyeler.ch; Baselstrasse 101, Riehen; adult/under 25yr Sfr25/free; ⏲10am-6pm Thu-Tue, to 8pm Wed; P) This astounding private-turned-public collection, assembled by former art dealers Hildy and Ernst Beyeler, is housed in a long, low, light-filled, open-plan building designed by Italian architect Renzo Piano. The varied exhibits juxtapose 19th- and 20th-century works by Picasso and Rothko against sculptures by Miró and Max Ernst and tribal figures from Oceania as well as regular visiting exhibitions.

**★Augusta Raurica** RUINS
(☎061 552 22 22; www.augustaraurica.ch; Giebenacherstrasse 17, Augst; adult/child Sfr8/6; ⏲10am-5pm; P 👪) About 17km east of Basel, on the Rhine's south bank, Switzerland's largest Roman ruins are the last remnants of a colony founded in 43 BCE, the population of which grew to 20,000 by the 2nd century AD. Today visitors can stroll at will through a hotchpotch of ruins, highlighted by one of the best-preserved Roman theatres in Central Europe. Take the S-bahn (S1) from Basel to Kaiseraugst (Sfr3.80, 11 minutes) then walk 10 minutes, following signs to the site.

At the entrance to the site, the **Römermuseum** (Roman Museum; ☎061 552 22 22; www.augustaraurica.ch; Giebenacherstrasse 17, Augst; adult/child Sfr8/6; ⏲10am-5pm; P) is also well worth a visit for its authentically restored Roman house and its unparalleled 270-piece collection of antique silver.

DON'T MISS

## GOING WITH THE FLOW

For a cheap thrill, take a ride on one of the city's four atmospheric old ferries, which ply the Rhine attached to cables that span the river. These age-old motorless boats are deftly guided across by expert ferry operators.

The two boats that will be of benefit to most are the **Klingentalfähre** (www.faehri.ch; adult/child Sfr1.60/0.80), located west of Mittlere Brücke, and the **Münsterfähre** (www.faehri.ch; adult/child Sfr1.60/0.80), whose patch of river is just beneath Münsterplatz. Both shuttle back and forth all day from about 9am till dusk.

## Activities

Swimming or floating down the rushing Rhine and sunbathing on its banks are popular summer pastimes. You can purchase a 'Wickelfisch' at Basel Tourismus (p229) offices and local boutiques – it's a watertight plastic 'fish' to put your clothes in to keep them dry as you whoosh down the river!

**Rehberger-Weg** WALKING
If you've got a smartphone, download the app for this 5km walking path between the Fondation Beyeler and Vitra Campus galleries. The walk features 24 colourful and unique public-art installations, designed by artist Tobias Rehberger, as waypoints/stops along the route, which ambles through countryside and crosses the Swiss border into Germany.

**Basler Personenschiffahrt** BOATING
(061 639 95 00; www.bpg.ch; Schifflände; boat cruises from Sfr19; 2pm Tue-Sat) Between mid-May and mid-October, Basler Personenschiffahrt operates 85-minute city/harbour boat cruises, as well as longer trips to Rheinfelden, or lunch, jazz and dinner jaunts. Cruises depart from Schifflände, near Mittlere Brücke.

## Festivals & Events

★**Fasnacht** CARNIVAL
(www.fasnachts-comite.ch; Feb or Mar) Basel's renowned 72-hour carnival kicks off at 4am on the Monday after Ash Wednesday with the **Morgestraich**, when streetlights are extinguished and a procession winds through the central district. Participants wear elaborate costumes and masks. The main parades are on Monday and Wednesday afternoons. Tuesday is devoted to children and an open-air display of colourful lanterns in Münsterplatz.

★**ART Basel** ART
(www.artbasel.ch; Jun) One of three international exhibits (the other two shows are in Miami and Hong Kong) showcasing the works of more than 4000 artists from almost 300 galleries, over a week in June.

**Vogel Gryff** CULTURAL
(Jan; ) This long-running January festival (the 'Festival of the Griffin') symbolically chases winter away from Kleinbasel. The three key figures – Vogel Gryff (the griffin), Wilder Mann (the savage) and Leu (the lion) – dance to the beat of drums on a raft on the Rhine and later in the streets of Kleinbasel.

**Herbstmesse** CULTURAL
(Autumn Fair; www.messen-maerkte.bs.ch; Oct; ) Artists, craftspeople, merchants and carnival rides fill the streets during Basel's massive autumn fair, which dates back more than 500 years.

## Sleeping

Basel's hotels fill fast during conventions and trade fairs, so book ahead whenever possible. When checking in, ask for your 'mobility ticket', which entitles all Basel hotel guests to free use of public transport for the duration of your stay. It's handy as you'll be hard pressed to find convenient hotel parking in the Old Town.

For Basel-area B&Bs, visit www.bbbasel.ch.

### Grossbasel

★**Basel Backpack** HOSTEL €
(061 333 00 37; www.baselbackpack.ch; Dornacherstrasse 192; 4-/8-bed dm Sfr39/31, s/d from Sfr75/89; ) Converted from a factory, this independent hostel has friendly staff, bright and roomy four- and eight- bed dorms and a selection of smart, simply stylish single and deluxe double rooms. Other perks include bike rental, breakfast, a bar, guest kitchen and laundry and two convivial lounges.

**SYHA Youth Hostel Basel** HOSTEL €
(061 272 05 72; www.youthhostel.ch; St Alban-Kirchrain 10; dm/s/tw with shared bathroom from Sfr41/70/93, s/d from Sfr120/132; ) Designed by Basel-based architects Buchner & Bründler, this swank, modern hostel is flanked by tree-shaded squares and a rushing

creek. It's only a stone's throw from the Rhine, and 15 minutes on foot from the SBB Bahnhof (or take tram 2 to Kunstmuseum.

**Hotel Basel** HOTEL €
(061 264 68 00; www.hotel-basel.ch; Münzgasse 12; s/d/tw from Sfr126/153/180; P ❄ 📶) In a great location in the heart of the Old Town, this smart, 72-room hotel has a range of simply but comfortably furnished compact single and more spacious double rooms. Due to the shape and size of the hotel, most have a feature wall, skylight or other pleasing particularity. Service is of an excellent standard.

**Au Violon** HOTEL €
(061 269 87 11; www.au-violon.com; Im Lohnhof 4; s/d from Sfr120/140; 📶) The doors are one of the few hints that quaint, atmospheric Au Violon was a prison from 1835 to 1995. Most of the rooms are two cells rolled into one and either look onto a delightful cobblestone courtyard or have views of the Münster. Sitting on a leafy hilltop, it also has a well-respected restaurant with outdoor seating in summer.

★ **Der Teufelhof** BOUTIQUE HOTEL €€
(061 261 10 10; www.teufelhof.com; Leonhardsgraben 49; s/d/ste from Sfr138/158/178; P 📶) One for lovers of art and design, 'The Devil's Court' self-bills as a 'guest and culture' house. It comprises two slick, themed hotels – the nine-room avant-garde Art hotel and larger Gallery hotel (in a former convent), each styled with high-end, locally made Vitra furnishings.

**Hotel Spalentor** HOTEL €€
(061 588 06 26; www.hotelspalentor.ch; Schönbeinstrasse 1; s/d from Sfr153/178; ❄ 📶) Just outside the Spalentor gate to the Old Town, you'll find this stylish hotel suited to both business and leisure travellers. Recently refurbished rooms feature sleek modern styling with plush leather chairs and large-screen TVs. Some have balconies. There's a lovely garden and polite, helpful staff.

**Steinenschanze Stadthotel** HOTEL €€
(061 588 12 13; www.steinenschanze.ch; Steinengraben 69; s/f from Sfr162/180) Well located between Basel SBB station and the Old Town, this great-value hotel has simple, compact rooms with fresh lines, comfortable beds, real wood parquetry floors and panelling, and lots of natural light. There's also a communal garden area and friendly, helpful staff.

★ **Les Trois Rois** LUXURY HOTEL €€€
(061 260 50 50; www.lestroisrois.com; Blumenrain 8; s/d from Sfr350/570; P ❄ 📶) Indisputably Basel's most prestigious address, this beautiful riverfront hotel blends the dignified elegance of bygone times (waltz in the ballroom, anyone?) with young moneyed style. Rooms range from classic to chic, but are hard to fault for comfort and appeal.

## Kleinbasel

★ **Hotel Krafft** HOTEL €€
(061 690 91 30; www.krafftbasel.ch; Rheingasse 12; s/d from Sfr110/175; 📶) Design-savvy urbanites gravitate to this renovated historic hotel for its smart, minimalist rooms, wonderfully fusing old and new; some have balconies. Free folding bikes, fresh fruit and water stations impress, but the hotel's key feature is its prime riverside position, adjacent Mittlere Brücke, peering out from Klienbasel across the Rhine onto Grosbasel's gorgeous townscape. Get a room with a view.

# Eating

Basel's culinary culture benefits from the city's long history of immigration and its proximity to the French and German borders, but there's no two ways about it: dining here can be expensive. For cheap/quick eats, hover around the station area, head to Marktplatz (p222) or nip across the border to France or Germany, where the euro keeps things reasonable.

## Grossbasel

★ **Markthalle** FOOD HALL €
(www.markthalle-basel.ch; Steinentorberg 20; dishes Sfr10-25; 8am-7pm Mon, to midnight Tue-Sat, 10am-5pm Sun; ) Around the corner from Basel SBB station you'll find this large indoor market/food hall, which is a popular spot for a cheap lunch on the go. Vendors are always changing and feature Swiss specialities and world flavours. Worth a look in.

**Latini** ITALIAN €€
(061 261 34 43; www.bindella.ch/de/latini.html; Falknerstrasse 31; pasta Sfr16-27, mains Sfr25-35; 11am-midnight Sun-Thu, to 1am Fri & Sat; ❄ ) This stylish but unpretentious and popular haunt on the fringe of the Old Town is a good local staple for reasonably priced Italian cuisine, including a variety of options for vegetarians. It's just off Barfüsserplatz.

**★Restaurant Stucki** EUROPEAN €€€
(☎061 361 82 22; www.tanjagrandits.ch; Bruderholzallee 42; ⏲3-/4-course lunch Sfr75/92, 8-/12-course aroma menu Sfr190/240; P❄) Under the tutelage of chef Tanja Grandits, this long-lauded restaurant remains one of Basel's finest – dining here is an absolute treat. The signature Aroma Menu, featuring the likes of juniper honey mountain lamb and buttermilk mousse with caramel puffed rice and melon is so beautifully presented that you'll feel guilty taking a knife to your plate. But you must.

**★Restaurant Schlüsselzunft** INTERNATIONAL €€€
(☎061 261 20 46; www.schluesselzunft.ch; Freie Strasse 25; mains Sfr34-56; ⏲9am-11.30pm Mon-Sat, 11am-10pm Sun, closed Sun Jun-Aug) Housed in a 15th-century guild house that had a neo-Renaissance remake early in the 20th century, this elegant restaurant includes an internal courtyard with sweeping staircase. The menu is replete with innovative flavour combinations such as perch fillet with pears and fennel, or veal in massaman curry sauce with fruit spring rolls.

**Acqua** ITALIAN €€€
(☎061 564 66 66; www.acquabasilea.ch; Binningerstrasse 14; 2/3 courses vegetarian Sfr45/62, regular Sfr65/82; ⏲noon-2pm & 7pm-midnight Tue-Fri, 7pm-midnight Sat; 🖉) A glam post-industrial atmosphere reigns at these converted waterworks, with brown-leather banquettes and chandeliers inside bare-stone and concrete walls, surrounded by candlelit outdoor patios. Build your own two- or three-course meal from the delectable menu of Tuscan-inspired meat, fish and vegetarian offerings.

**Atelier** SWISS, MEDITERRANEAN €€€
(☎061 261 10 10; www.teufelhof.com/en/eating-drinking/atelier; Leonhardsgraben 49; weekday lunch Sfr27, dinner mains Sfr24-52; ⏲noon-2pm & 6.30-10pm; 🖉) For excellent value at lunchtime, head to this bright, modern restaurant at the Teufelhof hotel (p227), with courtyard seating, superb Swiss and Mediterranean cuisine and top-notch service.

## Kleinbasel

**Lily's Maxim Basel** ASIAN €
(☎061 683 11 11; https://lilys.ch/eatery/maxim; Rebgasse 1; mains Sfr14-26; ⏲10am-midnight Mon-Fri, 11am-midnight Sat, 11am-10.30pm Sun; ❄🖉) A casual atmosphere, reasonable prices and all-day service make this pan-Asian restaurant a perennial Kleinbasel favourite. The menu features a mix of authentic Thai, Chinese and Indian dishes, from curries to noodles to soups, accompanied by draught beer or pots of tea and served at long informal tables or barstool-lined counters.

**★Volkshaus Basel** BRASSERIE, BAR €€
(☎061 690 93 10; www.volkshaus-basel.ch/en; Rebgasse 12-14; mains Sfr28-60; ⏲restaurant noon-2pm & 6-10pm Mon-Sat, bar 10am-midnight Mon-Wed, to 1am Thu-Sat) This stylish Herzog & de Meuron–designed venue is part resto-bar, part gallery and part performance space. For relaxed dining, head for the atmospheric beer garden in a cobblestoned courtyard decorated with columns, vine-clad walls and light-draped rows of trees. The menu ranges from brasserie classics *(steak frites)* to more innovative offerings.

## Drinking & Nightlife

For good bar-hopping, explore the area between Barfüsserplatz and Klosterberg or the Rheingasse/Utengasse neighbourhood in Kleinbasel.

**★Das Viertel** ROOFTOP BAR
(☎061 331 04 00; www.dasviertel.ch; Münchensteinerstrasse 81; ⏲terrace bar 6pm-midnight Mon-Sat, from 10am Sun, club 11pm-3am Fri & Sat) East from the SBB Bahnhof along the railway tracks, this rooftop bar draws crowds all week to its sun-drenched terrace. On weekends it morphs into a club.

**Cargo Bar** BAR
(☎061 321 00 72; www.cargobar.ch; St Johanns Rheinweg 46; ⏲4pm-1am Sun-Thu, to 2.30am Fri & Sat) Art installations, live gigs, video shows and DJ performances pepper this art bar's busy calendar. In summer, tables spill onto the pavement out front, providing prime views of sunset over the Rhine.

**Atlantis** BAR
(☎061 228 96 96; www.atlan-tis.ch/en/club; Klosterberg 13; ⏲11pm-4am Fri & Sat) Leather-topped stools are strung behind the long, curving and – on DJ weekend nights – packed bar. In summer there's a rooftop terrace.

**SUD** CLUB
(☎061 683 14 44; www.sud.ch; Burgweg 7; ⏲9pm-1am Thu, to 4.30am Fri & Sat, 10am-4pm Sun) This fun hybrid bar/club/event space occupying a former brewery in Kleinbasel has a welcoming, chilled vibe and hosts everything from DJ nights to poetry slams.

**Consum** WINE BAR

(☎061 690 91 35; www.consumbasel.ch; Rheingasse 19; ⊙5pm-midnight Sun-Thu, to 1am Fri & Sat) This relaxed bar is a marvellous spot for taking your taste buds on a wine journey around the world. Friendly staff will open one of more than 100 bottles for you if you order just three decilitres (about three glasses).

## Entertainment

For comprehensive entertainment listings, check out www.basellive.ch (in German). Annual musical events include the multiweek **Jazzfestival Basel** (www.offbeat-concert.ch) and **Baloise Session** (www.baloisesession.ch; ⊙Oct/Nov). In August, **Allianz Cinema Basel** (www.allianzcinema.com/basel) brings nightly outdoor film screenings (many in English) to the cobblestones of Münsterplatz.

**Bird's Eye Jazz Club** JAZZ

(☎061 263 33 41; www.birdseye.ch; Kohlenberg 20; ⊙8-11.30pm Tue-Sat Sep-May, Wed-Sat Jun-Aug) One of Europe's top jazz dens attracts local and headline foreign acts.

**Stadtcasino** CONCERT VENUE

(☎061 226 36 00; www.stadtcasino.ch; Steinenberg 14; ⊙show times vary) The Basel Symphony Orchestra and Basel Chamber Orchestra both play regularly at this 19th-century venue, which includes a 1500-seat concert hall, ballroom and chamber-music hall.

**FC Basel** SPECTATOR SPORT

(www.fcb.ch; St Jakob Park) Basel boasts one of Switzerland's top football teams, which plays at St Jakob Park, 3km east of SBB Bahnhof.

## Shopping

**Weihnachtshaus Johann Wanner** ARTS & CRAFTS

(☎061 261 48 26; www.johannwanner.ch; Spalenberg 14; ⊙12.30-6.30pm Mon, 10am-6.30pm Tue-Fri, 10am-5pm Sat) Weihnachtshaus Johann Wanner is a well-known Christmas store where you can pick up beautiful festive decorations year-round.

**Flohmarkt Petersplatz** MARKET

(www.messen-maerkte.bs.ch/flohmarkt.htm; Petersplatz; ⊙7.30am-4pm Sat) Petersplatz is the scene of Basel's popular Saturday flea market.

**Stadtmarkt** MARKET

(www.messen-maerkte.bs.ch; Marktplatz; ⊙8.30am-2pm Mon-Thu, to 6pm Fri & Sat) Marktplatz hosts this year-round food market.

### DISCOUNT CARDS

Pop into Basel Tourismus (Bahnhof) or Basel Tourismus (Stadtcasino) to pick up a BaselCard (Sfr20/30 for 24/48 hours) for a bunch of value-adds, including one free city walking tour and ferry crossing, and half-price tickets to all museums within the city limits.

## Information

**Basel Tourismus** (Stadtcasino; ☎061 268 68 68; www.basel.com; Steinenberg 14; ⊙9am-6.30pm Mon-Fri, to 5pm Sat, 10am-3pm Sun) This branch of Basel's tourist information association, in the Old Town, organises two-hour city walking tours (adult/child from Sfr18/9) in English, German and French, and has a wealth of information, maps and links to apps on the city's many museums. There's also a branch at Basel SBB station (☎061 268 68 68; www.basel.com; Centralbahnstrasse 10; ⊙8-6pm Mon-Fri, 9am-5pm Sat, 9am-3pm Sun).

## Getting There & Away

Basel is well served by road, rail and air.

The A35 freeway comes down from Strasbourg and passes by EuroAirport; the A3 heads east towards Zürich, while the A2 travels south towards Bern and Lucerne.

Basel has two main train stations: the main Swiss/French train station, SBB Bahnhof, to the south; and the German train station, Basel Bad Bahnhof, to the north.

Frequent direct trains run from SBB Bahnhof to Zürich (Sfr34, 55 minutes to 1¼ hours) and Bern (Sfr41, 55 minutes). Service to Geneva (Sfr77, 2¾ hours) requires a change of train in Bern, Biel/Bienne or Olten.

There's also a direct TGV service to Paris' Gare de Lyon (Sfr142, three hours) every other hour. Discounted tickets on this route start at Sfr78.

**EuroAirport** (MLH or BSL; ☎+33 3 89 90 31 11; www.euroairport.com) serves Basel (as well as Mulhouse, France and Freiburg, Germany). Located 5km north of the city, in France, it offers flights to numerous European cities on a variety of low-cost carriers.

## Getting Around

**Airport Bus 50** runs every seven to 30 minutes from 5am to midnight between the airport and SBB Bahnhof (Sfr4.70, 20 minutes). Buy tickets at the machine outside the arrivals hall (bills, coins and credit cards accepted). The trip by **taxi** (☎061 222 22 22; www.taxi-zentrale.ch) costs around Sfr40.

WORTH A TRIP

## FOUR CASTLES IN A DAY

If you love fairy tales or the general medieval vibe of TV series such as *Game of Thrones*, you might like to rent a car and explore the four robust, authentic castles found in the countryside between Baden and Aarau. The itinerary here takes you between the two towns, via the four castles, in a few easy hours. It can also be driven in reverse.

Starting in Baden, follow Rte 3 for 13km west to the town of Windisch with its one-time Roman garrison, the foundations and east gate of which remain intact, until you reach **Schloss Habsburg** (Habsburg Castle; ☎084 887 12 00; www.schloss-habsburg.ch; Habsburg; ⏲10am-11.30pm Apr-Oct, 11am-10pm Wed-Sun Nov-Mar; P) FREE. The house that built this fortress in 1020 would go on to become one of Europe's greatest dynasties.

From here take Rte 5 south for 8km to the neighbouring village of Wildegg and the eponymous **Schloss Wildegg** (☎062 887 12 30; www.schlosswildegg.ch; Effingerweg 5; adult/child Sfr14/8, gardens only Sfr7.50/2.50; ⏲10am-5pm Tue-Sun Apr-Oct; P). Crowning a hilltop, amid a working farm with gardens and orchards, the castle is chock-full of antiquities.

If you want something more medieval, head south via Rte 26 to **Schloss Lenzburg** (☎062 888 48 40; www.schloss-lenzburg.ch; Schlossstrasse, Lenzburg; adult/child Sfr14/8, gardens only Sfr5/2.50; ⏲10am-5pm Tue-Sun Apr-Oct), with its three museums and former dungeon: it's only another 6km down the road.

To round out your fantasy day, head south about 10km through the village of Seengen to the delightful **Wasserschloss Hallwyl** (☎062 767 60 10; www.schlosshallwyl.ch; Seengen; adult/child Sfr14/8; ⏲10am-5pm Tue-Sun Apr-Oct; P 👪), which is actually two small castles in a river joined by a bridge.

From here it's 19km northwest to Aarau, or just shy of 30km back to Baden.

Save money with the Schlösserpass (adult/child Sfr34/19), a single ticket that covers *three* of the four castles (Hallwyl, Lenzburg and Wildegg), which you can pick up from Tourist Office Info Baden and aarau info.

Trying to get to all four castles by public transport in a day is a stretch, but if you don't have a car there are options to visit one or two.



Basel hotel guests automatically receive a 'mobility ticket' pass, providing free transport throughout the city, operated by **BVB** (☎61 685 14 14; www.bvb.ch/en).

Without the pass, tram and bus tickets cost Sfr2.30 for short trips (maximum four stops), Sfr3.80 for longer trips within Basel and Sfr9.80 for a day pass.

# Baden

POP 16,118 / ELEV 388M

The Romans were the first bunch who came to Baden ('baths' in German) for its 18 mineral-rich thermal springs bubbling from beneath the earth at a scalding 47°C (116°F). They called the place Aquæ Helveticæ. But if this conjures up images of Japanese-style *rotemburo* (outdoor onsen baths) think again. By and large, Baden's springs have been channelled into a number of expensive- to overpriced thermal-spa hotels.

Baden's pièce de résistance is a sprawling public bath facility undergoing an impressive transformation. At the time of writing the reopening date had been pushed back from 2017 to 2019. Until it opens, the pretty town, with some excellent museums, makes for a nice excursion from nearby Zürich, but connoisseurs of luxury hotels or lovers of natural thermal pools might find better bang for their buck elsewhere.

## Sights & Activities

Baden's **Altstadt** (Old Town) is adorned by a fetching covered timber **bridge** (Holzbrücke), a beautifully restored **medieval tower** (Stadtturm), cobbled lanes and an assortment of step-gabled houses.

★**Stiftung Langmatt** GALLERY

(Langmatt Foundation; ☎056 200 86 70; www.langmatt.ch; Römerstrasse 30; adult/child Sfr12/free; ⏲2-5pm Tue-Fri, 11am-5pm Sat & Sun Mar-Nov) This gorgeous little museum is an ensemble of art, architecture and botany, housing a cornucopia of French impressionist art in a stately home surrounded by beautifully landscaped gardens. For your very own *déjeuner sur l'herbe,* pre-order one of the museum's picnic baskets (*Picknick-Korb*) to enjoy out on the lawn.

**Schweizer Kindermuseum** MUSEUM
(☎056 222 14 44; www.kindermuseum.ch; Ländliweg 7; adult/child Sfr12/4; ⏰2-5pm Tue-Sat, 10am-5pm Sun; 🅿👪) Occupying 20 rooms of a former mansion, this hands-on museum with a focus on educating kids about genealogy and generations past is a fun, free-for-all for inquisitive young minds. Although it's better suited to preteens, anyone with an imagination and a sense of play (including mum and dad) can enjoy a visit here.

## Sleeping & Eating

★**SYHA Jugendherberge Baden** HOSTEL €
(☎056 221 67 36; www.youthhostel.ch/baden; Kanalstrasse 7; dm/s/d from Sfr35/87/95; ⏰Apr-Dec; 🅿@) One of Switzerland's best-looking hostels, this has grey slate floors, earth-red walls and top-quality materials. To find it walk from the train station to the Altstadt, cross the Limmat river at Holzbrücke and take the first right into Kanalstrasse.

**Atrium-Hotel Blume** HOTEL €€
(☎056 200 02 00; www.blume-baden.ch; Kurplatz 4; s/d from Sfr170/185; 📶🏊) This atmospheric old place is a popular tourist choice for its inner courtyard with a fountain, plants and wrought-iron balconies. Rooms are pleasant and comfortably furnished. There's also a small thermal pool.

★**Goldener Schlüssel** INTERNATIONAL €€€
(☎056 221 77 21; www.goldenerschluessel.ch; Limmatpromenade 29; 2-/3-/4-/5-course tasting menu Sfr38/49/60/70; ⏰6pm-midnight Tue-Sat) Near the baths, this cosy eatery with beamed, painted ceilings invites diners to build their own dream menu from more than a dozen *Schneuggereien* (small plates akin to Spanish tapas). Choices range from Swiss classics to Italian- and Japanese-influenced options.

## Information

**Tourist Office Info Baden** (☎056 200 87 87; www.baden.ch; Bahnhofplatz 1; ⏰noon-6.30pm Mon, 9am-6.30pm Tue-Fri, to 4pm Sat) Castle fanatics can pick up their *Schlosser-passes* here, just opposite the train station.

## Getting There & Away

Baden is about 24km northwest of Zürich (on the A1).

The compact city is easily accessible from Zürich by regional train (Sfr13.40, 15 minutes) and even serviced by suburban S-Bahn lines S6 and S12 (30 to 40 minutes).

# Aarau

POP 20,782 / ELEV 383M

Perhaps Aarau's glory days are now, with visitors able to appreciate a trove of fascinating history in this charming medieval town – there's been a settlement here since the 1300s – draped on a spur of land overlooking the broad flow of the Aare River.

## Sights

★**Aargauer Kunsthaus** GALLERY
(☎062 835 23 30; www.aargauerkunsthaus.ch; Aargauerplatz; adult/child Sfr15/10; ⏰10am-5pm Tue, Wed & Fri-Sun, to 8pm Thu) To view centuries of Swiss art and regular temporary exhibitions, call by Aargau's impressive house of fine arts housed in a striking Herzog & de Meuron-designed glass and concrete building.

**Altstadt** AREA
(Old Town) Jutting high above the Aare River, Aarau's walled Old Town makes for a pleasant wander. Its grid of streets is lined with gracious, centuries-old buildings, more than 70 of which have grand roofs hanging out over the streets, with their timber undersides gaily decorated.

## Sleeping & Eating

There's a good selection of restaurants and bars in the medieval Old Town, which is popular with tourists and weekend day trippers.

★**Kettenbrücke Hotel** BOUTIQUE HOTEL €
(☎062 838 18 18; www.hotelkettenbruecke.ch; Zollrain 16; d/ste from Sfr140/290; 🅿❄) This lovely, historic, 27-room property with its own bar/restaurant offers some of the classiest rooms in town, featuring a calming palette of soothing greys and blues with birch floors and stylish furnishings and bedding. There are also two beautiful suites for long-stay guests.

★**Speck** SWISS €
(☎062 822 37 48; www.speck-metzgerei.ch; Zollrain 10; set menus Sfr16-17; ⏰10am-2pm & 5-11pm Mon-Fri, 10am-2pm Sat; 🅿❄) Finally, an unpretentious restaurant serving hearty Swiss cuisine at affordable prices! Stodgy, home-style, Germanic cooking featuring lots of local meat and potatoes affords excellent value.

## Information

**aarau info** (☎062 834 10 34; www.aarauinfo.ch; Metzgergasse 2; ⏰1.30-6pm Mon, 9am-6pm Tue-Fri, 9am-1pm Sat) In the heart of Aarau's Altstadt.

1

2

1. Horses graze near Gimmelwald (p133), Bernese Oberland
2. Corippo (p194), Ticino 3. Werdenberg (p269), Appenzell

# Alpine Villages

**Heidi may be fictional, but her Alpine village lifestyle isn't. Switzerland will meet all your storybook fantasies: from hilltop hamlets in the Bernese Oberland with cowbells as your wake-up call, to icicle hung log chalets in Valais where you can snuggle by a crackling fire as the flakes gently fall. Sound idyllic? You bet.**

## Val Fex

Lost in time and space, Val Fex nestles amid glacier-encrusted mountains, larch forests and meadows. Romantically reached on foot or by horse-drawn carriage, the tiny hamlets of Fex-Platta and Fex-Cresta are like the Alps before the dawn of tourism.

## Village Architecture

Pretty villages are in abundant supply in Appenzell's bucolic back country, but none matches Werdenberg (p269), with its perky medieval castle, geranium-studded timber chalets and pristine Alpine setting.

## Mürren & Gimmelwald

Mürren (p131) has scenery, skiing and hiking to make your heart sing. Pick a log chalet for dress-circle views of Eiger, Mönch and Jungfrau. To be at one with nature, tiptoe away from the crowds to cute-as-a-button Gimmelwald (p133) nearby.

## Corippo

With a population of 13, Switzerland's smallest hamlet, Corippo (p194), is more of a family than a village. Tumbling down a wooded hill in the Val Verzasca, its granite houses and mountain backdrop are the stuff of photographers' dreams.

## Aletsch Glacier

If you're looking for postcard Switzerland, car-free Riederalp and Bettmeralp (p173) are it, with their dreamy Matterhorn views and snuggly timber chalets perched on the edge of the Aletsch Glacier's icy wilderness.

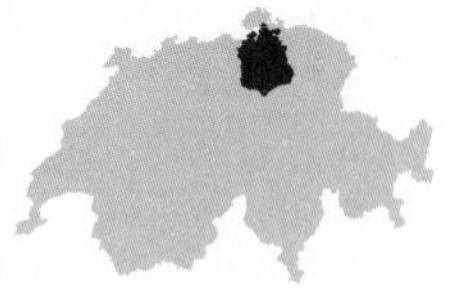

# Zürich

**Includes ➡**



## Best Places to Eat

- Alpenrose (p242)
- Didi's Frieden (p243)
- Kronenhalle (p244)
- Café Sprüngli (p242)
- Baltho Küche & Bar (p243)

## Best Places to Stay

- B2 Boutique Hotel & Spa (p241)
- Marktgasse (p242)
- Depot 195 (p251)
- Jakob (p249)
- Hotel Florhof (p241)
- Hotel Widder (p241)

## Why Go?

Naturally, the lakeside city of Zürich is the canton's centre of attention, with a clutch of excellent museums and restaurants in the walkable Altstadt (Old Town), not to mention happening bars, galleries and boutiques with urban edge in the revitalised Zürich-West neighbourhood.

But it's also worth venturing beyond Switzerland's financial capital for a day or two to delve deeper into this canton, where the Alps seem tantalisingly close on cloud-free days. Within half an hour of the city, you can try out walking trails or mountain-bike routes in the heights of 871m Uetliberg, or explore castle-topped Rapperswil and its medieval Old Town by the lake. Should art be more your bag, factor in a detour to Winterthur, something of a cultural hotspot, with a trio of terrific galleries and one of Europe's foremost photography museums.

## When to Go

- Celebrate spring's arrival by watching the Böögg snowman go up in flames at Sechseläuten.
- In August, live it up at one of Europe's biggest street carnivals, the Street Parade.
- In September, sample pop-ups, cookery workshops, brunches and starlit dinners at Food Zürich.

## Zürich Highlights

❶ **Fraumünster** (p236)
Basking in the glow of Marc Chagall's stained-glass windows.

❷ **Kunsthaus** (p236)
Admiring the extensive art collections in Zürich's impressive fine-arts gallery.

❸ **Street Parade** (p240)
Joining the throngs for the August Street Parade.

❹ **Frau Gerolds Garten** (p245) Sipping beers and mingling with locals in Zürich's favourite beer garden.

❺ **Seebad Enge** (p239)
Soaking up the sun or floating downstream at one of the city's lake and river swimming spots.

❻ **Uetliberg** (p247) Climbing this 871m-high mountain for stellar views of the city and countryside.

❼ **Café Sprüngli** (p242)
Indulging in pastries and chocolate at this epicentre of sweet.

❽ **Technorama** (p250)
Exploring the fun side of science at family-friendly Technorama in Winterthur.

# ZÜRICH

POP 396,955

Culturally vibrant, efficiently run and attractively set at the meeting of river and lake, Zürich is regularly recognised as one of the world's most liveable cities. Long known as a savvy, hard-working financial centre, Switzerland's largest and wealthiest metropolis has also emerged in the 21st century as one of central Europe's hippest destinations, with an artsy, post-industrial edge that is epitomised in its summer Street Parade (p240).

Much of the ancient centre, with its winding lanes and tall church steeples, has been kept lovingly intact. Yet Zürich has also wholeheartedly embraced contemporary trends, with the conversion of old factories into cultural centres and creative new living spaces. Nowhere is that clearer than in Züri-West (p245), the epicentre of the city's nightlife.

## History

Zürich started life as a Roman encampment called Turicum. Germanic tribes moved in by AD 400 and, in 1336, the already prosperous town underwent a minor revolution as craftspeople and traders took power, expelling the nobles and creating the 13 *Zünfte* (guilds) that long directed the city's fortunes. Many still exist today and come out to play for the Sechseläuten (p240) festival.

In 1351, Zürich joined the Swiss Confederation and, in the early 16th century, became a key player in the Reformation under Huldrych Zwingli. In the following centuries, it grew rich on textiles and banking.

Due to Switzerland's neutrality during both world wars, Zürich attracted all sorts of personalities, from James Joyce to Vladimir Lenin. The counter-cultural Dada art movement was born in Zürich in the wake of the horrors of WWI, and many Dadaist works are still on display in Zürich's Kunsthaus.

Since the early 1990s, the city has shed its image as a dour town of Protestant bankers and morphed into one of central Europe's hippest hang-outs.

## Sights

The city spreads around the northwest end of Zürichsee (Lake Zürich), from where the Limmat river runs further north still, splitting the city in two. The majority of Zürich's big-hitters cluster in and around the medieval centre, but the edgy Züri-West neighbourhood also has some terrific galleries. Best explored on foot, the narrow streets of the Niederdorf quarter on the river's east bank are crammed with restaurants, bars, shops and sights.

**★ Kunsthaus** MUSEUM

(Map p238; ☎044 253 84 84; www.kunsthaus.ch; Heimplatz 1; adult/child Sfr16/free, Wed free; ⏲10am-8pm Wed & Thu, to 6pm Tue & Fri-Sun; 🚋5, 8, 9, 10 to Kunsthaus) Zürich's impressive fine-arts gallery boasts a rich collection of largely European art. It stretches from the Middle Ages through a mix of Old Masters to Alberto Giacometti stick figures, Monet and van Gogh masterpieces, Rodin sculptures, and other 19th- and 20th-century art. Swiss Rail and Museum Passes don't provide free admission but the ZürichCard (p247) does.

**★ Fraumünster** CHURCH

(Map p238; www.fraumuenster.ch/en; Münsterhof; Sfr5 incl audioguide; ⏲10am-6pm Mar-Oct, to 5pm Nov-Feb; 🚋6, 7, 10, 11, 14 to Paradeplatz) This 13th-century church is renowned for its stunning stained-glass windows, designed by the Russian-Jewish master Marc Chagall (1887–1985), who executed the series of five windows in the choir stalls in 1971 and the rose window in the southern transept in 1978. The rose window in the northern transept was created by Augusto Giacometti in 1945. Admission includes a multilingual audioguide.

**Schweizerisches Landesmuseum** MUSEUM

(Swiss National Museum; Map p238; ☎058 466 65 11; www.nationalmuseum.ch/e/zuerich; Museumstrasse 2; adult/child Sfr10/free; ⏲10am-5pm Tue, Wed & Fri-Sun, to 7pm Thu; 🚋Zürich Hauptbahnhof, 🚆Zürich Hauptbahnhof) Inside a purpose-built cross between a mansion and a castle sprawls this eclectic and imaginatively presented museum. The permanent collection offers an extensive romp through Swiss history, with exhibits ranging from elaborately carved and painted sleds to domestic and religious artefacts, via a series of reconstructed historical rooms spanning six centuries. In August 2016 the museum celebrated a major expansion with the opening of its archaeology section in a brand-new wing.

**FIFA World Football Museum** MUSEUM

(www.fifamuseum.com; Seestrasse 27; adult/child Sfr24; ⏲10am-7pm Tue-Sat, 9am-6pm Sun; 🚋2, 5, 6, 7, 8, 11, 13, 14, 17 to Bahnhof Enge, 🚆Bahnhof Enge) Fans of the game won't want to miss out on the FIFA World Football Museum, which races you through the history of FIFA and the World Cup in a series of hands-on displays. Highlights include the original World Cup

## INDUSTRIAL CONVERSION

Symbolic of the renaissance of once-industrial western Zürich is the **Schiffbau** (Map p244; Schiffbaustrasse; 🚊3, 4, 6 to Schiffbau). Once a mighty factory churning out lake steamers and, until 1992, turbine-engine parts, this enormous shell has been turned into the seat of the **Schauspielhaus** (Map p244; ☎ticket office 044 258 77 77; www.schauspielhaus.ch; Schiffbaustrasse 4; 🚊3, 4, 6 to Schiffbau), a huge theatre with three stages. It's also home to a stylish restaurant and bar and the jazz den Moods (p246).

Other conversion projects around town include **Puls 5** (Map p244; www.puls5.ch; Giessereistrasse 18; 🚊17 to Förrlibuckstrasse), a one-time foundry now converted into a multi-use centre with restaurants, bars and offices, and the B2 Boutique Hotel (p241) in the old Hürlimann brewery, whose architects painstakingly retained the brewery's external structure and historic features such as the machine room.

Trophy and a giant pinball machine where you can put your own skills to the test.

**Museum für Gestaltung** MUSEUM
(☎043 446 67 67; www.museum-gestaltung.ch; Toni-Areal, Pfingstweidstrasse 96; adult/child Sfr12/free; ⏲10am-5pm Tue & Thu-Sun, to 8pm Wed; 🚊3, 4, 6 to Toni-Areal) Consistently impressive and wide-ranging, the revolving exhibitions at this design museum can include anything from works by classic photographers such as Henri Cartier-Bresson to advertising for the design furniture of yesteryear. Graphic and applied arts dominate the permanent collections.

**Beyer Museum** MUSEUM
(Map p238; ☎043 344 63 63; www.beyer-ch.com/uhrenmuseum; Bahnhofstrasse 31; adult/child Sfr8/3; ⏲2-6pm Mon-Fri; 🚊4, 10, 14, 15 to Paradeplatz) Inside the premises of a purveyor of fine timepieces is this small jewel of a museum, which chronicles the rise of timekeeping, from striated medieval candles to modern watches. To see short videos of the most creative pieces in action (Moses striking a rock with his staff to bring forth water, and a magician who lifts cups to reveal ever-changing geometric shapes), ask staff for a loaner iPad.

**Grossmünster** CHURCH
(Map p238; www.grossmuenster.ch; Grossmünsterplatz; ⏲10am-6pm Mar-Oct, to 5pm Nov-Feb; 🚊4, 15 to Helmhaus) Founded by Charlemagne in the 9th century (but heavily reworked since), Zürich's twin-towered landmark cathedral sits directly across the river from Fraumünster. The interior showcases stained-glass work by Augusto Giacometti. For far-reaching city views, climb the southern tower, the **Karlsturm** (adult/child Sfr4/2; ⏲10am-5pm Mon-Sat, 12.30-5.30pm Sun Mar-Oct, to 4.30pm daily Nov-Feb).

Firebrand preacher Huldrych Zwingli (1484–1531) began speaking out against the Catholic Church here in the 16th century, and thus brought the Reformation to Zürich. **Zwingli's house** (Map p238; Kirchgasse 13; 🚊2, 4, 15 to Helmhaus) is nearby.

**St Peterskirche** CHURCH
(St Peter's Church; Map p238; St Peterhofstatt; ⏲8am-6pm Mon-Fri, to 4pm Sat; 🚊4, 10, 11, 14, 15 to Paradeplatz) From any position in the city, it's hard to overlook the 13th-century tower of this church. Its prominent clock face, 8.7m in diameter, is the largest in Europe. Inside, the choir stalls date from the 13th century, but the rest of the church is largely an 18th-century reconstruction. Just below is one of Zürich's most picturesque spots: **St Peterhofstatt**, a lovely cobbled square surrounding a graceful old linden tree.

**James Joyce Foundation** MUSEUM
(Map p238; ☎044 211 83 01; www.joycefoundation.ch; Augustinergasse 9; ⏲10am-5pm Mon-Fri; 🚊4, 6, 7, 10, 11, 13, 14, 15, 17 to Rennweg) FREE James Joyce spent much of WWI in Zürich and wrote *Ulysses* here. This foundation, which boasts Europe's largest Joyce collection, hosts regular English-language readings of his work on Monday, Tuesday and Thursday afternoons.

**Cabaret Voltaire** GALLERY
(Map p238; ☎043 268 57 20; www.cabaretvoltaire.ch; Spiegelgasse 1; ⏲gallery 2-6pm Tue-Fri, noon-6pm Sat & Sun, bar from 6pm Tue-Fri, from 4pm Sat-Sun; 🚊2, 4, 15 to Rathaus) FREE Birthplace of the zany Dada art movement, this art space has come back to life as a hotbed of contentious art exhibitions and socially critical artistic ferment. Explore the history of Dada downstairs or head for the poster-plastered cafe-bar upstairs. Art books and Dada-related publications are sold in the shop.

# Central Zürich

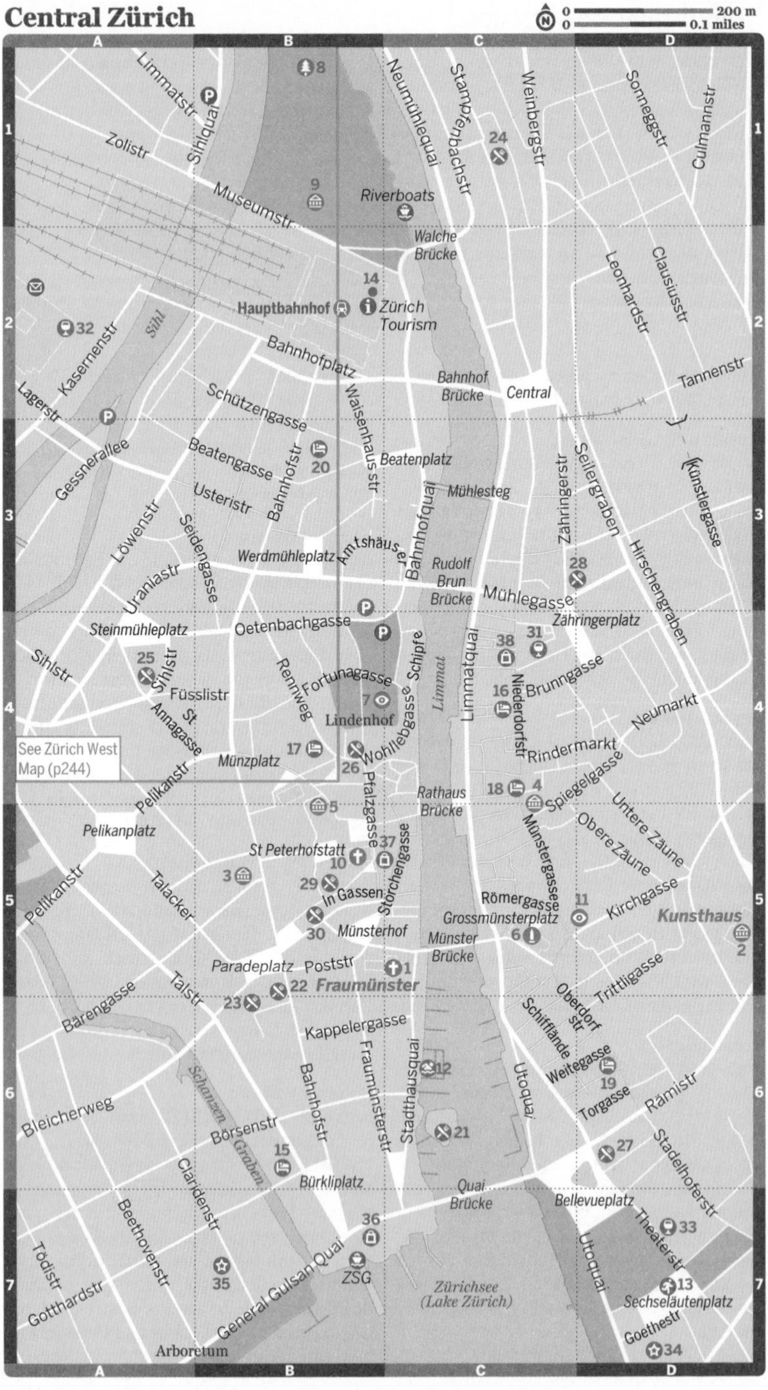

0 200 m
0 0.1 miles

A B C D

1 2 3 4 5 6 7



See Zürich West Map (p244)

Limmatstr
Sihlquai
Zolistr
Museumstr
Neumühlequai
Stampfenbachstr
Weinbergstr
Sonneggstr
Culmannstr
Riverboats
Walche Brücke
Leonhardstr
Clausiusstr
Hauptbahnhof
Zürich Tourism
Sihl
Kasernenstr
Lagerstr
Bahnhofplatz
Bahnhof Brücke
Central
Tannenstr
Schützengasse
Waisenhaus str
Beatengasse
Bahnhofstr
Beatenplatz
Gessnerallee
Usteristr
Bahnhofquai
Mühlesteg
Zähringerstr
Seilergraben
Künstlergasse
Löwenstr
Seidengasse
Werdmühleplatz
Amtshäuser
Rudolf Brun Brücke
Mühlegasse
Hirschengraben
Uraniastr
Zähringerplatz
Steinmühleplatz
Oetenbachgasse
Schipfe
Limmatquai
Sihlstr
Rennweg
Fortunagasse
Limmat
Niederdorfstr
Brunngasse
Füsslistr
St Annagasse
Lindenhof
Neumarkt
Wohllebgasse
Münzplatz
Rindermarkt
Pelikanstr
Pfalzgasse
Rathaus Brücke
Spiegelgasse
Untere Zäune
Pelikanplatz
Münstergasse
Obere Zäune
St Peterhofstatt
Talacker
Storchengasse
In Gassen
Römergasse
Kirchgasse
Grossmünsterplatz
Kunsthaus
Münsterhof
Münster Brücke
Paradeplatz
Poststr
Fraumünster
Trittligasse
Bärengasse
Talstr
Oberdorf str
Schifflände
Kappelergasse
Weitegasse
Fraumünsterstr
Stadthausquai
Utoquai
Rämistr
Torgasse
Bleicherweg
Schanzen Graben
Börsenstr
Stadelhoferstr
Bürkliplatz
Quai Brücke
Bellevueplatz
Claridenstr
Beethovenstr
Theaterstr
Tödistr
General Gulsan Quai
ZSG
Zürichsee (Lake Zürich)
Gotthardstr
Sechseläutenplatz
Goethestr
Arboretum

1 2 3 4 5 6 7 8 9 10 11 12 13 14 15 16 17 18 19 20 21 22 23 24 25 26 27 28 29 30 31 32 33 34 35 36 37 38

## Central Zürich





## Activities

Zürich comes into its own in summer, when the parks lining the lake are overrun with bathers, sunseekers, in-line skaters, footballers, lovers, picnickers, party animals and preeners. Police even patrol on rollerblades!

From May to mid-September, official swimming areas known as *Badis* (usually wooden piers with a pavilion) open around the lake and up the Limmat river. There are also plenty of free, unofficial places to take a dip.

**Thermalbad & Spa Zürich** SPA

(044 205 96 50; http://thermalbad-zuerich.ch; Brandschenkestrasse 150; thermal baths adult/child Sfr36/18, Irish-Roman spa Sfr60; 9am-10pm; 13 to Enge) To see Zürich's lights glimmer while being pummelled in a jetted open-air infinity pool, head across to this spa in the former Hürlimann brewery. The thermal waters are drawn from the mineral-rich Aqui springs deep below Zürich. In the vaults are the wonderfully atmospheric Irish-Roman baths (adults only), a series of beautifully lit pools and curative water treatments.

**Seebad Enge** SWIMMING

(044 201 38 89; www.seebadenge.ch; Mythenquai 9, 700m southwest of Bürkliplatz; swimming/sauna Sfr8/29; 9am-7pm May & Sep, to 8pm Jun-Aug; sauna 11am-11pm Mon-Sat, 10am-10pm Sun late Sep-early May; 2, 5, 10, 11 to Rentenanstalt) At this happening bath, the bar stays open until midnight when the weather is good. Other offerings include massage, yoga, stand-up paddleboarding and a winter sauna (women only on Mondays; mixed rest of week). No children.

**Seebad Utoquai** SWIMMING

(044 251 61 51; www.bad-utoquai.ch; Utoquai 49; adult/child Sfr8/4; 7am-8pm mid-May–late Sep; 2, 4, 10, 11, 14, 15 to Kreuzstrasse) Just north of leafy Zürichhorn park, about 400m south of Bellevueplatz, this is the most popular bathing pavilion on the Zürichsee's eastern shore.

**Frauenbad** SWIMMING

(Map p238; 044 211 95 92; Stadthausquai; adult/child Sfr8/4; 9am-7.30pm mid-May–mid-Sep; 2, 5, 8, 9, 10, 11, 14, 15 to Bürkliplatz) For a blast of nostalgia, take a dip in this art nouveau outdoor swimming pool on the banks of the Limmat. The pool is only open to women during the day. Its trendy bar opens to both sexes at night.

**Letten** SWIMMING

(Map p244; ☎044 362 92 00; Lettensteg 10; 🚋3, 4, 6, 10, 11, 13, 15, 17 to Limmatplatz) FREE North of the train station on the eastern bank of the Limmat (just south of Kornhausbrücke), this is where Züri-West trendsetters swim, dive off bridges, skateboard, play volleyball, or just drink at the riverside bars and chat on the grass and concrete steps.

## Tours

**eTuk Tuk** DRIVING

(Map p244; ☎044 514 33 44; www.etuktuk.ch; Lagerstrasse 107; ⏰9am-7pm) These eco-friendly tuk-tuk tours are a novel way to take a spin around Zürich. Clued-up guides run 40-minute 'Heart of Zürich' tours (Sfr29), taking in the Old Town and Niederdorf, hour-long tours of the city centre (Sfr36), a 90-minute tour of Zürich and its surrounds (Sfr45), plus wacky 90-minute chocolate fondue tours (Sfr154), including fruit, marshmallows, chocolate and dessert wine. Check ahead where the tours begin.

**Zürich Food Tour** FOOD & DRINK

(Map p238; ☎044 215 40 00; www.zuerich.com; Sfr85; ⏰4-7pm Fri; 🚋Zürich Hauptbahnhof, 🚆Zürich Hauptbahnhof) For the inside scoop on Zürich's food scene, try out this tour run by the tourist office. Leading through the industrial-turned-trendy Züri-West quarter, it's three hours of tastings in restaurants, bars, markets and breweries. The changing starting point is given when you book.

## Festivals & Events

**Street Parade** STREET CARNIVAL

(www.streetparade.com; Utoquai; ⏰2nd Sat in Aug; 🚋2, 5, 8, 9 to Bellevue) This techno celebration in mid-August has established itself as one of Europe's largest and wildest street parties since its first festive outing in 1992.

**Food Zürich** FOOD & DRINK

(www.foodzurich.com; ⏰late May–early Jun) Held over 11 days in May and June, this festival celebrates all things food and drink, with everything from pop-ups to cookery workshops, market brunches and dinners under the stars. Menus swing from Swiss to global flavours.

**Sechseläuten** PARADE

(Sächsilüüte; Map p238; www.sechselaeuten.ch; Sechseläutenplatz; ⏰3rd or 4th Mon in Apr; 🚋2, 4, 10, 11, 14 to Opernhaus) The highlight of this spring festival is the ignition of a fireworks-filled 'snowman' (the *Böögg*); the speed with which his head explodes is said to predict the weather for the coming summer (the quicker the explosion, the balmier the weather will be).

**Pride** LGBT

(Map p244; http://zurichpridefestival.ch; Kasernenareal; ⏰2nd weekend in Jun; 🚋3, 14 to Sihlpost) Zürich waves the rainbow flag at this massive LGBT street festival during the second weekend in June. It's held at the Kasernenareal festival grounds.

## Sleeping

Many hotels offer lower prices on weekends. Note that finding a room on the weekend of the August Street Parade is tough and prices skyrocket. Prices can also head north during various major trade fairs (including those in Basel).

**Kafischnaps** HOTEL €

(Map p244; ☎043 538 81 16; www.kafischnaps.ch; Kornhausstrasse 57; s Sfr69, d Sfr88-118; 📶; 🚋11, 14 to Schaffhauserplatz) Set in a one-time butcher's shop, this cool, bustling neighbourhood cafe-bar rents out a collection of five cheerful little upstairs rooms, each named and decorated after a fruit-based liquor. Book ahead online; it fills up fast. The cafe-bar (open 8am or 9am to midnight daily) is grand for a coffee, beer or brunch.

**City Backpacker** HOSTEL €

(Map p238; ☎044 251 90 15; www.city-backpacker.ch; Niederdorfstrasse 5; dm/s/d Sfr37/77/118; ⏰reception closed noon-3pm; @📶; 🚋2, 4, 15 to Rathaus) Attractively situated in the Old Town, this private hostel with a youthful party vibe is friendly and well equipped, if a trifle cramped. In summer, you can overcome the claustrophobia by hanging out on the rooftop terrace. Be prepared for a climb, as the reception area and hostel rooms are up several flights of stairs, and there's no lift.

**SYHA Hostel** HOSTEL €

(☎043 399 78 00; www.youthhostel.ch; Mutschellenstrasse 114; dm Sfr40.50, s Sfr82-118, d Sfr92-139; @📶; 🚋7 to Morgental, Ⓢ S8, S24 to Wollishofen) A pink 1960s landmark houses this busy, institutional hostel with 24-hour reception, dining hall, sparkling modern bathrooms and dependable wi-fi in the downstairs lounge. The included breakfast features miso soup and rice alongside all the Swiss standards. It's about 20 minutes south of the Hauptbahnhof.

**Oldtown Hostel Otter** HOSTEL €
(Map p238; ☎044 251 22 07; www.oldtownzurich.com; Oberdorfstrasse 7; dm/d from Sfr43/134; 🛜; 🚊2, 4, 15 to Helmhaus) Converted from a hotel to a hostel, the Otter offers one of Zürich's better price-to-location ratios. Tucked into a Niederdorf backstreet, it has seven dorms and eight private rooms in a variety of configurations, plus a shared guest kitchenette. It's a five-minute walk from several major attractions, including the Fraumünster, the Kunsthaus, the Limmat River and the Zürichsee.

**25hours Hotel Zürich West** DESIGN HOTEL €€
(☎044 577 25 25; www.25hours-hotels.com; Pfingstweidstrasse 102; d Sfr162-370; P🛜; 🚊3, 4, 6 to Toni-Areal) Belonging to the fresh-faced 25hours brand, this Züri-West hotel pairs ultra-slick design with exuberant playful touches, original art and pops of bright colour. Rooms are minimalist funky, with eco-cosmetics, Bluetooth speakers, geometric-patterned rugs, free minibars and recycled Freitag bags to borrow. Other nice touches include free Mini Cooper rental, ping-pong by the entrance and long, late breakfasts.

**Townhouse** BOUTIQUE HOTEL €€
(Map p238; ☎044 200 95 95; www.townhouse.ch; Schützengasse 7; s Sfr195-365, d Sfr225-395, ste Sfr315-425; 🛜; 🚊Zürich Hauptbahnhof, 🚆Zürich Hauptbahnhof) With a cracking location only steps from the train station and the shops of Bahnhofstrasse, this stylish five-storey hotel offers friendly service and a host of welcoming touches. The 21 rooms come in an assortment of sizes from 15 sq metres to 35 sq metres, with luxurious wallpaper, wall hangings, parquet floors, retro furniture, DVD players and iPod docking stations.

**Lady's First** HOTEL €€
(☎044 380 80 10; www.ladysfirst.ch; Mainaustrasse 24; r Sfr180-338; 🛜; 🚊2, 4, 10, 11, 14, 15 to Feldeggstrasse) Despite the name, discerning guests of all genders are welcome at this attractive hotel near the opera house and lake – though the attached wellness centre with a rooftop terrace is open to women only. The immaculate, generally spacious rooms abound in aesthetic touches such as traditional parquet flooring and designer furnishings.

**Hotel Ni-Mo** B&B €€
(☎044 370 30 30; www.hotel-nimo.ch; Seefeldstrasse 16; s Sfr180-200, d Sfr210-290; 🛜; 🚊2, 4, 10, 11, 14, 15 to Kreuzstrasse) Gregarious film producer Eva Stiefel has turned this 10-room B&B near the opera house into one of Zürich's most welcoming small hotels. Minimalist modern rooms with all-wood flooring and tiled bathrooms are complemented by a tiny downstairs breakfast room hung with local artwork. A Zürich native, Eva enjoys helping guests discover the city.

**Hotel Hottingen** HOTEL €€
(☎044 256 19 19; www.hotelhottingen.ch; Hottingerstrasse 31; dm Sfr50, s Sfr110-200, d Sfr160-300, s/d with shared bathroom from Sfr85/115; P🛜; 🚊3, 8, 9, 11, 15, 17 to Hottingerplatz) Fresh from a 2016 renovation, this place is more promising than outside appearances would suggest. The 32 rooms are clinical but good value, and some have a balcony. Each floor has showers and a communal kitchen, and the top floor houses a women-only dorm with a rooftop terrace.

★**Hotel Widder** BOUTIQUE HOTEL €€€
(Map p238; ☎044 224 25 26; www.widderhotel.ch; Rennweg 7; s/d from Sfr523/625; P❄@🛜; 🚊4, 6, 7, 10, 11, 13, 14, 15, 17 to Rennweg) A supremely stylish boutique hotel in the equally grand district of Augustiner, the Widder is a pleasing fusion of five-star luxury and 12th-century charm. Rooms and public areas across the eight individually decorated townhouses that make up this place are stuffed with designer furniture, art and original features – from oak beams to antique stoves and murals.

★**B2 Boutique Hotel & Spa** BOUTIQUE HOTEL €€€
(☎044 567 67 67; www.b2boutiquehotels.com; Brandschenkestrasse 152; s Sfr290-420, d Sfr295-555; @🛜🏊; 🚊13 to Enge) Removed from the city centre (but next door to Google's European headquarters), this hip boutique hotel in a renovated brewery abounds in seductive features, including a stupendous rooftop thermal pool, a spa (p239) and a fanciful library-lounge, filled floor to ceiling with 30,000 books purchased from a local antiquarian. Spacious rooms sport slick, urban-cool decor.

**Hotel Florhof** HOTEL €€€
(☎044 250 26 26; www.hotelflorhof.ch; Florhofgasse 4; s Sfr185-230, d Sfr300-360, junior ste Sfr540-640; 🛜🐾; 🚊3, 17 to Neumarkt) Set in a lovely garden, this former silk factory and noble family's mansion contains 32 tastefully appointed rooms and is a stone's throw from the Kunsthaus. A top-to-bottom renovation has restored many original features, including the patterned stone flooring and ceramic

wood stove in the reception area, and the parquet floors in the guest rooms.

**Marktgasse Hotel** BOUTIQUE HOTEL €€€
(Map p238; ☎044 266 10 10; www.marktgassehotel.ch; Marktgasse 17; s Sfr199-250, d Sfr259-385, ste Sfr359-535; 📶; 🚊4, 15 to Rathaus) Opened in late 2015 following a revamp, the Marktgasse Hotel sits in the historic Niederdorf quarter. It spins together 15th-century features like stucco, tiled ovens and wood panelling with pared-back modern design in the rooms – the higher you go, the better the views. Baltho bistro and bar, plus a wellness area with a hammam and gym, invite relaxation.

**Baur au Lac** HOTEL €€€
(Map p238; ☎044 220 50 20; www.bauraulac.ch; Talstrasse 1; s/d from Sfr570/680; P❄@; 🚊2, 5, 8, 9, 10, 11, 14, 15 to Bürkliplatz) This family-run lakeside jewel is set in a private park and offers all imaginable comforts and a soothing sense of privacy. Rooms are decorated in a variety of classic colours and styles, including Empire, Regency and art deco. Throw in the spa, restaurants and faultless service and you can see why VIPs flock here.

## Eating

**★ Haus Hiltl** VEGETARIAN €
(Map p238; ☎044 227 70 00; www.hiltl.ch; Sihlstrasse 28; per 100g Sfr4.90, mains Sfr25-35; ⏰6am-midnight Mon-Sat, 8am-midnight Sun; 🌿; 🚊4, 6, 7, 10, 11, 13, 14, 15, 17 to Rennweg) Guinness-certified as the world's oldest vegetarian restaurant (established 1898), Hiltl proffers an astounding smorgasbord of meatless delights, from Indian and Thai curries to Mediterranean grilled veggies, plus salads and desserts. You can opt for the buffet (charged per 100g) or for more substantial mains. Sit in the informal cafe or the spiffier adjoining restaurant. Good-value takeaway service is also available.

**★ Café Sprüngli** SWEETS €
(Map p238; ☎044 224 46 46; www.spruengli.ch; Bahnhofstrasse 21; sweets Sfr8-16; ⏰7.30am-6.30pm Mon-Fri, 8am-6pm Sat; 🚊4, 6, 7, 10, 11, 13, 14, 15, 17 to Paradeplatz) Sit down for cakes, chocolate, ice cream and exquisite coffee drinks at this epicentre of sweet Switzerland, in business since 1836. You can have a light lunch too, but whatever you do, don't fail to check out its heavenly chocolate shop, where you can buy delectable pralines and truffles, plus the house speciality – rainbow-bright Luxemburgerli macarons – to take home.

**Bauschänzli** CAFETERIA €
(Map p238; ☎044 212 49 19; www.bauschaenzli.ch; Stadthausquai 2; mains Sfr13-22; ⏰11am-11pm Apr-Sep; 🚊2, 4, 5, 8, 9, 10, 11, 14, 15 to Bürkliplatz) Location is the big draw at this beer garden/cafeteria-style eatery built atop 17th-century fortifications that jut into the middle of the Limmat River. Watch swans, boats and passersby as you nosh on bratwurst, fried perch, Wiener schnitzel and chips, and sip from cold mugs of beer. From early October to early November, it hosts Zürich's month-long version of Oktoberfest.

**Burgermeister** BURGERS €
(Map p244; www.burger-meister.ch; Langstrasse 238; burgers Sfr11-22; ⏰11am-10.30pm Mon-Wed, to 11pm Thu, to midnight Fri, noon-midnight Sat; 🚊3, 4, 6, 10, 11, 13, 15, 17 to Limmatplatz) Burgermeister dishes up seriously satisfying burgers – all homemade with Swiss beef and tangy sauces. For a dash of spice go for the chilli cheeseburger with jalapeño peppers, or for vegetarians there is the tofu burger with mango-curry sauce.

**Alpenrose** SWISS €€
(Map p244; ☎044 431 11 66; www.restaurantalpenrose.ch; Fabrikstrasse 12; lunch set menus Sfr23-27, dinner mains Sfr24-38; ⏰9am-11.30pm Tue-Fri, from 5pm Sat & Sun; 🚊3, 4, 6, 10, 11, 13, 15, 17 to Quellenstrasse) With its tall, stencilled windows, warm wood panelling and stucco ceiling ornamentation, the Alpenrose exudes cosy Old World charm, and the cuisine here lives up to the promise. Hearty Swiss classics, such as herb-stuffed trout with homemade *Spätzli* (egg noodles) and buttered carrots are exquisitely prepared and presented, accompanied by a good wine list.

**Raclette Stube** SWISS €€
(Map p238; ☎044 251 41 30; www.raclette-stube.ch; Zähringerstrasse 16; fondue Sfr29-32, raclette Sfr40; ⏰6-11pm; 🚊2, 4, 15 to Rudolf-Brun-Brücke) For the quintessential Swiss cheese experiences – fondue and raclette – pop by this warm and welcoming restaurant, which has three branches around town.

**Restaurant Zum Kropf** SWISS €€
(Map p238; ☎044 221 18 05; www.zumkropf.ch; In Gassen 16; mains Sfr25-43; ⏰11.30am-11.30pm Mon-Sat; 🚊4, 10, 11, 14, 15 to Paradeplatz) Notable for its historic interior, with wood panelling, marble columns, stained glass and ceiling murals, Kropf has been favoured by locals since 1888 for its hearty Swiss staples and fine beers.

## TOP PARKS FOR A PICNIC

For a city of its size, Zürich has an amazing wealth of green spaces. When the weather's good, pack a picnic – or grab a takeaway box from Hiltl – and head for one of these peaceful city spots.

**Lindenhof** (Map p238; 4, 6, 7, 10, 11, 13, 14, 15, 17 to Rennweg) Spectacular views across the Limmat to the Grossmünster from a tree-shaded hilltop park, smack in the heart of the Aldstadt (Old Town). Watch the *boules* players while you eat.

**Platzspitz** (Map p238; Zürich Hauptbahnhof, Zürich Hauptbahnhof) A green point of land where the Limmat and Sihl Rivers come together, just north of the train station and Landesmuseum. James Joyce was fond of this spot and included references to both rivers in *Finnegans Wake*.

**Josefswiese** (Map p244; ; 3, 4, 6 to Schiffbau) An atmospheric Kreis 5 park in the shadow of a towering smokestack and railway viaduct, this family-friendly place has huge grassy expanses and a fountain for kids to splash in, along with drinks and snacks for sale at the adjacent **Kiosk Josefswiese** (Map p244; www.josefswiese.ch; 10am-6pm Mar-May & Sep-Oct, 9am-10pm Jun-Aug; ).

**Zürichhorn** (2, 4, 10, 14, 15 to Fröhlichstrasse) This long and leafy lakeside park spreads down the eastern shore of the Zürichsee, south of the Opernhaus, with the Seebad Utoquai (p239) close at hand for an after-lunch dip.

**My Kitchen** MALAYSIAN €€

(043 810 06 78; Franklinstrasse 6; mains Sfr22.50-28.50; 11am-2pm Mon, 11am-2pm & 6-9pm Tue-Sat; 10, 11, 12, 14, 15 to Sternen Oerlikon) A way out of the centre in Oerlikon, My Kitchen is worth going the extra mile for its winningly fresh and authentic Malaysian food. It's always buzzing with locals chowing down on beef *redang* (spicy beef with coconut, cloves, cinnamon and kaffir lime) or mopping up coconut-laced curries with *roti* (a crisp flatbread). Trams to Sternen Oerlikon stop nearby.

**Baltho Küche & Bar** INTERNATIONAL €€

(Map p238; 044 266 10 14; www.balthokuechebar.ch; Marktgasse Hotel, Marktgasse 17; lunch set menus Sfr21-24, mains Sfr28-42; 11am-midnight Mon-Wed, to 2am Fri, to 11pm Sun; ; 4, 15 to Rathaus) Monochrome colours, plenty of light and well-spaced seating give Baltho at Marktgasse Hotel the look and feel of an urban-chic brasserie. Attentive staff serve attractively presented dishes with a nod to the seasons – from home-smoked salmon with pickles to burrata ravioli with date tomatoes and bang bang chicken. Kids get their own table and craft activities at weekends.

**Kindli** INTERNATIONAL €€

(Map p238; 043 888 76 78; www.kindli.ch; Rennweg; mains Sfr36-56; 11am-2pm & 6-10pm Mon-Sat; 4, 6, 7, 10, 11, 13, 14, 15, 17 to Rennweg) Kindli captures the warmth and grace of a bygone age in its warm, wood-panelled interior, with bistro tables laid neatly and lit by candles for intimate tête-à-têtes. Dishes include traditional Swiss fare, such as like *Zürcher Geschnetzeltes* (sliced veal with mushroom-cream sauce and rösti), as well as red Thai curry and rock lobster with Sardinian pasta, tomatoes and rosemary.

**Zeughauskeller** SWISS €€

(Map p238; 044 220 15 15; www.zeughauskeller.ch; Bahnhofstrasse 28a; lunch specials Sfr21.50, mains Sfr19-37; 11.30am-11pm; 4, 10, 11, 14, 15 to Paradeplatz) Tuck into the heartiest of Swiss grub under the heavy oak beams at this sprawling, atmospheric 15th-century beer hall with ample pavement seating. The menu (in eight languages) goes to town with a dozen varieties of sausage, along with other Swiss faves like pork roast with lashings of sauerkraut. Vegetarian options are also available.

★ **Didi's Frieden** SWISS €€€

(Map p238; 044 253 18 10; www.didisfrieden.ch; Stampfenbachstrasse 32; 4-/5-course menu Sfr98/108; 11am-2.30pm & 5pm-midnight Mon-Fri, 6pm-midnight Sat; 7, 11, 14, 17 to Stampfenbachplatz) With its unique blend of familiarity and refinement, Didi's Frieden features among Zürich's top tables. The look is understated elegance with wood floors, white tablecloths and wine-glass chandeliers. Service is discreet yet attentive, while menus sing of the seasons in dishes like venison

# Zürich West

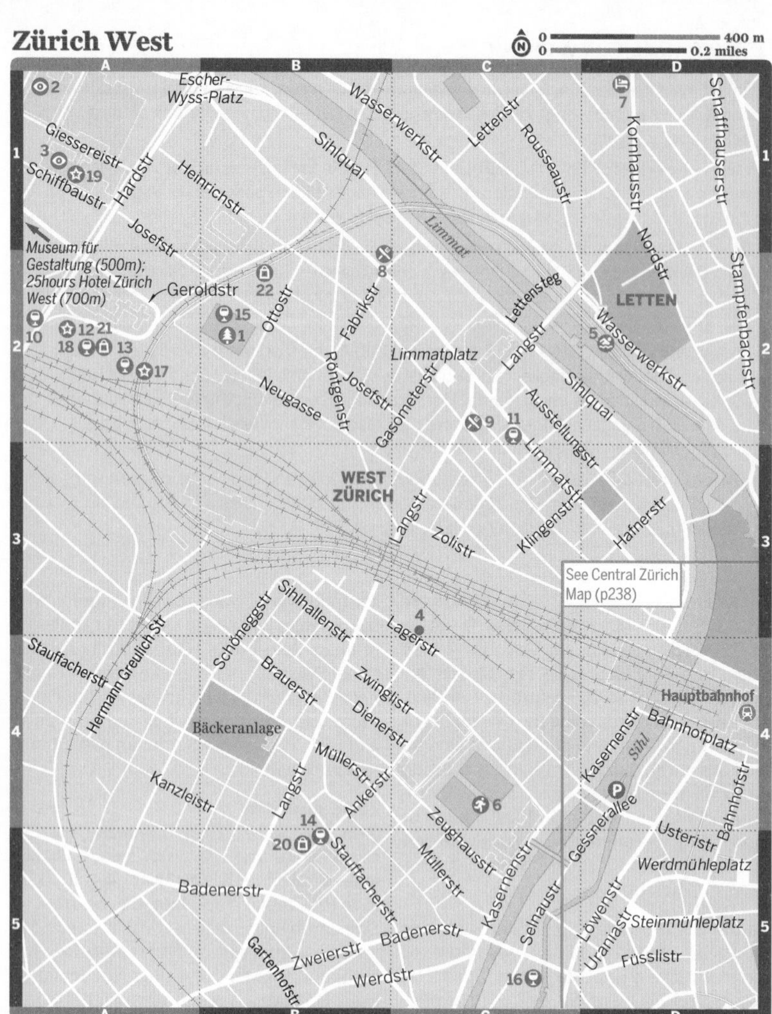


ravioli with dark chocolate and shallot jus – big on integral flavours and presented with panache.

**Coco** EUROPEAN €€€

(Map p238; ☎044 211 98 98; www.coco-grill.ch; Bleicherweg 1a am Paradeplatz; 2-course lunch menu Sfr25-45, 5-course dinner menu Sfr120-130; ⏰11am-3pm & 5pm-midnight Mon-Fri, 5.30pm-12.30am Sat; 🚋4, 6, 7, 10, 11, 13, 14, 15, 17 to Paradeplatz) Secreted down a short alley just off Paradeplatz, Coco features an ever-changing five-course 'surprise menu' in the evenings, revolving around the restaurant's trademark charcoal-grilled meat and fish. The atmosphere is romantic, with a teeny front bar, good for a predinner glass of wine, and an almost conspiratorial dining area out back.

**Kronenhalle** BRASSERIE €€€

(Map p238; ☎044 262 99 00; www.kronenhalle.ch; Rämistrasse 4; mains Sfr36-76; ⏰noon-midnight; 🚋4, 5, 8, 9, 10, 15 to Bellevue) A haunt of city movers and shakers in suits, the Crown Hall is a brasserie-style establishment with white tablecloths, dark wood and an Old World feel. Impeccably mannered waiters move discreetly below Chagall, Miró, Matisse

## Zürich West

**Sights**
1 Josefswiese ..... B2
2 Puls 5 ..... A1
3 Schiffbau ..... A1

**Activities, Courses & Tours**
4 eTuk Tuk ..... C3
5 Letten ..... D2
6 Pride ..... C4

**Sleeping**
7 Kafischnaps ..... D1

**Eating**
8 Alpenrose ..... B2
9 Burgermeister ..... C2

**Drinking & Nightlife**
10 Clouds ..... A2
11 Eldorado ..... C2
12 Frau Gerolds Garten ..... A2
13 Hive Club ..... A2
14 Kanzlei ..... B5
15 Kiosk Josefwiese ..... B2
16 Rimini Bar ..... C5

**Entertainment**
17 Bogen F ..... A2
18 Helsinki ..... A2
19 Moods ..... A1
Schauspielhaus ..... (see 3)

**Shopping**
20 Flohmarkt Kanzlei ..... B5
21 Freitag ..... A2
22 Im Viadukt ..... B2

and Picasso originals, serving a menu that regularly crosses international borders, from gazpacho to tuna sashimi, and curried prawn ravioli to Chateaubriand in Béarnaise sauce.

## Drinking & Nightlife

The reborn Züri-West district is made up of two former working-class neighbourhoods: Kreis 4 and Kreis 5. At night it becomes a hedonists' playground. Kreis 4, still something of a red-light district and centred on Langstrasse, is lined with bars. Across the railway tracks in Kreis 5, a number of other nightspots radiate off Hardstrasse.

### ★Frau Gerolds Garten — BAR

(Map p244; www.fraugerold.ch; Geroldstrasse 23/23a; bar-restaurant 11am-midnight Mon-Sat, noon-10pm Sun Apr-Sep, 6pm-midnight Mon-Sat Oct-Mar, market & shops 11am-7pm Mon-Fri, to 6pm Sat year-round; ; S Hardbrücke) Hmm, where to start? The wine bar? The margarita bar? The gin bar? Whichever poison you choose, this wildly popular focal point of Zürich's summer drinking scene is pure unadulterated fun and one of the best grown-up playgrounds in Europe.

Strewn with shipping containers, illuminated with multicoloured fairy lights and sandwiched between cheery flower beds and a screeching railyard, its outdoor seating options range from picnic tables to pillow-strewn terraces and a 2nd-floor sundeck. In winter, the restaurant moves indoors to a funky pavilion and great fondue warms the soul.

### ★Rimini Bar — BAR

(Map p244; www.rimini.ch; Badweg 10; 7.15pm-midnight Sun-Thu, 6.45pm-midnight Fri, 2pm-midnight Sat Apr-Oct; 2, 6, 7, 8, 9, 13, 17, 19 to Bahnhof Selnau) Secluded behind a fence along the Sihl River, this bar at the Männerbad public baths is one of Zürich's most inviting open-air drinking spots. Its vast wood deck is adorned with red-orange party lights, picnic tables and throw cushions for lounging, accompanied by the sound of water from the adjacent pools. Open in good weather only.

### Clouds — BAR

(Map p244; http://clouds.ch; Prime Tower, Maagplatz 5; 4pm-midnight Tue-Thu, to 2am Fri & Sat; S Hardbrücke) Zürich seems unfathomably tiny from the heights of this backlit, glass-fronted lounge bar on the 35th floor of the Prime Tower in the happening 5th district. Pick out city landmarks, the lake and Uetliberg over signature gin and tonics, antipasti and cocktails. The 'Martini in C' is a blend of Clouds' own gin, ginger liqueur, dry orange curacao and vermouth.

### Hive Club — CLUB

(Map p244; 044 271 12 10; www.hiveclub.ch; Geroldstrasse 5; cover Sfr35; 11pm-4am Thu, to 7am Fri, to 9am Sat; S Hardbrücke) Electronic music creates the buzz at this artsy, alternative club adjacent to Frau Gerolds Garten in Kreis 5. Enter through an alley strung with multicoloured umbrellas, giant animal heads, mushrooms and watering cans. Big-name DJs keep things going into the wee hours three nights a week.

**Eldorado** CRAFT BEER

(Map p244; www.eldorado-zh.ch; Limmatstrasse 109; ⌚5pm-midnight Mon-Tue, to 1am Wed-Thu, to 2am Fri, 8pm-2am Sat; 🚋3, 4, 6, 10, 11, 13, 15, 17 to Limmatplatz) A poster child for Zürich's emerging craft-beer scene, Eldorado is a cracking little bar, with a softly lit, retro-cool interior decorated with vintage furniture and a backlit chrome bar. Choose from 101 craft beers on the menu (including more than a dozen Swiss options).

**Mascotte** CLUB

(Map p238; ☎044 260 15 80; www.mascotte.ch; Theaterstrasse 10; cover free-Sfr25; ⌚9.30pm-late; 🚋2, 9, 11, 15 to Stadelhofen) The old variety hall 'Corso' has been revamped into one of Zürich's most popular clubs, with huge windows facing Sechseläutenplatz and the lake. A jam-packed calendar of events keeps things hopping all week; 'Cool Mondays' are a perennial favourite, featuring house, hip-hop, electropop, nu-disco and indie dance with no cover charge.

**Kanzlei** CLUB

(Map p244; ☎044 291 63 11; www.kanzlei.ch; Kanzleistrasse 56; cover free-Sfr23; ⌚11pm-5am Fri & Sat, 11pm-midnight Sun; 🚋8 to Helvetiaplatz) What is a school playground by day morphs into an outdoor bar and underground club by night. Reggae, dancehall, hip-hop and more appear regularly on the varied calendar.

**Heaven** LGBTIQ+

(Map p238; ☎078 667 80 01; www.heavenclub.ch; Spitalgasse 5; cover Sfr15-20; ⌚11pm-6am Fri, 9.30pm-7am Sat; 🚋2, 4, 15 to Rudolf-Brun-Brücke) This boisterous club playing an eclectic musical mix is the epicentre of LGBTIQ+ nightlife in Niederdorf.

**Loft Five** LOUNGE

(Map p238; www.loftfive.ch; Europaallee 15; ⌚8am-midnight Mon-Thu, 8am-2pm Fri, 10.30am-2pm Sat; 🚋Zürich Hauptbahnhof, 🚆Zürich Hauptbahnhof) Purple backlighting, eye-catching art, wacky chandeliers and vintage chairs create an air of shabby-chic decadence at Loft Five. There's a great terrace for sipping a zingy cocktail or craft beer in summer, plus occasional live music and DJ sets.

## ☆ Entertainment

**Rote Fabrik** LIVE MUSIC

(☎music 044 485 58 68, theatre 044 485 58 28; www.rotefabrik.ch; Seestrasse 395; 🚌161, 165) With a fabulous lakeside location, this multifaceted performing-arts centre stages rock, jazz and hip-hop concerts, original-language films, theatre and dance performances. There's also a bar and a restaurant. Take bus 161 or 165 from Bürkliplatz.

**Bogen F** LIVE MUSIC

(Map p244; ☎043 204 18 90; www.bogenf.ch; Viaduktstrasse 97; ⌚cafe from 3pm Thu & Fri, 11am Sat; performance times vary; Ⓢ Hardbrücke) This vibrant performance space, attached to its eponymous cafe in Kreis 5's Viadukt complex, brings in indie bands from all over the world (performers hail from as far away as the US, Canada, Sweden, South Africa and Japan).

**Helsinki** LIVE MUSIC

(Map p244; www.helsinkiklub.ch; Geroldstrasse 35; ⌚8pm-1.30pm Thu, 8am-4pm Fri & Sat, 8pm-2am Sun; Ⓢ Hardbrücke) A leftover hut from the area's industrial days, the Helsinki attracts people of all tastes and ages for its low-lit, relaxed band scene. On Sundays, catch house band Hollander Trio from Hell (country, rockabilly, rock, blues, even polka!); other nights, the eclectic mix ranges from soul and funk to hip-hop and tango. From Hauptbahnhof, take any train to Hardbrücke.

**Moods** LIVE MUSIC

(Map p244; ☎044 276 80 00; www.moods.ch; Schiffbaustrasse 6; ⌚7.30pm-late Mon-Sat, from 6pm Sun; 🚋3, 4, 6 to Schiffbau) Though this is one of Zürich's top jazz spots, other musical genres including funk, hip-hop, swing, Latin and world music also grab the occasional spot on its busy calendar.

**Tonhalle** CLASSICAL MUSIC

(Map p238; ☎044 206 34 34; www.tonhalle-orchester.ch; Claridenstrasse 7; 🚋2, 4, 5, 8, 9, 10, 11, 14, 15 to Bürkliplatz) An opulent venue used by Zürich's orchestra and chamber orchestra.

**Opernhaus** OPERA

(Map p238; ☎044 268 66 66; www.opernhaus.ch; Falkenstrasse 1; 👪; 🚋2, 4, 10, 11, 14, 15 to Opernhaus) Behind an opulent neoclassical facade, the city's premier opera house enjoys a worldwide reputation and stages top-drawer concerts, opera and ballet productions. There's also a terrific line-up of opera for children.

## 🔒 Shopping

For high fashion, head to Bahnhofstrasse. Elsewhere, funky boutiques abound in places like Niederdorf and Züri-West, Popular street markets include the **Bürkliplatz flea market** (Map p238; www.buerkli-flohmarkt.ch; Bürkliplatz; ⌚7am-5pm Sat May-Oct; 🚋2, 4, 5, 8, 9, 10, 11, 14, 15

WORTH A TRIP

## UETLIBERG

Marking the swift transition between the urban and the outdoors, 871m-high Uetliberg is the mountain on Zürich's doorstep, ablaze with wildflowers in spring and daubed with russets and golds in autumn. When city dwellers fancy stretching their legs, they head up here to hike, jog or mountain bike on the trails that criss-cross the woods and countryside. Topping the mountain is the **Aussichtsturm** (Uetliberg; S 10 to Uetliberg), a steel lattice observation tower with fine views over lake, city and – on clear days – the Alps beyond. Sunset is prime-time viewing.

From Uetliberg top station, follow the 1½- to two-hour **Planetenweg** (Planetary Path; www.uetliberg.ch; Uetliberg; ) FREE along the at-times heavily wooded mountain ridge as it gently dips and rises en route to Felsenegg and Buchenegg vantage points. You'll pass 1:1 billion scale models of the planets and enjoy lake views along the way.

Train line S10 runs from Hauptbahnhof to Uetliberg (Sfr8.80, 27 minutes) twice hourly. From here, it's a 10-minute uphill walk to the viewpoint. At Felsenegg vantage point, a cable car descends every 15 minutes to the town of Adliswill, from where frequent S4 trains return to Zürich (Sfr3.40, 23 minutes). Buy the Sfr17.60 Albis-Tageskarte, which gets you to Uetliberg and back with unlimited travel downtown.

to Bürkliplatz), **Flohmarkt Kanzlei** (Map p244; www.flohmarktkanzlei.ch; Kanzleistrasse 56; 8am-4pm Sat; 8 to Helvetiaplatz) and **Rosenhof crafts market** (Map p238; Rosenhof; 10am-8pm Thu, to 5pm Sat Mar-Dec; 4, 15 to Rathaus).

**★Freitag** FASHION & ACCESSORIES
(Map p244; 043 366 95 20; www.freitag.ch; Geroldstrasse 17; 10.30am-7pm Mon-Fri, 10am-6pm Sat; 3, 4, 6 to Schiffbau) The Freitag brothers recycle colourful truck tarps into water-resistant messenger bags in their factory. Every item, from purses to laptop bags, is original. Their outlet is pure whimsy – a pile of shipping containers that's been dubbed Kreis 5's first skyscraper. Shoppers can climb to the rooftop terrace for spectacular city views.

**Max Chocolatier** CHOCOLATE
(Map p238; www.maxchocolatier.com; Schlüsselgasse 12; 10.30am-7pm Tue-Fri, 10am-5.30pm Sat; 4, 10, 11, 14, 15 to Paradeplatz) Of all Zürich's tempting chocolatiers, Max has the edge. This chic Old-Town boutique has a fabulous array of beautifully packaged bars, truffles and pralines, made with 100% natural Swiss ingredients. Keep an eye out for seasonal one-offs such as Alpine hay, cassis and violets, elderflower, white peach and green pepper. Check the website for details on tasting workshops.

**Im Viadukt** SHOPPING CENTRE
(Map p244; www.im-viadukt.ch; Viaduktstrasse; 10am-8pm Mon-Thu, 8am-8pm Fri & Sat; 3, 4, 6, 10, 11, 13, 15, 17 to Dammweg) In a city enamoured with reinvention and repurposing, Im Viadukt stands proud. Once a down-at-heel storage facility under stone railway bridges, it has been reborn into a humming complex of numerous locally owned shops (clothes, furniture etc), restaurants, cafes and artisan food markets. Stroll the viaduct's three-block length between Limmatstrasse and Geroldstrasse and see what catches your eye.

## Information

**Bellevue Apotheke** (044 266 62 22; www.bazh.ch; Theaterstrasse 14) Twenty-four hour chemist.

**Police Station** (044 411 71 17; www.stadtpolizei.ch; Bahnhofquai 3)

**Post Office** (Map p238; Europaallee 11; 6.30am-10.30pm Mon-Fri, 6.30am-8pm Sat, 10am-10.30pm Sun) Just west of the Hauptbahnhof.

**UniversitätsSpital Zürich** (University Hospital; 044 255 11 11; www.en.usz.ch; Schmelzbergstrasse 8; 24hr) Casualty medical service.

**Zürich Tourism** (Map p238; 044 215 40 00, hotel reservations 044 215 40 40; www.zuerich.com; Hauptbahnhof; 8am-8.30pm Mon-Sat, 8.30am to 6.30pm Sun May-Oct, 8.30am-7pm Mon-Sat, 9am-6pm Sun Nov-Apr) This very helpful tourist office is located at Zürich's main station. You can book tours, reserve rooms and pick up the ZürichCard (www.zuerichcard.ch; adult/child 24hr Sfr24/16, 72hr Sfr48/32).

## Getting There & Away

**Zürich Airport** (ZRH; 043 816 22 11; www.zurich-airport.com) is 9km north of the centre, with flights to most European capitals as well as some in Africa, Asia and North America.

The A3 approaches Zürich from the south along the southern shore of Zürichsee. The A1 is the fastest route from Bern and Basel. It proceeds northeast to Winterthur.

Direct trains run frequently to Stuttgart (Sfr63, four hours), Munich (Sfr96, four to 4¼ hours), Innsbruck (Sfr76, 3½ hours) and other international destinations. There are regular direct departures to most major Swiss destinations, such as Lucerne (Sfr26, 45 to 50 minutes), Bern (Sfr51, one to 1½ hours) and Basel (Sfr34, 55 minutes to 1¼ hours).

## Getting Around

### TO/FROM THE AIRPORT

Several trains an hour connect Zürich's airport with the Hauptbahnhof between around 5am and midnight (Sfr6.80, 10 to 13 minutes). A taxi to the centre costs around Sfr60.

### BICYCLE

**Züri Rollt** (044 415 67 67; www.schweizrollt.ch) is an innovative program that allows visitors to borrow or rent bikes from a handful of locations, including **Velostation Nord** (Museumstrasse 2; 8am-11.30pm Mon-Fri, 8am-11pm Sat-Sun) across the road from the north side of the Hauptbahnhof. Bring ID and leave Sfr20 as a deposit. Rental is free if you bring the bike back on the same day and costs Sfr10 per day if you keep it overnight.

### BOAT

**ZSG** (Zürichsee-Schifffahrtsgesellschaft; Map p238; 044 487 13 33; www.zsg.ch) runs lake cruises from Bürkliplatz between April and October. A small circular tour *(kleine Rundfahrt)* takes 1½ hours (adult/child Sfr13.80/9.40) and departs every 30 minutes between 11am and 7.30pm. A longer tour *(grosse Rundfahrt)* lasts four hours (adult/child Sfr31/18). Pick tickets up at ZVV (local transport) ticket windows.

**Riverboats** (Map p238; adult/child Sfr9.40/8.10; every 30min Easter–mid-Oct) run by the same company head up the Limmat river and do a small circle around the lake (one hour). Board at the Schweizerisches Landesmuseum stop.

### BUS, TRAIN & TRAM

Operated by **ZVV** (0848 988 988; www.zvv.ch), Zürich's public transport system of buses, S-Bahn suburban trains and trams is completely integrated. Regular services run daily from 5.30am to shortly past midnight, with additional late-night services available for a surcharge on weekends.

Buy tickets in advance from dispensers at bus and tram stops. Either type in the four-figure code for your destination or choose your ticket type: a short single-trip *Kurzstrecke* ticket valid for five stops (Sfr2.70), a single ticket for greater Zürich valid for an hour (Sfr4.40) or a 24-hour city pass for the centre (Sfr8.80).

### CAR & MOTORCYCLE

Parking is tricky and garage prices run as high as Sfr45 for a 24-hour period. **Parking Zürich AG** (www.parkingzuerichag.ch) operates 13 garages within the city limits, the most useful of which are at Sihlquai 41 near the train station and at Uraniastrasse 3.

### TAXI

Taxis are expensive and usually unnecessary given the quality of public transport. Pick them up at the Hauptbahnhof or other ranks, or call **Taxi 444** (044 444 44 44; www.taxi444.ch).

# AROUND ZÜRICH

## Rapperswil-Jona

POP 26,034 / ELEV 405M

On Zürichsee's eastern shore, Rapperswil is a cultured little town with a castle-topped medieval centre, a forward-thinking art gallery and a history museum. The town flicks into holiday mode when the weather warms up and locals and visitors stroll along the lake promenade, or wander through gardens that play home to fallow deer and 15,000 rose varieties. The town even boasts its own wine, Rapperswiler Schlossberg AOC – a Pinot noir grown on the vine-clad slopes of the castle.

### Sights

**Schloss Rapperswil** CASTLE
(www.schlossrapperswil.com; Lindenhügel) FREE Rapperswil's Old Town is dominated by the sturdy turrets of its much-photographed 13th-century castle. Climb up to its terrace for views over a jigsaw of gables and the lake. On a cloudless day it's possible to make out the outline of the Glarus Alps. The castle now harbours the **Polenmuseum** (Polish Museum; www.muzeum-polskie.org; adult/child Sfr5/3; 1-5pm daily Apr-Oct, 1-5pm Sat & Sun Mar, Nov, Dec). Wander the lovely castle grounds and you might well come eye to eye with fallow deer.

**Stadtmuseum Rapperswil-Jona** MUSEUM
(www.stadtmuseum-rapperswil-jona.ch; Herrenberg 30/40; adult/child Sfr6/free; 2-5pm Wed-Fri, 11am-5pm Sat & Sun) Completely renovated in 2012, the town's biggest museum now sports a cool facade that's half modernist perforated bronze and half 14th-century stone tower. Inside, the wide-ranging historical and cultural artefacts span eight centuries, from the late Middle Ages to the

present. Highlights include its gold collection, a late-Gothic banquet room with vibrant murals and a beautifully wood-panelled Renaissance room. For a view out across the town and lake, head up to the top floor of the tower.

**Kunst(zeug)haus** GALLERY
(www.kunstzeughaus.ch; Schönbodenstrasse 1; adult/child Sfr10/free; ⌚2-6pm Wed-Fri, 11am-6pm Sat & Sun) This enormous art space, a converted weapons arsenal with a very 21st-century wavy roof bearing the hallmark of Züricher architects Isa Stürm und Urs Wolf, is devoted to exhibitions of cutting-edge, contemporary Swiss art.

## Sleeping & Eating

Restaurants line Rapperswil's Fischmarktplatz, Hauptplatz, Marktstrasse and lake-facing Seequai – from traditional taverns with historic clout to brunch cafes, plus Italian and Asian options.

**Jakob** HOTEL €€
(☎055 220 00 50; http://jakob-rapperswil.ch; Hauptplatz 11; s Sfr107-177, d Sfr169-223; 📶) Right in the heart of the Old Town, Jakob flaunts chic, minimalist-style rooms in neutral tones and with wood floors. The chef takes pride in local sourcing in the excellent downstairs restaurant (mains Sfr28 to Sfr58). Organic farm produce and delicious wood-fired breads appear on the buffet at breakfast.

## Information

**Tourist Office** (☎055 225 77 00; www.vvrj.ch; Fischmarktplatz 1; ⌚10am-6pm Apr-Oct, 1-5pm Nov-Mar) In a waterfront square midway between the train station and the boat dock.

## Getting There & Away

Rapperswil can be reached by the S5, S7 or S15 from Zürich's main train station (Sfr17.20, 36 minutes) or by boat from Bürkliplatz (two hours).

Best value for a day trip is the 9-Uhr Tagespass (Sfr26), which is valid Monday to Friday from 9am to 5am the following day, and for 24 hours on Saturdays, Sundays and holidays. The ticket is valid for trains; should you also wish to use the boats it costs an additional Sfr5.

If you're driving from Zürich, 40km north, the fastest route is via the A3 motorway that rims the lake's western shore. A more scenic (but longer) route is the lakefront Seestrasse (Route 17).

# Winterthur

POP 108,044 / ELEV 447M

Often eclipsed by the charms of nearby Zürich, Winterthur, Switzerland's sixth-largest city, packs a real cultural punch. It's home to truly stupendous art collections (p250) bankrolled by art collector Oskar Reinhart, one of Europe's foremost photography museums and a kid-pleasing science museum (p250) – not to mention an archetypal turreted castle (p250) topping a crag just south of town.

Beyond the evident appeal of its sights, Winterthur also has one of Switzerland's largest pedestrian-only old towns, lined with pastel-painted, terracotta-tiled cafes and bars, plus boutiques ideal for a leisurely mooch around.

## Sights

Winterthur owes much of its eminence as an art mecca to collector Oskar Reinhart, a scion of a powerful banking and insurance family. His collection was bequeathed to the nation and entrusted to his hometown when he died in 1965.

Ask the tourist office (p251) about the Winterthur Museum Pass (Sfr25 for one day, Sfr35 for two days), which gives you entry to almost all the sights.

**Fotomuseum** MUSEUM
(☎052 234 10 60; www.fotomuseum.ch; Grüzenstrasse 44 & 45; adult/child Sfr10/free; ⌚11am-6pm Tue & Thu-Sun, 11am-8pm Wed; 🚌2, 2E to Fotozentrum) The vast collection at Winterthur's outstanding photography museum features great names and styles from the 19th century to the present, zooming in on everything from fashion to art and architecture. Additional photo shows are staged across the street in the museum's two partner institutions, the Fotostiftung and Zentrum für Fotografie. Buy a Kombi ticket (Sfr19) to visit all three. Take bus 2 to Fotozentrum.

**Kunstmuseum** MUSEUM
(☎052 267 51 62; www.kmw.ch; Museumstrasse 52; adult/child Sfr15/free; ⌚10am-8pm Tue, 10am-5pm Wed-Sun; 🚌3, 10 to Stadthaus) For a satisfying stroll through a solid collection of the 19th- and 20th-century classics, head to Winterthur's city art museum. Many of the standard suspects, from Klee to Monet, van Gogh and

## Winterthur

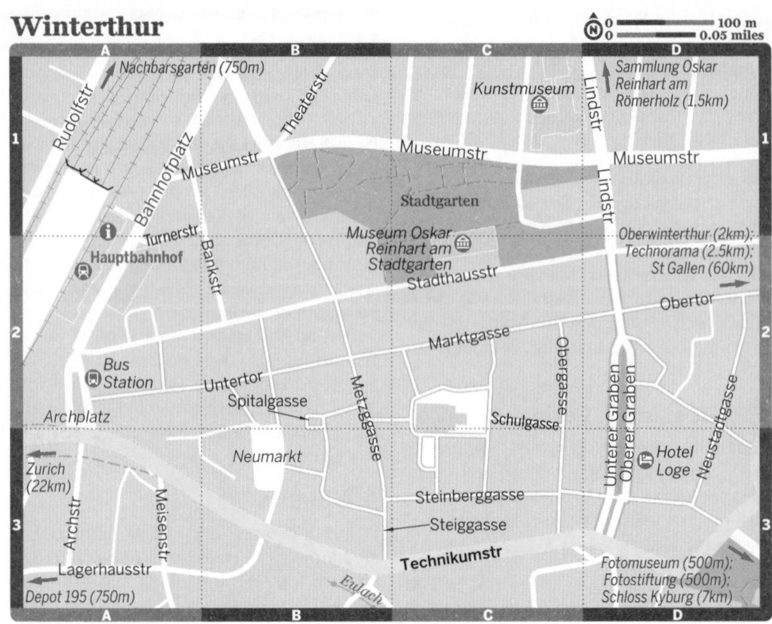


Rodin, are represented, along with figurative works by Swiss sculptor Alberto Giacometti and an impressive slew of contemporary creators. The museum also stages top-drawer temporary exhibitions, such as recent ones homing in on Renoir and Picasso. English-language audioguides cost Sfr3.

**Technorama** MUSEUM

(www.technorama.ch; Technoramastrasse 1; adult/child Sfr28/17; 10am-5pm Tue-Sun; ; 5 to Pfaffenwiesen) Had enough art? What about a science session? Technorama is an extraordinary voyage into the multiple worlds of hands-on science. Encompassing four jam-packed floors of exhibits, it offers some 500 interactive experiences (explained in English, French, German and Italian) that can't fail to fascinate kids, and plenty of adults too. Take bus 5 from the Hauptbahnhof. Swiss Museum Pass not accepted.

**Sammlung Oskar Reinhart am Römerholz** GALLERY

(www.roemerholz.ch; Haldenstrasse 95; adult/child Sfr15/free; 10am-5pm Tue & Thu-Sun, 10am-8pm Wed; 3 to Spital) The collection, housed in a charming country estate, is fascinating in the way it seeks to bridge the gap between traditional and modern art, juxtaposing the likes of Goya, Rembrandt, Bruegel and Rubens with Cézanne, Monet, Picasso, Renoir and van Gogh. The works you will get to see from the collection depend upon the exhibition showing.

**Museum Oskar Reinhart am Stadtgarten** MUSEUM

(http://museumoskarreinhart.ch; Stadthausstrasse 6; adult/child Sfr15/free; 10am-5pm Tue-Wed & Fri-Sun, 10am-8pm Thu; Winterthur Hauptbahnhof) Reinhart's 500-strong collection of Swiss, German and Austrian works of art from the 18th, 19th and 20th centuries is displayed in a museum on the edge of the central city's park. Star exhibits include works by German Romantic painter Caspar David Friedrich and Austrian Biedermeier painter Ferdinand Georg Waldmüller, alongside 18th-century Swiss landscapes by Caspar Wolf.

**Schloss Kyburg** CASTLE

(www.schlosskyburg.ch; Schloss 1, Kyburg; adult/child Sfr9/4; 10am-5.30pm Tue-Sun; 655 to Kyburg) On a rocky spur above the Töss River and with its riot of turrets, Schloss Kyburg is one of Eastern Switzerland's most important medieval feudal castles, first mentioned in 1027. The museum brings interactive fun to the castle buildings; try on a suit of armour – but not the torture instruments... Take the S-Bahn to Effretikon, then bus 655 to Kyburg.

## Sleeping & Eating

Anonymous chain hotels reign supreme in Winterthur, but there are a few notable exceptions. Cheap restaurants are clustered along Neumarkt, offering a wide array of different ethnic cuisines.

**Depot 195** HOSTEL €
(052 203 13 63; www.depot195.ch; Lagerplatz 4; dm/s/d/f Sfr36-41/99/129/194; P; 4, 11 to Wylandbrücke) A shining example of Winterthur's urban regeneration, this hip hostel takes shelter in a born-again factory. Backpackers are in their element here, with cool digs with exposed brick and wood floors, a common room, roof terrace and bike rental (Sfr7 per day). Breakfast costs an extra Sfr10.

**Hotel Loge** HOTEL €€
(052 268 12 00; www.hotelloge.ch; Oberer Graben 6; s Sfr155-220, d Sfr190-250; ; 2, 3 to Technikum) With its own bar, restaurant and even an arthouse cinema, this designer place provides comfort and style in understated rooms with parquet floors. Some of the 17 spacious rooms behind the Gothic entrance offer nice views across the leafy avenue to the Old Town.

**Nachbarsgarten** INTERNATIONAL €€
(052 534 89 47; http://nachbarsgarten.ch; Feldstrasse 22; mains Sfr25-49; 9am-2pm & 5-11.30pm Tue-Fri, 11.30am-2pm & 5-11.30pm Sat; 2, 2E to Tellstrasse) A one-man-band affair in the kitchen, this little restaurant on the fringes of Winterthur is wonderfully inviting, with warm wood, bistro lighting and cheek-by-jowl tables. On the menu: creative salads (Italian fennel with fig, Parma ham and fresh herbs, for instance), pasta dishes, *tarte flambée* and belly-warming classics like pork roast with port-wine jus and buttery *Spätzle* (egg noodles).

## Information

**Tourist Office** (052 267 67 00; www.winterthur-tourismus.ch; Hauptbahnhof; 9am-6.30pm Mon-Fri, 10am-4pm Sat) Conveniently located at the Hauptbahnhof.

## Getting There & Away

Several trains per hour run to Zürich (Sfr6.50, 22 to 32 minutes). Buses to Zürich depart from stands opposite the train station.

A Museumsbus minivan shuttle (Sfr5 return) leaves the train station hourly between 9.45am and 4.45pm for the Sammlung Oskar Reinhart am Römerholz, the Museum Oskar Reinhart am Stadtgarten and the Kunstmuseum (p249). On weekends the shuttle also stops at the Fotomuseum (p249).

If you're driving from Zürich, take the A1 motorway.

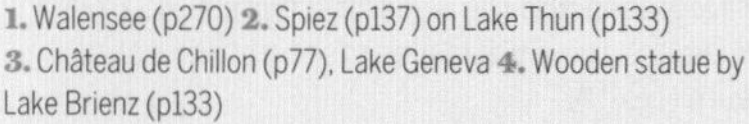

**1.** Walensee (p270) **2.** Spiez (p137) on Lake Thun (p133) **3.** Château de Chillon (p77), Lake Geneva **4.** Wooden statue by Lake Brienz (p133)

# Swiss Lakes

**Glacially cold and deliciously warm, palm-fringed and mountain-rimmed, Alpine and inner-city, green, blue and aquamarine – this little land has a lake for every style and season. Pedal around Lake Constance, sip sundowners by Lake Zürich, or watch the Alps' reflection in a crystal-clear tarn.**

## Lago Maggiore

Switzerland spills over into Italy on Lago Maggiore (p189), which offers the best of two worlds: the grandeur of the Alps, and the palm trees, pasta and sunshine of the south. Soak up the lake's unique style in Locarno (p190) and Ascona (p194).

## Lakes Thun & Brienz

These startlingly turquoise twin lakes (p133) at the foot of the Bernese Alps buzz with sightseers and water-sports enthusiasts in summer. Castle-topped Thun (p133), vine-strewn Spiez (p137) and woodcarving Brienz (p138) are standouts.

## Lake Geneva

Glide across Lake Geneva (p45) by boat as the soft dusk light paints Mont Blanc pink. Europe's biggest Alpine lake sparkles in cosmopolitan Geneva (p42), by fairy-tale Château de Chillon (p77) and below the steep Lavaux (p71) vine terraces.

## Lake Uri

Enigmatic in the morning mist and silhouettes of sunset, Lake Uri (p209) is a fitting backdrop for tales of Switzerland's greatest hero, William Tell. Turner liked to paint the lake from Brunnen (p210).

## Walensee

The Churfirsten mountains rise like an iron curtain behind Walensee (p270). Weesen makes a finebase for windsurfing, wakeboarding or lolling around the lake in summer. For breathtaking views, head to Seerenbachfälle (p271), Switzerland's highest waterfall.

# Northeastern Switzerland

POP 927,988

**Includes ➡**



## Best Places to Eat

- Romantik Hotel Säntis (p270)
- Bäumli (p267)
- Wirtschaft Zum Frieden (p259)
- Burg Hohenklingen (p261)

## Best Places to Stay

- B&B Stein am Rhein (p261)
- Schloss Wartegg (p264)
- Märchenhotel Bellevue (p272)
- Hotel Hecht (p269)
- Arcona Living (p257)

## Why Go?

Northeastern Switzerland is the place to tiptoe off the map and back to nature for a few days. Country lanes unravel like spools of thread, weaving through Appenzell's patchwork meadows, past the steel-blue waters of Walensee and south to remote hamlets engulfed by the glacier-licked peaks of the Glarus Alps. This region calls for slow touring, whether you're cycling through cornfields and apple orchards on a cloudless summer's day or walking through Klettgau's gold-tinged vineyards in the diffused light of autumn.

From the thunderous Rheinfall to the still waters of Lake Constance, nature here is on a grand scale. Completing the storybook tableau are castle-topped towns such as Stein am Rhein and Schaffhausen, their facades adorned with frescos and oriel windows, while in graceful St Gallen, the abbey library will take your breath away with its rococo splendour.

## When to Go

- St Gallen eases into summer with open-air music festivals and opera galore.
- Fireworks light up the Rheinfall and Kreuzlingen on Lake Constance in August.
- Winter's arrival brings twinkling Christmas markets to the region's towns, and skiers to its slopes.

## Northeastern Switzerland Highlights

❶ **Stein am Rhein** (p260) Gawping at one of Switzerland's loveliest squares in this town's half-timbered heart.

❷ **Rheinfall** (p259) Hearing the thunder of Europe's largest plain waterfall.

❸ **Stiftsbibliothek** (p264) Taking a fascinating romp through literary history at St Gallen's rococo masterpiece.

❹ **Zwinglipass** (p268) Hiking through the magnificent karst mountains above Appenzell on this Alpine trail.

❺ **Lake Constance** (p261) Pedalling, walking or canoeing over to Germany and Austria on Central Europe's third-largest lake.

❻ **Bolderhof** (p260) Meeting Daisy and co at this farm in Hemishofen, where you can cow trek to the Rhine.

❼ **Schaffhausen** (p256) Slipping back to the Middle Ages while exploring this town's fountains and oriel windows.

❽ **Piz Sardona** (p266) Seeking solitude in the remote Alpine wilderness around this 3056m mountain.

## Information

The tourist region of Ostschweiz (Eastern Switzerland) unites several easterly Swiss cantons and Liechtenstein. Information can be found on the pages of **Switzerland Tourism** (www.myswitzerland.com) or the official website of **Ostschweiz Tourismus** (www.ostschweiz.ch).

## Getting There & Around

Public transport connects Zürich and Friedrichshafen (Germany) airports to this region. Road and rail link Zürich with Schaffhausen, Stein am Rhein, St Gallen and Linthal (for Braunwald). Also, a ferry crosses the lake from Friedrichshafen to Romanshorn, which has good car and train links.

Several areas, such as the Bodensee region around Lake Constance and Appenzell, offer regional passes.

By road, the A1 motorway links St Gallen to Zürich, 86km west, while the A4 stretches from the German border south to Winterthur via Schaffhausen.

DON'T MISS

### FREEWHEELING ALONG THE RHINE

The Rhine flows swiftly through the heart of Schaffhausen and there's no better way to explore it than by hiring a bike. A number of well-marked trails shadow the river and weave through the surrounding countryside. Scenic rides include the 20km **Rheinfall-Rheinau** route, which leads past the thundering Rheinfall (p259) to the Benedictine monastery Kloster Rheinau. Or quaff wine as you pedal through vineyards and past half-timbered houses on the 43km **Klettgau Wine Route**. Details of these and other routes are given on www.veloland.ch.

At the train station, **Rent a Bike** (051 223 42 17; www.rentabike.ch) rents out Flyer e-bikes/city bikes for Sfr54/35 per day, respectively.

# Schaffhausen

POP 35,948 / ELEV 404M

Schaffhausen is the kind of quaint medieval town more readily associated with Germany – which is no coincidence, given its proximity to the border. Ornate frescos and oriel bay windows grace the pastel-coloured houses lining the pedestrian-only Old Town on the banks of the Rhine, while the circular Munot fortress lords it over a vineyard-streaked hill.

During WWII, Allied pilots mistook Schaffhausen for a German city, dropping bombs on the outskirts twice in April 1944 and giving it the dubious honour of being the only bit of Swiss soil to take a direct hit during the war.

## Sights

**★Allerheiligen Münster** CATHEDRAL
(All Saints' Cathedral; Münsterplatz; 10am-noon & 2-5pm Tue-Sun, cloister 7.30am-8pm Mon-Fri, 9am-8pm Sat & Sun) Completed in 1103, Schaffhausen's cathedral is a rare, largely intact specimen of the Romanesque style in Switzerland. It opens to a beautifully simple cloister. The herb garden has been lovingly tended since the Middle Ages and is a tranquil spot for contemplation. Walk through the cloister to reach the **Museum zu Allerheiligen** (www.allerheiligen.ch; Klosterstrasse 16; adult/child Sfr12/free; 11am-5pm Tue-Sun) for antiquities, artworks, and archaeological and natural history exhibitions.

**★Munot** FORTRESS
(8am-8pm May-Sep, 9am-5pm Oct-Apr) FREE Steps lead up through terraced vineyards to this fine specimen of a 16th-century fortress. The unusual circular battlements were built with forced labour following the Reformation and conceal an atmospheric vaulted casemate. Climb the spiral staircase for views over a patchwork of rooftops and spires to the Rhine and wooded hills fringing the city.

**Vorstadt** STREET
Schaffhausen is often given the nickname the Erkerstadt because of its 171 *Erker* (oriel bay windows), once a status symbol of rich merchants. Some of the most impressive line up along Vorstadt, including the 17th-century **Zum Goldenen Ochsen** (Vorstadt 17), whose frescoed facade displays an eponymous Golden Ox. The frescos of the 16th-century **Zum Grossen Käfig** (Vorstadt 45) present an extraordinarily colourful tale of the parading of Turkish sultan Bajazet in a cage by the triumphant Mongol leader Tamerlane.

A block east, the eye-catching **Haus zum Ritter** (Vordergasse 65), built in 1492, boasts a detailed Renaissance-style fresco depicting a knight.

**Fronwagplatz** SQUARE
At the very heart of the Altstadt lies this square, flanked by ornate facades. The 16th-century **Mohrenbrunnen** (Moor's Fountain) marks the northern end of the old

marketplace, while at the southern end stands the **Metzgerbrunnen** (Butcher's Fountain), a William Tell–type figure and a large clock tower. Facing the latter is the late-baroque **Herrenstube** (Fronwagplatz 3), built in 1748, which was once the drinking hole of quaffing nobles.

**Herrenacker** SQUARE

Framed by pastel-coloured houses with steep tiled roofs, this is one of Schaffhausen's prettiest squares. In August it's an atmospheric backdrop for music fest **Stars in Town** (www.starsintown.ch).

## Activities

**Rhybadi** SWIMMING

(www.rhybadi.ch; Rheinuferstrasse; adult/child Sfr4/2; 8am-9pm Sun-Thu, to 10.30pm Fri & Sat May-Sep) If you're itching to leap into the Rhine, do it at this rickety 19th-century wooden bathhouse. There are diving boards and old-fashioned changing rooms reminiscent of an era when 'proper' folk bathed fully clothed.

## Tours

**Altstadt Walks** WALKING

(adult/child Sfr14/10; 2pm Sat May–mid-Oct) These 1¼-hour tours of the Old Town kick off at the tourist office. The well-informed guides speak German, English and French.

**Untersee und Rhein** BOATING

(052 634 08 88; www.urh.ch; Freier Platz; one way to Stein am Rhein/Konstanz Sfr26/50; Apr-Oct) The 45km boat trip from Schaffhausen to Konstanz via Stein am Rhein and Reichenau takes in one of the Rhine's more beautiful stretches. The journey takes 3¾ hours downstream to Schaffhausen and 4¾ hours the other way. See the website for timetables.

## Sleeping

The tourist office can advise on B&Bs (expect to pay Sfr55 for a single and Sfr95 for a double) and holiday apartments.

**Arcona Living** DESIGN HOTEL €€

(052 631 00 00; http://schaffhausen.arcona.ch; Bleicheplatz 1; s/d/ste Sfr180/225/306; P) Sidling up to the train station, Arcona Living is a more contemporary addition to Schaffhausen's hotel scene. The look is new-wave functional and streamlined in the rooms, with pops of bright colour and ample space. There's an Asia-inspired spa area, plus a bistro serving regional food and wine.

**Hotel Kronenhof** HOTEL €€

(052 635 75 75; www.kronenhof.ch; Kirchhofplatz 7; s Sfr120-140, d 140-210, ste Sfr230-270; ) A guesthouse since 1489, the Kronenhof boasts a guestbook featuring the likes of Goethe and Tsar Alexander. The historic interior has been tastefully revampd over the past few years, with the best rooms now featuring dark wood floors, bold art and views of the Munot fortress. You can wind down with a steam in the little spa or a steak in the Ox bistro.

**Hotel Promenade** HOTEL €€

(052 630 77 77; www.promenade-schaffhausen.ch; Fäsenstaubstrasse 43; s Sfr135-175, d Sfr180-280; P) Polite service, a serene location and large, immaculately kept rooms set this hotel apart. There's a flower-dotted garden and a restaurant dishing up seasonal cuisine.

**Park Villa** HOTEL €€

(052 635 60 60; www.parkvilla.ch; Parkstrasse 18; s/d Sfr169/229, without bathroom Sfr98/130; P) The eclectic furniture in this faintly Gothic house resembles a private antiques



OFF THE BEATEN TRACK

### KLETTGAU WINE TRAIL

West of Schaffhausen spreads the red-wine-producing territory of Klettgau, which spills into neighbouring Germany. Like sheets of corduroy, the serried ranks of mostly Pinot Noir vineyards are draped over pea-green fields and gentle rises.

Sprinkled about this soothing countryside are engaging villages such as medieval **Neunkirch**, 13km from Schaffhausen. Others worth passing through include **Beringen**, **Hallau** and **Osterfingen**. Some of these slow-paced hamlets come to life in mid-October for wine festivals. In particular, look out for Osterfingen's **Trottenfest** (www.trottenfest.ch; mid-Oct), when vintners throw open their doors for tastings. If you come at any other time, head for **Bad Osterfingen** (052 681 21 21; www.badosterfingen.ch; Zollstrasse; mains Sfr30-45; 11am-11pm Wed-Sun) – going strong since 1472, this rustic tavern and wine estate pairs hearty local cooking with home-produced wines.

Buses from Schaffhausen serve these villages.

## Schaffhausen

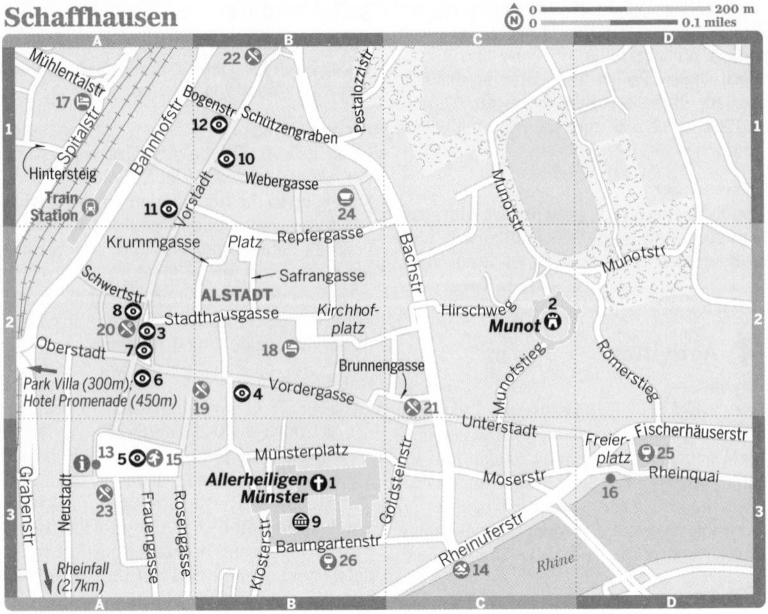

### Schaffhausen

**Top Sights**

1 Allerheiligen Münster ........ B3
2 Munot ........ C2

**Sights**

3 Fronwagplatz ........ A2
4 Haus zum Ritter ........ B2
5 Herrenacker ........ A3
6 Herrenstube ........ A2
7 Metzgerbrunnen ........ A2
8 Mohrenbrunnen ........ A2
9 Museum zu Allerheiligen ........ B3
10 Vorstadt ........ B1
11 Zum Goldenen Ochsen ........ A1
12 Zum Grossen Käfig ........ B1

**Activities, Courses & Tours**

13 Altstadt Walks ........ A3
14 Rhybadi ........ C3
15 Stars in Town ........ A3
16 Untersee und Rhein ........ D3

**Sleeping**

17 Arcona Living ........ A1
18 Hotel Kronenhof ........ B2

**Eating**

19 Café Vordergasse ........ B2
20 Chäs Marili ........ A2
21 D'Chuchi ........ C2
22 Gasthaus zum Adler ........ B1
23 Wirtschaft Zum Frieden ........ A3

**Drinking & Nightlife**

24 Fass-Beiz ........ B1
25 Güterhof ........ D3
26 Kammgarn ........ B3

collection, with an array of four-poster beds, Persian carpets, chandeliers, patterned wallpaper and fake Ming vases in rooms. Dine in Louis XVI splendour in the banquet room.

## Eating

**Chäs Marili** DELI €
(www.chaes-marili.ch; Fronwagplatz 9; 9am-noon & 1.30-6.30pm Mon, 8am-6.30pm Tue-Fri) Cheese, glorious cheese is what you'll find here, with 120 kinds from all over Switzerland and France, alongside other goodies for your picnic basket.

**Café Vordergasse** CAFE €
(052 625 50 30; Vordergasse 79; snacks & light meals Sfr10-20; 6am-7pm Mon-Fri, 7am-5pm Sat, 10am-5pm Sun) This art nouveau–style tearoom opens onto an ever-popular, flower-

bedecked pavement terrace. Try some of their sandwiches, salads and quiches with a homemade lemonade or smoothie, or head inside if you feel more like a leisurely Sunday brunch (Sfr20 to Sfr27).

**D'Chuchi** SWISS **€€**
(☎052 620 05 28; www.dchuchi.ch; Brunnengasse 3; mains Sfr28-44; ⏲6-11.30pm Tue, 11.30am-2pm & 6-11.30pm Wed-Fri, 6-11.30pm Sat) Petite and cosy, with exposed brick, soft lighting and banquette seating, D'Chuchi has just a handful of tables – so book ahead. The chef prides himself on using regional, seasonal ingredients, and there's a succinct but well-edited menu.

**Gasthaus zum Adler** SWISS **€€**
(☎052 625 55 15; www.gasthaus-adler.ch; Vorstadt 69; mains Sfr24.50-44.50; ⏲8.30am-11pm Tue-Sat, 9am-10pm Sun; ✍) Home to famous local painter Tobias Stimmer in the 16th century, the Adler has been doing a roaring trade as an inn for the past three centuries. The menu keeps things traditional and regional, with a nod to seasonal produce. Vegetarians are well catered for.

**Wirtschaft Zum Frieden** SWISS **€€**
(☎052 625 47 67; www.wirtschaft-frieden.ch; Herrenacker 11; mains Sfr35-50; ⏲11am-2.30pm & 5-11.30pm Tue-Fri, 10am-2.30pm & 5-11.30pm Sat; ✍) Rheinfall locals have been eating, drinking and making merry at this wood-panelled inn since 1445. It's still an incredibly cosy choice today, with a tiled oven, cheek-by-jowl tables and old black-and-white photos. Come in for regional fare with a Med-style twist, such as tartare of Aargau water buffalo with pecorino mash or lemon ravioli with wild-garlic pesto. There's always a handful of veggie picks, too.

## Drinking & Nightlife

**Kammgarn** LIVE MUSIC
(www.kammgarn.ch; Baumgartenstrasse 19; ⏲11.30am-11.30pm Tue-Fri, 4-11.30pm Sat) Tune into the local live-music and cultural scene at this textile factory turned arts centre. The line-up swings from blues, rock and jam sessions to disco nights and summer parties – see the website for details.

**Güterhof** LOUNGE
(☎052 630 40 40; www.gueterhof.ch; Freier Platz 10; ⏲8am-midnight Sun-Thu, to 3am Fri & Sat) This half-timbered building was once the goods depot for the many transport companies that relied on the Rhine river to move their cargo around Europe. It's now a super-sleek combination of bar, cafe, restaurant and sushi bar that spills out onto a lovely riverfront terrace. There's a great roster of events, too, from live music to themed party nights and DJ sets.

**Fass-Beiz** CAFE
(www.fassbeiz.ch; Webergasse 13; ⏲11.30am-11.30pm Tue-Thu, 11.30am-12.30am Fri, 10am-12.30am Sat) A laid-back, alternative cafe serving decent lunch specials (Sfr18 to Sfr23). More than just a cafe, gigs, theatre performances and art exhibitions take place in the cellar below. There's live music on Saturday evenings.

## Information

**Tourist Office** (☎052 632 40 20; www.schaffhausen-tourismus.ch; Herrenacker 15; ⏲1.30-6pm Mon, 10am-6pm Tue-Fri, 10am-3pm Sat May-Sep, shorter hours Oct-Apr) Hands out brochures and stocks cycling maps and guides.

## Getting There & Away

Direct trains run half-hourly to Zürich (Sfr23.20, 40 minutes) and Stein am Rhein (Sfr9.20, 24 minutes). Frequent trains to St Gallen (Sfr31, 1½ to two hours) usually involve a change at Winterthur or Romanshorn.

By road, Schaffhausen is off the A4 motorway, which sweeps north to the German border and south to Winterthur, where it meets the A1 to Zürich.

# Rheinfall

Formed by tectonic shifts during the last ice age, 15,000 years ago, the **Rheinfall** (Rhine Falls; www.rheinfall.ch) is an impressive sight, raging at a speed of around 700 cubic metres per second as it spills 23m into a basin in a series of swirling cascades, billowing plumes of spray and raging white water. Europe's biggest plain waterfall is best surveyed on the trail that wends down from medieval Schloss Laufen or on one of the boats that cross to the rock that rises above it.

## Sights

**Schloss Laufen am Rheinfall** CASTLE
(www.schlosslaufen.ch; adult/child Sfr5/3; ⏲8am-7pm Jun-Aug, shorter hours rest of year) Looking proudly back on 1000 years of history, this medieval castle offers a close-quarters view of the Rheinfall cascade. You can buy a ticket at its souvenir shop to walk or take the

panoramic lift down to the Känzeli viewing platform, where you can appreciate the full-on crash-bang spectacle of the falls.

## Activities

**Rhyfall Mändli** BOATING
(www.rhyfall-maendli.ch; adult/child return Sfr20/10) During summer, ferries flit in and out of the water at the bottom of the Rheinfall cascade. The best is the round trip that stops at the tall rock in the middle of the falls, from where you can climb to the top and watch the water rush all around you.

**Adventure Park** ADVENTURE SPORTS
(www.ap-rheinfall.ch; Nohlstrasse; adult/child Sfr40/26; ⏲10am-7pm Apr-Oct; 👪) For an above-the-treetops perspective of the Rheinfall waterfall, visit Adventure Park, one of Switzerland's biggest rope parks, with routes graded according to difficulty.

## Sleeping & Eating

**SYHA Dachsen am Rheinfall** HOSTEL €
(☎052 659 61 52; www.youthhostel.ch/dachsen; dm Sfr30.50; 📶) If the sound of the Rheinfall waterfall lulling you to sleep at night appeals, stay at the hostel inside Schloss Laufen.

**Schlössli Worth** INTERNATIONAL €€€
(☎052 672 24 21; www.schloessliwoerth.ch; Rheinfallquai 30; mains Sfr42-68; ⏲11.30am-11.30pm) Schlössli Worth, on the north bank of the Rheinfall waterfall, harbours a lounge-style restaurant with floor-to-ceiling windows affording magical views of the falls, which are strikingly illuminated after dark. Market-fresh cuisine is paired with fine local wines.

## Getting There & Away

Buses 1 and 6 run every 10 minutes between Schaffhausen and Neuhausen am Rheinfall (Sfr4.80, 15 minutes). From here, bear right towards Schlössli Worth or left across the combined train and pedestrian bridge to Schloss Laufen.

If you come by train from Schaffhausen or Winterthur to Schloss Laufen am Rheinfall, you'll need to climb the hill to the castle. By car, you'll pull up in the car park behind the castle. Neuhausen am Rheinfall is 4km southwest of Schaffhausen.

# Stein am Rhein

POP 3343 / ELEV 407M

Stein am Rhein, with its miniature steam train, leafy river promenade and gingerbready houses, looks as though it has leapt from the pages of a Swiss folk tale. The effect is most striking in its cobblestone Rathausplatz, where houses of all shapes and sizes, some half-timbered, others covered in frescos, line up for a permanent photo op. It's an enduring mystery why this place isn't on Unesco's World Heritage list.

## Sights & Activities

**Rathausplatz** SQUARE
Often hailed as Switzerland's most beautiful town square (no mean feat!), the elongated Rathausplatz often elicits little gasps of wonder because it's so darned ornate. The fresco-festooned **Rathaus** (town hall) soars above the 16th-century houses named after their elaborate murals, such as Sonne (Sun) and Der Weisse Adler (The White Eagle). Look up a level and you'll notice that many also sport intricately carved oriel windows and billowing flower boxes. It's pure fairytale stuff.

**Klostermuseum St Georgen** MUSEUM
(www.klostersanktgeorgen.ch; Fischmarkt 3; adult/child Sfr5/free; ⏲10am-5pm Tue-Sun Apr-Oct) This monastery museum sits between the Rathaus and the Rhine. A Benedictine monastery was built here in 1007, but what you see today,

DON'T MISS

### GET ON YOUR COW & RIDE

Forget horseback riding; the latest craze to sweep this corner of Switzerland is cow trekking – yes, really. It's all thanks to the madcap brainwave of local farmer Heinz Morgenegg, who runs the **Bolderhof** (www.bolderhof.ch; 90min trek per person Sfr95, half-day trek incl picnic Sfr150) in **Hemishofen**, 3km west of Stein am Rhein. Cow trekking is part of the Morgenegg family's experiential approach to organic dairy farming. Simply pick your brown-eyed beauty, saddle up and ride at cow pace through bucolic countryside to the banks of the Rhine. The cows can sense a soft touch and have been known to suddenly make a sprint for the freedom of a meadow full of luscious grass, so a firm hand (and riding crop) is needed.

including the cloister and the magnificent *Festsaal* (grand dining room), is largely a late-Gothic creation.

**Museum Lindwurm** MUSEUM
(Unterstadt 18; adult/child Sfr5/3; ⌚10am-5pm Mar-Oct) A four-storey house has been converted into this museum, whose living rooms, servants' quarters and kitchen replicate the conditions enjoyed in the mid-19th century by a bourgeois family.

**La Canoa** CANOEING
(☎052 741 27 82; www.lacanoa.com; Strandbad Niderfeld, Hemishoferstrasse 69; 3hr canoe/kayak/SUP rental Sfr14/18/30) If you fancy paddling along the Rhine, you can rent canoes, kayaks and stand-up paddleboards here.

## Sleeping

★**B&B Stein am Rhein** B&B €
(☎052 741 45 44; Bollstieg 22; s/d/f Sfr90/130/170; P 📶) Huddled in a quiet corner of town is this charming B&B. The kindly Keller family make you feel instantly at home in their chalet with bright, well-kept rooms kitted out with pine furnishings, a garden and a sauna. Families are *herzlich willkommen* (warmly welcomed), and cycling, mountain-biking and kayaking tours can be arranged.

**SYHA hostel** HOSTEL €
(☎052 741 12 55; www.youthhostel.ch/stein; Hemishoferstrasse 87; dm Sfr34-37, s/d/q Sfr52/100/152; 📶) On the banks of the Rhine, this neat and tidy hostel has attractive gardens, a barbecue area and a playground. It's a 15-minute stroll northwest of the central Rathausplatz.

**Hotel Adler** HISTORIC HOTEL €€
(☎052 742 61 61; www.adlersteinamrhein.ch; Adlergässli 4; s/d/ste Sfr135/185/205; 📶) Behind the frescoed exterior lie simple yet comfortable rooms, but the location on Rathausplatz is the big draw. The dining areas have a pleasingly old-fashioned feel about them and the food, while not outlandishly creative, hits the spot. Local fish is a safe bet. Service can be a tad on the surly side at times.

## Eating

Half-timbered houses serving Swiss grub line the Rhine, but the quality can be hit and miss.

**La P'tite Crêperie** CRÊPES €
(☎052 741 59 55; Unterstadt 10; crêpes Sfr8-17; ⌚11am-7pm) Feast on fabulously light crêpes with cheese and *Bündnerfleisch* (air-dried beef), maple syrup or – what could be more Swiss? – Toblerone at this hole-in-the-wall place with a boho feel. It's closed Tuesday and Wednesday in low season.

**Kafi und Me** CAFE €
(☎052 558 20 45; www.kafiundme.ch; Unterstadt 13; snacks & light meals Sfr5-15; ⌚10am-5pm Wed-Sun) With its mishmash of furniture, eye-catching knick-knacks and friendly service, this vintage-cool cafe is one of Stein am Rhein's best. Nip in for great coffee, speciality teas, homemade cakes and light bites from quiche to salads and toasties.

**Burg Hohenklingen** SWISS €€
(☎052 741 21 37; www.burghohenklingen.com; Hohenklingenstrasse 1; mains Sfr36.50-55; ⌚10am-midnight Tue-Sat, to 6pm Sun, closed late Dec-early Mar) For a dollop of medieval atmosphere, you can't beat this 12th-century hilltop fortress with cracking views over the rooftops of Stein am Rhein. Tuck into Swiss classics such as beef braised in Pinot Noir or local trout cooked in Riesling in the *Rittersaal* (Hall of Knights).

## Information

**Tourist Office** (☎052 632 40 32; www.steinamrhein.ch; Oberstadt 3; ⌚9.30am-noon & 1.30-5pm Mon-Fri, shorter hours winter) The tiny tourist office lies east of the central Rathausplatz.

## Getting There & Away

There are direct twice-hourly trains from Stein am Rhein to Schaffhausen (Sfr9.20, 24 minutes) and St Gallen (Sfr26.20, 1½ hours).

The B13, running along the southern shores of Lake Constance, passes through Stein am Rhein and heads west to Schaffhausen and the German border.

# LAKE CONSTANCE

Before package holidays began whisking the locals and their beach towels abroad in the '70s and '80s, Lake Constance (Bodensee) was the German Mediterranean, with its mild climate, flowery gardens and palm trees. The 'Swabian Sea', as it's nicknamed, is Central Europe's third-largest lake, straddling Switzerland, Germany and Austria. It's a relaxed place to wind down for a spell, whether cycling through apple orchards and vineyards, relaxing on the beach or taking to the lake by canoe.

WORTH A TRIP

### A SPIN AROUND LAKE CONSTANCE

Hopping across the Swiss–German border from Kreuzlingen brings you to the high-spirited, sunny university town of Konstanz, well worth a visit for its Romanesque cathedral, pretty Old Town and tree-fringed harbour. Edging north of **Konstanz**, you reach the Unesco-listed Benedictine monastery of **Reichenau** (www.reichenau-tourismus.de), founded in 724. Nearby is **Insel Mainau** (www.mainau.de; adult/child €20/11.50; ⏲dawn-dusk), a pleasantly green islet whose Mediterranean-style gardens include rhododendron groves, a butterfly house and a waterfall-strewn Italian garden.

The winegrowing town of **Meersburg** reclines on the northern shore of Lake Constance – cobbled lanes thread past half-timbered houses up to the perkily turreted medieval castle. Just east is **Friedrichshafen**, forever associated with the Zeppelin, the cigar-shaped craft that made its inaugural flight in 1900. The **Zeppelin Museum** (www.zeppelin-museum.de; adult/child €9/4; ⏲9am-5pm) traces the history of this bombastic but ill-fated means of air transport. Still on German turf is the postcard-perfect island town of **Lindau**, with its lavishly frescoed houses, palm-speckled promenade and harbour watched over by a lighthouse and a Bavarian lion.

Lindau sits just a few kilometres north of Austria and the town of **Bregenz**, which hosts the highly acclaimed **Bregenzer Festspiele** from mid-July to mid-August, in which opera and orchestral concerts are staged on a vast water-borne stage. Rising dramatically above the town is the Pfänder (1064m) – the **Pfänderbahn** (www.pfaenderbahn.at; Steinbruchgasse 4, Bregenz; adult/child return €12.70/6.40; ⏲8am-7pm) cable car glides to the summit, where panoramic views of Lake Constance and the not-so-distant Alps unfold.

Even if you don't have your own car, getting around by bike or boat is a breeze. Well signposted and largely flat, the 273km **Bodensee-Radweg** (www.bodensee-radweg.com) encircles the lake, weaving through fields of ripening wheat, vineyards, orchards and shady avenues of chestnut and plane trees. Most train stations in the region rent out bikes, and **La Canoa** (www.lacanoa.com) has canoe-rental points in all major towns on the lake.

## ℹ Information

For regional savings on sights, activities and ferry travel, invest in a **Bodensee Erlebniskarte** (www.bodensee-erlebniskarte.de; per 3/4/7 days Sfr81/109/158), sold from mid-April to mid-October. In its most expensive version (Seebären), it entitles the holder to free unlimited ferry travel, entrance to many museums and attractions (except Insel Mainau), and a return journey up the Pfänder cable car in Bregenz and the Säntisbahn.

## ℹ Getting There & Away

Frequent rail services link Zürich with Konstanz (Sfr33, 80 minutes) and Munich (Sfr96, five hours) in Germany. Trains run between Bregenz in Austria and St Margrethen in Switzerland (Sfr7, 17 minutes).

The A7 and A1 motorways link Swiss towns on the lake with destinations to the west such as St Gallen, Winterthur and Zürich.

## ℹ Getting Around

Various ferry companies, including Switzerland's **SBS Schifffart** (www.sbsag.ch), Austria's **Vorarlberg Lines** (www.bodenseeschifffahrt.at) and Germany's **BSB** (www.bsb-online.com), travel across, along and around the lake from mid-April to late October, with the more frequent services starting in late May. A Swiss Pass is valid only on the Swiss side of the lake.

Trains tend to be the easiest way to get around on the Swiss side, as buses are on the German bank. The B31 road hugs the north shore but can get busy. On the south shore, the N13 shadows the train line around the lake.

# Kreuzlingen

POP 21,524 / ELEV 404M

Kreuzlingen, in the Swiss canton of Thurgau, is often eclipsed by its prettier, more vivacious sister, Konstanz in Germany, just a few paces over the border. That said, its lake-front location is charming, with activities from swimming and kayaking to hiking and cycling on the excellent bike trail that makes a loop around the Bodensee (Lake Constance).

France's Napoleon III grew up at **Schloss Arenenberg** (www.napoleonmuseum.tg.ch; Salenstein; adult/child Sfr12/5; ⏲10am-5pm Apr-Oct, closed Mon rest of year), a handsome, powder-puff-pink mansion with beautiful grounds on Lake Constance. The little chateau dates to the 16th century but was given a total makeover in the 18th century by Hortense de Beauharnais, Napoleon's stepdaughter. The interior remains intact, and the lake-facing park, laid out in the formal French style, is a delight to wander in spring and summer.

Beautifully situated in lake-front parkland, this charming **SYHA Hostel** (☎071 688 26 63; www.youthhostel.ch/kreuzlingen; Promenadenstrasse 7; dm Sfr37.50, d Sfr75-80, q Sfr164; ⏲Mar-Nov; 📶) occupies an art nouveau villa and offers canoe and kayak rental.

The **tourist office** (☎071 672 38 40; www.kreuzlingen-tourismus.ch; Hauptstrasse 39; ⏲9.30am-12.30pm & 1.30-6pm Mon-Fri, 9.30am-2pm Sat May-Sep, shorter hours rest of year) is on Kreuzlingen's main drag, Hauptstrasse, several blocks east of the train station.

From Kreuzlingen, trains run frequently to St Gallen (Sfr19.20, 55 minutes) and Zürich (Sfr32, 1½ hours), as well as to destinations along the lake, including Arbon (Sfr12, 40 minutes). The A7 runs west of Kreuzlingen, connecting up with the A1 to Zürich.

# Arbon

POP 14,266 / ELEV 400M

Reclining on the southern shore of the Bodensee, Arbon makes an attractive base for exploring the lake, with a medieval Altstadt punctuated by lofty half-timbered houses and presided over by a 16th-century castle. On clear days there are views deep into the snowcapped Alps from the lakefront promenade, which attracts walkers, cyclists and in-line skaters.

## Sights

**Historisches Museum** MUSEUM

(http://museum-arbon.ch; Alemannenstrasse 4; adult/child Sfr6/free; ⏲2-5pm Tue-Sun May-Sep, shorter hours rest of year) Housed in 16th-century Schloss Arbon, this museum races you through 5500 years of history, from the Stone Age to the 18th-century linen trade. Among the finds on display are a Roman lead pig, an early medieval bronze belt buckle and Biedermeier furniture.

## Sleeping & Eating

**Hotel Brauerei Frohsinn** HOTEL €€

(☎071 447 84 84; www.frohsinn-arbon.ch; Romanshornerstrasse 15; s/d/f Sfr120/175/235; P📶) Set in a pretty half-timbered house, Hotel Frohsinn has light, airy rooms and its own microbrewery. Venture down to the vaulted cellar for a cold frothy one and hearty fare such as veal sausages with onion-beer sauce.

**Römerhof** INTERNATIONAL €€

(☎071 447 30 30; www.roemerhof-arbon.ch; Freiheitsgasse 3; mains Sfr44-52; ⏲noon-2pm & 6-10pm Tue-Fri, 6-10.30pm Sat) Lodged in a 16th-century building, the Römerhof paints a refined picture with its wood panelling, stained glass and white linen–draped tables. The menu has French and international overtones, with starters like wild-garlic cream with caramelised scallops seguing into mains like duck with kumquat sauce and black lentils. There's a terrace for warm-weather dining.

## Information

**Tourist Office** (☎071 440 13 80; www.arbon tourismus.ch; Schmiedgasse 5; ⏲9-11.30am & 2-6pm Mon-Fri, 9-11.30am Sat) The helpful tourist office is in Arbon's historic centre.

## Getting There & Away

Arbon is on the train line between Zürich (Sfr33, 1½ hours) and Rorschach (Sfr5.80, 10 minutes). The train station is 1km south of the historic centre.

The town is just off the A1 motorway that connects Lake Constance and Zürich.

# Rorschach

POP 9214 / ELEV 398M

Sitting serenely on the shores of Lake Constance, Rorschach is backed by a wooded hill. Although something of a faded beauty, the harbour town has some fine 16th- to 18th-century houses with oriel windows, a striking 18th-century granary that's a nod to its one-time importance as a trading centre, and a 1920s bathhouse that's a real blast from the past. Its lakefront promenade is a pleasure to stroll, cycle or skate.

## Sights

**Badhütte** NATURAL POOL

(Bathing Hut; Thurgauerstrasse; adult/child Sfr4/2; ⏲8am-7pm mid-May–mid-Sep) Out on the lake is the 1920s Badhütte, attached to land by a little covered bridge. It's a pleasant place for a refreshing dip in the water and a drink.

**Markthalle Altenrhein** ARCHITECTURE

(www.markthalle-altenrhein.ch; Knotternstrasse 2, Staad; adult/child Sfr5/2; ⏲10am-5.30pm) The wacky creation of Austrian artist Friedensreich Hundertwasser (1928–2000), who once called the straight line 'godless', this market hall bears his indelible hallmark with its wonky walls, rainbow-bright colours and golden onion domes – like a hallucinatory vision of legendary Arabia in small-town Switzerland.

## Sleeping

**Schloss Wartegg** HOTEL €€
(☎071 858 62 62; http://wartegg.ch; Rorschacherberg; s Sfr135-175, d Sfr195-355; P ☎) For an exceptional escape, book into this fantasy palace a 10-minute drive from Rorschach on the hillside above town. This 16th-century former royal Austrian castle is set in grounds with towering sequoias and Lake Constance views. There are nods to the 21st century in the slick rooms, which have iPod docks and minibars. Organic produce features at breakfast.

## Information

**Tourist Office** (☎071 841 70 34; www.tourist-rorschach.ch; Hauptstrasse 56; ⊙8.30am-6pm Mon-Fri, 9am-2.45pm Sat & Sun, shorter hours winter)

## Getting There & Away

Rorschach Hafen station is handily located on Haupstrasse, in the heart of the Old Town. Trains run frequently to lake destinations, including Arbon (Sfr5.80, nine minutes) and Kreuzlingen (Sfr14.40, 49 minutes). There are also speedy connections to St Gallen (Sfr7.20, 18 minutes).

The town is on the A1 motorway, which runs west to St Gallen, Winterthur and Zürich.

# St Gallen

POP 74,111 / ELEV 670M

One of northern Switzerland's most cultured towns, St Gallen is well worth the pilgrimage for the lavish history that unfurls as you step through its lattice of cobblestone backstreets and squares, past half-timbered houses embellished with turrets and intricately carved oriel windows.

## Sights & Activities

Multilingual guided tours of the **Old Town** and **abbey** (Sfr25 per person) kick off at the tourist office (p267) at 11.30am on Monday and Wednesday and 10.30am on Saturday from May to October. Tours from December to April take place at 11.30am on Saturday. All tours last around 90 minutes. There are also 90-minute audioguide tours available at the tourist office for Sfr15.

★ **Stiftsbibliothek** LIBRARY
(www.stibi.ch; Klosterhof 6d; adult/child Sfr12/9, audioguide Sfr5; ⊙10am-5pm) St Gallen's abbey library is one of the world's oldest and it's Switzerland's finest example of rococo architecture. Along with the rest of the Benedictine monastery, founded by St Gall in 612, the library forms a Unesco World Heritage Site. Filled with priceless leather-bound books and manuscripts painstakingly handwritten and illustrated by monks during the Middle Ages, it's a lavish confection of frescos, stucco, cherubs and parquetry. Multilingual audioguides are available, as are felt slippers, obligatory to protect the floor.

**Dom** CATHEDRAL
(Klosterhof; ⊙9am-6pm Mon, Tue, Thu & Fri, 10am-6pm Wed, 9am-4pm Sat, noon-5.30pm Sun) St Gallen's twin-towered, mid-18th-century cathedral is only slightly less ornate than the world-famous Stiftsbibliothek library nearby. The cathedral features dark and stormy frescos and mint-green stucco embellishments. The cupola shows a vision of paradise with the Holy Trinity at the centre. Oddly, entry is by two modest doors on the north flank – there is no door in the main facade, which is actually the cathedral's apse. Concerts are sometimes held; consult www.dommusik-sg.ch. The cathedral is closed during services.

**St Laurenzen-Kirche** CHURCH
(Zeughausgasse; tower adult/child Sfr5/2.50; ⊙9.30-11.30am & 2-4pm Mon, 9.30am-4pm Tue-Sat) St Gallen's cathedral gets all the attention, but this Protestant neo-Gothic church is also beautiful, with its mosaic-tiled roof, delicate floral frescos and star-studded ceiling resembling a night sky. Climb the tower for views over the town's terracotta rooftops and spires.

**Textilmuseum** MUSEUM
(www.textilmuseum.ch; Vadianstrasse 2; adult/child Sfr12/free; ⊙10am-5pm) St Gallen has long been an important hub of the Swiss textile industry, and this museum pays homage to that tradition. The collection brings together many centuries of textiles from all over the world – from fabrics taken from ancient Egyptian graves to medieval embroidery and impossibly intricate lace – and the machinery used to produce them.

**Stadtlounge** LANDMARK
(City Lounge; Schreinerstrasse; ⊙24hr) FREE Quite astonishingly, part of historic St Gallen is covered by a rubberised red tennis-court coating, with in-situ outdoor-furniture-like chairs, sofas and tables – even a car. This zany art-installation project by Pipilotti Rist and Carlos Martínez is intended as an 'outdoor living room'.

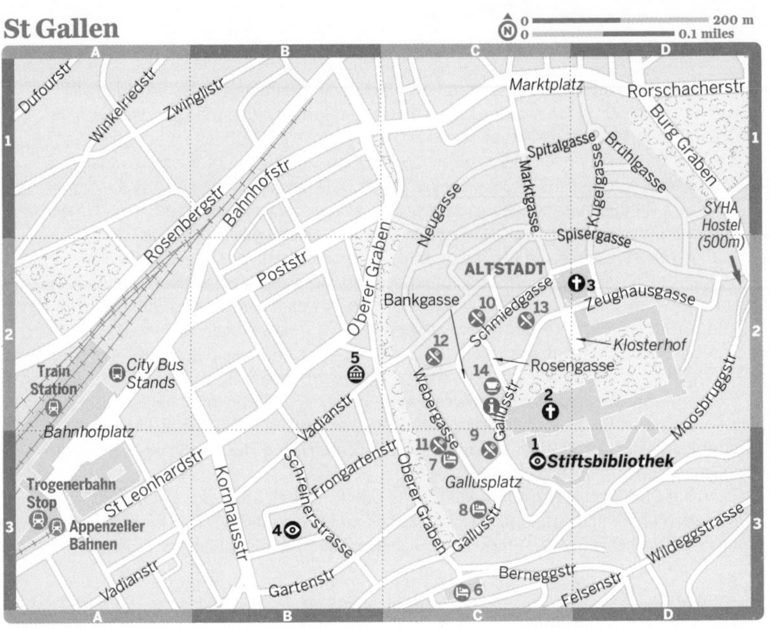


## St Gallen

**Top Sights**
1 Stiftsbibliothek........C3

**Sights**
2 Dom........C2
3 St Laurenzen-Kirche........D2
4 Stadtlounge........B3
5 Textilmuseum........B2

**Sleeping**
6 Einstein St Gallen........C3
7 Hotel Dom........C3
8 Hotel Vadian........C3

**Eating**
9 Am Gallusplatz........C3
10 Bäumli........C2
Einstein Gourmet........(see 6)
11 Lansin........C3
12 Metzgerei Gemperli........C2
13 Wirtschaft Zur Alten Post........C2

**Drinking & Nightlife**
14 Chocolaterie Kölbener........C2

**Maestrani's Chocolarium** FOOD
(☎071 228 38 11; www.chocolarium.ch; Toggenburgerstrasse 41, Flawil; adult/child Sfr14/8; ⊙9am-6pm Mon-Fri, 9am-5pm Sat, 10am-5pm Sun; 👪) For the inside scoop on the chocolate-making process from bean to bar, take an hour-long guided tour of the Maestrani's Chocolarium, housed in an architecturally innovative building. You can decorate your own chocolate (for an extra Sfr10) or simply indulge in the sweet stuff at the cafe and shop.

To reach it from St Gallen, take a train to Flawil, then change to the bus to Bütschwil (Maestrani stop).

## Festivals & Events

**St Galler Festspiele** MUSIC
(www.stgaller-festspiele.ch; ⊙late Jun-early Jul) Two-week outdoor opera season held in the square behind the cathedral.

## Sleeping

St Gallen is a business town, which can make beds scarce and prices high. It's blessed with a couple of charming places to stay, but not as many as you might expect in light of the beauty of its historic centre.

OFF THE BEATEN TRACK

**SARDONA**

A wild and wonderful area of sawtoothed, glaciated mountains springs up around **Piz Sardona** (3056m), the highest peak in St Gallen. Spread along the boundary with Graubünden, this remote Alpine region receives just a trickle of visitors, which makes it all the more alluring for hikers, bikers and anyone wanting to tiptoe off the radar and unplug for a few days. Its pride and joy is the 32,000-hectare **Swiss Tectonic Arena Sardona** (http://tourismus.unesco-sardona.ch), a Unesco World Heritage Site and one of the best places on earth to observe mountain creation and plate tectonics.

To get there, take one of two minor roads southwest from Bad Ragaz. Both climb rapidly, one passing via Pfäfers and the other via Valens and Vasön. Where they join, you enter the **Taminatal**, a spectacular valley that mixes high pastureland with dense forest (the autumn colours are nearly as vivid as in the USA's New England).

After 20km you reach the foot of the jewel-coloured, fjord-like **Gigerwaldsee** reservoir, flanked by sheer-sided mountains and laced with waterfalls. The road climbs to skirt its southern shore and reach the Walser settlement of St Martin im Calfeisental. Here you can stay at the peaceful **Sankt Martin guesthouse** (081 306 12 34; www.sanktmartin.info; dm Sfr40-45, s Sfr85, d Sfr130-140, tr Sfr180, q Sfr210), the perfect base for a couple of days' majestic walking.

An easy trail heads two hours west to the scenic lookout at Sardona Alp. Another hour is needed to reach the mountain refuge **Sardona Hütte** (081 306 13 88; www.sardonahuette.ch; dm per adult/child Sfr33/16, incl half-board Sfr68/49; Jul-Sep) at 2158m.

**Hotel Vadian** HOTEL €
(071 228 18 78; www.hotel-vadian.com; Gallusstrasse 36; s Sfr99-120, d Sfr160-170; ) You can't get much closer to the heart of St Gallen at this kind of price. Each room boasts individual furnishings meaning there's something for everyone here.

**SYHA Hostel** HOSTEL €
(071 245 47 77; www.youthhostel.ch/st.gallen; Jüchstrasse 25; dm/s/d/q Sfr34/64/90/150; P ) Nestled in leafy grounds, this modern hillside hostel is only a 15-minute walk from the Old Town – or take the Trogenerbähnli (S21) from the train station to Birnbäume.

**Hotel Dom** BOUTIQUE HOTEL €€
(071 227 71 71; www.hoteldom.ch; Webergasse 22; s Sfr85-185, d Sfr120-255, tr Sfr245-305; ) An almost startlingly modern hotel, plonked in the middle of the Old Town. The room decor is razor sharp, with clean lines, backlit walls and bold colours. The cheapest rooms are simple and have shared bathrooms. Light sleepers should be aware that noise travels. A 1st-floor lounge with complimentary tea, coffee and fruit and a generous breakfast buffet sweeten the deal.

**Einstein St Gallen** HISTORIC HOTEL €€€
(071 227 55 55; www.einstein.ch; Berneggstrasse 2; s Sfr185-275, d Sfr275-470, ste Sfr495-2500; P @ ) Silk curtains, cherry-wood furnishings and plush lamb's-wool rugs grace the spacious rooms at this grand 19th-century pile. Relax with a swim in the strikingly lit atrium pool or a massage in the spa. The panoramic rooftop restaurant emphasises regional cuisine.

## Eating & Drinking

St Gallen is noted for its *Erststock-Beizli* (traditional taverns situated on the 1st floor of half-timbered houses). You'll find these alongside cafes, patisseries, takeaways and restaurants dishing up global flavours in the lanes of the Altstadt.

**Lansin** VIETNAMESE €
(071 223 20 00; http://lansin.ch; Webergasse 16; mains Sfr17-20; 11.30am-2.30pm Mon-Sat, 5.30-10pm Tue-Thu, to 11pm Fri & Sat) If you're tired of traditional Swiss grub, swing across to this nicely chilled, bistro-style Vietnamese restaurant. Go for a classic bowl of belly-warming *pho bo* (rice-noodle soup with beef, bamboo shoots and herbs), or a fragrant curry.

**Metzgerei Gemperli** HOT DOGS €
(Schmiedgasse 34; sausages Sfr6.50-7.50; 8am-6.30pm Mon-Fri, 7am-5pm Sat) Bite into the best OLMA bratwurst – found only in St Gallen, this soft, white veal bratwurst is made with spices and bacon and has a crispy brown skin – served plain in a *Bürli* (bun), at this butcher–sausage stand combo.

**Wirtschaft Zur Alten Post** INTERNATIONAL €€
(☎071 222 66 01; www.apost.ch; Gallusstrasse 4; mains Sfr29-45; ⏰11.30am-2pm & 5.30-10.30pm Tue-Sat) Things are a little ritzy at this upmarket but historical *Beizl* (tavern), where St Gallen specialities like fat veal sausages with rösti are complemented by more original creations such as baby monkfish with warm vegetable salad, fresh herbs and buffalo mozzarella.

**Bäumli** SWISS €€
(☎071 222 11 74; www.weinstube-baeumli.ch; Schmiedgasse 18; mains Sfr25-47; ⏰11am-2pm & 5-11pm Tue-Fri, 11am-11pm Sat) Creaking with 500 years of personality, this late-medieval wine tavern houses a wood-panelled, candlelit restaurant that showcases all the typical *Erststock-Beizli* (1st-floor tavern) specialities, from bratwurst with fried onions to lamb cutlets, Wiener schnitzel, cordon bleu (pork schnitzel stuffed with ham and cheese) and *Geschnetzeltes* (a dish of sliced pork or veal).

**Am Gallusplatz** SWISS €€
(☎071 230 00 90; http://amgallusplatz-sg.ch; Gallusstrasse 24; mains Sfr38-44; ⏰10am-2pm & 5-11pm Tue-Sat) Opposite the cathedral, you can dine below atmospheric vaults at this tavern, which was a horse stable in a former life and still has a whiff of late-medieval charm about it. The menu plays up meaty classics such as beef stroganoff and Wiener schnitzel, with a superb selection of wines to match.

**Chocolaterie Kölbener** CAFE
(☎071 222 57 70; www.chocolaterie-koelbener.ch; Gallusstrasse 20; ⏰8.30am-6pm Mon-Fri, to 5pm Sat & Sun) For coffee, cake and chocolate, this half-timbered place opposite the cathedral is surely the devil's work.

## Information

**Tourist Office** (☎071 227 37 37; www.st.gallen-bodensee.ch; Bankgasse 9; ⏰9am-6pm Mon-Fri, 9am-3pm Sat, 10am-3pm Sun Apr-Oct, shorter hours rest of year; 📶) Right opposite the Dom, St Gallen's swish tourist office is well stocked with information on the city and region. It also has a gift shop and free wi-fi. You can book tours of the Altstadt here.

## Getting There & Away

St Gallen is a short train or bus ride from Romanshorn (Sfr12, 20 minutes). There are also regular trains to Bregenz in Austria (Sfr17, 35 to 50 minutes), Chur (Sfr36, 1½ hours) and Zürich (Sfr31, 65 minutes via Winterthur).

By car, the main link is the A1 motorway, which runs from Zürich and Winterthur to the Austrian border.

# Appenzell

POP 5822 / ELEV 785M

Appenzell looks as though it has been plucked straight from the pages of a children's bedtime story. Behind the gaily muralled facades of its gabled houses lie *Konditoreien* (cake shops), craft shops, delis, butchers, and taverns dishing up cheese-laden specialities. The Sitter River curves through the town and beyond to meadows of velvet green that pucker and rise to mountains sheer and ragged. This is Swiss dairy country par excellence: deeply traditional, endearingly authentic and still rooted in farming customs that have been honoured for generations.

## Sights

Countless hiking trails thread up into the surrounding pastures and Alps from Appenzell, including the family-geared Barfussweg (p269) from Jakobsbad to Gonten. The high-level trails at Säntis and Ebenalp can also be explored from here. For more details, consult www.appenzell.info, or pick up the *Wandern* booklet at the tourist office.

**Altstadt** AREA
Set against a backdrop of rolling hills that rise to rugged mountains, Appenzell's Altstadt is Grimm fairy-tale stuff. The carved gabled houses that grab the attention in the compact historic centre are liberally covered with frescoes and ornate shop signs. The centrepiece square is **Landsgemeindeplatz**, but you'll also find rows of photogenic houses and shopfronts on **Hauptgasse**, which is presided over by the village church.

**Pfarrkirche St Mauritius** CHURCH
(Hauptgasse 2; ⏰9am-6pm) Looking back on almost 1000 years of history, Appenzell's church is easily identified by its whopping great late-Gothic bell tower, embellished with a mural of the cantonal patron saint, St Maurice. If the facade is somewhat austere, the interior is the polar opposite, replete with frescoes, stained glass and gilding. The church is a potpourri of Gothic, baroque and neoclassical styles.

**Brauquöll Appenzell** BREWERY
(www.brauquoell.ch; Brauereiplatz 1; visitor centre free, beer tasting Sfr8.50; ⏰1-5pm Mon, 10am-12.15pm & 1-5pm Tue-Fri, 10am-5pm Sat & Sun

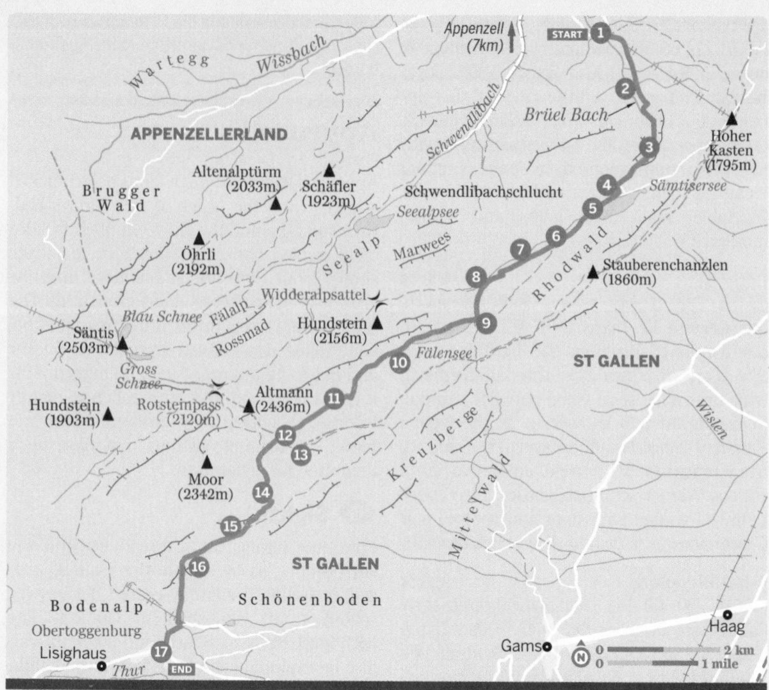


# Walking Tour Zwinglipass

**START** BRÜLISAU
**END** WILDHAUS
**LENGTH** 17.5KM; TWO DAYS

This moderately challenging hike leads through karst scenery and rural valleys to cross a pass at the northern foot of the Churfirsten. Buses run frequently from Appenzell to the trailhead in Brülisau.

From 1 **Brülisau**, follow the signposted road southeast to 2 **Pfannenstiel** (940m). Continue into the 3 **Brüeltobel** gorge, which rises over a watershed to reach 4 **Gasthaus Plattenbödeli** after 1¼ hours. Take the Waldabstieg down left to the 5 **Sämtisersee**, a striking lake. Bear right at 6 **Appenzeller Sämtis**, and head towards the towering peaks of the Alpstein. The dirt track peters out at 7 **Rheintaler Sämtis** (1295m), and a foot track leads up to the grassy 8 **Chalberweid** below the canyon-like Marwees Ridge. Ascend southward via a steep gully onto a tiny saddle from where the stark, elongated Fälensee (1446m) slides into view, 1½ hours from the Gasthaus Plattenbödeli.

Perched above Fälensee is 9 **Berggasthaus Bollenwees**, a scenic hut to spend the night.

Skirt the Fälensee's northern flank, sidling across broad scree fields to reach the 10 **Alphütte Fälenalp** dairy farm. Above you, spectacular needles protrude from the rock walls of the Hundstein (2156m). Make a steep ascent along a ridge to the stone shelters at 11 **Häderen**, 1¼ hours from Bollenwees. The route now rises more gently through karst fields with views to the bishop's mitre–shaped peak of Altmann (2436m). Cross the 12 **Zwinglipass** (2011m), a plateau pitted with depressions and sinkholes, then descend leftward to arrive at the 13 **Zwinglipasshütte**, 50 minutes on. From the terrace there are views of the Churfirsten's seven sawtooth peaks. Drop down the mountainside to pass 14 **Chreialp** (1817m). Steep switchbacks zigzag down to 15 **Teselalp** (1433m), at the end of a farm track, after one hour. Follow the dirt road for 1.25km, bear left onto a foot track, then head 400m down via 16 **Flürentobel** chasm before branching right through clearings in the spruce forest. Continue down to 17 **Wildhaus**, 50 to 60 minutes from Teselalp.

Apr-Oct, shorter hours winter) FREE Pure local spring water goes into the refreshing Appenzeller Bier that's brewed here. The hands-on visitor centre whisks you through brewing history and processes. At the front you can buy beers such as hoppy Vollmond (full moon) and alcohol-free Leermond (empty moon).

**Museum Appenzell** MUSEUM
(Hauptgasse 4; adult/child Sfr7/3; 10am-noon & 1.30-5pm Mon-Fri, 11am-5pm Sat & Sun Apr-Oct, shorter hours rest of year) This heritage museum gives the inside scoop on rural life and folk traditions in Appenzell. Occupying seven floors, it displays beautifully painted wooden furniture with pastoral scenes in the local Bauernmalerei style, lacework, costumes, weapons, religious art, flags and banners, cheesemaking equipment and more. Highlights include an intact *Stube* (parlour) complete with coffered ceiling, a 3000-year-old Egyptian sarcophagus, a 16th-century winged altar and touching paintings of farming life by local artist Carl August Liner.

**Appenzeller Schaukäserei** FARM
(www.schaukaeserei.ch; Dorf 711, Stein; entry to dairy free, iPad tour & tasting adult/child Sfr10/5, cheese tasting Sfr8.50; 9am-6.30pm May-Oct, to 5.30pm Nov-Apr) Cheese-lovers won't want to miss out on a visit to this dairy, where an iPad tour gives you a behind-the-scenes look at the cheesemaking process, including a peek in the cellar, where 12,500 rounds of cheese are regularly bathed in herb-infused brine. Or you can go it alone and end things with a tasting of five Appenzeller cheeses.

**Appenzeller Volkskunde Museum** MUSEUM
(www.appenzeller-museum-stein.ch; Stein; adult/child Sfr7/3.50; 10am-5pm Tue-Sun) This folklore museum, its collection spanning from pastoral paintings to embroidery, provides an insight into rural Appenzell life. From April to October there are daily live weaving demonstrations, as well as twice-weekly demonstrations of traditional cheesemaking in the museum's 400-year-old dairy.

**Werdenberg** VILLAGE
Blink and you'll miss this village and that would be a shame! Founded in 1289, it is said to be the oldest settlement of timber houses in Switzerland. The huddle of some 40-odd dwellings lies between an oversized pond and a grapevine-covered hill topped by a castle.

An easy day trip from Appenzell, Werdenberg is a 40-minute drive south via the A13.

## Activities

**Barfussweg** WALKING
(www.barfusspark.info; ) A great family walk is the 5km Barfussweg (barefoot trail), which skips through meadows and over mountain brooks from Jakobsbad to Gonten. The marked trail leads gently past kid-pleasing attractions like balancing beams, water-treading stations and arm baths.

## Festivals & Events

**Landsgemeinde** CULTURAL
(last Sun Apr) The Landsgemeinde open-air parliament takes place on this square, with locals wearing traditional dress and voting (in the case of the men, by raising a short dagger). A unique form of direct democracy, this tradition dates back to 1294 and attracts a turnout of around 3000 people – more than half the town's population.

**Alpabfahrt Urnäsch** CULTURAL
(mid-Sep) The cows and goats are paraded home from their summer pastures in style at the Alpabfahrt. There's also a farmers market where you can stock up on regional goodies. The event is held in Urnäsch, 10km west of Appenzell.

## Sleeping & Eating

★ **Null Stern Hotel** DESIGN HOTEL €€
(071 898 33 00; http://nullsternhotel.ch; Gonten; d Sfr295; P) As the name suggests, this hotel has zero stars – apart from the ones twinkling above you, that is... In one of Switzerland's most romantic ventures, you'll be collected from Gonten station and driven to your bed in the middle of nature. No walls. No roof. Just birdsong and the first light creeping over craggy Alpine summits as your wake-up call.

The location (near Gonten) is kept pretty hush-hush, so a butler (read: farmer) picks you up and escorts you to the hotel, brings your breakfast basket and provides a welcome drink. Never has the phrase 'room with a view' been more opportune. It's a six-minute train ride from Appenzell to Gonten.

**Hotel Hecht** HISTORIC HOTEL €€
(071 788 22 22; www.hecht-appenzell.ch; Hauptgasse 9; s/d/tr/q Sfr100/170-260/270/320; ) Straddling several higgledy-piggledy floors, this historic hotel is full of creaky charm and places you right in the thick of things. Elegantly furnished with drapes, warm colours and polished wood, the rooms are spacious, immaculate and peaceful. But it's the hospitality that sets this place apart.

WORTH A TRIP

### SÄNTIS & EBENALP

Small in Swiss terms, the jagged Säntis peak (2503m) is the highest in this part of Switzerland. It offers a marvellous panorama encompassing Lake Constance, Zürichsee, the Alps and the Vorarlberg Mountains. From Schwägalp, the cable car **Säntisbahn** (www.saentisbahn.ch; one way/return Sfr32/45; ⏲7.30am-6pm Mon-Fri, to 6.30pm Sat & Sun late May–mid-Oct, 8.30am-5pm rest of year) glides to the summit every 30 minutes.

From Säntis summit, you can walk along the ridge to the neighbouring peak of **Ebenalp** (1640m) in about 3½ hours. At Wildkirchli on Ebenalp there are prehistoric caves showing traces of Stone Age habitation.

A 1½-hour downhill walk from Ebenalp leads to the jewel-coloured Seealpsee, where the family-run dairy **Seealpchäs** (www.seealpchaes.ch; ⏲Jun-Aug) sells delicious cheese specialities, including varieties made with wild garlic and chilli. For a glowing complexion, you can bathe in whey in a wooden bathtub (Sfr45) and gaze up at the mountains.

The **Ebenalpbahn cable car** (www.ebenalp.ch; one way/return Sfr20/31; ⏲7.30am-7pm late May–mid-Oct, 9.30am-5pm rest of year) descends roughly every 15 minutes from Ebenalp summit to Wasserauen, where you can connect to Appenzell by rail (Sfr5.80, 11 minutes) or minor road.

To revel in the mountain views a bit longer, consider spending the night atop Säntis at the charming, down-to-earth, family-run hut **Berggasthaus Alter Säntis** (☎071 799 11 60; www.altersaentis.ch; dm Sfr44, d Sfr140-188, half-board Sfr24; ⏲mid-May–Oct) or chic, boutique-style **Säntis – das Hotel** (☎071 365 66 00; https://saentisbahn.ch; s Sfr135, d Sfr240-260, ste Sfr300-340; P).

**Hotel Appenzell** HOTEL €€
(☎071 788 15 15; www.hotel-appenzell.ch; Landsgemeindeplatz; s/d Sfr135/230; P 📶) With its broad, brightly decorated facade, this typical Appenzeller building houses generously sized rooms with wooden beds. Decor combines gentle pinks and blues with frilly lace on the picture windows. The restaurant offers a wide-ranging seasonal menu that includes vegetarian dishes. E-bike rental is offered for Sfr25 – perfect for zipping off into the hilly surrounds.

**Romantik Hotel Säntis** GASTRONOMY €€
(www.saentis-appenzell.ch; Landsgemeindeplatz 3; mains Sfr32-52) Romantik Hotel Säntis' 1st-floor restaurant is Appenzell's top table. Crisp white tablecloths, beautiful carved pine and views across Landsgemeindeplatz await. The ambience is formal and the service slick, delivering season-inflected dishes.

**Marktplatz** INTERNATIONAL €€
(☎071 787 12 04; www.marktplatz-appenzell.ch; Kronengarten 2; mains Sfr24-39; ⏲11am-2pm & 5.30-11pm Wed-Sat; 👪) Sit on the terrace on one of Appenzell's prettiest squares or in the intricately carved wooden interior of this restaurant. The menu swings with the seasons and has Italian and Swiss influences.

## ℹ Information

**Tourist Office** (☎071 788 96 41; www.appenzell.ch; Hauptgasse 4; ⏲9am-noon & 1.30-5pm Mon-Fri, 10am-5pm Sat, 11am-5pm Sun) Helpful office with stacks of information on Appenzell and the surrounding region, including maps and walking and cycling brochures. It has details on the money-saving Appenzeller Ferienkarte.

## ℹ Getting There & Away

From St Gallen, the narrow-gauge train to Appenzell (Sfr9.60, 48 minutes) leaves from the front and to the right of the main train station. Departures from St Gallen are approximately every half hour, and services run via Gais or Herisau (where you must occasionally change trains).

By car, Appenzell is 17.5km south of St Gallen, connected to Zürich by the A1 motorway.

# Walensee

Walensee is a long finger of a lake that points deep into the mountainous country on the cantonal borders of Glarus and Graubünden. The jagged limestone peaks of the Churfirsten range rise above the lake's green-blue, fjord-like expanse, occasionally interrupted by a coastal hamlet or upland pasture and, about halfway along the lake front, seemingly cracked open by Seerenbachfälle, one of Switzerland's highest falls.

## Sights & Activities

Windsurfers and wakeboarders breeze across Walensee's turquoise waters in summer, while the limestone mountains of the Churfirsten, topping out at 2306m, entice hikers, climbers, canyoneers and paragliders to their heights. When snow settles in winter, those same slopes attract skiers, boarders and freeriders.

**Flumserberg** MOUNTAIN
(www.flumserberg.ch; ) For a little Alpine fun, take the winding mountain road to Flumserberg, perched high above the lake and facing the impenetrable rock wall of the Churfirsten range. The mountain is the starting point for high-Alpine hikes like the 13km 7-Gipfel Tour. For families, there are buggy-friendly footpaths, adventure playgrounds and a toboggan run, Floomzer. In winter the same slopes lure skiers and snowboarders, who pound the powder on 65km of well-maintained pistes.

**Seerenbachfälle** WATERFALL
This series of three colossal waterfalls, thundering 585m from top to bottom, is fuelled by underground rivers running through the mountain rock from as far away as the peak of Säntis. Shooting over a sheer cliff face, the middle waterfall, a 305m single drop, is considered to be Switzerland's highest. The closest you can reach by car is the town of Betlis; the falls are a 30-minute hike from the road.

**7-Gipfel Tour** WALKING
A hike linking Flumserberg-Maschgenkamm to Flumserberg-Tannenbodenalp, the 13km 7-Gipfel Tour takes in seven peaks and affords mind-blowing views of the Swiss Alps and Walensee. Allow roughly 6½ hours for the return-trip hike.

**Murgsee** HIKING
A challenging, classic Alpine trail leads from Flumserberg's Maschgenkamm top station to the inky-blue Murgsee lakes. You'll hike through silent pastures cloaked in wildflowers, and forests of chestnuts and pines. The return-trip trek takes around seven hours.

**Amden** ADVENTURE SPORTS
(www.amden-weesen.ch; ) On the northwest shore of Walensee, the high pasture plateau of Amden has arresting lake and mountain views. There's some fine walking – for families too – amid the marmot burrow–dotted meadows and a bit of snow activity in winter. It's also a base for more adventurous sports in the wider area, including climbing, canyoning and paragliding.

**Schiffsbetrieb Walensee** BOATING
(www.walenseeschiff.ch; Unterterzen) Boats regularly cross the fjord-like Walensee, stopping at the villages, towns and resorts that hug the shores, including Murg, Quinten, Betlis, Weesen and Walenstadt. It's a relaxed way to see the mountain-rimmed lake from the water.

## Sleeping & Eating

**Flyhof** HOTEL €
(055 616 12 30; www.flyhof.ch; Betliserstrasse 16, Weesen; s Sfr85, d Sfr130-150; ) Sitting in mature gardens that slope picturesquely down to the lake, family-run Flyhof is a delight. Antique furniture and beams lend character to the quiet, comfy rooms. Regional ingredients are given a pinch of Mediterranean flavour in the wood-panelled restaurant.

**Lofthotel Murg** BOUTIQUE HOTEL €€
(081 720 35 75; www.lofthotel.ch; Alte Spinnerei, Murg; s Sfr120-170, d Sfr180-270; ) A 19th-century cotton mill has been reincarnated as the Lofthotel, affording fine views of the Churfirsten mountains and Walensee. Clean lines, polished concrete and bold artworks define the industrial-chic rooms. Farm-fresh produce and homemade preserves are served at breakfast.

**Fischerstube** SEAFOOD €€
(055 616 16 08; www.fischerstubeweesen.ch; Marktgasse 9, Weesen; mains Sfr40-59; 11.45am-3pm & 6-11pm Thu-Mon) Snowy-white linen and bottle-green wood panelling create a refined backdrop for well-executed fish dishes. Pair fine wines with local whitefish and perch.

## Information

For information on Walensee and its resorts, stop by **Heidiland Tourismus** (081 720 17 17; www.heidiland.com; Walenseestrasse 18; 9am-noon & 1-5pm Mon-Fri, 9am-1pm Sat) in Unterterzen.

## Getting There & Away

Walenstadt and Weesen are handily located on the A3 motorway (and railway line) that connects Zürich with Graubünden. By train from Zürich, get off at Ziegelbrücke (Sfr27.80, 43 minutes), a 15-minute walk from central Weesen. Trains also run regularly from Zürich to Walenstadt (Sfr29, one hour).

# Glarus

POP 12,570 / ELEV 472M

Crouching below the austerely beautiful Glarus Alps, Glarus is the capital of the eponymous canton. Two-thirds destroyed by fire in 1861, the town is a graceful 19th-century creation with a few typical rural timber houses that survived the flames.

Lording it over Glarus and the Alpine range of the same name, **Tödi's** file-shaped peak tops out at 3614m and is the sole preserve of proficient mountain climbers.

Taking pride of place in the heart of town is **Glarnerhof** (☎055 645 75 75; www.glarnerhof.ch; Bahnhofstrasse 2; s Sfr145-160, d Sfr170-190; ). What the rooms lack in character they more than make up for with space, comfort and Alpine views.

Check out **Glarner Tourismus** (☎055 610 21 25; www.glarnerland.ch; Raststätte A3, Niederurnen) for information on Glarus and the surrounding region.

Some trains from Zürich (Sfr27.80, one hour) require a change at Rapperswil or Ziegelbrücke. There are also frequent connections to St Gallen (Sfr28.40, 1¼ hours).

# Braunwald

POP 308 / ELEV 1256M

Slow travel is the watchword in the car-free mountain resort of Braunwald in the Glarus Alps, which can only be reached by funicular. Remarkably peaceful, Braunwald perches on the side of a sunny terrace that slopes down to pastures and fir forests. High peaks crowd the horizon to the south, dominated by the glaciated summit of Tödi (3614m). The resort has plenty of family and outdoors appeal, with hiking trails, mountain-biking routes and a *via ferrata* harnessing the heights.

## Sights & Activities

Braunwald is a terrific base for hiking in summer. In winter the resort has family appeal, with moderate skiing and off-piste fun from sledding to snow-tubing.

**Oberblegisee** LAKE

Formed by glacial moraine, this vivid blue lake is reached via a beautiful mountain trail from Braunwald. The moderate, 3½-hour walk leads through meadows and open forest and takes in an Alpine dairy. The lake is a great spot for a family picnic.

**Zwerg-Bartli Erlebnisweg** WALKING

() A sure-fire way to get kids walking, this adventure trail is themed after a dwarf named Bartli and takes in a tower, caves and hidden treasures. The 3½-hour trail begins in Gumen and ends at the Braunwaldbahn top station. Shorter variants are also possible – ask at the tourist office for a leaflet.

**Braunwald Via Ferrata** ADVENTURE SPORTS

A cable car rises from Braunwald to Gumen, the starting point for this demanding, three-peak *via ferrata* to Leiteregg, Mittler and Hintere Eggstock (2½ to 5½ hours). The heart-quickening climb offers giddy Alpine views and highlights such as a large suspension bridge. Equipment can be reserved by calling **Kessler Sport** (☎079 612 81 83; www.kesslersport.ch; Dorfstrasse 5; rental per day Sfr30).

## Sleeping

**Hostel Adrenalin** HOSTEL €

(☎079 347 29 05; www.adrenalin.gl; Alpinaweg 3; dm Sfr42-48, s Sfr52-64, d Sfr116) Hostel Adrenalin is the hub of the young snowboarding and adventure-sports community in winter, with video games and lots of parties. Breakfast costs an extra Sfr8, and be prepared to pay an extra Sfr5 each for towels and bed linen.

**Märchenhotel Bellevue** HOTEL €€€

(☎055 653 71 71; www.maerchenhotel.ch; Dorfstrasse 24; d incl half-board Sfr370-450, f Sfr390-510; P) Could this be kid heaven? A converted grand Victorian hotel, the 'fairy-tale hotel' combines a beautiful setting and modern rooms with all manner of child-pleasing fun – from alpacas and llamas to slides, climbing walls, trampolines and creative workshops.

## Information

You'll find the **tourist office** (☎055 653 65 65; www.braunwald.ch; Dorfstrasse 2; 8.15am-noon & 2-5pm Mon-Fri, 8.45am-12.45pm Sat) on the funicular station's top floor.

## Getting There & Away

Trains run hourly from Linthal Braunwaldbahn to Zürich (Sfr27.80, 1½ hours) via Ziegelbrücke (Sfr9.60, 43 minutes). It's a 1¼-hour drive from Zürich along the A3.

The **Braunwaldbahn** (one way/return Sfr7.20/14.40) climbs the hill from the Linthal Braunwaldbahn station at a 64% gradient. The funicular is the only means of access to the village. Cars are not allowed.

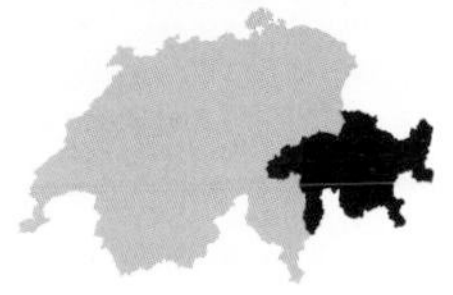

# Graubünden

POP 196,600

**Includes ➜**



## Best Places to Eat

➜ Hotel Albrici (p301)

➜ Kaffee Klatsch Easy (p288)

➜ Burestübli (p282)

## Best Places to Stay

➜ Berghaus Diavolezza (p300)

➜ Romantik Hotel Muottas Muragl (p300)

➜ Hotel Engiadina (p292)

➜ Berghotel Schatzalp (p290)

➜ Zunfthaus zur Rebleuten (p277)

## Why Go?

Ask locals what it is that makes their canton special and they'll wax lyrical about how, well, wild it is. In a country blessed with supermodel looks, Graubünden is all about raw natural beauty. Whether it's wind-battered plateaux in Engadine where clouds roll over big-shouldered mountains, the Rhine gouging out knife-edge ravines near Flims, or the brooding Alpine grandeur of the Swiss National Park, this wonderfully remote region begs outdoor escapades.

While you've probably heard about Davos' sensational downhill skiing, St Moritz' glamour and the tales of Heidi (fictionally born here), vast swaths of Graubünden remain little known and ripe for exploring. Strike into the Alps on foot or follow the lonely passes that corkscrew high into the mountains and the chances are you will be alone in exhilarating landscapes, where only the odd marmot or chamois and your own little gasps of wonder break the silence.

## When to Go

➜ Graubünden's slopes buzz with skiers from mid-December to Easter. Cross-country pros swish across to Davos for the FIS Cross-Country World Cup in December, while upper-crust St Moritz attracts a discerning crowd at January's Snow Polo World Cup.

➜ Summer cranks up the craziness: see men do battle with their beards at the Chur Festival and with their bulk *Schwingen* (Alpine wrestling) with Sertig Schwinget in Davos in August.

➜ Many resorts hibernate from May to mid-June and October to November. If you do rock up then, you might bag a good deal and some surprisingly nice weather.

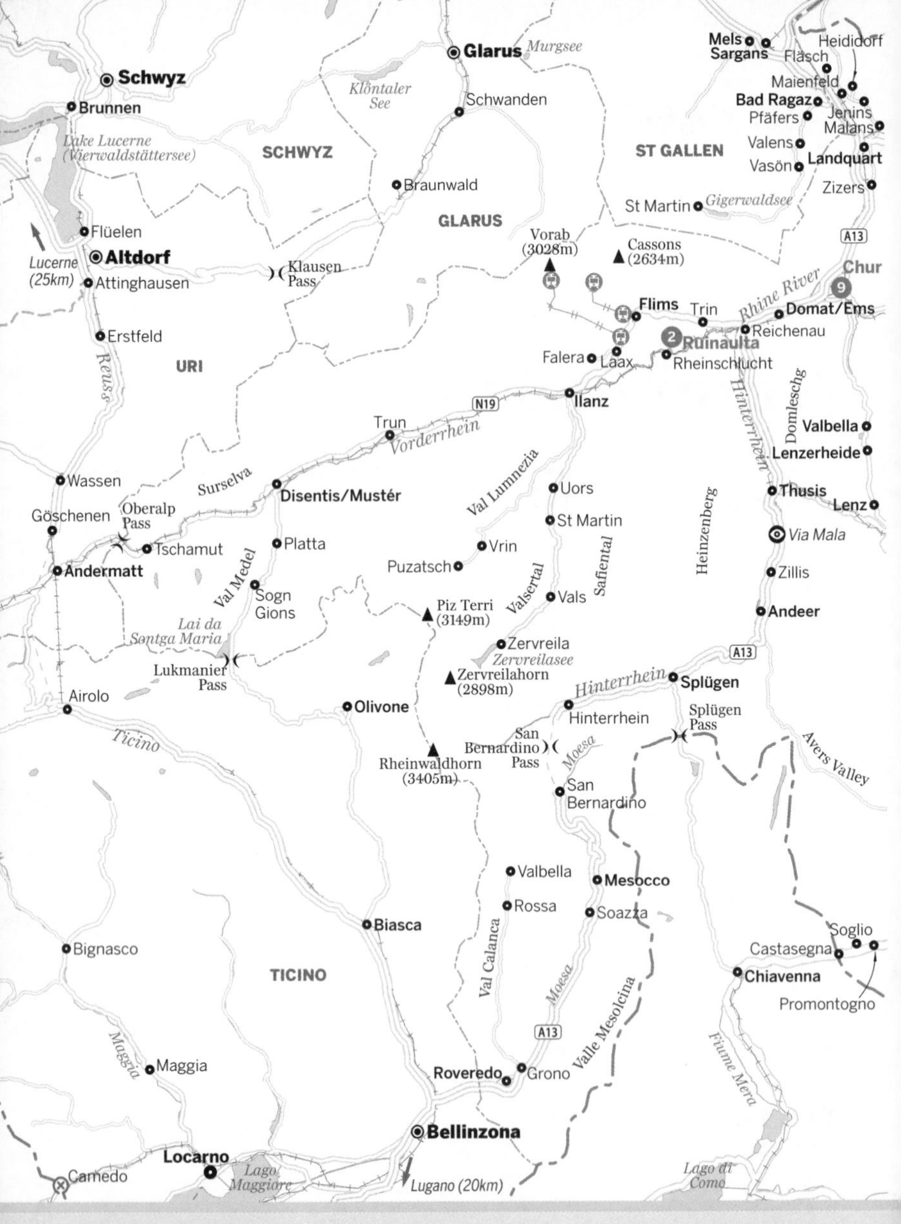


## Graubünden Highlights

❶ **Swiss National Park** (p298) Feeling elevated by high-altitude hiking and evocative Alpine scenery.

❷ **Ruinaulta** (p283) Rafting or hiking past bizarre limestone formations in the Rhine Gorge.

❸ **St Moritz** (p294) Skiing, dining and shopping in this exciting, ritzy winter resort.

❹ **Morteratsch Glacier Hike** (p300) Taking a guided hike down this spectacular glacier.

❺ **Corvatsch 3303** (p298) Gazing out over Silvaplana and

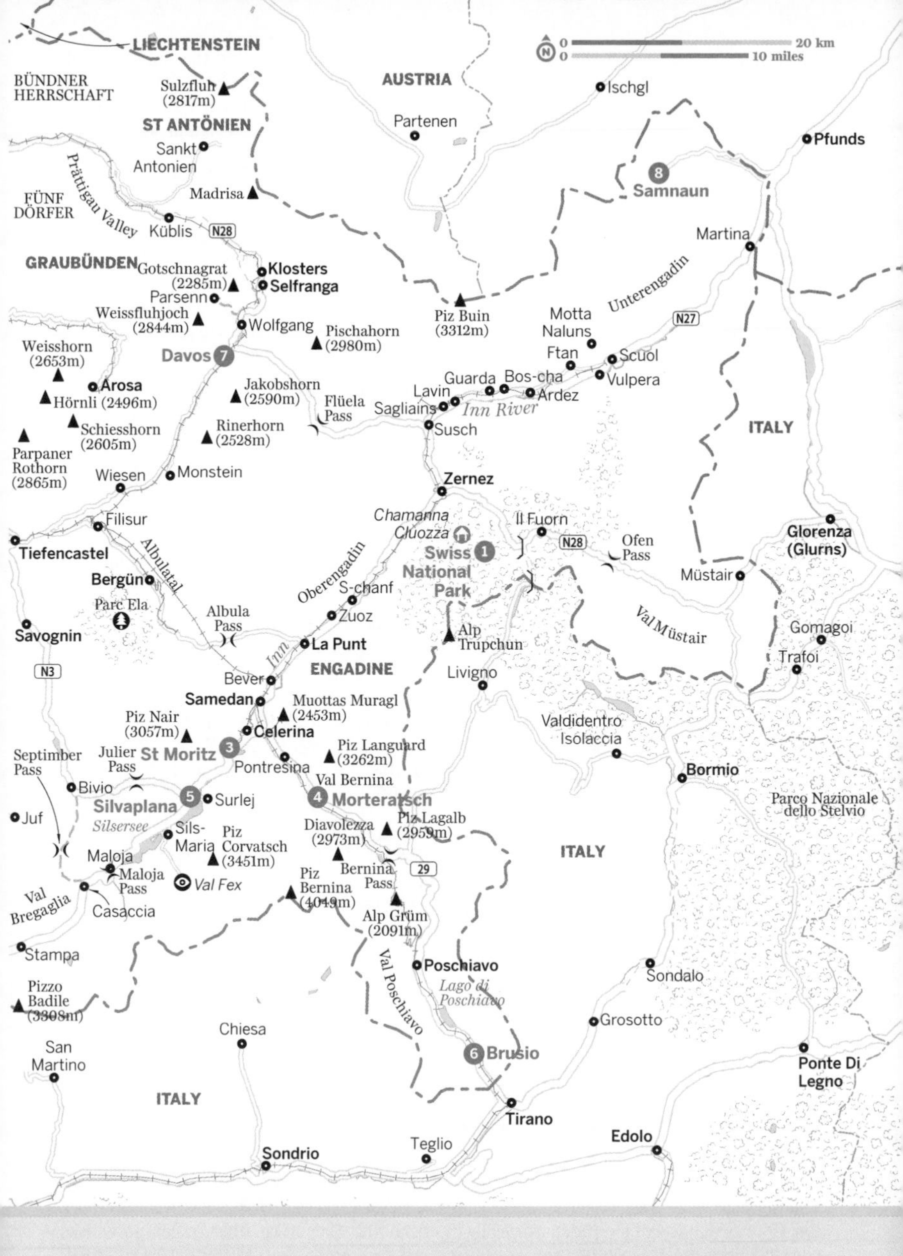


one of the most spectacular Alpine vistas on earth.

**6 Circular Viaduct of Brusio** (p301) Trying to photograph this amazing construction on the Bernina Express.

**7 Davos** (p288) Getting on your bike and riding heart-pulsing single tracks and mountain passes.

**8 ClauWau** (p293) See scores of wannabe Santas do festive battle in Samnaun.

**9 Chur** (p276) Wandering the streets of the Altstadt (Old Town) in the canton's capital.

## History

The canton's openness to all comers today is a far cry from its inward-looking, diffident past. Throughout the centuries, the people of this rugged area lived largely in isolated, rural pockets, mistrustful of outsiders and, aided by the near impregnable mountain terrain, able to resist most would-be conquerors.

In medieval times the region was known as Rhaetia, and was loosely bound by an association of three leagues (Drei Bünde). The modern name for the canton derives from the Grauer Bund (Grey League).

Graubünden joined the Swiss Confederation in 1803; however, much more important was the year 1864, when a hotel owner in St Moritz invited summer guests to stay for the winter – for free. In this way, winter tourism in Graubünden, and later all of Switzerland, was launched.

## Information

**Graubünden Ferien** (☎ 081 254 24 24; http://en.graubuenden.ch; Alexanderstrasse 24; ⏲ 8am-noon & 1-5pm Mon-Fri) Chur, the capital, houses the cantonal tourist office, Graubünden Ferien, located in the building marked 'Publicitas', 200m east of the train station.

## Getting There & Away

Graubünden's capital of Chur is a transport hub, with trains arriving from Zürich. Chur is a departure point for the Bernina Express to Tirano in Italy and is a major stop on the Glacier Express connecting St Moritz with Zermatt.

Three main passes lead from northern and western Graubünden into the southeast Engadine region: Julier (open year-round), Albula (summer only) and Flüela (year-round subject to weather). These approximately correspond to three exit points into Italy: Maloja, Bernina and Fuorn/Ofen (all open year-round). The Oberalp Pass west to Andermatt is closed in winter but, as at Albula, there's the option of taking the car-carrying train instead. In winter, use snow chains or winter tyres.

# Chur

POP 34,650 / ELEV 585M

The biggest city in Switzerland's largest canton, Chur is well worth a wander, especially if you walk up to the Altstadt (Old Town) and do some exploring. The city itself is like a vibrant gallery with arty boutiques, authentic restaurants and relaxed bars.

The Alps rise like an amphitheatre around Chur, the country's oldest city, inhabited since 3000 BC. When Chur was almost destroyed by fire in 1464, German-speaking artisans arrived to rebuild and, in the process, inadvertently suppressed the local Romansch language. What's spoken these days is a variant of the Alemannic Swiss-German dialect.

## Sights & Activities

**★ Altstadt** AREA

(Old Town) Near the Plessur River, the **Obertor** marks the entrance to Chur's alley-woven Altstadt. Along with the stout **Malteserturm** (once the munitions tower), and the **Sennhofturm** (nowadays the city's prison), it's all that remains of the old defensive walls.

**★ Martinskirche** CHURCH

(St Martin's Church; Kirchgasse 12) The city's most iconic landmark is Martinskirche with its distinctive spire and clock face. The 8th-century church was rebuilt in the late-Gothic style in 1491 and is dramatically lit by a trio of Augusto Giacometti stained-glass windows. St Martin presides over a burbling stone fountain in front of the church.

**Kathedrale St Maria Himmelfahrt** CATHEDRAL

(Hof; ⏲ 6am-7pm Mon & Wed-Sat, from 8am Tue, from 7am Sun) Chur's 12th-century cathedral, which took over a century to build, conceals a late-1400s Jakob Russ high altar containing a splendid triptych. First signs of settlement on this site date from the Bronze Age (1300 to 800 BCE).

**Bündner Kunstmuseum** GALLERY

(Museum of Fine Arts; ☎ 081 257 28 68; www.buendner-kunstmuseum.ch; Bahnhofstrasse 35; adult/child Sfr15/free; ⏲ 10am-5pm Tue-Sun, to 8pm Thu) This gallery reflects the history of art in Graubünden as well as artists linked with the canton. It gives an insight into the legacy of Graubünden-born Augusto Giacometti (1877–1947) and his contemporaries, including Giovanni Segantini. Chur-born Angelika Kaufmann's enigmatic Self Portrait (1780) is a standout.

**Brambrüesch** CABLE CAR

(☎ 081 250 55 90; www.facebook.com/brambruesch; Kasernenstrasse 15; adult/child return Sfr25/5, bike park Sfr39/20; ⏲ 8.45am-4.45pm mid-Jun–late Oct & mid-Dec–mid-Mar) Only a few minutes' walk from the Old Town, this cable car whisks you to Brambrüesch at 1600m for spectacular views. In summer, the 13km return-trip hike to **Feldis** is superb, leading through wildflower-strewn heights, woods and past glittering lakes. The peak also attracts mountain bikers to the exhilarating freeride and downhill trails in the **Alpenbikepark** (http://alpenbikepark.ch).

DON'T MISS

## GREAT RAIL JOURNEYS

Graubünden's rugged, high-Alpine terrain is harnessed by some of Switzerland's greatest railways. The panoramic **Rhätische Bahn** (RhB, Rhaetian Railway; www.rhb.ch) is a staggering feat of early-20th-century engineering, traversing viaducts and tunnels and commanding wide-screen views of forested slopes, jewel-coloured lakes and snow-capped peaks. See the website for advance bookings, seat reservations and special deals. The Half Fare, Swiss Card and Swiss Travel Pass give substantial discounts. The Rhätische Bahn's two flagship routes are the Glacier Express (p163) and the **Bernina Express** (www.berninaexpress.ch; one-way Chur–Tirano Sfr64; ⌚ mid-May–early Dec) One of Switzerland's classic trains, the Bernina Express connects the German- and Italian-speaking regions of Graubünden, climbing high into the glaciated realms of the Alps and traversing 55 tunnels and 196 bridges on its four-hour journey from Chur to Tirano. The Thusis–Tirano section is a Unesco World Heritage Site. From Tirano, a connecting bus (Sfr34) continues west to Lugano.

## Festivals & Events

**Churer Fest** CULTURAL

(www.churtourismus.ch; ⌚ mid-Aug) Chur's big summer bash involves three days of concerts, feasting, cow-milking marathons and kiddie fun. Top fun is the Alpine Beard Competition, where hairy men do battle.

## Sleeping

**VIVA Hostel** HOSTEL €

(☎ 081 868 83 48; https://viva-hostel.ch; Welschdörfli 19; dm/s from Sfr31/65; P 📶) VIVA is a backpacker's dream, offering spacious dorms, a drink voucher for the lobby bar on arrival, Sfr7 continental breakfast and, if you're into partying, the in-house VIVA Club (open Thursday to Saturday). It has a great location near the Old Town, even if the nearby area is a tad seedy.

★ **Zunfthaus zur Rebleuten** HISTORIC HOTEL €€

(☎ 081 255 11 44; www.rebleutenchur.ch; Pfisterplatz 1; s/d/q from Sfr75/140/210; P 📶) Housed in an imposing frescoed building on a pretty square in the Old Town, the Zunfthaus zur Rebleuten looks proudly back on 500 years of history. The 12 rooms are fresh and inviting. Especially romantic are those in the loft (watch your head). The restaurants are a joy and lots of non-guests turn up to dine.

**Hotel Freieck** HOTEL €€

(☎ 081 255 15 15; www.freieck.ch; Reichsgasse 44; s/d/tr from Sfr100/160/240; P 📶) Occupying a beautiful 16th-century building in a handy location, Freieck is a seamless blend of history and modernity. Exposed stone, beams and vaults lend character, while rooms are bright and contemporary.

**Romantik Hotel Stern** HISTORIC HOTEL €€

(☎ 081 258 57 57; www.stern-chur.ch; Reichsgasse 11; s/d/ste from Sfr120/220/320; P 📶) Part of Switzerland's romantic clan, this centuries-old hotel has kept its flair, with vaulted corridors and low-ceilinged, pine-filled rooms. As you'd expect, there's an excellent restaurant and well-stocked wine cellar. It's in a good location for exploring the Old Town.

## Eating

Eateries line Bahnhofstrasse, leading up from the train station to the Old Town, where you'll find plenty more options.

**Da Mamma** ITALIAN €

(☎ 081 252 14 12; www.damammabistro.com; Obere Gasse 35; lunch menu from Sfr16.50; ⌚ 8am-6.30pm Mon-Fri, to 5pm Sat) This neat little Italian job has what every bistro needs – people who cook with passion and serve with a pinch of soul. With its slick surrounds and friendly vibe, this is a terrific choice for an inexpensive lunch of salad followed by homemade pasta. The Sicilian pastries and desserts are divine.

**Evviva Plankis** CAFE €

(☎ 081 252 40 21; www.plankis.ch/de/betrieb/arbeitsstaetten/evvivaplankis; Kornplatz 9; snacks & mains from Sfr13; ⌚ 9am-6.30pm Tue-Thu, to 10pm Fri & Sat, 1-6pm Sun) An inviting cafe with a sunny terrace on a square in the Old Town, with delicious Italian gelato and authentic pasta, gnocchi and risotto on the menu.

★ **Bündner Stube** SWISS €€

(☎ 081 258 57 57; www.stern-chur.ch; Reichsgasse 11; mains from Sfr25; ⌚ 11am-midnight Mon-Sat, to 11pm Sun) Candlelight and wood panelling create a warm atmosphere in Romantik Hotel Stern's

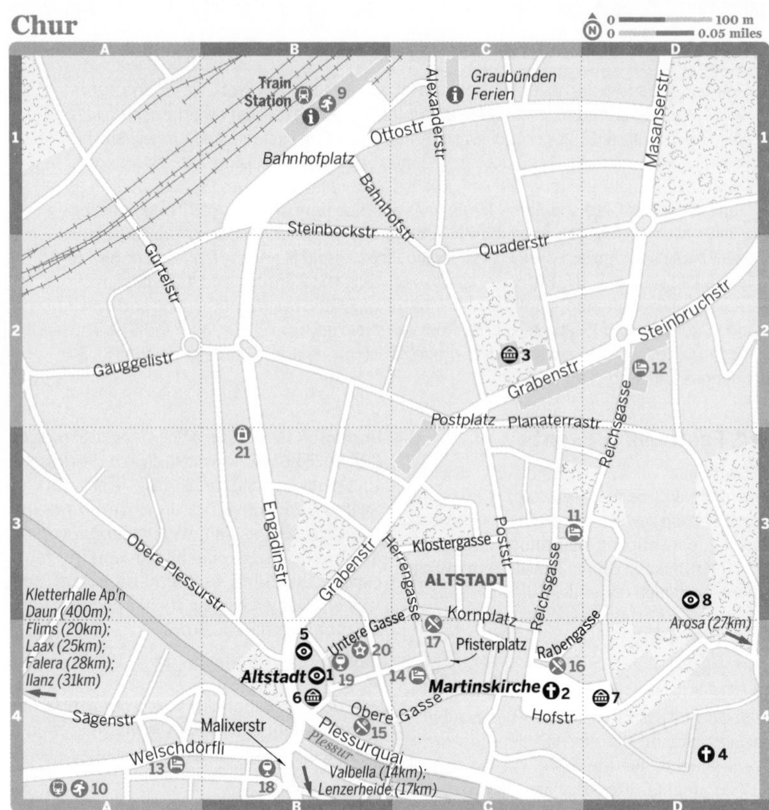


highly regarded restaurant. The chef keeps it fresh and seasonal, serving asparagus (from their own plantation, no less) in spring and game in autumn. Bündner specialities like *Capuns* (egg pasta and sausage wrapped in chard), *Maluns* (like rösti) and *Gerstensuppe* (barley soup) are beautifully cooked.

**Drei Bünde** SWISS €€

(☎081 252 27 76; www.dreibuende.ch; Rabengasse 2; mains from Sfr22; ⏲11am-2pm & 5.30-11pm Tue-Sat) Huddled down a sidestreet just off Martinsplatz, this warm, pine-clad wine tavern is an inviting spot for meaty classics – from spot-on schnitzel to beef medallions.

## Drinking & Entertainment

A buoyant student population keeps the bars and clubs pumping, especially on weekends around Untere Gasse in the Old Town and along Welschdörfli.

**Tom's Beer Box** PUB

(www.toms.ch; Untere Gasse 11; ⏲5pm-midnight Mon-Thu, 3pm-1am Fri & Sat) The bottle-top window is a shrine to beer at this chilled haunt in the Old Town, where locals spill outside to socialise and guzzle one of 140 brews.

**Felsenbar** BAR

(☎081 284 50 50; www.fels.bar; Welschdörfli 1; ⏲5pm-2am Tue-Thu, to 3am Fri & Sat, 1-8pm Sun) Themed parties from DJ battles to beer pong attract a vivacious bunch to this all-black haunt, set around a horseshoe bar just over the river from the Old Town.

**Werkstatt Chur** ARTS CENTRE

(☎081 525 42 46; http://werkstattchur.ch; Untere Gasse 9; ⏲5pm-midnight Mon-Thu, to 1am Fri & Sat) A coppersmith factory turned dynamic cultural centre, hosting gigs, jam sessions, arthouse film screenings, plays and parties. See the website for what's coming up.

## Chur

**Top Sights**
1 Altstadt....B4
2 Martinskirche....C4

**Sights**
3 Bündner Kunstmuseum....C2
4 Kathedrale St Maria Himmelfahrt....D4
5 Malteserturm....B4
6 Obertor....B4
7 Rätisches Museum....D4
8 Sennhofturm....D3

**Activities, Courses & Tours**
9 Bernina Express....B1
10 Brambrüesch....A4

**Sleeping**
11 Hotel Freieck....C3
12 Romantik Hotel Stern....D2
13 VIVA Hostel....A4
14 Zunfthaus zur Rebleuten....C4

**Eating**
Bündner Stube....(see 12)
15 Da Mamma....B4
16 Drei Bünde....C4
17 Evviva Plankis....C4

**Drinking & Nightlife**
18 Felsenbar....B4
19 Tom's Beer Box....B4

**Entertainment**
20 Werkstatt Chur....B4

**Shopping**
21 Rätische Gerberei....B3

## Shopping

**Rätische Gerberei** ARTS & CRAFTS
(081 252 52 42; www.felle.ch; Engadinstrasse 30; 1.30-6.30pm Mon, 8am-noon & 1.30-6pm Tue-Fri, 9am-noon & 1.30-4pm Sat) Upstairs at this shop between the train station and the Old Town are mountains of fluffy sheepskins, while downstairs are genuine cowbells for a fraction of the price you'd pay elsewhere.

## Information

**Tourist Office** (081 252 18 18; www.churtourismus.ch; Bahnhofplatz 3; 8am-8pm Mon-Fri, 9am-12.15pm & 1.15-6pm Sat, 10am-12.15pm & 1.15-6pm Sun) You'll find this office downstairs at the train station.

## Getting There & Away

There are frequent rail connections to Klosters (Sfr11, 1¼ hours) and Davos (Sfr15.50, 1½ hours), and fast trains to Sargans (Sfr11.40, 20 minutes), with onward connections to Liechtenstein and Zürich (Sfr41, 1¼ to 1½ hours). Postal buses leave from the terminus above the train station. The A13 freeway runs north from Chur to Zürich and Lake Constance.

## Getting Around

Bahnhofplatz is the hub for all local buses, which cost Sfr2.80 per journey (valid for changes for 30 minutes).

Aldstadt is mostly pedestrian only. Look for signs to several parking garages on the edge of the Old Town (eg on Gäuggelistrasse).

**Avis** (081 300 33 77; www.avis.com; Comercialstrasse 20; 7.30am-noon & 2-6pm Mon-Fri, to 2pm Sat) has rental cars.

# Lenzerheide & Valbella

POP 1540 / ELEV 1500M

Straddling the blue Heidsee, these twin Alpine resorts bombard you with mountainous wooded splendour, and appeal to families with their low-key atmosphere. Only 15km south of Chur, they're easily reached by postal bus or car, although it's a solid climb to get there. Lenzerheide is flooded with day trippers in summer, and most come to enjoy the outdoors, hiking in summer and skiing in winter. To add to the excitement, it's possible to ski or hike over to the neighbouring resort town of Arosa, in the next valley to the east.

## Activities

Among the area's 170km of hiking trails, the five- to seven-hour trek to 2865m Parpaner Rothorn (p281) stands out as one of the best. Head over to Arosa, or start there and hike to Lenzerheide.

Kids can let off excess energy on the **Globi Trail**, with activities from pine-cone throwing to splashy water games. In high season, kid-friendly activities range from circus days to llama trekking and igloo building – ask the tourist office for details.

### Mountain Biking

Lenzerheide is one of the top mountain-biking and freeriding centres in the country, with 305km of marked routes, 1000km of self-guided GPS tours and several knuckle-whitening downhill tracks.

**Activ Sport Baselgia** MOUNTAIN BIKING

(www.activ-sport.ch; Voa Sporz 19; ⌚ 8.30am-noon & 2-6.30pm Mon-Fri, to 5pm Sat) Activ Sport Baselgia rents mountain bikes/downhill bikes/e-bikes/kids bikes for Sfr42/70/49/28 per day in summer, plus snowshoes/cross-country skis for Sfr19/40. Enquire about its winter snowshoeing tours (around Sfr50).

### Winter Sports

**Skiing in Lenzerheide** SKIING

(http://lenzerheide.com; ski pass adult/child 1 day Sfr72/24, 6 days Sfr332/111, cross-country day/week pass Sfr8/25) Lift queues are a rare sight in Lenzerheide with skiing on 225km of slopes that link with neighbouring Arosa, mostly geared towards beginners and intermediates, as well as some glorious off-piste skiing. Snowboarders hit the rails, boxes and kickers at the snow park. Cross-country skiers can glissade along 56km of tracks. Family-oriented activities include 80km of winter walking trails and a 3km toboggan run.

## Sleeping & Eating

These busy Alpine resorts live on visitors and there are lots of places to stay. Pop into the tourist office for a list of holiday apartments and chalets.

**Camping St Cassian** CAMPGROUND €

(☎ 081 384 24 72; www.st-cassian.ch; Voia Principala 106, Lenz; sites per adult/child/tent/car Sfr8.40/4.70/9.50/2.50; P 📶) Popular with cyclists, this tree-shaded campground is 3km south of Lenzerheide. Expect pin-drop peace, mountain vistas and first-rate facilities, including barbecue areas and a restaurant.

★ **Berghotel Tgantieni** HOTEL €€

(☎ 081 384 12 86; www.tgantieni.ch; Voa Tgantieni 17; r per person winter/summer from Sfr130/90; P 📶) The cowbells are your wake-up call at this hotel, high on a hill above Lenzerheide, with a dreamy mountain panorama and the slopes and trails right on your doorstep. The light, spacious rooms open onto balconies or terraces. Maximise the view with drinks and snacks at the hotel's Marola hut.

**Hotel Kurhaus** BOUTIQUE HOTEL €€

(☎ 081 384 11 34; www.kurhaus-lenzerheide.ch; Voa Principala 40, Lenzerheide; d/apt from Sfr160/400; P 📶) Historic meets modern at this young-at-heart hotel on the main road through Lenzerheide. The pick of the rooms sport razor-sharp decor, with monochrome hues, funky log tables and mountain-facing balconies. Downstairs you'll find a rustic-chic restaurant and a cinema-turned-nightclub.

★ **La Riva** INTERNATIONAL €€

(☎ 081 384 26 00; www.la-riva.ch; Voa Davos Lai 27; mains from Sfr26; ⌚ 11.30am-11pm Wed-Sun; 👪) Hailed for the freshness of its regional produce and its inventive menus, La Riva has an elegant pine interior and views across Heidsee lake. It's a highly atmospheric setting for exquisitely presented specialities, like chanterelle soup with venison ham and Thai-style breast of guinea fowl.

## Information

**Lenzerheide Tourist Office** (☎ 081 385 57 00; http://lenzerheide.com; Voa Principala 37; ⌚ 8.30am-6pm Mon-Sat, 8.30am-noon & 3-6pm Sun Dec-late Apr, shorter hours May-Nov) This office is on the main road, opposite the bus stop.

## Getting There & Around

Either resort is easily reached by an hourly bus from Chur (Sfr10.60, 30 minutes). In the high summer and winter seasons, a free bus operates between Lenzerheide and Valbella.

# Arosa

POP 3350 / ELEV 1800M

If you're into the outdoors and mountain resorts, Arosa is like a dream come true. Framed by the peaks of Weisshorn, Hörnli and moraine-streaked Schiesshorn, it is a superb Alpine all-rounder: perfect for downhill and cross-country skiers in winter, hikers and downhill bikers in summer, and families year-round with heaps of activities to amuse kids. It's also possible to ski and hike over to the neighbouring resort of Lenzerheide.

Getting there is plenty of fun too. Although only 30km southeast of Chur, the journey is nothing short of spectacular. The road zigzags up from Chur in a series of 365 hairpin bends so challenging that Arosa cannot be reached by postal buses. Alternatively, the one-hour scenic train ride from Chur will keep you on the edge of your seat.

## Activities

**Tschuggen Bergoase Spa** SPA

(Sonnenbergstrasse; http://en.tschuggen.ch/spa; Tschuggen Grand Hotel; nonguest morning/evening pass Sfr65, massage from Sfr80; ⌚ 7am-9pm) The Tshuggen Bergoase is not only a grand spa but also an architectural statement, thanks to Mario Botta, one of the country's best-known 'starchitects'. Bold, beautiful and respectful to its surrounds with its leaf-inspired forms and wood and granite textures, you could do worse than book a treatment or entry pass to this special spot.

### Winter Activities

Arosa attracts skiers of all levels with 225km of pistes, combined with Lenzerheide, rising as high as Weisshorn at 2653m. Big-air fans should check out the half-pipe and fun park. Cross-country skiing is equally superb, with 30km of prepared *Loipen* (tracks) stretching from Maran's gentle forest trails to challenging routes at La Isla and Ochsenalp.

There's plenty to amuse families and non-skiers in winter. You can stomp through the snow on 40km of prepared winter walking trails, twirl across an open-air ice rink, or rock up for a game of curling.

**Swiss Ski and Snowboard School** SKIING
(081 378 75 00; www.sssa.ch; Seeblickstrasse; 8.30am-5.30pm) The downhill ski school in Arosa, at the bottom of the Hörnli Express.

**Langlauf- und Skiwanderschule Geeser** SKIING
(081 377 22 15; www.geeser-arosa.ch; Maranerstrasse; 9am-noon & 1-6pm) Langlauf- und Skiwanderschule Geeser offers equipment rental and instruction, with cross-country and snowshoe taster sessions from Sfr55. You can also book guided snowshoe hikes (Sfr50 to Sfr70).

**Prätschli** SNOW SPORTS
Prätschli is the start of a floodlit 1km toboggan run through twinkling woodlands.

### Summer Activities

Arosa's backyard has 200km of maintained **hiking trails**. Scenic options include the 3½-hour uphill trudge to **Weisshorn** and the easy forest rambles shadowing the Plessur to **Litzirüti** (one hour) and **Langwies** (two hours). Kids love to spot red squirrels on the **Eichhörnchenweg**.

**Mountain bikers** are in their element with 700km of trails to explore. For knuckle-whitening thrills, hire a downhill bike to race from Mittelstation to Litzirüti or from Hörnli to Arosa; both tracks involve descents of more than 500m.

**Parpaner Rothorn** HIKING
The 18km, five- to seven-hour trek to Parpaner Rothorn begins at the Hörnli Express gondola station. This hike climbs up through meadows, past the lakes of Schwellisee and Älplisee, to the rust-red peak of Parpaner Rothorn, then down the other side to Lenzerheide.

OFF THE BEATEN TRACK

### PARC ELA

Switzerland's biggest nature park is **Parc Ela** (www.parc-ela.ch). Spanning nearly 600 sq km and encompassing 19 communities in the Albula-Bergün and Savognin-Bivio areas, the park is over three times the size of the Swiss National Park. Three cultures and three languages (German, Romansh and Italian) feature here in this area of historic transport routes. If you have the time and inclination, the spectacular 15-day **Veia Parc Ela** hike takes you through the park's most enchanting Alpine landscapes.

## Festivals & Events

Look out for horse racing and football on the snow in January.

**Arosa Classic Car** RACE
(www.arosaclassiccar.ch; Sep) Vintage motors make a mad dash on the winding road from Langwies to Arosa.

## Sleeping

**Arosa Vetter Hotel** HOTEL €€
(081 378 80 00; www.arosa-vetter-hotel.ch; Seeblickstrasse; s/d Sfr165/210; P) Looking sharp, Vetter has rustic-chic rooms done out in dark wood and stone. Breakfast is a treat with local yoghurt, cheese, eggs, bread and homemade jam. The restaurant dishes up seasonally inspired fare. This place is extremely convenient to the train station and lifts.

**Hotel Arlenwald** HOTEL €€
(081 377 18 38; www.arlenwaldhotel.ch; Prätschli; s/d Sfr140/280; P) Direct access to Burestübli is just one of the perks of staying at this hotel at Prätschli (1908m). The spacious, light-flooded rooms feature loads of chunky pine, antique family heirlooms and mountain-facing balconies. Venture down to the sauna for views of snow-capped peaks.

★**Waldhotel** HISTORIC HOTEL €€€
(081 378 55 55; www.waldhotel.ch; s/d/ste from Sfr200/430/660; P) This forest hideaway is where Nobel Prize–winning German novelist Thomas Mann spent the first weeks of his exile. The luxurious chalet exudes old-world charm with its warm pine-clad rooms and guests arriving by horse-drawn carriage.

## Eating & Drinking

**Hörnlihütte** MEDITERRANEAN €
(☎081 377 15 04; http://hoernliarosa.ch; snacks & light meals Sfr8.50-20; ⏲9am-5pm) This top-of-the-mountain hut at 2511m at the peak of the Hörnli Express is a scenic spot for a bowl of goulash or macaroni.

**Sennerei Maran** CHEESE €
(☎081 377 22 77; www.sennerei-maran.ch; Maranerstrasse; snacks & light meals Sfr8-14.50; ⏲10am-6pm) Fill your picnic basket with award-winning cheese from this dairy. Or refuel over a cheese platter or a slice of cheesecake in the cafe.

★ **Burestübli** SWISS €€
(☎081 377 18 38; www.arlenwaldhotel.ch; Hotel Arlenwald, Prätschli; mains from Sfr25; ⏲8am-midnight) This woodsy chalet on the forest edge affords magical above-the-treetop views. Come winter, it's beloved by ruddy-faced sledders who huddle around pots of gooey fondue, butter-soft steaks and mugs of glühwein before a floodlit dash through the snow. The marvellously eccentric chef prides himself on using first-rate local produce.

**Grischuna Arosa** SWISS €€
(☎081 377 17 01; www.grischuna-arosa.ch; Poststrasse; mains from Sfr18.50; ⏲noon-2pm & 7-10pm) The enormous cowbells hanging in the window of this low-beamed, antique-filled tavern grab your attention. It's a convivial spot for Graubünden specialities, such as homemade *Capuns,* cheese-topped rösti and fresh game in season.

**Los Arosa** BAR
(☎081 356 56 10; www.losbar.ch; Poststrasse, Haus Madrisa; ⏲4pm-2am Mon-Fri, 2pm-2am Sat & Sun) Slope-side imbibing aside, this is where the party is in winter. Expect a laid-back crowd, DJs, foosball and shots aplenty.

## Information

**Tourist Office** (☎081 378 70 20; www.arosa.ch; Poststrasse, Sport- und Kongresszentrum; ⏲8am-6pm Mon-Fri, 9am-noon & 1-4pm Sat & Sun) Helpful tourist office with details on bike and scooter rental.

## Getting There & Around

The only way to reach Arosa is from Chur: take the hourly narrow-gauge train that leaves from in front of the train station (Sfr15.40, one hour). It's a winding journey chugging past mountains, pine trees, streams and bridges. The train crosses the oldest steel-and-concrete rail bridge ever built. At 62m high, it's a dizzying engineering feat, completed in 1914.

By car, it's a winding 30km drive from Chur that will take 40 minutes with good road conditions.

Buses in the resort are free. Drivers should note a traffic ban from midnight to 6am.

# Flims, Laax & Falera

POP 4200

They say that if the snow ain't falling elsewhere, you'll surely find some around Flims, Laax and Falera. This high-altitude trio forms the Weisse Arena (White Arena), with 220km of slopes catering for all levels. Host of the Laax Open in January, Laax is a mecca for party-loving snowboarders seeking big air.

Both Flims and Laax have witnessed a design explosion in recent years, with architects eschewing cutesy Alpine kitsch in favour of contemporary cool. There's history here too, though. The oldest surviving building in Laax was built in 1580 and the first hotel went up in 1880.

## Sights

**Caumasee** LAKE
Ringed by thick woods, this exquisitely turquoise lake is a 15-minute stroll and then short lift ride south of Flims Waldhaus. It's an attractive spot for a cool summer swim. You can hire a rowboat and eat at a restaurant terrace overlooking the lake. It's known as 'Lag la Cauma' in Romansh, meaning Lake Siesta.

**St Remigiuskirche** CHURCH
(Falera) This Romanesque church is perched on a hill that has been a site of worship since prehistoric times, as attested by the line-up of modest menhirs leading up to it. Inside the shingle-roofed church is a striking mid-17th-century fresco depicting the Last Supper. From the cemetery you can see deep into the Vorderrhein Valley.

## Activities

### Winter Activities

**Skiing in Laax** SKIING
(www.laax.com; adult/child 1-day pass incl ski buses Sfr75/50) Laax is a riders' mecca, boasting both Europe's smallest and largest half-pipe, excellent freestyle parks and many off-piste opportunities. Skiers can bash the pistes in the interlinked resorts, with 235km of varied slopes (most above 2000m) to suit all but the most hard-core black-run freaks. You'll probably spy the unfortunately named Crap da Flem (crap means 'peak' in Romansch).

### Summer Activities

In summer, the hiking network spans 250km.

**★Ruinaulta** HIKING

(Rhine Gorge) A dramatic 3½-hour trek leads through the glacier-gouged, 400m-deep Ruinaulta, hailed the 'Swiss Grand Canyon'. Beginning in Trin, 7km east of Flims, the trail shadows the swiftly flowing Vorderrhein River and shimmies past limestone cliffs that have been eroded into a veritable forest of pinnacles and columns.

**Pinut Via Ferrata** VIA FERRATA

(www.flims.com; guided tour per person Sfr135; ⏲mid-May–Oct) Traverse soaring rock faces and get an eagle's-eye view of the valley on the Pinut *via ferrata*, considered the oldest *via ferrata* in Switzerland still in use. First mention of it was in 1739, but don't worry, it's been fully renovated of late. It costs around Sfr25 to hire the gear from sports shops or the tourist office in Flims.

**Alpine Nature Trail** WALKING

The 6km Alpine Nature Trail at the summit of Cassons provides information on geology and the flora and fauna of the region, and is brilliant for spotting wild Alpine flowers and critters.

**Swissraft** RAFTING

(☎081 911 52 50; www.swissraft.ch) Taking you through the Rhine Gorge, the turbulent 17km stretch of the Vorderrhein between Ilanz and Reichenau is white-water-rafting heaven. This company organises half-/full-day rafting trips for Sfr115/165, as well as canoeing (Sfr125) and hydrospeeding (Sfr140).

## Sleeping & Eating

There are lots of places to stay in this trio of resort villages. Ask the tourist office for a list of good-value holiday houses and apartments.

**Riders Palace** HOSTEL €

(☎081 927 97 00; www.riderspalace.ch; Via Murschetg 1, Laax Murschetg; dm/d from Sfr45/190; P 📶) Sleep? Dream on. This design-focused boutique hostel draws party-mad riders to its strikingly lit, bare concrete spaces. Choose between basic five-bed dorms, slick rooms with Philippe Starck tubs, and hi-tech suites complete with PlayStation and Dolby surround sound. It's 200m from the Laax lifts. Rates are cheaper outside the main season.

**★Posta Veglia** HISTORIC HOTEL €€

(☎081 921 44 66; www.postaveglia.ch; Via Principala 54, Laax; d & ste Sfr180-230; P 📶) Today this 19th-century post office delivers discreet service and rustic flavour. The eight country-cottage-style rooms and suites are filled with wooden furnishings, while suites up the romance (and price) with everything from beams to waterbeds and star-gazing bathtubs. The restaurant (mains from Sfr29) is feted for Bündner classics like *Gerstensuppe* (Swiss barley soup) and *Capuns* (egg pasta and sausage wrapped in chard).

**Arena Flims** GUESTHOUSE €€

(☎081 911 24 00; www.arenaflims.ch; Via Prau da Monis 2, Flims; lodge/guesthouse per person from Sfr55/85; P 📶) At the base station in Flims, this place lures snowboarders with its designer digs, DJs and gigs. There are lots of sleeping options here with a lodge, guesthouse and penthouse. Throw in the restaurant and the lively **Arena Bar** and these guys have got it covered.

**Fidazerhof** HOTEL €€

(☎081 920 90 10; www.fidazerhof.ch; Via da Fidaz 34, Flims-Fidaz; s/d from Sfr145/190; P 📶) This dark-wood chalet is a relaxing escape, with its expansive Alpine views, sunny rooms sporting hardwood floors and a spa where Ayurveda treatments invite a post-ski unwind. Slow food is the word in the restaurant, which prepares wonderful regional and vegetarian food. Snuggle by the fireplace in winter.

**★Cavigilli** MEDITERRANEAN €€

(☎081 911 01 25; www.cavigilli.ch; Via Arviul 1, Flims Dorf; mains from Sfr37; ⏲11.30am-2pm & 6.30-10.30pm Mon-Fri, 11.30am-10.30pm Sat & Sun) Flims' oldest house, dating from 1453, comprises a Gothic parlour and an elegant beamed dining room. The accent is on market-fresh produce in refined dishes that list primary ingredients, along the lines of scallops with watermelon, chickpeas, mango and herbs, and pigeon with May turnip, blackcurrant, almond and star anise.

## Drinking & Nightlife

**Riders Palace Club** BAR

(www.riderspalace.ch; Laax Murschetg; ⏲4pm-4am) The favourite hang-out of freestyle dudes, this too-cool bar in the lobby of the eponymous hostel rocks to gigs and DJs spinning beats into the blurry-eyed hours.

**Crap Bar** BAR
(☎081 927 99 45; Laax-Murschetg lifts; ⏰4pm-2am) Crap by name but not by nature, this après-ski hot spot is shaped from 24 tonnes of granite. It's the place to slam shots, check your email and shimmy in your snow boots after a day pounding powder.

## Information

**Main Tourist Office** (☎081 920 92 00; www.alpenarena.ch; Via Nova 62, Flims; ⏰8am-6pm Mon-Fri, to noon Sat mid-Jun–mid-Aug, to 5pm Mon-Sat mid-Dec–mid-Apr) The main tourist office is in Flims.

## Getting There & Around

Postal buses run to Flims and the other villages in the White Arena area hourly from Chur (Sfr14.20 to Flims Dorf, 35 minutes), which lies 20km to the east. A free local shuttle bus connects the three villages.

# Vals

POP 990 / ELEV 1252M

The gorgeous Graubünden village of Vals (1252m) sits in the Valsertal (Vals Valley), 20km south of Ilanz. While the village itself is full of attractive weathered wooden buildings and shingle roofs, the mountainsides above are green Alpine pastures, liberally scattered with chalets and shepherds' huts.

Swiss people will tell you that Vals is the home to Valser mineral water and the company's factory greets you as you enter the village, but it is also known for its soothing warm waters, especially since Basel-born architect Peter Zumthor worked his magic to transform Therme Vals' thermal baths into a temple of cutting-edge cool. There's history here, though; Vals' first spa hotel opened in 1893.

Valstertal is a tributary valley with the Glogn River flowing north to join the Vorderrhein at Ilanz. It's a dead-end, so you go out the same way you came in.

## Activities

There is some modest downhill skiing in the heights above Vals in winter, plus some good hiking in summer.

**7132 Therme** SPA
(☎058 7132 011; http://7132therme.com; adult/child Sfr80/52, with Vals guest card Sfr45/30; ⏰11am-8pm) Using 60,000 slabs of local quartzite, Peter Zumthor created one of Switzerland's most enchanting thermal spas. Aside from heated indoor and outdoor pools, this grey-stone labyrinth hides watery nooks and crannies; it's cleverly lit and full of cavernous atmosphere. Enjoy bath-warm Feuerbad (42°C; 107.6°F) and perfumed Blütenbad, sweat it out in the steam room and cool down in the teeth-chattering Eisbad.

**Zervreilasee** HIKING
Eight kilometres south of Vals, this lake was formed when a 151m-high dam was completed in 1957, flooding the village of Zervreila. The lake is overshadowed by the frosted 3402m peak of Rheinwaldhorn. Access is usually only possible from June to October, when there are some excellent trails to hike. Ask for advice at the tourist office.

## Sleeping

As well as a few hotels and B&Bs, there are holiday apartments – check out www.vals.ch.

★**Brücke 49** B&B €€
(☎081 420 49 49; www.brucke49.ch; Poststrasse 49; d from Sfr200; P 📶) A clean Nordic aesthetic is paired with Alpine warmth at this incredibly chic little B&B, which Ruth and Thomas run with heartfelt passion. The individually decorated rooms feature bare-wood floors, muted colours and a designer flourish. An open fireplace, garden and reading room invite lingering. Breakfast is as special as the rest, with top-quality, local farm produce and homemade bread.

**7132 Hotel** DESIGN HOTEL €€€
(☎058 7132 000; http://7132.com; Vals; d from Sfr533; P 📶) This 1960s colossus has had a rebrand and its rooms have been revamped under the design skills of world-famous architects Peter Zumthor from Switzerland, Tadao Ando and Kengo Kuma from Japan, and American Thom Mayne. Check out the website and pick your package. 7132 also features three restaurants and a bar.

## Information

**Tourist Office** (☎081 920 70 70; www.vals.ch; ⏰9-11.30am & 2-5pm Mon-Sat) Located on the main road into the village on the right.

## Getting There & Away

Postal buses run more or less hourly to Vals (Sfr13.20, 40 minutes) from Ilanz (itself reached by regular train from Chur; Sfr16.60, 35 minutes).

By a winding road, Vals is 20km south of Ilanz.

## Disentis/Mustér

POP 2070 / ELEV 1130M

This small village in western Graubünden – Disentis in German and Mustér in Romansh – is officially called Disentis/Mustér. It's part of the Surselva region of the canton, and it and the surrounding valleys and highlands are home to some 20,000 Romansh speakers.

Rising like a vision above Disentis/Mustér and easily visible from the train station if you're passing through on the Glacier Express (p163) is the massive Benedictine monastery, Kloster Disentis. Glacier Express riders get to hop off the train here for about 15 minutes as engines are changed – cogwheel engines take over for the steep climb to the Oberalp Pass at 2044m, about 21km to the west. While few make the effort to stay here, heading either west to Andermatt or east to Chur, it makes an attractive stopover.

### Sights

**Kloster Disentis** MONASTERY

(www.kloster-disentis.ch; Via Claustra 1; museum adult/child Sfr10/5; museum 8.30-5pm) This Benedictine monastery, which towers above Disentis/Mustér, has a lavishly stuccoed baroque church attached. A monastery has stood here since the 8th century, but the present immense complex dates from the 18th century. The **Klostermuseum** is crammed with memorabilia on the monastery's history.

### Sleeping

**Hotel Alpsu** HOTEL €

(081 947 51 17; www.hotelalpsu.ch; Via Alpsu 4; s/d/tr/q from Sfr75/120/165/200; P ) Festooned with geraniums in summer, central Hotel Alpsu has individually decorated rooms. It's ideally located: a five-minute walk from the train station and a similar distance to the monastery. The restaurant does fine renditions of *Capuns* and *Pizokel* (noodles).

### Information

**Tourist Office** (081 920 40 30; www.disentis-sedrun.ch; Disentis/Mustér train station; 7.30am-5.45pm Mon-Fri, from 7.50am Sat & Sun) This office is located at the train station.

### Getting There & Away

Trains travel west to Andermatt (Sfr21.20, one hour) over the Oberalp Pass and east to Chur (Sfr30, 1¼ hours).

Disentis/Mustér is on the N19, 32km east of Andermatt and 60km west of Chur.

# BÜNDNER HERRSCHAFT

North of Chur, Bündner Herrschaft is known as wine country, especially the region east of the Rhine River called **Fünf Dörfer** (Five Villages) – Fläsch, Maienfeld, Jenins, Malans and Zizers. This is the canton's premier wine region, dominated by the Blauburgunder (Pinot noir) grape variety that yields some memorable reds. A gentle wander through this area of vineyards is most enjoyable.

The peaceful town of Bad Ragaz with its numerous sculptures and thermal waters is the centre for what is now being marketed as 'Heidiland' – the surrounding region of 17 communities and 37 small towns. Although Heidi was a fictional figure, the region has laid claim to her and you're likely to run into all sorts of Heidi-related places.

## Bad Ragaz & Around

POP 4950 / ELEV 502M

The graceful little town of Bad Ragaz sits beside the Rhine River and features a spa that opened in 1840, attracting the bath-loving likes of Douglas Fairbanks and Mary Pickford. The fabled waters are said to boost the immune system and improve circulation. While visitors still come to bathe, today they also come to ski, hike, play golf, peruse the neighbouring vineyards and enjoy the genteel nature of the region and the town, which has gone out of its way to fill itself with lovely and intriguing sculptures.

Just across the river, the neighbouring village of Maienfeld makes a good spot to sample the local wine – and indulge your personal 'Heidi' fantasy (p286), if you're so inclined.

### Activities

**Fünf Seen Wanderung** HIKING

(Five Lake Walk) One of the region's top day hikes, the Fünf Seen Wanderung begins at the 2227m Pizolhütte. The five-hour walk takes in a crest of limestone peaks, glaciers and five jewel-coloured lakes. The views of the Swiss and Austrian Alps are incredible.

**Tamina Therme** SPA

(081 303 27 40; www.taminatherme.ch; Hans-Albrecht-Strasse; weekday ticket adult/child Sfr36/22; 8am-10pm Sun-Thu, to 11pm Fri) Bad Ragaz' ultra-sleek Tamina Therme has several pools for wallowing in the 36.5°C (97.7°F) thermal waters, as well as massage jets, whirlpools, saunas, and an assortment of treatments and massages.

WORTH A TRIP

### HEIDIDORF

**Maienfeld**, 3km east of Bad Ragaz, is where to start your Heidiland experience. Johanna Spyri (1827–1901) had the idea of basing the story of Heidi in the countryside around Maienfeld, and the locals had the worse idea of identifying one local village as Heidi's. It is now called – you guessed it! – Heididorf. There's a 1½-hour **Heidi Loop Trail** from Maienfeld across idyllic country to get you there. There's not much to be found except Heidihaus, where of course, she never lived because she never existed.

You can also visit the **Heidi Shop** (www.heididorf.ch; Bahnhofstrasse 1; 10am-5pm Mar-Nov) in central Maienfeld for all your Heidi-related needs. When you're done, you might be in the mood for some Heidiwein for your Heidiheadache. Even more extreme, the whole surrounding region is now doing its tourism marketing under the banner 'Heidiland' (www.heidiland.com).

**Pizol** SKIING
(081 300 48 20; www.pizol.com; adult/child day pass Sfr54/27) The forest-cloaked slopes of Pizol, rising up above Bad Ragaz, attract beginner and intermediate skiers with 40km of runs in winter. Those same slopes buzz with hikers in summer.

**Sculpture Promenade** WALKING
Drop by the tourist office and pick up a map for Bad Ragaz's unique Sculpture Promenade. This peaceful town is know for having art and sculptures dotted all over the place, with the main attraction being its Sculpture Promenade, which will take you about an hour to stroll around.

**Vinothek Von Salis** WINE
(081 300 60 60; www.vonsalis-wein.ch; Kruseckgasse 3, Maienfeld; 2-6pm Mon-Fri, 9.30am-4pm Sat) For some wine tasting and to brush up on your knowledge of local tipples, make sure that you head to convivial Vinothek von Salis.

## Sleeping & Eating

★**Schlaf Fass** GUESTHOUSE €€
(http://schlaf-fass.ch; Weingut zur Bündte, Maienfeld; per person from Sfr90; P) Should you have overindulged on the local plonk, for a unique experience, you can spend the night in one of two giant wine barrels at Schlaf Fass, among the vineyards northeast of Maienfeld. You'll want to check out the website to see how this works!

**Hotel Krone** HOTEL €€
(081 303 84 44; www.kroneragaz.ch; Kronenplatz 10; s Sfr84-97, d Sfr160; P) The lovely place, right in the centre of Bad Ragaz, has slickly renovated, individually decorated rooms, plus its own excellent restaurant. You're sure to end up taking photos not only of the rooms, but of the building itself as it's so cute and has been around, operating as a hotel, since the late 19th century.

**Hotel Schloss Ragaz** HOTEL €€
(081 303 77 77; www.hotelschlossragaz.ch; Schlossstrasse; s/d from Sfr160/280; P) This historic hotel is a petite, turreted castle with spacious and quiet quarters framed by beautifully manicured gardens. The restaurant is very popular and lots of non-guests come to dine. Treat yourself to a day at the spa to soothe away your stress with back-to-nature treatments.

**Weinstube Alter Torkel** SWISS €€
(081 302 36 75; www.torkel.ch; Jeninserstrasse 3, Malans; mains from Sfr30; 9am-11pm) Stop off for a glass of the local Pinot noir and have lunch on the vine-facing terrace at Weinstube Alter Torkel in Malans. Working with seasonal produce, the rustic wine cellar churns out terrific local fare along the lines of crispy roast pork served with Pinot noir sauce and potato gratin.

## Information

**Tourist Office** (081 300 40 20; www.heidiland.com; Am Platz 1; 8.30am-noon &1-5pm Mon-Fri, 9am-2pm Sat) Located in the middle of town, 900m south of the train station down Bahnhofstrasse.

## Getting There & Away

Bad Ragaz is on the Chur–Zürich railway line. Trains from Chur via Maienfeld run hourly (Sfr9, 15 minutes). Zürich is 1¼ hours away (Sfr34).

It's 21km by road from Bad Ragaz to Chur and 99km to Zürich.

# Klosters

POP 4280 / ELEV 1194M

No matter whether you come in summer to hike in the flower-speckled mountains or in winter when the log chalets are veiled in snow and icicle-hung – Klosters is postcard stuff. Indeed, the village has attracted a host of slaloming celebrities and royals with its gorgeous looks and paparazzi-free slopes. This is where a 14-year-old Prince Charles learned to ski, and where Harry and William whizzed down the slopes as tots.

Often paired with Davos, 12km away, it may surprise to find that Klosters is in the valley at 1194m, while Davos is up high at 1560m.

## Activities

### Winter Activities

**Skiing in Klosters** SKIING
(www.davos.ch; Regional Pass 2/6 days Sfr139/332) Davos and Klosters, who work together, share 320km of ski runs covered by the Regional Pass. If you're staying in Klosters, **Parsenn** beckons up to the west and easily connects through to Davos (p288). The vast area reaches as high as Weissfluhjoch (2844m), from where you can ski to Küblis, more than 2000m lower and 12km away.

**Madrisa**, up the eastern side of the valley, is family-friendly, with long, sunny runs, mostly above the treeline.

**Toboggan Run** SNOW SPORTS
(Madrisa; day ticket adult Sfr37, child Sfr15-26; ⏲8.15am-4pm Dec-Apr) Kid-friendly winter activities include this bumpy downhill dash from Madrisa to Saaseralp.

**Horse-Drawn Sleigh** SNOW SPORTS
(☎081 422 18 73; www.pferdekutschen.ch; Doggilochstrasse 1) When the flakes are falling, nothing beats a horse-drawn sleigh ride. Organise this through the tourist office.

### Summer Activities

Hikers can hit the trail on one of the region's 700km of well-maintained footpaths, which range from gentle family strolls to high-altitude, multiday treks. Would-be climbers can tackle the rope bridges and climbing trees at Madrisa.

Mountain and downhill biking are equally popular. See www.davos.ch for inspiration.

**Bardill** CYCLING
(☎081 422 10 40; www.bardill-sport.ch; Landstrasse 185; ⏲8.30am-noon & 2-6.30pm Mon-Fri, 8.30am-12.30pm & 2-5pm Sat) Mountain/electro/tandem bikes cost Sfr30/49/75 per day. It also offers ski rental in winter.

**Gotschna Freeride** MOUNTAIN BIKING
(www.davos.ch/en/summer/activities/bike/mountainbike/gotschna-freeride; ⏲Jun-Oct) This breathtakingly steep 5.7km trail from Gotschna middle station to Klosters is freeride heaven with over 200 banked curves, jumps and waves. Warm up at the skill centre before tackling it.

**R&M Adventure** ADVENTURE SPORTS
(☎079 384 29 36; www.ramadventure.ch; Landstrasse 171) Tailor your own adventure with this reputable company offering white-water rafting and canyoning. Visit the website for options and prices.

**Strandbad Klosters** SWIMMING
(Doggilochstrasse 51; adult/child Sfr7/5; ⏲9am-7pm May-Sep) Enjoy views of the Silvretta Alps as you splash at this heated outdoor pool. There's a kids' play area, volleyball court and a climbing wall suspended above the diving pool.

**Madrisa Land** AMUSEMENT PARK
(www.madrisa-land.ch; Madrisastrasse 7; adult/child incl cable car Sfr24/10; ⏲10am-4.45pm Jul-Oct) This kiddie wonderland on Madrisa has a fairy-tale-themed adventure playground with a flying fox, petting zoo, pony riding, scooters, tree houses and all sorts of family fun.

## Sleeping & Eating

Klosters lives off the tourist franc. Pick up a list of private rooms and apartments from the tourist office. Prices are 30% to 50% cheaper in summer.

**R&M Adventure Hostel** HOSTEL €
(☎081 422 12 29; www.ramadventure.ch; Landstrasse 171; dm/s/d from Sfr45/75/110; P 📶) Bang in the heart of Klosters, R&M has colourful digs, a lounge where you can prepare tea and snacks, and a TV and playroom in the attic. It also offers all sorts of winter and summer adventure activities, such as rafting – check its website for details.

**Steinbock** HOTEL €€
(☎081 422 45 45; www.steinbock-klosters.ch; Landstrasse 146; d from Sfr250; P 📶) The Steinbock has a real up-in-the-mountains feel with its expansive mountain views, rooms clad in honeyed pine and a trio of restaurants dishing up heart-warming Swiss fare. Up the budget and you'll even get your own open fire. All guests can get warm in the whirlpool, sauna and steam room.

★**Romantik Hotel Chesa Grischuna** HISTORIC HOTEL €€€
(☎081 422 22 22; www.chesagrischuna.ch; Bahnhofstrasse 12; s/d/ste from Sfr126/198/234; P 📶) An archetypal vision of a Swiss chalet, this family-run pad has toasty pine rooms with antique flourishes and ornately carved ceilings. The lantern-lit restaurant (mains from Sfr42) is an Alpine charmer, too. Dirndl-clad waitresses bring fresh, seasonal dishes from local trout to roast beef to the table.

★**Kaffee Klatsch Easy** CAFE €
(☎081 422 66 30; www.kaffeeklatsch-klosters.ch; Bahnhofstrasse 8; lunch mains from Sfr16.50; ⏰8am-6pm Mon-Sat; 📶) Catchy Kaffee Klatsch has two operations in Klosters, with Easy, next to the Co-op on Bahnhofstrasse, being a cafe, open during the day for breakfast, lunch, snacks and divine desserts. Everything is homemade. **Kaffee Klatsch Lounge** (☎081 417 68 40; Gotschnastrasse 21; lunch mains from Sfr11.90), on the other side of the tracks next to the Goschna Ski Lift, is open 8.30am to 6pm Friday to Sunday.

## Information

**Tourist Office** (☎081 410 20 20; www.davos.ch/klosters; Alte Bahnhofstrasse 6; ⏰8.30am-noon & 2-6pm Mon-Fri, 9am-5pm Sat, 9am-1pm Sun) Located in the centre of the village.

## Getting There & Around

Klosters is split into two sections. Klosters Platz is the main resort, grouped around the train station. Two kilometres to the left of the station is smaller Klosters Dorf and the Madrisa cable car.

Klosters is on the same train route between Landquart and Filisur as Davos. They are linked by free buses for those with Guest Cards or ski passes.

# Davos

POP 11,700 / ELEV 1560M

Unlike its little sister Klosters, Davos is more cool than quaint. But what the resort lacks in Alpine prettiness, it makes up for with seductive skiing, including monster runs descending up to 2000m, and après-ski parties. The first visitors came to Davos from 1865, when it was discovered that the high-altitude climate proved effective in fighting tuberculosis. These days they come for the excitement of this Alpine resort, both in winter and summer.

Davos is the annual meeting point for the crème de la crème of world capitalism: the World Economic Forum. Global chat fests aside, Davos inspired Sir Arthur Conan Doyle (of Sherlock Holmes fame) to don skis and Thomas Mann to pen *The Magic Mountain*. Davos comprises two contiguous areas, each with a train station: Davos Platz and the older Davos Dorf.

## Sights

★**Kirchner Museum** MUSEUM
(☎081 410 63 00; www.kirchnermuseum.ch; Promenade 82; adult/child Sfr12/5; ⏰11am-6pm Tue-Sun) This giant cube of a museum showcases the world's largest Ernst Ludwig Kirchner (1880–1938) collection. The German expressionist painted extraordinary scenes of the area. When the Nazis classified Kirchner a 'degenerate artist' and emptied galleries of his works, he was overcome with despair and took his own life in 1938.

**Wintersportmuseum** MUSEUM
(☎081 413 24 84; www.wintersportmuseum.ch; Promenade 43; adult/child Sfr5/3; ⏰4.30-6.30pm Tue & Thu Dec-Mar & Jul-Oct) This ski-obsessed museum races you back to an age when skis were wooden planks and snowshoes improvised tennis rackets.

## Activities

### Winter Activities

**Skiing in Davos** SKIING
(www.davos.ch; Regional Pass 2/6 days Sfr139/332) Davos and Klosters (p287) share 320km of ski runs, covered by the Regional Pass, as well as some glorious off-piste terrain. They operate together, but if you're staying in Davos, the **Jakobshorn** lifts on the south side of the valley are superb. Also on the south side is family-friendly **Rinerhorn**.

On the north side, **Parsenn**, with a huge variety of terrain, is accessible from both Davos and Klosters. **Schatzalp/Strela** focuses on 'decelerated' skiing on gentle slopes. It's all magnificent!

Davos is a cross-country hot spot, with 75km of well-groomed trails, including classic and skating options, plus a floodlit track for starlit swishing. It is also laced with toboggan runs, such as the 2.5km floodlit track from Schatzalp to Davos Platz; hire your sled at base station Schatzalp.

**Schweizer Schneesportschule** SKIING
(☎081 416 24 54; www.ssd.ch; Promenade 157) This is one of the best ski and snowboard schools in the country.

## Davos

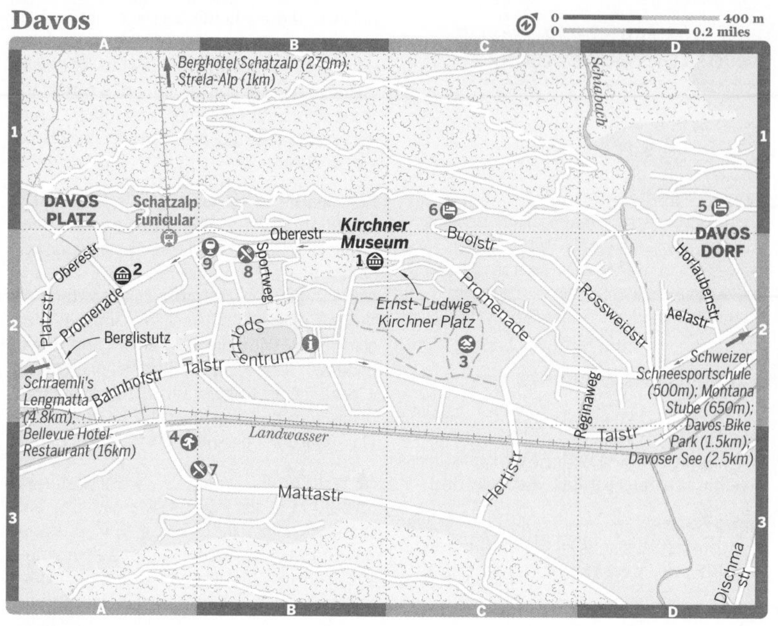




### Summer Activities

Together Davos and Klosters provide 700km of marked hiking paths and 1300km of mountain-bike tracks, including some challenging descents and single-track trails; see www.bike-davos.ch for routes, maps and rental outlets.

Summer water sports include windsurfing and sailing on the **Davoser See** (Davos Lake).

**Flüela Pass** SCENIC DRIVE

Fourteen kilometres southeast of Davos, the road over the magnificent Flüela Pass (2383m) links Davos (1560m) with Susch (1438m) in the lower Engadin Valley. The pass is marked by a beautiful Alpine lake, a hospice and small restaurant. The pass generally opens in June and presents gorgeous Alpine views.

**Davos Bike Park** MOUNTAIN BIKING

(☎081 416 18 68; www.davos.ch/bikepark; Flüelastrasse; ⊙dawn-dusk Jul-Oct) Test your skills on the tables, curves and jumps. Dirt bikes can be hired for Sfr20 per hour.

**Luftchraft – Flugschule Davos** PARAGLIDING

(☎079 623 19 70; www.luftchraft.ch; Mattastrasse 9) Daredevils eager to leap off Jakobshorn or Gotschnagrat can book tandem flights for Sfr175 at this reputable school. Call ahead.

**Eau-là-là** SWIMMING

(www.eau-la-la.ch; Promenade 90; pool adult/child Sfr10/7, day spa Sfr28; ⊙10am-10pm Mon-Sat, to 6pm Sun) If you prefer horizontal sightseeing to vertical drops, try this leisure centre, with heated outdoor pools, splash areas for the kids and a spa with mountain views.

**SUMMER SAVER: DAVOS-KLOSTERS GUEST CARD**

Stay overnight in Davos or Klosters in summer and you'll receive the Guest Card, which entitles you to free use of buses and cable cars, limited travel on the **Rhätische Bahn** (p277), plus free entry to Schatzalp botanical gardens and Davos' artificial ice rink. The card also gives discounts on activities from guided hikes to introductory climbing sessions. See www.davos.ch for details.

## Festivals & Events

**Schwingen** CULTURAL
(www.davos.ch; Aug) Swiss craziness peaks at Sertig Schwinget, with *Schwingen* (Swiss wrestling) champs battling in the sawdust.

**Davos Festival** MUSIC
(www.davosfestival.ch; Aug) Classical music resounds for two weeks at the Davos Festival.

**FIS Cross-Country World Cup** SPORTS
(www.davosnordic.ch; Dec) Davos hosts a round of the FIS Cross-Country World Cup each December.

## Sleeping

Davos is full-on in winter and room rates can plunge by up to 30% in summer.

**Davos Youthpalace** HOSTEL €
(081 410 19 20; www.youthhostel.ch; Horlaubenstrasse 27; dm/s/d from Sfr39/110/114; P) This one-time sanatorium has been transformed into a groovy backpacker palace. Budget-conscious skiers dig the bright, modern dorms with pine bunks (balconies cost a few francs extra), the relaxed lounge and ski storage.

★ **Berghotel Schatzalp** MOUNTAIN HOTEL €€
(081 415 51 51; www.schatzalp.ch; Schatzalp; s/d from Sfr125/230; ) There's something cool about staying at a historic mountain hotel, 300m above Davos, that is reached by its own funicular railway that runs from 8am until midnight. The hotel features both a villa (built in 1907) and a chalet, plus there are two restaurants, a terrace and a piano bar. Good family and beginner skiing is right outside the door.

**Bellevue Hotel-Restaurant** HOTEL €€
(081 404 11 50; http://bellevuewiesen.com; Hauptstrasse 9, Davos Wiesen; d/ste from Sfr139/349; P) In the tranquil village of Wiesen, the Bellevue flaunts boutiquey interiors and extends the warmest of welcomes. Rooms are kitted out in modern Alpine-chic style, with eye-catching wallpaper, muted colours and wood floors. An enticingly cosy lounge, excellent restaurant and mountain-facing terrace seal the deal.

**Schraemli's Lengmatta** B&B €€
(081 413 55 79; www.lengmatta-davos.ch; Lengmattastrasse 19, Davos Frauenkirch; per person from Sfr80; P) Big mountain views await at this sun-blackened timber chalet, which fits the bill nicely. You'll feel bug-snug in pine-clad rooms with checked fabrics and downy bedding. There's a children's playground, a peak-facing terrace and a fine restaurant dishing up Bündner specialities (from Sfr17). Half-board per person is Sfr35.

★ **Waldhotel Davos** HISTORIC HOTEL €€€
(081 415 15 15; www.waldhotel-davos.ch; Buolstrasse 3; s/d from Sfr205/390; P) *The Magic Mountain* in Thomas Mann's eponymous 1924 novel, this built-in-1911 sanatorium-turned-hotel has had a stylish facelift, and even standard rooms come with sunny balconies. When you tire of mountain views, head down to the spa's saltwater pools and saunas. The restaurant matches Grisons cuisine with wines drawn from the award-winning cellar. This hotel is only open in winter.

## Eating

**Kaffee Klatsch** CAFE €
(081 413 30 16; Promenade 72; light meals from Sfr19; 7.30am-9pm Mon-Sat, 8am-9pm Sun) Mellow music creates a relaxed feel in this arty cafe. Try the delicious homemade Swiss muesli for breakfast, filled focaccia or organic salad, or stop by for cake with a speciality coffee like vanilla bean or Heidi latte (made with roasted organic oats). Opens shorter hours in the low season.

**Strela-Alp** SWISS €
(081 413 56 83; www.schatzalp.ch; Schatzalp; mains from Sfr17; 9am-6pm Jul–mid-Oct, to 5pm mid-Oct–Jun; ) Expansive mountain views, a sunny terrace and Swiss grub like rösti and fondue await at this rustic haunt, a 10-minute walk from Schatzalp funicular top station. This is a superb spot to come for lunch.

**Hänggi's** ITALIAN €€
(081 416 20 20; www.haenggis.ch; Mattastrasse 11; pizza/mains from Sfr16/23; 11.30am-2pm & 6-9pm; ) Wood-fired pizza, crisp and delicious, is what this cosy beamed restaurant

is known for. Or go for well-executed Italian-inspired dishes, such as tagliatelle with fresh chanterelles, market-fresh fish and tangy homemade sorbet.

**Montana Stube** SWISS €€
(081 420 71 77; www.montanastube.ch; Bahnhofstrasse 2, Davos Dorf; mains from Sfr24; 5-11pm Wed-Sat; ) Warm and woody, the Montana Stube is a convivial spot for dinner in Davos Dorf. Heavy on the meat and cheese, the menu is Swiss through and through. The fondue chinoise is highly recommended.

## Drinking & Nightlife

**Jatzhütte** BAR
(081 413 73 61; www.jatzhuette.ch; Jakobshorn; from 2.30pm) Perched at 2560m at the top of Jakobshorn, this is Davos' wackiest après-ski joint. Those who dare to partially bare can soak in a 39°C (102.2°F) whirlpool framed by icy peaks.

**Mountain's Akt** BAR
(079 829 79 16; www.facebook.com/mountainsakt; Promenade 64; 3pm-1am Tue-Thu & Sun, to 4am Fri & Sat; ) DJs spin house and electro at the weekend at this funky bar. There's a great selection of beers from Kilkenny to Leffe. The summer beer garden becomes a snow bar in winter.

## Information

**Tourist Office** (081 415 21 21; www.davos.ch; Tourismus- und Sportzentrum, Talstrasse 41; 8.30am-6pm Mon-Fri, 1-5pm Sat, 9am-1pm Sun) The most central branch of the tourist office is in Davos Platz. It's well stocked with maps and brochures.

## Getting There & Away

For trains to Chur (Sfr15.50, 1½ hours) or Zürich (Sfr28, 2½ hours), you will change at Landquart. For St Moritz (Sfr30, 1½ hours), take the train at Davos Platz and change at Filisur. For the hourly service to Scuol (Sfr32, 1¼ hours) in the Unterengadin, take the train from Davos Dorf and change at Klosters.

# THE ENGADINE

The almost-3000km-long Inn River (En in Romansch) springs up from the snowy Graubünden Alps around the Maloja Pass and gives its name to the Engadine.

This is the stuff of Swiss dreams. St Moritz, possibly the slickest resort in Switzerland, is joined by a string of other piste-pounding hotspots along the Oberengadin (Upper Engadine) Valley and nearby Pontresina. Further east in the Unterengadin (Lower Engadine), you'll find loads of rural charm, thick woods and the spectacular Swiss National Park. The whole valley is a mix of majestic vistas of snowy Alpine crags, valleys and silvery mountain streams.

If that's not enough, it's a joy to explore gorgeous valleys such as Val Bregaglia, Val Poschiavo and Val Müstair that extend over mountain passes and stretch like fingers towards Italy.

The Engadine's unique cultural roots are reflected in festivals such as **Schlittéda** (Jan), when lads on flamboyant horse-drawn sleds whisk girls (to their delight or dismay) through the snow to neighbouring villages, and **Chalandamarz** (1 Mar), when winter is ceremoniously chased away with chanting, whip-cracking and the clanging of cowbells.

## Scuol

POP 4690 / ELEV 1250M

The last biggish town in the Lower Engadine Valley before you hit Austria (25km away), Scuol is surrounded by rippling peaks and dense forests, and is ideal for remote Alpine hikes in summer, crowd-free cruising in winter and relaxation in its thermal baths year-round. It's a joy to stroll the Old Town (Lower Scuol), an attractive jumble of frescoed chalets, cobbled squares, and fountains that spout mineral water tapped from one of 20 springs in the region.

### Sights & Activities

**★Guarda** VILLAGE
With its twisting cobbled streets, Hobbit-like houses and numerous fountains, Guarda, 11km west of Scuol, has much appeal and many Swiss turn up to stroll. With a population of 160, it sits on a terrace, 30 minutes' walk uphill from its valley-floor station. **Hotel Piz Buin** (081 860 30 40; https://pizbuin.ch; Chantun Sura 21; s/d from Sfr100/150; ) is great if you're keen to stay. A trail leads 8km north from Guarda to the foothills of 3312m Piz Buin (of sunscreen fame), dominating the glaciated Silvretta range on the Swiss–Austrian border.

**Schloss Tarasp** CASTLE
(081 864 93 68; www.schloss-tarasp.ch) Perched on a clifftop, this 1000-year-old turreted castle stands high over the valley and is definite

fairy-tale material. In 2016, the castle was purchased by Swiss artist Not Vital, who plans to turn it into a cultural attraction of national and international importance. The castle can only be visited by guided tour; check the website for the latest details.

**Motta Naluns** SKIING
(www.bergfex.com/scuol; adult/child 1-day pass Sfr56/28) There's skiing on 80km of runs and fun for boarders at the snow park at Motta Naluns. In summer the same slopes attract hikers and downhill bikers. At the cable-car station you can hire scooters (Sfr18), mountain bikes (Sfr35), downhill bikes (Sfr48) and e-bikes (Sfr43) to whizz through meadows and forests.

**Engadin Bad Scuol** SPA
(www.engadinbadscuol.ch; Via dals Bogns 323; adult/child Sfr26.50/16; ⏲8am-9.45pm Mon-Sun) Saunas, massage jets, waterfalls and whirlpools pummel you into relaxation at these thermal baths. Linger for a starlit soak in the snail-shaped outdoor pool by night. For full-on pampering, book a 2¼-hour Roman-Irish bath (Sfr66), combining different baths and massages, all done naked.

**Engadin Adventure** ADVENTURE SPORTS
(☎081 861 14 19; www.engadin-adventure.ch; Via da Ftan 495) Tailors outdoor adventures that include half-day rafting trips (from Sfr95) and knuckle-whitening, single-track bike tours from Motta Naluns (Sfr69).

## Sleeping & Eating

Scuol has several attractive hotels, especially down in the Old Town, below the main road through town. There are also some budget options.

**Chasa Valär** B&B €
(☎081 864 19 59; www.ferienhaus364.ch; Vi 364; r per person from Sfr55; P 📶) This place above the main street in Scuol makes an excellent budget option. Cheaper rooms share bathrooms, while slightly more expensive rooms have their own facilities. The 400-year-old building has real character, a cobbled street and a fresh-water fountain right outside the front door. Parking is about 300m away.

★**Hotel Engiadina** HISTORIC HOTEL €€
(☎081 864 14 21; www.engiadina-scuol.ch; Rablüzza 152; d Sfr184-264; P 📶) Each of the light-filled rooms is different at the Engiadina – some whitewashed, some vaulted and some with intricate timber ceilings. Best of all is the award-winning restaurant (mains from Sfr27), serving specialities like regional game and homemade peppermint *Pizokel* with Engadine mountain cheese. Nicely placed in the middle of the Old Town.

## Information

**Tourist Office** (☎081 861 88 00; www.scuol.ch; ⏲8am-6.30pm Mon-Fri, 9am-noon & 1-5.30pm Sat, 9am-noon Sun) Located on the main street through Scuol.

## Getting There & Away

This is as far east as trains go in Switzerland. The train from St Moritz (Sfr29, 1¼ hours), with a change at Samedan, terminates at Scuol-Tarasp train station. There are direct trains from Klosters (Sfr24, 45 minutes). Postal buses from the station operate year-round to Samnaun (Sfr11, 1¼ hours).

If you're driving, Scuol is 60km northeast of St Moritz and 47km east of Davos. It's 25km further east to the Austrian border.

# Samnaun

POP 793 / ELEV 1844M

Virtually right on the Austrian border, in Switzerland's remote northeast corner, is the duty-free Alpine resort of Samnaun. Through a bizarre quirk of history and law, Samnaun was excluded from the Swiss customs territory in the 19th century, since although it was part of Switzerland, the only way into this remote valley was from Austria. Even when a road was built in 1905 from Swiss territory, Samnaum kept its duty-free status, albeit a tad controversially. What that means today is that Samnaum is Switzerland's only duty-free zone and claims to be Europe's highest (in altitude!) shopping centre with over 50 stores emblazoned with 'Duty-Free' selling cosmetics, perfumes, alcohol, cigarettes and designer goods.

## Information

**Tourist Office** (☎081 861 88 30; www.samnaun.ch; Dorfstrasse 4; ⏲8.30am-6pm Mon-Fri, 8.30am-noon & 1-5.30pm Sat, 1-5.30pm Sun) The tourist office is at the entrance to Samnaun-Dorf.

## Getting There & Away

Take the hourly postal bus from Scuol-Tarasp station (Sfr11, 1¼ hours) to Samnaun-Dorf.

Samnaun is up its own tributary valley curling west (surprisingly) from the Inn River valley. By car, it's 36km (45 minutes) from Scuol. If you're driving, buy petrol in the duty-free zone as it's incredibly cheap.

# Müstair

POP 764 / ELEV 1273M

In a remote corner of Switzerland, at the country's most easterly point, Müstair sits barely a kilometre from the Italian border. It is one of Europe's early Christian treasures and a Unesco World Heritage Site to boot. When Charlemagne supposedly founded a monastery and a church here in the 8th century, it was a strategically placed spot below the Ofen (or Fuorn) Pass (2149m), separating northern Europe from Italy and the heart of Christendom.

The Müstair Valley follows the Rom River, which flows out into Italy. You'll need to head southeast from Zernez, through the Swiss National Park and over the Ofen Pass. A brown bear was seen and photographed near the pass in 2005, the first sighting of a wild bear in Switzerland since 1923.

Vibrant Carolingian (9th century) and Romanesque (12th century) frescos smother the interior of the church of Benedictine **Kloster St Johann** (St John's Convent; www.muestair.ch). Beneath Carolingian representations of Christ in Glory in the apses are Romanesque stories depicting the grisly ends of St Peter (crucified), St Paul (decapitated) and St Steven (stoned). There's no cost to enter the church; guided tours can be arranged.

The village and valley **tourist office** (081 861 88 40; www.val-muestair.ch; 9am-6pm Mon-Sat, 1.30-6pm Sun) is at the museum.

Postal buses run along the valley between Zernez and Müstair (Sfr22, one hour).

It's a 38km drive from Zernez to Müstair, passing through the Swiss National Park and over the Ofen Pass. If heading into Italy, it's a 65km drive out to Merano.

# Zernez

POP 1570 / ELEV 1474M

Perched on the doorstep of the Swiss National Park, Zernez is a cluster of stone chalets, outlined by the profile of its baroque church and the stout medieval tower of its castle, Schloss Wildenberg. A main gateway to the Alps' oldest national park, this slow-paced village is the perfect base for exploring the surrounding mountains, lakes and river valleys. It's home to the informative Swiss National Park Centre (p298), with 21 walking trails readily accessible along the main park road just east of town towards Pass dal Fuorn (Ofenpass).

### YOU'D BETTER WATCH OUT

For most of the year, Samnaun is but a sleepy little town. Yet on the last weekend in November, it steals Lapland's reins by staging **ClauWau** (www.clauwau.ch; Nov), aka the Santa Claus World Championships. Some 100 pseudo–Father Christmases compete for the title of world's best Santa, proving their X-mas factor in disciplines like chimney climbing, gingerbread decorating and snow sculpting. It's an event full of Yuletide cheer and ho-ho-ho-ing overkill.

## Sleeping & Eating

**Hotel Bär & Post** HOTEL €
(081 851 55 00; www.baer-post.ch; dm/s/d from Sfr25/90/150; P) Welcoming all comers since 1905, these central digs have inviting rooms with lots of stone, pine and downy duvets, plus basic bunk rooms. There's also a sauna, and a rustic restaurant dishing up good steaks and pasta.

★ **Hotel Parc Naziunal Il Fuorn** HOTEL €€
(081 856 12 26; www.ilfuorn.ch; s/d Sfr120/196, without bathroom Sfr95/150, half-board extra Sfr35; closed Nov, 2nd half Jan & Easter-late Apr; P) Bang in the heart of the national park, this guesthouse shelters light, comfy rooms with pine furnishings. Fresh trout and game are big at the excellent on-site restaurant. There's plenty of history here as Il Fuorn was already being referred to as in 'inn' in 1509.

## Information

**Tourist Office** (081 856 13 00; www.zernez.ch; Via d'Urtatsch 2; 8.30am-6pm) Located at the Swiss National Park Centre.

## Getting There & Away

Trains run regularly from Zernez to St Moritz (Sfr19.60, 45 to 55 minutes) and to Scuol-Tarasp (Sfr14.20, 30 minutes).

Postal bus 811 runs every hour or two from Zernez train station to Il Fuorn in the heart of the national park (Sfr9.80, 25 minutes).

# Celerina

POP 1534 / ELEV 1714M

To many, Celerina (Schlarigna in Romansh) is synonymous with the Cresta Run toboggan run and its Olympic bobsleigh course, two terrifying icy hurtles that have been luring speed freaks and daredevils for decades. You no longer need to be a fearless gold medalist to skim and skid down either, but if cheek-wobbling g-force really isn't your idea of an entertaining 75 seconds, the delightfully sunny resort always has something going on thanks to the local hoteliers attempting to put their village in the spotlight.

The family-friendly ski area of Corviglia/Piz Nair is part of the St Moritz Ski Resorts group with the glizty, royal-welcoming village just a three-minute train ride away.



## Activities

**Bob Run** SNOW SPORTS
(☎081 830 02 00; www.olympia-bobrun.ch) Celerina is synonymous with its 1722m Olympic bobsleigh run, which is the world's oldest, dating from 1904, and made from natural ice. A hair-raising 75-second, 135km/h guest ride costs a cool Sfr250, but the buzz is priceless. Don't worry, you'll be safely ensconced between a pilot and a brakeman.

**Cresta Run** SNOW SPORTS
(www.cresta-run.com) The heart-stopping, head-first 1km tobogganing course, Cresta Run, was created by British visitors in 1885. A set of five rides, including tuition, costs Sfr600 (and Sfr51 per ride thereafter). This is different from a bobsleigh run. Here, the rider goes down solo in a lying position head first, using rakes on the end of special boots to brake and steer.

## Information

**Tourist Office** (☎081 830 00 11; www.celerina.ch; Plazza da la Staziun 8; ⏲8.30am-6pm Mon-Fri, 9am-noon & 2-6pm Sat, plus 4-6pm Sun high season) The tourist office is at the train station.

## Getting There & Away

Celerina is easily reached from St Moritz by train (Sfr3, three minutes).

# St Moritz

POP 5067 / ELEV 1856M

Switzerland's original winter wonderland and the cradle of Alpine tourism, St Moritz has been luring royals, celebrities and moneyed wannabes since 1864. With its shimmering aquamarine lake, emerald forests and aloof mountains, the town looks a million dollars.

Yet despite the string of big-name designer boutiques on Via Serlas and celebs bashing the pistes, this resort isn't all show. The real riches lie outdoors in the mountains with superb carving on Corviglia, hairy black runs on Diavolezza and miles of hiking trails when the snow melts. St Moritz has hosted the Winter Olympics twice, and most are surprised to hear that the town first gained fame due to its mineral springs, which were discovered 3000 years ago and established the town as a summer spa resort.

## Sights

**Segantini Museum** MUSEUM
(www.segantini-museum.ch; Via Somplaz 30; adult/child Sfr10/3; ⏲10am-noon & 2-6pm Tue-Sun, closed 20 Oct-10 Dec & 20 Apr-20 May) Housed in an eye-catching stone building topped by a cupola, this museum shows the paintings of Giovanni Segantini (1858–99). The Italian artist beautifully captured the dramatic light and ambience of the Alps on canvas.

**Engadiner Museum** MUSEUM
(☎081 833 43 33; www.engadiner-museum.ch; Via dal Bagn 39; adult/child Sfr13/free; ⏲10am-6pm Wed-Mon 20 May-20 Oct, 2-6pm Dec-Apr) For a peek at the archetypal dwellings and humble interiors of the Engadine Valley, visit this museum showing traditional stoves and archaeological finds.

## Activities

### Winter Activities

Skiing in St Moritz is superb with one ski pass covering a huge area of lifts and slopes around St Moritz village and the Engadine and Bernina valleys. Either stick close to town using the **Corviglia Funicular** to access the ski areas above St Moritz-Dorf or head further afield for a mind-boggling array of places to play on the snow. There's also an abundance of cross-country ski trails in the valleys.

**St Moritz Ski Resorts** SKIING
(www.engadin.stmoritz.ch; 2-/6-day high-season downhill ski pass Sfr156/376, day/week cross-country pass Sfr8/25) With 350km of slopes, ultramodern lifts and spirit-soaring views, skiing in St Moritz is second to none. The general ski pass covers all the slopes, including Silvaplana, Sils-Maria, Celerina, Zuoz, Pontresina and Diavolezza.

If cross-country skiing is more your scene, you can glide across sunny plains and through snowy woods on 220km of groomed trails.

For groomed slopes with big mountain vistas, head to **Corviglia** (2486m), accessible by funicular from St Moritz-Dorf. From St Moritz-Bad a cable car goes to **Signal** (shorter queues), giving access to the slopes of Piz

## St Moritz

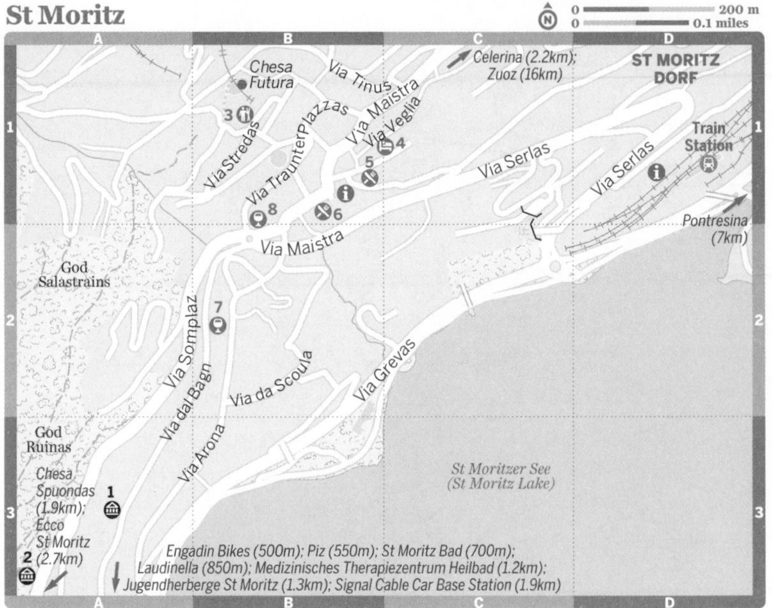


## St Moritz

**Sights**
1 Engadiner Museum ........ A3
2 Segantini Museum ........ A3

**Activities, Courses & Tours**
3 Schweizer Skischule ........ B1

**Sleeping**
4 Hotel Eden ........ C1

**Eating**
5 Chesa Veglia ........ B1
6 Hanselmann ........ B1

**Drinking & Nightlife**
7 Bobby's Pub ........ B2
8 Roo Bar ........ B1

Nair. There's varied skiing at **Corvatsch** (3303m), above nearby Silvaplana, including spectacular glacier descents and the gentle black run Hahnensee. Silhouetted by glaciated four-thousanders, **Diavolezza** (2973m) is a must-ski for freeriders and fans of jaw-dropping descents.

**Schweizer Skischule** SKIING
(☎081 830 01 01; www.skischool.ch; Via Stredas 14; ⏲8am-noon & 2-6pm Mon-Sat, 8-9am & 4-6pm Sun) The first Swiss ski school was founded in St Moritz in 1929. Today, you can arrange skiing or snowboarding lessons here – check out the website for details.

### Summer Activities

In summer, get out and stride one of the region's excellent hiking trails, such as the Corvatsch *Wasserweg* (water trail) linking six mountain lakes. Soaring above St Moritz, **Piz Nair** (3057m) commands views of the jewel-coloured lakes that necklace the valley below. For head-spinning views of the Pers glacier and the Bernina Alps, tackle the vertiginous, 2½-hour **Piz Trovat** *via ferrata* at Diavolezza; equipment rental is available at the base station. The tourist office has a map providing more suggestions (in English) for walking in Oberengadin.

From Piz Nair, another interesting hike is the eco-friendly 2½-hour **Clean Energy Tour** (www.clean-energy.ch), which showcases different kinds of renewable energy in natural settings. Descend from Chantarella along the flower-speckled Heidi Blumenweg, then along Schellenursliweg past Lord Norman Foster's wood-tiled, pumpkin-shaped **Chesa Futura** (www.fosterandpartners.com/projects/chesa-futura;

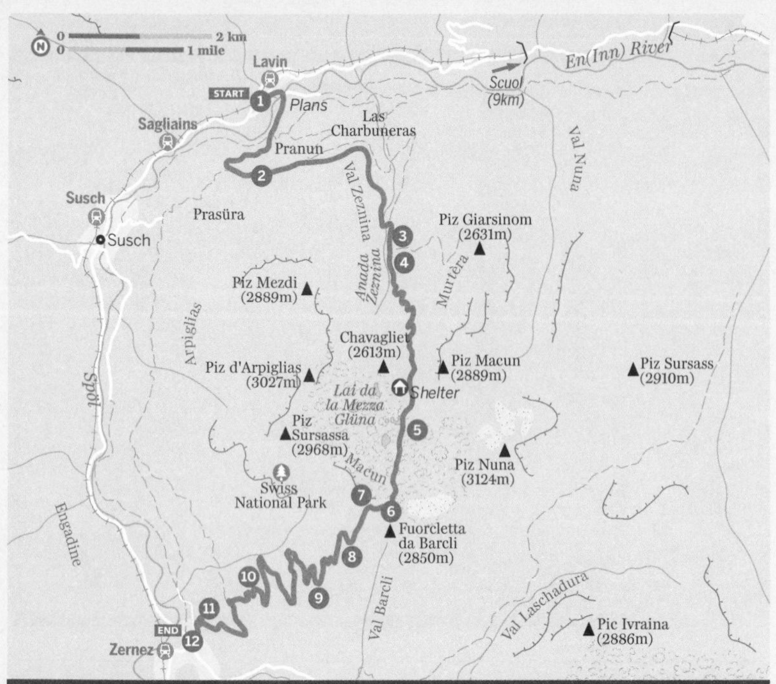


# Walking Tour Lakes of Macun

**START** LAVIN
**FINISH** ZERNEZ
**LENGTH** 16KM; 7½ TO 8½ HOURS

This highly rewarding day walk leads from the main valley of the Engadine into the lakeland of the Macun Basin. Hourly trains operate between Zernez and Lavin (Sfr6.20, 15 minutes).

From the village of 1 **Lavin**, cross the En (Inn) River on a wooden bridge. Head along a gravelled lane, then left on a track twisting up eastward through forest to 2 **Plan Surücha** (1577m). The trail veers gradually southward to cross the Aua da Zeznina. The 2889m Piz Macun and 2850m Fuorcletta da Barcli slide into view as you approach 3 **Alp Zeznina Dadaint** (1958m) around two hours from Lavin. Scenes from *Heidi* were shot at this idyllic Alpine spot.

Make your way into the 4 **Val Zeznina**, negotiating steep switchbacks through rhododendron-flecked meadows. The gradient eases as you rise to a rustic shelter built against cliffs beside a tarn. Cross the streamlet and continue along its rocky western banks to enter the national park. The upper valley opens into the basin of 5 **Macun**, 1½ to two hours from Alp Zeznina Dadaint. Like a natural amphitheatre, the cirque is ringed by craggy, 3000m peaks and sprinkled with almost two dozen Alpine lakes and tarns.

Cross the stream and follow the white-red-white markings southward up sparsely vegetated ridges of glacial debris. Ascend steep slopes of loose rock to 6 **Fuorcletta da Barcli**, a gap in the range at 2850m. From here traverse west along an exposed ridgetop to reach a minor peak at 2945m, one to 1½ hours from Macun. The 7 **lookout** commands top-of-the-world views.

Trace a prominent spur running southwest directly from the summit, then drop away rightward out of the national park. The route descends through rows of avalanche grids on the open slopes of 8 **Munt Baselgia** to meet an Alpine track at 9 **Plan Sech** (2268m). Make a long serpentine descent into the coniferous forest via 10 **La Rosta** and 11 **God Baselgia**. The final stretch leads out onto grassy fields just above the town, then down to arrive in 12 **Zernez** after 2½ to three hours.

Via Tinus 25), whose Romansch name means 'House of the Future.'

**Medizinisches Therapiezentrum Heilbad** SPA
(☎081 833 30 62; www.heilbad-stmoritz.ch; Plazza Paracelsus 2; mineral bath from Sfr35; ⊙8am-7pm Mon-Fri, to 12.30pm Sat) After exerting yourself on the slopes, rest in a mineral bath or with an Alpine herb pack here. Oh, so many options!

## Sleeping

Book early for the winter season. Many hotels throw in free mountain transport when you stay more than two nights in summer, when you can expect rates to drop up to 30%. St Moritz virtually shuts down in the shoulder seasons.

**Jugendherberge St Moritz** HOSTEL €
(☎081 836 61 11; www.youthhostel.ch/st.moritz; Via Surpunt 60; dm/s/d/q Sfr47/148/188/268; P) On the edge of the forest, this modern hostel has clean, quiet four-bed dorms and doubles. Considered a top family hostel, there's a children's toy room, bike hire and laundrette. Bus 3 offers door-to-door connections with the town centre and train station (10 minutes).

**Chesa Spuondas** HOTEL €€
(☎081 833 65 88; www.chesaspuondas.ch; Via Somplaz 47; s/d/f incl half-board Sfr155/280/330; P) This family hotel nestles amid meadows at the foot of forest and mountains, 3km southwest of the town centre. Rooms have high ceilings and parquet floors. Kids are the centre of attention here, with dedicated meal times, activities and play areas, plus a children's ski school a 10-minute walk away.

**Hotel Eden** HOTEL €€
(☎081 830 81 00; www.eden.swiss; Via Veglia 12; s/d from Sfr171/341; P) Right in the heart of town, the Eden centres on an attractive central atrium and antique-strewn lounge where a fire crackles in winter. The old-style, pine-panelled rooms are cosy and those on the top floor afford terrific views.

**Piz** HOTEL €€
(☎081 832 11 11; www.piz-stmoritz.ch; Via dal Bagn 6; s/d/apt from Sfr110/190/280; ) Splashes of crimson, hardwood floors and clean lines define this contemporary B&B in St Moritz-Bad. Fitted with rain showers and flat-screen TVs, the wood-floored rooms are sleek and comfy. The sauna and steam room invite relaxation after a day on the trails or slopes.

## Eating

**Laudinella Pizzeria Caruso** PIZZA €
(☎081 836 06 29; www.laudinella.ch; Via Tegiatscha 17; pizza from Sfr13.50; ⊙noon-2am; ) Pizza lovers rave about the thin-crust Neapolitan numbers that fly out of the wood-oven at Hotel Laudinella's pizzeria, which range from a simple Margherita to the gourmet Domenico with truffles and beef. Laudinella also offers delivery service.

**Hanselmann** CAFE €
(☎081 833 38 64; www.hanselmann.ch; Via Maistra 8; pastries & cakes Sfr3-6, snacks & light meals Sfr12-24; ⊙7.30am-7pm) You can't miss the lavishly frescoed facade of St Moritz' celebrated bakery and tea room, famous for its caramel-rich, walnut-studded Engadine nut tart.

**Chesa Veglia** ITALIAN €€€
(☎081 837 28 00; www.badruttspalace.com; Via Veglia 2; pizza/mains from Sfr25/45; ⊙noon-11.30pm) This slate-roofed, chalk-white chalet restaurant dates from 1658. The softly lit interior is all warm pine and creaking wood floors, while the terrace affords lake and mountain views. Go for pizza or regional specialities such as *Bündner Gerstensuppe* (creamy barley soup) and venison medallions with *Spätzli* (egg noodles).

**Ecco St Moritz** ITALIAN €€€
(☎081 836 63 00; www.giardino-mountain.ch; Giardino Mountain, Champfèr; menus Sfr190-240; ⊙7pm-midnight Wed-Sun) The pinnacle of St Moritz' dining scene, Ecco St Moritz is where chef Rolf Fliegauf gives flight to culinary fantasy when the flakes fall in winter. A sublime gold-and-white interior is the backdrop for exquisitely presented dishes with strong, assured flavours that revolve around primary ingredients.

## Drinking & Nightlife

**Bobby's Pub** PUB
(☎081 834 42 83; www.bobbys-pub.ch; Via dal Bagn 50a; ⊙9am-1am Mon-Fri, 11am-1am Sat, noon-1am Sun) This friendly English-style watering hole serves 20 different international brews and is one of the few places open year-round.

**Roo Bar** BAR
(☎081 837 50 50; www.facebook.com/RooBarStMoritz; Via Traunter Plazzas 7; ⊙2-10pm) Snow bums fill the terrace of this après-ski joint at Hauser's Hotel. Hip-hop, techno and hot chocolate laced with rum fuel the party.

DON'T MISS

## SWISS NATIONAL PARK

The Engadine's pride and joy is the **Swiss National Park** (www.nationalpark.ch) FREE, easily accessed from Scuol, Zernez and S-chanf. Spanning 172 sq km, Switzerland's only national park was the first national park to be established in the Alps in 1914.

Given that nature has been left to its own devices for a century, the park is a glimpse of the Alps before the dawn of tourism. There are some 80km of well-marked hiking trails, where, with a little luck and a decent pair of binoculars, ibex, chamois, marmots, deer, bearded vultures and golden eagles can be sighted. The **Swiss National Park Centre** (081 851 41 41; www.nationalpark.ch; exhibition adult/child Sfr7/3; 8.30am-6pm Jun-Oct, 9am-noon & 2-5pm Nov-May) should be your first port of call for information on activities and accommodation. It sells an excellent 1:50,000 park map (Sfr14, or Sfr20 with guidebook), which covers 21 walks through the park.

You can easily head off on your own, but you might get more out of one of the informative guided hikes (Sfr25) run by the centre from late June to mid-October. These include wildlife-spotting treks to the Val Trupchun and high-Alpine hikes to the Offenpass and Lakes of Macun. Most are in German, but many guides speak a little English. Book ahead by phone or at the park office in Zernez.

Entry to the park and its car parks is free. Conservation is paramount here, so stick to footpaths and respect regulations.

### Information

The main **tourist office** (081 837 33 33; www.stmoritz.ch; Via Maistra 12; 9am-6.30pm Mon-Fri, to 6pm Sat) is in St Moritz-Dorf, but if you're coming by train, visit the **sub-office** (St Moritz train station; 10am-2pm & 3-6.30pm) in the train station.

### Getting There & Away

St Moritz-Bad is about 1.5km south of the main town, St Moritz-Dorf.

Trains run at least hourly from Zürich to St Moritz (Sfr77, three to 3½ hours), with one change (at Landquart or Chur).

Between mid-December and late October, one of Switzerland's most celebrated trains, the Glacier Express (p163), makes the scenic eight-hour journey from St Moritz to Zermatt.

Postal buses run frequently in high season from St Moritz southwest to Maloja (Sfr6, 30 minutes) with stops at Silvaplana (Sfr2.80, 20 minutes) and Sils-Maria (Sfr4.20, 25 minutes).

### Getting Around

Local buses and postal buses shuttle between St Moritz-Bad and St Moritz-Dorf.

## Silvaplana

POP 915 / ELEV 1815M

With a startlingly turquoise and wind-buffeted lake only 5km southeast of St Moritz, the lively resort village of Silvaplanasee is a gorgeous spot to play both in the winter and summer. Silvaplana, or Silvaplauna in Romansch, is known as a kite-surfing and windsurfing mecca and brightly coloured kites and sails dot the lake once things warm up a bit. In winter, slopes beckon on the far side of the lake with the **Corvatsch 3303 cable cars** (081 838 73 73; www.corvatsch.ch; Via dal Corvatsch; return adult/child Sfr60/30) whisking skiers and boarders up to 3303m from Silvaplana-Surlej for spectacular skiing. And, of course, there's some great hiking in summer.

### Sights & Activities

**Murtèl to Val Roseg Hike** HIKING

For superb day hike, ride the Corvatsch cable cars to 3303m, check out the views, then return down to the mid-station of Murtèl (2702m). Hike east for 45 minutes to Fuorcla Surlej (2760m), the hut you can see on the ridge line. From there, it's a 1½ hour hike down to Hotel Roseg Gletscher (p301) in the Roseg Valley.

From there, either walk (1½ hours) or take a **horse-drawn carriage** (81 842 60 57; www.stalla-costa.ch; per person from Sfr25; 50 minutes) out to Pontresina station.

**Kite Sailing School Silvaplana** WATER SPORTS

(081 828 97 67; www.kitesailing.ch; Silvaplana; intro/2-day/5-day course Sfr190/350/800; 9am-6.30pm) Slip into a wetsuit at this outfit, offering instruction and equipment rental. It has introductory lessons for kite-surfing, plus windsurfing and stand-up paddleboarding in summer and snow-kiting in winter. Check its website for details.

## Sleeping

**Camping Silvaplana** CAMPGROUND €
(081 828 84 92; www.campingsilvaplana.ch; sites per adult/child Sfr11/8, tent Sfr7-10; P) Right on Silvaplanasee at the south end of town, this popular campground is the haunt of kite- and windsurfers in summer. Everything you could want is here, including a shop, covered picnic area, billiards table and hot tub.

★ **Aparthotel Chesa Bellaval** APARTMENT €€
(081 838 74 00; www.chesa-bellaval.ch; Via suot Pignia 9; P) At the back of town, these roomy apartments are perfect for long-stayers, especially if you turn up out of high season. There's a mix of options, but one-bedroom apartments have a living room, fully equipped kitchen, bathroom and bedroom.

## Information

**Tourist Office** (081 838 60 00; www.engadin.stmoritz.ch; Via dal Farrèr 2; 8.30am-noon & 1.30-6pm) Located in the middle of the village; it has reduced hours out of high seasons.

## Getting There & Around

Silvaplana is only 5km from St Moritz by postal bus (Sfr2.80, 12 minutes). To reach the high country above Silvaplana, catch a postal bus from St Moritz to Surlej-Corvatschbahn (Sfr2.80, 25 minutes), then take the spectacular Corvatsch 3303 cable cars to the 3303m summit via the Murtèl mid-station (2702m).

# Sils-Maria

POP 760

Sitting peacefully between Lake Sils and Lake Silvaplana, only 10km southeast of St Moritz, Sils-Maria (Segl in Romansch) is a peaceful enclave of pastel-painted, slate-roofed chalets set against a dramatic backdrop of rugged, glacier-capped mountains. Fans through the ages have included such luminaries as Nietzsche, Chagall, Strauss and David Bowie.

The village acts as the entrance for Val Fex, which can be explored on foot or by horse-drawn carriage, and a cable car ascends to Furtschellas (2312m), where there is a network of hiking trails and ski slopes.

## Sights

**Nietzsche Haus** HOUSE
(081 826 53 69; www.nietzschehaus.ch; Via da Marias 67; adult/child Sfr8/free; 3-6pm Tue-Sun Jun-Oct & Dec-Apr) Sils-Maria might be a sleepy lakeside village now, but the rumble of existential philosophy once reverberated around these peaks, courtesy of Friedrich Nietzsche who spent his summers here from 1881 to 1888 writing texts concerning the travails of modern man. The little museum contains a collection of photos, memorabilia and letters.

## Sleeping & Eating

★ **Hotel Fex** HOTEL €€
(081 832 60 00; www.hotelfex.ch; Via da Fex 73; per person incl half-board from Sfr155; ) If you fancy staying in the remote Val Fex, south of Sils-Maria, book into the grand 19th-century Hotel Fex, a mountain retreat with sensational views and a restaurant serving top-quality regional dishes. Reaching the valley is an experience in itself, whether you hike (2½ hours from Sils-Maria) or arrive by horse-drawn carriage. For the latter, head to Dorfplatz in Sils-Maria where carriages depart for Val Fex. The scenic journey costs Sfr22.50 to Sfr40 to Hotel Fex; times and prices depend on group numbers.

**Hotel Privata** HOTEL €€
(081 832 62 00; http://hotelprivata.ch; Via da Marias 83; s/d incl half-board from Sfr170/280; P) This family-run (since 1921), dreamy, country-style hotel is a terrific choice, with huge pine-clad rooms, antique-style furniture and forest views from the herb and flower garden. The restaurant focuses on the best cuisine of both Italy and the Engadine.

**Hotel Waldhaus** LUXURY HOTEL €€€
(081 838 51 00; www.waldhaus-sils.ch; Via da Fex 3; s/d incl half-board from Sfrr290/580; P) For five-star grandeur, try the palatial Hotel Waldhaus, set on a rise amid the woods. Along with modern comforts (pool, Turkish baths, tennis courts), the owners have retained the opulence of the 1908 building. It's a great family choice with its connecting rooms, childcare, and activities and menus geared towards kids.

## Information

**Tourist Office** (081 838 50 50; www.engadin.stmoritz.ch; Via da Marias 93; 9am-noon & 1-6pm Mon-Sat, 3-6pm Sun) Located in the middle of the village.

Sils-Maria can be reached by postal bus from St Moritz (Sfr4.20, 20 minutes).

# BERNINA PASS

Bare, brooding mountains and glaciers that sweep down to farmland give the landscape around the Bernina Pass (2323m; Passo del Bernina in Italian) austere grandeur. A road and railway both twist their way up to the pass from the Engadine Valley, cross it, then drop into Val Poschiavo. This is high Alpine stuff, with superb skiing and hiking.

The stretch of track that crosses the pass, known as the Bernina Line, was added to the Unesco World Heritage list in 2008. Constructed in 1910, it is one of the world's steepest narrow-gauge railways, negotiating the highest rail crossing in Europe and taking in glaciers, gorges and rock pinnacles.

## Sights & Activities

High up the Bernina Valley, 2973m Diavolezza is a must-ski for freeriders and fans of jaw-dropping descents. Skiing here is covered under the general St Moritz area ski pass.

**Diavolezza** CABLE CAR
(081 838 73 73; www.diavolezza.ch; return adult/youth/child Sfr36/24/12) This cable car, with its own station on the Bernina Line (Bernina Diavolezza) and a huge car park at its base, whisks passengers up from 2093m to Diavolezza where you'll find stupendous views of the highest peaks in the Bernina range, including Piz Bernina (4049m) and Piz Palü (3905m). It's absolutely stunning on a good day. Stay at Berghaus Diavolezza (p300) or take a guided glacier hike (p300) down to Morterasch. There is superb skiing here in winter.

★**Diavolezza to Morteratsch Glacier Hike** HIKING
(081 842 82 82; http://bergsteiger-pontresina.ch; guided hike Sfr60; Jun-Oct) For a unique guided glacier hike, take the Diavolezza cable car up to Berghaus Diavolleza at 3000m, then hike down 1100 vertical metres on the Pers and Morteratsch Glaciers to Morteratsch train station. The hike covers 12km and takes around five hours. Bring your own refreshments, boots or hiking shoes, rain and sun protection, gloves and walking sticks.

**Ospezio Bernina to Alp Grum Hike** HIKING
This is a great easy walk from the Ospizio Bernina train station (2253m) on the Bernina Pass to Alp Grüm (2091m) to the south. It takes about 2½ hours through wildflower-cloaked pastures and affords crisp views of Lago Bianco and the Palü Glacier.

## Sleeping

★**Berghaus Diavolezza** MOUNTAIN HOTEL €
(081 839 39 00; www.diavolezza.ch; dm/s/d per person from Sfr80/131/228; P) Perched at 3000m at the top of the Diavolezza cable car, this mountain hotel offers both dormitory and private rooms, an excellent restaurant, sun terrace, outdoor Jacuzzi, and some of the best mountain and glacier views in the Alps. Rates include dinner and breakfast, plus the cable car (return).

## Getting There & Away

From St Moritz, frequent trains run via Pontresina (Sfr5.40, 10 minutes) direct to Tirano (Sfr30, 2½ hours) in northern Italy. The station at the pass is Ospezio Bernina (Sfr7.60, 45 minutes).

There are also postal buses from St Moritz to Ospezio Bernina (Sfr7.60, 40 minutes).

By car, the Bernina Pass is 22km from St Moritz and 41km from Tirano, Italy.

# Pontresina

POP 2080 / ELEV 1805M

At the mouth of Val Bernina, Pontresina is a low-key alternative resort to St Moritz, only 8km away. It's a brilliant place to stay, especially if you are into the outdoors. There is a lively main street, great hiking and skiing right above the town, and easy access to the spectacular heights of Punt Muragl at the top of the Muottas Muragl Bahn funicular. Val Roseg, with its hiking, cross-country skiing trails and horse-drawn carriage rides, is just across the valley, and the amazing Morterasch glacier is also close by.

## Sights & Activities

**Muottas Muragl Bahn** FUNICULAR
This fun old funicular railway, the first in the Engadine Valley dating from 1907, takes its passengers up over 700 vertical metres to Punt Muragl (2454m) and wonderful views out over the Upper Engadine, including St Moritz, Piz Palü and Piz Bernina. There's a first-rate **hotel** (www.muottasmuragl.ch; per person from Sfr141; P) and restaurant, and in summer, great hiking opportunities. For winter, there's no skiing, but snowshoeing and a toboggan-run are popular.

**Muottas Muragl to Pontresina Hike** HIKING
Save this spectacular hike, known as the Climate Trail, for a good day. It involves taking the Muottas Muragl Bahn funicular up to Punt Muragl at 2454m, then hiking across the mountains above Pontresina to Alp Languard (2330m), then taking the chairlift down into Pontresina. There are 18 information boards along the 9km route, which will take around 2½ to three hours.

## Sleeping & Eating

**★Hotel Roseg Gletscher** HOTEL €
(081 842 64 45; www.roseg-gletscher.ch; per person from Sfr85; ) This family-run, remote hotel and restaurant sits in the Roseg Valley. There's a free shuttle bus, but access by horse-drawn carriage (p298) or sleigh from Pontresina train station is more fun. Alternatively, hike or bike in, or arrive on the Murtèl to Val Roseg hike (p298). Rooms are stylish and modern, and shared rooms are also available.

**★Gondolezza** SWISS €€
(081 839 36 26; www.hotelsteinbock.ch/en/kulinarik/en-gondolezza; Via Maistra 219; fondue/raclette from Sfr29/32; from 5pm/2pm winter/summer) It's not often you can sit in a former Diavolezza gondola car and dine out on top-notch fondue or raclette. Head up to the back of Pontresina to find this yellow cable-car cabin and accompanying sun terrace.

## Information

**Tourist Office** (081 838 83 00; www.pontresina.ch; Via Maistra 133; 8.30am-6pm Mon-Fri, 8.30am-noon & 3-6pm Sat, 4-6pm Sun) From the train station, walk east, cross the two rivers, Rosegg and Bernina, and the tourist office is on the main street in the middle of town.

## Getting There & Away

Pontresina's train station is across the valley, a 10- to 15-minute walk from the middle of town. It's only 10 minutes by train (Sfr2.80) to St Moritz.

Postal buses also run from St Moritz to the middle of Pontresina (Sfr2.80, 10 minutes).

# Val Poschiavo

Italian-speaking Val Poschiavo stretches from south of the Bernina Pass (2323m) all the way to the Swiss–Italian border, just short of the Italian town of Tirano (441m). There's a 1900m vertical drop over the length of the valley, making the grade breathtakingly steep at times. The valley is hemmed in by towering peaks and occasionally is so narrow that the rail line runs down the middle of the road.

There's great hiking in the vicinity of the pass, gorgeous little villages dotted with atmospheric buildings, and impressive engineering marvels such as the **Brusio Viaduct**, a 360-degree spiral bridge built in 1908 to limit the railway's grade to the required maximum of 7% and prevent the engine from going too fast on the way down.

The village of **Poschiavo** (population 3500; altitude 1014m) is the valley's main settlement. Its Old Town, characterised by pastel-hued town houses and the lovely Church of San Vittore, is under special protection. Cross the Poschiavino river to central Plazza da Cumün, where you'll find the charming **Hotel Albrici** (www.hotelalbrici.ch; Plazza da Cumün 137; s/d from Sfr140/190; ), a 17th-century lodging with free bicycle use, and a spa area with sauna and steam room.

At 962m, a few kilometres down the valley, gorgeous **Lago di Poschiavo** was formed naturally by rock slides on both sides of the valley meeting to form a natural dam.

## Getting There & Away

From St Moritz, frequent trains run via Pontresina (Sfr5.40, 10 minutes) direct to Tirano (Sfr30, 2½ hours) in northern Italy. The station at the pass is Ospezio Bernina (Sfr7.60, 45 minutes).

There are also postal buses from St Moritz to Ospezio Bernina (Sfr7.60, 40 minutes).

By car, the Bernina Pass is 22km from St Moritz and 41km from Tirano, Italy.

# Val Bregaglia

This wildly beautiful valley tumbles southeast towards Italy from the **Maloja Pass** (1815m) at the head of the Engadine Valley. It is dominated by horn-shaped granite peaks, chestnut forests and stone villages crowned by Italianate churches.

Italian-speaking Val Bregaglia is also known as the valley of artists. The village of **Stampa** was the home of Alberto Giacometti (1901–66), and is now the location of the **tourist office** (www.bregaglia.ch; Strada Principale 101; 9-11.30am & 2-5.30pm Mon, Tue & Thu, 9-11.30am Wed & Fri). The nearby **Palazzo Castelmur** (www.palazzo-castelmur.ch; Coltura; adult/child Sfr8/4; 11am-5pm Tue-Sun Jun-Aug) castle-museum houses a photography collection and other displays about the valley's history.

Another beautiful stopover near the Italian border is the hamlet of **Soglio**, a warren of lanes and stone houses facing 3308m Pizzo Badile. **Hotel Palazzo Salis** (www.palazzo-salis.ch; Villaggio 131; per person incl half-board from Sfr152; ), dating from 1630, makes an appealing base here, with beautiful gardens and a restaurant focusing on local produce. Soglio is the starting point for hiking trails, most notably the historic 11km **La Panoramica** route to Casaccia down in the valley.

Hourly postal buses depart from St Moritz for Chiavenna In Italy, travelling the length of Val Bregaglia and dropping passengers off at various points in the valley.

# Liechtenstein

POP 38,000

**Includes ➡**



## Best Places to Eat

- Torkel (p305)
- Adler Vaduz (p305)
- Bergrestaurant Sareis (p306)
- Vanini Café Bar (p306)

## Best Places to Stay

- Parkhotel Sonnenhof (p305)
- Familienhotel Gorfion (p306)
- Gasthof Löwen (p305)
- Hotel Kulm (p305)
- Camping Mittagspitze (p305)
- Schaan-Vaduz Youth Hostel (p305)

## Why Go?

A pipsqueak of a country, Liechtenstein snuggles between Switzerland and Austria, among mountain ranges that rise steep and rugged above the Rhine. Besides the sheer novelty value of visiting one of the world's tiniest and richest countries, Liechtenstein is pure fairy-tale stuff – a mountain principality governed by an iron-willed monarch, embedded deep in the Alps and crowned by turreted castles.

Only 25km long by 12km wide (at its broadest point), Liechtenstein doesn't have an international airport, and access from Switzerland or Austria is by local bus. The western, more populated side of the country is in the Rhine Valley and relatively flat; the east is mountainous.

Outdoor enthusiasts are in their element here, with a remarkable number of trails to hike and slopes to ski given the country's size. Strike out into the Alpine wilderness beyond Vaduz and, suddenly, this landlocked sliver of a micronation no longer seems quite so small.

## When to Go

- You can visit pocket-sized Liechtenstein at any time of the year. That said, different months and seasons boast different charms.
- Wildflowers bring a burst of spring colour, while golden autumn days are a fine time to sample new wine and game in Liechtenstein's top restaurants.
- Slow travel is the word at cycle-happy Slow Up Liechtenstein in May.
- The country strums to Guitar Days in July and celebrates National Day with fireworks on 15 August.
- Come in summer for high-Alpine hiking, and cycling along the Rhine.
- Downhill and cross-country skiers glide along Malbun's slopes in winter.

## Liechtenstein Highlights

1. **Schloss Vaduz** (p303) Hiking up to the perky turrets for postcard views of the Alps.
2. **Malbun** (p306) Strapping on walking boots or skis and heading to the slopes.
3. **Vaduz** (p303) Wandering the pedestrianised zone of this bustling little capital.
4. **Fürstensteig** (p305) Playing among the peaks on Liechtenstein's vertiginous flagship walk.
5. **Drei Länder Tour** (p306) Pedalling along the sprightly Rhine and over to Switzerland and Austria.

## History

Austrian prince Johann Adam Von Liechtenstein purchased the counties of Schellenberg (1699) and Vaduz (1712) from impoverished German nobles and gave them his name. Long a principality under the Holy Roman Empire, Liechtenstein gained independence in 1866. In 1923 it formed a customs union with Switzerland.

Even then, none of the ruling Liechtensteins had bothered to leave their Viennese palace to see their acquisitions. It wasn't until 1938, in the wake of the Anschluss (Nazi Germany's takeover of Austria) that Prince Franz Josef II became the first monarch to live in the principality; together with his wife, Gina, he set about transforming a poor rural nation into today's rich banking state. Their son, Prince Hans Adam II, ascended the throne on the prince's death in 1989.

The country's use of the Swiss franc encourages people to see it as a mere extension of its neighbour, but Liechtenstein has very different foreign policies, having joined the UN and the European Economic Area (EEA) relatively early, in 1990 and 1995, respectively.

Long known as a tax haven, the principality banned customers from stashing away money anonymously in 2000. Recently it has implemented tougher reforms in a bid to shrug off its reputation for banking secrecy and recast its image as a legitimate financial centre.

# Vaduz

POP 5430 / ELEV 455M

A tiny capital for a tiny country, Vaduz is a postage-stamp-sized city with a postcard-perfect backdrop. Crouching at the foot of forested mountains, hugging the banks of the Rhine and crowned by a turreted castle, its location is visually stunning. Vaduz is mostly on the flat, with its castle clinging to the side of the mountain, high above town, and towering peaks soaring further up.

The bustling centre itself is curiously modern, with its mix of tax-free luxury-goods stores and cube-shaped concrete buildings. There are plenty of older buildings though, making it an intriguing wander, especially in the pedestrianised zone below the castle. Just a few minutes' walk brings you to traces of the quaint village that existed just 50 years ago and quiet vineyards where the Alps seem that little bit closer.

## Sights

### ★Schloss Vaduz — CASTLE

Vaduz Castle looms over the capital from the hill above and, although closed to the public, is worth the climb for the vistas. Trails ascend the hill from the end of Egertastrasse. For a rare peek inside the castle grounds, arrive on 15 August, Liechtenstein's National

## Vaduz

**Top Sights**

1 Kunstmuseum Liechtenstein ............. B2
2 Liechtensteinisches Landesmuseum ............. B3
3 Schloss Vaduz ............. B2

**Sights**

4 Mitteldorf ............. A1
5 Parliament Building ............. B3
6 Postmuseum ............. B2
7 Treasure Chamber ............. B3

**Sleeping**

8 Gasthof Löwen ............. A1

**Eating**

9 Adler Vaduz ............. B2
10 Torkel ............. A1

**Drinking & Nightlife**

11 Vanini Café Bar ............. B2

Day, when there are magnificent fireworks and the prince invites all Liechtensteiners over to his place for a glass of wine or beer.

### ★Liechtensteinisches Landesmuseum — MUSEUM

(www.landesmuseum.li; Städtle 43; adult/child Sfr8/free, incl Kunstmuseum Liechtenstein Sfr15/free; ⏲10am-5pm Tue & Thu-Sun, to 8pm Wed) This well-designed museum provides a surprisingly interesting romp through the principality's past, heritage and natural history, from medieval witch trials to the manufacture of false teeth and stuffed Alpine animals.

### ★Kunstmuseum Liechtenstein — MUSEUM

(www.kunstmuseum.li; Städtle 32; adult/child Sfr12/free, incl Liechtensteinisches Landesmuseum Sfr15/free; ⏲10am-5pm Tue, Wed & Fri-Sun, to 8pm Thu) This black concrete and basalt cuboid on Städtle hosts temporary exhibitions, revolving around the gallery's collection of contemporary art, which includes Ernst Ludwig Kirchner, Paul Klee and Joseph Beuys originals.

### Postmuseum — MUSEUM

(www.landesmuseum.li; 1st fl, Städtle 37; ⏲10am-noon & 1-5pm) FREE Liechtenstein once made a packet producing souvenir stamps for enthusiasts, but that market has been hit by the rise of email. Here you'll find all national stamps issued since 1912 in a surprisingly interesting little museum.

The adjacent **Treasure Chamber** (adult/child Sfr8/free; ⏲10am-5pm) houses a collection of jewels, hunting knives, Russian Easter eggs and other gifts presented to Liechtenstein by various kings and emperors.

### Mitteldorf — AREA

To see how Vaduz once looked, amble north of town to Mitteldorf. Its streets form a charming quarter of traditional houses and rose-strewn gardens. Particularly eye-catching is the late-medieval, step-gabled **Rote Haus** perched above the vineyards.

### Parliament Building — NOTABLE BUILDING

Since 2008, Liechtenstein's 25-member parliament has been convening in this somewhat startlingly modern building. Munich-based architect Hansjörg Göritz designed both it and the central Peter-Kaiser-Platz square, named after the famous local historian Peter Kaiser. The building is made up of the 'Long House', the 'High House' and the 'Joining House'.

## Activities

**Planetenweg** WALKING

You can spot Jupiter, Mars and Pluto on the so-called 'Planet Trail', which starts at the car park by the Rheinpark stadium. The 5km trail shadows the Rhine and maps out the solar system on a scale of 1:1 billion.

## Sleeping

Visit www.tourismus.li for details on B&Bs and holiday apartments.

### Vaduz

★**Gasthof Löwen** HISTORIC HOTEL €€

(☎238 11 44; www.hotel-loewen.li; Herrengasse 35; s/d from Sfr199/299; P 🛜) Historic and creakily elegant, this 600-year-old guest house has eight spacious rooms with antique furniture and modern bathrooms. There's a cosy bar, a fine-dining restaurant, and a rear outdoor terrace overlooking grapevines.

**Parkhotel Sonnenhof** BOUTIQUE HOTEL €€€

(☎239 02 02; www.sonnenhof.li; Mareestrasse 29; s/d from Sfr195/380; P 🛜 ≋) The Sonnenhof's landscaped gardens command a breathtaking vista of the Alps and Rhine Valley. This boutique hotel piles on the luxury with its oriental-style pool and spa, plush rooms and polished service. The Michelin-starred Restaurant Maree emphasises seasonal cuisine.

### Around Vaduz

★**Hotel Kulm** HOTEL €

(☎237 79 79; www.hotelkulm.li; Schlossstrasse 3, Triesenberg; s/d/tr Sfr80/130/160; P 🛜) In Triesenberg, at 888m, a 10-minute drive up from Vaduz, Hotel Kulm offers stunning views of both the mountains and the Rhine Valley. A buffet breakfast is included, and the 20 rooms are nicely fitted out.

**Camping Mittagspitze** CAMPGROUND, HOSTEL €

(☎392 36 77; www.campingtriesen.li; Sägastrasse 29; sites per adult/child/car Sfr9/4/5, per tent Sfr6-8; P 🛜 ≋) This well-equipped, year-round campground is excellent for families, with a playground and pool as well as a restaurant, TV lounge and kiosk. There is also a hostel building here, perfect for backpackers.

**Schaan-Vaduz Youth Hostel** HOSTEL €

(☎232 50 22; www.youthhostel.ch/schaan; Under Rüttigass 6; dm/s/d Sfr35/66/92; ⏲Mar-Oct; P 🛜) A stay in Liechtenstein need not break the bank. This hostel is particularly geared for cyclists and families. Halfway between Schaan and Vaduz, it's within easy walking distance of either city.

WORTH A TRIP

#### FÜRSTENSTEIG

The country's most famous trail is the **Fürstensteig** (www.tourismus.li/en/activities/summer/hiking/hikes-in-Liechtenstein.html), a rite of passage for nearly every Liechtensteiner. You must be fit and not suffer from vertigo, as in places the path is narrow and falls away to a sheer drop. The 12km hike, including the Drei Schwestern (Three Sisters) track, takes about five hours, begins at Gaflei and ends in Planken.

You can stay at the **Gafadurahütte** (☎787 14 28; www.gafadurahuette.li; dm adult/child Sfr22/10; ⏲mid-May–mid-Oct) at 1428m, above Planken. Check the tourist office for info on track conditions, weather forecasts and up-to-date bus timetables between Gaflei and Planken.

**Hotel Garni Säga** HOTEL €

(☎392 43 77; www.saega.li; Alte Landstrasse 17, Triesen; s/d/tr Sfr89/148/180; P 🛜) Nestled in gardens and with fine mountain views, this family-run pension is a great base for walkers and cyclists. The pick of the comfortable, quiet rooms have balconies overlooking the Rhine Valley.

## Eating & Drinking

Cafes, pizzerias and nondescript restaurants vie for your franc along Städtle, the pedestrianised main street.

**Adler Vaduz** SWISS €€

(☎232 21 31; www.adler.li; Herrengasse 2; mains from Sfr18; ⏲8.30am-midnight Mon-Fri) Creaking wood floors and lilac walls create a rustic-chic backdrop for Swiss classics at the Adler. Dishes like *Zürcher Geschnetzeltes* (sliced veal in a creamy mushroom sauce) go nicely with a glass of Vaduz Pinot Noir.

★**Torkel** SWISS €€€

(☎232 44 10; www.torkel.li; Hintergasse 9; mains from Sfr49; ⏲11.30am-1.30pm & 6.30-9pm Mon-Fri, 6.30-9pm Sat) Just above the prince's vineyards sits His Majesty's ivy-clad restaurant. The garden terrace enjoys a wonderful perspective of the castle above, while the ancient, wood-lined interior is fantastcially cosy in winter. Food moves from local and seasonal to international.

**Vanini Café Bar** BAR
(☎232 21 31; www.adler.li/en/vanini-cafe-bar; Herrengasse 2; ⏰8am-11pm Mon-Fri; 📶) Directly behind the restaurant Adler Vaduz, Vanini is a superb spot to chill out with a beer, wine or coffee and contemplate life.

## Information

For general information on the country, visit www.liechtenstein.li and www.tourismus.li.

**Liechtenstein Center** (☎239 63 63; www.tourismus.li; Städtle 39, Vaduz; ⏰9am-5pm Nov-Apr, 9am-6pm May-Oct) Offers brochures, souvenir passport stamps (Sfr3) and screens with scenes from all over the country.

## Getting There & Away

The Postbus station is in the middle of town. There are frequent buses to Vaduz from the Swiss towns of Buchs (Sfr4, 20 minutes) and Sargans (Sfr5.80, 25 minutes) and from Feldkirch in Austria. Liechtenstein buses are light green; purchase tickets from the driver.

Arriving by car is easy as Vaduz is only 1km from the Swiss border and there are no immigration formalities. The roads from Vaduz to the north and south of Liechtenstein are excellent.

Vaduz is mostly on the flat Rhine Valley making bicycle travel viable.



# Malbun

POP 75 / ELEV 1600M

At the end of the road and a big climb into the mountains from Vaduz (455m), the 1600m-high resort of Malbun feels – in the nicest possible sense – like the end of the world. It's definitely the end of the road and the only way out is back the way you came. It's not really as remote as it seems though, and in the high season Malbun is mobbed. Generally, however, it's perfect for unwinding, especially with the family. The skiing is inexpensive, if not too extensive, while the hiking is beautiful.

## Activities

Skiing is aimed at beginners, with a few intermediate and cross-country runs thrown in. Indeed, older British royals learnt to ski here. A general ski pass (including the Sareis chairlift) for a day/week costs Sfr48/215 for adults and Sfr29/127 for children. Equipment rental is available from Malbun Sport.

**Furstin-Gina Path** HIKING
The 12km Furstin-Gina Path has arresting views over Austria, Switzerland and Liechtenstein. This walk starts at the top of the Sareis chairlift (Sfr9.80/15.30 single/return in summer) and returns to Malbun.

### TWO WHEELS, THREE COUNTRIES

Liechtenstein's location on the border to Austria and Switzerland makes it easy to pedal across borders by bike in a day. One of the most scenic and memorable rides is the 59km **Drei Länder Tour** (Three Countries Tour), which leads from Vaduz to the medieval town of Feldkirch in Austria. The route then heads on to Illspitz and down along the Rhine to Buchs in Switzerland – dominated by its 13th-century castle, Schloss Werdenberg – before heading back to Vaduz.

Maps and e-bikes are available from the tourist office in Vaduz.

## Sleeping & Eating

**Alpenhotel Vögeli** GUESTHOUSE €
(☎263 11 81; www.alpenhotel.li; r per person Sfr90; P📶🏊) With speedy access to the slopes in winter and trails in summer, this welcoming guesthouse has bright, comfy rooms in the classic Alpine mould. There's a mountain-view pool, sauna and pine-clad restaurant.

★ **Familienhotel Gorfion** HOTEL €€
(☎265 90 00; http://en.gorfion.li; Stubistrasse 8; r per adult/child from Sfr135/50; P📶🏊) Tots in tow? This is your place. Kids are kept amused with a playground, petting zoo and activities. Parents, meanwhile, can enjoy a lie-in with the (like it!) sleep-in service, and relax in the whirlpool. Kids' mealtimes are supervised and the hotel will let you borrow buggies, backpacks, highchairs – you name it.

**Bergrestaurant Sareis** SWISS €
(☎263 46 86; www.bergrestaurant-sareis.li; light meals Sfr9.50-21.50; ⏰8am-5pm Jun–mid-Oct, 9am-4pm mid-Dec–Apr) For amazing mountain views while eating, it is hard to beat this woodsy hut, at the top of the Sareis chairlift.

## Information

**Tourist Office** (☎263 65 77; www.malbun.li; ⏰9am-noon & 1-4pm mid-Dec–mid-Apr, 9am-noon Mon-Fri, 9am-1.30pm Sat & Sun Jul–mid-Oct) The tourist office is on the main street.

## Getting There & Away

Bus 21 travels more or less hourly from Vaduz to Malbun between 7.15am and 8.15pm daily (Sfr3.50, 30 minutes), returning between 8.20am and 7.20pm. It's a 14km drive (uphill!) from Vaduz to Malbun. There is plenty of parking.

# Understand Switzerland

# History

**Switzerland is unique, and nowhere is this more explicit than in its history. An exception to the nation-state norm, this small, landlocked country is a rare and refined breed, born out of its 1874 constitution and tried and tested by two world wars (during which it remained firmly neutral). Despite the overwhelming presence of global institutions and moves towards greater international cooperation, modern-day Switzerland remains insular, idiosyncratic and staunchly singular.**

## Clans & Castles: Swiss Roots

Modern Swiss history might start in 1291, but that's not to say that the thousands of years leading up to Switzerland's birth are not significant – this was the period that gave Switzerland the best of its châteaux and *schlösser* (castles).

The earliest inhabitants were Celtic tribes, including the Helvetii of the Jura and the Mittelland Plain, and the Rhaetians near Graubünden. Their homelands were first invaded by the Romans, who had gained a foothold under Julius Caesar by 58 BCE and established Aventicum (now Avenches) as the capital of Helvetia (Roman Switzerland). Switzerland's largest Roman ruins are at Augusta Raurica, near Basel. By 400CE, Germanic Alemanni tribes arrived to drive out the Romans.

Switzerland's neutrality is actually the world's second longest: Sweden has been neutral since it ended its involvement in the Napoleonic Wars in 1814.

The Alemanni groups settled in eastern Switzerland and were later joined by another Germanic tribe, the Burgundians, in the western part of the country. The latter adopted Christianity and the Latin language, sowing the seeds of division between French- and German-speaking Switzerland. The Franks conquered both tribes in the 6th century, but the two areas were torn apart again when Charlemagne's empire was partitioned in 870.

When it was reunited under the pan-European Holy Roman Empire in 1032, Switzerland initially was left to its own devices. Local nobles wielded the most influence: the Zähringen family, who founded Fribourg, Bern and Murten, and built a fairy-tale castle with soaring towers and red turrets in Thun in the Bernese Oberland; and the Savoy clan, who established a ring of castles around Lake Geneva, most notably Château

**TIMELINE**

**58 BCE**

Julius Caesar establishes Celtic tribe the Helvetii between the Alps and the Jura to watch over the Rhine frontier and keep Germanic tribes out of Roman territory.

**1032 CE**

Clans in western Switzerland, together with the kingdom of Burgundy, are swallowed up by the Holy Roman Empire but left with a large degree of autonomy.

**1291**

Modern Switzerland officially 'begins' with an independence pact at Rütli Meadow. Many historians consider the event, and the accompanying William Tell legend, to have actually taken place in 1307.

de Morges and the magnificent Château de Chillon, right on the water's edge near Montreux.

When the Habsburg ruler Rudolph I became Holy Roman Emperor in 1273, he sent in heavy-handed bailiffs to collect more taxes and tighten the administrative screws. Swiss resentment grew quickly.

## Confoederatio Helvetica: Modern Switzerland

Rudolph I died in 1291, prompting local leaders to make an immediate grab for independence. On 1 August that year, the forest communities of Uri, Schwyz and Nidwalden – so the tale goes – gathered on Rütli Meadow in the Schwyz canton in Central Switzerland to sign an alliance vowing not to recognise any external judge or law. Historians believe this to be a slightly distorted version, but, whatever the scenario, a pact does exist, preserved in the town of Schwyz. Displayed at the Bundesbrief-museum, the pact is seen as the founding act of the Swiss Confederation, whose Latin name, Confoederatio Helvetica, survives in the 'CH' abbreviation for Switzerland (used, for example, on oval-shaped car stickers and as an internet domain extension).

In 1315, Duke Leopold I of Austria dispatched a powerful army to quash the growing Swiss nationalism. Instead, the Swiss inflicted an epic defeat on his troops at Morgarten, which prompted other communities to join the Swiss union. The next 200 years of Swiss history was a time of successive military wins, land grabs and new memberships. The following cantons came on board: Lucerne (1332), Zürich (1351), Glarus and Zug (1352), Bern (1353), Fribourg and Solothurn (1481), Basel and Schaffhausen (1501), and Appenzell (1513). In the middle of all this, the Swiss Confederation gained independence from Holy Roman Emperor Maximilian I after a victory at Dornach in 1499.

**Best Castles**

*Château de Chillon (p77), Montreux*

*Château de Morges (p69), Morges*

*Schloss Thun (p134), Thun*

*Medieval castles (p180), Bellinzona*

*Burg Hohenklingen (p261), Stein am Rhein*

*Wasserschloss Hallwyl (p230), Aargau Canton*

## No More Stinging Defeats: Swiss Neutrality

Swiss neutrality was essentially born out of the stinging defeat that the rampaging Swiss, having made it as far as Milan, suffered in 1515 against a combined French and Venetian force at Marignano, 16km southeast of Milan. After the bloody battle, the Swiss gave up their expansionist dream, withdrew from the international arena and declared neutrality for the first time. For centuries since, the country's warrior spirit has been channelled solely into mercenary activity – a tradition that continues today in the Swiss Guard that protects the pope at the Vatican.

When the religious Thirty Years' War (1618–48) broke out in Europe, Switzerland's neutrality and diversity combined to give it some protection.

**1315**

Swiss irregular troops win a surprise victory over Habsburg Austrian forces at the Battle of Morgarten. It was the first of several Swiss victories over imperial invaders.

**1499**

The Swiss Confederation wins virtual independence from the Habsburg-led Holy Roman Empire after imperial forces are defeated in a series of battles along the Rhine and on Swiss territory.

**1515**

After Swiss forces take Milan and Pavia in Italy in 1512, the Swiss are defeated at Marignano by a French-Venetian army. Chastised, the Swiss withdraw and declare neutrality.

**1590–1600**

Some 300 women in Vaud are captured, tortured and burned alive on charges of witchcraft, even as Protestants in other Swiss cantons strive to end witch hunts.

Protestant Swiss first openly disobeyed the Catholic Church during 1522's 'affair of the sausages', when a printer and several priests in Zürich were caught gobbling *Würste* on Ash Wednesday, when they should have been fasting.

The Protestant Reformation led by preachers Huldrych Zwingli and Jean Calvin made some inroads in Zürich and Geneva, while Central Switzerland (Zentralschweiz) remained Catholic. Such was the internal division that the Swiss, unable to agree even among themselves as to which side to take in the Thirty Years' War, stuck to neutrality.

The French invaded Switzerland in 1798 and established the brief Helvetic Republic, but they were no more welcome than the Austrians before them, and internal fighting prompted Napoleon (then in power in France) to restore the former Confederation of Cantons in 1803 – the cantons of Aargau, St Gallen, Graubünden, Ticino, Thurgau and Vaud joined the confederation at this time.

Swiss neutrality as it exists today was formally established by the Congress of Vienna peace treaty in 1815 that, following Napoleon's defeat by the British and Prussians at Waterloo, formally guaranteed Switzerland's independence and neutrality for the first time. (The same treaty also added the cantons of Valais, Geneva and Neuchâtel to the Swiss bow.)

Despite some citizens' pro-German sympathies, Switzerland's only involvement in WWI lay in organising Red Cross units. After the war, Switzerland joined the League of Nations, but on a strictly financial and economic basis (which included providing its headquarters in Geneva) – it would have no military involvement.

WWII likewise saw Switzerland remain neutral, the country unscathed bar some accidental bombings on Schaffhausen in April 1944, when Allied pilots mistook the town in northeastern Switzerland for Germany, twice dropping bombs on its outskirts. Indeed, the most momentous event of WWII for the Swiss was when Henri Guisan, general of the civilian army, invited all top military personnel to Rütli Meadow (site of the 1291 Oath of Allegiance) to show the world how determined the Swiss were to defend their own soil.

**Best Swiss History Museums**

- *Bundesbriefmuseum (p211), Schwyz*
- *Schweizerisches Landesmuseum (p236), Zürich*
- *Historisches Museum Bern (p104), Bern*
- *Château de Prangins (p70), Nyon*
- *Château de Chillon (p77), Montreux*

## Give Cantons a Voice: the Swiss Constitution

In 1847, civil war broke out. The Protestant army, led by General Dufour, quickly crushed the Sonderbund (Special League) of Catholic cantons, including Lucerne. The war lasted a mere 26 days, prompting German chancellor Otto von Bismarck to subsequently dismiss it as 'a hare shoot', but for the peace-loving Swiss, the disruption and disorder were sufficient to ensure they rapidly consolidated the victory by Dufour's forces with the creation of a new federal constitution. Bern was named the capital.

The 1848 constitution, largely still in place today, was a compromise between advocates of central control and conservative forces who

**1847**

'Hare shoot' civil war between Protestants and Catholics lasts just 26 days, leaving 86 dead and 500 wounded, and paving the way for the 1848 federal constitution.

**1863**

After witnessing slaughter and untended wounded at the Battle of Solferino in 1859 in northern Italy, businessman and pacifist Henri Dunant co-founds the International Red Cross in Geneva.

**1918**

With a sixth of the population living below the poverty line and 20,000 dead of a flu epidemic, workers strike; the 48-hour week is among the long-term results.

**1940**

General Guisan's army warns off WWII invaders; 430,000 troops are placed on borders but most are put in Alpine fortresses to carry out partisan war in case of German invasion.

wanted to retain cantonal authority. The cantons eventually relinquished their right to print money, run postal services and levy customs duties, ceding these to the federal government, but they retained legislative and executive control over local matters. Furthermore, the new Federal Assembly was established in a way that gave cantons a voice. The lower national chamber, the Nationalrat, has 200 members, allocated from the 26 cantons in proportion to population size. The upper states chamber, the Ständerat, comprises 46 members, with two per canton.

Opposition to political corruption sparked a movement for greater democracy. The constitution was revised in 1874 so that many federal laws had to be approved by national referendum – a phenomenon for which Switzerland remains famous today. A petition with 50,000 signatures can challenge a proposed law; 100,000 signatures can force a public vote on *any* new issue.

## THE MAGIC FORMULA: SWISS GOVERNMENT

The make-up of Switzerland's Federal Council, the executive government, is determined not by who wins the most parliamentary seats (ie the winning party rules), but by the 'magic formula' – a cosy power-sharing agreement made between the four main parties in 1959:

- The Federal Council consists of seven ministers, elected one by one by the parliament.
- The four largest parties in parliament are guaranteed seats in the Federal Council in accordance with their share of the popular vote.
- The president is drawn on a rotating basis from the seven federal ministers, so there's a new head of state each year.
- Each councillor takes charge of one of seven federal executive departments (finance, foreign affairs etc).
- Many federal laws must first be approved by public referendum; several are held every year.

For decades, the three biggest political parties (the Free Democratic Party, the Christian Democrats and the Social Democrats) had two seats each, with the fourth party – the right-wing Swiss People's Party (SVP) – having one seat. This 'grand coalition' was altered in 2003, when the SVP gained a seat on the council (and the Christian Democrats lost one), and once more in 2008, when the SVP split and the Conservative Democrats was formed.

At the last federal elections in 2019, strong gains were made by the left-wing Green Party, which received 13.2% of the vote, surpassing expectations and reflected the heightened importance of climate change and environmental issues. Despite a drop in support, the right-wing, anti-immigration SVP (Swiss People's Party) remained the largest party in parliament, with 25.6% of the overall vote.

**1979**

Five years after a first vote in favour in 1974, the Jura (majority French-speaking Catholics), absorbed by Bern in 1815, leaves Bern (German-speaking Protestants), becoming an independent canton.

**1990**

The internet is 'born' at Geneva's CERN, where Tim Berners-Lee develops HTML, the language used to prepare pages for the World Wide Web and link text to graphics.

**2001**

National airline Swissair collapses, a gun massacre in Zug parliament kills 14 politicians, 21 people perish in a canyoning accident and 11 die in a fire in the St Gotthard Tunnel.

**2008**

The world financial crisis affects Switzerland's two biggest banks, UBS and Credit Suisse. The government bails out UBS with a US$60-billion package, while Credit Suisse seeks funds elsewhere.

## Famously Secret: Swiss Banking

Even in a new, fiscally transparent world, neutral Switzerland remains an exceedingly attractive place to stash cash. Every Swiss canton sets its own tax rates, encouraging individuals and businesses to 'play' the canton market; Zug entices tycoons with Switzerland's lowest income and corporate tax rates and tax breaks.

Banking confidentiality, dating back to the Middle Ages, was enshrined in Swiss law in 1934 when numbered (rather than named) bank accounts were introduced. The Swiss banking industry has, for the most part, thrived ever since, thanks mainly to the enviable stability that guaranteed neutrality brings. When the Bank for International Settlements (BIS; the organisation that facilitates cooperation between central banks) chose Basel as its base in 1930 it was for one good reason: Switzerland was a neutral player.

In the late 1990s, a series of scandals erupted, forcing Switzerland to start reforming its secretive banking industry, born when a clutch of commercial banks was created in the mid-19th century. In 1995, after pressure from Jewish groups, Swiss banks announced that they had discovered millions of dollars lying in dormant pre-1945 accounts and belonging to Holocaust victims and survivors. Three years later, amid allegations they'd been sitting on the money without seriously trying to trace its owners, Switzerland's two largest banks, UBS and Credit Suisse, agreed to pay US$1.25 billion in compensation to Holocaust survivors and their families.

Switzerland has long been a favourite spot for the wealthy to deposit their fortunes in private banks, hence the immense pressure on Switzerland since 2009 from the US, Britain, Germany and other high-tax countries to change its 1934 banking law protecting depositors accused of tax evasion by their home countries.

The Swiss conceded, prompting critics to triumphantly ring the death knell for Swiss banking secrecy. Amid the hand-wringing, Wegelin, Switzerland's oldest bank, shut up shop in 2013, after pleading guilty in the US to aiding tax evasion. That same year, Switzerland and the US signed a joint statement allowing Swiss banks to voluntarily cooperate with US authorities on the issue of tax evasion. In 2014 Switzerland's second-largest bank, Credit Suisse, pleaded guilty to criminal wrongdoing in the form of conspiring to aid tax evasion over many years. The bank agreed to pay US$2.6 billion in penalties.

Visit www.parliament.ch and www.admin.ch for insight into Switzerland's unusual political system, with its 'direct democracy', 'magic formula' and part-time politicians.

In 2018, the era of secret Swiss bank accounts finally came to an end, with new rules introduced to ensure that account details are shared with the tax authorities of other nations, in line with international transparency standards.

## Forever Neutral: a Nation Apart

Since the end of WWII, Switzerland has enjoyed an uninterrupted period of economic, social and political stability – thanks, in predictable Swiss fashion, to the neutrality that saw it forge ahead from an already powerful commercial, financial and industrial base while the rest of

**2009**

The first experiments in the world's largest particle accelerator are successfully conducted with the Large Hadron Collider at CERN, the European Centre for Nuclear Research in Geneva.

**2014**

A popular initiative to set immigration quotas is successful at the Swiss polls.

**2016**

The Gotthard Base Tunnel, the world's longest at 57km, opens for operation in December, speeding up connections between the Alps and Italy.

**2017**

The Swiss vote in favour of phasing out nuclear energy and switching to renewables.

Europe was still picking up and rebuilding the pieces broken during the war. Zürich developed as an international banking and insurance centre, and the World Health Organization and a range of other international bodies set up headquarters in Geneva. To preserve its neutrality, however, Switzerland chose to remain outside the UN (although Geneva has hosted its second-largest seat after the main New York headquarters from the outset) and, more recently, the European Union.

A hefty swing to the conservative right in the 2003 parliamentary elections served to further enhance Switzerland's standing as a nation staunchly apart. In 2006, the anti-EU, anti-immigration Swiss People's Party (SVP) called for the toughening of immigration and political-asylum laws; the policies were passed with an overwhelming majority at a national referendum. Then there was the rumpus over the right-wing bid to ban the building of new minarets for Muslim calls to prayer – an idea that aroused much anger internationally but was approved by the constitution after 57.7% of voters said yes to the ban in a referendum. During the campaign, the SVP published anti-immigrant posters featuring three white sheep kicking one black sheep off the striking white cross of the Swiss flag.

In spite of the SVP's tough conservative line, there have been many positive signs that Switzerland is opening up to embrace the wider world. The country became the 190th member of the UN in 2002 (a referendum on the issue had last been defeated in 1986) and three years later it voted to join Europe's passport-free travel zone, Schengen (finally completing the process at the end of 2008). The Swiss put an end to banking secrecy in 2018, and in 2019, the Green Party made impressive gains in the parliamentary elections. In a 2021 referendum, the majority of Swiss (two thirds) voted to allow same-sex marriage.

Yet few expect Switzerland to even consider joining either the EU or the euro zone any time soon (if ever). Traditionally, the western, French-speaking cantons are more sympathetic to the idea, while the German-speaking cantons (and Ticino) have generally been opposed. In 2021, after years of talks, the country scrapped the idea of an over-arching treaty with the EU, citing protection of wages, state aid, and the right of EU citizens working in Switzerland to claim welfare benefits as reasons.

Switzerland has always been a step ahead of the game environmentally, with the Swiss government aiming to halve emissions by their 1990 levels by 2030 and committing to achieving climate neutrality by 2050. It came as a shock, therefore, when voters narrowly rejected key climate change measures in a law to limit emissions (including government plans for a car fuel levy and air ticket tax) in a 2021 referendum.

When Switzerland finally joined the UN in 2002, officials mistakenly ordered a rectangular Swiss flag to fly outside the organisation's New York headquarters. Swiss functionaries strenuously objected, insisting the UN run up the proper square flag pretty damn quick.



**2018**
Swiss bank secrecy comes to an end as Swiss start sharing account data.

**2019**
Green parties make significant gains in Switzerland's parliamentary election, though the anti-immigration Swiss People's Party (SVP) comes top.

**2021**
The Swiss vote overwhelmingly to allow same-sex couples to marry in a referendum that aligns the country with others in Western Europe.

**2021**
Following years of talks, Switzerland rejects efforts aimed at finding an over-arching treaty with the EU.

# Swiss Way of Life

**Chocolate, cheese, cuckoo clocks, precision watches, banking secrecy, bircher muesli, Heidi, William Tell, yodelling and the Alps: a swath of stereotypes envelops Switzerland and the Swiss. This perfectly well-behaved country is hard-working, super organised, efficient, orderly, obedient (have you ever seen a Swiss pedestrian cross the road when the little man is red?), overly cautious and ruthlessly efficient – a mother-in-law's dream. Or maybe not...**

## Special-Case Switzerland

The Swiss see themselves as different, and they are. Take their country's overwhelming cultural diversity, eloquently expressed in four languages and attitudes; German-, French- and Italian-speaking Swiss all display similar characteristics to German, French and Italian people respectively, creating an instant line-up of reassuringly varied, diverse and oftentimes surprising psyches. Then there are those in Graubünden who speak Romansch. One cookie-cutter shape definitely does not fit *Sonderfall Schweiz* (literally 'special-case Switzerland') and its different inhabitants.

Given their comfortable and privileged lifestyle, it's hardly surprising that the Swiss have such impressive life-expectancy figures: women live to an average 84.7 years and men to 80.5.

Quite the contrary: from centuries-old Alpine traditions that are positively wild in nature, such as wrestling and stone throwing, to new-millennium Googlers in Zürich who shimmy into work down a fire pole, to Geneva jewellers who make exclusive watches from moon dust or ash from Iceland's Eyjafjallajökull volcano, to fashionable 30-somethings sporting bags made of recycled truck tarps, the Swiss like to innovate.

They also have the determination to complement their creativity – keenly demonstrated by their restless quest to test their limits in the sporting arena, and the extraordinarily tough, independent spirit with which Swiss farmers resolutely work the land to create a sustainable lifestyle. That *Sonderfall Schweiz* halo might not shine quite as brightly as it did a few decades back, but Switzerland definitely still glows.

## A Quality Lifestyle

To be born Swiss is to be born lucky, thanks to a combination of universal health care, quality education and a strong economy (not to mention one hell of a backyard in the form of all those lakes and mountains). No less an authority than the Economist Intelligence Unit declared Switzerland the best place in the world to be born in 2013, based on 11 indicators (including geography, job security and political stability). In addition to this, Swiss cities – such as Zürich and Geneva – regularly appear on 'world's best cities' lists. In the Mercer Consulting 2017 quality-of-life report, these cities were ranked second and eighth respectively.

The Swiss are conservative with money and their currency. Since the Swiss franc went into circulation in the 1850s, it has rarely been tampered with; there are (rare) 10-centime coins minted in 1879 that are still in circulation and legal tender.

Yet the Swiss don't necessarily enjoy a particularly different lifestyle from other Westerners; they just enjoy it more. They can rely on their little nation, one of the world's 10 richest in terms of GDP per capita, to deliver excellent health services, efficient public transport and all-round security. Spend a little time among them and you realise their sportiness and concern for the environment is symptomatic of another condition: they simply want to extract as much as possible from life.

The Swiss lifestyle is not all hobnobbing on the ski slopes during weekend visits to the chalet. Rural regions – particularly Appenzellerland, Valais and the Jura – are not about money-driven glam but traditional culture that lives and breathes. The people mark the seasons with time-honoured local traditions and rituals, such as the autumnal grape harvest, celebrated with ancient feasts, or spring shepherds decorating their cattle with flowers and bells to herd them in procession to mountain pastures for the summer.

## Alpine Tourism

The geography of Switzerland is what gives the country its sporting backbone and makes its people so outrageously outdoor-oriented. It's also how little Switzerland put itself on the map as a big tourist destination. In the 19th century, during the golden age of Alpinism, it was the Swiss Alpine peaks that proved particularly alluring to British climbers. Alfred Wills made the first ascent of the Wetterhorn (3692m) above Grindelwald in 1854, which was followed by a rash of ascents up other Swiss peaks, including Edward Whymper's famous Matterhorn expedition in 1865. This flurry of pioneering activity in the Swiss Alps prompted the world's first mountaineering club, the Alpine Club, to be founded in London in 1857, followed by the Swiss Alpine Club in 1863.

With the construction of the first mountain hut on Tödi (3614m) the same year and the emergence of St Moritz and its intoxicating 'champagne climate' a year later as *the* place to winter among British aristocracy, winter Alpine tourism was born. Hotels, railways and cable cars followed, and by the time St Moritz hosted the second Winter Olympics in 1928, Switzerland was the winter-wonderland-action buzzword on everyone's lips. Not surprisingly, one year on, the first ski school in Switzerland opened its doors in St Moritz.

Fast forward almost a century and the Swiss Olympic Committee is backing Sion in its bid for the 2026 Winter Olympics.

### Alpine History Museums

*Matterhorn Museum (p161), Zermatt*

*Schweizerisches Alpines Museum (p103), Bern*

*Engadiner Museum (p292), St Moritz*

*Rätisches Museum (www.raetisches museum.gr.ch), Chur*

*Ballenberg Open-Air Museum (p136), near Brienz*

*Saaser Museum (p168), Saas Fee*

## Wacky Sports

Swiss specialist sports include *Hornussen,* a game of medieval origin played between two 16- to 18-strong teams. One launches a 78g *Hornuss* (ball) over a field; the other tries to stop it hitting the ground with a *Schindel,* a 4kg implement resembling a road sign. To add to the game's bizarre quality, the *Hornuss* is launched by whipping it around a steel ramp with a flexible rod in a motion that's a cross between shot putting and fly-fishing. The *Schindel* can be used as a bat to stop the 85m-per-second ball or simply tossed into the air at it.

*Schwingen* is a Swiss version of sumo wrestling. Two people, each wearing short hessian shorts, face off across a circle of sawdust. Through a complicated combination of prescribed grips (including crotch grips), jerks, feints and other manoeuvres, each tries to wrestle their opponent onto his or her back. See it at mountain fairs and Alpine festivals, most notably the phenomenal Unspunnenfest (www.unspunnenfest.ch), held every 12 years in Interlaken – the last one was held from late August to early September in 2017.

For wacky sports, head to French-speaking Valais, where cow fighting is a mighty serious business – watch it in the Val d'Hérens.

## E=mc², WWW & LSD: the Scientific Swiss

The Swiss have more registered patents and Nobel Prize winners (mostly in scientific disciplines) per capita than any other nationality.

It was while he was working in Bern (between 1903 and 1905) that Albert Einstein developed his theory of relativity. German born, Einstein studied in Aarau and later in Zürich, where he trained to be a physics and maths teacher. He was granted Swiss citizenship in 1901 and, unable to find a suitable teaching post, wound up working as a low-paid clerk in the

## SOLAR MOBILITY

In typical green-thinking Swiss fashion, the Swiss are playing around with solar power – and setting new ground-breaking records in sustainable technology along the way. In 2016, *Solar Impulse 2* (www.solarimpulse.com), an ultra-light solar-powered aeroplane, made history by becoming the first plane to journey 40,000km around the world without a single drop of fuel. For pioneering Lausanne adventurers, explorers and scientists André Borschberg and Bertrand Piccard, it was a dream come true. A remarkable achievement that involved overcoming many logistical challenges, it marked firsts in the history of aviation and in renewable energy.

The Swiss don't restrict their solar-transport innovations to the air. On water, *Planet-Solar,* the world's largest solar-powered boat, set sail in 2010 from Monaco on a world tour covering 50,000km. The catamaran, flying the Swiss flag, is energised by 536 sq metres of photovoltaic panels on deck and is headed by Swiss expedition leader and project founder Raphaël Domjan. Since 2015 it has been operated by the Swiss-based Race for Water Foundation as a scientific platform in the fight against plastic pollution in the oceans. Follow the boat at www.planetsolar.org.

Bern patent office. He gained his doctorate in 1905 and subsequently became a professor in Zürich, remaining in Switzerland until 1914, when he moved to Berlin. Bern's Einstein-Haus museum (p103) tells the full story.

**Science Trips**

*CERN (p47), Geneva*

*Technorama (p248), Winterthur*

*Einstein-Haus (p103), Bern*

*Maison d'Ailleurs (www.ailleurs.ch), Yverdon-les-Bains*

The internet, meanwhile, was born in Geneva at the European Organization for Nuclear Research, better known as CERN, on Christmas Day 1990. The genius behind the global information-sharing tool was Oxford graduate Tim Berners-Lee, a software consultant for CERN who started out creating a program for the research centre to help its hundreds of scientists share their experiments, data and discoveries. Two years on it had become a dramatically larger and more powerful beast than anyone could have imagined.

Equally dramatic, large and powerful is CERN's Large Hadron Collider, where Geneva scientists play God with Big Bang experiments. A guided tour of the world's biggest physics experiment, quietly conducted in a Geneva suburb, is phenomenal.

Other great Swiss science forays include the ground-breaking glacial research carried out by courageous 19th-century scientists on the extraordinary 23km-long Aletsch Glacier in the Upper Valais, and a chemist in Basel called Albert Hofmann inadvertently embarking on the world's first acid trip – ingesting lysergic acid diethylamide (LSD) – in 1943.

## Forever Innovating: Architecture

Switzerland's contribution to modern architecture has been pivotal thanks to Le Corbusier (1887–1965), born in the small Jura town of La Chaux-de-Fonds. Known for his radical economy of design, formalism and functionalism, Le Corbusier spent most of his working life in France but graced his country of birth with his first and last creations.

CERN's most recent headline-grabbing breakthrough came in 2012, when scientists revealed that they had identified the subatomic particle known as the Higgs boson (aka the 'God particle').

Swiss architects continue to innovate. Basel-based partners Jacques Herzog and Pierre de Meuron are the best known. Strings in their bow include London's Tate Modern gallery and the main stadium for the 2008 Beijing Olympics. In Switzerland you can admire their work at an art gallery in Basel and – hopefully in the next decade – in Davos, in the shape of a 105m-tall pencil twisting above the famous Schatzalp hotel, should the debate ever end over whether to start construction.

The other big home-grown architect is Ticino-born Mario Botta, who basks in the international limelight as creator of San Francisco's Museum of Modern Art. Closer to home, his Chiesa di San Giovanni Battista in Mogno in Ticino's Valle Maggia and his cathedral-style Tschuggen Bergoase spa hotel in Arosa, Graubünden, are soul-soothing creations, while his futuristic remake of Leuk's Romanesque *schloss* (castle) in Upper Valais is nothing short of wacky. His latest Swiss creation is Fiore di Pietra (Stone Flower), which opened in spring 2017, with astonishing views of Lago di Lugano and the Alps from its fabulous Monte Generoso perch in Ticino.

Then there's the award-winning 7132 Therme in Vals by Basel-born Peter Zumthor, Davos' Kirchner Museum by Zürich's Annette Gigon and Mike Guyer, and a clutch of design hotels in Zermatt by resident avant-garde architect Heinz Julen.

In true Swiss fashion, contemporary Swiss architects don't confine their work to urban Switzerland. Increasingly their focus is on the mountain hut and how it can be modernised in keeping with nature, ecology and the environment. Stunning examples are the Tschierva Hütte (2753m) in the Engadine Valley; Chetzeron, a concrete 1960s cable-car station turned hip piste hangout on the slopes in Crans-Montana; and, most significantly, the visionary Monte Rosa Hütte (2883m) on Monte Rosa.

**Architectural Pilgrimages**

*La Maison Blanche (p96), La Chaux-de-Fonds*

*Villa Le Lac (p72), Corseaux*

*Schaulager (p223), Basel*

*Pavillon Le Corbusier (www.museen-zuerich.ch), Zürich*

*7132 Therme (p282), Vals*

*Ballenberg Open-Air Museum (p136), near Brienz*

## Heidi & Co: Literature

Thanks to a 1930s Shirley Temple film, Johanna Spyri's *Heidi* is Switzerland's most famous novel. The story of an orphan living with her grandfather in the Swiss Alps who is ripped away to the city is unashamedly sentimental and utterly atypical for Swiss literature, which is otherwise generally quite serious and gloomy.

Take German-born, naturalised Swiss Hermann Hesse (1877–1962). A Nobel Prize winner, he fused Eastern mysticism and Jungian psychology to advance the theory that Western civilisation is doomed unless humankind gets in touch with its own essential humanity – as in *Siddharta* (1922) and *Steppenwolf* (1927). Later novels such as the cult *The Glass Bead Game* (1943) explore the tension between individual freedom and social controls.

*Ich bin nicht Stiller* (I'm Not Stiller/I'm Not Relaxed; 1954), by Zürich-born Max Frisch (1911–91), is a dark, Kafkaesque tale of mistaken identity. More accessible is the work of Friedrich Dürrenmatt (1921–90), who created a wealth of detective fiction.

*Green Henry* (1854), by Gottfried Keller (1819–1900), is a massive tome revolving around a Zürich student's reminiscences and is considered one of the masterpieces of Germanic literature.

## Pastoral to Pop: Music

Yodelling and alpenhorns are the traditional forms of Swiss music. Yodelling began in the Alps as a means of communication between peaks, but it became separated into two disciplines: *Juchzin* consists of short yells with different meanings, such as 'it's dinner time' or 'we're coming', while *Naturjodel* sees one or more voices sing a melody without lyrics. Yodelling is fast becoming the trendy thing to do in urban circles, thanks in part to Swiss folk singers like Nadja Räss who yodel with great success.

James Joyce spent much of WWI in Zürich, where he wrote *Ulysses*. Listen to weekly readings of excerpts from *Ulysses* and *Finnegan's Wake* at the James Joyce Foundation (p235).

'Dr Schacher Seppli' is a traditional song reyodelled by Switzerland's best-known yodeller, farmer and cheesemaker Rudolf Rymann (1933–2008). The other big sound is Sonalp, a nine-person band from the Gruyères/Château d'Œx region, whose vibrant ethno-folk mix of yodelling, cow bells, musical saw, classical violin and didgeridoo is contagious.

The alpenhorn, a pastoral instrument used to herd cattle in the mountains, is 2m to 4m long with a curved base and a cup-shaped mouthpiece; the shorter the horn the harder it is to play. Catch a symphony of a hundred-odd alpenhorn players blowing in unison on the 'stage' – usually alfresco and invariably lakeside between mountain peaks – if you can. Key dates include September's Alphorn in Concert festival (www.alphorninconcert.ch) in Oesingen near Solothurn and July's

## COMPLETELY DADA

Antibourgeois, rebellious, nihilistic and deliberately nonsensical, Dada grew out of revulsion to WWI and the mechanisation of modern life. Its proponents paved the way for nearly every form of contemporary art by using collage, extracting influences from indigenous art, applying abstract notions to writing, film and performance, and taking manufactured objects and redefining them as art.

Zürich was the movement's birthplace. Hugo Ball, Tristan Tzara and Emmy Jennings' creation of the Cabaret Voltaire in February 1916 kicked off a series of raucous cabaret and performance-art events in a bar at Spiegelgasse 1 (still in place today). The name Dada was allegedly randomly chosen by stabbing a knife through a French-German dictionary.

By 1923 the movement was dead, but its spirit lives on in the works of true Dadaists like George Grosz, Hans Arp and Max Ernst and those infected with its ideas, such as Marcel Duchamp (whose somewhat damaged urinal-as-art piece conveys the idea succinctly) and photographer Man Ray. See Dadaist works in Zürich's Kunsthaus (p234) and Museum für Gestaltung (p235).

International Alphorn Festival (www.nendaz.ch), emotively held on the Alpine shores of Lac de Tracouet in Nendaz, 13km south of Sion in Valais; hike or ride the cable car up for a complete Alpine experience.

If jazzy-folky-pop's more your cup of tea, the fragile voice of Bern-born singer Sophie Hunger, who flips between English, German and Swiss German, will win you over. Her recent albums, *1983* (2010), *The Danger of Light* (2012) and *Supermoon* (2015), were huge successes. For some (much) harder beats, Stress, Switzerland's hottest hip-hop artist, is known for his at times controversial and political lyrics.

## Painting, Sculpture & Design

Dada aside, Switzerland has produced little in the way of 'movements'. In terms of Swiss 'themes', the painter Ferdinand Hodler (1853–1918) depicted folk heroes like William Tell, and events from history, such as the first grassroots Swiss vote. Unlike many of his fellow Swiss artists, Bern-born Hodler remained resident in Switzerland. His colourful landscapes of Lake Geneva and the Alps are worth seeking out in Swiss museums.

> Climb to the top of the country's coolest skyscraper in Zürich's trendy Kreis 5 district, aka a pile of containers inside the Freitag factory shop. Pioneers in Swiss design, the Freitag brothers turn truck tarps into chic, water-resistant bags for every occasion.

The country's best-known artist, abstract painter and colour specialist Paul Klee (1879–1940), spent most of his life in Germany, including with the Bauhaus school, but the largest showcase of his work is at the striking and fascinating Zentrum Paul Klee (p102) in Bern. Likewise, sculptor Alberto Giacometti (1901–66) was born in Graubünden and worked in Paris, but many of his trademark wiry sculpted figures (often walking or standing) can be seen in Zürich's Kunsthaus (p234). Quirky meta-mechanic sculptures by Paris-based Jean Tinguely (1925–91) are clustered around Basel (where there's a museum dedicated to his work) and Fribourg.

The Swiss excel in graphic design. The 'new graphics' of Josef Müller-Brockmann (1914–96) and Max Bill (1908–94) are still well regarded, as is the branding work by Karl Gerstner (1930–2017) for IBM and the Búro Destruct studio's typefaces, a feature of many album covers.

Product design and installation art are Switzerland's other fortes. It gave the world Europe's largest urban lounge in St Gallen in Northeastern Switzerland, courtesy of Pipilotti Rist (b 1962), and *Cow Parade,* processions of life-size, painted fibreglass cows trotting around the globe. The first 800-head herd had its outing in Zürich in 1998 and stray animals in different garb continue to lurk around the country.

# The Swiss Table

**There's more to Swiss cuisine than cheese and chocolate. The food in this largely rural country is driven by season and setting: air-dried meats on a farm, fondue in a forest – you name it. If Alpine tradition gives Swiss food its soul, geography gives it an unexpected edge. Cooks in French-speaking cantons take cues from France, Ticino kitchens turn to Italy and a fair chunk of the country looks to Germany and Austria for culinary clues.**

## Not Only Holes: Cheese

First things first: not all Swiss cheese has holes. Emmental, the hard cheese from the Emme Valley east of Bern, does – as does the not dissimilar Tilsiter from the same valley. But, contrary to common perception, most of Switzerland's 450 types of cheese (*käse* in German, *fromage* in French, *formaggio* in Italian) are hole-less. Take the well-known hard cheese Gruyère, made in the town of Gruyères near Fribourg, the overwhelmingly stinky Appenzeller used in a rash of tasty, equally strong-smelling dishes in the same-name town in Northeastern Switzerland, or Sbrinz, Switzerland's oldest hard cheese and the transalpine ancestor to Italian Parmesan, ripened for 24 months to create its distinctive taste – eat it straight and thinly sliced like carpaccio or grated on top of springtime asparagus.

Another distinctive Swiss cheese with not a hole in sight is hard, nutty-flavoured Tête de Moine (literally 'monk's head') from the Jura that comes in a small round and is cut with a flourish in a flowery curl using a special handled cutting device known as a *girolle* (a great present to take back home – look for them in supermarkets).

As unique is L'Etivaz, which, in the finest of timeless Alpine traditions, is only made up high on lush summer pastures in the Alpes Vaudoises (Vaud Alps). As cows graze outside, shepherds inside their century-old *chalets d'alpage* (mountain huts) heat up the morning's milk in a traditional copper cauldron over a wood fire. Strictly seasonal, the Appellation d'Origine Contrôllée (AOC) cheese can only be made from May to early October, using milk from cows that have grazed on mountains between 1000m and 2000m high.

This is by no means the only cheese to be made at altitude using traditional methods; when travelling around the Valais, Bernese Alps, Ticino and other predominantly rural mountain areas in summer, look for signs pointing to isolated farmsteads where *fromage d'alpage* (mountain cheese; *hobelkäse* in German, *fromaggio d'Alpe* in Italian) is made and sold.

On the Swiss–Italian border, Zincarlìn is a raw-milk, cup-shaped cheese that, unusually, is made from unbroken curds.

The Swiss consume on average 8g to 12g of salt per day (the WHO recommends 5g of salt per day), and some medicos believe that the locals' love of cheese with a high salt content (such as Gruyère) is to blame.

### HOT BOX

Connoisseurs dig a small hole in the centre of the soft-crusted cheese, fill it with finely chopped onions and garlic, pour white wine on top, wrap it in aluminium foil and bake it for 45 minutes to create a *boîte chaude* (hot box) – into which bread and other tasty titbits can be dunked to create an alternative fondue.

## Fondue & Raclette

It is hard to leave Switzerland without dipping into a fondue (from the French verb *fondre,* meaning 'to melt'). The main French contribution to the Swiss table, fondue entails a pot of melted cheese being placed on the table and kept on a slow burn while diners dip in cubes of crusty bread using slender two-pronged fondue forks. If you lose your chunk in the cheese, you buy the next round of drinks or, should you be in Geneva, get thrown in the lake. It's traditionally a winter dish, and the Swiss tend to eat it mostly if there's snow around or they're at a suitable altitude.

The classic fondue mix in Switzerland is equal amounts of Emmental and Gruyère cheese, grated and melted with white wine and a shot of kirsch (cherry-flavoured liquor), then thickened slightly with potato or cornflour. It is served with a basket of bread slices (which are soon torn into small morsels), and most people order a side platter of cold meats and tiny gherkins to accompany it. *Fondue moitié moitié* (literally 'half-half fondue') mixes Gruyère with Vacherin Fribourgeois, and *fondue savoyarde* sees equal proportions of Comté, Beaufort and Emmental thrown into the pot. Common variants involve adding ingredients such as mushrooms or tomato.

Switzerland's other signature Alpine cheese dish, another fabulous feast of a meal in itself, is raclette. Unlike fondue, raclette – both the name of the dish and the cheese at its gooey heart – is eaten year-round. A half-crescent slab of the cheese is screwed onto a specially designed 'rack oven' that melts the top flat side. As it melts, cheese is scraped onto plates for immediate consumption with boiled potatoes, cold meats and pickled onions or gherkins.

When buying your own tangy wheel of raclette (or, indeed, discussing the topic with a born-and-bred Valaisian), be aware of the difference between *raclette Suisse* (Swiss raclette), made industrially with pasteurised milk anywhere in Switzerland, and Raclette du Valais, produced in the Valais using *lait cru* (raw milk) since the 16th century. In 2007 Raclette du Valais – never other than 29cm to 31cm in diameter and 4.8kg to 5.2kg in weight – gained its own AOC, much to the horror of cheesemakers in other cantons, who vehemently argued, to no avail, that raclette (from the French verb *racler,* meaning 'to scrape') refers to the dish, not the cheese, and thus shouldn't be restricted to one region.

### Best Fondues

- *La Tour de Gourze (p72), Lavaux – lake and vineyard views*
- *Café Tivoli (p73), Châtel-St-Denis – Fribourgeois fondue temple*
- *Café du Midi (www.cafedumidi.ch), Martigny – with beer or goat's cheese*
- *Le Namasté (p150), Verbier – ski, eat, sledge*
- *Bains des Pâquis (p50), Geneva – winter-only Champagne-based fondue*
- *Le Chalet (p77), Château-d'Œx – touristy but traditional*
- *Burestübli (p280), Arosa – sled down the valley afterwards*

## Spätzli, Rösti, Meat & Wild Game

For a quintessential Swiss lunch, nothing beats an alfresco platter of air-dried beef, a truly sweet and exquisitely tender delicacy from Graubünden that is smoked, thinly sliced and served as *Bündnerfleisch.* Eat it neat or in *Capuns,* a rich mix of *Spätzli* dough, air-dried beef, ham and herbs cooked, cut into tiny morsels, wrapped with spinach and mixed with yet more *Spätzli* (a Germanic cross between pasta and dumplings). The same wafer-thin slices of *viande séchée* (air-dried beef) are a staple in the Val d'Hérens, a delightfully remote valley in the Valais where fertile pastures are mowed by silky black Hérens cattle and local gourmets feast on butter-soft Hérens beef served in every imaginable way. Au Vieux Mazot (p153) in Evolène and Au Cheval Blanc (p153) in Sion are two Swiss-simple but superb insider addresses to sample this local beef any way you like it.

Drinking water while dipping into a fondue is said to coagulate the warm cheese in your stomach and bring on unpleasant gut ache – not necessarily true, but why risk it (or upsetting your hosts)? Opt instead for a local white wine like Fendant from the Valais.

Travel east and *Würste* (sausages) become the local lunch feast, typically served with German-speaking Switzerland's star dish: rösti (a shredded, oven-crisped potato bake), perhaps topped with a fried egg. (If only to prove they're different, Swiss French cook it in oil, while Swiss Germans throw a lump of butter or lard into the frying pan.) As common and cheap as chips it might be these days, but be aware that the vacuum-sealed packs of rösti sold in supermarkets cannot be compared to the

## HARVEST SUPPERS

Nothing prompts a celebration more than a harvest, and every village and region has its own way of partying in thanks.

In the Valais' French-speaking vineyards, grapes are harvested as *châtaignes* (chestnuts) tumble from the trees – prompting family and friends to gather for La Brisolée, a copious feast unchanged for centuries. It comprises hot roasted chestnuts, five local cheeses – *d'alpage* (high pasture), *de laiterie* (dairy), *tomme* (semi-hard and made from raw milk), *sérac* (whey) and Tête de Moine – ham, air-dried beef, *lard sec* (air-dried bacon face), buttered rye bread, grapes and apples. All this is washed down with *vin nouveau* (the first wine of the year) and *le moût* (must; wine that is still fermenting).

Around Fribourg, centuries-old harvest festival Le Bénichon is another marathon affair, with much eating, drinking and merriment. The traditional meal starts with *cuchaule*, a saffron-scented bread served with *moutarde de Bénichon* (a thick condiment made of cooked wine must, spices, sugar and flour).



real McCoy dish cooked up in authentic mountain restaurants. Baked to a perfect crisp, often in a wood-fuelled oven, the shredded potato is mixed with seasonal mushrooms and bacon bits to create a perfect lunch, paired with nothing more than a simple green salad. This is Swiss Alpine heaven.

Veal is highly rated and is usually thinly sliced and smothered in a cream sauce as *geschnetzeltes Kalbsfleisch* in Zürich. Horse meat is also eaten. Two unusual Swiss salami to look out, sufficiently rare to be on Slow Food's list of endangered world food products (see www.slowfoodfoundation.com), are *sac* (made from pork, liver, lard and spices aged for 12 months) and *fidighèla* (packed in veal intestine when straight, and pork intestine if curved; and aged for two to three weeks).

For true, blue-blooded meat-lovers there's no better season to let taste buds rip in this heavily forested country than autumn, when restaurants everywhere cook up *Wildspezialitäten/chasse/cacciagione* (fresh game). Venison and wild boar are deservedly popular.

One typically Swiss snack worth trying is the *cervelat* (or *cervelas*), a short beef-and-pork sausage with a smoky flavour and a natural casing enjoyed by locals in salads, roasted over an open fire or raw. Pick them up in any supermarket; they make handy hiking snacks.

## Time to Pig Out

Autumn, with its fresh game, abundance of wild mushrooms, chestnuts and grape harvests, is exquisitely gourmet in Switzerland, and as the days shorten this season only gets better. Fattened over summer, the family pig – traditionally slaughtered on the feast of St Martin (11 November) marking the end of agricultural work in the fields and the start of winter – is ready for the butcher. On farms and in villages for centuries, the slaughter would be followed by the salting of meat and sausage-making. Their work done, people would then pass over to feasting to celebrate the day's toil. The main dish for the feast: pork, of course.

In the French-speaking Jura, in particular, the feasting tradition around Fête de la St-Martin lives on with particular energy and enthusiasm in Porrentruy. Local bars and restaurants organise feasts for several weekends on the trot in October and November. A typical pork feast consists of seven copious courses, kicking off perhaps with *gelée de ménage,* a pork-gelatine dish. *Boudin, purée de pommes et racines rouges* (black pudding, apple compote and red vegetables) and piles of sausages accompanied by rösti and *atriaux* (a dish based on pork fat, sausage and liver, all roasted in sizzling fat) follows. Next up is the main course, with *rôti, côtines et doucette* (roast pork, ribs and a green salad). A liquor-soaked sorbet might follow to aid digestion, followed by a serving of *choucroute* (boiled cabbage enlivened by bacon bits). Finally, a traditional dessert, such as *striflate en sauce de vanille* (strings of deep-fried pastries in vanilla sauce), is served.

Traditionally it was not with a pig but with onions that medieval townsfolk in German-speaking Bern celebrated Martinmas (St Martin's Day). Today's Zibelemärit (Onion Fair), on the fourth Sunday in November, is an extravaganza of onion-themed produce.

### SWISS CHOCOLATE

In the early centuries after Christ's death, as the Roman Empire headed towards slow collapse on a diet of rough wine and olives, the Mayans in Central America were pounding cocoa beans, consuming the result and even using the beans as a system of payment.

A millennium later, Spanish conquistador Hernán Cortés brought the first load of cocoa to Europe, in 1528. He could not have anticipated the subsequent demand for his cargo. The Spaniards, and soon other Europeans, developed an insatiable thirst for the sweetened beverage produced from it. The solid stuff came later.

Swiss chocolate (www.chocolat.ch) built its reputation in the 19th century, thanks to pioneering spirits such as François-Louis Cailler (1796–1852), Philippe Suchard (1797–1884), Henri Nestlé (1814–90), Jean Tobler (1830–1905), Daniel Peter (1836–1919) and Rodolphe Lindt (1855–1909). Cailler established the first Swiss chocolate factory in 1819 near Vevey. Daniel Peter added milk in 1875 and Lindt invented conching, a rotary aeration process that gives chocolate its melt-in-the-mouth quality.

Pork dishes to look out for year-round include *Rippli* (a bubbling pot of pork-rib meat cooked up with bacon, potatoes and beans) in and around Bern, and in the canton of Vaud, *papet vaudois* (a potato, leek, cabbage and sausage stew) and *taillé aux greubons* (a crispy savoury pastry, studded with pork-lard cubes). In the Engadine, sausage is baked with onions and potato to make *pian di pigna*.

## Around the Lake: Fish

Fish is the speciality in lakeside towns. Perch (*perche* in French) and whitefish *(féra)* fillets are common, but don't be fooled into thinking the *filets de perche* chalked on the blackboard in practically every Lake Geneva restaurant are from the lake; the vast majority cooked around its shores, and in Geneva too, come frozen from Eastern Europe.

## Ever-Fabulous Fruit & Sweets

Sensible Swiss: they don't simply eat the plump Valais apricots, plums, pears and sweet black cherries that fill their orchards with a profusion of pretty white blossoms in April and May. As their 19th-century cookbook spells out, the Swiss also dry, preserve and distil their abundance of fruit to create fiery liqueurs, winter compotes and thick-as-honey syrups for baking or spreading on bread.

*Müsli* (muesli) was invented in Switzerland at the end of the 19th century. The most common form of this very healthy breakfast is *Birchermüsli*, sometimes served with less-than-slimming dollops of cream.

*Berudge eau de vie* is made from Berudge plums grown on the slopes of Mont Vully in the Fribourg canton, and cherries from around Basel go into thick *Chriesimues* syrup and sweet cherry kirsch – the ingredient that gives Zug's to-die-for *Zuger Kirschtorte* (cherry cake made from pastry, biscuit, almond paste and butter cream, all infused with cherry liqueur) its extra-special kick. (There are fears for genuine Swiss kirsch as fruit farmers replace ancient cherry varieties with less aromatic modern equivalents.) Apple or pear juice is simmered for 24 hours to make Fribourgois *vin cuit* (a dense, semi-hard concentrate used in tarts and other fruity desserts) and Vaudois *raisinée*; *Buttemoscht* is a less common rose-hip equivalent.

The Botzi pear cultivated around Gruyères is deemed precious enough to have its own AOC. Bite into it as nature intended or try it with local *crème de Gruyères,* the thickest cream ever, traditionally eaten by the spoonful with sugary-sweet meringues. *Cuisses de dame* (lady's thighs) are sugary, deep-fried, thigh-shaped pastries, found in French-speaking cantons next to *amandines* (almond tarts). Apart from the ubiquitous *Apfelstrudel* (apple pie), typically served with vanilla sauce, German cantons cook up *Vermicelles,* a chestnut-cream creation resembling spaghetti.

# Swiss Wine

**Savouring local wine in Switzerland is a rare joy in this globalised world: Switzerland exports just a tiny percentage of its wine (around 1.5%), meaning that most of its quality reds, whites and rosé vintages can only be tasted in situ. Most wines hail from the French-speaking cantons, with vineyards on the shore of Lake Geneva rising sharply up hillsides in tightly packed terraces knitted together by ancient drystone walls.**

## Lake Geneva & Vaud

Some small family producers on the fringes of Geneva open their doors for *dégustation* (tasting) – the canton's annual Caves Ouvertes (Open Cellars) day, held one weekend in late May, is a fabulous opportunity to discover the wines of cellars and *domaines viticoles* (estates) otherwise closed to visitors. However, most of Lake Geneva's winemaking estates are further east, lying either side of Lausanne in the canton of Vaud. Whites from the pea-green terraced vineyards of the Lavaux wine region between Lausanne and Montreux are outstanding, and the area is a Unesco World Heritage Site. Lavaux' two *grands crus* are Calamin and Dézaley.

When ordering wine in a wine bar or restaurant, use the uniquely Swiss approach of *déci* (décilitre – ie a tenth of a litre) multiples. Or just order a bottle...

The generic Vaud red is the Salvagnin, divided into several labels and generally combining Pinot noir and Gamay grapes. A home-grown offshoot is the Gamaret or Garanoir, a throaty red created in the 1970s that ages particularly well. Straddling Vaud is the small Chablais winemaking area, best known for its Yvorne whites.

Winemakers around Lausanne party hard in late September and October, when the grapes are harvested and the *vin nouveau* (new wine) is tasted.

## Valais

Drenched in extra sunshine and light from above the southern Alps, much of the land north of the Rhône River in western Valais is planted with vines – this is where some of Switzerland's best wines are produced. Unique to the Valais are the *bisses* (narrow irrigation channels) that traverse the vineyards.

Dryish white Fendant, the perfect accompaniment to fondue and raclette, and best served crisply cold, is the region's best-known wine, accounting for two-thirds of Valais wine production. Johannisberg is another excellent white and comes from the Sylvaner grape, while Petite Arvine and Amigne are sweet whites.

Dôle, made from Pinot noir and Gamay grapes, is the principal red blend and is full bodied, with a firm fruit flavour. Reds from Salgesch are generally excellent and the region increasingly uses innovative blends to create exciting wines such as Maîtresse de Salquenen, an assemblage of 13 grape varieties.

Tasting and exploring opportunities abound. Year-round, the region's many gentle walking trails through the vines make a perfect introduction: top trails include the Chemin du Vignoble (www.cheminduvignoble.ch) from Martigny (Lower Valais) to Leuk (Upper Valais), which

### Best Wine Tasting

*Domaine du Daley (p70), Lutry*

*Lavaux Vinorama (p71), Rivaz*

*Musée de la Vigne et du Vin (p76), Aigle*

*Le Cube Varone (153), Bisse de Clavaux*

*Château de Villa (p155), Sierre*

*Vinothek Von Salis (p284), Maienfeld*

## SOMETHING STRONGER

Locally produced fruit brandies are often served with or in coffee. Kirsch is made from the juice of compressed cherry pits. Appenzeller Alpenbitter (Alpine Bitters) is a liqueur made from the essence of 67 flowers and roots. Damassine (most likely found in the French cantons) is made of small prunes and is a good digestive. A pear-based drop is the popular Williamine, and Pflümli is a typical plum-based schnapps in the German cantons.

After a century on the index of banned beverages, absinthe – aka the green fairy – is legal again. Try it in Neuchâtel canton, where the wormwood drink was first distilled in the 18th century.

passes the world's highest drystone walls, ensnaring green vines near Sion; the Sierre-Salgesch Sentier Viticole (6km), linking a twinset of wine museums and host to September's fabulous Marché des Cépages; and the 2½-hour trail from Visp up to Europe's highest vineyards (1150m) in Visperterminen.

The Vinea wine fair (www.vinea.ch), held for three days in early September in Sierre, Valais, is a brilliant opportunity to meet winegrowers from around Switzerland and taste their wines.

## Lacs de Neuchâtel & Bienne

The fruity rosé Œil-de-Perdrix (literally 'Partidge's Eye') comes from the scenic shores of Lake Neuchâtel: taste and drink it along the Route du Vignoble, a wine itinerary that trails the 30km of steeply terraced water-facing vineyards between Lac de Neuchâtel and the western shore of Lac de Bienne (Bieler See) in Mittelland.

For stunning scenery sufficiently delightful to rival Lavaux and sublime vineyard trails and tasting, the enchanting hamlet of Ligerz on Lake Biel's northern shore is a magnificent winegrowing area.

### Best Vineyard Sleeps

*Auberge de Dully (www.aubergedully.ch), La Côte*

*Hotel Lavaux (p71), Cully*

*Hôtel Masson (p75), Montreux*

*Hotel Arkanum (p155), Salgesch*

*Schlaf Fass (p284), Maienfeld*

## Ticino

Switzerland's Italianate climes produce wonderful merlot, which accounts for almost 90% of Ticino's wine production. Some white merlots are also produced, as well as wines made from a handful of other grape varieties. The main areas for winemaking are between Bellinzona and Ascona, around Biasca and between Lugano and Mendrisio (with its lovely September wine festival).

## Swiss-German Wines

Less known than their Swiss-French counterparts and produced in substantially smaller quantities, Swiss-German vintages are nonetheless worth tasting. About 75% are reds and are predominantly Pinot noir (Blauburgunder) – taste and enjoy in wine taverns and tasting rooms in Bündner Herrschaft, Graubünden's premier wine region north of Chur.

Gewürztraminer is a dry white variety. The main white is Müller-Thurgau (a crisp mix of riesling and Sylvaner), produced in the town of Spiez on Lake Thun in Bernese Oberland. The best time to taste is at the nearby Läset-Sunntig wine festival (late September).

# Survival Guide

# Directory A–Z

## Accommodation

Switzerland offers accommodation in every price range. Tourist information offices have listings and can make reservations.

**Hotels** Hotels range from chains to luxury retreats in the Alps and city hotels with all the five-star trappings.

**B&Bs** Small and usually family-run, B&Bs reach from simple country places to boutique-style pads with first-class facilities.

**Farmstays** Family-friendly *Bauernhöfe* (farms) in country or mountain locations, often with homegrown produce and animals to pet.

**Campgrounds** Swiss campgrounds are generally well maintained and often have beautiful lake or mountain settings.

**Mountain huts** Bare-bones *Hütten* are dotted throughout the Alps. Most have basic dorms or *Matratzenlager* (bunkhouses with mattresses on the floor).

### B&Bs

Some of Switzerland's most charming accommodation comes in the form of a B&B: a room in a private home (anything from castle to farm), which includes breakfast, often made from homemade produce. Some hosts will also, if you order in advance, cook up an evening meal, served for an additional Sfr30 to Sfr40 per person including wine.

Tourist offices have lists of B&Bs in their area – they're rare in cities but plentiful in the countryside – and hundreds can be tracked through **BnB** (www.bnb.ch). In rural areas, private houses frequently offer inexpensive 'room(s) vacant' (*Zimmer frei* in German, *chambres libres* in French, *camere libere* in Italian), with or without breakfast.

### Camping

Campgrounds have one to five stars depending on amenities and location. They are often scenically situated out of the way by a river or lake. Charges per night are from around Sfr10 per person plus Sfr8 to Sfr15 for a tent, and from an additional Sfr5 for a car.

Wild camping (*wildes camping* in German, *camping sauvage* in French) is not strictly allowed, but it's viable in the wide-open mountain spaces.

Useful resources include:

**www.camping.ch** Directory with 350 detailed listings, plus practical info, tips and news on camping and caravanning in Switzerland.

**www.sccv.ch** Search online for the perfect pitch for you with the Swiss Camping and Caravanning Federation (SCCV).

**www.tcs.ch** Road and traffic conditions in real time, insurance, campground listings and everything else you could possibly require to organise camping trips in Switzerland.

### Farmstays

A unique way to experience life on a Swiss farm is Switzerland's **Agrotourismus Schweiz** (☎031 359 50 30; www.agrotourismus.ch) – the ultimate adventure in the straw. When the cows are out to pasture in summer, Swiss farmers charge travellers Sfr20 to Sfr30 per adult and Sfr10 to Sfr20 per child under 15 to sleep on straw in their hay barns or lofts (listen to the jangle of cow bells!). Farmers provide cotton undersheets (to avoid straw pricks) and woolly blankets for extra warmth, but guests need their own sleeping bags and – strongly advisable – a

**BOOK YOUR STAY ONLINE**

For more accommodation reviews by Lonely Planet authors, check out http://lonelyplanet.com/hotels/. You'll find independent reviews, as well as recommendations on the best places to stay. Best of all, you can book online.

pocket torch. Nightly rates include a farmhouse breakfast, and a morning shower and evening meal are usually available for an extra Sfr2 and Sfr20 to Sfr30, respectively. Reservations are necessary in summer. A list of the 170-odd farms across Switzerland offering this accommodation is available on the website.

Should you prefer a room in the farmhouse rather than above the cows, try **Swiss Holiday Farms** (☎031 329 66 99; www.bauernhof-ferien.ch), an association of about 200 farms countrywide that open their doors to both overnight B&B guests and self-caterers keen to rent a renovated barn or farmhouse cottage for a week or longer.

### Hostels

Swiss youth hostels (*Jugendherberge* in German, *auberge de jeunesse* in French, *alloggio per giovanni* in Italian) range from older, institutional affairs to modern establishments bordering on designer accommodation – Saas Fee's dazzling **WellnessHostel 4000** (p171) with pool and spa is a striking example.

➡ Most are run by Switzerland's national hostelling organisation **Swiss Youth Hostels** (www.youthhostel.ch), affiliated with Hostelling International (HI). Non-HI members must take out an annual membership (Sfr22/33 for those under/over 18, Sfr44 per family) or pay Sfr6 a night extra to stay in an HI hostel.

➡ Hostels charge Sfr30 to Sfr45 for a dorm bed with breakfast and sheets (sleeping bags are forbidden in HI-affiliated hostels for fear of bedbugs).

➡ Hostels with a **Swiss Hostels** (formerly 'Backpacker'; www.swisshostels.com) tag tend to be more flexible with their regulations (some hostels allow sleeping bags, for example), reception times and opening hours; membership is not required.

➡ Hostels take bookings via their websites; few accept telephone reservations. During busy times a three-day maximum stay may apply.

### Hotels & Pensions

➡ The cheapest hotel rooms have a sink but share a toilet and shower in the corridor; these rooms cost around Sfr70 for a single and Sfr100 for a double in a small town, and around Sfr90 for a single and Sfr140 for a double in cities or mountain resorts. Add a private shower and the nightly rate rises by at least Sfr20. Rates usually include breakfast.

➡ A *Frühstückspension* or *Hotel-Garni* serves only breakfast. Small pensions with a restaurant often have a 'rest day' when guest check-in at the hotel may not be possible except by prior arrangement (telephone ahead).

➡ Hotels displaying the 'Green Living' label are eco-hotels with sustainable credentials.

### Rental Accommodation

Self-caterers can opt for a chalet or an apartment, both of which need to be booked in advance; for peak periods, reserve at least six to 12 months ahead. A minimum stay of one week (usually from Saturday to Saturday) in season is common.

Useful resources include **REKA** (www.reka.ch), **Interhome** (www.interhome.ch) and **Switzerland Tourism** (www.myswitzerland.com). For self-catering chalets and apartments in ski resorts – summer and winter – surf **Ski Suisse** (http://en.skisuisse.com).

### SLEEPING PRICE RANGES

The following price ranges refer to a double room with a private bathroom, except in hostels or where otherwise specified. Quoted rates are for high season and include breakfast, unless otherwise noted.

**€** less than Sfr170

**€€** Sfr170 to Sfr350

**€€€** more than Sfr350

## Children

Orderly, clean and not overly commercial, Switzerland is a dream for family travel.

➡ The Swiss tourist board's meaty *Families* brochure is packed with ideas; its website, www.myswitzerland.com, lists kid-friendly accommodation, family offers and so on.

➡ Family train travel with **Swiss Railways** (www.sbb.ch) is staggering value. Kids under six years travel free and those aged six to 16 years get free unlimited rail travel with an annual **Junior Card** (Sfr30) or – should it be grandparents travelling with the kids – the **Grandchild Travelcard** (Sfr30). Otherwise, buy a one-day child's **travelpass** (Sfr16), which allows unlimited rail travel. Cards include travel on many cable cars in mountain resorts.

➡ Switzerland's mountain of scenic journeys by train and boat enchant children of all ages. Upon arrival at point B, dozens of segments of the perfectly signposted hiking, biking, inline-skating and canoeing trails designed strictly for non-motorised traffic by **Switzerland Mobility** are flagged as suitable for younger children.

➡ In mountain resorts, tourist offices have information on pushchair-accessible walking trails and dozens of other activities for children of every age, toddler to teen.

➡ Staying in a B&B is family fabulous: little kids can slumber sweetly upstairs while weary parents wine and dine in peace downstairs (don't forget your baby monitor!). Pick a B&B on a farm or sleep on straw in the hay barn for adventurous kids to have the time of their life.

➡ Those with kids aged six to 12 years should buy Dianne Dicks' *Ticking Along with Swiss Kids*, part children's book about Switzerland, part guide for parents on what to see, where to eat and what to do. Also check out Lonely Planet's *Travel with Children*.

### Practicalities

The Swiss are mostly very accommodating when it comes to families.

➡ Many large hotels have dedicated family or interconnecting rooms, and even some smaller places will often squeeze in a cot or an extra bed at a moment's notice.

➡ Most of the major car-hire companies rent out child, baby and booster seats equipped to the latest safety standards for an extra fee of around Sfr45 to Sfr65.

➡ Nappy-changing facilities are widespread and disposable nappies (diapers) can be readily purchased in pharmacies and supermarkets.

**EATING PRICE RANGES**

The following price ranges refer to a main course.

**€** less than Sfr25

**€€** Sfr25 to Sfr50

**€€€** more than Sfr50

➡ The Swiss are generally tolerant when it comes to breastfeeding in public provided it is done discreetly.

➡ Many hotels and tourist offices can point you in the direction of local childcare agencies and babysitting services.

➡ Some – but by no means all – restaurants provide high chairs and special children's menus. If in doubt, check ahead.

## Discount Cards

### Senior Cards

Senior citizens are not entitled to discounts on Swiss railways, but discounts are available on museum admission, ski passes and some cable cars. Discounts often start for those as young as 62 (proof of age necessary), although sometimes a higher limit is observed. The abbreviation for senior citizens is AHV in German and AVS in French.

### Student & Youth Cards

An International Student Identity Card (ISIC) yields discounts on admission prices, air and international train tickets, and even some ski passes. If you're under 31 but not a student, apply for the IYTC (International Youth Travel Card). Cards are issued by student unions and youth-oriented travel agencies in your home country.

### Swiss Museum Pass

Regular or long-term visitors to Switzerland may want to buy the **Swiss Museum Pass** (www.museumspass.ch; per adult/family Sfr166/288), which grants a year's free entry to 500 Swiss museums.

### Visitors' Cards

In many resorts and cities there's a *Gästekarte* (visitors' card), which provides various benefits such as reduced prices for museums, swimming pools or cable cars, as well as free use of public transport within city limits. Cards are issued by your accommodation.

## Electricity

The electrical current in Switzerland is 230V, 50Hz. Swiss sockets are recessed, three-holed, hexagonally shaped and incompatible with many plugs from abroad. They usually, however, take the standard European two-pronged plug.

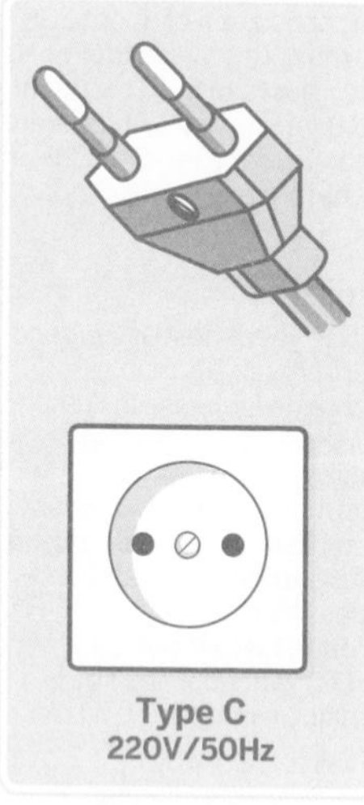


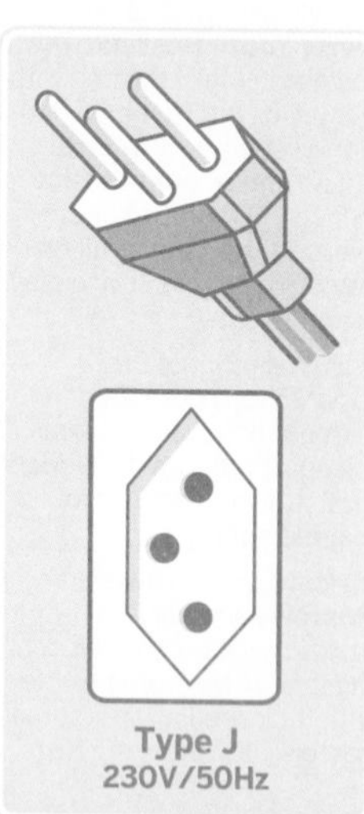

## Embassies & Consulates

For a list of Swiss embassies abroad and embassies in Switzerland, see www.eda.admin.ch. Embassies are in Bern, but Zürich and Geneva have several consulates.

## Health

Health care in Switzerland is of high quality, but it's expensive. An embassy, consulate or hotel can usually recommend a local doctor or clinic.

A European Health Insurance Card (EHIC) enables European citizens to access state-provided health care in Switzerland at a reduced cost. Otherwise, expect to pay around Sfr150 for a straightforward, non-urgent consultation with a doctor. Over-the-counter medications are available at a local *Apotheke* (pharmacy), where staff usually speak English and are well informed.

### Altitude Sickness

This disorder can occur above 3000m, but few treks or ski runs in the Swiss Alps reach such heights. Headache, vomiting, dizziness, extreme faintness, and difficulty in breathing and sleeping are signs to heed. Treat mild symptoms with rest and simple painkillers. If symptoms persist or get worse, descend to a lower altitude and seek medical advice.

### Hypothermia

Hypothermia occurs when the body loses heat faster than it can produce it and the core temperature of the body falls. It is surprisingly easy to progress from very cold to dangerously cold due to a combination of wind, wet clothing, fatigue and hunger, even if the air temperature is above freezing. It is best to dress in layers of good insulating materials and to wear a hat and a strong, waterproof outer layer when hiking or skiing. A 'space' blanket for emergencies is essential. Carry basic supplies, including food containing simple sugars and fluid to drink.

Symptoms of hypothermia are exhaustion, numb skin (particularly toes and fingers), shivering, slurred speech, irrational or violent behaviour, lethargy, stumbling, dizzy spells, muscle cramps and violent bursts of energy.

To treat mild hypothermia, get the person out of the wind and/or rain, remove their clothing if wet and replace it with dry, warm clothing. Give them hot liquids – not alcohol – and high-kilojoule, easily digestible food. Do not rub victims; allow them to slowly warm themselves. The early recognition and treatment of mild hypothermia is the only way to prevent severe hypothermia (a critical condition).

### Ticks

These small creatures can be found throughout Switzerland up to an altitude of 1200m, and live in underbrush at the forest edge or beside walking tracks.

Always check your whole body if you've been walking through a potentially tick-infested area. If a tick is found attached, press down around the tick's head with tweezers, grab the head and gently pull upwards. Avoid pulling the rear of the body, as this may squeeze the tick's gut contents through the attached mouth-parts into the skin, increasing the risk of infection and disease. Smearing chemicals on the tick is not recommended.

#### LYME DISEASE

This is an infection transmitted by ticks that may be acquired in Europe. The illness usually begins with a spreading rash at the site of the tick bite and is accompanied by fever, headache, extreme fatigue, aching joints and muscles, and mild neck stiffness. If untreated, these symptoms usually resolve over several weeks, but over subsequent weeks or months, disorders of the nervous system, heart and joints may develop. Seek medical help.

#### TICK-BORNE ENCEPHALITIS

This disease is a cerebral inflammation carried by a virus. Tick-borne encephalitis can occur in most forest and rural areas of Switzerland. If you have been bitten, even having removed the tick, you should keep an eye out for symptoms, including blotches around the bite, which is sometimes pale in the middle. Headache, stiffness and other flu-like symptoms, as well as extreme tiredness, appearing a week or two after the bite, can progress to more serious problems. Medical help must be sought. A vaccination is available.

## Insurance

If you're skiing, snowboarding or trekking, ensure your policy covers helicopter rescue and emergency repatriation. Most standard policies don't cover many outdoor activities; you'll need to pay a premium for winter-sports cover and further premiums for adventure sports such as bungee jumping and skydiving.

## Internet Access

- Public wireless access points can be found at major airports, at dozens of train stations, and in business seats of 1st-class train carriages on many routes.
- Most hotels have free wi-fi, as do many cafes and public spaces.
- Public hot spots, like those provided by **Swisscom** (www.swisscom.ch), levy a charge – from Sfr5 per day to Sfr35 per month, payable by credit card or prepaid card sold at Swisscom's 3400 hot

spots; locate them at http://hotspotlocator.swisscom.ch.

➡ The odd internet cafe can be found in larger towns and cities.

## Legal Matters

Police have wide-ranging powers of detention, allowing them to hold a person without charge. If you're approached by them, you will be required to show your passport, so always carry it.

There are some minor legal variations between the 26 cantons: busking (playing music in the streets) is allowed in some places but not in others. If in doubt, ask.

## LGBTIQ+

Attitudes to homosexuality are progressive. Same-sex partnerships are recognised (although same-sex couples are not permitted to adopt children or have fertility treatment). Major cities have gay and lesbian bars, and pride marches are held in Geneva (early July) and Zürich (mid-July).

Useful websites include:

**www.gay.ch** (in German)

**www.myswitzerland.com** Information on LGBTIQ+ friendly accommodation and events if you type 'Gay & Lesbian' into the search function.

**www.pinkcross.ch** (in German and French)

## Maps

**Hallwag, Kümmerly + Frey** (www.swisstravelcenter.ch) has a vast range of road atlases, city maps and hiking maps, which can be bought online. **Swiss Alpine Club** (www.sac-cas.ch) maps, **Kompass** (www.kompass.de) maps and maps produced by the **Bundesamt for Topographie** (www.swisstopo.admin.ch) – sometimes down to 1:15,000 scale – are found in travel bookshops.

The 48-page *Swiss Travel System* brochure, free from Switzerland Tourism and major train stations, has an A3 map of bus and train routes. Tourist offices also have free maps and brochures.

### PRACTICALITIES

**Newspapers** German readers can gen up with Zürich's *Neue Zürcher Zeitung* (www.nzz.ch) and *Tages Anzeiger* (www.tagesanzeiger.ch); Geneva's *Le Temps* (www.letemps.ch) and *La Tribune de Genève* (www.tdg.ch) are sold in Suisse Romande; Lugano-based *Corriere del Ticino* (www.cdt.ch) is in Italian.

**Radio** WRS (World Radio Switzerland; FM 101.7; www.worldradio.ch) is a Geneva-based English-language station broadcasting music and news countrywide.

**Twitter** For a dose of daily news and insights into Swiss cultural affairs and happenings, follow @Switzerland, @TheLocalSwitzer, @swissinfo_en and @MySwitzerland_e.

**Websites** Swissinfo (www.swissinfo.org) is the national news website.

**Smoking** Illegal in all indoor public spaces, including restaurants, pubs, offices and transport. It is allowed in separate smoking rooms and on pavement terraces.

**Weights & Measures** The metric system is used. Like other continental Europeans, the Swiss indicate decimals with commas and thousands with full points.

## Money

### ATMs

ATMs – called *Bancomats* in banks and *Postomats* in post offices – are widespread and accessible 24 hours. They accept most international bank or credit cards and have multilingual instructions. Your bank or credit-card company will often charge a 1% to 2.5% fee, and there may also be a small charge at the ATM end.

### Cash

Swiss francs are divided into 100 centimes (*Rappen* in German-speaking Switzerland). There are notes for 10, 20, 50, 100, 200 and 1000 francs, and coins for five, 10, 20 and 50 centimes, as well as for one, two and five francs.

Businesses throughout Switzerland, including most hotels and some restaurants and souvenir shops, will accept payment in euros. Change will be given in Swiss francs at the rate of exchange calculated on the day.

### Credit Cards

Credit cards are widely accepted at hotels, shops and restaurants. EuroCard/MasterCard and Visa are the most popular.

### Moneychangers

Change money at banks, airports and nearly every train station until late into the evening. Banks tend to charge about 5% commission; some money-exchange bureaus don't charge commission at all.

### Tipping

Tipping is not necessary, given that hotels, restaurants, bars and even some taxis are legally required to include a 15% service charge in bills.

**Restaurants** You can round up the bill after a meal for good service, as locals do.

**Hotels** Hotel and railway porters expect a franc or two per bag.

## Opening Hours

Each Swiss canton decides how long shops and businesses can stay open. With the exception of convenience stores at 24-hour service stations and shops at airports and train stations, businesses shut completely on Sunday. High-season opening hours appear in listings for sights and attractions; hours are almost always shorter during low season.

**Banks** 8.30am–4.30pm Monday to Friday

**Restaurants** noon–2.30pm and 6pm–9.30pm; most close one or two days per week

**Shops** 10am–6pm Monday to Friday, to 4pm Saturday

**Museums** 10am–5pm, can close Mondays and open late Thursdays

## Public Holidays

Some cantons observe their own special holidays and religious days, eg 2 January, Labour Day (1 May), Corpus Christi, Assumption (15 August) and All Saints' Day (1 November).

**New Year's Day** 1 January

**Good Friday** March/April

**Easter Sunday and Monday** March/April

**Ascension Day** 40th day after Easter

**Whit Sunday and Monday (Pentecost)** 7th week after Easter

**National Day** 1 August

**Christmas Day** 25 December

**St Stephen's Day** 26 December

## Safe Travel

- Street crime is relatively uncommon. As in any urban situation, though, watch your belongings; pickpockets thrive in city crowds.
- Swiss police aren't very visible but have a reputation for performing random street searches of questionable necessity on people of non-European background or appearance.

## Telephone

Search for phone numbers online at http://tel.local.ch/en.

National telecom provider **Swisscom** (www.swisscom.ch) provides public phone booths that accept coins and major credit cards.

### Mobile Phones

Most mobile phones brought from overseas will function in Switzerland; check with your provider about costs. Prepaid local SIM cards are widely available.

Prepaid local SIM cards are available from network operators **Salt** (www.salt.ch), **Sunrise** (www.sunrise.ch) and **Swisscom Mobile** (www.swisscom.ch/mobile) for as little as Sfr10. You can also purchase (and recharge) SIM cards at newsagents throughout Switzerland. Prepaid cards must be officially registered, so bring your passport.

### Phone Codes

- The country code for Switzerland is 41. When calling Switzerland from abroad, drop the initial zero from the number; hence to call Bern, dial 41 31 (preceded by the international access code of the country you're dialling from).
- The international code from Switzerland is 00.
- Telephone numbers with the code 0800 are toll free; those with 0848 are charged at the local rate. Numbers beginning with 0900, 156 or 157 are premium rate.
- Mobile-phone numbers start with the code 076, 078 or 079.

**WARNING: DIAL ALL NUMBERS**

Area codes do not exist in Switzerland. Although the numbers for a particular city or town share the same three-digit prefix (for example Bern 031, Geneva 022), numbers must always be dialled in full, even when calling from next door.

## Time

Swiss time is GMT/UTC plus one hour. Daylight-saving time starts at midnight on the last Saturday in March, when the clocks are moved forward one hour, making Switzerland two hours ahead of GMT/UTC; clocks go back on the last Saturday in October.

Note that, in German, *halb* is used to indicate the half-hour before the hour, hence *halb acht* (half eight) means 7.30, not 8.30.

The following table shows the time difference between Bern and major cities around the world; times do not take daylight saving into account.

| CITY | LOCAL TIME |
|---|---|
| **Auckland** | 11pm |
| **Bern** | noon |
| **London** | 11am |
| **New York** | 6am |
| **San Francisco** | 3am |
| **Sydney** | 9pm |
| **Tokyo** | 8pm |
| **Toronto** | 6am |

## Toilets

- Public toilets are, as a rule, clean and in reasonable supply.
- Urinals are often free, and many cubicles are too, but some of the latter may have a charge of Sfr0.50.

➡ The spotless Mr Clean range of facilities in big train stations is more expensive – Sfr2 to pee.

## Tourist Information

Prepare for your Swiss travels by browsing the in-depth, multilingual Switzerland Tourism website (www.myswitzerland.com), which gives the inside scoop on destinations, accommodation, getting around, sights and attractions, sports, culture, events and much more. Tune in to what's happening across the country with news, weather and webcams, or download brochures and mobile apps.

Switzerland's tourist offices are invariably helpful. Information and maps are free and somebody always speaks English; many offices book hotel rooms, tours and excursions for you. In German-speaking Switzerland tourist offices are called *Verkehrsbüro,* or *Kurverein* in some resorts. In French they are called *office du tourisme* and in Italian *ufficio turistico*.

## Travellers with Disabilities

Switzerland ranks among the world's most easily navigable countries for travellers with physical disabilities. Most train stations have a mobile lift for boarding trains, city buses are equipped with ramps, and many hotels have disabled access (although budget pensions tend not to have lifts).

**Switzerland Tourism** (www.myswitzerland.com) has excellent travel tips for people with physical disabilities. Or get in touch with **Mobility International Switzerland** (MIS; ☎062 212 67 40; www.mis-ch.ch).

Download Lonely Planet's free Accessible Travel guide from http://lptravel.to/AccessibleTravel.

## Visas

For up-to-date details on visas and entry requirements in light of COVID-19, go to the Swiss State Secretariat for Migration (www.sem.admin.ch).

Visas are not required if you hold a passport from the UK, Ireland, the USA, Canada, Australia or New Zealand, whether visiting as a tourist or on business. Citizens of the EU, Norwegians and Icelanders may also enter Switzerland without a visa. A maximum 90-day stay in a 180-day period applies, but passports are rarely stamped.

Other non-European citizens wishing to come to Switzerland have to apply for a Schengen Visa, named after the agreement that has abolished passport controls between 26 European countries. It allows unlimited travel throughout the entire Schengen zone for a 90-day period. Apply to the consulate of the country you are entering first, or your main destination.

In Switzerland, carry your passport at all times. Swiss citizens are required to always carry ID, so you will also need to be able to identify yourself at any time.

## Volunteering

Though volunteering might not be as big in Switzerland as it is elsewhere, a number of places allow you to immerse yourself in local life by getting involved in projects lasting from a week to 18 months. You can hook up with the networks in your home country and/or, if you speak German, French, or Italian, approach a Swiss organisation directly.

**Bergwaldprojekt** (www.bergwaldprojekt.ch) Do your bit to save Switzerland's magnificent forests at one of the free week-long work camps run by this eco-aware initiative.

**SCI – International Voluntary Service** (https://ivsgb.org/sci) Search online for volunteer work, which might be anything from building new hiking trails to promoting biodiversity and cultural projects.

**Service Civil International** (www.sci.ngo) Promoting peace, this worldwide organisation has local networks and volunteer work camps (short, mid- and long term) that range in theme from sustainable living to raising awareness for asylum seekers.

**Swiss Volunteers** (www.swissvolunteers.ch) The first port of call for anyone who wants to get involved in Swiss sporting events.

**TravelnStudy** (http://travelnstudy.com) Offers programs in Lugano (Ticino) that combine travel, voluntary work and study.

## Work

Nationals of the EU-25, plus Norwegians and Icelanders, may work in Switzerland for up to 90 days a year without a permit. Other foreigners and EU citizens on longer assignments will need a permit. For details check the **State Secretariat for Migration** (www.sem.admin.ch).

Language skills are crucial for work in service industries and usually necessary for work in ski resorts and chalets. *Working in Ski Resorts: Europe & North America* by Victoria Pybus provides detailed information about how to organise winter work. Or consult **Rolling Pin** (www.rollingpin.at) for jobs in the hospitality industry. Two good websites for contacts and tips are **Season Workers** (www.seasonworkers.com) and **Natives** (http://jobs.natives.co.uk/switzerland).

In October, work is available in vineyards in Vaud and Valais.

# Transport

## GETTING THERE & AWAY

Landlocked between France, Germany, Austria, Liechtenstein and Italy, Switzerland is well linked, especially by train. Formalities are minimal when entering the country by air, rail or road, thanks to the Schengen Agreement.

Flights, tours and rail tickets can be booked online at www.lonelyplanet.com/bookings.

### Entering the Country/Region

Formalities are minimal when arriving in Switzerland by air, rail or road thanks to the Schengen Agreement, which allows passengers coming from the EU to enter without showing a passport. When arriving from a non-EU country, you'll need your passport or EU identity card – and visa if required – to clear customs.

#### Passport

All non-EU travellers must carry a passport valid for at least three months beyond the planned departure date from Switzerland.

Switzerland has no explicit entry restrictions based on nationality or previous passport stamps, but citizens of some countries may require a visa.

### Air

Switzerland's national carrier is Swiss (www.swiss.com), commonly known as Swissair. In addition to many national carriers, the following budget and/or smaller airlines connect Switzerland with the rest of Europe.

**EasyJet** (www.easyjet.com) Low-cost flights to Geneva, Zürich and EuroAirport (Basel) from destinations across Europe and the UK.

**Etihad Regional** (www.etihadregional.com) Connections from Geneva, Lugano and Zürich to Spain, France, Italy, Germany, Asia and the United Arab Emirates.

**Eurowings** (www.eurowings.com) German low-cost carrier flying from Zürich and Geneva to Europe and the UK.

**Flybe** (www.flybe.com) Flights from Geneva and Zürich to Manchester, Birmingham and other UK cities.

**Helvetic Airways** (www.helvetic.com) Budget Swiss airline, with flights from Zürich to Shannon (Ireland) and Bordeaux (France), and from Bern to Olbia (Sardinia) and Palma de Mallorca (Spain).

**Hop** (www.hop.com) Low-cost carrier of Air France, with flights from Geneva to/from Biarritz and Calvi (Corsica).

**Jet2.com** (www.jet2.com) Connections between Geneva and UK destinations London Stansted, Birmingham, East Midlands, Edinburgh, Leeds Bradford and Manchester.

#### CLIMATE CHANGE & TRAVEL

Every form of transport that relies on carbon-based fuel generates $CO_2$, the main cause of human-induced climate change. Modern travel is dependent on aeroplanes, which might use less fuel per kilometre per person than most cars but travel much greater distances. The altitude at which aircraft emit gases (including $CO_2$) and particles also contributes to their climate change impact. Many websites offer 'carbon calculators' that allow people to estimate the carbon emissions generated by their journey and, for those who wish to do so, to offset the impact of the greenhouse gases emitted with contributions to portfolios of climate-friendly initiatives throughout the world. Lonely Planet offsets the carbon footprint of all staff and author travel.

**FLY-RAIL BAGGAGE SERVICE**

Travellers bound for Geneva or Zürich airports can send their luggage directly to any one of 50-odd Swiss train stations, without waiting for their bags at the airport. Upon departure, they can also check their luggage in at any of these train stations up to 24 hours before their flight and collect it upon arrival at their destination airport. The cost is Sfr22 per item of luggage; maximum weight per item is 32kg and bulky items such as bicycles and surfboards are a no go. Similar luggage forwarding is possible within Switzerland; see www.sbb.ch.

**SkyWork Airlines** (www.flyskywork.com) Airline based in **Bern** (BRN; ☎031 960 21 11; www.flughafenbern.ch) with flights to European cities including London, Amsterdam, Berlin, Munich and Vienna.

## Land

### Bus

**Eurolines** (www.eurolines.com), a group of 29 long-haul coach operators, runs buses all over Europe from most large towns and cities in Switzerland, including Basel, Bellinzona, Bern, Bulle, Fribourg, Geneva, Lausanne, Lucerne, Lugano, Martigny, Sion, St Gallen and Zürich. Discounts are available to people under 26 and over 60. Make reservations, especially in July and August.

### Car & Motorcycle

Fast, well-maintained roads run from Switzerland through to all bordering countries; the Alps present a natural barrier, meaning that main roads generally head through tunnels to enter Switzerland. A foreign motor vehicle entering the country must display a sticker or licence plate identifying its country of registration.

➡ An EU driving licence is acceptable throughout Europe.

➡ Third-party motor insurance is a minimum requirement; get proof of this in the form of a Green Card issued by your insurers. Also ask for a 'European Accident Statement' form. Taking out a European breakdown-assistance policy is a good investment.

➡ If using Switzerland's motorways, drivers must purchase and display a special sticker (*vignette* in French and German, *contrassegno* in Italian), available for Sfr40 at major border crossings.

➡ A warning triangle, to be displayed in the event of a breakdown, is compulsory.

➡ Recommended accessories include first-aid kit, spare-bulb kit and fire extinguisher.

### Train

Ecofriendly Switzerland makes rail travel a joy.

➡ Book tickets and get train information from **Rail Europe** (www.raileurope.com). In the UK contact **Railteam** (www.railteam.eu), an alliance of several high-speed-train operators in Europe, including Switzerland's very own **Swiss Federal Railways** (www.sbb.ch), commonly abbreviated to SBB in German, CFF in French and FFS in Italian. The latter accepts internet bookings but does not post tickets outside Switzerland.

➡ A very useful train-travel resource is the information-packed website **The Man in Seat 61** (www.seat61.com).

➡ From the UK, hourly **Eurostar** (www.eurostar.com) trains scoot from London (St Pancras International) to Paris (Gare du Nord) in 2¼ hours, then onward by French TGV from Paris (Gare de Lyon) to Basel, Bern, Geneva, Lausanne, Zürich and more; passengers aged under 26 and over 60 get slight discounts.

➡ Zürich is Switzerland's busiest international terminus, with trains to Munich and Vienna, from where there are extensive onward connections to cities in Eastern Europe.

➡ Most connections from Germany pass through Zürich or Basel.

➡ Nearly all connections from Italy pass through Milan before branching off to Zürich, Lucerne, Bern or Lausanne.

## River & Lake

Switzerland can be reached by steamer from several lakes, but it's a slightly more unusual option. From Germany, arrive via Lake Constance; from France, via Lake Geneva. You can also cruise down the Rhine to Basel.

**CGN** (☎0848 811 848; www.cgn.ch) has ferry connections on Lake Geneva.

# GETTING AROUND

## Air

Switzerland's compact size and excellent rail transport render internal flights almost unnecessary.

**Swiss** (www.swiss.com) serves the hub airports of Geneva and Zürich, along with Basel's EuroAirport, with return fares fluctuating wildly.

## Bicycle

### Hire

**SBB Rent a Bike** (☎041 925 11 70; www.rentabike.ch; half/full day from Sfr27/35), the super-efficient bike-rental service run by Swiss railways,

## SCENIC JOURNEYS

Swiss trains, buses and boats are more than a means of getting from A to B. Stunning views invariably make the journey itself the destination. No matter how you travel, you'll never look at public transport in the same way again. Switzerland has it down to a fine art, with even bog-standard buses taking you up to remote mountain passes for eye-to-eye wildlife encounters.

The **Swiss Travel System** (www.swisstravelsystem.co.uk) is an interconnected web of trains, boats, cable cars and postal buses that puts almost the entire country within easy car-free reach – and, naturally, with its famous precision you can set your watch by it.

### Panorama Trains

The first three trains on this list have panoramic coaches with extended-height windows:

**Glacier Express** (p163)

**Golden Pass Route** (www.goldenpass.ch) Travels between Lucerne and Montreux. The journey is in three legs, and you must change trains twice. Regular trains, without panoramic windows, work the whole route hourly.

**Bernina Express** (p277)

**Chocolate Train** (www.mob.ch) Return trip in a belle époque Pullman car from Montreux to the chocolate factory at Broc.

**Mont Blanc/St Bernard Expresses** (www.tmrsa.ch) From Martigny to Chamonix, France, or over the St Bernard Pass.

**Voralpen Express** (www.voralpen-express.ch) Lake Constance to Lake Lucerne, through St Gallen, Rapperswil and Romanshorn.

### Postal Buses

Beginning in St Moritz, the four-hour **Palm Express** (www.palmexpress.ch) takes travellers from the glacier-capped peaks of the Engadine via the Maloja Pass, through the Val Bregaglia valley to Chiavenna, Italy, then further along Lakes Como and Lugano.

Another half a dozen scenic Alpine routes can be found at **Postbus** (www.postauto.ch).

### Rail & Boat: The Gotthard Panorama Express

The **Gotthard Panorama Express** (www.sbb.ch; ⏲Sat & Sun mid-Apr–May, daily Jun-Oct) starts with a wonderful 2½-hour cruise across Lake Lucerne to Flüelen, from where a train winds its way through ravines and past mountains to Bellinzona or Lugano.

offers bike hire at 100-odd train stations. Reserve online or by phone and – for a Sfr10 surcharge – can be collected at one station and returned to another. In addition to regular adult and child bikes, most train stations have e-bikes and tandems, trailer bikes for kids unable to pedal alone, and trailers to tow little kids in. Rates include helmets.

If you're staying awhile, it's worth registering for public bike-sharing scheme **PubliBike** (www.publibike.ch/en), with almost 100 'pick-up and return' stations dotted around Switzerland and a low yearly membership fee. You can also purchase a 'DayBike' card from most tourist information centres located near the stations. Use the website to order and check sales and station locations.

From May to October, the ecofriendly initiative **Schweiz Rollt** (Suisse Roule; www.schweizrollt.ch) offers free bike hire in Bern, Geneva, Zürich and the cantons of Valais and Neuchâtel.

### Transport

Bikes can be taken on slower trains, and sometimes even on InterCity (IC) or EuroCity (EC) trains, when there's room in the luggage carriage. A one-day bike ticket costs Sfr20 (Sfr13 with Swiss Travel Pass). Between 21 March and 31 October, you must book (Sfr5) to take your bike on ICN (intercity tilting) trains.

Trains that don't permit accompanied bikes are marked with a crossed-out pictogram in the timetable. Sending a standard bike unaccompanied costs Sfr20. Taking your bike as hand luggage in a transport bag is free.

## Boat

All the larger lakes are serviced by steamers operated by **Swiss Federal Railways** (www.sbb.ch), or allied private companies for which Swiss national travel passes are valid. These include Lakes Geneva, Constance, Lucerne, Lugano, Neuchâtel, Biel,

## SWISS TRAVEL PASSES

The following Swiss national travel passes offer fabulous savings on extensive travel within Switzerland. Passes can be purchased at train stations in Switzerland. For comprehensive information, check www.swisstravelsystem.ch and http://traintickets.myswitzerland.com.

**Swiss Travel Pass** This entitles the holder to unlimited travel on almost every train, boat and bus service in the country, and on trams and buses in 41 towns, plus free entry to 500-odd museums. Reductions of 25% to 50% apply on funiculars, cable cars and private railways. Different passes are available, valid between three (Sfr216) and 15 (Sfr458) consecutive days. There's a 15% discount for young adults under age 26.

**Swiss Travel Pass Flex** This pass allows unlimited travel for a certain number of days within a one-month period – from three (Sfr248) to 15 (Sfr502) days. A 15% discount applies for those under age 26.

**Swiss Half-Fare Card** As the name suggests, you pay only half the fare on trains with this card (Sfr120 for one month), plus you get some discounts on local-network buses, trams and cable cars.

**Junior Travelcard** This card (Sfr30), valid for one year, gets a child aged six to 16 years free travel on trains, boats and some cable cars when travelling with at least one parent. Children travelling with a grandparent can buy an equivalent **Grandchild travelcard**. Childen not travelling with a relative can get unlimited travel for one day with a one-day **children's travel pass** (Sfr16).

**Regional Passes** Network passes valid only within a particular region are available in several parts of the country. Such passes are available from train stations in the region.

Murten, Thun, Brienz and Zug, but not Lago Maggiore. Rail passes are not valid for cruises that are offered by smaller boat companies.

# Bus

Canary-yellow PostBuses supplement the Swiss rail network, following postal routes and linking towns to the less accessible mountain regions. Departures are synchronised with train arrivals, with bus stops conveniently located next to train stations. Travel is one class only and fares are comparable to train fares.

- National travel passes are valid on postal buses, but a few tourist-oriented Alpine routes levy a surcharge.
- Tickets are purchased from the driver, though on some scenic routes that travel over the Alps (eg the Lugano–St Moritz run) reservations are necessary. See www.postauto.ch for details.

# Car & Motorcycle

Public transport is good in city centres – unlike parking cars, which can be hard work.

## Automobile Associations

The Swiss Touring Club (www.tcs.ch) provides information and services for motorists, including a Swiss national 24-hour emergency breakdown service, free for members of TCS and its affiliates. The **Swiss Automobile Club** (www.acs.ch) offers a similar Europe-wide service.

## Car Sharing

**Mobility** (☎0848 824 812; www.mobility.ch) has more than 2950 cars at 1500 points located throughout Switzerland and you can use the cars from one hour to up to 16 days, although one-way travel is not permitted. Make car reservations online or by phone, collect it at the reserved time, and drive off. If you don't want to take out an annual subscription (Sfr290), you can pay a single-use subscription (Sfr25) plus Sfr1 per hour on top of the standard hourly rates (from Sfr2.80 per hour, plus Sfr0.50 per kilometre).

## Fuel

Unleaded *(bleifrei, sans plomb, senza piombo)* petrol is standard, at green pumps, and diesel is also widely available. Expect to pay around Sfr1.41 per litre for unleaded and Sfr1.43 for diesel.

## Hire

- Major car-rental companies have offices at airports and in major cities and towns.
- Reserve cars online. If you're flying into Geneva Airport, note that it's cheaper to rent a car on the French side.
- The minimum rental age is usually 25 but falls to 20 at some local firms; you always need a credit card.
- In winter, rental cars are usually equipped with winter tyres.

## Road Conditions

- Swiss roads are well built, well signposted and well maintained.
- Phone ☎163 for up-to-the-hour traffic conditions (recorded information in French, German, Italian and English).
- Most major Alpine passes are negotiable year-round, depending on the weather. However, you will often have to use a tunnel instead at the Great St Bernard, St Gotthard and San Bernardino passes.
- Passes that are open only from June to October: Albula, Furka, Grimsel, Klausen, Oberalp, Susten and Umbrail. Other passes are Lukmanier (open May to November), Nufenen (June to September) and Splügen (May to October).

## Road Rules

- Headlights must be on at all times, day and night; the fine for not doing so is Sfr40.
- The minimum driving age for cars and motorcycles is 18 and for mopeds it's 14.
- The Swiss drive on the right-hand side of the road.
- Give priority to traffic approaching from the right. On mountain roads, the ascending vehicle has priority, unless a postal bus is involved, as it always has right of way.
- The speed limit is 50km/h in towns, 80km/h on main roads outside towns, 100km/h on single-lane freeways and 120km/h on dual-lane freeways.
- Car occupants must wear a seatbelt at all times and vehicles must carry a breakdown-warning triangle.
- Headlights must be dipped (set to low beam) in all tunnels.
- Motorcyclists and passengers must wear helmets.
- The blood alcohol content (BAC) limit is 0.05%.
- If you're involved in a car accident, the police must be called if anyone receives more than superficial injuries.
- Proof of ownership of a private vehicle should always be carried.

## Road Signs

There are road signs in Switzerland that you may not have seen before.

- A criss-crossed white tyre on a blue circular background means that snow chains are compulsory.
- A yellow bugle on a square blue background means that you should obey instructions given by postal-bus drivers.

## Tolls

Drivers of cars and motorcycles have to pay an annual one-off charge of Sfr40 in order to use Swiss freeways

### ROAD DISTANCES (KM)

| | Basel | Bellinzona | Bern | Biel-Bienne | Brig | Chur | Fribourg | Geneva | Interlaken | Lausanne | Lucerne | Lugano | Neuchâtel | St Gallen | St Moritz | Schaffhausen | Sion |
|---|---|---|---|---|---|---|---|---|---|---|---|---|---|---|---|---|---|
| Bellinzona | 241 | | | | | | | | | | | | | | | | |
| Bern | 97 | 253 | | | | | | | | | | | | | | | |
| Biel-Bienne | 93 | 247 | 41 | | | | | | | | | | | | | | |
| Brig | 190 | 161 | 91 | 129 | | | | | | | | | | | | | |
| Chur | 228 | 115 | 242 | 237 | 174 | | | | | | | | | | | | |
| Fribourg | 132 | 285 | 34 | 71 | 179 | 274 | | | | | | | | | | | |
| Geneva | 267 | 420 | 171 | 209 | 214 | 409 | 138 | | | | | | | | | | |
| Interlaken | 153 | 195 | 57 | 92 | 73 | 209 | 92 | 230 | | | | | | | | | |
| Lausanne | 203 | 359 | 107 | 146 | 151 | 346 | 72 | 62 | 167 | | | | | | | | |
| Lucerne | 103 | 140 | 115 | 107 | 149 | 140 | 147 | 280 | 71 | 218 | | | | | | | |
| Lugano | 267 | 28 | 279 | 273 | 187 | 141 | 331 | 446 | 221 | 383 | 166 | | | | | | |
| Neuchâtel | 141 | 294 | 46 | 31 | 141 | 283 | 43 | 123 | 104 | 73 | 156 | 320 | | | | | |
| St Gallen | 191 | 217 | 204 | 197 | 288 | 102 | 236 | 371 | 225 | 307 | 138 | 243 | 244 | | | | |
| St Moritz | 313 | 150 | 327 | 321 | 241 | 85 | 359 | 494 | 294 | 430 | 225 | 176 | 368 | 178 | | | |
| Schaffhausen | 161 | 246 | 173 | 167 | 259 | 182 | 205 | 340 | 228 | 276 | 108 | 272 | 214 | 80 | 266 | | |
| Sion | 252 | 214 | 160 | 195 | 53 | 399 | 128 | 161 | 86 | 98 | 271 | 240 | 166 | 356 | 294 | 329 | |
| Zürich | 113 | 195 | 125 | 119 | 208 | 118 | 157 | 292 | 177 | 229 | 57 | 221 | 166 | 81 | 203 | 51 | 281 |

## Major Swiss Rail Routes

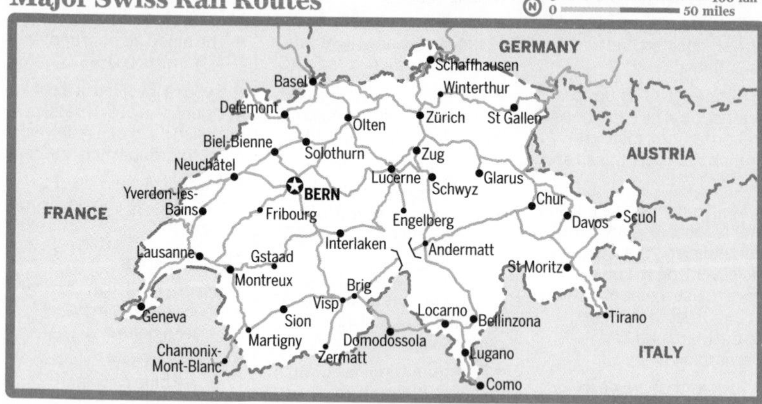


and semi-freeways, identified by green signs. The charge is payable at the border (in cash, including euros), at Swiss petrol stations and post offices, and at Swiss tourist offices abroad. Upon paying the tax, you'll receive a sticker (*vignette* in French and German, *contrassegno* in Italian) that must be displayed on the windscreen and is valid for 14 months, from 1 December to 31 January. If you're caught without it, you'll be fined Sfr200.

On the Swiss–Italian border you'll need to pay an additional toll if using the Great St Bernard Tunnel between Aosta, Italy, and Valais (car and passengers single/return Sfr29.30/46.90).

### Tunnels

Take your car on trains through these tunnels all year:

**Furka Tunnel** (☎0848 642 442; www.mgbahn.ch; car & up to 9 passengers Sfr33) From Oberwald to Realp in just 15 minutes through this 15.4km-long tunnel.

**Lötschberg Tunnel** (☎0900 553 333; www.bls.ch; car & up to 9 passengers Kandersteg-Iselle Sfr98, Kandersteg-Goppenstein Mon-Thu Sfr27, Fri-Sun Sfr29.50) From Kandersteg to Goppenstein (15 minutes, year-round), or Iselle (Italy; one hour, April to mid-October), which must be booked in advance.

**Vereina Tunnel** (☎081 288 37 37; www.rhb.ch; car & up to 9 passengers low/mid/high season Sfr34/39/44) Alternative to the Flüela Pass, which is closed in winter; from Selfranga outside Klosters to Sagliains in the Engadine. Trains run half-hourly and the journey time is 18 minutes.

## Mountain Transport

The Swiss have many words to describe mountain transport: funicular (*Standseilbahn* in German, *funiculaire* in French, *funicolare* in Italian), cable car (*Luftseilbahn, téléphérique, funivia*), gondola (*Gondelbahn, télécabine, telecabina*) and chairlift (*Sesselbahn, télésiège, seggiovia*). All are subject to regular safety inspections.

Check what time the last cable car goes down the mountain – in winter it's as early as 4pm in resorts.

## Train

The Swiss rail network combines state-run and private operations. The **Swiss Federal Railway** (www.sbb.ch) is abbreviated to SBB in German, CFF in French and FFS in Italian.

- Second-class compartments are perfectly acceptable but are often close to full; 1st-class carriages are more spacious and have fewer passengers. Power points for laptops let you work aboard and some seats are in wi-fi hot spots.
- Standard 2nd-class fares cost about Sfr40 per 100km; 1st-class fares average 75% more. Return fares are only cheaper than two singles for longer trips.
- Train schedules, revised every December, are available online and at train stations. For information, see www.sbb.ch or call **Rail Service** (☎0900 300 300; calls per min Sfr1.19).
- Larger train stations have 24-hour left-luggage lockers (per day Sfr3 to Sfr6), usually accessible 6am to midnight.
- Seat reservations (Sfr5) are advisable for longer journeys, particularly in high season.
- European rail passes such as Eurail and Interrail passes are valid on Swiss national railways. However, you cannot use them on postal buses, city transport, cable cars or private train lines (eg the Zermatt route and the Jungfraubahn routes in the heart of the Bernese Oberland), which makes Swiss travel passes better for those exploring scenic Switzerland.

# Language

Switzerland *(Schweiz/Suisse/Svizzera)* has three official federal languages: German (the native language of about 64% of the population), French (20%) and Italian (7%). A fourth language, Romansch, is spoken by less than 1% of the population, mainly in the canton of Graubünden. Since 1996 it has enjoyed status as a semi-official federal language, with guarantees for its preservation and promotion.

If you read the coloured pronunciation guides in this chapter as if they were English, you shouldn't have problems being understood. The stressed syllables are indicated with italics. Masculine, feminine, informal and polite forms are indicated with (m), (f), (inf) and (pol) where needed.

## FRENCH

Nasal vowels (pronounced 'through the nose') are indicated with o or u followed by an almost inaudible nasal m, n or ng. Note also that air is pronounced as in 'fair', eu as the 'u' in 'nurse', ew as ee with rounded lips, r is a throaty sound, and zh is pronounced as the 's' in 'pleasure'. Syllables in French words are, for the most part, equally stressed.

### Basics

| | | |
|---|---|---|
| **Hello.** | *Bonjour.* | bon·zhoor |
| **Goodbye.** | *Au revoir.* | o·rer·vwa |
| **Excuse me.** | *Excusez-moi.* | ek·skew·zay·mwa |
| **Sorry.** | *Pardon.* | par·don |
| **Please.** | *S'il vous plaît.* | seel voo play |
| **Thank you.** | *Merci.* | mair·see |
| **Yes./No.** | *Oui./Non.* | wee/non |

**What's your name?**
*Comment vous appelez-vous?* — ko·mon voo·za·play voo

**My name is ...**
*Je m'appelle ...* — zher ma·pel ...

**Do you speak English?**
*Parlez-vous anglais?* — par·lay·voo ong·glay

**I don't understand.**
*Je ne comprends pas.* — zher ner kom·pron pa

**WANT MORE?**

For in-depth language information and handy phrases, check out Lonely Planet's *Western Europe Phrasebook*. You can easily find it with a quick search at **shop.lonelyplanet.com**

### Accommodation

| | | |
|---|---|---|
| **campsite** | *camping* | kom·peeng |
| **guesthouse** | *pension* | pon·syon |
| **hotel** | *hôtel* | o·tel |
| **youth hostel** | *auberge de jeunesse* | o·berzh der zher·nes |

| | | |
|---|---|---|
| **Do you have a ... room?** | *Avez-vous une chambre ...?* | a·vey·voo ewn shom·bre ... |
| **single** | *à un lit* | a un lee |
| **double** | *avec un grand lit* | a·vek un gron lee |

**How much is it per night/person?**
*Quel est le prix par nuit/personne?* — kel ey le pree par nwee/pair·son

### Eating & Drinking

**What would you recommend?**
*Qu'est-ce que vous conseillez?* — kes·ker voo kon·say·yay

**Do you have vegetarian food?**
*Vous faites les repas végétariens?* — voo fet ley re·pa vey·zhey·ta·ryun

**I'll have ...**
*Je prends ...* zhe pron ...

**Cheers!**
*Santé!* son·tay

| | | |
|---|---|---|
| **I'd like the ..., please.** | *Je voudrais ..., s'il vous plaît.* | zhe voo·drey ... seel voo pley |
| **bill** | *l'addition* | la·dee·syon |
| **menu** | *la carte* | la kart |
| **beer** | *bière* | bee·yair |
| **coffee** | *café* | ka·fay |
| **tea** | *thé* | tay |
| **water** | *eau* | o |
| **wine** | *vin* | vun |

## Emergencies

**Help!**
*Au secours!* o skoor

**Leave me alone!**
*Fichez-moi la paix!* fee·shay·mwa la pay

**Call a doctor.**
*Appelez un médecin.* a·play un mayd·sun

**Call the police.**
*Appelez la police.* a·play la po·lees

**I'm lost.**
*Je suis perdu/perdue.* (m/f) zhe swee pair·dew

**I'm ill.**
*Je suis malade.* zher swee ma·lad

**Where are the toilets?**
*Où sont les toilettes?* oo son ley twa·let

## Shopping & Services

**I'd like to buy ...**
*Je voudrais acheter ...* zher voo·dray ash·tay ...

**How much is it?**
*C'est combien?* say kom·byun

**It's too expensive.**
*C'est trop cher.* say tro shair

| | | |
|---|---|---|
| **market** | *marché* | mar·shay |
| **post office** | *bureau de poste* | bew·ro der post |
| **tourist office** | *office de tourisme* | o·fees der too·rees·mer |

### Signs – French

| | |
|---|---|
| **Entrée** | Entrance |
| **Sortie** | Exit |
| **Ouvert** | Open |
| **Fermé** | Closed |
| **Interdit** | Prohibited |
| **Toilettes** | Toilets |

### Numbers – French

| | | |
|---|---|---|
| **1** | *un* | un |
| **2** | *deux* | der |
| **3** | *trois* | trwa |
| **4** | *quatre* | ka·trer |
| **5** | *cinq* | sungk |
| **6** | *six* | sees |
| **7** | *sept* | set |
| **8** | *huit* | weet |
| **9** | *neuf* | nerf |
| **10** | *dix* | dees |

## Transport & Directions

**Where's ...?**
*Où est ...?* oo ay ...

**What's the address?**
*Quelle est l'adresse?* kel ay la·dres

**Can you show me (on the map)?**
*Pouvez-vous m'indiquer (sur la carte)?* poo·vay·voo mun·dee·kay (sewr la kart)

| | | |
|---|---|---|
| **One ... ticket, please.** | *Un billet ..., s'il vous plaît.* | um bee·yey ... seel voo pley |
| **one-way** | *simple* | sum·ple |
| **return** | *aller et retour* | a·ley ey re·toor |

| | | |
|---|---|---|
| **boat** | *bateau* | ba·to |
| **bus** | *bus* | bews |
| **plane** | *avion* | a·vyon |
| **train** | *train* | trun |

# GERMAN

Vowels in German can be short or long. Note that in the following air is pronounced as in 'fair', aw as in 'saw', eu as the 'u' in 'nurse', ew as ee with rounded lips, ow as in 'now', kh as in Scottish *loch* (pronounced at the back of the throat), r is also a throaty sound, and zh is pronounced as the 's' in 'pleasure'.

## Basics

| | | |
|---|---|---|
| **Hello.** | *Grüezi.* | *grew*·e·tsi |
| **Goodbye.** | *Auf Wiedersehen.* | owf *vee*·der·zey·en |
| **Excuse me.** | *Entschuldigung.* | ent·*shul*·di·gung |
| **Sorry.** | *Entschuldigung.* | ent·*shul*·di·gung |
| **Please.** | *Bitte.* | *bi*·te |
| **Thank you.** | *Danke.* | *dang*·ke |
| **Yes./No.** | *Ja./Nein.* | yaa/nain |

**What's your name?**
*Wie ist Ihr Name?* vee ist eer *naa*·me

**My name is ...**
*Mein Name ist ...* main *naa*·me ist ...

**Do you speak English?**
*Sprechen Sie Englisch?* *shpre*·khen zee *eng*·lish

**I don't understand.**
*Ich verstehe nicht.* ikh fer·*shtey*·e nikht

## Accommodation

| | | |
|---|---|---|
| **campsite** | *Campingplatz* | *kem*·ping·plats |
| **guesthouse** | *Pension* | paang·*zyawn* |
| **hotel** | *Hotel* | ho·*tel* |
| **youth hostel** | *Jugend-herberge* | *yoo*·gent·her·ber·ge |

| | | |
|---|---|---|
| **Do you have a ... room?** | *Haben Sie ein ...?* | *haa*·ben zee ain ... |
| **single** | *Einzelzimmer* | *ain*·tsel·tsi·mer |
| **double** | *Doppelzimmer mit einem Doppelbett* | *do*·pel·tsi·mer mit *ai*·nem *do*·pel·bet |

**How much is it per night/person?**
*Wie viel kostet es pro Nacht/Person?* vee feel *kos*·tet es praw nakht/per·*zawn*

## Eating & Drinking

**What would you recommend?**
*Was empfehlen Sie?* vas emp·*fey*·len zee

**Do you have vegetarian food?**
*Haben Sie vegetarisches Essen?* *haa*·ben zee ve·ge·*taa*·ri·shes e·sen

**I'll have ...**
*Ich hätte gern ...* ikh *he*·te gern ...

**Cheers!**
*Prost!* prawst

| | | |
|---|---|---|
| **I'd like the ..., please.** | *Bitte bringen Sie die ...* | *bi*·te *bring*·en zee dee ... |
| **bill** | *Rechnung* | *rekh*·nung |
| **menu** | *Speisekarte* | *shpai*·ze·kar·te |
| **beer** | *Bier* | beer |
| **coffee** | *Kaffee* | *ka*·fey |
| **tea** | *Tee* | tey |
| **water** | *Wasser* | *va*·ser |
| **wine** | *Wein* | vain |

### Signs – German

| | |
|---|---|
| **Eingang** | Entrance |
| **Ausgang** | Exit |
| **Offen** | Open |
| **Geschlossen** | Closed |
| **Verboten** | Prohibited |
| **Toiletten** | Toilets |

## Emergencies

| | | |
|---|---|---|
| **Help!** | *Hilfe!* | *hil*·fe |
| **Go away!** | *Gehen Sie weg!* | *gey*·en zee vek |

| | | |
|---|---|---|
| **Call ...!** | *Rufen Sie ...!* | *roo*·fen zee ... |
| **a doctor** | *einen Arzt* | *ai*·nen artst |
| **the police** | *die Polizei* | dee po·li·*tsai* |

**I'm lost.**
*Ich habe mich verirrt.* ikh *haa*·be mikh fer·*irt*

**I'm ill.**
*Ich bin krank.* ikh bin krangk

**Where are the toilets?**
*Wo ist die Toilette?* vo ist dee to·a·*le*·te

## Shopping & Services

**I'm looking for ...**
*Ich suche nach ...* ikh *zoo*·khe nakh ...

**How much is it?**
*Wie viel kostet das?* vee feel *kos*·tet das

**That's too expensive.**
*Das ist zu teuer.* das ist tsoo *toy*·er

| | | |
|---|---|---|
| **market** | *Markt* | markt |
| **post office** | *Postamt* | *post*·amt |
| **tourist office** | *Fremden-verkehrs-büro* | *frem*·den·fer·kairs·bew·raw |

## Transport & Directions

**Where's ...?**
*Wo ist ...?* vaw ist ...

**What's the address?**
*Wie ist die Adresse?* vee ist dee a·*dre*·se

**Can you show me (on the map)?**
*Können Sie es mir (auf der Karte) zeigen?* *keu*·nen zee es meer (owf dair *kar*·te) *tsai*·gen

| | | |
|---|---|---|
| **One ... ticket, please.** | *Einen ..., bitte.* | *ai*·nen ... *bi*·te |
| **one-way** | *einfache Fahrkarte* | *ain*·fa·khe *faar*·kar·te |

**Numbers – German**

| | | |
|---|---|---|
| 1 | *eins* | ains |
| 2 | *zwei* | tsvai |
| 3 | *zdrei* | drai |
| 4 | *vier* | feer |
| 5 | *fünf* | fewnf |
| 6 | *sechs* | zeks |
| 7 | *sieben* | zee·ben |
| 8 | *acht* | akht |
| 9 | *neun* | noyn |
| 10 | *zehn* | tseyn |

| | | |
|---|---|---|
| **return** | *Rückfahr-karte* | rewk·faar·kar·te |

| | | |
|---|---|---|
| **boat** | *Boot* | bawt |
| **bus** | *Bus* | bus |
| **plane** | *Flugzeug* | flook·tsoyk |
| **train** | *Zug* | tsook |

# ITALIAN

Italian vowels are generally shorter than in English. The consonants sometimes have a more emphatic pronunciation – if the word is written with a double consonant, use the stronger form. Note that ow is pronounced as in 'how', dz as the 'ds' in 'lads', and r is rolled and stronger than in English.

## Basics

| | | |
|---|---|---|
| **Hello.** | *Buongiorno.* | bwon·jor·no |
| **Goodbye.** | *Arrivederci.* | a·ree·ve·der·chee |
| **Excuse me.** | *Mi scusi.* (pol)<br>*Scusami.* (inf) | mee skoo·zee<br>skoo·za·mee |
| **Sorry.** | *Mi dispiace.* | mee dees·pya·che |
| **Please.** | *Per favore.* | per fa·vo·re |
| **Thank you.** | *Grazie.* | gra·tsye |
| **Yes./No.** | *Sì./No.* | see/no |

**What's your name?**
*Come si chiama?* (pol) ko·me see kya·ma
*Come ti chiami?* (inf) ko·me tee kya·mee

**My name is ...**
*Mi chiamo ...* mee kya·mo ...

**Do you speak English?**
*Parla inglese?* par·la een·gle·ze

**I don't understand.**
*Non capisco.* non ka·pee·sko

## Accommodation

| | | |
|---|---|---|
| **campsite** | *campeggio* | kam·pe·jo |
| **guesthouse** | *pensione* | pen·syo·ne |
| **hotel** | *albergo* | al·ber·go |
| **youth hostel** | *ostello della gioventù* | os·te·lo de·la jo·ven·too |

| | | |
|---|---|---|
| **Do you have a ... room?** | *Avete una camera ...?* | a·ve·te oo·na ka·me·ra ... |
| **single** | *singola* | seen·go·la |
| **double** | *doppia con letto matri-moniale* | do·pya kon le·to ma·tree·mo·nya·le |

| | | |
|---|---|---|
| **How much is it per ...?** | *Quanto costa per ...?* | kwan·to kos·ta per ... |
| **night** | *una notte* | oo·na no·te |
| **person** | *persona* | per·so·na |

## Eating & Drinking

**What would you recommend?**
*Cosa mi consiglia?* ko·za mee kon·see·lya

**Do you have vegetarian food?**
*Avete piatti vegetariani?* a·ve·te pya·tee ve·je·ta·rya·nee

**I'll have ...**
*Prendo ...* pren·do ...

**Cheers!**
*Salute!* sa·loo·te

| | | |
|---|---|---|
| **I'd like the ..., please.** | *Vorrei ..., per favore.* | vo·ray ... per fa·vo·re |
| **bill** | *il conto* | eel kon·to |
| **menu** | *il menù* | eel me·noo |

| | | |
|---|---|---|
| **beer** | *birra* | bee·ra |
| **coffee** | *caffè* | ka·fe |
| **tea** | *tè* | te |
| **water** | *acqua* | a·kwa |
| **wine** | *vino* | vee·no |

**Signs – Italian**

| | |
|---|---|
| **Entrata** | Entrance |
| **Uscita** | Exit |
| **Aperto** | Open |
| **Chiuso** | Closed |
| **Proibito** | Prohibited |
| **Gabinetti** | Toilets |

### Numbers – Italian

| | | |
|---|---|---|
| 1 | *uno* | oo·no |
| 2 | *due* | doo·e |
| 3 | *tre* | tre |
| 4 | *quattro* | kwa·tro |
| 5 | *cinque* | cheen·kwe |
| 6 | *sei* | say |
| 7 | *sette* | se·te |
| 8 | *otto* | o·to |
| 9 | *nove* | no·ve |
| 10 | *dieci* | dye·chee |

## Emergencies

| | | |
|---|---|---|
| **Help!** | *Aiuto!* | ai·yoo·to |
| **Go away!** | *Vai via!* | vai vee·a |
| **Call ...!** | *Chiami ...!* | kya·mee ... |
| **a doctor** | *un medico* | oon me·dee·ko |
| **the police** | *la polizia* | la po·lee·tsee·a |

**I'm lost.**
*Mi sono perso/a.* (m/f) mee so·no per·so/a

**I'm ill.**
*Mi sento male.* mee sen·to ma·le

**Where are the toilets?**
*Dove sono i gabinetti?* do·ve so·no ee ga·bee·ne·tee

## Shopping & Services

**I'm looking for ...**
*Sto cercando ...* sto cher·kan·do ...

**How much is it?**
*Quant'è?* kwan·te

**That's too expensive.**
*È troppo caro.* e tro·po ka·ro

| | | |
|---|---|---|
| **market** | *mercato* | mer·ka·to |
| **post office** | *ufficio postale* | oo·fee·cho pos·ta·le |
| **tourist office** | *ufficio del turismo* | oo·fee·cho del too·reez·mo |

## Transport & Directions

**Where's ... ?**
*Dov'è ... ?* do·ve ...

**What's the address?**
*Qual'è l'indirizzo?* kwa·le leen·dee·ree·tso

**Can you show me (on the map)?**
*Può mostrarmi (sulla pianta)?* pwo mos·trar·mee (soo·la pyan·ta)

| | | |
|---|---|---|
| **One ... ticket, please.** | *Un biglietto ..., per favore.* | oon bee·lye·to ... per fa·vo·re |
| **one-way** | *di sola andata* | dee so·la an·da·ta |
| **return** | *di andata e ritorno* | dee an·da·ta e ree·tor·no |

| | | |
|---|---|---|
| **boat** | *nave* | na·ve |
| **bus** | *autobus* | ow·to·boos |
| **plane** | *aereo* | a·e·re·o |
| **train** | *treno* | tre·no |

### ROMANSCH

Derived from Latin and part of the Rhaeto-Romanic language family, Romansch dialects tend to be restricted to their own particular mountain valley. Usage is gradually declining with German taking over as the lingua franca in the Romansch areas. The main street in villages is usually called Via Maistra.

| | |
|---|---|
| **Hello.** | *Allegra.* |
| **Goodbye.** | *Adieu./Abunansvair.* |
| **Please.** | *Anzi.* |
| **Thank you.** | *Grazia.* |
| **bed** | *letg* |
| **closed** | *serrà* |
| **cross-country skiing** | *passlung* |
| **left** | *sanester* |
| **right** | *dretg* |
| **room** | *chombra* |
| **tourist office** | *societad da traffic* |
| **bread** | *paun* |
| **cheese** | *chaschiel* |
| **fish** | *pesch* |
| **ham** | *schambun* |
| **milk** | *latg* |
| **wine** | *vin* |
| **1** | *in* |
| **2** | *dus* |
| **3** | *trais* |
| **4** | *quatter* |
| **5** | *tschinch* |
| **6** | *ses* |
| **7** | *set* |
| **8** | *och* |
| **9** | *nouv* |
| **10** | *diesch* |

# Behind the Scenes

## SEND US YOUR FEEDBACK

We love to hear from travellers – your comments keep us on our toes and help make our books better. Our well-travelled team reads every word on what you loved or loathed about this book. Although we cannot reply individually to your submissions, we always guarantee that your feedback goes straight to the appropriate authors, in time for the next edition. Each person who sends us information is thanked in the next edition – the most useful submissions are rewarded with a selection of digital PDF chapters.

Visit **lonelyplanet.com/contact** to submit your updates and suggestions or to ask for help. Our award-winning website also features inspirational travel stories, news and discussions.

Note: We may edit, reproduce and incorporate your comments in Lonely Planet products such as guidebooks, websites and digital products, so let us know if you don't want your comments reproduced or your name acknowledged. For a copy of our privacy policy visit lonelyplanet.com/privacy.

## OUR READERS

**Many thanks to the travellers who used the last edition and wrote to us with helpful hints, useful advice and interesting anecdotes:** Ben Campbell, Liesbeth Cobbaut, Loreto Corrales, Scott Hall ,Paul Hodgen, Ted Keener, Ueli Münger, Kathy Piro, Robert Rachofsky, Polly Seidler, Sam Sharp, Andrew Smith, Jens Stollburges, Anton van Veen, Patrizia Vollmar

## WRITER THANKS

### Kerry Walker

*Merci vielmal* to all the Swiss locals, tourism professionals and timely train and cable car drivers who made the road to research silky smooth and provided valuable insight. Special thanks go to Sara Roloff (Switzerland Tourism UK), Lucia Filippone (Zürich Tourism), Janine Zingg (Swiss Travel System) and Remo Käser (Jungfraubahnen). Big thanks too go to my fellow authors – Benedict Walker and Craig McLachlan – for being such stars to work with.

### Craig McLachlan

A hearty thanks to everyone who helped out during my research trip around Switzerland and Liechtenstein, but especially to my exceptionally beautiful wife, Yuriko, who kept me on track, focused and constantly smiling. Switzerland is a joy to explore, and a big part of that joy comes from meeting and talking to happy people! Thanks to you all.

### Benedict Walker

A big thanks to Daniel Fahey for his patience and flexibility in taking me on for this project, to Michal Greenberg in Leipzig for helping me find a home to work from, and to my 'Foster' mum, Vicki Kirkman, for being a champion of strength in the face of her own adversity. Special thanks to my real mum, Trish Walker, the ultimate font of patience, love and support, and to all the aunties, uncles and cuzzies that helped pack up Bonnie's place while I was away. Finally, thanks to Switzerland for stealing my heart, twice in a lifetime.

## ACKNOWLEDGEMENTS

Climate map data adapted from Peel MC, Finlayson BL & McMahon TA (2007) 'Updated World Map of the Köppen-Geiger Climate Classification', *Hydrology and Earth System Sciences*, 11, 1633-44.

Cover photograph: Alps, Lucerne canton (p199); Xantana/Getty Images ©

## THIS BOOK

This 10th edition of Lonely Planet's *Switzerland* guidebook was curated by Gregor Clark, and was researched and written by Kerry Walker, Craig McLachlan and Benedict Walker. The previous edition was written by Kerry, Gregor, Craig and Benedict. This guidebook was produced by the following:

**Destination Editor** Daniel Fahey

**Senior Product Editor** Kate Chapman

**Product Editors** Alex Conroy, Jenna Myers, Genna Patterson

**Cartographers** Corey Hutchison, Rachel Imeson

**Book Designer** Virginia Moreno

**Assisting Editors** Sarah Bailey, Andrew Bain, Lucy Cowie, Peter Cruttenden, Andrea Dobbin, Victoria Harrison, Clare Healy, Alison Killilea, Jodie Martire, Kristin Odijk, Alison Ridgway

**Cover Researcher** Ania Bartoszek

**Thanks to** Ronan Abayawickrema, Sonia Kapoor, Anne Mason, Vicky Smith

# Index



Map Pages **000**
Photo Pages **000**

Map Pages **000**
Photo Pages 000

Map Pages **000**
Photo Pages **000**

# Map Legend

## Sights

- Beach
- Bird Sanctuary
- Buddhist
- Castle/Palace
- Christian
- Confucian
- Hindu
- Islamic
- Jain
- Jewish
- Monument
- Museum/Gallery/Historic Building
- Ruin
- Shinto
- Sikh
- Taoist
- Winery/Vineyard
- Zoo/Wildlife Sanctuary
- Other Sight

## Activities, Courses & Tours

- Bodysurfing
- Diving
- Canoeing/Kayaking
- Course/Tour
- Sento Hot Baths/Onsen
- Skiing
- Snorkelling
- Surfing
- Swimming/Pool
- Walking
- Windsurfing
- Other Activity

## Sleeping

- Sleeping
- Camping
- Hut/Shelter

## Eating

- Eating

## Drinking & Nightlife

- Drinking & Nightlife
- Cafe

## Entertainment

- Entertainment

## Shopping

- Shopping

## Information

- Bank
- Embassy/Consulate
- Hospital/Medical
- Internet
- Police
- Post Office
- Telephone
- Toilet
- Tourist Information
- Other Information

## Geographic

- Beach
- Gate
- Hut/Shelter
- Lighthouse
- Lookout
- Mountain/Volcano
- Oasis
- Park
- Pass
- Picnic Area
- Waterfall

## Population

- Capital (National)
- Capital (State/Province)
- City/Large Town
- Town/Village

## Transport

- Airport
- Border crossing
- Bus
- Cable car/Funicular
- Cycling
- Ferry
- Metro station
- Monorail
- Parking
- Petrol station
- S-Bahn/Subway station
- Taxi
- T-bane/Tunnelbana station
- Train station/Railway
- Tram
- U-Bahn/Underground station
- Other Transport

## Routes

- Tollway
- Freeway
- Primary
- Secondary
- Tertiary
- Lane
- Unsealed road
- Road under construction
- Plaza/Mall
- Steps
- Tunnel
- Pedestrian overpass
- Walking Tour
- Walking Tour detour
- Path/Walking Trail

## Boundaries

- International
- State/Province
- Disputed
- Regional/Suburb
- Marine Park
- Cliff
- Wall

## Hydrography

- River, Creek
- Intermittent River
- Canal
- Water
- Dry/Salt/Intermittent Lake
- Reef

## Areas

- Airport/Runway
- Beach/Desert
- Cemetery (Christian)
- Cemetery (Other)
- Glacier
- Mudflat
- Park/Forest
- Sight (Building)
- Sportsground
- Swamp/Mangrove

*Note: Not all symbols displayed above appear on the maps in this book*

# OUR STORY

A beat-up old car, a few dollars in the pocket and a sense of adventure. In 1972 that's all Tony and Maureen Wheeler needed for the trip of a lifetime – across Europe and Asia overland to Australia. It took several months, and at the end – broke but inspired – they sat at their kitchen table writing and stapling together their first travel guide, *Across Asia on the Cheap*. Within a week they'd sold 1500 copies. Lonely Planet was born.

Today, Lonely Planet has offices in the US, Ireland and China, with a network of over 2000 contributors in every corner of the globe. We share Tony's belief that 'a great guidebook should do three things: inform, educate and amuse'.

# OUR WRITERS

**Kerry Walker**

Bernese Oberland; Northeastern Switzerland; Ticino; Zürich

Kerry is an award-winning travel writer, photographer and Lonely Planet author, specialising in Central and Southern Europe. Based in Wales, she has authored/co-authored more than a dozen Lonely Planet titles. An adventure addict, she loves mountains, cold places and true wilderness. She features her latest work at kerrywalker.com and tweets @kerrywalker. Kerry also wrote the Plan, Understand and Survival Guide sections.

**Gregor Clark**

Since 2000, Gregor has regularly contributed to Lonely Planet guides, with a focus on Europe and the Americas. Titles include *Italy*, *France*, *Brazil*, *Costa Rica*, *Argentina*, *Portugal*, *Switzerland*, *Mexico*, *South America on a Shoestring*, *Montreal & Quebec City*, *France's Best Trips*, *New England's Best Trips*, cycling guides to Italy and California, and coffee-table pictorials such as *Food Trails*, *The USA Book* and *The Lonely Planet Guide to the Middle of Nowhere*.

**Craig McLachlan**

Central Switzerland; Graubünden; Liechtenstein; Valais

Craig has covered destinations all over the globe for Lonely Planet for two decades. Based in Queenstown, New Zealand for half the year, he runs an outdoor activities company and a sake brewery, then moonlights overseas for the other half, leading tours and writing for Lonely Planet. Craig has completed a number of adventures in Japan and his books are available on Amazon. Describing himself as a 'freelance anything', Craig has an MBA from the University of Hawai'i and is also a Japanese interpreter, pilot, photographer, hiking guide, tour leader, karate instructor and budding novelist.

**Benedict Walker**

Fribourg, Drei-Seen-Land & the Jura; Geneva; Lake Geneva & Vaud; Mittelland; Northwestern Switzerland

Benedict was born in Newcastle, New South Wales, Australia, and grew up in the 'burbs spending weekends and long summers by the beach whenever possible. Although he is drawn magnetically to the kinds of mountains he encountered in the Canadian Rockies and the Japan and Swiss Alps, beach life is in his blood. Japan was Benedict's first gig for Lonely Planet in 2008/9 and he has been blessed to have been asked back three more times. He has since worked on numerous Lonely Planet titles, including guides to Australia, Canada, Germany and the USA. Join him on his journeys on Instagram: @wordsandjourneys.

**Published by Lonely Planet Global Limited**
CRN 554153
10th edition – May 2022
ISBN 978 1 78701 663 7

10 9 8 7 6 5 4 3 2 1
Printed in China

# BEST TRANSPORT FROM ZÜRICH AIRPORT TO CITY CENTRE

## Train

CHEAPEST

**9-12 mins, Sfr6.80**

Up to nine SBB trains run hourly to Hauptbahnhof from around 5am to midnight. Tram line 10 also makes the same journey but is considerably slower (48 minutes).

## Taxi & Ride Share

### Taxi

**10–20mins, Sfr45–70**

Taxis are expensive and usually not worth it unless you're arriving on a late flight or have a lot of luggage. Pick them up at Arrivals/the Hauptbahnhof.

### Uber

**10–20mins, Sfr35–60**

Uber is only marginally cheaper than a taxi, but becomes a better deal if you can share the cost of the ride.

## Car & Motorcycle

**10–20mins**

If you're hiring a car or motorcycle at the airport, the A3 approaches Zürich from the south along the southern shore of Zürichsee. The A1 is the fastest route from Bern and Basel. It proceeds northeast to Winterthur.

TEAR OUT, FOLD UP & KEEP WITH YOUR PASSPORT

# JUST LANDED • ZÜRICH •

*Easy steps from airport to city*

## Zürich Airport

## Get Connected

**Free airport wi-fi** Passengers get four hours of free wi-fi, supported by Monzoon. You can register by phone, text or with your boarding pass on any device.

**Charging stations** Located throughout the airport; free for passenger use. A locking technique means you can leave your device to charge while using other airport services.

**SIM card** These are available at standard prices at Swisscom in the public area of the airport, open daily from 8am to 9pm.

## Money

**Money** Around Sfr500 per person should cover transport and meals for a few days.

**Credit cards** Widely accepted.

**ATMs** You'll find several 24-hour ATMs at the airport both landside and airside, including Credit Suisse and UBS.

**Currency exchange** You can change money in arrivals and airside at Travelex (6am to 6pm). However, banks in the centre generally offer better rates.

## Helpful Phrases

Zürich Airport has English-language signs and some English-speaking staff in Arrivals, but here are a few German phrases if you get stuck.

| | | |
|---|---|---|
| **Do you speak English?** | Sprechen Sie Englisch? | *shpre*·khen zee *eng*·lis |
| **I don't understand.** | Ich verstehe nicht | ikh fer·*shtey*·e nikht |
| **Can you show me (on the map)?** | Können Sie es mir (auf der Karte) zeigen? | *ker*·nen zee es meer (owf dair *kar*·te) *tsai*·gen |
| **I'm looking for ...** | Ich suche nach ... | ikh *zoo*·khe nakh ... |
| **One return ticket, please.** | Einen rückfahrkarte, bitte | *ai*·nen *rewk*·-faar·kar·te, *bi*·te |
| **How much is it?** | Wie viel kostet das? | vee feel *kos*·tet da |
| **Please take me to (this address).** | Bitte bringen Sie mich zu (dieser Adresse). | *bi*·te *bring*·en zee mikh tsoo (dee·zer a·*dre*·se) |
| **At what time's the ...bus?** | Wann fährt van fairt der ... Bus? | van fairt dair... bus |
| **first** | erste | *ers*·te |
| **last** | letzte | *lets*·te |

Find great travel tips at
**www.lonelyplanet.com**

Take me to this address:

..............................................................................

# • GENEVA •

## Geneva Airport

### Get Connected

**Free airport wi-fi** Geneva Airport offers 90 minutes of free wi-fi. Connect by SMS, boarding pass or by presenting your passport or ID card at the visitor centre (Arrivals level).

**Charging stations** You can charge mobile phones at the airside business corner (USB and standard socket).

**SIM card** The exchange desk as you exit Arrivals sells SIM cards.

### From Geneva Airport to City Center

**Train**

7mins, Sfr4

Geneva Airport SBB trains run at least every 10 minutes to Gare de Cornavin.

**Shuttle**

28mins, Sfr4

Bus 10 departs from the Rive stop (four to nine hourly).

**Taxi**

20mins, Sfr40

Fares depend on the traffic and time of day.